W9-AFI-301

Crusade
in Europe

A Da Capo Press Reprint Series

THE POLITICS AND STRATEGY OF WORLD WAR II

General Editor: Manfred Jonas

Union College

DWIGHT D. EISENHOWER

Crusade in Europe

With a New Introduction
by **Manfred Jonas,** *Union College*

DA CAPO PRESS · NEW YORK · 1977

Library of Congress Cataloging in Publication Data

Eisenhower, Dwight David, Pres. U.S., 1890-1969.
    Crusade in Europe.

    (The Politics and strategy of World War II)
    Reprint of the 1st ed. published by Doubleday,
Garden City, N. Y., with a new introd.
    Includes bibliographical references.
    1. World War, 1939-1945–Campaigns. I. Title.
D743.E35 1976   940.54'2   76-25037
ISBN 0-306-70768-3

This Da Capo Press edition of *Crusade in Europe* is, except for the addition of a new Introduction by Manfred Jonas, an unabridged republication of the first edition published in New York in 1948. It is reprinted with the permission of Doubleday & Company, Inc.

Published by Da Capo Press, Inc.
A Subsidiary of Plenum Publishing Corporation
227 West 17th Street, New York, N. Y. 10011

INTRODUCTION

Military memoirs are all too often designed either to demonstrate the genius of victorious commanders or to rescue the reputations of defeated ones. *Crusade in Europe* remains a happy exception to that rule. More than twenty-five years after its original publication, it occupies a secure place, alongside the *Memoirs of Ulysses S. Grant*, as one of the outstanding examples of its genre. It remains a valuable, accurate and highly readable account of the North African and Western European campaigns of the Second World War; an astute and revealing description of the opportunities and pitfalls of modern coalition warfare; and best of all, a thoughtful, personal account of the problems of military command in a democratic society.

The meteoric rise of Dwight D. Eisenhower from relative obscurity in America's peacetime army to chief of the War Department's War Plans (later Operations) Division, to commanding general for the European Theater, to Allied Commander in chief for the North African invasion, to Supreme Allied Commander for the invasion and reconquest of Western Europe made him, among other things, a prime target for ambitious publishers seeking the rights to his memoirs. By the time LeBaron Barker, Jr., the editor-in-chief at Doubleday, Doran and Company, made his initial inquiry on January 6, 1944, Eisenhower had already developed a standard response which he promptly instructed his naval aide, Lt. Cmdr. (later Capt.) Harry C. Butcher, to prepare. "Your suggestion is most complimentary," it ran in part, "but I shall have to tell you, as I have answered other inquiries, that not only am I too busy now to write, but cannot determine whether I shall wish to do so after the war."

Eisenhower remained too busy at war's end, first as commander of American occupation forces in Europe and then, from late 1945 to early 1948, as George C. Marshall's successor in the office of U.S. Army Chief of Staff. But public interest in the man who had played a major role in bringing victory in World War II continued to increase. By 1947 his services were being sought by some of the country's largest business firms, and prestigious institutions of all description hoped to benefit not only from his demonstrated managerial skills but also from his towering and still growing reputation. More and more, too, elements in both of the major political parties saw Eisenhower, whose political views were entirely unknown, as a promising prospect for the presidency of the United States.

Under these circumstances it is hardly surprising that the interest of publishers in his memoirs continued to increase. In the middle of 1947, when he had decided to leave active Army service at the conclusion of his term as chief of staff, and to accept the presidency of Columbia University, Eisenhower succumbed to the pleadings and entered into negotiations with Doubleday. Three months of terminal leave prior to assuming his duties at Columbia would, he thought, finally give him the time to write.

Once he had decided to write the book, Eisenhower set out to complete the task with efficiency and dispatch. He began almost immediately after the start of his terminal leave on February 7, 1948, and quickly put the project on an assembly line basis. Working twelve or more hours a day, five or six days each week, he dictated the chapters to a series of secretaries. While the first secretary transcribed the dictation, he would dictate the next section to a second stenographer. And, while the second transcribed, he would dictate to a third. In the meantime, the typed drafts were sent to the Pentagon, where an army historian checked them for factual accuracy. Eisenhower then made final corrections in longhand, before turning the parts of the manuscript back to the secretaries for retyping. The final editing was performed both by Joseph Barnes, the foreign news editor of the New York *Herald-Tribune,* and by Kenneth McCormick, the editor-in-chief at Doubleday. In what must be close to record time for such an enterprise, the total span between beginning the writing and the publication date was a mere nine months.

Crusade in Europe was greeted with almost unanimous critical acclaim, along with praise for its author's modesty, candor, fairness, tact, and general humanity. It was called the best American military reminiscence (with the possible exception of Grant's), and "the work of the best soldier-historian since, perhaps, Caesar and his commentaries." The public responded to the book by propelling it to the top of the best-seller lists. 239,265 copies were sold in less than six weeks, with total hard-cover sales eventually topping the million mark.

Neither the critical nor the public acclaim were misplaced. Though subsequent accounts have added a good deal to our knowledge and understanding of events, they have challenged neither the essential accuracy nor the value of Eisenhower's book. General De Gaulle, to be sure, protested in a letter to the New York *Times* on December 7, 1948, that he had *not* asked Eisenhower to parade American troops through Paris on August 29, 1944 as a sign of support for him. He had not needed such support, the proud Frenchman insisted, because his authority had already been recognized in Paris "by unanimous and indescribable enthusiasm." In the same vein, Lord Alanbrooke denied having praised Eisenhower for sticking to his plan to clear the west bank of the Rhine before authorizing a deep penetration east of that river early in 1945—a strategy that Alanbrooke had vigorously opposed. But these are minor matters of no substantive consequence. The editors of the wartime papers of General Eisenhower detected no discrepancies between the book and the documents and, indeed, they found much helpful supporting information in *Crusade in Europe.*

Eisenhower clearly did not relish the role of author and surely did not need the additional fame that a book might bring. But there were two considerations, one practical and the other ideological, that led him to write *Crusade in Europe.* The practical consideration was financial. As a junior officer in America's peacetime army, Eisenhower had been ill-paid for many years, and, at the time the United States entered the Second World War, he had only attained the rank of lieutenant-colonel. The rapid promotions and consequent salary increases that followed had been accompanied by even greater increases in his personal expenses. As he contemplated the end of his active army service, therefore, Eisenhower, though assured of an annual income of $20,000 for life, had few tangible assets. His decision to pass up lucrative offers from industry for the much more modest compensation offered by Columbia University made the prospect of a possible windfall from the publication of his memoirs all the more appealing. Nor were his expectations in this regard to be disappointed. The $625,000 in royalties his best-selling volume produced, combined with a ruling by the Internal Revenue Service that allowed him to keep three-fourths of that sum, made him a wealthy man.

Yet Eisenhower had a more compelling reason for writing his book. Although he was in every sense a professional soldier and, as such, without either training or particular interest in politics and political policymaking, he had nevertheless acquired in the course of his wartime activities certain well-defined conceptions of the world role of the United States. In particular, he had become convinced that world order and stability, and indeed the safety of the United States, required a continuing commitment on the part of this country to international cooperation and the principles of collective security. From this perspective, he viewed with mounting concern the evidences of a new isolationism, of whose existence his experience with the demobilization process had convinced him.

There can be no question but that this concern was a deep and abiding one with Eisenhower. In 1948 it led him to keep alive the possibility of accepting the Democratic presidential nomination, despite his strong inclination to decline at once, until after the Republicans had nominated Governor Thomas E. Dewey of New York, by then a good internationalist and thus had made certain that no isolationist would succeed to the White House in 1949. Four years later he agreed to seek the Republican presidential nomination only when it appeared certain that that nomination would otherwise go to the isolationist Senator Robert A. Taft of Ohio.

In 1947, the same concern about America's role in world politics led him to the decision to present his views to the public. It is no accident that *Crusade in Europe* not only places a heavy emphasis on the role of international cooperation in the winning of the Second World War, but ends with a chapter, entitled "Russia," concluding that the "democracies must learn that the world is now too small for the rigid concepts of national sovereignty that developed in a time when nations were self-sufficient and self-dependent for their own well-being and safety. None of them today can stand alone."

The lasting value of the Eisenhower volume lies in a number of elements that he was able to combine with considerable skill. In the first place, the book remains, despite the plethora of subsequent Eisenhower literature, the best clue to the character, abilities and limitations of the man who became the thirty-fourth president of the United States. Beyond that, it contains a series of balanced, judicious, and quintessentially fair assessments not only of Churchill, Montgomery and Patton, with whom Eisenhower had considerable difficulties, but also of other actors in the drama of the Second World War: Roosevelt, De Gaulle, Marshall, Portal, Giraud and many others. Eisenhower here details better and more convincingly than any outside critic could the mistakes in strategy and tactics that were made, but at the same time he brings out the magnitude and scope of the effort, the energy and imagination that were harnessed in a common cause and the remarkable achievement in coalition warfare this represented.

Eisenhower, to be sure, was a soldier, and he tells us less about the navy and the air force than we might like to know. His various commands were in and around Western Europe, and the Pacific War is therefore largely ignored. He dealt only sporadically with the Russians, and, aside from his friendship with Marshal Zhukov, which developed late in the war, had no better means of unraveling the Russian enigma than the other American leaders of the day. But Eisenhower saw the Second World War from a unique point of vantage, and his account of that momentous upheaval, tempered as it is by his own essential humanity, will maintain its place on the very small shelf of military memoirs that are worth rereading.

MANFRED JONAS

Schenectady, New York
May, 1976

CRUSADE IN EUROPE

DWIGHT D. EISENHOWER

Crusade in Europe

DOUBLEDAY & COMPANY, INC.   1950

GARDEN CITY, NEW YORK

To the Allied Soldier,
Sailor, and Airman of World War II

CONTENTS

MAPS

CARTOGRAPHY BY RAFAEL PALACIOS

ix

*does not appear in this edition.
**reproduced in black and white in this edition.

ILLUSTRATIONS

PHOTOGRAPHS SELECTED BY EDWARD STEICHEN

interrupted by bridges and culverts that the enemy invariably destroyed as he drew back fighting."

Infantrymen Advance Along Sicilian Cliff
(Photo by U. S. Army Signal Corps)

In Italy, "head-on attacks against the enemy on his
mountainous frontiers would be slow and extremely
costly." Only by utter destruction of his strongholds
could the battle toll be tolerable.

Smoke Pall Shrouds Cassino as Bombing Begins
(Photo by U. S. Army Signal Corps)

" 'You will enter the continent of Europe and . . .
undertake operations aimed at the heart of Germany and
the destruction of her Armed Forces.' "

Assault Troops Hit Normandy Beach on D-day
(Photo by U. S. Army Signal Corps)

". . . we had . . . to build up on the beaches the reserves in troops, ammunition, and supplies that would
enable us, within a reasonable time, to initiate deep
offensives . . ."

Ships, Troops, Trucks, Supply Crowd French Beach
(Photo by U. S. Coast Guard)

"Some soldier once said, 'The weather is always neutral.'
Nothing could be more untrue." In Tunis, Italy, and
across the Continent, mud was a formidable barrier to
Allied advances.

Even the Jeep Succumbed to Italian Mud
(Photo by U. S. Army Signal Corps)

On Red Ball Highways, "every vehicle ran at least twenty

hours a day . . . allowed to halt only for necessary loading, unloading, and servicing."

Tank Transporters Rush Armored Supply
(Photo by U. S. Army Signal Corps)

NAKEDNESS OF THE BATTLEFIELD   *facing page* 305

". . . each man feels himself so much alone, and each is prey to the human fear and terror that to move or show himself may result in instant death."

German 88 Pounds Paratroopers Near Arnhem
(Photo by U. S. Army Signal Corps)

ISOLATE, THEN ANNIHILATE   *facing page* 336

". . . battles of annihilation are possible only against some isolated portion of the enemy's entire force. Destruction of bridges, culverts, railways, roads, and canals by the air force tends to isolate the. force under attack . . ."

Ulm Rail Yards After December 1944 Raid
(Photo by U. S. Air Force)

SUPREME OVER GERMANY   *facing page* 337

"By early 1945 the effects of our air offensive against the German economy were becoming catastrophic . . . there developed a continuous crisis in German transportation and in all phases of her war effort."

Bremen Is Target of B-17 and B-24 Flight
(Photo by U. S. Air Force)

THESE WERE HITLER'S ELITE   *facing page* 440

". . . within eighteen days of the moment the Ruhr was surrounded it had surrendered with an even greater number of prisoners than we had bagged in the final Tunisian collapse . . ."

Nazis Taken Prisoner in the Ruhr Pocket
(Photo by U. S. Army Signal Corps)

DOUBLE-LOADED FOR HOME   *facing page* 441

This plan required "one man to sleep in the daytime so

that another could have his bunk during the night. . . .
I never afterward heard of a single complaint . . ."
The Queen Elizabeth Brings Them Home
(Photo by U. S. Coast Guard)

SURVIVING BOMBS AND HITLER   *facing page* 456
But no edifice, however sacred, will survive atomic war.
"Even the bombed ruins of Germany . . . provide but
faint warning of what future war could mean to the
people of the earth."
The Cathedral Stands Amid Cologne's Rubble
(Photo by U. S. Army Signal Corps)

PARTNERS IN VICTORY   *facing page* 457
"The Russians are generous. They like to give presents
and parties . . . the ordinary Russian seems to me to
bear a marked similarity to what we call an 'average
American.' "
East and West Celebrate at Torgau
(Photo by U. S. Army Signal Corps)

CRUSADE IN EUROPE

Chapter 1

PRELUDE
TO WAR

IN THE ALLIED HEADQUARTERS AT REIMS,
Colonel General Jodl signed the instrument of German surrender on
May 7, 1945. At midnight of the next day there ended, in Europe,
a conflict that had been raging since September 1, 1939.

Between these two dates millions of Europeans had been killed.
All Europe west of the Rhine had, with minor exceptions, lived for
more than four years under the domination of an occupying army.
Free institutions and free speech had disappeared. Economies were
broken and industry prostrated. In Germany itself, after years of seeming invincibility, a carpet of destruction and desolation had spread
over the land. Her bridges were down, her cities in ruins, and her
great industrial capacity practically paralyzed. Great Britain had exhausted herself economically and financially to carry on her part of
the war; the nation was almost entirely mobilized, with everybody of
useful age, men and women alike, either in the armed forces or engaged in some type of production for war. Russian industry west of the
Volga had been almost obliterated.

America had not been spared: by V-J Day in the Pacific, 322,188
of her youth had been lost in battle or had died in the service and
approximately 700,000 more had been wounded.[1] The nation had
poured forth resources in unstinted measure not only to support her
own armies and navies and air forces but also to give her Allies equipment and weapons with which to operate effectively against the
common enemy. Each of the Allies had, according to its means, contributed to the common cause but America had stood pre-eminent as
the arsenal of democracy. We were the nation which, from the war's
beginning to its end, had achieved the greatest transformation from

almost complete military weakness to astounding strength and effectiveness.

Europe had been at war for a full year before America became alarmed over its pitifully inadequate defenses. When the nation began, in 1939, first steps toward strengthening its military establishment, it started from a position as close to zero as a great nation could conceivably have allowed itself to sink.

That summer the Germans were massing against the Polish frontiers 60 infantry divisions, 14 mechanized and motorized divisions, 3 mountain divisions, more than 4000 planes, and thousands of tanks and armored cars. To oppose them the Poles could mobilize less than a third that strength in all categories.[2] Their force was doomed to quick destruction under the fury and weight of the German assault. But the Polish Army, easy victim though it was to Hitler's war machine, far surpassed the United States Army in numbers of men and pieces of equipment.

On July 1, 1939, the Army's enlisted strength in the United States —air, ground, and service—was less than 130,000; of three organized and six partially organized infantry divisions, not one approached its combat complement; there were two cavalry divisions at less than half strength; but there was not one armored division, and the total number of men in scattered tank units was less than 1500; the entire Air Force consisted of approximately 1175 planes, designed for combat, and 17,000 men to service, maintain, and fly them. Overseas, to hold garrisons from the Arctic Circle to the Equator and from Panama to Corregidor, eight thousand miles away, there were 45,300 soldiers.[3]

Two increases, authorized during the summer and fall of 1939, raised the active Army at home and overseas to 227,000. But there it remained during the eight months that Germany, brutally triumphant over Poland, was readying her full might for the conquest of western Europe.

The American people still believed that distance provided adequate insulation between us and any conflict in Europe or Asia. Comparatively few understood the direct relationship between American prosperity and physical safety on the one hand, and on the other the existence of a free world beyond our shores. Consequently, the only Americans who thought about preparation for war were a few professionals in the armed services and those far-seeing statesmen who understood that American isolation from any major conflict was now completely improbable.

In the spring of 1940, with the German seizure of Denmark and Norway, the blitz that swept from the Rhine through France to the Bay of Biscay, and the crippled retreat of the British Army from Dunkirk, America began to grow uneasy. By the middle of June the Regular Army's authorized strength had been increased to 375,000. By the end of August, Congress had authorized mobilization of the National Guard; six weeks later Selective Service was in operation. By the summer of 1941 the Army of the United States, composed of regulars, Guardsmen, and citizen soldiers, numbered 1,500,000. No larger peacetime force had ever been mustered by this country. It was, nevertheless, only a temporary compromise with international fact.[4]

The million men who had come into the Army through the National Guard and Selective Service could not be required to serve anywhere outside the Western Hemisphere or for more than twelve months at home. In the summer of 1941, consequently, with the Germans racing across Russia and their Japanese ally unmistakably preparing for the conquest of the far Pacific, the Army could only feebly reinforce overseas garrisons.

The attack at Pearl Harbor was less than four months away when, by a one-vote margin in the House of Representatives, the Congress passed the Selective Service Extension Act, permitting the movement of all Army components overseas and extending the term of service.[5] The congressional action can be attributed largely to the personal intervention of General George C. Marshall, who had already attained a public stature that gave weight to his urgent warning. But even he could not entirely overcome the conviction that an all-out effort for defense was unnecessary. Limitations on service, such as the release of men of the age of twenty-eight, reflected a continuing belief that there was no immediate danger.

Thus for two years, as war engulfed the world outside the Americas and the Axis drove relentlessly toward military domination of the globe, each increase in the size, efficiency, and appropriations of the armed services was the result of a corresponding decrease in the complacency of the American people. But their hesitation to abandon compromise for decisive action could not be wholly dispelled until Pearl Harbor converted the issue into a struggle for survival.

Thereafter, in the space of three and a half years, the United States produced the fighting machine that played an indispensable role in beating Germany to its knees, even while our country, almost single-handed, was conducting a decisive war against the Japanese Empire.

The revolutionary transformation of America was not achieved overnight; the fact that it was ever achieved at all was due to the existence of staunch allies and our own distance from the scene of combat. At the outset none of us could foresee the end of the struggle; few of us saw eye to eye on what was demanded of us as individuals and as a nation; but each began, step by step, to learn and to perform his allotted task.

America's transformation, in three years, from a situation of appalling danger to unparalleled might in battle was one of the two miracles that brought Jodl to our headquarters to surrender on May 7, 1945. The other was the development, over the same period, of near perfection in allied conduct of war operations. History testifies to the ineptitude of coalitions in waging war. Allied failures have been so numerous and their inexcusable blunders so common that professional soldiers had long discounted the possibility of effective allied action unless available resources were so great as to assure victory by inundation. Even Napoleon's reputation as a brilliant military leader suffered when students in staff colleges came to realize that he always fought against coalitions—and therefore against divided counsels and diverse political, economic, and military interests.

Primarily the Allied task was to utilize the resources of two great nations with the decisiveness of single authority.

There was no precedent to follow, no chart by which to steer. Where nations previously had been successful in concert against a common foe, one member of the coalition had usually been so strong as to be the dominating partner. Now it was necessary to produce effective unity out of concessions voluntarily made. The true history of the war, and more especially the history of the operations Torch and Overlord, in the Mediterranean and northwest Europe, is the story of a unity produced on the basis of this voluntary co-operation. Differences there were, differences among strong men representing strong and proud peoples, but these paled into insignificance alongside the miracle of achievement represented in the shoulder-to-shoulder march of the Allies to complete victory in the West.

On the day the war began, in 1939, I was in the Philippines, nearing completion of four years' duty as senior military assistant to General Douglas MacArthur, who had been charged with building and training an independent Filipino military establishment.

Local interest in the war was heightened by outbreaks in Manila clubs of arguments and fist fights among members of foreign consulates —Hitler was a deep-dyed villain to most but a hero to a small though vociferous element. Hirohito was rarely if ever mentioned: all attention centered on the next move of the Nazi dictator.

The news of the invasion of Poland reached us and we heard that the Prime Minister of Great Britain was to make a radio address. With my friend, Colonel Howard Smith, I listened to the declaration that Britain and Germany were again at war. It was a solemn moment, particularly so for me because I was convinced that the United States would soon find it impossible to retain a position of neutrality.

I was certain that the United States would be drawn into the whirlpool of the war, but I was mistaken as to the manner of our entry. I assumed that Japan would make no move against us until after we were committed to the European war. Moreover, I was wrong as to time. It seemed to me that we would be compelled to defend ourselves against the Axis within a year of the war's outbreak.

From 1931 onward a number of senior officers of the Army had frequently expressed to me their conviction that the world was heading straight toward another global war. I shared these views. It seemed clear that every action of the dictatorships in Japan, Germany, and Italy pointed to their determination to seize whatever territories they might happen to want, and that these ambitions would early force democratic nations into conflict. Many believed, however, that in pushing England and France to war Hitler had at last miscalculated.

They reasoned that the French Army and the British Navy together would beat him into submission; not only did they scorn the reports of skilled observers who cast suspicion on the legend of French military efficiency but they failed to consider the record of the German General Staff for striking only when cold-blooded calculations gave promise of quick success.

I called upon the President of the Philippines and told him I wanted to return home to take part in the work of intensive preparation which I was now certain would begin in the United States. President Manuel Quezon urged me to stay, but my mind was made up. I requested permission to leave the islands before the end of the year.

When my wife, my son John, and I left Manila in December, General MacArthur saw us off at the pier. It was the last time I was to see him until my postwar visit, as Chief of Staff, to his Tokyo headquarters. We talked of the gloominess of world prospects, but our forebodings turned toward Europe—not Asia.

Our trip home took us through Japan, where we spent a few days in the coastal cities. At that time numbers of American Army officers made casual tours of Japan and there was nothing unusual about a transitory visit from another lieutenant colonel. Yet a rather unusual incident occurred. Scarcely had we gone through the formalities of landing when we met, apparently by pure chance, a Japanese graduate of an American university, who described himself as an assistant postmaster general. He said he knew, from friends of his, of the nature of my work in the Philippines and, while he asked no specific questions, he was much interested in my impressions of the Filipino people. He attached himself to us as a guide for the duration of our stay. He helped us shop, taking the lead in beating down prices; he took us to vantage points for interesting views, and in a dozen ways made himself agreeable and helpful. The burden of his conversation was the need for friendly understanding between his country and ours, for which he professed great admiration and affection. He seemed to have unlimited time to devote to us and I assumed that he made it a practice to meet and talk with visiting Americans, possibly in nostalgic memory of his student days. Some weeks later, however, when I mentioned him to others who had passed through Japan shortly before or after that period, I found no one who had met him or any other governmental official.

In early January 1940, I arrived in the United States and was assigned to troop duty with the 15th Infantry at Fort Lewis, Washington. After eight years of desk and staff duty in the rarefied atmosphere of military planning and pleading, I was again in daily contact with the two fundamental elements of military effort—men and weapons.

No better assignment than mine could have been asked by a professional soldier at a time when much of the world was already at war and the eventual involvement of the United States daily became more probable. In large part the troops of the 15th were either seasoned veterans who had been with the regiment in China before its 1938 return to the States, or volunteers who had recently enlisted; the officers were all professionals.

In case of war such outfits would be the bulwark of American defense and the spearhead of our retaliation, should there be a sudden attack on us. Given time to expand our military forces, they would provide the cadres around which would be built hundreds of battalions, and from their ranks would come instructors to convert recruits by the hundred thousand into trained soldiers. In either instance there was unlimited opportunity for men and officers to prove their professional worth.

In early 1940, however, the United States Army mirrored the attitudes of the American people, as is the case today and as it was a century ago. The mass of officers and men lacked any sense of urgency. Athletics, recreation, and entertainment took precedence in most units over serious training. Some of the officers, in the long years of peace, had worn for themselves deep ruts of professional routine within which they were sheltered from vexing new ideas and troublesome problems. Others, bogged down in one grade for many years because seniority was the only basis for promotion, had abandoned all hope of progress. Possibly many of them, and many of the troops too, felt that the infantryman's day had passed.

The number of infantrymen assigned to organized units in the Army had been reduced from 56,000 on July 1, 1939, to 49,000 on January 31, 1940.[6] On the face of things, to the average foot soldier who could not foresee his role in Europe or the Pacific, this reduction might with reason have been interpreted as a sign of his early disappearance from the military scene.

The situation in weapons and equipment added little to the infantryman's esprit. The Springfield rifle was outmoded; there was no dependable defense against a modern tank or plane; troops carried wooden models of mortars and machine guns and were able to study some of our new weapons only from blueprints. Equipment of all sorts was lacking and much of that in use had been originally produced for the national Army of World War I.

Moreover, military appropriations during the thirties had restricted training to a unit basis. Even small-arms ammunition for range firing had to be rationed in occasional doles. The Army concentrated on spit and polish, retreat formations, and parades because the American people, in their abhorrence of war, denied themselves a reasonable military posture.

Military doctrine and theory, consequently, could not be supplemented with practical application; officers and men did not have the assurance that comes only with field experience and the tests of use. Nevertheless, it was apparent that the War Department was moving as rapidly as possible to be ready for the inevitable climax. Laborious preparation, against almost unbelievable difficulties, went on under the determined leadership of General Marshall. The handicaps were many.

The greatest obstacle was psychological—complacency still persisted! Even the fall of France in May 1940 fa ed to awaken us—and by "us" I mean many professional soldiers as well as others—to a full realization of danger. The commanding general of one United States division, an officer of long service and high standing, offered to bet, on the day of the French armistice, that England would not last six weeks longer—and he proposed the wager much as he would have bet on rain or shine for the morrow. It did not occur to him to think of Britain as the sole remaining belligerent standing between us and starkest danger. His attitude was typical of the great proportion of soldiers and civilians alike. Happily there were numerous exceptions whose devoted efforts accomplished more than seemed possible.

Despite the deepening of congressional concern, the nation was so unprepared to accept the seriousness of the world outlook that training could not be conducted in realistic imitation of the battlefield. We had to carry it on in soothing-syrup style calculated to rouse the least resentment from the soldiers themselves and from their families at home. Many senior officers stood in such fear of a blast in the headlines against exposing men to inclement weather or to the fatigue of extended maneuvers that they did not prescribe the only type of training that would pay dividends once the bullets began to fly. Urgent directives from above and protest from the occasional "alarmist" could not eliminate an apathy that had its roots in comfort, blindness, and wishful thinking.

The induction of the National Guard sharply increased the Army's numerical strength, particularly in infantry and anti-aircraft. Although undermanned, underequipped, and undertrained, the organizational structure of the Guard outfits was complete; only recruits, equipment, time, and the right kind of training were needed to make them effective.

Bright spots in the military picture gradually emerged. Congress in the fall of 1940 provided some money for critically needed field training. This training, under the supervision of Major General, later Lieutenant General, Lesley J. McNair, one of our ablest officers, became the chief preoccupation of the Army. From Fort Lewis the 15th Infantry, as part of the 3d Infantry Division, went on extended field maneuvers to outlying districts in the state of Washington and to the Monterey Peninsula, some distance south of San Francisco. The attendant marches, logistic planning, tactical problems, and necessary staff work provided the best possible schools for officers and men, both Regular and emergency. One of these problems involved an eleven-hundred-mile motor march, from Fort Lewis to the Jolon Ranch, south of Monterey, California. We assumed tactical conditions and during the movement tested out our control procedures, communication systems, and march discipline.

While serving in the 3d Division, I renewed a friendship of my cadet days with Major Mark W. Clark. He and I worked together constantly in many phases of the field exercises we both so much enjoyed, and I gained a lasting respect for his planning, training, and organizing ability, which I have not seen excelled in any other officer. But in answer to the rapidly expanding needs of the new headquarters springing up all over the country he soon went to Washington as an assistant to General McNair, while, in November, I was again removed from direct command duty to become the chief of staff of the 3d Division. That post was to be mine only four months, when again I was transferred, this time to be chief of staff of the IX Army Corps, which had shortly before been established at Fort Lewis. This assignment brought me my first emergency promotion; I became a temporary colonel in March 1941.

The corps commander was Major General Kenyon A. Joyce. On his staff I met an exceptionally keen group of men, three of whom I tried, with some success, to keep close to me throughout the ensuing war years. These were all of relatively low rank at the time but they emerged from the war as Lieutenant General Lucian K. Truscott, Major General Willard G. Wyman, and Colonel James Curtis. Such men as these were ready, even anxious, to support every measure that promised to add realism and thoroughness to training, but it was an uphill fight.

During the spring of 1941 every post and camp was astir with the business of building the Army of the United States, into which had been fused all elements of the country's military front—Regular, Guard, and Reserve, augmented by the hundreds of thousands of men inducted through Selective Service. For us at Fort Lewis the process of development began on September 16, 1940, when the advance echelon of the 41st Infantry Division arrived on the post. Within a short time the entire division and other units of the National Guard were encamped there.

By the following spring the entire West Coast area was in a state of almost endless movement—men arriving in groups for assignment to units; cadres of men being withdrawn from units to form new organizations; officers and men leaving for and returning from specialist schools; cities of tents and barracks with all the multiple utilities of modern living—hospitals, water systems, light and power plants—springing up overnight where before had been open fields.

Our objective was to turn out physically fit men, schooled in their military and technical jobs, adjusted to discipline and unit teamwork, with the greatest possible measure of a soldier's pride in his mission; because of public unreadiness to support true battle training we could not hope to turn out masses of toughened fighting men, emotionally and professionally ready for warfare.

But even our limited objective absorbed all the energy officers and men could give it. For those on staff work the days became ceaseless rounds of planning, directing, inspecting; compromising what had been commanded with what could be done; adjusting assignments of men and quotas of vehicles to the shortages that continually plagued us; striving always to keep pace in our area with the Army-wide pace.

In June 1941, I was assigned to Lieutenant General Walter Krueger's Third Army as his chief of staff at San Antonio headquarters. There I was brought closer to the problems of the Army of the United States as a whole. The four tactical armies, into which the ground forces were divided, varied in numerical strength; but all were alike in their core of Regular units, around which had been assembled the Guard outfits, with vacancies in all units filled by Reserve officers and soldiers from Selective Service. Consequently the reports coming across my desk at Fort Sam Houston on the training, morale, and capacity of our divisions and units in the field were accurate indications of our progress throughout the United States.

The situation contrasted favorably to that of a year earlier. The Army of the United States now totaled approximately 1,500,000 officers and men. However, grave deficiencies still existed. Vehicles, modern tanks, and anti-aircraft equipment were critically short. Supporting air formations were almost non-existent. Moreover, the approaching expiration of a year's service for National Guard units and Selective Service soldiers was a constant worry, not to be relieved until two months later. In June we feared the exodus of men, beginning in September, would not be matched by a comparable inflow.

But even the rapid growth of the Army and the latest manifestations of Axis military power had not jolted some Regular officers out of their rigid devotion to obsolete tenets and routine. For their blindness there was no longer an acceptable excuse. In the civilian components another type of difficulty was encountered. Many Guard and Reserve officers had grown old in the prewar struggle to maintain a citizen security force, and now that their efforts of the twenties and thirties were bearing fruit, they themselves were physically unable to meet the demands of field duty in combat echelons.

General Krueger himself was one of the senior officers of the Army. A private, corporal, and sergeant in the late 1890s, he had an Army-wide reputation as a hard-bitten soldier. But through more than forty years of service he had kept pace with every military change, and few officers had a clearer grasp of what another war would demand of the Army; few were physically tougher or more active. Relentlessly driving himself, he had little need of driving others—they were quick to follow his example.

His Third Army was now directed to concentrate in Louisiana for a great maneuver, with Lieutenant General Ben Lear's Second Army as its opponent. Not one of our officers on the active list had commanded a unit as large as a division in the first World War. Like a vast laboratory experiment, the maneuvers would prove the worth of ideas, men, weapons, and equipment. More than 270,000 men—the largest army ever gathered in the United States for a single tactical operation—were assembled by General Krueger that September. Moving out of Second Army camps at the same time were another 130,000.[7]

The beneficial results of that great maneuver were incalculable. It accustomed the troops to mass teamwork; it speeded up the process of eliminating the unfit; it brought to the specific attention of seniors certain of the younger men who were prepared to carry out the most difficult assignments in staff and command; and it developed among responsible leaders skill in the handling of large forces in the fields. Practical experience was gained in large-scale field supply of troops. No comparable peacetime attempt had ever been made by Americans in the road movement of food, fuel, and ammunition from railhead and depot to a constantly shifting front line. Advance planning, consequently, was thorough and intensive; as is always the case, it paid off.

"The essential effectiveness of supply," General McNair, expert in the conduct and assessment of maneuvers, told the assembled staffs in a critique of the operations, "was an outstanding feature of the maneuvers. The magnitude of the problem alone was sufficient to warrant apprehension as to whether the troops would be supplied adequately. Combat commanders and the services alike deserve the highest praise for the results achieved." The efficiency of American trucks in the movement of troops and supply, demonstrated so magnificently three years later in the race across France, was forecast on the roads of Louisiana in September 1941.

In the Third Army the officer directly responsible for supply efficiency was Lieutenant Colonel LeRoy Lutes. His brilliance in this type of work was to bring him, long before the end of this war, the three stars of a lieutenant general.

Many of the military faults revealed in the maneuvers, General McNair believed, had their root in discipline. "There is no question," he said, "that many of the weaknesses developed in these maneuvers are repeated again and again for lack of discipline. Our troops are capable of the best of discipline. If they lack it, leadership is faulty. A commander who cannot develop proper discipline must be replaced."[8]

During this time I had my first important introduction to the press camera, which, since the days of Brady, has been a prominent feature of the American military scene. In the fall of 1941, however, flash bulbs were a fairly novel element in my daily life and I was only an unknown face to the men who used them. During the critique at Camp Polk a group shot was made of General Krueger, Major A. V. Golding, a British military observer, and me; in the caption my two companions were correctly identified, but I appeared as "Lt. Col. D. D. Ersenbeing" —at least the initials were right.

The maneuvers provided me with lessons and experience that I appreciated more and more as subsequent months rolled by. We conducted in Louisiana an extensive test of the usefulness of the cub plane for liaison and observation purposes. Its worth was demonstrated so conclusively that later, in the War Department, I was able to argue successfully, under the leadership of Assistant Secretary of War John J. McCloy, for its inclusion in the normal equipment of every division. These planes enabled our heavy and long-range artillery to gain an accuracy and quickness of adjustment previously restricted to the light guns within eyeshot of the target; and field commanders could get a grasp of the tactical situation—terrain, avenues of movement, concentrations of troops and artillery—almost as complete as in the eighteenth century, when the opposing commanders, from horseback or a hillock, could view all the regiments committed to battle.

At the end of the maneuvers I was promoted to the temporary grade of brigadier general.

October and November were as busy as the months preceding maneuvers. Measures to correct defects revealed in Louisiana were begun at the unit level; in many cases the return movement offered an immediate opportunity. Some officers, both Regular and National Guard, had of necessity to be relieved from command; controversies and rumors, following on this step, required quick action to prevent injury to morale among officers and troops.

Although the Washington negotiations with the Japanese ambassadors were nearing their dramatic climax at the beginning of December, a relaxation of tenseness among the civilian population was reflected within the Army. It seemed that the Japanese bluff had been called and war, at least temporarily, averted in the Pacific. On the Russian front the Germans had been stopped before Leningrad, Moscow, and Sevastopol. My daily paper, on December 4, editorialized that it was now evident the Japanese had no desire for war with the United States. A columnist a few days later reported that in Washington there was a strong feeling that the crisis in the Pacific had been postponed, although a week earlier betting odds in Washington circles had been 10 to 1 on immediate war.

On the afternoon of December 7 at Fort Sam Houston, Texas, tired out from the long and exhausting staff work of the maneuvers and their aftermath, I went to bed with orders that under no circumstances was I to be disturbed. My dreams were of a two weeks' leave I was going to take, during which my wife and I were going to West Point to spend Christmas with our plebe son, John. But even dreams like these—and my strict orders—could be shattered with impunity by the aide who brought the news that we were at war.

Within an hour of the Pearl Harbor attack orders began pouring into Third Army Headquarters from the War Department. There were orders for the immediate transfer of anti-aircraft units to the West Coast, where the terrified citizens hourly detected phantom bombers in the sky; orders for the establishment of anti-sabotage measures; orders for careful guarding of industrial plants; orders for reconnaissance along our Southern border to prevent the entrance of spies; and orders to insure the safety of ports along the Gulf of Mexico. There were orders for rushing heavy bodies of troops to the West in anticipation of any attacks the Japanese might contemplate. In turn General Krueger's headquarters had to send out instructions to a hundred stations as rapidly as they could be prepared and checked. It was a period of intense activity.

Immediacy of movement was the keynote. The normal channels of administration were abandoned; the chain of command was compressed at meetings where all echelons got their instructions in a single briefing; the slow and methodical process of drawing up detailed movement orders that specified to the last jot of equipment what should be taken with the troops, how it should be crated and marked, was ignored. A single telephone call would start an infantry unit across the continent; troops and equipment entrained with nothing in writing to show by what authority they moved. Guns were loaded on flatcars, if flatcars were available; on gondolas if they could be had; in freight cars if nothing else was at hand. The men traveled in de luxe Pullmans, in troop sleepers, in modern coaches, and in day cars that had been obsolete and sidetracked in the yards for a generation and were now drafted for emergency troop movements.

I had five days of this. Early in the morning of December 12 the telephone connecting us directly to the War Department in Washington began to jangle. I answered and someone inquired, "Is that you, Ike?"

"Yes."

"The Chief says for you to hop a plane and get up here right away. Tell your boss that formal orders will come through later." The "Chief" was General Marshall, and the man at the other end of the line was Colonel Walter Bedell Smith, who was later to become my close friend and chief of staff throughout the European operations.

This message was a hard blow. During the first World War every one of my frantic efforts to get to the scene of action had been defeated —for reasons which had no validity to me except that they all boiled down to "War Department orders." I hoped in any new war to stay with troops. Being ordered to a city where I had already served a total of eight years would mean, I thought, a virtual repetition of my experience in World War I. Heavyhearted, I telephoned my wife to pack a bag, and within the hour I was headed for the War Department.

I had probably been ordered to Washington, I decided, because of my recently completed tour in the Philippines. Within a matter of hours after their assault on Pearl Harbor the Japanese had launched against the Philippines an air attack that quickly reduced our inadequate air forces to practical impotence.[9] It was the spot upon which official and public interest was centered, and General Marshall undoubtedly wanted someone on his staff who was reasonably familiar with conditions then current in the islands, who was acquainted with both the Philippines Department of the United States Army and the defense organization of the Philippines Commonwealth, which war had caught halfway in its planned development.

The Commonwealth defense organization dated back to 1935, when General MacArthur was asked by newly elected President Quezon to plan and build a military force able to defend the islands; on July 4, 1946, when the Commonwealth was to become an independent republic, United States troops were to be withdrawn and armed defense would thereafter be a Philippines function. On General MacArthur's acceptance, a military mission of American officers was formed and I was assigned to it as his senior assistant.

In 1935 we planned to turn out each year during the coming ten, through a program of universal military training, approximately 30,-000 soldiers with five and a half months' basic experience. At first we would form units of only platoon size, but within four or five years we hoped to produce regiments and by 1946, with a total of 300,000 men who had the minimum basic training, we would be able to form thirty divisions.

During the same transitional period the Philippines Department of the United States Army, while working closely with the Commonwealth defense force and supplying it with officer and enlisted instructors, arms, and equipment, was planning also for its own part in defense should war come before Philippine independence. In such a contingency it was planned to withdraw our troops on the main island of Luzon into the Bataan Peninsula across from Corregidor so that the two areas would constitute one almost impregnable position where our forces could hold until reinforcements arrived. In 1938, I witnessed a maneuver demonstrating this plan, and shortly after I left the islands it was repeated on a larger scale.

Traveling to Washington on December 12, 1941, I had no clear idea of the progress of fighting in the Philippines. The reports we had received at Fort Sam Houston were fragmentary and obscure. Undoubtedly the Japanese would not dare by-pass the islands. But the direction and weight of their assault was still unknown when I arrived at the War Department.

Chapter 2

GLOBAL
WAR

WASHINGTON IN WARTIME HAS BEEN VARIOUSLY
described in numbers of pungent epigrams, all signifying chaos. Tradi-
tionally the government, including the service departments, has always been as unprepared for war and its all-embracing problems as
the country itself; and the incidence of emergency has, under an
awakened sense of overwhelming responsibility, resulted in confusion,
intensified by a swarming influx of contract seekers and well-meaning
volunteers. This time, however, the War Department had achieved a
gratifying level of efficiency before the outbreak of war. So far as my
own observations during the months I served there would justify a
judgment, this was due to the vision and determination of one man,
General Marshall. Naturally he had support. He was backed up by
the President and by many of our ablest leaders in Congress and in
key positions in the Administration. But it would have been easy for
General Marshall, during 1940–41, to drift along with the current, to
let things slide in anticipation of a normal end to a brilliant military
career—for he had earned, throughout the professional Army, a reputation for brilliance. Instead he had for many months deliberately followed the hard way, determined that at whatever cost to himself or to
anyone else the Army should be decently prepared for the conflict
which he daily, almost hourly, expected.

I reported to General Marshall early on Sunday morning, December
14, and for the first time in my life talked to him for more than two
minutes at a time. It was the fourth time I had ever seen him. Without
preamble or waste of time the Chief of Staff outlined the general
situation, naval and military, in the western Pacific.

The Navy informed him that the Pacific fleet would be unable for some months to participate in major operations. The Navy's carriers remained intact because they had not been at Pearl Harbor at the time of the attack,[1] but supporting vessels for the carriers were so few in number that great restrictions would have to be placed upon their operation. Moreover, at that moment there was no assurance that the Japanese would not quickly launch a major amphibious assault upon Hawaii or possibly even upon the mainland, and the Navy felt that these carriers should be reserved for reconnaissance work and defense, except only when some great emergency demanded from them other employment. The Navy Department had given General Marshall no estimate of the date when they expected the fleet to be sufficiently repaired and strengthened to take offensive action in the Pacific area.

The garrison in Hawaii was so weak that there was general agreement between the War and Navy Departments that its air and ground strength should be reinforced as rapidly as possible and should take priority over other efforts in the Pacific.[2]

At the time of the Japanese attack American army and air forces in the Philippines had reached an aggregate of 30,000, including the Philippine Scouts,[3] formations integrated into the United States Army, but with all enlisted personnel and some of the officers native Filipinos.

United States outfits provided the garrison for Corregidor and its smaller supporting forts. Other American units were organized into the Philippine Division, which consisted of Philippine Scout units and the 31st Infantry Regiment. National Guard units—three field artillery regiments, one anti-aircraft artillery regiment, one infantry regiment, two tank battalions, and service troops—had recently arrived as reinforcements.[4]

The air strength had been increased during 1941, and on the day of attack there were 35 modern bombers, B-17s, stationed in the Philippines. Present also were 220 airplanes of the fighter type, not all of them in operating readiness.[5] General Marshall knew that this air detachment had been hit and badly damaged during the initial Japanese attack, but he had no report upon the circumstances of that action.

There were known to be shortages in essential items of supply, but in the matter of food and normal types of ammunition it was thought there would be little difficulty, provided the garrison was given time to concentrate these at their points of greatest usefulness.

The Navy Yard at Cavite, just outside Manila, had been damaged very severely by Japanese bombers on December 10. That portion of the modest task force comprising the Asiatic Fleet which was disposed at or near Manila consisted mainly of small divisions of submarines. The largest warship in the Asiatic Fleet was the heavy cruiser, *Houston,* at Iloilo.⁶

Against a strong and sustained attack, forces such as these could not hold out indefinitely. All the evidence indicated that the Japanese intended to overrun the Philippines as rapidly as possible, and the problem was to determine what could now be done.

General Marshall took perhaps twenty minutes to describe all this, and then abruptly asked, "What should be our general line of action?"

I thought a second and, hoping I was showing a poker face, answered, "Give me a few hours."

"All right," he said, and I was dismissed.

Significantly and characteristically, he did not even hint at one of the most important factors in the problem: the psychological effects of the Philippine battle upon people in the United States and throughout the Pacific. Clearly he felt that anyone stupid enough to overlook this consideration had no business wearing the star of a brigadier general.

I took my problem to a desk assigned me in the division of the War Department then known as "War Plans," headed by my old friend Brigadier General Leonard T. Gerow. Obviously, if I were to be of any service to General Marshall in the War Department, I would have to earn his confidence: the logic of this, my first answer, would have to be unimpeachable, and the answer would have to be prompt. A curious echo from the long ago came to my aid.

For three years, soon after the first World War, I served under one of the most accomplished soldiers of our time, Major General Fox Conner. One of the subjects on which he talked to me most was allied command, its difficulties and its problems. Another was George C. Marshall. Again and again General Conner said to me, "We cannot escape another great war. When we go into that war it will be in company with allies. Systems of single command will have to be worked out. We must not accept the 'co-ordination' concept under which Foch was compelled to work. We must insist on individual and single responsibility—leaders will have to learn how to overcome nationalistic considerations in the conduct of campaigns. One man who can do it is Marshall—he is close to being a genius."

With that memory I determined that my answer should be short, emphatic, and based on reasoning in which I honestly believed. No oratory, plausible argument, or glittering generality would impress anyone entitled to be labeled genius by Fox Conner.

The question before me was almost unlimited in its implications, and my qualifications for approaching it were probably those of the average hard-working Army officer of my age. Naturally I had pursued the military courses of the Army's school system. Soon after completing the War College in 1928, I went to serve as a special assistant in the office of the Assistant Secretary of War, where my duties were quickly expanded to include confidential work for the Chief of Staff of the Army.

In these positions I had been forced to examine world-wide military matters and to study concretely such subjects as the mobilization and composition of armies, the role of air forces and navies in war, tendencies toward mechanization, and the acute dependence of all elements of military life upon the industrial capacity of the nation. This last was to me of especial importance because of my intense belief that large-scale motorization and mechanization and the development of air forces in unprecedented strength would characterize successful military forces of the future. On this subject I wrote a number of studies and reports. Holding these convictions, I knew that any sane preparation for war involved also sound plans for the prompt mobilization of industry. The years devoted to work of this kind opened up to me an almost new world. During that time I met and worked with many people whose opinions I respected highly, in both military and civil life. Among these an outstanding figure was Mr. Bernard Baruch, for whom my admiration was and is profound. I still believe that if Mr. Baruch's recommendations for universal price fixing and his organizational plans[7] had been completely and promptly adopted in December 1941 this country would have saved billions in money—possibly much in time and therefore in lives.

From tasks such as these I had gone, in 1935, to the Philippines. Now, six years later, I was back in the War Department, the nation was at war, and the Philippines were in deadly danger.

So I began my concentration on General Marshall's question. Our naval situation in the western Pacific, as outlined by the Chief of Staff, was at that moment completely depressing. The fleet could not attempt any aggressive action far from a secure base and dared not venture with surface vessels into Philippine waters. The clamor of ground and air commanders in Hawaii and on the West Coast for defensive strength—clamors emphasized in hysterical terms by mayors, city

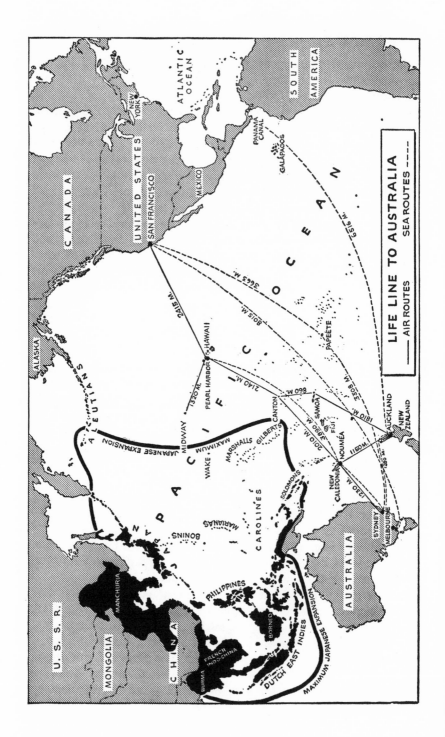

LIFE LINE TO AUSTRALIA
AIR ROUTES ———
SEA ROUTES -----

councils, and congressmen—would, if answered, have absorbed far more than all United States shipping, troops, and immediately available anti-aircraft force then in existence.

It was painfully clear that the Philippines themselves could not, at that time, be reinforced directly by land and sea forces. Any hope of sending major reinforcements into the islands had to be based upon such future rehabilitation of our Navy as would permit it to operate safely in the Philippines area. At the moment there was no way of estimating when this could be done.

To prolong the duration of the defense while the Navy was undergoing repair, there was the possibility that we could ship to the islands vitally needed items by submarine and blockade runners, and, provided we could keep open the necessary line of communications, something could be shipped by air. Australia was the base nearest to the Philippines that we could hope to establish and maintain, and the necessary line of air communications would therefore follow along the islands intervening between that continent and the Philippines.

If we were to use Australia as a base it was mandatory that we procure a line of communications leading to it. This meant that we must instantly move to save Hawaii, Fiji, New Zealand, and New Caledonia, and we had to make certain of the safety of Australia itself.

It seemed possible, though not probable, that the Netherlands Indies, in some respects the richest area in the world in natural resources, could be denied to the Jap invader, who would soon be desperately in need of Indies oil to continue his offensives. Unless this could be done short-range fighter planes could not be flown into the Philippines; and fighter planes were vital to successful defense.

In spite of difficulties, risks, and fierce competition for every asset we had, a great nation such as ours, no matter how unprepared for war, could not afford cold-bloodedly to turn its back upon our Filipino wards and the many thousand Americans, troops and civilians, in the archipelago. We had to do whatever was remotely possible for the hapless islands, particularly by air support and by providing vital supplies, although the end result might be no more than postponement of disaster. And we simply had to save the air life line through Australia, New Zealand, Fiji, and Hawaii.

With these bleak conclusions I marched back to the Chief of Staff. "General," I said, "it will be a long time before major reinforcements can go to the Philippines, longer than the garrison can hold out with any driblet assistance, if the enemy commits major forces to their reduction. But we must do everything for them that is humanly possible. The people of China, of the Philippines, of the Dutch East Indies will be watching us. They may excuse failure but they will not excuse abandonment. Their trust and friendship are important to us. Our base must be Australia, and we must start at once to expand it and to secure our communications to it. In this last we dare not fail. We must take great risks and spend any amount of money required."

He merely replied, "I agree with you." His tone implied that I had been given the problem as a check to an answer he had already reached. He added, "Do your best to save them." With that I went to work; my partner was Brigadier General, later General, Brehon Somervell, War Department supply and procurement chief. Every day—no matter what the other preoccupation—I met with him in the desperate hope of uncovering some new method of approach to a problem that defied solution. General Marshall maintained an intensive interest in everything we did and frequently initiated measures calculated to give some help, particularly on the morale side. He awarded unit citations to every organization serving in the Philippines, he promptly directed the highest promotions and decorations for General MacArthur, and he supported without stint every idea and scheme our imagination could suggest.

On my desk memorandum pad, which by accident survived, I find this note, made on January 1, 1942: "I've been insisting that the Far East is critical—and no sideshows should be undertaken until air and ground there are in satisfactory state. Instead we are taking on Magnet, Gymnast, etc." Three days later appeared: "At last we're getting some things on the road to Australia. The air plan includes four pursuit groups, and two heavy, two medium, and one light bombardment groups. But we've got to have ships—and we need them now! Tempers are short. There are lots of amateur strategists on the job. I'd give anything to be back in the field." My obvious irritation was possibly caused by the knowledge that much time would elapse before the "air plan" could be implemented.

On December 22, when the Pensacola Convoy arrived at Brisbane, we began the establishment of our Australian base.[8] This quick start was largely the result of accident. On the day of the Pearl Harbor attack numbers of our ships were en route to the Philippines with troops, pianes, and supplies. The Navy counseled that they be ordered to return to the United States or seek refuge in Hawaii, since no one could be sure that the Japanese would not set up an interceptive net for them; those only a few days out of port did return. But the War Department insisted that one convoy of five ships—the *Holbrook* and the *Republic,* with 5000 troops aboard, and the *Meigs, Holstead,* and *Bloemfontein,* loaded with equipment and supplies—be ordered to proceed with all possible speed to Australia.[9] This was the beginning of the great base that was eventually to be General MacArthur's launching platform for the liberation of the Philippines.

Reinforcement of this Australian base and the island steppingstones to it was a continuous process throughout the winter. By February 21 our overseas strength in officers and men exceeded 245,000, the largest concentrations being in the Pacific, where there were on that date 115,877, exclusive of 29,566 in Alaska and the Aleutians. In the Caribbean the garrisons by then numbered 79,095. In the European theater there were as yet only 3785 officers and men, but two divisions were en route. The overseas garrisons of the Eastern Defense Command numbered 15,876, most of whom were in Iceland.[10]

Although at that time American forces were fighting only in the Philippines, there was literally almost no spot throughout the length and breadth of the continents and the oceans that did not present at least one problem for the planning staff of the War Department. In Alaska we were wide open to attack and there existed the definite possibility that the enemy might succeed in establishing himself in an Alaskan airfield, from which he could bomb, with one-way attacks, numbers of our important cities. The coast of Brazil was needed so that we could secure on the shoulder of the South American continent a base from which to combat submarines. That area had an added importance because it provided also a steppingstone for airplane flights across the Atlantic. With the Mediterranean closed, the shortest route to the Middle East theater of war was over central Africa; we had to establish an air route across that undeveloped continent.

Russia, of course, was now an Ally; and another problem was to determine the ways and means through which effective help could be given her so that she could successfully maintain herself against the common enemy. The Middle East, with its vast oil resources, was still another region whose safety was important to America. It provided one of the avenues by which supplies might be sent to Russia and we had the problem of early establishment of communications northward from the Persian Gulf into Russian territory. Dozens of islands in the Pacific had to be garrisoned if we were to maintain the security of communications to our Australian base. Burma was an·

other area in which we had a great interest because running through it was the last remaining line of supply for China.

As a prerequisite to everything else we had to stop the Jap short of countries that were vital to our successful prosecution of the war—Australia and India.[1] And all of us tirelessly sought ways and means of helping the defenders of the Philippines.

Problems of disposing troops, including anti-aircraft defenses, at key points within the United States itself; of making distribution and allocations of such weapons as we then possessed; of establishing bases, particularly air bases, in South America, Africa, and throughout the world; of attending to our own reorganization within the War Department; and of developing outline plans into actual directives for operations, required eighteen-hour days for all of us.

Fortunately for me, at this hectic time my youngest brother, Milton, and his wife, Helen, were living just outside Washington at Falls Church. During the weeks following my arrival in the War Department, until my wife could pack our belongings at San Antonio and re-establish a home in Washington, they insisted that their home be mine. My brother was already in war work in the government and his hours were scarcely less exhausting than mine. Yet every night when I reached their house, regardless of the hour, which averaged something around midnight, both would be waiting up for me with a snack of midnight supper and a pot of coffee. I cannot remember ever seeing their house in daylight during all the months I served in Washington.

Constantly General Somervell and I sought for one more hope to hold out to the Philippines garrison. In the final result all our efforts proved feeble enough, but after many months of contemplation I do not yet see what more could have been done. One proposition that was frequently advanced, both in the public press and by enthusiastic but ignorant professionals, was to dispatch fighter craft by carrier to some point within flying range of the islands and from that point to fly them in to land bases for operations against the Japanese invader. The first difficulty encountered was final in itself.

The Navy Department stated flatly that none of the carriers they then had could be supported with the necessary cruisers and destroyers to risk an operation that could place it, even for the required fleeting moment, within fighter range of the Philippines. Other obstacles, almost equally decisive, were exposed by a full examination of the proposal, but this one alone obviously made further entertainment of the idea completely futile.

Many months later I read the assertion that while the Philippines were forlornly battling for their existence United States bombers were flying in endless streams to Great Britain and materials needed in the islands were being saved for the North African campaign. That was far from the actual fact.

We had only one light bombardment squadron in England, which arrived in May 1942, and there was no American heavy bomber unit there until the following month.[12] The African campaign was not even an approved project until July of the same year. Both these dates were after the surrender of Bataan and Corregidor. The crux of the matter was that Japan had command of the seas surrounding the Philippines; we could not furnish substantial help until we could develop strength to break the encirclement.

As early as December 1941 we determined to try a system of blockade running into the Philippines. We sent officers to Australia with money to hire, at no matter what fantastic prices, the men and ships needed to carry supplies into the islands and to smuggle them into the beleaguered garrison.[13]

The man we sent to Australia to head up this particular effort was a former Secretary of War, Colonel, soon Brigadier General, Patrick J. Hurley. He had reported to the Operations Division one noon to volunteer his services to the government. At that moment we were in search of a man of his known energy and fearlessness to invigorate our filibustering attempts out of Australia and his offer was immediately accepted.

I asked him, "When can you be ready to report for duty?"

"Now."

"Be back here at midnight," I instructed him, "prepared for extended field service."

Although he seemed to change color slightly, he never batted an eye but replied, "That will give me time to see my lawyers and change my will."

Immediately he was recommended for the grade of brigadier general. Knowing that he would be confirmed as such before he could reach Australia, Gerow and I each donated a star from our uniforms, and—pinning them on the ex-Secretary's shoulders—sent him happily from our office. At one o'clock that night he was on a plane for Australia.

For the transport of a few very critical items the Navy provided submarines. The Philippines garrison was always short of proper fuses for their anti-aircraft and artillery, but we did succeed in sending them small quantities by this means.[14]

We began the assembly in Australia of fifty-two dive bombers, which we hoped to be able to fly to the Philippines via staging fields on the intervening islands.[15] While all this was going on we continued to rush driblets of ground reinforcements to many threatened spots in the Pacific, from Alaska southward. They went to Hawaii, the Fiji Islands, New Caledonia, Tonga Tabu, New Zealand, Australia, and many smaller places.

To give one example of the desperate extremes to which we were reduced: I learned by sheer accident late one evening that the Navy, in order to place a small garrison at Efate in the New Hebrides, considered an important spot, had directed bluejackets to be detached from a carrier and temporarily used for the purpose. This was unthinkable. Each of our few carriers was worth its weight in gold. By scurrying about we determined, within a few minutes, that an Army battalion was available in the critical area to do the job, and it was moved in,[16] but this was the type of thing to which all of us had to resort. The incident, small as it was, also brought home to me the sketchy and unsatisfactory character of our contacts with the Navy.

Mr. Quezon, then in Corregidor with General MacArthur, radioed to President Roosevelt in early February a plea for him to seek the neutralization of the Philippines, with each contestant agreeing to withdraw its troops.[17] In view of our helpless situation there at that time, neutralization of the islands would have been an immediate military advantage and would, of course, have prevented tremendous suffering and privation on the part of the defending garrison and the population. However, its public proposal would not only have been greeted with scorn by the Japanese: such a confession of weakness would have had unfortunate psychological reverberations. None of us believed for a moment that the proposal represented a betrayal on the part of President Quezon. We felt that he was sturdily loyal but merely submitting for consideration a plan that, in his helpless situation, appeared to him as the possible salvation of his country. Receipt of the proposal was a bombshell—but the idea was instantly repudiated by the President and the Chief of Staff.

A principal duty of War Department planners was to recommend a scheme of operations for the Army in the waging of war against Germany and Japan. Our enemies, widely separated geographically, were each in possession of a rich empire. We had to attack to win.

In late December, Prime Minister Churchill came to Washington, accompanied by the British Chiefs of Staff. These were Admiral Sir Dudley Pound for the Navy, General Sir Alan Brooke for the Army, and Air Chief Marshal Sir Charles Portal for the Air Force. At that time the old War Plans Division, under General Gerow, was still in existence and most of the staff liaison work with the British group was carried on by him and other members of the staff.

The conference[18] had two principal purposes, the first of which was to organize a workable system by which the American and British Chiefs of Staff could operate effectively as a team. The gist of the arrangement made was that each of the British Chiefs of Staff designate a representative to serve in Washington, in close contact with the American staffs. The British named Sir John Dill as the head of this mission and in that capacity he continued to render outstanding service until his death in 1944. A second purpose of the conference was to confirm earlier agreements[19] upon the region in which should first be concentrated major forces of the two nations. The staffs saw no reason to change prior conclusions that the European enemy should be the first object of our attacks. There were, of course, numerous and important other subjects of discussion but from my place on the fringe of the conference it seemed to me that these were the two greatest accomplishments.

Stated in simple form, the basic reasons for first attacking the European members of the Axis were:

The European Axis was the only one of our two separated enemies that could be attacked simultaneously by the three powerful members of the Allied nations, Russia, Great Britain, and the United States. The United States was the only one of the coalition free to choose which of its enemies to attack first. But if we should decide to go full out immediately against Japan, we would leave the Allies divided, with two members risking defeat or, at the best, struggling indecisively against the great European fortress. Meanwhile America, carrying the war alone to Japan, would always be faced with the necessity, after a Pacific victory, of undertaking the conquest of Hitler's empire with prostrated or badly weakened Allies. Further, and vitally important, it was not known at that time how long Russia could hold out against the repeated attacks of the Wehrmacht. No effort against Japan could possibly help Russia stay in the war. The only way aid could be given that country, aside from shipping her supplies, was by engaging in the European conflict in the most effective way possible. Finally, the defeat of the European Axis would liberate British forces to apply against Japan.

As far as I know, the wisdom of the plan to turn the weight of our power against the European enemy before attempting an all-out campaign against Japan has never been questioned by any real student of strategy. However—and here was the rub—it was easy enough to state this purpose as a principle but it was to prove difficult indeed to develop a feasible plan to implement the idea and to secure its approval by the military staffs of two nations.

Within the War Department staff basic plans for European invasion began slowly to take shape during January and February 1942.[20] As always, time was the critical element in the problem. Yet everywhere delay was imposed upon us! It profited nothing to wail about unpreparedness. It is a characteristic of military problems that they yield to nothing but harsh reality; things must be reduced to elemental simplicity and answers must be clear, almost obvious. Everywhere men and materials were needed. The wave of Japanese aggression had not then reached full tide, and everything upon which we in the United States could lay our hands had necessarily to go to the Southwest Pacific to prevent complete inundation. Aside from preserving lines of air and sea communications to Australia, we had to hold the Indian bastion at all costs; otherwise a junction between Japanese and German forces would be accomplished through the Persian Gulf. Prevention of this catastrophe became the chief preoccupation of our British partners.

The prospect of the two industrial empires of Japan and Germany drawing freely upon the vast resources of rubber, oil, and the other riches of the Netherlands Indies was too black a picture to contemplate. The Middle East, of course, had to be held; if it should fall and the German U-boats were able to proceed through the Red Sea into the Indian Ocean, it was doubtful that India could be saved. Moreover, Middle East oil was a great prize.

In the late winter of 1941–42 the U-boat campaign in the Atlantic was at almost the height of its effectiveness. We were monthly losing ships, including valuable tankers, by the score. A typical month was March 1942, when we lost in the Atlantic and Arctic areas 88 Allied and neutral ships of 507,502 tonnage. During May 1942, when 120 Allied and neutral vessels were sunk in the same waters, the United States sustained its highest loss of merchant shipping in any one month of the war—40 vessels.[21] For a time even our vital sea lines to South

America were in peril. Shipping was at a premium; simultaneously we needed every type of fighting vessel, cargo and personnel ship.

Already we had learned the lesson that, while air power alone might not win a victory, no great victory is possible without air superiority. Consequently the need for airplanes in vast numbers competed with all other needs—shipping, cannon, tanks, rifles, ammunition, food, clothing, heavy construction material, and everything from beeswax to battleships that goes to make up a nation's fighting power.

We had to do the best we could, with almost nothing to distribute but deficits, in stemming the onslaughts of our enemies, but plans for victory had to look far ahead to the day when the airplanes, the battle fleets, the shipping, the landing craft, and the fighting formations would allow us to pass to the offensive and to maintain it. It was in this realm of the future—a future so uncertain as to be one almost of make-believe—that the projected plan for European invasion had to take its initial form.

Plans for the future could not take priority over the needs of the day. In a desperate attempt to save the Netherlands Indies and Singapore, General Sir Archibald P. Wavell, in late December 1941, was sent to Java from India to become the first Allied commander in chief.[22] The directive for his organization was laboriously written in Washington by the Combined Chiefs of Staff, in the hope that out of unified effort might spring a miracle. Wavell never had a chance.

Yet the Washington effort itself was a valuable lesson. For the first time we had the concrete task of writing a charter for a supreme commander, a charter that would insure his authority in the field but still protect the fundamental interests of each participating nation. We found it necessary to go painstakingly into rights of appeal and scope of authority in operations and service organizations. Procedures to be followed if major differences should be encountered were a matter of concern. We had not yet come to appreciate fully the nature of an allied command.

No written agreement for the establishment of an allied command can hold up against nationalistic considerations should any of the contracting powers face disaster through support of the supreme commander's decisions. Every commander in the field possesses direct disciplinary power over all subordinates of his own nationality and of his own service; any disobedience or other offense is punishable by such measures as the commander believes appropriate, including the court-martial of the offender. But such authority and power cannot be given by any country to an individual of another nation. Only trust and confidence can establish the authority of an allied commander in chief so firmly that he need never fear the absence of this legal power.

Success in such organizations rests ultimately upon personalities; statesmen, generals, admirals, and air marshals—even populations—must develop confidence in the concept of single command and in the organization and the leader by which the single command is exercised. No binding regulation, law, or custom can apply to all its parts —only a highly developed sense of mutual confidence can solve the problem. Possibly this truth has equal applicability in peace.

Throughout the first winter of war the news from the East Indian region was increasingly bad and the Navy did not have sufficient strength to undertake major operations far from a friendly base. Every troop and cargo ship upon which we could lay our hands was dispatched hurriedly to the Southwest Pacific. But we had so little!

The transport of personnel without heavy equipment did not involve elaborate arrangements when fast ships were available. These vessels depended solely on their speed for safety against the submarine. The British gave us the use of some of the fastest and largest passenger ships afloat. Among these was the *Queen Mary*.

One day we dispatched her, without escort, from an Eastern port in the United States to Australia, loaded with 14,000 American troops. It would have been only bad luck of the worst kind if a submarine had got close enough to attack her successfully. Moreover, we believed that even if one torpedo should strike her she would probably have enough remaining speed to escape from any submarine of the type then possessed by the Germans. However, such probabilities could provide no assurance that she would get through.

On that trip the *Queen Mary* had to put into a Brazilian port for fuel. We were horrified to intercept a radio from an Italian in Rio who reported her presence to the Italian Government and upon her departure actually gave the direction upon which she set out to sea. For the next week we lived in terror, fearing that the Axis might be able to plant across her path such a nest of submarines in the South Atlantic as to make it almost impossible for her to evade them completely. I do not remember whether General Marshall knew of this incident at the time, but it was the type of thing that we kept from him when possible. There was no use burdening his mind with the worries that we were forced to carry to bed with us. He had enough of his own.

Chapter 3

COMMAND POST
FOR MARSHALL

EARLY IN JANUARY 1942 THE CHIEF OF STAFF had announced a determination to reorganize the War Department for the efficient waging of war. Foreseeing that the War Department as set up under peacetime laws could not stand the strain of a long and bitter conflict, he had a year before assigned Colonel William K. Harrison to investigate its organizational weaknesses and search out a remedy for them. Although the studies were completed by early winter and a corrective plan tentatively adopted, the attack on Pearl Harbor delayed its execution. The task of actual reorganization was now placed in the hands of Major General Joseph T. McNarney, possessed of an analytical mind and a certain ruthlessness in execution which was absolutely necessary to uproot entrenched bureaucracy and streamline and simplify procedures.

At the same time it was evident that somewhere on the War Department level there would have to be an agency which could assemble and concentrate the sum total of strategic information for General Marshall's attention and through which, after he had reached a decision, his commands could be implemented. This agency, in other words, would be the Chief of Staff's personal command post. The creation of the Operations Division of the War Department General Staff was the answer to this need; it replaced the War Plans Division, where I had succeeded General Gerow as assistant chief of staff on February 16. On March 9, I became the first chief of OPD.[1] Almost simultaneously I was promoted to a temporary major generalcy.

As I remember it, I was far too busy then to take the time to thank General Marshall for advancement to the grade which, in our prewar Army, represented the virtual apex of a professional military career.

Within the War Department a shocking deficiency that impeded all constructive planning existed in the field of Intelligence. The fault was partly within and partly without the Army. The American public has always viewed with repugnance everything that smacks of the spy: during the years between the two World Wars no funds were provided with which to establish the basic requirement of an Intelligence system—a far-flung organization of fact finders.

Our one feeble gesture in this direction was the maintenance of military attachés in most foreign capitals, and since public funds were not available to meet the unusual expenses of this type of duty, only officers with independent means could normally be detailed to these posts. Usually they were estimable, socially acceptable gentlemen; few knew the essentials of Intelligence work. Results were almost completely negative and the situation was not helped by the custom of making long service as a military attaché, rather than ability, the essential qualification for appointment as head of the Intelligence Division in the War Department.

The stepchild position of G-2 in our General Staff system was emphasized in many ways. For example the number of general officers within the War Department was so limited by peacetime law that one of the principal divisions had to be headed by a colonel. Almost without exception the G-2 Division got the colonel. This in itself would not necessarily have been serious, since it would have been far preferable to assign to the post a highly qualified colonel than a mediocre general, but the practice clearly indicated the Army's failure to emphasize the Intelligence function. This was reflected also in our schools, where, despite some technical training in battlefield reconnaissance and Intelligence, the broader phases of the work were almost completely ignored. We had few men capable of analyzing intelligently such information as did come to the notice of the War Department, and this applied particularly to what has become the very core of Intelligence research and analysis—namely, industry.

In the first winter of the war these accumulated and glaring deficiencies were serious handicaps. Initially the Intelligence Division could not even develop a clear plan for its own organization nor could it classify the type of information it deemed essential in determining the purposes and capabilities of our enemies.[2] The chief of the division could do little more than come to the planning and operating sections of the staff and in a rather pitiful way ask if there was anything he could do for us.

An example of the eagerness with which we seized upon every bit of seemingly authentic information was provided by the arrival in Washington of Colonel John P. Ratay, who at the beginning of the war had been our military attaché in Rumania. The colonel was an extremely energetic officer, one of our better attachés. After Rumania joined the Axis in November 1940, he had been interned and eventually transferred through a neutral port to the United States.

The Operations Division learned of his arrival and immediately called upon him for such information as he could provide. He was thoroughly convinced that the German military power had not yet been fully exerted and was so great that Russia and Great Britain would most certainly be defeated before the United States could intervene effectively. He believed that the Germans then had 40,000 combat airplanes in reserve, ready with trained crews to operate at any moment. He considered that these were being withheld from immediate employment with the intention of using them to support an invasion of the United Kingdom. He also believed that Germany had sufficient numbers of reserve divisions, still uncommitted to action, to carry out a successful invasion of the British Isles.

In the Operations Division we refused to give credence to Ratay's information concerning the 40,000 operational airplanes. The German Army had just been halted in front of Moscow and we were convinced that no army possessing a weapon of this overwhelming strength would have withheld it merely because of a future plan for its use, particularly when its employment would have insured the destruction and capture of such an important objective as Moscow. It was obvious, of course, that if the Germans did possess such a tremendous reserve any attempt to invade the European continent by amphibious landings would certainly be abortive.

However, information that reached us only after the war was over did show that Ratay's information and conclusions concerning the reserve divisions had a reasonable basis. Postwar reports from Germany[3] show that, in the summer of 1941, Hitler was planning to employ only sixty divisions as an occupation force for conquered Russia. He planned to use a portion of the large number of divisions, thus freed, for movement into the Middle East. It seems evident that the German high command considered the German ground forces completely adequate for any task.

No one was more keenly aware of our shortcomings in Intelligence than General Marshall. In his search for improvement he assigned, on May 5, 1942, as head of the Intelligence Division Major General George V. Strong, a senior officer possessed of a keen mind, a driving energy, and ruthless determination.

No longer handicapped by lack of money, the Chief of Staff did everything possible to repair the neglect of many years; but no amount of money or emergency effort could rapidly establish throughout the world the essential base of observers and fact finders. However, together with General William Donovan's Office of Strategic Services, General Strong gradually began building a system that was eventually to become a vast and effective organization. Fortunately in the early days of the war the British were able to provide us, out of their prior war experience, much vital information concerning the enemy.

The nature of the work in the War Department threw all of us in constant contact with other American services and with Washington representatives of other members of the Allied nations. The necessity for co-ordination in production and in operations, and the realization that all theaters were interrelated, at least in so far as their demands upon the industrial capacity of the country were involved, were obvious. Meetings between the Chief of Staff and Admiral Harold R. Stark, and later Admiral Ernest J. King, were frequent.

The Chief of Staff's assistants, among whom the principal members were General Somervell, Lieutenant General, later General of the Army, Henry H. Arnold, General McNarney, and the chief of his planning and operations staff, met almost daily with their opposite numbers in the Navy Department in an effort to achieve balanced objectives, in keeping with the output of training organizations and American industry. Thus service in the War Department inevitably produced a complete picture of the global war.

General Marshall gave long and earnest attention to the selection of individuals to occupy key spots in overseas commands and in the reorganized department. In the process he sometimes gave clear indication of the types of men who in his opinion were unsuited for high position. Foremost among these was the one who seemed to be self-seeking in the matter of promotion. Pressure from any source, in favor of any individual in the Army, was more likely than not to boomerang if the Chief of Staff became aware of its existence. I was in his office one day when someone called him on the telephone, apparently to urge the promotion of some friend in the Army. His answer was, "If the man is a friend of yours, the best service you can do him is to avoid mentioning his name to me."

Another thing that annoyed him was any effort to "pass the buck," especially to him. Often he remarked that he could get a thousand men to do detailed work but too many were useless in responsible posts because they left to him the necessity of making every decision. He insisted that his principal assistants should think and act on their own conclusions in their own spheres of responsibility, a doctrine emphasized in our Army schools but too little practiced in peacetime.

By the same token he had nothing but scorn for any man who attempted "to do everything himself"—he believed that the man who worked himself to tatters on minor details had no ability to handle the more vital issues of war. Another type General Marshall disliked was the truculent personality—the man who confused firmness and strength with bad manners and deliberate discourtesy. He also avoided those with too great a love of the limelight. Moreover, he was irritated by those who were often in trouble with others or who were too stupid to see that leadership in conference, even with subordinates, is as important as on the battlefield.

Again, General Marshall could not stand the pessimist—the individual who was always painting difficulties in the darkest colors and was excessively fearful of the means at hand for overcoming them. He would never assign an officer to a responsible position unless he believed that the man was an enthusiastic supporter of the particular project and confident of the outcome. He believed in the offensive.

Sometimes, of course, selections were necessarily made from among officers who did not, in all respects, fully conform to these ideas. But when he made exceptions it was clear that General Marshall always maintained a positive, and permanent, mental reservation.

In the development of strategic, logistic, and operational plans for the Army and its Air Forces, the Operations Division worked closely with the Joint and the Combined Chiefs of Staff. From estimates of the current military situation—our available strength against the enemies' proved capacity and staggering territorial advances—it was our duty to determine military policy in terms of objectives, requirements in men and materials for the attainment of those objectives, and the most effective means of quickly meeting these requirements.

Behind this technical language was an immense amount of pick-and-shovel activity in the accumulation, study, and co-ordination of data affecting military operations. The preparation of a single directive on a proposed operation might require information that ranged from the projected production rate of a specific item in a particular key factory to an encyclopedic presentation of all factors—military, political, geographical, and climatic—influencing the composition of a major task force. The basic principles of strategy are so simple that a child may understand them. But to determine their proper application to a given situation requires the hardest kind of work from the finest available staff officers. In this particular resource, at least, we were well off. The selected body of officers, which had, between the two world wars, truly absorbed the teachings of our unexcelled system of service schools, was splendidly prepared, except in the field of practical Intelligence training, to carry on the vital task of operational planning. In Operations Division this planning meant the toilsome drudgery of grinding countless unrelated facts into the homogeneous substance of a military policy; everything that remotely concerned the business of war and its conduct was grist to our planning mill. But even while we plotted the future and looked toward the day when great offensives could be mounted, the pressure of present demands for action never relaxed and the evidence of our weakness was always with us.

Through the twenty-four hours of each day a steady stream of reports on action taken, appeals for reinforcements and supply, requests for decisions, summaries of intelligence, poured into Operations Division from every continent and from the islands of the Pacific still held by us and our Allies. Occasionally trivial in content, most often far-reaching in strategic import, sometimes inspiring and sometimes calamitous, the decoded messages that crossed my desk during those days were constant reminders that America was engaged in a global war, fighting a desperate delaying battle in some places where heroic men still held out, in others building the bases and extending the air and sea pathways for a counteroffensive, persistently striving to inch forward on a front that circled the earth.

A typical day was April 7—and a tragic one, too, for the surrender of Bataan was becoming hourly more imminent.

The first message to come in that morning was from Fort Mills on Corregidor, announcing that the food situation on Bataan had become desperate. To heartbreaking messages of this sort we had seldom been able to respond with any more than the cold comfort of a promise to do our best. But this time—if Bataan could be held a little while longer—at least a trickle of relief would reach the troops. An answer was immediately sent to Lieutenant General Jonathan M. Wainwright that some supplies were on their way by submarine and should arrive within a few days; we asked that he report their arrival as well as information on his further plans and any change in the situation. A request was radioed to General MacArthur in Sydney for a summary of his plans to maintain supply in Manila Bay by submarine from Australia and the probable dates that he could make delivery. Another radio went to Lieutenant General Joseph W. Stilwell in Burma, asking him to investigate the possibility of flying food concentrates from his area to Bataan.

A second message from General Wainwright reported that heavy attacks were continuing on the Bataan front and the enemy was making progress against our center positions. The hospital there had again been bombed and this time, he added, intentionally—the Japanese had apologized for an earlier bombing.

In rapid sequence came messages notifying us that additional airports would be developed in Central and South America and in Liberia under the supervision of the Chief of Engineers; that the Coast Guard would assign four guards to each vessel during transit of the Soo Canal between Lakes Superior and Michigan, where we had long feared sabotage at the most critical transportation bottleneck in the United States; that Lieutenant General John L. De Witt requested authority to issue 3000 rifles to the Alaskan Territorial Guard; that Lieutenant General Delos C. Emmons, having inspected the New Zealand defense measures in the Fiji Islands, found them inadequate against a major Japanese attack; that General MacArthur asked shipment of personnel to organize five staging areas and one replacement camp in Australia; that Major General Charles H. Bonesteel wanted confirmation of a report that the convoy bringing American reinforcements to Iceland in mid-April would be used to transport relieved British troops to the United Kingdom; that the Caribbean Defense Command recommended installation of a coastal battery on Patos Island; that the Southern Defense Command was activating a new headquarters on the coastal frontier along the Gulf of Mexico, where it was feared Axis submarine activity was likely to increase.

Outgoing instructions concerning defense in the Pacific were radioed to Australia and to our commanders on Christmas, Bora-Bora, Canton, and Fiji Islands. To Iceland a directive was sent that General Bonesteel would assume command of the forces there when American units reached two thirds of the total troop strength on the island. To General Wainwright we relayed President Roosevelt's congratulations upon the Bataan garrison's magnificent resistance to Japanese mass assaults during the previous week. To General MacArthur went a message asking information on the inclusion of Dutch officers on his staff in the Southwest Pacific.

The study of messages received and the preparation of those to be sent were interrupted constantly by conferences on a multitude of topics with representatives of all the armed services, with government officials and industrial leaders, and with Allied agents.

Most of the conferences were held in my own office. Out of them were developed decisions, many minor but some of great significance. Each required action at some point within the Operations Division or the War Department or at some remote point where troops of the Army were stationed. To insure that none would be forgotten and that records for subordinates would always be available, we had resorted to an automatic recording system that proved most effective.

The method was a complete wiring of my war room with dictaphones so placed as to pick up every word uttered in the room. Conversations were thus recorded on a machine just outside my office where a secretary instantly transcribed them into notes and memoranda for the benefit of my associates in the Operations Division. As a consequence, and often without further reference to me, the staff was able to translate every decision and agreement into appropriate action and to preserve such records as were necessary.

I made it a habit to inform visitors of the system that we used so that each would understand its purpose was merely to facilitate the execution of business. It saved me hours of work in the dictation of notes and directives and relieved my mind of the necessity of remembering every detail of fact and opinion that was presented to me.

On April 7 there was also a conference of the Combined Chiefs at which I had to represent OPD. Before we adjourned the discussion covered topics as specific as the allocation of planes originally intended for the Dutch East Indies while resistance continued there and as nebulous as the German intentions in Syria, Turkey, and Iraq.

By nightfall of April 7 an average day had been spent by everyone in Operations Division. Directly or indirectly, we had been in touch with the principal sectors of our war effort and with many distant places that a year before had been only place names on a map.

As early as February 1942 we were worrying about the production of landing craft. Landing craft are primarily designed for offensive operations; it was difficult to develop a widespread interest in them when everyone was desperately concerned with defense. Although the Navy would have to take charge of building landing craft, it informed us that it could not even provide crews for them. General Somervell promptly retorted that he would do so. With characteristic energy he set about the task and performed it successfully. Months later, when he tried to transfer the organization to the Navy, we ran up against the curious proposition that the Navy could not take *drafted* men.

What a difference it would have made if we had had a co-ordinated policy and a single head at that time! Throughout the spring of 1942 attempts were made, through joint conferences and interoffice visits, to reach an agreement on the character and volume of our needs in landing craft and to get some one person to assume the responsibility for procuring them. Naturally such a program had to be articulated with general naval construction so that it would develop without interfering fatally with the production of the escort vessels, submarines, and other types of equipment vital to the execution of plans. At that time, however, the Navy was thinking only in terms of restoring the fleet. They were not particularly interested in landing craft for future offensives. But if we didn't start building we would never attack.

About this time President Quezon became the head of yet another government-in-exile when he was evacuated from the Philippines by submarine before the final capitulation.[4] He eventually made his way to the United States. Within a week of his arrival he called at my office in the War Department and gave to me and my staff many of the intimate details of the Philippines mobilization, campaign, and final defeat. His gratitude to America was profound; he clearly understood all the reasons why more effective help could not be rendered at that moment, but he knew the Philippines would again live under its own flag. From this conviction he never wavered.

The history of those days of the Pacific war will one day be written in detail. The various decisions, movements, and actions will all be brought into their proper perspective and might-have-beens will be weighed against what was actually accomplished by Washington and by commanders in the field. This brief recitation is necessary only because, in some of its aspects, the Southwest Pacific situation had a bearing upon plans for the conduct of war in the Atlantic theater, with which I was to be closely associated. But, strive as we did, we could not save the Philippines. The epic of Bataan came to a tragic end on April 9; Corregidor surrendered on May 6.

Naturally I saw and conferred with General Marshall periodically. We fell into a practice of holding at least one general review a week, during which we often sat alone to evaluate the changing situation; sometimes others were called in, so that the conference took the form of a general orientation for key members of the staff. Marshall's rapid absorption of the fundamentals of a presentation, his decisiveness, and his utter refusal to entertain any thought of failure infused the whole War Department with energy and confidence. His ability to delegate authority not only expedited work but impelled every subordinate to perform beyond his own suspected capacity.

True delegation implies the courage and readiness to back up a subordinate to the full; it is not to be confused with the slovenly practice of merely ignoring an unpleasant situation in the hope that someone else will handle it. The men who operate thus are not only incompetent but are always quick to blame and punish the poor subordinate who, while attempting to do both his own and his commander's jobs, has taken some action that produces an unfortunate result.

One problem that gave the War Department continuing concern was that of securing practical battlefield experience for portions of the Army before the whole of it should finally be thrown into a life-and-death struggle. In Asia and Africa our Allies were conducting active operations and it appeared logical to take advantage of these circumstances to obtain experience on a wider scale than could be accomplished through the mere assignment of American military observers to various areas.

One morning we received a suggestion that appeared so completely sensible that the entire operations staff started to work on it. The idea was to ship one of our armored divisions to reinforce the British Army in the Egyptian desert. Then when definite American need for this division arose, we would bring out only the personnel, leaving its equipment as replacement items for the British forces.[5] The proposition seemed all the more attractive because we were then engaged in producing an improved tank, and by the time we should be ready to use the division ourselves, we counted on having the new equipment ready for issue.

For commander of such a unit my mind turned instantly to one of my oldest friends, Major General George S. Patton, Jr., who was not only a tank expert but an outstanding leader of troops. I was astonished to find my choice flatly opposed by a considerable portion of the staff, but I was convinced that this was due entirely to Patton's rather bizarre mannerisms and his sometimes unpredictable actions. He conformed to no pattern—a circumstance that made many fearful of his ability to fit into a team. Such doubts had no influence with me because of my confidence in his fighting heart and my conviction that he would provide effective leadership for combat troops. I felt that I knew him well because, at the end of the first World War, he and I had formed a fast friendship that could even include heated, sometimes almost screaming, argument over matters that more often than not were doctrinal and academic rather than personal or material.

With approval of the Chief of Staff, I called Patton to Washington and, though I knew the answer in advance, asked him whether he was willing to step down from command of his training corps to take a division into actual battle. His answer was in pleasing contrast to that of another corps commander who, when asked to take command of an American combat corps in the Pacific, declined on the basis that it was not fitting that he, a senior corps commander, should serve under an Australian "amateur" soldier.

The desert project for the employment of Patton's division was defeated largely by lack of available shipping. To transport an armored division by sea there are required, entirely aside from escorting combat vessels, a total of 45 troop and cargo ships.[6] In this instance the convoy would have had to reach Cairo by the long route circling the Cape of Good Hope. The absence of so many ships from other vital supply missions could not be tolerated at the moment.

The incident was a valuable lesson to me, however. I realized that selection of personnel for key positions would, even in war, frequently be opposed only on the basis of routine consideration and commonly accepted standards, and would sometimes be influenced by nothing more important than the single factor of deportment. Also I learned that combat commanders must be selected from among those who preferred a battle-line position to any other, regardless of lesser considerations.

Development of the Operations Division went so well that my key assistants and I gradually gained more time for thinking and study. We could safely leave routine operations in the hands of a group of outstanding young staff officers, supervised by Brigadier Generals Thomas T. Handy, Matthew B. Ridgway, and Robert W. Crawford and Colonels John E. Hull and Albert C. Wedemeyer, all of whom came into deserved Army prominence before the end of the war.

In the security of victory and with the benefit of hindsight it is easy to point out instances in which the War Department made mistakes. But none of us, not even the most sincere and analytical, can recapture in his own heart and mind the fears and worries of those days. These were reflected in the intensity of emotional and mental strain to which responsible officials were subjected. Time was vital—decisions had to be made promptly on whatever estimates and information were available at the time.

For instance, there were projects for building a pipe line into Alaska and an international highway into South America. Both ideas were born out of the very lively fear that we could never produce the tankers and naval escorts needed for all war requirements, and that these two developments might prove the saviors of important areas and the means of preserving access to vital oil supplies. The Operations Division gave the snap judgment that neither would prove decisive in the war effort, but those who made the positive decision had the advice of experts in the particular problem of petroleum supply.

In the development of a concrete plan to implement the approved Allied policy of defeating the European Axis first, we attempted to study and analyze each step and each important factor so thoroughly that no opportunity, risk, or needed preparation would be overlooked. Always, in war, whether problems of tactics, strategy, or logistics are involved, concentration for positive, offensive purposes must be calculated in the light of minimum needs in areas where the enemy might damage us decisively. This meant that during January, February, and March 1942 basic strategic plans had to be drawn in cognizance of the irreducible requirements of the Southwest Pacific.

Among the United Nations, only America could produce great amounts of disposable reserves. Great Britain's air force and, to a lesser extent, her ground and sea forces were largely pinned down to the defense of her home country, a base that had to be protected at all costs if ever any offensive action was to be undertaken across northern Europe. Britain's war effort was already creating a definite strain on her manpower, and only by resorting to the conscription of women was she able to meet her commitments and to maintain herself precariously in the Middle East, Persia, and India. The Soviet forces, though vast in numbers, were committed against an enemy that was threatening Russia's very existence.

The question before the War Department resolved itself into the selection of the exact line of operations along which the potential power of the United States would be best directed against the European Axis. This decision, once reached, would be the guiding principle of the war until Germany was defeated; all other operations and efforts would necessarily be considered as auxiliary or secondary to the main thrust, and would be designed either to defend vital links in our defensive structure or to support the principal effort when once the main attacking forces should be ready.

To use American forces for an attack on Germany through the Russian front was impossible. The only lines of approach were the long, tortuous, and difficult routes through Murmansk on the north and the Persian Gulf on the south, via the Cape of Good Hope. These lines could carry nothing additional to the equipment and supplies that were necessary to keep the Russian forces in the struggle until their own badly torn industrial fabric could be repaired.

Plans for attacking through Norway, through Spain and Portugal, and even for not attacking with ground forces at all but depending exclusively on the effect of sea and air superiority, were all studied in infinite detail.[7]

Another area to be considered as a possible theater of operations for the main effort against Germany was the Mediterranean. In the early spring of '42 the British situation in the Middle East was not too bad. Auchinleck was standing in the Western Desert with the hope that the arrival of reinforcements from England, together with promised equipment from America, would eventually allow him to undertake an offensive that might drive Rommel out of Africa. But the central Mediterranean was closed to the Allies. Malta was beleaguered, pounded incessantly by bombers based in Sicily and Italy. Any attack that attempted to move straight in from Gibraltar against Italy and Sicily was doomed to failure from the start because the invading forces, without defensive air support, would have to pass directly under an overwhelming strength of land-based aviation.

Even at that early date we studied the possibility of launching an expedition to seize French holdings on the Atlantic coast of North Africa and make that area a principal base from which to attack *Festung Europa*.[8] One senior officer seriously proposed that we make our initial landing in Liberia, and begin from there to fight our way laboriously up the coast of Africa toward Europe.[9]

For a number of reasons the Mediterranean route was rejected as the principal avenue of attack. The first disadvantage was the distance of the North African bases from the heart of Germany. While con-

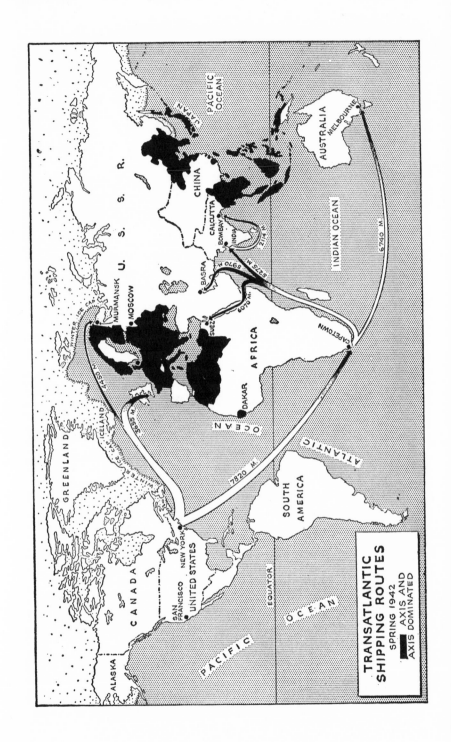

TRANSATLANTIC
SHIPPING ROUTES

SPRING 1942

AXIS AND
AXIS DOMINATED

ceivably Italy might readily be eliminated as an enemy, the heart of the opposition was Germany—an Italian collapse would not be decisive. The difficulty of attacking Germany through the mountainous areas on her southern and southwestern flanks was obvious, while we always had to face the fact that the full might of Great Britain and the United States could not possibly be concentrated in the Mediterranean. This could be done only in an operation which used England as a base. The remaining strength of her land armies and, above all, the air and naval strength required for the defense of England could be employed offensively only if it were hurled across the Channel directly at the continent of Europe. Moreover, between the coast line of northwest Europe and the border of Germany there was no natural obstacle to compare in importance with the Alps.

Another very important reason for making Great Britain the principal base from which to launch the attack was that the transatlantic journey from New York was shortest when terminated in the United Kingdom. This would permit the most rapid turn-around of ships and would utilize the great British ports, already constructed and in good working order. Selection of this base would save shipping in another way. The U-boat packs then infesting the North Atlantic could best be combated by means of heavy escorts.[10] No matter what line of military operations might be selected, we still had to keep open Britain's life line.

For her minimum existence needs she had to import something between twenty and twenty-five million tons per year—her peacetime imports were over fifty million—and a considerable portion of this amount came from the United States.[11] This line, therefore, had to be maintained, and by placing our troops and military cargo convoys on the same route we could achieve a greater safety from the U-boat until such time as that menace could be nullified.

By comparison with other possible avenues of approach, considering the need for concentration, quick access to the heart of the enemy country, avoidance of impassable terrain obstacles, and rapidity of build-up, the best choice was invasion of northwest Europe, using England as a base.

All these things were so obvious as to be axiomatic; there was no quarrel. But from that point on we encountered the obstacle on which all discussions split and practically exploded in our faces. This was a very definite conviction, held by some of our experienced soldiers, sailors, and airmen, that the fortified coast of western Europe could not be successfully attacked. Already much was known of the tremendous effort the German was making to insure integrity of his Atlantic wall. Moreover, a considerable amount of the German Air Force could still be disposed in those areas, and important elements of his fleet were lying in the harbors of northern France, in Norway, and in the Baltic Sea. The coast line was crowded with U-boat nests, while undersea mining was rapidly covering every possible approach.

Many held that attack against this type of defense was madness, nothing but military suicide. Even among those who thought direct assault by land forces would eventually become necessary, the majority believed that definite signs of cracking German morale would have to appear before it would be practicable to attempt such an enterprise.

A very few—initially a very, very few—took a contrary view. General Marshall, who had already been informed of the basic conception on which we were working, was one of the believers. Others were Major Generals McNarney and Carl Spaatz of the Air Corps, while my little band of faithful assistants in the Operations Division, including Generals Handy and Crawford, and Colonels Hull and Wedemeyer, were nothing less than enthusiasts. In the aggregate, not many officers were really aware of the existence of the project, nor had they heard any of the great arguments pro and con that went into its making. Many with whom we had to consult were always ready to express doubts of the blackest character, but these never discouraged the group responsible for the preparation of the project.

This group held that if we would plan for an operation on the assumptions that our Air Force would be, at the chosen moment, over- whelming in strength; that the German air forces would be virtually swept from the skies and our air bombers could practically isolate the attack area from rapid reinforcement; that the U-boat would be so effectively countered that our convoys could count with comparative certainty on making a safe Atlantic crossing; that our supporting naval vessels would be present in strength to batter down local de- fenses and that specialized landing craft could be available in such numbers as to make possible the rapid pouring ashore of a great army through an initial breach—then the assault against the Atlantic wall was not only practicable but would lead to the definite defeat of Ger- many. Moreover, this tiny group solidly held that no other operation could do more than peck at the outer perimeter of the German de- fense; that unless this particular campaign were undertaken the pros- pect of defeating Germany on land was completely black.

We felt we were bringing a new concept, almost a new faith, to strategic thinking, one which envisioned the air co-ordinated with ground operations to the extent that a ground-air team would be developed, tending to multiply the effectiveness of both.

Many ground soldiers belittled the potentialities of the airplane against ground formations. Curiously enough, quite a number of Air Force officers were also antagonistic to the idea, thinking they saw an attempt to shackle the air to the ground and therefore a failure to realize the full capabilities of air attack. It was patiently explained over and over again that, on the contrary, the results of co-ordination would constantly advance the air bases and would articulate strategic bombing effects with ground strategy, so that as the air constantly assisted the advance of the ground forces its long-range work would not only be facilitated but destruction of its selected targets would contribute more effectively and directly to Nazi defeat. All this—so easy now to see—was then the subject of prolonged and earnest argument, extending over days and weeks.

These reasons and supporting arguments, coupled with a great number of technical papers, were finally drawn up in a tentative strategic outline for presentation to the Chief of Staff.[12] He had been aware, of course, of its preparation.

With his usual receptiveness and openmindedness, General Marshall invited a full explanation of the scheme. The burden of proof was on us, but the critical point, the very basis of the whole plan, had to be taken almost on faith. This basis was the conviction that through an overpowering air force, numbering its combat strength in thousands rather than in hundreds, the German's defenses could be beaten down or neutralized, his communications so badly impaired as to make counterconcentration difficult, his air force swept from the skies, and that our ground armies would have an ever-present asset of incalculable power. Without this conviction the whole plan was visionary. Yet there was no way of proving this particular point because, among other things, the airplanes we needed did not then exist.

The Chief of Staff listened patiently through long presentations and at the end said, "This is it. I approve." He immediately conferred with Admiral King and General Arnold, who also approved. The next step was to secure the approval of the President.[13] Then our Allies would have to be convinced. It was manifest that the wholehearted support of the British Government must be obtained or the scheme would fall of its own weight. Without unstinted co-operation by the

British there was no possibility of turning that country into an armed camp of Americans, much less of obtaining British naval, air, ground, and logistic support. The President directed General Marshall to proceed to London. With him went Mr. Harry L. Hopkins, intimate assistant of the President. They departed on April 7.[14]

During the succeeding months I was to have many meetings with Mr. Hopkins. Preoccupied with the war, I never learned, at first hand, much about his personal political philosophy, a subject of bitter argument throughout his tour of public service in Washington. But he was almost fanatically loyal to the President and his loyalty did not hesitate to express itself, when he deemed it necessary, in opposition and prolonged argument. He had a grasp of the broad factors in military problems that was almost phenomenal and he was selflessly devoted to the purpose of expediting victory. He never spared himself, even during those periods when his health was so bad that his doctors ordered him to bed. His function as a lieutenant to the President with an endless variety of jobs, mainly concerned with the prosecution of the war, absorbed his full attention and made him a most important figure.

Concerning the details of the negotiations in London, General Marshall has never talked to me. I do know that he came back with the agreement between the British and American governments to make the attack across the English Channel the principal offensive effort of the two governments in Europe. This decision was made in April 1942.[15]

History has proved that nothing is more difficult in war than to adhere to a single strategic plan. Unforeseen and glittering promise on the one hand and unexpected difficulty or risk upon the other present constant temptation to desert the chosen line of action in favor of another. This one was no exception—realization of the plan was far removed from its making, and countless occasions were to arise when argument, blandishment, and exhortation would seek its abandonment. But the war in Europe was finally won because through every trial and every temptation—in spite of difficulty, delay, pressure, and profitable preliminary operations in the Mediterranean which themselves offered a temptation to forsake the original concept—the President, General Marshall, and many others never wavered from their purpose of launching a full-out invasion of Europe across the English Channel at the earliest practicable moment.

"In Germany . . . a carpet of destruction and desolation had spread over the land. Her bridges were down, her cities in ruins . . ." *Page 1*

Infantry Patrol Advances Through Zweibrücken

PEACEFUL IS BATTLE'S EVE

"During those hours that we paced away among Gibraltar's caverns, hundreds of Allied ships, in fast- and slow-moving convoys, were steaming across the North Atlantic . . . ," *Page 96*

U. S. Navy Escorted Convoy Near North Afri...

Chapter **4**

PLATFORM
FOR INVASION

VERY SHORTLY AFTER GENERAL MARSHALL RE-
turned from the April conference in London he called me to his office.
He said that during his visit he had found little chance to look over
American activity but had become concerned because American officers on duty in London were not familiar with the broader problems
and objectives of the War Department.[1] Specifically, they seemed to
know nothing about the maturing plans that visualized the British Isles
as the greatest operating military base of all time. Marshall directed me
to visit London to see what I could do about correcting this situation
and to bring back recommendations involving future organization and
development of our European forces. I requested permission to take
with me Major General Mark Clark, then chief of staff for General
McNair, head of the ground forces. I felt that Clark's observations
regarding the suitability of the United Kingdom as a training and staging ground would prove valuable.

We started just after the middle of May. Our trip took us over the
Northern Air Route, developed by the Army Air Forces and destined
to become a significant factor in the final defeat of the European Axis.
Airfields in Maine, Newfoundland, Labrador, Greenland, Iceland, and
Scotland eventually made it possible to ferry all our planes, even
fighters, to Europe. Without that route, built in spite of difficulty, discouragement, and even great skepticism as to its usability, we could
scarcely have maintained the forces we put into Europe.

Upon our arrival in England we met the United States commander,
Major General James E. Chaney, who had been assigned there as a
"military observer" before our entry into the war.[2] He and his small
staff had been given no opportunity to familiarize themselves with the

revolutionary changes that had since taken place in the United States and were completely at a loss in their earnest attempts to further the war effort. They were definitely in a back eddy, from which they could scarcely emerge except through a return to the United States. Up to that time American preoccupation with the Pacific war had been so great that the very existence of the London group was all but forgotten—the spotlight had not yet turned toward Europe.

Our inspection team spent ten days in the United Kingdom. I returned home to report to the Chief of Staff that in my opinion the individual to take charge of the American effort in Europe should be someone thoroughly indoctrinated in the plans of the United States Government, with a working knowledge of our capabilities in the production of land, air, and naval units and materials to support them in offensive fighting. In his quick way General Marshall asked me who should take the job, and this time I had my answer ready. I recommended General McNarney. I knew that McNarney had previously served some months in London, was thoroughly familiar with the workings of the British service departments, and was acquainted with many of the key officers therein. Moreover, it was apparent that the earliest operations of the United States out of Great Britain would be limited to air raids, because the building up of the great air forces visualized in the invasion plan would have as a first result the initiation of a long and vigorous bombing campaign. Finally, I knew that General McNarney firmly believed in the Air Force's ability to make ground invasion of France possible.

The Chief of Staff rejected this recommendation. He had just appointed McNarney Deputy Chief of Staff for the War Department and there was no other suitable officer to take over the post.[3] To insure integration and to build up mutual confidence, General Marshall felt it essential that, at that time, his deputy should be from the Air Corps.

On June 8, I submitted to the Chief of Staff a draft of a "Directive for the Commanding General, European Theater of Operations," which provided for unified command of all American forces allocated to the European area.[4] I remarked to General Marshall that this was one paper he should read in detail before it went out because it was likely to be an important document in the further waging of the war. His reply still lives in my memory: "I certainly do want to read it. You may be the man who executes it. If that's the case, when can you leave?" Three days later General Marshall told me definitely that I would command the European theater.

Naturally I have often wondered what led to that particular and apparently sudden decision. General Marshall has never volunteered a word but of course I did realize that it was sudden only to me; he had thought the matter over carefully. The transfer from staff to command duty would have been welcomed by any soldier; but the weight of responsibility involved was so great as to obliterate any thought of personal elation and so critical as to compel complete absorption in the job at hand. In any event, the unexpected orders started me on a hurried round of preparation, most of which involved the transfer of War Department duties to my successor, General Handy.

I had several meetings with important officials. In a short talk with Secretary of War Stimson, I gained the impression that he was counting on the start of active operations very soon. I commented that a long period of build-up would have to precede any attack on the European continent, but I did learn that he was a firm supporter of the plan.

A later call on President Roosevelt and Prime Minister Churchill, a guest at the White House, was no more than an informal chat. It had no military significance, but it was the first time I ever had a personal talk with either of these two men. Tobruk, in the African desert, had just fallen to the Germans and the whole Allied world was thrown into gloom. These two leaders, however, showed no signs of pessimism. It was gratifying to note that they were thinking of attack and victory, not of defense and defeat.

I also went to see Admiral King. He was a naval officer of the fighting type, abrupt, decisive, and frequently so blunt as to frighten his subordinates. In our conversation he stressed the point that the venture on which I was going to Britain would mark the first deliberate attempt by the American fighting services to set up a unified command in the field for a campaign of indefinite length. He assured me that he would do everything within his power to sustain my status of actual "commander" of American forces assigned to me. He said that he wanted no foolish talk about my authority depending upon "co-operation and paramount interest." He insisted that there should be single responsibility and authority and he cordially invited me to communicate with him personally at any time that I thought there might be intentional or unintentional violation of this concept by the Navy.

All this was of vital importance to me because, before that time, Joint Regulations for the control of Army-Navy forces in the field had stressed the principle of "paramount interest"[5] in determining which service should have directing authority and responsibility.

General Clark and I, with a few assistants, left Washington in late June 1942.[6] This time the parting from my family seemed particularly difficult although it was, in a sense, a mere repetition of previous instances covering many years. Our son came down from West Point; he, my wife, and I had two days together, and then I left.

Our party landed in England without incident and I immediately assumed command of the European Theater of Operations, United States Army, which then comprised only the United Kingdom and Iceland. Since it was a wartime habit to manufacture new words from group initials, it was inevitable that the theater should quickly acquire the popular name of ETOUSA.

The United States theater in Europe was established for the purpose of preparing the American part of the invasion of the Continent, agreed upon between the British and American governments as the main strategical effort in defeating Germany. Here are short excerpts from the directive:

> The Commanding General . . . European Theater, . . . will command all U. S. Army Forces and personnel now in, or hereafter dispatched to, the European Theater of Operations, including any part of the Marine Corps therein which may be detached for service with the Army.
>
> By agreement between Navy and War Departments, planning and operational control . . . will be exercised by the Commanding General . . . over all U. S. Navy Forces assigned to this Theater.
>
> Subject to such limitations within the British Isles as are necessary to avoid any violation of British sovereignty, the Commanding General, European Theater, is charged with the tactical, strategical, territorial and administrative duties of a theater commander.
>
> The mission of the Commanding General, European Theater, will be to prepare for and carry on military operations in the European Theater against the Axis Powers and their Allies.[7]

In late June 1942 the press of the United States and Great Britain was echoing the Russian cry for a "second front." To the professional soldier this was disturbing, not because of any quarrel with the soundness of the idea but because the impatience of the public clearly demonstrated a complete lack of appreciation of the problems involved, particularly of the time that must elapse before any such operation could be launched. Unless there is some understanding of the vastness of those problems, any account of what happened during the ensuing two years will remain meaningless and unintelligible. To help toward such an understanding, here are a few statistics.

When the actual invasion of northwestern Europe took place on June 6, 1944, there were in England ready for use:

17 British Empire divisions, including 3 Canadian
20 American divisions
1 French division
1 Polish division
5049 fighter aircraft
3467 heavy bombers
1645 medium, light, and torpedo bombers
698 other combat aircraft
2316 transport aircraft
2591 gliders

233 LSTs (a large vessel capable of unloading tanks and heavy trucks directly on the beach)
835 LCTs
6 battleships and 2 monitors
22 cruisers
93 destroyers
159 smaller fighting craft, not including motor torpedo boats, PT boats, and mine layers
255 mine sweepers
72 LCIs

The combat planes enumerated here comprise only those actually with squadrons. The total of the landing craft, merchant ships, and naval fighting vessels was more than 6000. This figure does not include "ducks" or swimming tanks.[8]

There were heavy contingents of base troops, transport units, ground crews, hospitals, and every type of repair and maintenance organization. The Allied strength in land, sea, and air on that day was 2,876,439 officers and men assigned to the Expeditionary Forces. Added to this were forty-one divisions which would be ready to sail from the United States with their equipment and supplies at as rapid a rate as ports in Britain, and those that could be gained on the Continent, could receive them. Moreover, ten additional divisions, some of them French, were scheduled to join in the attack from the Mediterranean sector.[9] Some of our most important and vitally essential equipment did not arrive until May 1944, on the eve of the invasion.

But consider the picture in June 1942.

The United States was just getting into its stride in the mobilization and training of its armies, navies, and air forces. Only the 34th Division, the 1st Armored Division, and small detachments of the United States Air Forces had arrived in northern Ireland.[10] They were still only partially trained. The great bulk of the fighting equipment, naval, air, and ground, needed for the invasion did not exist. Some of the landing craft were not yet in the blueprint stage. Production limitations alone ruled out any possibility of a full-scale invasion in 1942 or early 1943. Indeed, it soon became clear that unless practically all American and British production could be concentrated on the single purpose of supporting the invasion of Europe that operation could not take place until early 1944.

Manifestly these things could not be explained to the public. The enemy would have given much to know just what were our prospects in the impedimenta of invasion, and we went to every length to deny him any possible access to this information. So while uninformed, homeland strategists could and did shout "timidity, procrastination, indecision," we at least had the satisfaction of hoping that the Nazi likewise overestimated our capabilities.

The United States Army had already taken over, for headquarters purposes, a large apartment building in the heart of London. I disliked the idea of establishing an operating headquarters in a great city but for the moment there seemed no alternative. Housing was a problem and the largest number of available hotel and other quarters was near Grosvenor Square, the site of our building. The great portion of our early activity would involve constant conferences with civil and military officers in the British Government and transport was so lacking that proximity to our principal points of contact was a necessity. Add to this the fact that we simply could not find accommodations outside the city big enough to house the staff and were not yet in position to build hut camps, and it is easy to see why I accepted defeat in my first organizational idea and settled down in London, temporarily.

General headquarters for American naval interests in Europe was commanded by Admiral Stark, previously Chief of Naval Operations.[11] His office was independent of mine, but immediately upon my arrival he came to me and said, "The only real reason for the existence of my office is to assist the United States fighting forces in Europe. You may call on me at any hour, day or night, for anything you wish. And when you do, call me 'Betty,' a nickname I've always had in the service."

United States naval forces allocated to me for the proposed operation were commanded by Rear Admiral Andrew C. Bennett, who reported as my immediate subordinate soon after my own arrival in London. The naval contingent was expected to be little more than a training organization for many months. This was, however, a most important feature of our plans: amphibious training on a large scale would have to precede any invasion of the Continent.

My first job was to collect and organize a working team. General Marshall approved my request for Brigadier General Walter B. Smith as my chief of staff. He was a godsend—a master of detail with clear comprehension of main issues. Serious, hard-working, and loyal, he proved equally as capable in difficult conference as he was in professional activity. Strong in character and abrupt by instinct, he could achieve harmony without appeasement, and earned for himself an enviable standing throughout the armies and governments of Europe. He reached London on September 7 and there began a personal friendship and official association which lasted throughout the war.

While plans visualized an eventual force to be numbered in the millions, I was determined to avoid the curse of early over-organization in the ground forces. To begin with, we brought over, as the highest ground headquarters, only the II Corps, to the command of which I assigned General Clark.[12] I knew that during the months that must elapse before troops and supplies could be accumulated in sufficient numbers for a major attack we would have time to bring over the several army headquarters we would need. Thus was avoided the confusion certain to ensue from the immediate presence of many senior staffs, each with little to do except add to general congestion. By building up from the bottom we kept all our preparatory work concrete and specific and had time for the careful selection of high commanders. We established II Corps in Salisbury Plain, the best training ground in the United Kingdom.

Major General John C. H. Lee reported to me to command our Services of Supply. He at once began the appalling task of preparing ports and building warehouses, camps, airfields, and repair facilities, all of which would be needed before we could start an offensive from the British base. The work accomplished under his direction was so vital to success and so vast in proportion that its description would require a book in itself. By the time the cross-Channel assault was launched, two years later, the United Kingdom was one gigantic air base, workshop, storage depot, and mobilization camp. It was claimed facetiously at the time that only the great number of barrage balloons floating constantly in British skies kept the islands from sinking under the seas.

In the American headquarters in Europe organizational plans followed the conventional pattern of a general and special staff. One problem that arose early and bothered us throughout the campaigns in Europe was how to separate administrative from operational matters without setting up an additional headquarters. American law and regulations give a theater commander a vast amount of administrative responsibility and authority, much of which he must exercise personally. How to free a mobile, tactical staff from the vast bulk of this

work, which ordinarily must be performed at a fixed, stable headquarters, and still observe economy in highly trained personnel is
always a problem. It was difficult from the beginning, but did not become really bothersome until I was given the additional assignment
of Allied commander. For the moment we adopted a temporary solution, realizing that England itself would eventually be merely a base,
not a theater of operations. General Lee, as commander of our Services of Supply and the British base, was charged with handling administration.

The organizational plan for air was pressing in point of time. We intended to participate as quickly as possible in the bombing campaign
against Germany. The Eighth Air Force was allocated to our theater,
with General Spaatz assigned to me as its commander.[13] From the time
of his arrival at London in July he was never long absent from my
side until the last victorious shot had been fired in Europe. On every
succeeding day of almost three years of active war I had new reasons
for thanking the gods of war and the War Department for giving me
"Tooey" Spaatz. He shunned the limelight and was so modest and retiring that the public probably never became fully cognizant of his
value.

All these preliminary organizational tasks were normal to such
enterprises. They had been anticipated and therefore were soon disposed of, so far as immediate needs were concerned. Another task for
which we had to organize very specifically was almost unique in
character. It involved the fitting of our training, building, and organizational activities into British life.

The plan to bring large fighting forces to Great Britain required
those highly populated islands to ready themselves for the absorption
of 2,000,000 Americans and to provide for them necessary facilities,
including training grounds, in which to prepare for the great invasion.
England's insufficiency in food supplies had already led to a program
of placing even submarginal ground under intensive cultivation, while,
to save fuel and power, all unnecessary transportation and power
facilities had been eliminated. Our friendly invasion would vastly increase the strain on the population. The whole of the British Isles is
only slightly larger than Colorado. Certain portions were either un-
usable or unsuited to our purpose. Southern Ireland was neutral, while
Scotland was short of suitable areas for training. Almost the entire
burden was thrown onto the crowded sections of middle and southern
England, with some troops stationed in North Ireland. We had to ex-

pect inevitable clashes with civilian processes, and in spite of the best will in the world on both sides, we had to anticipate, and do our best to prevent, mutual irritations that would naturally lead to misunderstandings and could not fail to impede the war effort.

Except during World War I, the United States public has habitually looked upon Europe's quarrels as belonging to Europe alone. For this reason every American soldier coming to Britain was almost certain to consider himself a privileged crusader, sent there to help Britain out of a hole. He would expect to be treated as such. On the other hand, the British public looked upon itself as one of the saviors of democracy, particularly because, for an entire year, it had stood alone as the unbreakable opponent of Nazism and the European Axis. Failure to understand this attitude would of course have unfortunate results.

If the United Kingdom had possessed great open spaces in which to concentrate the American forces, the problem would have been less acute, but because of the density of population every soldier arriving in England made living conditions just that much more difficult. Every American truck on the streets, and every piece of ground withdrawn from cultivation, added to the irritations.

Fortunately all this was foreseen and discussed frankly with the leaders of the British war effort. Our principal collaborator was Mr. Brendan Bracken, head of the Ministry of Information. He seemed to be as controversial a figure in British life as Harry Hopkins was in ours, but he was always helpful to us and, equally important, he was decisive and energetic. He had another characteristic particularly noticeable among a people normally regarded as conservative and correct. Until I met him I had always regarded the American cowpuncher as the world's greatest master of picturesque expression. The effect of Bracken's language was always heightened by the rasping intensity of his voice.

Intensive programs were devised with Bracken's splendid organization to fit the newly arrived Americans into the highly complex life of a thickly populated area in such a way as to minimize trouble. Of these programs, probably the most successful was education of both sides, coupled with intermingling in homes and public places. Through Brendan Bracken the British public was constantly informed as to what to expect. He explained the necessity for further accommodation and sacrifices among the whole population, and the need for tolerance. At the same time educational pamphlets and literature were distributed to American troops before their embarkation from the United States.[14] These were written in the vernacular and contained specific suggestions to facilitate the adjustment of American soldiers to the new environment.

Wherever possible, newly arrived American personnel were taken on a short tour through Britain's bombed areas. The American Red Cross and the several relief and welfare organizations of Great Britain helped institute a system of home entertainment of American GIs by British families.[15] I have never yet met an American soldier who, after spending a week end with a British family, did not feel that America had a staunch and sturdy Ally. We found, however, that a British family, inspired by a determination to show real hospitality, was likely to utilize an entire week's rations to entertain an American over Sunday. At once we encouraged visiting soldiers to carry rations with them on these home visits, while a publicity campaign explained the matter to the British hosts, so as to save their pride and preclude embarrassment. In every direction where we expected trouble we instituted preventive measures—generally with success. The keynote of the campaign was avoidance of mawkish sentimentality and the basing of all our programs on facts—with emphasis on opportunity for personal discovery of facts. Everyone who occupied a responsible position in Britain during that time will always have a feeling of gratitude and admiration for the almost universal spirit of co-operation, tolerance, and friendship displayed by both sides.

This type of problem brought immediately to the fore the need for an effective Public Relations Section of the headquarters. Our concern was emphasized by the necessity for keeping two populations, the American and the British, informed on a variety of subjects. I began the practice of holding short, informal conferences with the press, for the purpose of discussing our mutual problems and finding common solutions for them. I insisted that they occupy positions as quasi-staff officers on my staff, and I respected their collective responsibilities in the war as they did mine.

My first press conference had a curious result. Prior to my arrival in England censorship had been established by American headquarters on stories involving minor difficulties between Negro troops and other soldiers, or civilians. These incidents frequently involved social contacts between our Negro soldiers and British girls. The British population, except in large cities and among wealthy classes, lacks the racial consciousness which is so strong in the United States. The small-town British girl would go to a movie or dance with a Negro quite as readily as she would with anyone else, a practice that our white soldiers could not understand. Brawls often resulted and our white soldiers were further bewildered when they found that the British press took a firm stand on the side of the Negro.

When I learned at the press conference that stories of this kind were on the censored list I at once revoked the order and told the pressmen to write as they pleased—urging them only not to lose their perspective. To my astonishment, several reporters spoke up to ask me to retain the ban, giving me a number of arguments in support of their recommendations. They said that troublemakers would exaggerate the importance of the incidents and that the reports, taken up at home, would cause domestic dissension. I thanked them but stuck to my point, with the result that little real excitement was ever caused by ensuing stories. It was a lesson I tried always to remember.

Progress in these matters of administration, preparation, training, planning, had to go forward simultaneously. An early deficiency in our wartime Army involved a dismaying lack of comprehension on the part of our soldiers as to fundamental causes of the war. Differences between democracy and totalitarianism were matters of academic rather than personal interest; soldiers saw no apparent reason why conflict between the two was any concern of America. No matter what clash of opinion had existed on the point before the war began, a clear, simple, and commonly held understanding was now essential among our troops. An attendant deficiency was a similar lack of comprehension as to the need for battle discipline and for incessant training in teamwork and in the employment of weapons.

Both subjects evoked frequent comment by observant press representatives. The matter could not be dismissed—as some commanders tried to do—with the complacent statement that all of this came about because the troops were not yet "blooded." There has always existed a curious notion that instant perfection in these matters comes about with the first whistle of a hostile bullet. Admittedly there are certain things to be learned from battle experience that can be absorbed in no other way. On the other hand, any commander who permits a unit to enter battle lacking any advantage, any needed instruction, or any useful understanding that could be imparted to that unit beforehand, is guilty of a grave crime against the soldiers he leads.

That a soldier should understand why he is fighting would not seem to be an arguable point. Yet I have heard commanders attempt to oversimplify this psychological problem with the assertion that soldiers fight for only a few simple and essentially local reasons. Among these they include pride in a unit, respect for the opinion of comrades, and blind devotion to an immediate leader. These things are important and the wise commander will neglect none of them in his effort to produce a first-class fighting unit in which all the members are so trained that chances of success—and individual survival—are raised to the maximum. But the American soldier, in spite of wisecracking, sometimes cynical speech, is an intelligent human being who demands and deserves basic understanding of the reasons why his country took up arms and of the conflicting consequences of victory or defeat. Von Steuben commented vividly on this point during the American Revolution. He explained in a letter to a friend that in Europe you tell a soldier to do thus, and he does it; and that in America it is necessary also to tell him why he does it.

Once the recruit of 1941 was inducted into the service the military leader had to shoulder almost exclusive responsibility for imparting such an understanding, but there was implied a glaring deficiency in our country's educational processes. It seemed to me that constant stressing of the individual rights and privileges of American citizenship had overshadowed the equally important truth that such individualism can be sustained only so long as the citizen accepts his full responsibility for the welfare of the nation that protects him in the exercise of these rights.

Belief in an underlying cause is fully as important to success in war as any local esprit or discipline induced or produced by whatever kind of command or leadership action. Cromwell's "Ironsides" marched into battle singing hymns. Their iron discipline was matched by an inner conviction that never deserted them in any kind of dramatic crisis.

Grosvenor Square, where our headquarters and the American Embassy were located, through the soldier's love of nicknames soon became "Eisenhowerplatz," and was so referred to, at times, in the press.

This was merely amusing, but the location made it difficult to lead a quiet personal life. British hospitality and the presence in London of a number of American friends combined to bring me innumerable invitations of all kinds. Finally, to avoid the inescapable incidents of hotel life, I moved my personal quarters to a quiet little cottage on the edge of the city. I lived there with my naval aide, Commander Harry C. Butcher, and my orderly, Sergeant Michael McKeogh. Two Negro soldiers, Sergeants John Moaney and John Hunt, joined us to take care of the house and a simple mess. They stayed with me throughout the war.

From July onward I did not, during the war, accept any invitations except from the Prime Minister or from members of the American or British armed services. These always had business as their primary object.

Visits to the troops had not yet assumed their later proportions on my schedule; there were still relatively few units in the United Kingdom to visit. One of the earliest trips of this sort was in connection with our first offensive operation against the enemy—a bombing raid to celebrate July 4, 1942. The targets were four German airdromes in Holland. Six Bostons under command of Captain Charles C. Kegelman, included as part of a larger British formation, ran into severe flak and two failed to return.[16] To mark our entry into the European fighting I took time to visit the crews immediately before the take-off, and talked with the survivors after their return.

During the war Mr. Churchill maintained such close contact with all operations as to make him a virtual member of the British Chiefs of Staff; I cannot remember any major discussion with them in which he did not participate.

An inspirational leader, he seemed to typify Britain's courage and perseverance in adversity and its conservatism in success. He was a man of extraordinarily strong convictions and a master in argument and debate. Completely devoted to winning the war and discharging his responsibility as Prime Minister of Great Britain, he was difficult indeed to combat when conviction compelled disagreement with his views. In most cases problems were solved on a basis of almost instant agreement, but intermittently important issues arose where this was far from true. He could become intensely oratorical, even in discussion with a single person, but at the same time his intensity of purpose made his delivery seem natural and appropriate. He used humor and pathos with equal facility, and drew on everything from the Greek classics to Donald Duck for quotation, cliché, and forceful slang to support his position.

I admired and liked him. He knew this perfectly well and never hesitated to use that knowledge in his effort to swing me to his own line of thought in any argument. Yet in spite of his strength of purpose, in those instances where we found our convictions in direct opposition, he never once lost his friendly attitude toward me when I persisted in my own course, nor did he fail to respect with meticulous care the position I occupied as the senior American officer and, later, the Allied commander in Europe. He was a keen student of the war's developments and of military history, and discussion with him, even on purely professional grounds, was never profitless. If he accepted a decision unwillingly he would return again and again to the attack in an effort to have his own way, up to the very moment of execution. But once action was started he had a faculty for forgetting everything in his desire to get ahead, and invariably tried to provide British support in a greater degree than promised. Some of the questions in which I found myself, at various periods of the war, opposed to the Prime Minister were among the most critical I faced, but so long as I was acting within the limits of my combined directive he had no authority to intervene except by persuasion or by complete destruction of the Allied concept. Nevertheless, in countless ways he could have made my task a harder one had he been anything less than big, and I shall always owe him an immeasurable debt of gratitude for his unfailing courtesy and zealous support, regardless of his dislike of some important decisions. He was a great war leader and he is a great man.

Our planning and organizational work sometimes involved differences in national conceptions that struck at the very foundation of our basic plan. These points were discussed in an atmosphere of cordiality and objectivity, but they were none the less serious. Whenever I found myself opposed to the views of the Prime Minister, he was, of course, supported by his War Cabinet and technical advisers. That differences should occur was inescapable and natural. Varying situations in national geography bring with them differences in military doctrine, and special war experiences bring with them strong differences in projected strategy. An early instance involved the proposed employment of our slowly developing bombing force.

The U. S. Army Air Forces believed in daylight bombing with the heavily defended Fortress type of bomber as the backbone of the organization.[17] I emphatically agreed. Each of these planes carried ten .50-caliber machine guns for defense. We believed that, in suitable close formations permitting concentration of a terrific fire power, they could proceed well outside of the area in which they could be protected by their own fighters and could carry out daylight bombing operations without undue losses.

The Prime Minister was convinced that this view was false and that the United States was merely wasting its effort and resources in making the attempt. General Spaatz knew, of course, that the United

States was already developing long-range fighters which would become available by the time his Eighth Air Force could reach its scheduled strength. However, for some months his forces would have to employ the P-39 and P-40 fighters, which had a very limited operational radius, roughly about three hundred miles.[18] The Prime Minister urged us to give up the whole idea of daylight bombing and start training our crews for night work. British air experience at that time was far greater than ours. Following hard upon the Battle of Britain in 1940, they had begun laboriously to build up a bomber force that could strike deep into the heart of Germany. Their experience had driven them to bomb only at night; otherwise they suffered unsupportable losses. The British staged their first 1000-plane raid in an attack against Cologne on the night of May 30–31, 1942. Losses amounted to 42 planes.[19]

The British bombers could not, in daylight, have undertaken such an operation except with prohibitive losses. We believed that this was due to the fact that they were designed for range and weight lifting at the expense of speed and defensive fire power. The British fighter called the Spitfire was handicapped by very short range, although in other respects it was one of the finest then in existence. While acknowledging the superior defensive power of our Fortress formations, the British still held that unless we quickly turned to night bombing our losses would be prohibitive and our effort futile.

The arguments on this point were long, with neither side convinced. It was granted by all that daylight precision bombing, if successful, would be far superior to night area bombing in ton-for-ton effect. Consequently discussions centered exclusively around the one point of feasibility. General Spaatz and I were supported in our position by the United States Chiefs of Staff and we insisted that our system should first be thoroughly and completely tested before anything could lead us to deviate from it.

In the final outcome, months later, both sides were proved to be partially right. When our heavy bombers first began operating in formation outside fighter range, the volume of their defensive fire so astonished the enemy that for a period we enjoyed a considerable degree of immunity. Gradually, however, the German devised new tactics and methods and began to use his fighters in large concentrations against our units. Our percentage of losses began to mount rapidly. On June 13, 1943, the U. S. Eighth Air Force attacked Kiel with 76 planes, without fighter support, and lost 22.[20] A later raid by 291 planes suffered a loss of 60. With each plane shot down went also

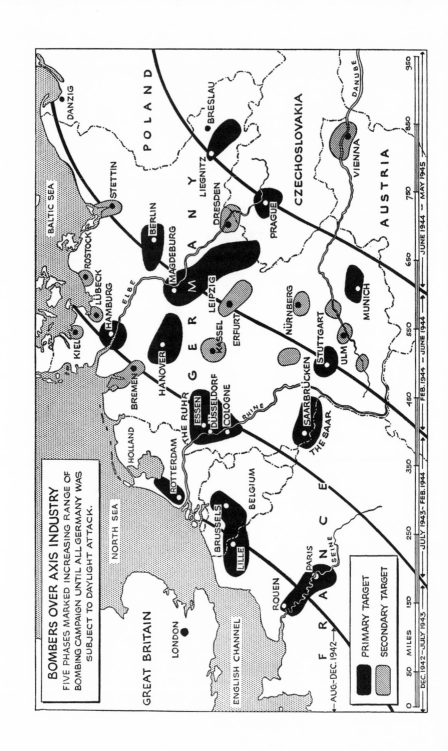

BOMBERS OVER AXIS INDUSTRY

FIVE PHASES MARKED INCREASING RANGE OF
BOMBING CAMPAIGN UNTIL ALL GERMANY WAS
SUBJECT TO DAYLIGHT ATTACK.

PRIMARY TARGET

SECONDARY TARGET

0   50   MILES   150   250   350   450   550   650   750   850   950

AUG.-DEC. 1942 — DEC. 1942-JULY 1943 — JULY 1943-FEB. 1944 — FEB.1944-JUNE 1944 — JUNE 1944-MAY 1945

GREAT BRITAIN

LONDON

NORTH SEA

ENGLISH CHANNEL

BALTIC SEA

DANZIG

POLAND

STETTIN

ROSTOCK

LÜBECK

KIEL

HAMBURG

BREMEN

HOLLAND

ROTTERDAM

BRUSSELS

LILLE

BELGIUM

PARIS

ROUEN

SEINE

F R A N C E

THE RUHR

ESSEN

DÜSSELDORF

COLOGNE

RHINE

HANOVER

ELBE

BERLIN

MAGDEBURG

G E R M A N Y

KASSEL

ERFURT

LEIPZIG

DRESDEN

LIEGNITZ

BRESLAU

PRAGUE

CZECHOSLOVAKIA

SAARBRÜCKEN

THE SAAR

SAARBRÜCKEN

NÜRNBERG

STUTTGART

ULM

MUNICH

VIENNA

AUSTRIA

DANUBE

a minimum of ten officers and men. In the face of such percentage losses it became certain that but for the mass production of the long-range efficient fighter we would have had to modify our bombing program and could have proceeded into Germany itself only under cover of darkness or bad weather.

But in the initial arguments these experiences still belonged to the future. A great factor in my own calculations was the degree of dependence I placed upon the operation of the precision bomber in preparing the way for a ground invasion of France.

This was the keynote of the invasion plan. Unless accurate daylight bombing was feasible, I believed, large-scale invasion of the Continent would be exceedingly risky. Therefore I maintained that even if we could carry on precision bombing only to the extreme range of our fighters we must continue to develop the United States forces on that basis, so as to have available the great force that would be needed to carry out the preparatory work in the areas selected for invasion.

The upshot was that the United States Air Forces stuck to their program of precision bombing, while the British Bomber Force continued to concentrate on increasing the efficiency of night bomber operations. While the question was raised again, on the highest levels, at the Casablanca Conference in January 1943, the result was merely to confirm this earlier decision.[21]

Coupled with our organizational and preparatory program was the task of developing an operational plan to carry out the agreed-upon strategical concepts of the two governments. At that time General Sir Bernard Paget was commanding the Home Forces of Great Britain, from which would have to come the British contingent of the invading army. His troops included a number of Canadian divisions serving under the command of General Andrew McNaughton. Air Chief Marshal Sir Sholto Douglas was designated as the commander for the British Expeditionary Air Forces. Admiral Sir Bertram Ramsay was named to head British naval forces. It was in co-operation with these men that the original work of developing a European invasion plan was undertaken by United States headquarters.

It is difficult now to recapture the sober, even fearful, atmosphere of those days: the state of the public mind which was reflected in the thinking of so many people in and out of the service. Except for the early June defeat of the Japanese fleet at Midway, Allied fortunes were at low ebb. Prospects were bright only in their long-range aspect, and were contingent on Russia's maintaining herself in the war with the material help that could be given her while the United States developed her latent power. Moreover, it was essential that Great Britain hang on grimly in India and the Western Desert in order to keep our two principal enemies divided and to deny them the Middle East oil.

In the summer of 1942 it took a very considerable faith, not to say optimism, to look forward to the day when the potentialities of the United States would be fully developed and the power of the three great Allies could be applied simultaneously and decisively against the European Axis. This attitude of faith was demanded at all superior headquarters. Any expression of defeatism or any failure to push ahead in confidence was instant cause for relief from duty, and all officers knew it.

At the time of my first visit to London, in May, no detailed study of tactical plans for an invasion of the coast line of northwestern Europe had been made. Requirements in troops, airplanes, supplies, and equipment were all yet to be determined. In general terms I was thinking of an assault to be launched early in 1943, conducted during its initial stages by British troops supported by possibly ten or twelve American divisions. This general idea presupposed the existence in England of an air force capable with some reinforcement of carrying out the preliminary and supporting action that we believed to be necessary. It presupposed, also, British capacity for assisting materially in the quick delivery of all the amphibious equipment we would need, and, of course, contemplated the regular arrival of new divisions from the United States in sufficient strength to support the attack constantly and to enlarge the operations against the enemy.

With these general ideas in mind but with no detailed studies upon which to make a firm conclusion, I went to an informal meeting with the British Chiefs of Staff. Shortly after the conference began I was invited to present my general views concerning the nature of the projected operation. Speaking as an American planner assigned to the War Department in Washington, and with no idea that I would later be assigned to Britain, I said in substance, "The first thing to do is to name a commander for the operation. That man must be given every bit of power that both governments can make available to him. He must be directed to plan for an invasion of Europe on the basis that it will certainly be successful, at least to the extent of establishing on the Continent a solid front capable of carrying out effective operations against the German. He must be directed instantly to prepare his outlined plan and to submit to the Chiefs of Staff his requirements not only in troops of all kinds but in all types of additional equipment—-land, sea, and air."

The first question asked me was, "And who would you name as commander of this expedition?"

Still thinking of an operation in early 1943, when the British would necessarily provide the major portion of the forces during initial stages, I replied, "In America I have heard much of a man who has been intensively studying amphibious operations for many months. I understand that his position is Chief of Combined Operations, and I think his name is Admiral Mountbatten.[22] Anyone will be better than none; such an operation cannot be carried out under committee command. But I have heard that Admiral Mountbatten is vigorous, intelligent, and courageous, and if the operation is to be staged initially with British forces predominating I assume he could do the job."

My remarks were greeted with an amazed silence. Then General Brooke said, "General, possibly you have not met Admiral Mountbatten. This is he sitting directly across the table from you." My failure to recognize him when I entered the meeting and my later personal remarks about him naturally caused a moment of embarrassment. Nevertheless, I stuck to my guns and retorted, "I still say that the key to success is to appoint a commander and give him the necessary authority and responsibility to carry out the planning and preparatory work that otherwise will never be done."

The meeting was merely for an exchange of ideas and nothing was done. Almost needless to add, however, from then on Admiral Lord Louis Mountbatten was my warm and firm friend.

Upon my permanent assignment to London, there began a series of meetings among the commanders concerned to examine into the detailed requirements of the projected operation. Ordinarily these discussions involved General Paget, Admiral Ramsay, Air Chief Marshal Douglas, General Spaatz, Admiral Mountbatten, and myself, together with groups from our respective staffs. No one was in authority so no decisive action could be planned. Dozens of different ideas affecting strategy, tactics, organization, and supply were discussed interminably. These discussions were complicated by service and personal prejudices and by varying convictions regarding the usefulness of the air in ground operations.

But through these studies and conferences the Americans became more fully acquainted with the details of the strategic, tactical, and logistic problems involved in an invasion of Europe on a decisive scale.

We gained access to all the British intelligence and learned the exact strength and commitments of British land, sea, and air forces. Further mobilization of British power, in any significant amount, was impossible; they had already organized their full strength, including women between the ages of eighteen and fifty-two.

We learned a number of things that caused us to revise radically our earlier general ideas of the operation. The first of these was that the British Air Force was not equipped either in types and numbers of planes or in training of personnel to carry out the intensive preparatory work by air that we deemed a prerequisite to successful invasion. The second was that the British fleet, necessarily holding itself in reserve at all times to meet any threat of a sortie by the German surface fleet, could not provide the amount of direct support and the intensity of naval bombardment that would be required for successful landings.

In land forces, also, the British were badly stretched. Considering their commitments in India, the Middle East, and their precarious position in the Western Desert, they could not possibly provide for the new invasion more than some fifteen divisions.[23] Finally, we found that in the matter of landing craft, special equipment, and the great stores of material reserves that would be necessary the British were not much better off than we. All this meant that there was no hope of beginning a major invasion of Europe until America could produce the necessary land, sea, and air power to participate in the initial operation on at least an equal basis and be prepared, thereafter, to provide the great bulk of the ground and air units that would be needed. Moreover, the attack could not take place until American industry could largely supply the vast amount of special equipment and supplies that would be necessary.

It became increasingly doubtful to the American headquarters that a full-out attack could be launched in the early spring of 1943, and because it would be extremely hazardous to begin a major operation across the English Channel in the fall of the year, we began to realize that a large-scale invasion might not be possible before the spring of 1944.

This was a bitter possibility to contemplate. It was bitter for ourselves, for our Chiefs of Staff, and far more so for the political heads of the two countries: they not only had the burden of directing the industrial effort to produce the ships and guns and tanks and planes and of mobilizing millions of men, but they had also to maintain civilian morale during the period of preparation. Moreover, most of these delays could not be explained to the public. To do so would be to expose our own current weaknesses, with the danger of intensifying the gloom and despondency that were then so heavy, owing to the rapidity of the Japanese conquest and the misfortunes which had overtaken the British forces in the desert during the early summer.[24]

At the very least it was clear to the Chiefs of Staff that no significant invasion of western Europe was possible in 1942. We kept General Marshall informed of our developing conclusions, primarily through verbal communications carried by trusted staff officers. In mid-July 1942, General Marshall and Admiral King came to London to meet with the British Chiefs of Staff.[25] They were to discuss problems arising out of realization that a very considerable period must elapse before a full-blooded, decisive operation could be undertaken against the coasts of northwest Europe. They had to reckon with these factors:

The agreed-upon major strategical operation to be carried out jointly by Great Britain and the United States could not be put into effect, because of lack of forces and equipment, before late 1943 at the earliest, and, since the fall of the year would be a most unpropitious time to begin such a campaign, the prospective D-day, in the absence of some unforeseen, radical change in the situation, might be postponed until the spring of 1944.

Russia was insistently demanding an offensive move by Great Britain and the United States during 1942, and there was a lively fear that unless such a move was undertaken the gravest consequences might ensue on the Russian front.

The psychological reaction in the United States and Great Britain and in all the occupied countries of Europe might be little short of disastrous if positive action of some kind were not undertaken during 1942.

Whatever was attempted in 1942 would necessarily be on a much smaller scale than the contemplated invasion of Europe and, so far as possible, it should not seriously cut into the production and preparatory program then getting under way to make possible the final major operation.

The President had specifically ordered the United States Chiefs of Staff to launch some kind of offensive ground action in the European zone in 1942.[26]

In view of these circumstances there seemed to be three lines of action deserving of earnest study.

The first was the direct reinforcement of the British armies in the

Middle East via the Cape of Good Hope route, in an effort to destroy Rommel and his army and, by capturing Tripolitania, to gain secure control of the central Mediterranean.

The second was to prepare amphibious forces to seize northwest Africa with the idea of undertaking later operations to the eastward to catch Rommel in a giant vise and eventually open the entire Mediterranean for use by the United Nations.

The third was to undertake a limited operation on the northwest coast of France with a relatively small force but with objectives limited to the capture of an area that could be held against German attack and which would later form a bridgehead for use in the large-scale invasion agreed upon as the ultimate objective. The places indicated were the Cotentin Peninsula or the Brittany Peninsula. This proposed operation was called Sledgehammer.

No other course of action seemed feasible at the moment. The discussions were long and exhaustive. A major factor in all American thinking of that time was a lively suspicion that the British contemplated the agreed-upon cross-Channel concept with distaste and with considerable mental reservations concerning the practicability of ever conducting a major invasion of northwest Europe. So, though we could not plead for a do-nothing policy while all the impedimenta of major invasion were being produced and accumulated, we looked askance on any project that seemed to be an effort to lead us to indefinite commitment to a strategy in which we did not believe. I was well aware of sincere British misgivings—often voiced in a general way by Mr. Churchill, but definitely and specifically by General Paget—concerning the major cross-Channel venture, then known as Roundup. General Marshall heartily agreed that, no matter what decision should be reached by the London Conference then in progress, we must secure from the British unequivocal reaffirmation of the cross-Channel strategy.

Influenced by these considerations, I personally favored, at that time, the third course of action; that is, the attempt to seize a small bridgehead on the northwest coast of France. However, I told General Marshall that the project was a hazardous one and that my only real reason for favoring it was the fear of becoming so deeply involved elsewhere that the major cross-Channel attack would be indefinitely postponed, possibly even canceled. Almost certainly any 1942 operation in the Mediterranean would eliminate the possibility of a major cross-Channel venture in 1943.

Later developments have convinced me that those who held the Sledgehammer operation to be unwise at the moment were correct in their evaluation of the problem. Our limited-range fighter craft of 1942 could not have provided sufficiently effective air cover over the Cotentin or Brittany peninsulas, against the German air strength as it then existed. At least, the operation would have been very costly. Another reason is that out of the northwest African operation flowed benefits to the Allied nations that were felt all through the war and materially helped to achieve the great victory when the invasion actually took place in 1944. Only meager advantages would have followed capture of Cherbourg; the desirable features of that project were merely that it would have initiated a small "second front" at once and would have launched our first offensive effort in the direction and along the same line that would later be taken by our full-out assault.

In any event the Combined Chiefs of Staff first concluded that it would be unprofitable and uneconomical to attempt direct reinforcement of the British Eighth Army then in Egypt. On this there was unanimous agreement. The British and American Chiefs of Staff had therefore to decide, in late July 1942, between the northwest African invasion and the seizing of a bridgehead in northwest France.

As far as I know, there was no argument based upon nationalistic lines. The conferees were merely searching for the most profitable line of combined action to be undertaken in 1942.

On July 24 it was determined to proceed with the planning for the invasion of northwest Africa with an Allied force of all arms, to be carried out under an American commander.[27] The operation received the name Torch. Its execution was approved by the President on July 25. Both governments agreed that the whole venture should have, initially at least, a completely American complexion. The hope was that French North Africa would receive the invading troops with no more than a nominal show of resistance, and the chances of this favorable development were considered to be much brighter if the operation was advertised as purely American. British standing in France was at a low ebb because of the Oran, Dakar, and Syrian incidents, in which British forces had come into open conflict with the French.

In his headquarters in the Claridge Hotel on July 26, General Marshall informed me that I was to be the Allied commander in chief of the expedition. He stated that while this decision was definite some little time would be necessary to accomplish all the routine of official designation. In August the appointment as commander in chief was made official in a directive from the Combined Chiefs of Staff.[39]

The decision to invade North Africa necessitated a complete reversal in our thinking and drastic revision in our planning and preparation. Where we had been counting on many months of orderly build-up, we now had only weeks. Instead of a massed attack across narrow waters, the proposed expedition would require movement across open ocean areas where enemy submarines would constitute a real menace. Our target was no longer a restricted front where we knew accurately terrain, facilities, and people as they affected military operations, but the rim of a continent where no major military campaign had been conducted for centuries. We were not to have the air power we had planned to use against Europe and what we did have would be largely concentrated at a single, highly vulnerable base— Gibraltar—and immediate substantial success would have to be achieved in the first engagements. A beachhead could be held in Normandy and expanded, however slowly; a beachhead on the African coast might be impossible even to maintain.

This violent shift in target, timing, and the circumstances of attack might have had a serious psychological effect on all those who were convinced that victory could not be attained except by an offensive aimed directly at the enemy's continental vitals. But fortunately the decision to attack Africa definitely did not constitute or imply any abandonment by the Combined Chiefs of Staff of their determination to carry out, when practicable, the invasion of Europe by the route across the English Channel. The African venture was looked upon as diversionary in character but necessitated by the circumstances of the moment and in the hope that from it we would achieve great results. The least of these results was that northwest Africa would be denied to the Axis for a submarine and aircraft base. Next, it was expected that through an advance to the eastward Malta would be succored. The final hope expressed at that early date was that all North Africa might be cleared of the Axis; and that the Mediterranean, at least along its southern shores, could be used by the convoys of the Allied nations, thus eliminating the long route around the Cape of Good Hope to reach both the Middle East and India.

Curiously enough, it was believed by some officers that even if we succeeded in driving Rommel out of Africa we would not be able to use the Mediterranean because the Germans would still have aircraft in south Europe. One lieutenant general of the United States Army had been convinced from the beginning of the war that any hope of using the Mediterranean was completely illusory. Even before I went to London he several times urged me to resist the attempt, which he labeled as "idiocy." This pessimistic attitude was flatly repudiated by the Navy, particularly by the British Navy, which insisted that, given some land-based fighter craft along the north coast of Africa, they would guarantee to put the convoys through the Mediterranean without abnormal loss.

Immediately the decision to invade North Africa had been taken, General Marshall and Admiral King left for Washington and I remained in command of the American forces in the European theater. But I now had the additional task of organizing and leading an Allied force into northwest Africa.

We were definitely embarked upon the type of Allied problem that would engage my attention and that of my close associates for the remainder of the war.

Chapter 5

PLANNING TORCH

THE FIRST TASK WAS TO SELECT AMERICAN AND British officers to fill key positions in the command and staff organizations we would need for the African invasion.

In modern war, battle areas frequently extend over hundreds of miles of front and are equally extensive in depth. Throughout such a theater are combat troops, replacement camps, hospital centers, lines of communication, repair shops, depots, ports, and a myriad of service organizations, both air and ground. In the same region dwells a civil population, sometimes friendly, sometimes hostile, sometimes neutral or mixed in attitude. All these units, individuals, and activities must be carefully controlled, so that everything is co-ordinated toward the achievement of the commander's strategic plan. Even when all this is done the task of the highest headquarters is not finished. Everything needed by the theater commander comes from his supporting nation or nations. Daily there are exchanged between his staff and the governments to his rear hundreds of messages dealing with plans, estimates, losses, requisitions, individuals, shipping, and all the other things necessary to carry out the purposes assigned him by his superiors. The military methods and machinery for making and waging war have become so extraordinarily complex and intricate that high commanders must have gargantuan staffs for control and direction. Because of this it is sometimes assumed that the influence of the individual in war has become submerged, that the mistakes of one responsible officer are corrected or concealed in the mass action of a great number of associates. This is not true.

The individual now works differently; indeed, one of the most important characteristics of the successful officer today is his ability to continue changing his methods, almost even his mental processes, in order to keep abreast of the constant change that modern science, working under the compelling urge of national self-preservation, brings to the battlefield. But personal characteristics are more important than ever before in warfare. The reasons for this are simple. It was not a matter of great moment if a Wellington happened to be a crusty, unapproachable individual who found one of his chief delights in penning sarcastic quips to the War Office. He was the single head, who saw the whole battlefield and directed operations through a small administrative staff and a few aides and orderlies. As long as he had the stamina and the courage to make decisions and to stand by them, and as long as his tactical skill met the requirements of his particular time and conditions, he was a great commander. But the teams and staffs through which the modern commander absorbs information and exercises his authority must be a beautifully interlocked, smooth-working mechanism. Ideally, the whole should be practically a single mind; consequently misfits defeat the purpose of the command organization essential to the supply and control of vast land, air, sea, and logistical forces that must be brought to bear as a unit against the enemy. The personalities of senior commanders and staff officers are of special importance. Professional military ability and strength of character, always required in high military position, are often marred by unfortunate characteristics, the two most frequently encountered and hurtful ones being a too obvious avidity for public acclaim and the delusion that strength of purpose demands arrogant and even insufferable deportment. A soldier once remarked that a man sure of his footing does not need to mount a horse!

Staffs develop plans from basic decisions made by responsible commanders. The planning process sometimes, as in the case of a vast triphibious undertaking, takes weeks and months. As a consequence these plans must be founded in fact and intelligent conclusion, and once made they must be fixed and clear. Deviation from fundamental concepts is permissible only when significant changes in the situation compel it. The high commander must therefore be calm, clear, and determined—and in all commands, especially allied organizations, his success will be measured more by his ability to lead and persuade than by his adherence to fixed notions of arbitrary command practices. This truth applies with particular force during the time necessary to build up confidence—a confidence that reaches back into the governments at home as well as throughout the length and breadth of the command.

But whenever any incident or problem requires the commander to exert and maintain his authority, then compliance must be exacted promptly and fully.

An early, happily minor, break of security by an American officer who had taken too much to drink brought to my attention the need for exercising particular care as to the habits of every individual assigned to an important post. Loyalty and efficiency were not enough —discretion, reliability, and sobriety were mandatory. Where individuals were relatively unknown or untested our highly efficient Secret Service organization was called upon to conduct a confidential investigation. All on my personal staff, without their knowledge, were so checked and tested over a period of weeks. The issues were too great to trust to chance; even chauffeurs had occasional opportunity to pick up information of value to the enemy.

In the organization, operation, and composition of my staff we proceeded as though all its members belonged to a single nation. Nevertheless we tried to include in every section individuals from both nationalities, and certain modifications in normal United States organization were compelled by differences in the staff procedures of the two countries. In the early days officers of the two nationalities were apt to conduct their business in the attitude of a bulldog meeting a tomcat, but as time went on their own discoveries of mutual respect and friendship developed a team that in its unity of purpose, devotion to duty, and absence of friction could not have been excelled if all its members had come from the same nation and the same service.

Because of the chance that through accident something might incapacitate me, particularly in the early stages of the operation, it was decided best to have the deputy also an American, so that the fiction of a practically exclusively American operation would be preserved as long as possible. To this post was named General Clark, who had come to England as commander of the II Corps.[1] He was a relatively young man but an extremely able professional, with a faculty for picking fine assistants and for developing a high morale within his staff. During the planning stages of Torch, General Clark acted as deputy and, until the arrival of General Smith in early September, as chief of staff. More than any other one person, Clark was responsible for the effective co-ordination of detail achieved in this, the first Allied plan for amphibious attack in the Mediterranean.

Considering our problem in London in early August 1942, it was obvious that if we were to launch a serious attack during that year there was not a moment to waste in preparation. Summer was already fading and good campaigning weather would soon be gone. The need for haste was so great as to admit of no opportunity for planning for the surest or the best—the satisfactory had to become the ideal.

A thousand intricacies had to be solved in close co-ordination with the British Ministry of Transport, the Director of Movements, the War Office, the Admiralty, the Air Ministry, the Director of Shipping, and the Prime Minister. In the United States these processes were equally involved. The venture was new—it was almost new in conception. Up to that moment no government had ever attempted to carry out an overseas expedition involving a journey of thousands of miles from its bases and terminating in a major attack.

One of our earliest and continuing problems was the determination of exactly what ground, air, and naval forces could and would be made available for the operation. Ordinarily a commander is given, along with a general objective, a definite allocation of force upon which to construct his strategical plan, supported by detailed tactical, organizational, and logistical programs. In this case the situation was vague, the amount of resources unknown, the final object indeterminate, and the only firm factor in the whole business our instructions to attack. We were still existing in a state of scarcity; there was no such thing as plenty of anything. A diary of the time quotes excerpts of dozens of messages, most of them transatlantic, on the one subject of possible availability of United States ground, air, and naval forces.[2] The United States Navy, in particular, was loath to commit itself firmly to an estimate of the vessels it could provide for the expedition. It was a nerve-racking state of uncertainty in which we had to work and plan.

Any narration of the problems that faced us during the late summer and fall of 1942 must take them up in turn; but solutions had to evolve together. Grand strategy, tactics, procurement of landing craft and ships, allocation of supporting naval forces, organization of air forces, provision of staging and training areas, arrangements for early and later supply, and determination of actual composition of each element of each assault force—all these were matters that had to be handled progressively and simultaneously. Difficulty in any of these produced at once difficulties in all the others.

The first requisite was to determine the areas and the general strength of the attack. As early as January 1942 our governments had briefly considered, but laid aside, a plan for an American attack, labeled Gymnast, against Casablanca alone.[3] It had as its object the mere denial of West Africa to the Axis as a submarine base. Later the scope of the initial plan for Gymnast was enlarged to include an attack within the Mediterranean by the British. Parenthetically, I should here remark that in all our later campaigning we never found, in West Africa, any evidence that the ports on that coast had ever been used as submarine bases by the Axis.

In fixing upon the landing areas for our expedition a primary consideration was the practicability of providing adequate air cover for our convoys, from the moment they should come within range of the hostile bombers until landings were successful. The danger range included the western Mediterranean up to Gibraltar, and extended even far west of that for the enemy's long-range bombers. Allied carriers were not available in significant numbers; indeed, during our entire experience in the Mediterranean we never had available more than two or three carriers at any time.

Land-based aircraft had to take almost the entire load of providing air protection, and the only available spot from which this could be done was Gibraltar. This made Gibraltar the focal point of our air umbrella and this in turn fixed the distance to which we could safely proceed into the Mediterranean with surface ships. Availability of shipping limited the size of the force that could be carried, while shortages in naval escorting and support vessels limited our attack to three major points; during early planning weeks it appeared that we would be limited to two.

Four important ports or port areas, within the extreme limits of our capabilities, were indicated as desirable objectives. These were, from west to east, Casablanca on the Atlantic coast, and Oran, Algiers, and the Bône area on the Mediterranean. A successful direct landing in the Bizerte-Tunis area would have yielded great results, but that locality was far outside the range of fighter support, and since British experiences in running convoys to Malta had been only little short of disastrous, this particular project was quickly given up as beyond the bounds of justifiable risk.

However, it was extremely desirable to capture the Bizerte-Tunis area at the earliest possible moment so that we could succor Malta and by land, sea, and air operate against Rommel's line of supply, thus assuring a victorious end to the war in Africa.

At the other end of the line, Casablanca was important at that moment for two reasons only. First, Casablanca was the terminus of a long, rickety railway line that wound its way through the Atlas

Mountains and on to the eastward through Oran, Algiers, and finally into Tunisia. The capacity of the railway was small but it did offer a weak life line to our forces if the enemy should decide to advance down through Spain, which was friendly to him, and, with bombers and artillery, render the Strait of Gibraltar useless to us for maintenance purposes. Without the rail line, bad as it was, from Casablanca to Oran, all the troops sent inside the Mediterranean would then have been cut off; even their escape might have been hazardous.

The other factor that made Casablanca important was the antici-pated influence of a strong landing at that point upon Spain and the Moroccan tribes. If we failed to land there it was possible that the Vichy French would carry those warlike tribes into open conflict against us, and this circumstance would almost certainly give Spain greater reason for intervening on the Axis side.

There was an unusual operational hazard connected with the Casablanca project. During the late fall and winter the northwest African coast is a forbidding one from the standpoint of small-boat landings. The long Atlantic swells break up on the beaches in terrifying fashion and even in relatively good autumn weather this condition exists, on the average, four days out of five.[4] From a naval viewpoint, the risk involved in this operation would be many times greater than inside the Mediterranean, where relatively good weather was to be expected.

From the first it was clear that Oran and Algiers must be attacked under any plan of operation. Both were important ports and the airfields near Oran were essential for later operations, particularly for staging short-range fighter aircraft from Gibraltar to front lines, wherever they might happen to be. Algiers, of course, was the center of political, economic, and military activity in the area.

Fixing the flanks of the assault, then, was what we had to decide. In the one case we could attack Casablanca, Oran, and Algiers; in the other, Oran, Algiers, and Bône.

Over this question we studied long and earnestly. I came to favor, personally, taking the entire force inside the Mediterranean. I believed that Tunis was so great a prize that we should land initially as far east as Bône. Admittedly, to pass inside the Mediterranean without establishing a base at Casablanca involved additional hazard, but I felt that as long as we were risking so much we might as well put all our chips on one number with the idea that Casablanca, when cut off from the eastward, would either fall of its own weight or could be captured by columns moving back down the railway from Oran. I was influenced also by the desire to avoid the very great natural hazards involved in landing at Casablanca.

We communicated this scheme to the Combined Chiefs of Staff and found that the United States Chiefs of Staff were opposed to omitting Casablanca from the original attack plan.[5] They were of the belief that the risks involved in depending entirely upon the Strait of Gibraltar for a line of communications were too great and that, in spite of the limited capacity of the Casablanca–Oran railway, we must quickly secure it as partial insurance against possible Axis attempts against the Gibraltar bottleneck. Moreover, they believed that unless a strong force landed instantly in Morocco the Spanish would be much more inclined to enter the war or to permit the Germans to use Spain as an avenue of advance against our rear. Another objection to the Bône operation was doubt as to our ability to provide adequate air cover so close in under the Axis air forces stationed in Italy and Sicily. Later losses to the hostile bombers in that port and others in the neighborhood tended to support the validity of this doubt.[6] Since this decision by the Combined Chiefs of Staff made it impossible to attack Bône initially, any later advance eastward from Algiers could be accomplished only by land marches, coupled with local seaborne attacks against the smaller ports along the coast toward Tunis.

As far as I can recall, this was the only instance in the war when any part of one of our proposed operational plans was changed by intervention of higher authority. We cheerfully accepted the decision because the governing considerations were political more than tactical, and political estimates are the function of governments, not of soldiers. However, we did point out that the early capture of Tunis was, by this decision, removed from the realm of the probable to the remotely possible.[7]

The next major decision concerned the timing of the attack. Meteorological reports indicated that a steady deterioration of weather was to be anticipated, beginning in the early fall. Naturally, therefore, time became of the essence. Everything was done to launch the attack at the earliest possible date, even to the point of sacrificing desired strength in sea, air, and ground formations when to secure any greater strength than that having a fighting chance for success would have meant delay.

In organizing the venture one of the most important factors was the estimated political situation in North Africa. This was an extremely complicated question, which had been under study by both the United

PUNCHING OUT A SNIPER

"The trained American possesses qualities that are almost unique. Because of his initiative and resourcefulness, his adaptability to change and his readiness to resort to expedient . . ." *Page 453*

Anti-Tank Gun Gets New Normandy Role

CONQUEST IN SINGLE FILE
"In the advance eastward from Palermo . . . the only road was of the 'shelf' variety, a mere niche in the cliffs interrupted by bridges and culverts that the enemy invariably destroyed as he drew back fighting." *Pages 176–77*

Infantrymen Advance Along Sicilian Cliff

States and British governments for a considerable length of time. Both governments were convinced that the expedition should be as exclusively American in complexion as it was possible to make it,[8] but it was deemed equally important to make the expedition so large in numerical strength that the local French government and military commanders could logically plead "overwhelming strength" to the Vichy government and its Nazi overlords, as an excuse for the prompt surrender and later co-operation we hoped to obtain.

Fundamentally the expedition was conceived in the hope that the French forces, officials, and population of northwest Africa would permit our entry without fighting and would join with us in the common battle against Germany. However, there was nothing in the political history of the years 1940–42 to indicate that this would occur; it was a hope rather than an expectation. Consequently we had to be prepared to fight against forces which, in all, were estimated to number 200,000.[9] But our governments were clear in their instructions that we were to strive to create an ally in North Africa; we were not to act as if we were conquering a hostile territory unless this attitude should be forced upon us by continued French resistance.[10] Everything that might induce the French forces in Africa to join us was incorporated into our plans, including careful wording of pronouncements and proclamations to be issued coincidentally with the beginning of the invasion.

To provide an entirely American façade to the attacking force was easy enough at Casablanca and Oran. All the attacking forces at the former place were to come directly from the United States. The Oran assault involved the U. S. 1st Infantry Division and parts of the U. S. 1st Armored Division, both then stationed in the United Kingdom. Since lack of shipping did not permit us to bring more forces directly from the United States, the only American troops that could be committed to the Algiers attack were part of the 34th Division, then in Ireland, reinforced by a regiment of the U. S. 9th Division and a Ranger battalion. This was not strong enough for the task in the event that any real resistance should be met, but British supporting units were so distributed in the landing tables that in only a few instances were they in the actual assault waves.[11]

Obviously the French African forces and the population would learn, soon after the initial landings, of British participation but it was believed that if entry could be gained and our friendly attitude promptly and clearly proved, possible complications would be minimized. American flags would identify our men and vehicles.

Out of study, revision, checking, and rechecking finally evolved the essentials of the attack plan, and these, regardless of changing details, were adhered to religiously. We would attack Casablanca, Oran, and Algiers. United States forces would then protect our rear in Morocco, and the British forces, as rapidly as they could land and the situation might permit, would rush for Tunis.[12]

I notified General Marshall of my desire to have General Patton command the Casablanca expedition and within a short time George reported to me in London, where he was thoroughly briefed on his portion of the plan.[13] Hardly had he returned to Washington before I received a message stating that he had become embroiled in such a distressing argument with the Navy Department that serious thought was being given to his relief from command. Feeling certain that the difficulty, whatever its nature, was nothing more than the result of a bit of George's flair for the dramatic, I protested at once, suggesting that if his personality was causing any difficulty in conferences the issue could be met by sending him out with his troops and allowing some staff member to represent him in the completion of planning details. In any event the matter was passed over.

I well knew that Patton delighted to startle his hearers with fantastic statements; many men who believed they knew him well never penetrated past the shell of showmanship in which he constantly and carefully clothed himself. But he was essentially a shrewd battle leader who invariably gained the devotion of his subordinates. From early life his one ambition was to be a successful battlefield commander. Because of this he was an inveterate reader of military history and his heroes were the great captains of past ages.

All the mannerisms and idiosyncrasies he developed were of his own deliberate adoption. One of his poses, for example, was that of the most hard-boiled individual in the Army. Actually he was so softhearted, particularly where a personal friend was concerned, that it was possibly his greatest fault. Later in the war he once vehemently demanded that I discharge eighty of his officers because, as he said, of inefficiency and timidity bordering on cowardice. He was so exercised and so persistent that I agreed, contingent upon his sending me a report in writing. Apparently astonished by my acquiescence, he began postponing from week to week, on one excuse or another, the submission of his list. Finally he confessed, rather sheepishly, that he had reconsidered and wanted to discharge no one.

The Center Task Force, the U. S. II Corps, to attack Oran, was under command of Major General Lloyd R. Fredendall. I had known him only slightly before the beginning of the African operation but his reputation as a fine trainer and organizer was unexcelled.

The Eastern Task Force, to capture Algiers, had a somewhat curious organization. To preserve the American character of the assaulting forces they were placed under Major General Charles W. Ryder, the commanding general of the U. S. 34th Division. He had established a splendid record in the first World War, in which he won battlefield promotions to the grade of lieutenant colonel at a very early age and had enjoyed a reputation as a sound soldier throughout the years intervening between the two wars. He was a man of sterling character and great gallantry in combat. Ryder was to lead the attack only until the city was captured. Once our Eastern Task Force was firmly established, command was to be taken over by Lieutenant General Sir Kenneth A. N. Anderson, commanding the British First Army. It was his mission to dash eastward as rapidly as the situation might permit, in an effort to secure Tunis. General Anderson was a gallant Scot, devoted to duty and absolutely selfless. Honest and straightforward, he was blunt, at times to the point of rudeness, and this trait, curiously enough, seemed to bring him into conflict with his British confreres more than it did with the Americans. His real difficulty was probably shyness. He was not a popular type but I had real respect for his fighting heart. Even his most severe critics must find it difficult to discount the smashing victory he finally attained in Tunisia.

From the inception of the invasion project, our governments carefully considered the possibility of including General de Gaulle, then in London, in Torch planning. Units under his command had taken part in the ill-fated Dakar expedition, where the attacking forces had to retire in confusion in the face of local French resistance. The British always believed that this fiasco resulted from leaks in De Gaulle's London headquarters. Our instructions from the two governments, possibly colored by this unfortunate early experience, were to the effect that under no circumstances was any information concerning the proposed expedition to be communicated to General de Gaulle.[14]

There was confirmation of the assumption that General de Gaulle's presence in the initial assaulting forces would incite determined opposition on the part of the French garrisons. During the course of our planning in London a constant stream of information came to us from consuls and other officials whom our State Department maintained in

Africa throughout the war. All of this information was to the effect that in the regular officer corps of the French Army De Gaulle was, at that time, considered a disloyal soldier. His standing with the resistance elements of the civil population was vastly different. But at that moment resistance elements, particularly in Africa, were inarticulate and ineffective—and we had to win over the armed services as a first objective.

It is possible to understand why De Gaulle was disliked within the ranks of the French Army. At the time of France's surrender in 1940 the officers who remained in the Army had accepted the position and orders of their government and had given up the fight. From their viewpoint, if the course chosen by De Gaulle was correct, then every French officer who obeyed the orders of his government was a poltroon. If De Gaulle was a loyal Frenchman they had to regard themselves as cowards. Naturally the officers did not choose to think of themselves in this light; rather they considered themselves as loyal Frenchmen carrying out the orders of constituted civilian authority, and it followed that they officially and personally regarded De Gaulle as a deserter.

Nevertheless, it was known that there was a strong anti-German and anti-Vichy sentiment in North Africa, even among some of the Army officers. It was believed possible that if a sufficient show of force could be made in the initial attack all these officers might find that their honor had been satisfied by token resistance and, bowing to the inevitable, would join in the fight against the traditional foe that had humiliated them in 1940. It was a complicated and hazy situation, but keeping the expedition entirely secret from the French in London was the fixed policy of the Allied governments. An added and most important motive in doing so was the fact that only through perfect surprise could the expedition succeed. The fewer people who knew anything at all about the matter the better.

Each day brought new difficulties in the development of plans for the operation. Among these intricate problems was, for example, interference with shipments to Russia. The withdrawal of shipping from the sea lanes in time to refit, load, assemble, and make the transit to the Mediterranean was certain to cut seriously into the Murmansk convoys; this interference began as early as September 1942.[15] This same consideration applied to other vital shipping commitments of Britain and America but it was, of course, one of the inescapable costs of undertaking the operation.

Another complication arose out of the fact that all of the earliest shipments of American supplies and equipment into England were in anticipation of an eventual cross-Channel attack. Since haste in unloading ships and speeding up their turn-around was initially the pressing consideration, supplies and equipment were thrown into warehouses and open storage without regard for segregation and inventories. We had thought there would be ample time for this as the organization grew. Now we were suddenly faced with an immediate need for the things we had already brought over but without the necessary records under which required supplies could be selected, packaged, and loaded in the least possible time.[16] We should have paid more attention to "red tape" and paper work.

Still another complication involved our air forces. In the summer of 1942 we had made only a good beginning at organizing a bomber and accompanying fighter command for conducting air operations against Germany. A considerable number of air units had to be hastily called away from their original tasks, retrained, and reshaped toward participation in the African invasion. Some American fighter organizations had to be equipped with the British Spitfire.[17] Similar problems arose with respect to the internal transportation systems of England, the use of her crowded ports, and the training of ground troops.

Each week brought us records of additional ships sunk or damaged by enemy U-boats, ships that were included in our programs for the transport of troops, equipment, and supplies. Each sinking caused revisions in operational and tactical plans.

All these things called for constant conferences, usually with members of the tactical staffs and services in Great Britain but frequently also with the Prime Minister. During this time, at his request, I fell into the habit of meeting with the Prime Minister twice each week. On Tuesdays we would have luncheon at 10 Downing Street, usually present at which were one or more members of the British Chiefs of Staff or the War Cabinet. On Friday nights I would have dinner with him at his country house, Chequers, and this would sometimes be prolonged into an overnight stay, during which there would be an unending series of meetings with officials, both military and civil. Almost always the Foreign Minister, Mr. Anthony Eden, was present.

After some six weeks of intensive planning we were notified that Mr. Robert D. Murphy, the senior American State Department officer in North Africa, would pay us a secret visit to discuss with us the political implications and possibilities in that region.[18] These factors remained among the great question marks of the entire operation. Vichy France was a neutral country and during the entire period of the war the United States had maintained diplomatic connection with the French Government. Never, in all its history, had the United States been a party to an unprovoked attack upon a neutral country and even though Vichy was avowedly collaborating with Hitler, there is no doubt that American political leaders regarded the projected operation, from this viewpoint, with considerable distaste.

Both the British and American governments believed that North African public opinion favored the Allies, and naturally desired to make the invasion appear as an operation undertaken in response to a popular desire for liberation from the Vichy yoke. Not only did we definitely want to avoid adding France to our already formidable list of enemies; we wanted, if possible, to make it appear that we had come into Africa on invitation rather than by force.

It was realized that, officially, some opposition would have to be made to the landing because within Europe itself the French dwelt constantly under the German heel. But if we could show that popular opinion was definitely in opposition to the Vichy rulers, any political antagonism to the invasion in Great Britain or America would be mollified.

Mr. Murphy, who had long been stationed in Africa, was early taken into the confidence of the President of the United States and informed of the possibility of military action in that region. With his staff of assistants he not only conducted a continuing survey of public opinion, but he did his best to discover among the military and political leaders those individuals who were definitely hostile to the Axis and occupying their posts merely out of a sense of duty to France. Affable, friendly, exceedingly shrewd, and speaking French capably, he was admirably suited for his task. Unquestionably his missionary work between 1940 and late 1942 had much to do with eventual success.

His trip to my headquarters in London, in the fall of 1942, was conducted in the greatest secrecy. In Washington, where he went first, he was placed in uniform, given a fictional commission as lieutenant colonel, and came to see me under the name of McGowan.[19] I met him at a rendezvous outside the city and within a matter of twenty-four hours he was again on the way to Washington.

From Mr. Murphy we learned the names of those officers who had pro-Allied sympathies and those who were ready to aid us actively.

We learned much about the temper of the Army itself and about feeling among the civil population. He told us very accurately that our greatest resistance would be met in French Morocco, where General August Paul Noguès was Foreign Minister to the Sultan.[20] He gave us a number of details of French military strength in Africa, including information concerning equipment and training in their ground, air, and sea forces. From his calculations it was plain that if we were bitterly opposed by the French a bloody fight would ensue; if the French should promptly decide to join us we could expect to get along quickly with our main business of seizing Tunisia and attacking Rommel from the rear. It was Mr. Murphy's belief that we would actually encounter a mean between these two extremes. Events proved him to be correct.

On another point, however, he was, through no fault of his own, completely mistaken. He had been convinced by the French Generals Charles Emmanuel Mast, chief of staff of the French XIX Corps in Algeria, Marie Emile Bethouart, commander of the Casablanca Division, and others who were risking their lives to assist us, that if General Henri Giraud could be brought into North Africa, ostensibly to aid in an uprising against the Vichy government, the response would be immediate and enthusiastic and all North Africa would flame into revolt, unified under a leader who was represented as being intensely popular throughout the region.[21] Weeks later, during a crisis in our affairs, we were to learn that this hope was a futile one.

Mr. Murphy was certain that much more effective co-operation with our known friends in North Africa would be achieved if a high-ranking officer from my staff could go to Africa for a conference. Naturally the meeting had to be arranged clandestinely because, if discovered, my emissaries would certainly be interned, while any French officer found engaged in such an affair would probably be tried by Vichy as a traitor. It was immediately decided that it was worth the risk to send a small group to confer with General Mast and others. Since manifestly I could not go myself, I chose, from many volunteers, my deputy, General Clark, to make the journey. He was accompanied by a small staff.

The trip was made by airplane and submarine and was carried out exactly as planned except that local suspicion finally was aroused and the French conspirators were forced to escape very hurriedly, while General Clark and his group had to hide until they could re-embark in their submarine. Rough weather made the re-embarkation a difficult affair but, except for a ducking and the loss of a small amount of money, no great damage was done.[22] This expedition was valuable in gathering more details of information. These did not compel any material change in our planned operations.

The conference with Mr. Murphy gave most of us, particularly the Americans, our first vicarious acquaintanceship with a number of French officials. He discussed at length the characteristics and political leanings of the principal generals and the officials we were likely to encounter.[23] He especially emphasized that at that time the American Government and people were held in high esteem by the French as compared to the antagonism that had developed toward the British.

The Prime Minister accepted this view and gave his personal attention to assuring that the operation should bear the appearance, so far as was humanly possible, of an exclusively American force. He even seriously considered, at one time, requiring all British units that had to participate in the initial landing to wear the uniform of the American Army. In discussions involving political possibilities Mr. Eden, as head of the Foreign Office, was almost always present, as was frequently Mr. John Winant, our wartime ambassador to Great Britain. Our concern over these affairs illustrates forcibly the old truism that political considerations can never be wholly separated from military ones and that war is a mere continuation of political policy in the field of force. The Allied invasion of Africa was a most peculiar venture of armed forces into the field of international politics; we were invading a neutral country to create a friend. Important as were these political problems, they constituted only a fraction of the difficult matters with which we daily wrestled.

We were gambling for high stakes, but this is a constant characteristic of war and in itself was not a particularly disturbing factor. But uncertainty prevailed in many directions: uncertainty as to the attitude of the Spanish and the knowledge that the enemy had of our plans; uncertainty as to the exact number of ships that would be available when the expedition should sail; and uncertainty as to the ability of the Air Force to give proper protection to our convoys as they neared the African coast.

Another hazard involved a project for dispatching from England by transport planes a parachute force to capture the airfields of Oran.[24] These planes had to wing their relatively slow course over a distance of more than twelve hundred miles, through areas from which they might be attacked by enemy planes. Parachutists had to drop, or the planes had to land, on fields of which we had only sketchy information. Many experienced officers literally threw up their hands in the face of such a "harebrained" scheme. Other projects involved direct and admittedly desperate assaults by selected forces against the docks of Algiers and Oran, in an effort to prevent sabotage and destruction and so preserve port facilities for our future uses.

The whole basis of our higher organization was new. Time and again during the summer old Army friends warned me that the conception of Allied unity which we took as the foundation of our command scheme was impracticable and impossible; that any commander placed in my position was foredoomed to failure and could become nothing but a scapegoat to carry the odium of defeat for the whole operation. I was regaled with tales of allied failure starting with the Greeks, five hundred years before Christ, and coming down through the ages of allied quarrels to the bitter French-British recriminations of 1940. But more than counterbalancing such doleful prophecy was a daily and noticeable growth of co-operation, comradeship, faith, and optimism in Torch headquarters. British and Americans were unconsciously, in their absorption in common problems, shedding their shells of mutual distrust and suspicion.

In the early fall Admiral Ramsay was relieved by the British Chiefs of Staff as the naval commander of the expedition and in his place was assigned Admiral Sir Andrew B. Cunningham, whom I then met for the first time. He was the Nelsonian type of admiral. He believed that ships went to sea in order to find and destroy the enemy. He thought always in terms of attack, never of defense. He was vigorous, hardy, intelligent, and straightforward. In spite of his toughness, the degree of affection in which he was held by all grades and ranks of the British Navy and, to a large extent, the other services, both British and American, was nothing short of remarkable. He was a real sea dog. There will always live with me his answer when I asked him in the fall of 1943 to send the British battle fleet, carrying a division of soldiers, into Taranto Harbor, known to be filled with mines and treachery.

"Sir," he said, "His Majesty's Fleet is here to go wherever you may send it!"

The terrific pressure under which we worked is hard to appreciate now for any who have not shared in the experience of planning a great allied operation in modern war. Yet this pressure remains a persistent and vivid memory for anyone who was a part of it.

It is equally difficult to classify our time-absorbing problems. There were, above all, people to see, most of them engaged in preparing the details of Torch but many others concerned with problems ranging from Red Cross affairs to the need for shipping white cloth to the Arabs, who insist on it for burial shrouds and will kill to get it. Press conferences were almost obligatory, since the problem of morale, both at home and in England, was never far from our minds.

We had to co-ordinate our plans not only with the British but also with the United States Navy. This was by no means simple, and it required a great many conferences. Two of the Navy's capable officers had been assigned by Admiral King to assist in planning, and they were welcomed by Brigadier General Alfred M. Gruenther, chief American planner, with the statement that there were a thousand questions the Navy could help answer. "We are here only to listen," was their answer. I knew that if I could talk personally to Admiral King there would be no difficulty, but under the circumstances these snarls had to be worked out with care and patience.

The Navy could remind us, after all, that we were asking for what was one of the greatest fighting armadas of all times—approximately 110 troop and cargo ships and 200 warships.[25] The Navy was conscious of the need for watching the German fleet, which they thought at that time included at least one aircraft carrier and possibly two. Some American officers seemed at times to feel a resentment toward the operation, apparently regarding it as a British plan into which America had been dragged by the heels. I stated and restated at conferences during this planning phase that Torch was an order from the Commander in Chief, the President of the United States, and the Prime Minister, and that I proposed to move into West and North Africa, as the order instructed me, whether we had protective warships or not.

Axis attacks on British convoys in the Mediterranean continued to bring us bad news.[26] One heavily escorted convoy of fourteen cargo vessels, attempting to take supplies to Malta, arrived there with only three of the supply ships still afloat. Of these, one was sunk at the dock. The aircraft carrier *Eagle,* which had been earmarked for Torch, was torpedoed and sunk. The naval staff brought us such news from time to time, and each time further revision of plans became necessary.

In the middle of September I sent a message to General Marshall on how the invasion's chances looked to us some seven weeks before it took place:

"Tentative and unofficial details of contemplated British carrier-borne air support are as follows: In the covering force east of Gibraltar, one carrier with twenty fighters and twenty torpedo planes; at Algiers in direct support sixty-six fighters and eighteen torpedo planes. In addition to above one old carrier with thirteen planes may possibly be available.

"The following are the particular factors that bear directly upon the degree of hazard inherent in this operation:

"(a) *The sufficiency of carrier-borne air support during initial stages.*

"The operational strength of the French Air Force in Africa is about 500 planes. Neither the bombers nor the fighters are of the most modern type, but the fighters are superior in performance to the naval types on carriers. Consequently, if the French make determined and unified resistance to the initial landing, particularly by concentrating the bulk of their air against either of the major ports, they can seriously interfere with, if not prevent, a landing at that point. The total carrier-borne fighter strength (counting on 100 U.S. fighters on *Ranger* and auxiliary) will apparently be about 166 planes in actual support of the landings. Only twenty to thirty will be with the naval covering forces to the eastward. These fighters will be under the usual handicaps of carrier-based aircraft when operating against land-based planes.

"(b) *Efficiency of Gibraltar as an erection point for fighter aircraft to be used after landing fields have been secured.*

"Since Gibraltar is the only port available to Allies in that region, the rapid transfer of fighter craft to captured airdromes will be largely dependent upon our ability to set up at Gibraltar a reasonable number for immediate operations and a flow thereafter of at least thirty planes per day. The vulnerability of Gibraltar, especially to interference by Spanish forces, is obvious. If the Spaniards should take hostile action against us immediately upon the beginning of landing operations, it would be practically impossible to secure any land-based fighter craft for use in northern Africa for a period of some days.

"(c) *Another critical factor affecting the air will be the state of the weather.*

"It is planned to transfer by flying to captured airdromes in North Africa the American units now in Great Britain except the Spitfire groups. These last will necessarily be shipped and set up at Gibraltar or captured airdromes. A spell of bad weather would so weaken the anticipated air support in the early stages of the operation as to constitute another definite hazard to success.

"(d) *The character of resistance of the French Army.*

"In the region now are some fourteen French divisions rather poorly equipped but presumably with a fair degree of training and with the benefit of professional leadership. If this Army should act as a unit in contesting the invasion, it could, in view of the slowness with which Allied forces can be accumulated at the two main ports, so delay and hamper operations that the real object of the expedition could not be achieved, namely, the seizing control of the north shore of Africa before it can be substantially reinforced by the Axis.

"(e) *The attitude of the Spanish Army.*

"While there have been no indications to date that the Spaniards would take sides in the war as a result of this particular operation, this contingency must be looked on as a possibility, particularly if Germany should make a definite move toward entering Spain. In any event, Spain's entry would instantly entail the loss of Gibraltar as a landing field and would prevent our use of the Strait of Gibraltar until effective action could be taken by the Allies. In view of available resources, it would appear doubtful that such effective action is within our capabilities.

"(f) *The possibility that the German air forces now in western Europe may rapidly enter Spain and operate against our line of communications.*

"This would not be an easy operation for the Germans except with the full acquiescence and support of Spain. Gasoline, bombs, and lubricants do not exist at the Spanish airfields and the transfer to the country of ground and maintenance crews and supplies would require considerable time. Certain facts that bear upon the likelihood of such enemy action are, first, that Germany already has excellent landing fields in Sicily, from which their long-range aircraft can operate without going to the trouble of establishing new bases. Secondly, the advantages to Germany of occupying the Iberian Peninsula in force have always existed. The fact that Germany has made no noticeable move in this direction, even under the conditions lately existing when substantial parts of the British naval strength have been inside the Mediterranean, is at least some evidence that the enemy does *not* consider this an easy operation.

"(g) *Other factors* that we have considered in arriving at the conclusions given below are the experiences of the recent Malta convoy and the assumption that Allied naval losses within the past ten days have been considerable. The Malta convoy did not come under air attack until it was practically south of Sardinia and its difficulties west of that point were from submarine action.

"Based on all the above, we consider that the operation has more than a fair chance of success provided Spain stays neutral and the French forces either offer only token resistance or are so badly divided by internal dissension and by Allied political maneuvering that effective resistance will be negligible. It is our opinion that Spain will stay neutral, at least during the early stages of the operation, provided we are successful in maintaining profound secrecy in connection with our intentions. She has done so in the past when similar large convoys passed through the strait. We believe, on the other hand, that we will encounter very considerable resistance from certain sections of the French forces. We believe the area in which the French will be most favorable to us is around Algiers, with the areas in which we will probably encounter resistance those between Oran and Casablanca and near Tunis.

"We believe that the chances of effecting initial landings are better than even but that the chances of over-all success in the operation, including the capture of Tunis before it can be reinforced by the Axis, are considerably less than fifty per cent. This takes into account the great difficulty surrounding the building up of a land-based air force, the low capacity of ports and consequent slowness in building up of land forces, the very poor character of the long line of communications from Casablanca to Oran, and finally the uncertainty of the French attitude.

"Further eventualities which might involve a change in Spanish attitude, as well as increasing naval and shipping difficulties and consequent slowing up in our reinforcements, are difficult to evaluate. Any sign of failure at this stage and a delay of reinforcements to arrive might be seized upon by the Axis as a reason for coming into Spain, and if Spain should then enter the war the results would be most serious."[27]

Week after week this sort of thing went on. Although the essentials of our operational plan had been crystallized early, every day brought some slight change in detail until almost the final day before sailing.

Along with planning went inspections of training and physical preparation. Our final and most ambitious training exercise in landing operations took place in western Scotland, during abominable weather. A group of the staff accompanied me to observe the operation and were far from encouraged by the evident lack of skill, particularly among ship companies and boat crews. However, since these had been assembled at the last minute, to minimize interference in Allied shipping programs, we hoped and believed that major errors revealed by the exercises would not be repeated in actual operations. This proved to be the case.

While on this trip I received a piece of information that carried me back again to America's traditional peacetime indifference toward preparedness. I was told by a troop commander that his unit had just received its final consignment of "bazookas," the infantryman's best weapon of defense against tanks. Since his command was to begin embarking the next day, he was completely at a loss as to how to teach his men the use of this vitally needed weapon. He said, "I don't know anything about it myself except from hearsay."

Nothing more could now be done in London. It was a relief to lock up a desk. To account for my absence from London an elaborate story was circulated that I was making a visit to Washington. Even the President helped out in this particular deception. Actually we took off for Gibraltar, in a flight of five Fortresses, on November 5, 1942.[28] At Gibraltar we were greeted by the governor, Lieutenant General Sir F. N. Mason MacFarlane, who most hospitably welcomed us to Government House for quarters. By a series of minor mishaps the plane in which I was flying was unreported in London for several hours after the safe arrival of the others in the group had been reported. This caused some consternation among the staff, the larger portion of which was still in the United Kingdom, but of this we were unaware at the moment. One plane, which had failed to take off with us, made the flight on the following day and was attacked by two German JU-88s.[29] One man was wounded but the gunners on the Fortress finally drove off the attacking planes.

I went to the tunnels of the Fortress, where our offices were located and where I met Admiral Cunningham, who had made the journey from London in a fast cruiser. He and I began to scan the reports of weather and of operation, to check and recheck everything we had done, and to talk over all the things that have so far been related in this book.

Chapter 6

INVASION
OF AFRICA

AT GIBRALTAR OUR HEADQUARTERS WAS ESTAB-
lished in the most dismal setting we occupied during the war. The
subterranean passages under the Rock provided the sole available
office space, and in them was located the signal equipment by which
we expected to keep in touch with the commanders of the three assault
forces. The eternal darkness of the tunnels was here and there partially
pierced by feeble electric bulbs. Damp, cold air in block-long passages
was heavy with a stagnation that did not noticeably respond to the clat-
tering efforts of electric fans. Through the arched ceilings came a constant drip, drip, drip of surface water that faithfully but drearily ticked
off the seconds of the interminable, almost unendurable, wait which
occurs between completion of a military plan and the moment action
begins.

There was no other place to use. In November 1942 the Allied nations possessed, except for the Gibraltar Fortress, not a single spot of
ground in all the region of western Europe, and in the Mediterranean
area, nothing west of Malta. Britain's Gibraltar made possible the invasion of northwest Africa. Without it the vital air cover would not
have been quickly established on the North African fields. In the early
phases of the invasion the small airdrome there had necessarily to
serve both as an operational field and as a staging point for aircraft
making the passage from England to the African mainland. Even
several weeks before D-day it became jammed with fighter craft. Every
inch was taken up by either a Spitfire or a can of gasoline. All this was
exposed to the enemy's reconnaissance planes and not even an attempt
at camouflage could be made. Worse, the airfield itself lay on the
Spanish border, separated from Spanish territory only by a barbed-

wire fence. Politically, Spain was leaning toward the Axis, and, almost physically, leaning against the barbed-wire fence were any number of Axis agents. Every day we expected a major attack by hostile bombers; as each day went by without such an attack we went to bed puzzled, even astonished.

The only explanation for it was that our measures for deceiving the enemy were working well. We knew that long before the attack could take place the Axis would learn of increased activity at Gibraltar. We hoped the enemy would conclude that we were making another, unusually ambitious attempt to reinforce Malta, which had been in dire straits for months.

Yet in spite of the certain consequences of any enemy air attack, of dreary surroundings, and of all the thousand and one things that could easily go wrong in the great venture about to be launched, within the headquarters there was a definite buoyancy. Soldiers, sailors, and airmen congregated there were stimulated by that feeling of exhilaration that invariably ensues when one leaves months of grinding preparation and irksome inaction behind and turns his eyes expectantly to the outcome of a bold venture.

True, there was tenseness—one could feel it in every little cave makeshifting for an office. It was natural. Within a matter of hours the Allies would know the initial fate of their first combined offensive gesture of the war. Aside from the seesaw campaigns of advance and retreat that had been going on in the Western Desert for two full years and the island battle of Guadalcanal, nowhere in the world had the Allies been capable of undertaking on the ground anything more than mere defense. Even our defensive record was tragically draped in defeats, of which Dunkirk, Bataan, Hong Kong, Singapore, Sourabaya, and Tobruk were black reminders.

During those hours that we paced away among Gibraltar's caverns, hundreds of Allied ships, in fast- and slow-moving convoys, were steaming across the North Atlantic toward a common center on the coast of northwest Africa. To attack Algiers and Oran, most of these ships would pass through the narrow Strait of Gibraltar, flanked by guns that might at any moment speak up in favor of the Nazis. Other ships, coming from America, were to proceed directly against Casablanca and port towns to its north and south.

The three main expeditions were plowing through seas infested with U-boats. At Gibraltar most of our separate convoys would enter an area where they would come under the threat of enemy bombers. Our

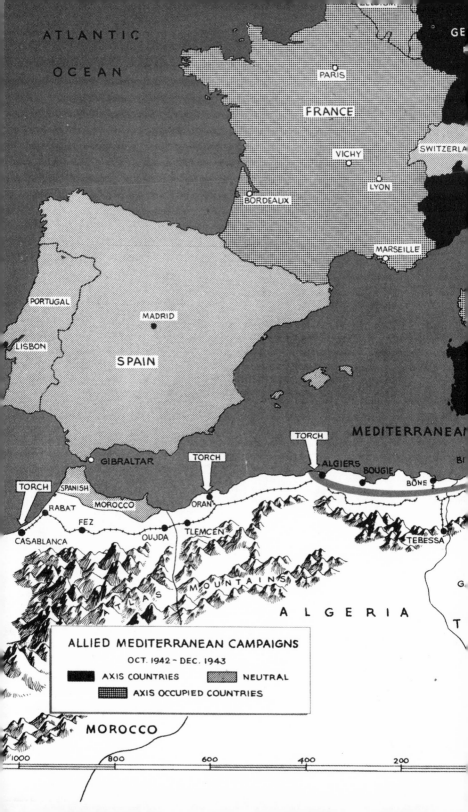

troops had been only hastily trained for this complicated type of landing operation and, for the most part, had never participated in battle. Available shipping did not permit us to carry along all the forces and equipment necessary to assure success. Of course we were tense.

Even our flight to Gibraltar had been hazardous. It had been accomplished only after two previous attempts to make the passage from England had been frustrated by foul weather. Before we finally took off from England the officer commanding the six Fortresses assigned to take our party to Gibraltar deliberately placed before me, together with his technical advice against making the flight, the decision as to whether or not he should take off. It was the only time in my life I was faced with that situation because normally the air commander's decision is final. It did not seem a propitious omen for the great adventure, but we had to go through. We flew at an average height of a hundred feet. When the great Rock of Gibraltar finally loomed out of its concealing haze my pilot remarked, "This is the first time I have ever had to climb to get into landing traffic at the end of a long trip!"

In spite of the inaction imposed upon us at Gibraltar, there was work we could do. Already we were planning steps to follow a successful landing, including the early transfer of headquarters to Algiers. There was no lack of future problems to attract our interest, but each could be solved, could even be undertaken, only if the initial attack proved successful. So back and back again to the immediate issue our minds and our talk inevitably came.

We had three days to wait. Finally the leading ships steamed in at night through the narrow strait and we stood on the dark headlands to watch them pass. Still no news of air or submarine attack! We became more hopeful that the enemy, following his tactics of the past against Malta convoys, would keep his air, submarine, and surface forces concentrated to the eastward around Sicily, in anticipation of making a devastating attack as ships approached the narrow passage between that island and the African mainland.

In the original planning the probability of encountering impossible conditions at Casablanca was one of the factors that made me reluctant to commit the largest of our contingents to this particular operation.[1] The danger of last-minute postponement at Casablanca was a lively one, and if this should happen there were only two alternatives.

The first was merely to direct that great convoy to delay its landing and to steam in circles through the adjacent sea areas, awaiting a favorable moment. The disadvantages of this scheme were several. All surprise in the western attack would be lost; secondly, the ships would remain exposed to the attacks of hostile submarines which swarmed in the Bay of Biscay and southward; thirdly, the appearance of overwhelming power resulting from simultaneous assault of all three ports would be greatly diminished. Finally, there is a limit to the fuel capacity of ships.

The alternative was to bring the entire western convoy inside the Mediterranean to cluster about the already crowded port of Gibraltar. Here it could save fuel and be ready to return to Casablanca for the landing as originally planned, or the troops could follow in the assault at Oran and push backward down the railway toward the northwest coast. Neither alternative was attractive, since each required hasty revision and adjustment of plans already in execution. But the law of probabilities indicated that we would have to adopt one of them.

Even as late as the afternoon before the attack the weather reports from one of our submarines in the Casablanca region were gloomy, and I tentatively decided, unless conditions should improve, to divert the expedition into Gibraltar. All our plans would thus be badly upset, but this seemed better than to steam aimlessly around the ocean, dodging submarines.

At no time during the war did I experience a greater sense of relief than when, upon the following morning, I received a meager report to the effect that beach conditions were not too bad and the Casablanca landing was proceeding as planned.[2] I said a prayer of thanksgiving; my greatest fear had been dissipated.

An unexpected difficulty involved radio communication. In the early stages of the campaign the Allied Headquarters would have to depend exclusively upon the radio for communication with the several expeditions, and it was little short of dismaying to find that our radios constantly functioned poorly, sometimes not at all. The trouble was attributed largely to the overloading of the naval channels on our headquarters ships and of the signal center at Gibraltar. But whatever the cause, the result was that I determined to move headquarters to the mainland as quickly as possible.

Our first battle contact report was disappointing. The USS *Thomas Stone,* proceeding in convoy toward Algiers and carrying a reinforced battalion of American troops, was torpedoed on November 7, only one hundred and fifty miles from its destination.[3] Details were lacking and there existed the possibility of a very considerable loss of life. Though our good fortune to this point had been amazing, this did not lessen our anxiety for the men aboard. We could get no further information of their fate that evening but later we learned that the incident had a happy outcome so far as the honor of American arms was concerned. Casualties were few and the ship itself was not badly damaged. There was no danger of sinking. Yet officers and men, unwilling to wait quietly until the ship could be towed to a convenient port, cheered the decision of the commander[4] to take to the boats in an attempt to reach, on time, the assault beach to which they were assigned. Heavy weather, making up during the afternoon, foiled their gallant purpose and they had to be taken aboard destroyers and other escort vessels, but they were finally placed ashore some twenty hours behind schedule.[5] Fortunately the absence of these troops had no appreciable effect upon our plans.

That same afternoon, November 7, brought to me one of my most distressing interviews of the war.

Because of the earnest conviction held in both London and Washington that General Giraud could lead the French of North Africa into the Allied camp, we had started negotiations in October, through Mr. Murphy, to rescue the general from virtual imprisonment in southern France. An elaborate plan was devised by some of our French friends and Mr. Murphy, who had returned to Africa after his visit to London. General Giraud was kept informed of developments through trusted intermediaries and at the appointed time reached the coast line in spite of the watchfulness of the Germans and the Vichyites. There he embarked in a small boat, in the dark of night, to keep a rendezvous with one of our submarines, lying just offshore. A British submarine, commanded for this one trip by Captain Jerauld Wright of the United States Navy, made a most difficult contact with General Giraud and put out to sea. At another appointed place the submarine met one of our flying boats, and the general, with but three personal aides and staff officers, flew to my headquarters during the afternoon of November 7. The incident, related thus briefly, was an exciting story of extraordinary daring and resolution.[6]

General Giraud, though dressed in civilian clothes, looked very much a soldier. He was well over six feet, erect, almost stiff in carriage, and abrupt in speech and mannerisms. He was a gallant if bedraggled figure, and his experiences of the war, including a long term of imprisonment and a dramatic escape, had not daunted his fighting spirit.

It was quickly apparent that he had come out of France laboring under the grave misapprehension that he was immediately to assume command of the whole Allied expedition. Upon entering my dungeon he offered himself to me in that capacity. I could not accept his services in such a role. I wanted him to proceed to Africa, as soon as we could guarantee his safety, and there take over command of such French forces as would voluntarily rally to him. Above all things, we were anxious to have him on our side because of the constant fear at the back of our minds of becoming engaged in a prolonged and serious battle against Frenchmen, not only to our own sorrow and loss, but to the detriment of our campaign against the German.

General Giraud was adamant; he believed that the honor of himself and his country was involved and that he could not possibly accept any position in the venture lower than that of complete command. This, on the face of it, was impossible. The naming of an Allied commander in chief is an involved process, requiring the co-ordinated agreement of military and political leaders of the responsible governments. No subordinate commander in the expedition could legally have accepted an order from General Giraud. Moreover, at that moment there was not a single Frenchman in the Allied command; on the contrary, the enemy, if any, was French.

All this was laboriously explained to the general. He was shaken, disappointed, and after many hours of conference felt it necessary to decline to have any part in the scheme. He said, "General Giraud cannot accept a subordinate position in this command; his countrymen would not understand and his honor as a soldier would be tarnished." It was pitiful, because he had left his whole family in France as potential hostages to German fury and had himself undergone great personal risks in order to join up with us.

My political advisers at that time were Mr. H. Freeman Matthews of the American State Department and Mr. William H. B. Mack of the British Foreign Office.[7] So concerned were they over this development that they suggested placing General Giraud in nominal command, while reserving to myself the actual power of directing operations. They felt that the difference between public association and non-association of the Giraud name with the operation might well mean the difference between success and disaster. To such a subterfuge I would not agree, and adhered to my decision that, unless General Giraud could content himself with taking charge of such French forces in North Africa as might come over to our side in the fight against Germany, we would proceed with the campaign exactly as if we had never met or conferred with him. The conversation with General Giraud lasted, intermittently, until after midnight. Though I could understand General Giraud's French fairly well, I insisted on using an interpreter, to avoid any chance of misunderstanding. When we had worn out more expert ones, General Clark volunteered to act in this capacity, and though he is far from fluent in the language, we made out fairly well. One reason for this was that after the first hour of talk each of us merely repeated, over and over again, the arguments he had first presented. When, finally, General Giraud went off to bed there was no sign of his modifying, in any degree, his original demands. His good-night statement was, "Giraud will be a spectator in this affair." He agreed, however, to meet me at the governor general's house the next morning. The political faces in our headquarters that night were long.

Before stopping work for the night I sent to the Combined Chiefs of Staff a detailed account of the conference and was grateful to receive prompt word from them that they fully supported my position.[8] The ending of the message was garbled but we could make out, "Our only regret is that you have been forced to devote so much of your time to this purpose during a period . . ." How fortunate I was that I could not foresee just how much of my time in ensuing weeks would be taken up with irritating and frustrating conferences on North African political affairs!

Fortunately a night's sleep did something to change General Giraud's mind and at the next morning's meeting he decided to participate on the basis we desired.[9] I promised that if he were successful in winning French support I would deal with him as the administrator of that region, pending eventual opportunity for civil authorities to determine the will of the population.

In further talks with General Giraud it developed that there was a radical difference between his conception and mine of what, at that moment, should be done strategically. He was in favor of turning immediately to the attack on southern France, paying no attention to northern Africa. I showed him that even as he spoke the troops were landing on their selected beaches; that there was no possibility of providing air support for the landing he proposed; and that the Allied shipping then in existence would not provide a build-up for an invasion of southern France that could withstand the force the Germans would assuredly bring against it. Finally, I explained that the campaign on which we were embarking was backed up by such intricate and de-

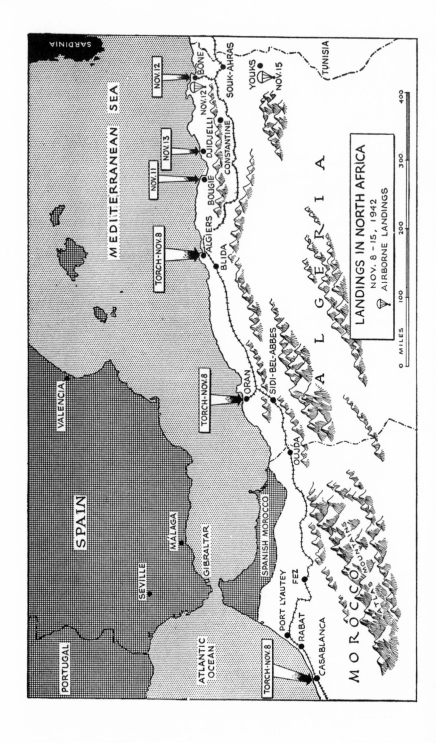

LANDINGS IN NORTH AFRICA
NOV. 8 - 15, 1942
AIRBORNE LANDINGS

tailed maintenance arrangements that the change he proposed was completely impossible.

He could not see the need of North Africa as a base—the need for establishing ourselves firmly and strongly in that region before we could successfully invade the southern portion of Europe.

He was not aware of the lessons the war had brought out as to the effect of land-based aviation upon unprotected seaborne craft. He had probably never assessed, in terms of tactical meaning, the loss in the Southwest Pacific of the two great British ships, the *Prince of Wales* and the *Repulse,* when they were heedlessly exposed to attack by land-based aviation. He assumed, moreover, that if the Allies chose to do so they could place 500,000 men in the south of France in a matter of two or three weeks. It was difficult for him to understand that we had undertaken an operation that stretched our resources to the limit, and that because of the paucity of these resources our initial strategic objectives had to be carefully calculated.

During the course of the night and in the early morning hours of November 8 operational reports began to come in that were encouraging in tone. As anticipated, the landings at Algiers met almost no opposition and the area was quickly occupied.[10] This was largely due to the prior accomplishments of Mr. Murphy, working through General Mast of the French Army, and to the sympathy, even if cloaked in official antagonism, of General Alphonse Pierre Juin.

Always in the back of our minds was the need for haste in getting on to the Tunis area. On the night of the eighth I scrawled a penciled memorandum which I still have. In it appears the notation, "We are slowed up in eastern sector when we should be getting toward Bône-Bizerte at once."

At Oran we got ashore, but the French forces in that region, particularly the naval elements, resisted bitterly.[11] Some hard fighting ensued and the U. S. 1st Division, which was later to travel such a long battle road in this war, got its first taste of conflict. In spite of incomplete training, the 1st Division, supported by elements of the 1st Armored Division, made progress and on November 9 we knew we would soon be able to report victory in that area. On the tenth all fighting ceased at Oran.[12] Generals Fredendall and Terry de la M. Allen met their initial battle tests in good fashion.

We knew that the attack on the west coast was launched, but there was no news of its progress. Actually at certain points, notably Port Lyautey, fierce fighting developed.[13] The treacherous sea had given us the one quiet day in the month necessary to make the landing feasible, but the period of calm lasted only a short time and later reinforcing was most difficult. I tried every possible means to get in communication with the western commanders, Rear Admiral H. K. Hewitt of the Navy and General Patton of the Army. The radio again failed and gave us nothing but unintelligible signals. Thereupon we tried sending light bomber craft to Casablanca to gain contact, but after French fighters had shot down several of them we knew that this method was futile. In desperation I asked Admiral Cunningham if he had a fast ship in port. By good fortune one of the speediest afloat was then at Gibraltar getting up steam to rush some vital supplies into Malta, and without hesitation the admiral offered her to me for the necessary time to make contact with the Western Task Force. I chose Rear Admiral Bernhard H. Bieri of the United States Navy to head a staff group, and they took off within the hour.[14]

On the morning of November 9, General Clark and General Giraud went by air to Algiers in an effort to make some kind of agreement with the highest French authorities. Their mission was to end the fighting and to secure French assistance in projected operations against the Germans.[15]

General Giraud's cold reception by the French in Africa was a terrific blow to our expectations. He was completely ignored. He made a broadcast, announcing assumption of leadership of French North Africa and directing French forces to cease fighting against the Allies, but his speech had no effect whatsoever. I was doubtful that it was even heard by significant numbers. Radio communications with Algiers were very difficult but eventually a message came through that confirmed an earlier report: Admiral Darlan was in Algiers!

We discounted at once the possibility that he had come into the area with a prior knowledge of our intentions or in order to assist us in our purpose. Already we had evidence, gathered in Oran and Algiers, that our invasion was a complete and astonishing surprise to every soldier and every inhabitant of North Africa, except for those very few who were actively assisting us. Even these had not been told the actual date of the attack until the last minute. There was no question that Darlan's presence was entirely accidental, occasioned by the critical illness of his son, to whom he was extremely devoted.

In Darlan we had the commander in chief of the French fighting forces! A simple and easy answer would have been to jail him. But with Darlan in a position to give the necessary orders to the very considerable French fleet, then in Toulon and Dakar, there was hope of reducing at once the potential naval threat in the Mediterranean and of gaining welcome additions to our own surface craft. Just before I left England, Mr. Churchill had earnestly remarked, "If I could meet Darlan, much as I hate him, I would cheerfully crawl on my hands and knees for a mile if by doing so I could get him to bring that fleet of his into the circle of Allied forces."

But we had another and more pressing reason for attempting to utilize Darlan's position. In dealing with French soldiers and officials General Clark quickly ran afoul of the traditional French demand for a cloak of legality over any action they might take. This was a fetish with the military; their surrender in 1940, they asserted, had been merely the act of loyal soldiers obeying the legal orders of their civil superiors.

Without exception every French commander with whom General Clark held exhaustive conversation declined to make any move toward bringing his forces to the side of the Allies unless he could get a legal order to do so. Each of them had sworn an oath of personal fealty to Marshal Pétain, a name that at that moment was more profound in its influence on North African thinking and acting than any other factor. None of these men felt that he could be absolved from that oath or could give any order to cease firing unless the necessary instructions were given by Darlan as their legal commander, to whom they looked as the direct and personal representative of Marshal Pétain.

It was useless then, and for many days thereafter, to talk to a Frenchman, civilian or soldier, unless one first recognized the Marshal's overriding influence. His picture appeared prominently in every private dwelling, while in public buildings his likeness was frequently displayed in company with extracts from his speeches and statements. Any proposal was acceptable only if "the Marshal would wish it."

General Clark radioed that without Darlan no conciliation was possible, and in this view he was supported by General Giraud, who was then in hiding in Algiers. Clark kept me informed of developments as much as he possibly could but it was obvious that he was having a difficult time in his attempt to persuade the French to stop fighting our troops.[16] While preoccupied with all these matters, I received a message from my chief of staff, who had temporarily remained in London, which stated that, in view of the initial successes and apparently certain outcome of Torch, a high-level suggestion had come to him that we cut down our planned build-up for Torch, so as to proceed with other strategic purposes. Before the war was over I became accustomed to this tendency of individuals far in the rear to overevaluate early success and to discount future difficulty. But at that moment receipt of the message irritated me and I dashed off a prompt reply, from which the following is extracted:

"Unalterably opposed to reducing contemplated Torch strength. The situation is not crystallized. On the contrary, in Tunisia, it is touch and go. Country is not pacified completely, communications are a problem of first magnitude, and two principal ports in North Africa are seriously blocked. Every effort to secure organized and effective French co-operation runs into a maze of political and personal intrigue and the definite impression exists that none really wants to fight or to co-operate wholeheartedly.

"Rather than talk of possible reduction we should be seeking ways and means of speeding up the build-up to clean out North Africa. We should plan ahead in orderly fashion on strategic matters but for God's sake let's get one job done at a time. We have lost a lot of shipping in the past three days and provision of air cover for convoys is most difficult. The danger of German intervention through Spain has not ceased. I am not growing fearful of shadows nor am I crying wolf. I merely insist that if our beginning looks hopeful, then this is the time to push rather than to slacken our efforts. We are just started working on a great venture. A good beginning must not be destroyed by any unwarranted assumptions."[17]

That day, the twelfth, General Clark reported that apparently Darlan was the only Frenchman who could achieve co-operation for us in North Africa.[18] I realized that the matter was one that had to be handled expeditiously and locally. To have referred it back to Washington and London would have meant inevitable delays in prolonged discussions. So much time would have been consumed as to have cost much blood and bitterness and left no chance of an amicable arrangement for absorbing the French forces into our own expedition.

Already we had our written orders from our governments to co-operate with any French government we should find existing at the moment of our entry into Africa.[19] Moreover, the matter at the moment was completely military. If resulting political repercussions became so serious as to call for a sacrifice, logic and tradition demanded that the man in the field should take complete responsibility for the matter, with his later relief from command becoming the symbol of correction. I might be fired, but only by making a quick decision could the essential unity of effort throughout both nations be preserved and the immediate military requirements met.

We discussed these possibilities very soberly and earnestly, always remembering that our basic orders required us to go into Africa in the attempt to win an ally—not to kill Frenchmen.

I well knew that any dealing with a Vichyite would create great revulsion among those in England and America who did not know the harsh realities of war; therefore I determined to confine my judgment in the matter to the local military aspects. Taking Admiral Cunningham with me, I flew to Algiers on November 13, and upon reaching there went into conference with General Clark and Mr. Murphy, the American consul general in the area.[20] This was the first time I had seen Murphy since his visit to London some weeks before.

They first gave me a full account of events to date. On November 10, Darlan had sent orders to all French commanders to cease fighting.[21] Pétain, in Vichy, immediately disavowed the act and declared Darlan dismissed. Darlan then tried to rescind the order, but this Clark would not allow. Next the news was received in Algiers that the Germans were invading southern France, and now Darlan said that because the Germans had violated the 1940 armistice he was ready to co-operate freely with the Americans. In the meantime General Giraud, at first shocked to discover that the local French would not follow him, had become convinced that Darlan was the only French official in the region who could lead North Africa to the side of the Allies. When the Germans entered southern France Giraud went to Darlan to offer co-operation. The fighting at Casablanca had ceased because of Darlan's order; at other places the fighting was over before the order was received. The French officers who had openly assisted us, including Generals Bethouart and Mast, were in temporary disgrace; they were helpless to do anything.

After exhaustive review of the whole situation Mr. Murphy said, "The whole matter has now become a military one. You will have to give the answer."

While we were reaching a final decision he stepped entirely aside except to act upon occasion as interpreter. It was squarely up to me to decide whether or not the procurement of an armistice, the saving of time and lives, and the early development of workable arrangements with the French were worth more to the Allied forces than the arbitrary arrest of Darlan, an action certain to be accompanied by continued fighting and cumulative bitterness. Local French officials were still officially members of a neutral country, and unless our governments were ready formally to declare war against France we had no legal or other right arbitrarily to establish, in the Nazi style, a puppet government of our own choosing.

The arrangement reached was set forth in a document that outlined the methods by which the French authorities engaged to assist the Allied forces.[22] It accorded to the Allied commander in chief, in a friendly, not an occupied, territory, all the necessary legal rights and privileges that were required in the administration of his forces and in the conduct of military operations. We were guaranteed the use of ports, railways, and other facilities.

The Allies merely stated that, provided the French forces and the civil population would obey Darlan's orders to co-operate militarily with us, we would not disturb the French administrative control of North Africa. On the contrary, we affirmed our intention of co-operating with them in preserving order. There was no commitment to engage our governments in any political recognition of any kind and Darlan was simply authorized, by the voluntary action of the local officials, and with our consent, to take charge of the French affairs of North Africa while we were clearing the Germans out of that continent. He agreed also to place our friend General Giraud in command of all French military forces in northwest Africa.

An important point was that we could not afford a military occupation, unless we chose to halt all action against the Axis. The Arab population was then sympathetic to the Vichy French regime, which had effectively eliminated Jewish rights in the region, and an Arab uprising against us, which the Germans were definitely trying to foment, would have been disastrous. It was our intention to win North Africa only for use as a base from which to carry on the war against Hitler. Legally our position in Africa differed from our subsequent status in Sicily, just as the latter differed from our status in Italy and, later, in Germany. Theoretically we were in the country of an ally. The actual effect of Darlan's commitment was to recognize and give effect to our position of dominating influence—but we would have to use this position skillfully if we were to avoid trouble.

Darlan's orders to the French Army were obeyed, in contrast to the disdain with which the earlier Giraud pronouncement had been received. Darlan stopped the fighting on the western coast, where the United States forces had just been concentrated against the defenses of

Casablanca and were preparing to deliver a general assault. General Patton's earlier experiences in Morocco indicated that this would have been a bloody affair.

Final agreement with the French Army, Navy, and Air officials, headed by Darlan, was reached at Algiers on November 13.[23] Flying back that night, Admiral Cunningham and I had a nasty experience with bad weather and poor landing conditions at Gibraltar. We flew around the Rock in complete blackness, making futile passes at the field. I saw no way out of a bad predicament and still think the young lieutenant pilot must have depended more upon a rabbit's foot than upon his controls to accomplish the skillful landing that finally brought us safely down. This experience strengthened my previously formed intention to shift headquarters to Algiers quickly, a decision that threw the Signal Corps into a panic. The signal officer said he could provide no communications at Algiers before the first of the year. But we moved on November 23.[24]

Official reports of all political problems had of course been periodically submitted to our two governments. Nevertheless, the instant criticism in the press of the two countries became so strong as to impel both the President and the Prime Minister to ask for fuller explanation. They got it in the form of a long telegram, which was given wide circulation among government officials in Washington and London. Even after long retrospective study of the situation I can think of little to add to the telegraphic explanation. I quote it here, paraphrased to comply with regulations designed to preserve the security of codes:

"November 14

"Completely understand the bewilderment in London and Washington because of the turn that negotiations with French North Africans have taken. Existing French sentiment here does not remotely agree with prior calculations. The following facts are pertinent and it is important that no precipitate action at home upset the equilibrium we have been able to establish.

"The name of Marshal Pétain is something to conjure with here. Everyone attempts to create the impression that he lives and acts under the shadow of the Marshal's figure. Civil governors, military leaders, and naval commanders agree that only one man has an obvious right to assume the Marshal's mantle in North Africa. He is Darlan. Even Giraud, who has been our trusted adviser and staunch friend since early conferences succeeded in bringing him down to earth, recognizes this overriding consideration and has modified his own intentions accordingly.

"The resistance we first met was offered because all ranks believed this to be the Marshal's wish. For this reason Giraud is deemed to have been guilty of at least a touch of insubordination in urging non-resistance to our landing. General Giraud understands and appears to have some sympathy for this universal attitude. All concerned say they are ready to help us provided Darlan tells them to do so, but they are not willing to follow anyone else. Admiral Esteva in Tunis says he will take orders from Darlan. Noguès stopped fighting in Morocco by Darlan's order. Recognition of Darlan's position in this regard cannot be escaped.

"The gist of the agreement is that the French will do what they can to assist us in taking Tunisia. The group will organize for effective co-operation and will begin, under Giraud, reorganization of selected military forces for participation in the war. The group will exhaust every expedient in an effort to get the Toulon fleet. We will support the group in controlling and pacifying country and in equipping selected units. Details still under discussion.

"Our hope of quick conquest of Tunisia and of gaining here a supporting population cannot be realized unless there is accepted a general agreement along the lines which we have just made with Darlan and the other officials who control the administrative machinery of the region and the tribes in Morocco. Giraud is now aware of his inability to do anything by himself, even with Allied support. He has cheerfully accepted the post of military chief in the Darlan group. He agrees that his own name should not be mentioned until a period of several days has elapsed. Without a strong French government we would be forced to undertake military occupation. The cost in time and resources would be tremendous. In Morocco alone General Patton believes that it would require 60,000 Allied troops to keep the tribes pacified. In view of the effect that tribal disturbance would have on Spain, you see what a problem we have."[25]

At no time in the long negotiations did Darlan state confidently that he could bring the French fleet over to our side. He thought that possibly, owing to lack of fuel oil and also to the confusion and uncertainty that were sure to prevail in southern France, the fleet commander would not actually attempt to bring the ships out to sea and join us, but he did say with complete conviction that the French admiral in Toulon would never allow his ships to fall into the hands of the Germans. He repeated this time and again, and later events proved him to be completely correct.[26]

On the other hand, Darlan felt sure that Admiral Jean Pierre Esteva, commanding in Tunis, would join with the rest of the French officials of North Africa in observing any orders he might issue. The first thing that defeated this great hope was the length of time consumed in the negotiations at Algiers. This created uncertainty on the part of Admiral Esteva, who, while informed of the nature of the conversations then going on in Algiers, was also in receipt of orders from Vichy to resist the Allies and, we were told, to admit the Germans into his area.[27] Military commanders in that region, Generals Louis Marie Koeltz at Algiers and Louis Jacques Barre at Tunis, were in a similar state of indecision and we were informed that General Koeltz was definitely opposed to making any agreement with the Allies.

In this state of doubt and indecision, the Germans began to make landings in the Tunisia area. The first German contingent reached the area by air on the afternoon of November 9. From that moment onward they reinforced as rapidly as possible[28] and by the time a tentative agreement was reached with Darlan in Algiers it was no longer possible for Admiral Esteva to act independently. In a final telephone conversation between him and a French official in Algiers he said, "I now have a guardian." This we took to mean that the Germans were really holding him as a hostage. On the other hand, both Generals Koeltz and Barre obeyed Darlan's orders without question, and the former, particularly, eventually became a fine fighting leader in the Allied forces.

After the receipt of my telegram in London and Washington both governments assured our headquarters of their complete understanding of the matter. They informed me that they would back up the arrangement so long as its terms were faithfully carried out by the French and until hostilities in Africa should draw to a close.[29]

This arrangement was of course wholly different from that we had anticipated, back in London. But it was not only with respect to personalities and their influence in North Africa that our governments had miscalculated. They had believed that the French population in the region was bitterly resentful of Vichy-Nazi domination and would eagerly embrace as deliverers any Allied force that succeeded in establishing itself in the country. The first German bombing of Algiers—and there were many—proved the fallacy of this assumption. Of course there were many patriots, and after the Tunisian victory was assured their number increased, but in the early days of touch and go and nightly bombing the undercurrent of sentiment constantly transmitted to me was, "Why did you bring this war to us? We were satisfied before you came to get us all killed." In his final dispatch, written after the completion of the campaign, General Anderson had this to say about the early attitude of the inhabitants:

. . . Many mayors, station- and post-masters and other key officials with whom we had dealings as we advanced (for instance, the civil telephone was, at first, my chief means of communicating with my forward units and with Allied Force Headquarters) were lukewarm in their sympathies and hesitant to commit themselves openly, while a few were hostile. I can safely generalize by saying that at first, in the Army, the senior officers were hesitant and afraid to commit themselves, the junior officers were mainly in favour of aiding the Allies, the men would obey orders; amongst the people, the Arabs were indifferent or inclined to be hostile, the French were in our favour but apathetic, the civil authorities were antagonistic as a whole. The resulting impression on my mind was not one of much confidence as to the safety of my small isolated force should I suffer a severe setback.[30]

This was a far cry from the governmental hope that the people of North Africa would, upon our entry, blaze into spontaneous revolt against control by Nazi-dominated Vichy!

Through Darlan's assumption of the French administration post in North Africa and his influence in French West Africa, the great center of Dakar soon fell to Allied hands.[31] The governor of that section was Pierre Boisson, an old soldier who had lost a leg and his hearing in the first World War and who was obviously honest in his hatred of everything German. He had a fanatical devotion to France and conceived his single duty to be the preservation of French West Africa for the French Empire. He had earlier in the war driven off from the shores of Dakar an attempted invasion by British and Free French forces[32] and announced that he would fight anyone who might challenge his sphere of responsibility. However, with the invasion of southern France by the Germans, he announced himself ready to take military orders from me, through Admiral Darlan, but from no one else.

Because Dakar was not then within the territorial limits of my theater, where I was busy enough with my own problems of fighting a campaign, and also because the press of both Britain and America was seriously disturbed by the military arrangements I had made with Darlan, I reminded my superiors that I had no responsibility to secure Boisson's adherence to the general capitulation and would take no part in it unless ordered. I did report to them, however, that I could have Dakar for the asking, and reported to them what Boisson had said.[33] My return orders were speedily received; they were to the effect that I was to proceed toward securing the West African region for the use of the Allies exactly as I had the North African.[34]

My decisive conference with Governor Boisson verged on the dramatic. There were many important details to be settled. Then interned in West Africa were numbers of British sailors who had been landed there from ships sunk earlier in the war. The British insisted upon instant release of these men, while, as a counterdemand, Boisson insisted that Free French radio propaganda from areas bordering upon West Africa should cease at once. He said that this propaganda was constantly charging him and his government with every kind of crime and was causing him trouble with the natives. He said the British Government should order this stopped immediately. Similar points arose, none of which was specifically covered in the document to be signed. Admiral Darlan and other French officials were present, as were Mr. Murphy and additional members of my staff. As the conversations progressed the participants grew excited and the French seemed all to be talking at once. Finally I took Governor Boisson, who could understand some English, to a corner to talk to him personally. The substance of what I said was:

"Governor, there is no possibility that I can tell you in detail exactly what the British Government will do, just as I cannot tell you in detail what the American Government will do. But this I can say with confidence: my two governments have directed me to make an agreement with you on the general basis that French West Africa is to join with North Africa in the war against the Axis. They have stated that they would not interfere in the local governmental arrangements. They will expect the co-operation from you that they would from any other friendly region, and this will involve the prompt release of any of our citizens who may now be interned in your area. They will attempt to stop whatever propaganda may be directed against you and your regime and they will unquestionably use their good offices to get other co-operating organizations, including the Free French forces under General de Gaulle, likewise to cease such practices. However, they obviously cannot give General de Gaulle orders in this matter. We want to use the air routes through your area and we want you on our side, and we want these things quickly. It would take weeks to get every one of these little details ironed out and we cannot waste the time. You sign the agreement and I assure you on my honor as a soldier that I will do everything humanly possible to see that the general arrangements between us are carried out on the co-operative basis that my governments intend, just as we are doing in North Africa. As long as I am kept in my present position by my two governments you may be certain that the spirit of our agreement will never be violated by the Allies."

Without another word he walked over to my desk and, while the chatter was still going on in other parts of the room, sat down and affixed his name to the agreement.[35] As soon as he had signed I said to him: "Governor, when can our airplanes start using the airfield at Dakar?" He looked at me and instantly replied in French, "But now." In his further remarks Boisson emphasized the importance he placed on my pledge as a soldier to avoid unnecessary disturbances of French institutions in West Africa and to assist in the task of reorganizing a French army to participate in the war on our side. It was easy to oversimplify the French problem as it then existed. Only patience and persistence could bring us valuable and, eventually, democratic allies. On the other hand, violence and disregard of the sense of humiliation felt by the French would have produced nothing but discord and a fair charge that we were Nazis.

Therefore, because of the power of our own arms and the acceptance of a temporary French administration in North Africa, all fighting in the entire area, west of Algiers inclusive, had ceased by November 12.

In the eastern sector, Tunisia, it was different.

Chapter 7

WINTER
IN ALGIERS

THE MINIMUM OBJECTIVE OF THE NORTH AFRI-
can invasion was to seize the main ports between Casablanca and Algiers, denying their use to the Axis as bases for submarines, and from
them to operate eastward toward the British desert forces. The successful action of the first few days assured attainment of the minimum
object and we immediately turned all our attention to the greater
mission assigned us of co-operating with General Sir Harold R. L. G.
Alexander's forces, then twelve hundred miles away at the opposite
end of the Mediterranean. Between us we would destroy all Axis forces
in northern Africa and reopen the sea for the use of Allied shipping.

On October 23, in Egypt, General Alexander had launched the
British Eighth Army, under General Sir Bernard L. Montgomery, in
an assault on the enemy lines at El Alamein,[1] and within two weeks the
enemy was in headlong flight to the westward, hotly pursued by the
victorious British. If we could advance to the Axis line of communications we could assure that the brilliant tactical victory of the Eighth
Army would result in even greater strategic gain.

British air and sea forces based on Egypt and Malta denied the
Axis any practicable and dependable line of communications crossing
the Mediterranean east of Tripoli.

Our own position, occupying French North Africa west of Bône,
imposed a western limit upon the sea areas that the Axis could use.
Thus there were available to Hitler and Mussolini only the ports lying
between Bône in Algeria and Tripoli in northwest Libya, from which
to support Rommel. Every advance by the Allies from either flank
would tend to squeeze the Axis channel of supplies and with continuation of this process eventual strangulation would result.

The air power of the Axis in Sicily, Pantelleria, and southern Italy was still so strong as to preclude the possibility of Allied naval advance into that region; final success in cutting the Axis communications would demand land advance, with continuous build-up of forward air bases and air power.

By far the most important of the African ports then available to the Axis were Bizerte and Tunis, with the secondary ones of Sfax and Gabès lying farther to the southward. Tripoli itself, while a good enough port, required Axis vessels to pass almost under the guns of Malta, where the British air forces were growing sufficiently strong to inflict severe loss. Obviously, if the ports of Tunis and Bizerte could be taken quickly further reinforcements of the Axis armies in Africa would be almost impossible and their destruction would be expedited.

Our main strategic purpose was, therefore, the speedy capture of northern Tunisia. This guided every move we made—military, economic, political. Through success and disappointment, through every incident and accident, through every difficulty that habitually dogs the footsteps of soldiers in the field, this single objective was constantly held before all eyes, in the certainty that its attainment would constitute the end of the Axis in Africa.

The first move was made in mid-November while we were still in Algiers urging Darlan to order the French to cease fighting our troops and to co-operate with us. General Anderson's British First Army had been organized for the specific purpose of undertaking the campaign to the eastward, using Algiers as an initial base.[2] He was directed to proceed with the operation as planned, and to exert every effort to capture Bizerte and Tunis with the least possible delay. However, he was beset with very great difficulties.

The first of these was the over-all weakness of his force. Lack of shipping had prevented us from bringing along the strength that could have solved the problem quickly and expeditiously. Consequently General Anderson's plans had to be based upon speed and boldness rather than upon numbers.

The second difficulty was our great shortage in motor equipment,[3] which was rendered all the more serious because of the very poor quality of the single-line railway running eastward from Algiers to Tunis, a distance as great as from New York to Cleveland.

The third major problem was the weather. Unseasonable rains soon overtook us, and since none of the scattered air strips that we had hoped to use boasted of a paved runway, our small air forces were

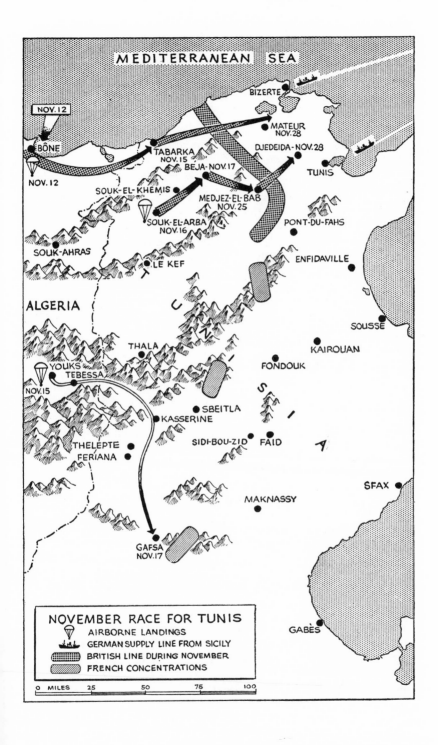

NOV. 12

MEDITERRANEAN SEA

BIZERTE

MATEUR
NOV. 28

BÔNE

TABARKA
NOV. 15

DJEDEIDA - NOV. 28

NOV. 12

BEJA - NOV. 17

TUNIS

SOUK-EL-KHEMIS

MEDJEZ-EL-BAB
NOV. 25

SOUK-EL-ARBA
NOV. 16

PONT-DU-FAHS

SOUK-AHRAS

LE KEF

ENFIDAVILLE

ALGERIA

T

U

SOUSSE

THALA

N

I

S

KAIROUAN

YOUKS
TEBESSA

FONDOUK

NOV. 15

I

SBEITLA

KASSERINE

A

SIDI-BOU-ZID

FAID

THELEPTE
FERIANA

SFAX

MAKNASSY

GAFSA
NOV. 17

GABÈS

NOVEMBER RACE FOR TUNIS
AIRBORNE LANDINGS
GERMAN SUPPLY LINE FROM SICILY
BRITISH LINE DURING NOVEMBER
FRENCH CONCENTRATIONS

O   MILES   25   50   75   100 handicapped and for days at a stretch were rendered almost completely helpless. The enemy was far better situated, since his large fields at Bizerte and Tunis were suitable for operations in all kinds of weather.

The next disadvantage was the proximity of the Tunisia area to the Axis forces in Sicily and in Italy. The day after we began our landings in northwest Africa the Axis started pouring troops into Tunisia, and they were reinforcing rapidly.

Another initial difficulty was the undetermined attitude of the French forces lying in the area between Constantine and Tunis. These were commanded by General Barre, and at the time General Anderson began his advance it was not known whether these forces and the local population would actively oppose him, would be neutral, or would cooperate with him in his advance toward Tunisia.

Under these conditions only a thoroughly loyal and bold commander would have undertaken without protest the operation that General Anderson was called upon to carry out. In response to my urgent orders he began the campaign on November 11 as soon as he put foot on shore.

Remembering that General Anderson and his troops were almost exclusively British, it has always seemed to me remarkable that he uttered not a single word of protest in accepting this bold order from an American. He was a true ally—and a courageous fighter. From Algiers he started his forces eastward by land and sea and in a series of rapid movements took the ports of Djidjelli, Philippeville, and Bône, at the same time moving farther inland to seize the towns of Sétif and Constantine.[4] Axis air and submarine action both took a constant toll of our shipping and caused material damage in the small harbors we were able to seize, but there was never any hesitation on the part of the Navy, under Admiral Cunningham, fully to support the operations, nor on the part of General Anderson to continue his advance in spite of these threats. From the general region of Bône and Constantine the British First Army kept pushing eastward through Souk-Ahras and Souk-el-Arba, where they made the first contacts with Axis ground forces.[5]

When I transferred headquarters from Gibraltar to Algiers on November 23, I took advantage of the journey to begin inspections of our troops and facilities. At the Oran airfield I came squarely up against conditions that were to plague us throughout that bitter winter. We landed on a hard-surfaced strip but then could not taxi a foot off the runway because of the bottomless mud. A huge tractor appeared and, with men placing great planks under the wheels of our Fortress, pulled us off a few yards so that incoming craft would still be able to land. Tactical operations were at a standstill so I spent the morning inquiring into problems of supply, housing, and food. It was on that occasion that I first met Lieutenant Colonel Lauris Norstad, a young air officer who so impressed me by his alertness, grasp of problems, and personality that I never thereafter lost sight of him. He was and is one of those rare men whose capacity knows no limit.

On arriving at Algiers that evening I found that previously issued orders to support Anderson's British army with whatever American contingents could be brought up to him from the Oran area were not clearly understood nor vigorously executed. In the office when I arrived was Brigadier General Lunsford E. Oliver, commander of Combat Command B, a portion of the U. S. 1st Armored Division. He had made a reconnaissance to the front, had determined that railway communications were inadequate to get him to the battle area promptly, and was seeking permission to march a part of his command in half-tracks over the seven hundred miles between Oran and Souk-el-Arba. The staff officer to whom he was appealing was well informed as to the characteristics of the half-track and refused permission on the ground that the march would consume half of the useful life of the vehicle!

The young staff officer was not to blame for this extraordinary attitude. He had been trained assiduously, through years of peace, in the eternal need for economy, for avoiding waste. Peacetime training was possible, as he well knew, only when the cost would be inconsequential. He had not yet accepted the essential harshness of war; he did not realize that the word is synonymous with waste, nor did he understand that every positive action requires expenditure. The problem is to determine how, in space and time, to expend assets so as to achieve the maximum in results. When this has been determined, then assets must be spent with a lavish hand, particularly when the cost can be measured in the saving of lives.

General Oliver's insistence, his desire to get to the battle, his pleading to take on a grueling march rather than to accept the easy solution with himself entirely absolved of responsibility, all impressed me greatly. Within five minutes he was on his way with the orders he sought.

During that night and the following one Algiers was bombed incessantly.[6] No great numbers of the Luftwaffe came over at any one time but the continuous din made sleep impossible and the lack of it soon showed plainly in the faces of headquarters personnel. The principal targets were the ships in the harbor, a quarter of a mile below our hotel, but bombs landing in the city caused some casualties and abundant consternation.

Our air defenses were only slowly developed; one of the ships we had lost to enemy submarines had been carrying most of the warning and control equipment vital to fighter defense. But by the end of the month we had partially corrected the deficiencies, and after the Luftwaffe had taken several nasty knocks it abandoned its attacks against our principal ports except for attempted sneak and surprise forays. One night we got unmistakable proof that the enemy's bombing crews had developed a healthy respect for the quality of our defenses. We intercepted a radio report from the commander of a bombing squadron to his home base. He said, "Bombs dropped on Algiers as ordered." But we knew he had dropped his bombs thirty miles out to sea because we had a plane in contact with him at the time. This evidence of weakening enemy morale was instantly circulated to our own people. It was astounding to see its buoyant effect.

After but three days' intensive work at headquarters I started for the front by automobile, taking General Clark with me. Because of hostile domination of the air, travel anywhere in the forward area was an exciting business. Lookouts kept a keen watch of the skies and the appearance of any plane was the signal to dismount and scatter. Occasionally, of course, the plane would turn out to be friendly—but no one could afford to keep pushing ahead on the chance that this would be so. All of us became quite expert in identifying planes, but I never saw anyone so certain of distant identification that he was ready to stake his chances on it. Truck drivers, engineers, artillerymen, and even the infantrymen in the forward areas had constantly to be watchful. Their dislike of the situation was reflected in the constant plaint, "Where is this bloody Air Force of ours? Why do we see nothing but Heinies?" When the enemy has air superiority the ground forces never hesitate to curse the "aviators."

Clark and I found Anderson beyond Souk-Ahras, and forward of that place we entered a zone where all around us was evidence of incessant and hard fighting. Every conversation along the roadside brought out astounding exaggerations. "Béja has been bombed to rubble." "No one can live on this next stretch of road." "Our troops will surely have to retreat; humans cannot exist in these conditions."

Yet on the whole morale was good. The exaggerations were nothing more than the desire of the individual to convey the thought that he had been through the ultimate in terror and destruction—he had no thought of clearing out himself.

Troops and commanders were not experienced, but the boldness, courage, and stamina of General Anderson's forces could not have been exceeded by the most battle-wise veterans. Physical conditions were almost unendurable. The mud deepened daily, confining all operations to the roads, long stretches of which practically disintegrated. Winter cold was already descending upon the Tunisian highlands. The bringing up of supplies and ammunition was a Herculean task. In spite of all this, and in spite of Anderson's lack of strength—his whole force numbered only about three brigades of infantry and a brigade of obsolescent tanks—he pushed on through Souk-el-Khemis, Béja, and finally reached a point from which he could look down into the outskirts of Tunis.[7]

Day by day, following the first contact, fighting grew more bitter, more stubborn, more difficult, and the enemy was more rapidly reinforced than were our own troops.

Very early I determined to take whatever additional risks might be involved in weakening our rear in order to strengthen Anderson. Shortage of transport prevented anything but movement by driblets—and the inherent dangers of such reinforcement are understood by the rawest of recruits. There was no lack of advisers to warn me concerning public reaction to "dissipation" of the American Army! "How," I was often asked, "did Pershing make his reputation in World War I?" What such advisers did not recall was Pershing's famous statement when stark crisis faced the Allies in March 1918. At that time, realizing the size of the stakes, he postponed integration of an American Army and said to Foch, "Every man, every gun, everything we have is yours to use as you see fit." I felt that here in Tunisia, on a small scale, we had a glowing opportunity comparable to the crisis of 1918, and I was quite willing to take all later criticism if only the Allied forces could turn over Tunis to our people as a New Year's present!

The gamble was great but the prize was such a glittering one that we abandoned caution in an effort to bring up to General Anderson every available fighting man in the theater. There still existed the fear that the German might thrust air forces down across the Pyrenees into Spain, to attack us from the rear. Nevertheless, as a beginning, the American air forces were directed to move as far to the eastward as possible to join in the air battle in support of General Anderson and to assist in cutting Axis sea communications between Tunis and Italy.[5] This was a definite change from the preconceived plan to retain the United States air forces in the western end of the Mediterranean. The move brought them into close proximity to the British air forces and created a need for daily co-ordination.

I had left General Spaatz in England and now I called him forward to take on this particular task. We merely improvised controlling machinery and gave General Spaatz the title of "Acting Deputy Commander in Chief for Air." Initially, the commander of the American Air Force in North Africa was Major General James Doolittle, who had sprung into fame as the leader of the raid on Tokyo. He was a dynamic personality and a bundle of energy. It took him some time to reconcile himself to shouldering his responsibilities as the senior United States air commander to the exclusion of opportunity for going out to fly a fighter plane against the enemy. But he had the priceless quality of learning from experience. He became one of our really fine commanders.

All during late November and early December the piecemeal process of reinforcing our eastern lines, principally by American troops, went on. Because of the critical nature of the day-by-day fighting and the lack of transport we could not wait to bring up any large unit as an entity nor could we wait to assemble such units before committing them to action. If we should fail to take Tunis we would suffer severely for this procedure, but General Anderson was given positive orders to use everything possible to gain his objective before the increasingly bad weather and the Axis reinforcements should compel us to settle down to a long winter campaign in such uninviting and inhospitable circumstances.

From Oran we brought up elements of the U. S. 1st Armored Division and part of the 1st Infantry Division. The U. S. 34th Division was distributed along the line of communication to protect critical points and to make sure of the security of the vast areas in which we were otherwise completely defenseless. We could use Allied troops for this purpose only on the most vital points, and as the enemy quickly resorted to a system of sabotage by night landing of paratroopers we were forced to rely on French contingents to protect hundreds of culverts, bridges, tunnels, and similar places where a few determined men could have inflicted almost decisive damage upon our lines of communication.

Courage, resourcefulness, and endurance, though daily displayed in overwhelming measure, could not completely overcome the combination of enemy, weather, and terrain. In early December the enemy was strong enough in mechanized units to begin local but sharp counterattacks and we were forced back from our most forward positions in front of Tunis.

As soon as we ceased attacking, the situation in northern Tunisia turned bleak for us, even from a defensive standpoint. Through a blunder during a local withdrawal we had lost the bulk of the equipment of Combat Command B, of the U. S. 1st Armored Division.[9] The 18th Infantry of the U. S. 1st Infantry Division took severe losses, and practically an entire battalion of a fine British regiment was wiped out.[10] General Anderson soon thought he would have to give up Medjez-el-Bab, a road center and a junction point with the French forces on his right. Since this spot was the key to our resumption of the offensive when we should get the necessary strength, I forbade this move—assuming personal responsibility for the fate of its garrison and the effect of its possible capture upon the safety of the command.[11]

We were still attempting to mount an attack of our own. Work continued twenty-four hours a day to build up the strength that we believed would, with some temporary improvement in the weather, give us a good fighting chance to capture northeastern Tunisia before all operations were hopelessly bogged down. December 24 was chosen as the date for our final and most ambitious attack.[12] Our chief hope for success lay in our temporary advantage in artillery, which was relatively great. But reports from the Tunisian front were discouraging; the weather, instead of improving, continued to deteriorate. Prospects for mounting another attack grew darker.

I was determined not to give up unless personally convinced that the attack was an impossibility. Weather prohibited flying and I started forward by automobile on December 22, encountering miserable road conditions from the moment we left Algiers. Traveling almost incessantly, I met General Anderson at his headquarters in the early morning of December 24 and with him proceeded at once to Souk-el-Khemis.[13] At that point was located the headquarters of the British 5 Corps, which was to make the attack and which was commanded by Major General C. W. Allfrey of the British Army. The preliminary moves of the attack had already been made by small detachments, attempting to secure critical points before the beginning of the major maneuver, scheduled for the following night.

The rain fell constantly. We went out personally to inspect the countryside over which the troops would have to advance, and while doing so I observed an incident which, as much as anything else, I think, convinced me of the hopelessness of an attack. About thirty feet off the road, in a field that appeared to be covered with winter wheat, a motorcycle had become stuck in the mud. Four soldiers were struggling to extricate it but in spite of their most strenuous efforts succeeded only in getting themselves mired into the sticky clay. They finally had to give up the attempt and left the motorcycle more deeply bogged down than when they started.

We went back to headquarters and I directed that the attack be indefinitely postponed.[14] It was a bitter decision. Immediately it was reached, we were faced with the problem of tidying up and straightening out our lines, assembling units into proper formations, collecting local reserves, and protecting our southern flank where the terrain would permit operations throughout the winter. General Anderson was to do all this while holding firmly the gains we had already made, pending the arrival of better weather in the spring.

In such circumstances it is always necessary for the commander to avoid an attitude of defeatism; discouragement on the part of the high commander inevitably spreads rapidly throughout the command and always with unfortunate results. On that occasion it was exceedingly difficult to display any particular optimism.

As early as the middle of November the French forces in Tunisia had cast their lot with us and were maintaining a precarious hold on the hilly masses stretching to the southward from Tunis, where their total lack of modern equipment did not so badly expose them to destruction.[15] With the giving up of our plan for immediate capture of Tunis, the line that we selected for defense was one that would cover the forward airfields located at Thelepte, Youks-les-Bains, and Souk-el-Arba. As long as these fields were in our possession we could, with our growing air forces, constantly pound away, at least in decent weather, at Axis communications. We would be in perfect position to resume the assault once conditions of weather and terrain and our growing strength permitted. For the rest of the winter, therefore, our defensive plan embraced the covering of these forward areas. Without them we would be forced back into the Bône-Constantine region and would be faced in the following spring with the problem of fighting our way forward, without suitable air support, through difficult mountainous areas at the cost of great numbers of lives. I was convinced that no disadvantage of supply or of danger in these forward positions was to be considered for a second above the dangers that would follow a general retirement to a more secure and convenient position. We had also to consider the moral effect of retreat upon the population of North Africa, a matter of grave concern to Giraud and other French leaders.

Up to this time the only flank protection we had been able to establish in all the great region stretching from Tebessa southward to Gafsa had been provided by scattered French irregulars reinforced and inspired by a small United States parachute detachment under the command of a gallant American, Colonel Edson D. Raff.[16] The story of his operations in that region is a minor epic in itself. The deceptions he practiced, the speed with which he struck, his boldness and his aggressiveness, kept the enemy completely confused during a period of weeks. But with the cessation of our attacks in the north the enemy was immediately enabled, behind the coastal mountain barrier, to concentrate his troops at will. It was unreasonable to assume that he would fail to realize our great weakness in the Tebessa region; it was likely that he would quickly strike us a damaging blow unless we took prompt measures to prevent it.

To provide the necessary protection the II Corps Headquarters, under General Fredendall, was brought up from Oran and directed to take station in the Tebessa region.[17] To it was assigned the U. S. 1st Armored Division, by this time largely brought up to strength, even though some of its equipment was already of an obsolete type. Logistics staffs opposed my purpose of concentrating a full corps east of Tebessa. They wailed that our miserable communications could not maintain more than an armored division and one additional regiment. But, convinced that the enemy would soon take advantage of our obvious weakness there, I nevertheless ordered the concentration of the corps of four divisions to begin and told the logistics people they would have to find a way to supply it.

The U. S. 1st Infantry Division was to be assigned to this corps as quickly as it could be assembled from its scattered positions on the front and brought into this sector. The U. S. 9th Division, less the 39th Regimental combat team which had participated in the Algiers assault, was gradually transferred eastward from the Casablanca area and was to go under command of II Corps when the movement could be completed. The 34th Division received similar orders, its duties in the line of communication to be taken over by the French.[18]

The instructions given to the American II Corps were to provide a strategic flank guard for our main forces in the north.[19] Fredendall was directed to hold the mountain passes with light infantry detachments and to concentrate the assembled 1st Armored Division in rear of the infantry outposts, ready to attack in force any hostile column that might attempt to move through the mountains toward our line of communications. General Fredendall was further authorized, upon completion of the assembly of his corps, to undertake offensive action in the direction of Sfax or Gabès in an effort to sever Rommel's line of communications with Tunisia.[20] A portion of the staff became obsessed with the idea of the potential results of such an operation and desired to order it forthwith. I disapproved: our immediate capacity for an offensive was nil. So that there could be no misunderstanding I held a personal conference with General Fredendall and completely outlined my purpose in concentrating his corps in the Tebessa area. These purposes were, as stated, to provide a mobile, strategic flank guard on our right, with its striking force represented principally in the concentrated armored division, which was stronger in tanks than anything the enemy could bring against it. Only when he could be assured that the whole region was safe from attack was he to be allowed to undertake offensive action in the direction of the coast line, and even under those conditions he was not to place any isolated infantry garrison in any coast town he might take.

In this incident I came squarely up against the love of staffs for expressing operational ideas in terms of geographical points and objectives. The idea of fighting to protect ourselves where necessary and of concentrating at chosen points to destroy the enemy is difficult to express. Such an idea implies great fluidity and flexibility in operations, and consequently planners find it difficult to reduce the conception to writing. Because of this they resort to the habit of laying out a plan based upon the capture or holding of specific geographical points, and sometimes, particularly in strategic planning, this is necessary. Nevertheless such plans are dangerous because they are likely to impose a rigidity of action upon the commander who receives them for execution. A qualified commander should normally be assigned only a general mission, whether it be of attack or defense, and then given the means to carry it out. In this way he is completely unfettered in achieving the general purpose of his superior.

During all these weeks it had been impossible to set up a unified command for the battle line, except that of Allied Force Headquarters itself. The French refused to serve under British command and maintained that there would be a rebellion in their Army if I insisted upon this arrangement, because of ill feeling still enduring from the British-French clashes in Syria, Oran, and Dakar.[21] The British First Army was on the left, the French forces in the center, and the American forces on the right, but all occupying parts of a single, closely interrelated battle front, and all dependent upon a single, inadequate line of communications. It was an exasperating situation, full of potential danger. The best I could do was to set up a forward command post of my own, where I spent as much time as I could. I left there permanently a small staff under General Truscott, whose task it was to represent me in the co-ordination of details on the front.

This condition persisted until French forces in the center, giving way in mid-January before small but determined German attacks, created a critical situation that demanded renewed dispersion of the assembling American troops in order to plug holes in the leaky front.[22] Under these conditions, just after the middle of January, I peremptorily ordered General Anderson to take charge of the entire battle line.[23] I personally visited General Juin, in command of the French forces in the line, to assure myself that he would take orders from General Anderson. Later I informed General Giraud of what I had done. He interposed no objection—the need had become too obvious.

The picture, then, when General Anderson took over the entire battle front, was that of a long tenuous line stretching from Bizerte to Gafsa, with units badly mixed and with no local reserves. To support this long front there was nothing available until the American II Corps could be fully concentrated in the Tebessa region and until additional troops from England should be able to perform a similar service in the northern Tunisia area. The process of sorting out units and providing the mobile reserves started before Christmas but received a bad setback when the French forces gave way in mid-January and American units had to rush in to close the gaps.[24] The French defeat could not be traced to any lack of gallantry or courage; it was merely the total lack of modern equipment, a deficiency we were struggling to correct.

Through all this period the tangled political situation kept worrying us; it was difficult to pierce the web of intrigue, misinformation, misunderstanding, and burning prejudice that surrounded even the minor elements of the whole problem. A principal factor in the situation was the Arab population and its explosive potentialities. The French general in Morocco, Noguès, was untrustworthy and worse, but he was the Foreign Minister to the Sultan; all reports indicated that he enjoyed the full confidence and friendship of the Moroccans. The fierce tribesmen of that area were a force to be reckoned with; General Patton was fearful of the whole situation and still adhered to his estimate that if the Moroccans should grow antagonistic to us it would require 60,000 fully equipped Americans to keep order in that region alone. We could not afford—and did not have—any such force. Patton strongly counseled us to let Noguès alone!

One complication in the Arab tangle was the age-old antagonism existing between the Arab and the Jew. Since the former outnumbered the latter by some forty to one in North Africa, it had become local policy to placate the Arab at the expense of the Jew; repressive laws had resulted and the Arab population regarded any suggestion for amelioration of such laws as the beginning of an effort to establish a Jewish government, with consequent persecution of themselves. Remembering that for years the uneducated population had been subjected to intensive Nazi propaganda calculated to fan these prejudices, it is easy to understand that the situation called more for caution and evolution than it did for precipitate action and possible revolution. The country was ridden, almost ruled, by rumor. One rumor was to the effect that I was a Jew, sent into the country by the Jew, Roosevelt, to grind down the Arabs and turn over North Africa to Jewish rule. The political staff was so concerned about this one that they published material on me in newspapers and in special leaflets to establish evidence of my ancestry. Arab unrest, or, even worse, open rebellion, would have set us back for months and lost us countless lives.

So far as the Frenchman in the cafés was concerned—the individual who talked incessantly to newspaper reporters—the answer was beautifully simple. It was merely to throw out, arbitrarily, every official who had been identified with or had taken orders from Vichy and to put in their places those who now claimed to be sympathetic to us. But since all the hated Vichy officials had carefully ingratiated themselves with the Arab population it was manifest that only through progressive changes and careful handling of personnel could we prevent the Arab-French-Jewish pot from boiling over.

To illustrate the delicacy of the situation: very early we had insisted that the French authorities ameliorate anti-Jewish laws and practices, going far beyond the bounds of "Allied co-operation" in the forcefulness of our demands. Appropriate proclamations were issued and we felt that some progress had been achieved. Imagine my astonishment when Darlan came to my office with a letter signed by a man whom he identified as the "Rabbi of Constantine," which implored the authorities to go very slowly in relaxation of anti-Jewish practices, else, the letter said, the Arabs would undoubtedly stage a pogrom! This minor example of the confused nature of the racial and political relationships was multiplied daily in innumerable directions.

Politics, economy, fighting—all were inextricably mixed up and confused one with the other.

On the political side Murphy and his British counterpart, Mr. Harold Macmillan, worked tirelessly, but they had had to deal with the dangerous Darlan, later with the gallant and honest but politically uninterested Giraud, the weak Yves Chatel, the notorious Noguès, and men of similar stripe. We insisted upon liberalization of the political systems but every day brought new complaints, most of them well founded, of continued injustices, lack of good faith, and lip service without performance. We determined to begin elimination of the most objectionable characters but were desperate over our failure to find satisfactory substitutes. Moreover, always we had to move in the knowledge that we were ostensibly in the land of an ally: we had neither the authority nor the responsibilities implicit in a military occupation. Nevertheless we early told Darlan he had to get rid of Chatel, governor of Algeria, and Noguès, minister to the Sultan of Morocco.

In this type of problem General Giraud was no help. He hated politics; not merely crookedness and chicanery in politics, but every part of the necessary task of developing an orderly, democratic system of government applicable to the North African kaleidoscope. He merely wanted supplies and equipment to develop fighting divisions and, provided he could get these, he had no interest in the governmental organization or its personnel. His purpose was pure but his capacity for larger administrative and organizational tasks was doubtful.

Darlan was assassinated on December 24, the same day that I was compelled to abandon all thought of immediate attack in northern Tunisia. I was at the headquarters of British 5 Corps near Béja when notice of his death reached me and I immediately started for Algiers. I arrived there after thirty hours of non-stop driving through rain, snow, and sleet.

My entire acquaintanceship with Darlan covered a period of six weeks. His reputation was that of a notorious collaborator with Hitler, but during the time that he served as the administrator of French North Africa he never once, to our knowledge, violated any commitment or promise. On the other hand, his mannerisms and personality did not inspire confidence and in view of his reputation we were always uneasy in dealing with him. In any event, his death presented me with new problems.

While it was known, of course, that the person in the French Government I trusted most was General Giraud, my headquarters was still in no position to sponsor a puppet government. Such a resort to Nazi methods would have been a far more serious violation of the principles for which we were fighting than would the mere temporary acceptance of some individual whose past record was, from our viewpoint, distasteful. Moreover, in our inner councils we doubted Giraud's ability to establish himself firmly in the chief position—but no one else was both acceptable and immediately available. Without delay the French local officials named General Giraud as the temporary administrator of North Africa to succeed Darlan.[25] Giraud visited my headquarters and his first request was that I "cease treating North Africa as a conquered territory and treat it more as the ally which it was trying to become." This attitude, on the part of one who, I thought, understood our motives so well, was something of a shock.

The governor in Algeria, Chatel, was a weakling who held the trust of none of us. He and General Noguès were two individuals we were determined to get rid of quickly, even though in the case of the latter General Patton constantly insisted that he was working effectively for the Allies in Morocco. My own belief was that General Noguès might co-operate with us as long as he thought we were winning but at the first sign of weakness he would unhesitatingly turn against us. Darlan had met every expression of our dissatisfaction with these two men by replying, "I don't want them either but the governing of Arab tribes is a tricky business that requires much experience with them. As quickly as you can produce any men, of your own choice, who are experienced in this regard and are loyal Frenchmen, I will instantly dismiss the incumbents and appoint the men you desire."

In the search for satisfactory individuals we decided to bring Marcel Peyrouton to Algiers. It was reported to me that Peyrouton was then a virtual exile in Argentina, unable to go back to France because of the bitter enmity of Pierre Laval toward him. It was also reported that he had previously established a reputation in North Africa as a skillful colonial administrator. Nevertheless he had been, for a considerable time, a member of the Vichy government and was therefore regarded in the democratic world as a Fascist. We explained our problem to the State Department and after some exchange of messages on the subject were informed that the State Department was in agreement with us.[26]

Bringing Peyrouton to Algeria as governor was a mistake, even though he was a vast improvement over his soft and vacillating predecessor. It was difficult indeed to find men who had any experience in French colonial administration and at the same time bore no trace of the Vichy trademark. Our first thought had been to use Mast, Bethouart, and a few others who had, by their actions, proved their friendliness to us. Here the difficulty was the attitude of the French Army, whose assistance we badly needed. We forced official acceptance, even the promotion, of Mast and Bethouart, but we could not force social acceptance at that time. Their wives were coldly treated, even insulted, by the wives of other officers. The feeling against them was initially so strong that they themselves, and Giraud, counseled against the attempt to use them in administrative positions.

In this period I made another error, even though from a good motive. It was the application of censorship to political news from North Africa for a period of six weeks. Because of personal dislike of censorship, I had to be convinced that the reason for such action was important. In this case it was. The plan of my political advisers and myself was to promote an eventual union between the local French administration and the De Gaulle forces in London. It was, we felt, a difficult but necessary development.

The local antagonism in the French Army and in all echelons of government against De Gaulle was intense, but he enjoyed a distinct popularity with the civilians and this sentiment progressively increased as prospects of Allied success brightened. Through every possible outlet open to them the De Gaulle forces in London and central Africa were fiercely attacking every French military and civil official in Africa, and the latter wanted to reply, publicly, in terms no less harsh. I believed that to permit the growth of such a public name-calling contest would create conditions which would make future reconciliation impossible. By imposing political censorship on all I prevented local French officials from participating in the public quarrel. They argued bitterly, as did the press representatives in the theater. I think the censorship had some of the desired effect, and it was lifted the second I learned that Giraud and De Gaulle had agreed to meet at Casablanca.

The reasons for the censorship could not be explained, however, and were of course misinterpreted at home.

The intricacies of the situation, military and political, were complicated by the economic situation. North Africa was stripped of usable goods, and shipping was so scarce that every available ton was required for military uses. Wheat, coal, cloth, medicine, soaps, and a myriad other items were sorely needed. While we took military needs as our criterion—that is, every problem was decided upon the basis of its bearing upon the military situation—still it was frequently difficult to tell, for example, whether military requirements would be best satisfied by a shipload of bombs or an equal amount of coal!

The Christmas season brought to me the dismaying realization that there are certain limits of physical stamina that cannot safely be exceeded. I inherited a hardy constitution from sturdy forebears and, heretofore always careful of health requisites, I had come to believe myself immune from the fatigues and exhaustions that I frequently observed in others. Long hours and incessant work were easily enough sustained, I thought, so long as one refused to fall victim to useless worry or to waste his strength in any kind of excess. But as the December weeks kept me constantly on the road or in the air and shorter and shorter hours of sleep became broken by an unaccustomed nervousness, I definitely felt a deterioration in vigor that I could not overcome. On Christmas Day I contracted a severe case of flu, and, convinced that I must not go to bed, I finally became really ill.

The doctors then took charge. For four days they would not let me move, and during that time I not only recovered my health, I learned a lesson I did not thereafter violate: a full measure of health is basic to successful command. I did not have another sick day—aside from minor accidents—during the war.

In December we received our first consignment of Women's Army Corps personnel, then known as Women's Auxiliary Army Corps. Until my experience in London I had been opposed to the use of women in uniform. But in Great Britain I had seen them perform so magnificently in various positions, including service in active anti-aircraft batteries, that I had been converted. In Africa many officers were still doubtful of women's usefulness in uniform—the older commanders in particular were filled with misgivings and open skepticism. What these men had failed to note was the changing requirements of war. The simple headquarters of a Grant or a Lee were gone forever. An army of filing clerks, stenographers, office managers, telephone operators, and chauffeurs had become essential, and it was scarcely less than criminal to recruit these from needed manpower when great numbers of highly qualified women were available. From the day they first reached us their reputation as an efficient, effective corps continued to grow. Toward the end of the war the most stubborn die-hards had become convinced—and demanded them in increasing numbers. At first the women were kept carefully back at GHQ and secure bases, but as their record for helpfulness grew, so did the scope of their duties in positions progressively nearer the front. Nurses had, of course, long been accepted as a necessary contingent of a fighting force. From the outset of this war our nurses lived up to traditions tracing back to Florence Nightingale; consequently it was difficult to understand the initial resistance to the employment of women in other activities. They became hospital assistants, dietitians, personal assistants, and even junior staff officers in many headquarters. George Patton, later in the war, was to insist that one of his most valuable assistants was his Wac office manager.

By late December my own personal staff, starting from a total of two individuals eight months before, had achieved the composition that it was substantially to maintain throughout the remainder of the war. Commander Harry Butcher of the Navy and Captain Ernest Lee were personal aides. Nana Rae, Margaret Chick, and Sue Sarafian were personal and office secretaries. Kay Summersby was corresponding secretary and doubled as a driver. Sergeants Leonard Dry and Pearlie Hargreaves were chauffeurs. Sergeants Popp, Moaney, Hunt, Novak, and Williams, with Sergeant Farr as a later replacement, ran the house, field camp, and mess. Colonel James Gault of the Scots Guard shortly joined me and thereafter remained with me throughout the war as British Military Assistant.

Sergeant Michael McKeogh was my orderly, who accompanied me always and was close by my side, day and night. One day in Africa I had to make a hurried trip to the front and I telephoned to Sergeant McKeogh to bring a bag to the airfield. Flying conditions were deplorable and, in the total absence of flying aids in the mountainous country of Tunisia, the prospect of the flight was not enjoyable. When I got to the plane I found Sergeant McKeogh also prepared to make the journey. I said, "Mickey, I intend to return tomorrow, and I doubt that I will need you before then. Flying conditions are not comfortable and there is no use in both of us being miserable. You may go on back to quarters."

The sergeant seemed to pale a bit but he looked me squarely in the eye and said, "Sir, my mother wrote me that my job in this war was to take care of you. And she said also, 'If General Eisenhower doesn't come back from this war, don't you dare to come back.' "

The impact of such loyalty and devotion, not only on the part of the sergeant but on the part of the mother who could say such a thing to her son, left me almost speechless. All I did say was, "Well, hop into the plane. We're late."

Many months after the war was over I heard that a landlady had denied Sergeant McKeogh and his family permission to stay temporarily in one of her apartments on the ground that "after all, he was merely General Eisenhower's valet. I must maintain the proper social atmosphere in my properties." I trust that the lady is not concerned over the relative standing of herself and Sergeant McKeogh in my affections, respect, and admiration!

One of my finest memories of the war is the service rendered me by my personal staff. Seemingly by common consent they gave my affairs and welfare, even my comfort and convenience, complete priority over any consideration of their personal desires or ambitions.

On the official level I had an outstanding staff, many members of which served with me throughout the war. Under General Smith, the chief of staff, were such men as Generals Sir Humfrey Gale, J. F. M. Whiteley, and Kenneth Strong of the British Army, and Everett S. Hughes, Ben M. Sawbridge, Lowell W. Rooks, and Arthur S. Nevins of the American Army. They and their many associates mastered, during the African campaigns, the art of dealing with large Allied forces, operating under single command. Without men of their caliber in the important staff positions of AFHQ, the unification of the Allied forces could not have been achieved. Their names are virtually unknown to the public. But they and their counterparts in many other high headquarters were as responsible for the teamwork out of which came the victories in Tunisia, Sicily, Italy, and northwest Europe as were many others whose more spectacular accomplishments often made headlines.

Every commander is always careful to select only the best officers he can find for key staff positions in his headquarters. Yet these men, who in the average case would do anything to obtain a field command and who could serve brilliantly in such positions, devote their talents to the drudgery of the staff with few of the rewards that go to their comrades of the line.

Chapter 8

TUNISIAN CAMPAIGN

IN DECEMBER WE RECEIVED WORD THAT THE
President of the United States and the Prime Minister of Great Britain,
each accompanied by a considerable civil and military staff, would
hold a meeting in Casablanca during the month of January. We were
directed to make all preparations for the meeting.

I have never learned the exact reasons that led the President and
the Prime Minister to choose Casablanca as the location for the conference. Possibly the spot was selected with the idea that Premier Stalin
might be induced to come that far to join in a conference; possibly
the President and Prime Minister saw certain psychological advantages
in meeting at a place so lately seized by Allied forces. At the time it
seemed to us a risky thing to do, both because hostile bombers were
occasionally visiting that area and because there were many dissident
elements in the population, including numbers of fanatics who might
be expected to undertake any kind of extreme action.[1] Preparations for
the meeting involved anxious care and a very considerable amount of
work, not the least of which was spent to preserve secrecy.

The conference convened on schedule. During the course of its
deliberations a number of British and American officers of all services
were called before it in the role of professional witnesses. I spent a
complete day at the conference, after a journey that suddenly and
unexpectedly became somewhat hazardous owing to the loss of two
engines. Under orders of the pilot, Captain Jock Reedy, we flew the
last fifty miles of the journey with all the passengers standing by
the nearest exits, equipped in parachutes and ready to jump on an instant's notice. With an anxious thought for an old football knee, I was
delighted that I did not have to adopt this method of disembarkation.

That was my only day at the conference. I was already far too busy elsewhere to stay for a single moment longer than my presence was required. I learned of most of the happenings and decisions when General Marshall later came to visit me at Algiers.[2] However, at the one staff session I did attend the military situation in North Africa was thoroughly discussed.

I described the conditions that had compelled us to suspend our offensive in the north and outlined our current effort to establish the II Corps in the Tebessa region. I told the conference that provided we could establish and maintain the entire corps there, and if the enemy should remain quiescent, we could later attempt an advance toward Gabès or Sfax, but we could not predict that this would happen. We regarded it as a most desirable move if it should prove possible, and were building up as rapidly as we could, but our first concern was and would remain the safety of our exposed right flank.[3]

Alexander here interrupted to say that we could drop consideration of the offensive move because the British forces would be quickly in Tripoli and, if that port was at all usable, the British Eighth Army would be at the southern border of Tunisia in the first week in March. This was great news!

I had long talks with General Marshall, the Prime Minister, and others. In the early evening the President sent word that he would like to see me alone. This was one of several intimate and private conversations I had with Mr. Roosevelt during the war. His optimism and buoyancy, amounting almost to lightheartedness, I attributed to the atmosphere of adventure attached to the Casablanca expedition. Successful in shaking loose for a few days many of the burdens of state, he seemed to experience a tremendous uplift from the fact that he had secretly slipped away from Washington and was engaged in a historic meeting on territory that only two months before had been a battleground. While he recognized the seriousness of the war problems still facing the Allies, much of his comment dealt with the distant future, the post-hostilities tasks, including disposition of colonies and territories.

He speculated at length on the possibility of France's regaining her ancient position of prestige and power in Europe and on this point was very pessimistic. As a consequence, his mind was wrestling with the questions of methods for controlling certain strategic points in the French Empire which he felt that the country might no longer be able to hold.

He was especially interested in my impressions of some of the more prominent French personalities, particularly Boisson, Giraud, De Gaulle, and Flandin; the last-named I had not met.

We went over in detail the military and political developments of the preceding ten weeks; he was obviously and outspokenly delighted with the progress we had made. However, when I outlined some of the possibilities for reverses that the winter held for us, his manner indicated that he thought I took this too seriously. While both of us were aware that the Axis forces in Africa could not permanently withstand the pincers effect that General Sir Harold R. L. G. Alexander's forces and our own were developing, President Roosevelt's estimate of the final collapse was, in my opinion, too sanguine by many weeks. Under his insistence that I name a date I finally blurted out my most miraculous guess of the war. "May 15," I said. Shortly thereafter I told Alexander of this and he, with a smile, said that in answer to the same question at the conference he had replied, "May 30."

I found that the President, in his consideration of current African problems, did not always distinguish clearly between the military occupation of enemy territory and the situation in which we found ourselves in North Africa.[4] He constantly referred to plans and proposals affecting the local population, the French Army, and governmental officials in terms of orders, instructions, and compulsion. It was necessary to remind him that from the outset we had operated under policies requiring us to gain and use an ally—that, far from governing a conquered country, we were attempting only to force a gradual widening of the base of government, with the final objective of turning all internal affairs over to popular control. He, of course, agreed—realizing that he had personally collaborated in the original formulation of the policy long before the invasion—but he nevertheless continued, perhaps subconsciously, to discuss local problems from the viewpoint of a conqueror. It would have been so much easier for us could we have done the same! He shrewdly remarked, however, that it was entirely proper to condition the supply of the considerable amounts of military equipment the French ardently desired upon their compliance with American convictions regarding European strategy, utilization of French bases, and the progressive replacement of French officials who were objectionable to the American Government.[5] Unless they generally supported us in these important matters, it was obviously futile to arm them. He was particularly anxious to retain Boisson in control of French West Africa.

To me, the most satisfying part of the whole conversation was the assurance I gained that the President firmly adhered to our basic concept of European strategy, namely the cross-Channel invasion. He was certain that great results would flow from the spring and summer campaigns in the Mediterranean but he properly continued to look upon these as preliminaries to, and in support of, the great venture which had been agreed upon almost a year before as the true line of Allied effort for accomplishing the defeat of Germany.[6]

When I later called upon the Prime Minister I was delighted to get a similar assurance. He said, "General, I have heard here that we British are planning to scuttle Roundup. This is not so. I have given my word and I shall keep it. But we now have a glorious opportunity before us; we must not fail to seize it. When the time comes you will find the British ready to do their part in the other operation." Roundup was the code name that was later changed to Overlord.

The President was hopeful of a quick settlement of the French political situation through a reconciliation between Giraud and De Gaulle, feeling that he could convince both that the best interests of France would be served by their joining forces. During the conversation, which turned frequently to the personal, I was struck with his phenomenal memory for detail. He recalled that my brother Milton had visited Africa and he told me the reasons why he had assigned Milton to the OWI, which was headed by Elmer Davis. He repeated entire sentences, almost paragraphs, from the radiogram I had sent home to explain the Darlan matter and told me the message had been most useful in calming fears that all of us were turning Fascist.

It was some time after I had returned to Algiers that the "unconditional surrender" formula was announced by the President and the Prime Minister.[7] Of more immediate importance to me was the decision that the British Eighth Army and the Desert Air Force, coming up through Tripoli and lower Tunisia, would be assigned to the Allied forces under my command when once they had entered the latter province. During the day I spent at Casablanca I was informed of this general plan, but not until General Marshall later came to Algiers did I learn that it had been definitely approved. General Alexander was to become the deputy commander of the Allied forces. Admiral Cunningham was to remain as my naval C. in C. and Air Chief Marshal Sir Arthur W. Tedder was assigned as the C. in C. of air forces. It was contemplated that this organization would become effective in early February.[8]

This development was extraordinarily pleasing to me because it meant, first and foremost, complete unity of action in the central Mediterranean and it provided needed machinery for effective tactical and strategical co-ordination. I informed the President and the Chief of Staff that I would be delighted to serve under Alexander if it should be decided to give him the supreme authority. I made this suggestion because the ground strength of the Allied Force, after amalgamation with the desert units, would be even more predominantly British. All of us announced ourselves as satisfied and thus there began what was, for me, an exceptionally gratifying experience in the unification of thought and action in an allied command. Other decisions of the Casablanca Conference affected later phases of our operations, the chief of which, so far as we were concerned, was to prepare to attack Sicily as soon as Africa should be cleared.[9]

The remainder of the month of January and early February were employed in haste to get the battle line properly organized, to improve our airfields, and to bring up reinforcements, both in men and in supplies.[10] A succession of relatively small enemy attacks along our front prevented full realization of our plan to assemble our larger units into proper formations. This was particularly serious in its effect upon the U. S. 1st Armored Division, which the army commander thought necessary to use in relatively small packets along a considerable portion of his front.

General Marshall and Admiral King came on to Algiers upon the completion of the Casablanca Conference and the three of us carefully analyzed the situation. All understood the inherent risks resulting from the temporary failure of my all-out gamble but they enthusiastically approved the attempt, Admiral King saying, "We've seen what happens when commanders sit down and wait for the enemy to attack. Keep slugging!"

I expected General Alexander and Air Chief Marshal Tedder to join us in Tunisia about February 4 or 5 and I was looking forward to their arrival, anticipating an opportunity to secure better unification of the several sectors of the battle line. Because General Anderson, commanding the British First Army, had originally been engaged entirely in the north, his communications and command post were so situated as to make most difficult his effective control of the central and southern portions of the long line.[11] On the other hand, the meager quality of the signal communications from west to east across North Africa made it impossible for me to stay permanently on what was essentially a single battle front. The arrival of Alexander would auto-matically correct this situation.

I was still concerned that both Anderson and Fredendall should clearly understand that my intentions in southern Tunisia were, tem-porarily, defensive and that our dispositions were made so as to insure our own safety and to secure the forward airfields. On January 18, I flew to Constantine, where I held a conference with Generals Ander-son, Fredendall, and Juin, and a number of staff officers.[12] I again instructed Anderson to hold as much of the II Corps as possible in mobile reserve, especially the U. S. 1st Armored Division.[13] I reiterated, also, that defenses in the southern sector should be perfected. I told the conference that what I had learned at Casablanca concerning the speed of Alexander's westward advance across the desert merely em-phasized the need for us to protect ourselves effectively in the area of eventual junction of the two forces. Small raids and minor tactical action were to be encouraged, but no moves were to be made that could throw us off balance.

In one of my later trips to the front, on February 1, I again met Anderson and repeated my instructions that, in the southern sector, there must be a strong, mobile reserve.[14] However, the inability of the poorly equipped French forces to withstand repeated, though light, attacks in the mountains between the British and American forces continued to defeat Anderson's efforts to comply with these orders. He was constantly forced to plug gaps in the central sector by drawing on British and American strength.

In early February we received information that the enemy was pre-paring for a more ambitious counterattack against our lines than any he had yet attempted. To provide additional strength for this counter-attack, some of Rommel's forces were hurried back from Tripoli to join Von Arnim and Messe in Tunisia. Our early information was that the attack was to be expected through the pass at Fondouk. Watchful-ness was of course indicated everywhere and it became more than ever important that our mobile reserves, particularly our armored elements, be kept well concentrated in order to meet the coming attack, no matter through which of the several available passes it might be launched.

The most dangerous area was that held by the American II Corps, stretching throughout a long line from Gafsa on the south to approxi-mately Fondouk on the left. As quickly as possible after conferences in Algiers with various individuals who had previously attended the

Casablanca meeting, I departed for that part of the front to spend a week satisfying myself that everything was in good order to receive the expected attack. I had received disappointing word from General Alexander that he could not arrive in the theater before the sixteenth or seventeenth of the month, and I felt it imperative to take personal action in the matter even though General Anderson had then been in command of the battle line for several weeks.

I departed from Algiers just after midnight on February 12 and, holding several conferences on the way, arrived at General Fredendall's headquarters on the afternoon of the thirteenth.[15] It was my first trip as a four-star general, to which temporary grade I was promoted on February 11. I was still a lieutenant colonel in the Regular Army.

Second Corps Headquarters had established itself in a deep and almost inaccessible ravine, a few miles east of Tebessa. It was a long way from the battle front, but, considering the length of the lines and the paucity of roads, it was probably as good a site for the main headquarters as was available. When I reached the headquarters there was a din of hammers and drills. Upon inquiring as to the cause, I learned that the corps engineers were engaged in tunneling into the sides of the ravine to provide safe quarters for the staff. I quietly asked whether the engineers had first assisted in preparing front-line defenses but a young staff officer, apparently astonished at my ignorance, said, "Oh, the divisions have their own engineers for that!" It was the only time, during the war, that I ever saw a divisional or higher headquarters so concerned over its own safety that it dug itself underground shelters.

In company with Lieutenant Colonel Russell F. (Red) Akers, one of Fredendall's staff officers, I promptly started on an all-night inspection of the front lines. At that time the II Corps consisted of the U. S. 1st Armored Division, the 1st Infantry Division, with the U. S. 34th Division assembling in the area. The 9th Division was under orders to join when it could come up.[16]

I found a number of things that were disturbing. The first of these was a certain complacency, illustrated by an unconscionable delay in perfecting defensive positions in the passes. Lack of training and experience on the part of commanders was responsible. At one point where mine fields were not yet planted the excuse was given that the defending infantry had been present in the area only two days. The commander explained, with an air of pride, that he had prepared a map for his mine defense and would start next day to put out the mines. Our experience in north Tunisia had been that the enemy was able to prepare a strong defensive position ready to resist counter-attack within two hours after his arrival on the spot. The enemy's invariable practice upon capture of a hill or other feature was to plant his mines instantly, install his machine guns, and locate troops in nearby reserve where they could operate effectively against any force that we might send against them. These tactical lessons had apparently been ignored by commanders, even by those who had been in the theater for three months. I gave orders for immediate correction.

But by far the most serious defect was the fact that the U. S. 1st Armored Division was still not properly concentrated to permit its employment as a unit.[27] At the moment General Anderson had such meager reserves throughout his long line that he felt compelled to station half the division near Fondouk, where he expected the main enemy attack to fall, and he held this force in army reserve by keeping in his own hands the authority to commit it to action. The remainder was scattered in small detachments to the southward throughout the II Corps front. As a result the 1st Armored Division commander, Major General Orlando Ward, had nothing left under his own command except minor detachments of light tanks.

During the night I visited along the front between Maknassy and Faid Pass. Near the latter place I decorated an American officer for gallantry only two or three hours before the German attack fell upon the positions outside the pass at Sidi-Bou-Zid.

Brigadier General Paul McD. Robinett, an old friend of mine, was commanding an armored unit in the valley, near Fondouk. He was sure that there would be no attack at that point, and pointed out for me on the map the distance to which his reconnaissance patrols had penetrated. He said he had reported those facts several times to his superiors. I was convinced of the accuracy of his report and told him I would take the matter up the next day with the corps and army commanders.

I spent the remainder of an exhausting night conferring with commanders and noting the matters that I wanted to take up with General Fredendall. Our little inspecting party started back before dawn, but we were delayed at Sbeitla by an outbreak of sporadic firing ahead of us. After a reconnaissance in force, in which my aide, Captain Lee, and Lieutenant Colonel Akers composed the assault wave, while I with a .45 formed the mobile reserve, we remounted our cars and made our way through the town without incident. A short time later my driver fell asleep and we ended up in a shallow ditch, but with no casualties. Upon arrival at corps headquarters I found that the German attack had already struck.[18] It was too late to make changes in dispositions.

Although during the morning frequent and, as it later turned out, very accurate reports were submitted by the American troops to General Anderson concerning the strength and direction of the German attack through Faid, these reports were discounted by the Army and AFHQ Intelligence divisions as the exaggeration of green, untried troops. The belief that the main attack was still to come through Fondouk persisted, both at Army headquarters and, as I later learned, in the G-2 Division at AFHQ.[19] The G-2 error was serious. After the battle I replaced the head of my Intelligence organization at AFHQ. The result of this misconception was that the penetration gained a tremendous headway before General Anderson could understand what was actually taking place.

Realizing by nightfall that reinforcements in men and equipment would be needed quickly and urgently, I hastened back to headquarters to hurry them forward. We scraped the barrel and then I started back to the front.

During the withdrawal the Americans fought a series of ineffective, though gallant, delaying actions on the way back toward Kasserine Pass, a spot clearly indicated as one to be strongly held. But there was a local lack of appreciation of exactly what was happening and the troops assigned were neither numerous enough nor skillful enough to hold that strong position. The enemy armor pushed on through the hastily constructed defense in the pass.

Finally, however, in spite of surprise and relatively large losses, our troops rallied in good fashion and fell back to cover the important center of Tebessa and the routes leading northward from Kasserine toward Le Kef.

Our forward airfields at Thelepte had to be temporarily abandoned but the air force pulled out with no loss of personnel or machines and with immaterial losses in fuel and other supplies. Just behind Tebessa was the field of Youks-les-Bains, and it was therefore doubly important for the II Corps to hold this center of communications. Farther to the north it had to resist a German penetration in the direction of Thala, toward Le Kef. The 34th Division was in position on the northern flank and, in spite of its long period of inactivity and dispersion, did good work in the defense. To help stop the enemy's

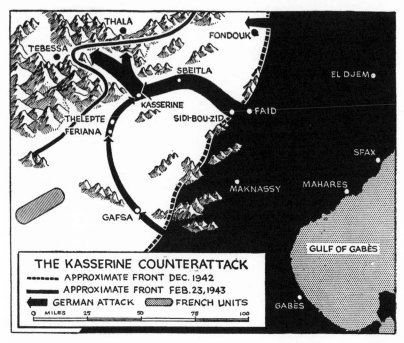

THE KASSERINE COUNTERATTACK
- - - - - - - APPROXIMATE FRONT DEC. 1942
—————— APPROXIMATE FRONT FEB. 23, 1943
GERMAN ATTACK   FRENCH UNITS
0   MILES   25   50   75   100

northward thrust, British artillery and tanks were rushed down from the north, where the enemy had somewhat thinned his lines in order to secure the strength for the Kasserine offensive. The artillery of the U. S. 9th Division also participated effectively in this action.[20] By the evening of the twenty-first it was apparent that the enemy had stretched himself to the limit and his supply was becoming difficult. More than this, his line of communications ran through the vulnerable Kasserine Gap and his troops to the west of that point were becoming precariously exposed to attack by any forces we could bring up.

The enemy's advance, by the twenty-second, was completely stalled. George Patton, who always liked to bring up historical precedent, remarked, "Well, Von Arnim should have read about Lee's attack at Fort Stedman." There, outside Petersburg, the last desperate Confederate counterattack was stopped and driven back in bloody retreat by strong Union reserves.

The staff, always charged with presenting the gloomy side of the picture, devised a plan to cover our movements in case the enemy should penetrate to the First Army's main line of communications. I told them that it was useless to consider the plan further—the enemy was substantially stopped—but finally agreed that there was no objection to letting subordinates know what would have to be done should some entirely unforeseen circumstance like this occur. Alexander, Spaatz, and others agreed that the immediate danger was over, and all of us turned our attention to punishing the enemy.

At that moment the weather, which had been so abominable as to prevent the effective use of our growing air force, took a turn for the better and all the combat planes we had were put into the fight. An embarrassing incident arose during these air attacks which, while admittedly due to lack of experience on the part of combat crews, still illustrates the technical difficulties of which critics, fighting battles from the comfort of an armchair, know nothing.

A group of Fortresses was ordered to bomb Kasserine Pass. They took off in cloudy weather and spent some time searching for the target. Completely dependent upon dead reckoning for navigation, they became badly lost. When they finally concluded they were over the target they dropped their bombs on Souk-el-Arba, an important town within our lines and more than a hundred miles from Kasserine Pass.[21] A number of Arabs were killed and wounded, and much property destroyed. We had to act fast to avoid disagreeable consequences. We had already learned that the native population would amicably settle almost any difficulty for money, and here we were so clearly in the wrong that I quickly approved the expenditure of a few thousand dollars to support our apologies; in war there frequently arise such contingencies, requiring instant availability of funds. The War Department, recognizing this, gave to each theater commander considerable credits to be used when needed.

On the evening of the twenty-second I discussed the situation personally with General Fredendall and told him that the enemy was no longer capable of offensive action. I informed him that he was perfectly safe in taking any reasonable risk in launching local counterattacks that could be properly supported by his artillery. I was so certain of this evaluation that I told the corps commander that I would assume full responsibility for any disadvantage that might result from vigorous action on his part. Fredendall felt that the enemy had "one more shot in his locker" and believed that he should spend the next twenty-four hours in perfecting and strengthening his defenses, rather than in the attempt to concentrate enough strength for a counterattack in the direction of Kasserine. No one could quarrel violently with this decision; my own convictions and desires were based upon an anxiety to take instant advantage of the fleeting opportunity for trouncing the enemy before he could recover from his embarrassing position.

By next morning it became apparent to everybody that the German was beginning his retreat. The enemy moved rapidly by night and, favored again by cloud cover during the day, successfully withdrew a large part of his attacking force. However, the Allies all along the front now kept up a constant pressure and the enemy was soon pushed back to his original positions, from which he never again attempted to launch a serious counterattack.[22]

During the final few days of this battle General Alexander was on the ground and in command of the actual battle line. I quickly formed a great respect and admiration for his soldierly qualities, an esteem that continued to grow throughout the remainder of the war. Certain of our battle-front weaknesses, which favored early German success in the battle, were my responsibility. Had I immediately, upon the acceptance of French troops into the Allied command in November 1942, insisted unequivocally upon their battle-line subordination to General Anderson, later confusion would have been less. There would have been resentment and increased difficulty for a period, but the over-all effect would have been advantageous. Moreover, pending the closer approach of Montgomery's army from the desert, I should have definitely limited the area on our southern flank in which the II Corps would be permitted to operate in strength. We were unquestionably attempting to do too much with too little by the southward extension of the II Corps front to include Gafsa.

That place, in itself, would not become important to us until the desert forces should approach the southern borders of Tunisia and active co-operation between the two armies become possible. However, it was the best position from which to cover, from the south, any raid or attack against the important airfield at Thelepte. We had a crying need for forward airfields and the best of all these was the one at Thelepte. It lay in a sandy plain, and operations from it were never interrupted by rain; only the occasional sandstorm impeded its use. Because of the advantages of this airfield, we placed on it large air formations with comparable quantities of supplies and repair facilities. A better disposition would have been to send to Gafsa only a reconnaissance detachment, and to keep defending forces farther to the rear. The holding of Gafsa tended to weaken other portions of the long front held by the II Corps, and since the U. S. 1st Armored Division was not held in one body for active and powerful counter-attack, the whole situation presented obvious risks.

Technically, our embarrassment resulted from four principal causes. The first and vastly most important of these was the inescapable conditions resulting from failure in our long-shot gamble to capture Tunis quickly. This gamble had been made on my personal orders. Afterward, dispersed units could not quickly be brought together and prepared for the hostile reactions we were certain would follow. Had I been willing, at the end of November, to admit temporary failure and pass to the defensive, no attack against us could have achieved even temporary success.

The second major reason was faulty work by Intelligence agencies. Staffs were too prone to take one isolated piece of intelligence in which they implicitly believed and to shut their eyes to any contrary possibility. They decided that the German attack was to come through Fondouk, and although we had reconnaissance units in the Ousseltia Valley, near Fondouk, who insisted the German was not concentrating in that area, the Intelligence section blindly persisted in its conviction. This caused the army commander to make faulty dispositions.

The third reason was the failure to comprehend clearly the capabilities of the enemy and the best measures for meeting them. The situation on the II Corps front called for the holding of mountain passes with light reconnaissance and delaying elements, with the strongest possible mobile reserves immediately in rear to strike swiftly and in strength at any penetration of the mountain barrier. Instructions for the general nature of the defense were positive in this regard but local fears, and again faulty intelligence, led to a dispersion of the mobile reserves that rendered them ineffective when the attack came.[23]

A fourth cause was greenness, particularly among commanders. The American divisions involved had not had the benefit of the intensive training programs instituted in the United States following the actual outbreak of the war. They were mainly divisions that had been quickly shipped to the United Kingdom, and since transportation facilities had not yet acquired their later efficiency, they had been separated from their organic equipment for long periods. Training, during a major part of 1942, was for them a practical impossibility. Commanders and troops showed the effects of this, and although there was no lack of gallantry and fortitude, their initial effectiveness did not compare with that of the American divisions later brought into action after a full year's intensive training.

These lessons were dearly bought, but they were valuable. Eventually the cost was reduced, since most of our personnel losses were in prisoners, whom we largely recovered at the end of the war. We suffered casualties in personnel and equipment, but by the time the enemy had succeeded in retiring to his former positions his losses in both categories were equal to ours. American losses from February 14 to 23 were 192 killed, 2624 wounded, 2459 prisoners and missing.[24]

The week of the hostile offensive was a wearing and anxious one. Whenever the initiative is lost to the enemy there is bound to be tension and worry, because it is always possible for anything to happen. No one escapes; in spite of confidence in the over-all situation and eventual outcome, there is always the possibility of local disasters.

The Kasserine battle marked the end of a phase of the campaign. With the defeat of the German attack it was obvious that his last chance of major offensive action was ended, but he did, within a short time, begin a series of savage local attacks against the British First Army in the north.[25] All through March this bitter battling continued, the German attempting to deepen and strengthen his defensive zone covering Tunis and Bizerte, the British trying to hold and regain positions favoring a final smashing offensive. The incessant fighting and the length of the front to be covered by depleted formations finally compelled Alexander to use a part of the U. S. 1st Division to help the First Army. However, the German attacks were largely frontal and held no danger of the enemy's achieving any momentous advantage. This certainty permitted us to resume the process of sorting and reorganizing our battle lines, improving our administration, and otherwise preparing for a major offensive as soon as weather conditions should be favorable.

From the close of the Kasserine battle our position steadily improved in a number of ways. First, as a result of the battle the entire American II Corps of four divisions was finally concentrated in the Tebessa region.[26] There it could form a solid link between the Allied forces in northern Tunisia and the advancing Eighth Army, coming from the desert. Troops, commanders, and staffs gained a vast measure of battle wisdom that remained with them always.

Moreover, as a result of splendid action in Washington, an extra shipment of 5400 trucks had been brought into the theater. This shipment immeasurably improved our transport and supply situation and had a profound effect in all later operations. It was accomplished under circumstances that should give pause to those people who picture the War and Navy Departments as a mass of entangling red tape. The shipment demanded a special convoy at a time when both merchant shipping and escort vessels were at a premium. General Somervell happened to be visiting my headquarters and I explained to him our urgent need for this equipment. He said he could be loading it out of American ports within three days, providing the Navy Department could furnish the escorts. I sent a query to Admiral King, then in Casablanca, and within a matter of hours had from him a simple "Yes."[27] The trucks began arriving in Africa in less than three weeks after I made my initial request.

General Somervell was still at my headquarters when the message came from the War Department that the last of the trucks had been shipped. The telegram from Somervell's assistant, Major General Wilhelm D. Styer, eloquently told the story of unending hours of intensive work to arrange this emergency shipment. In a plaintive final sentence it said, "If you should happen to want the Pentagon shipped over there, please try to give us about a week's notice."[28]

The tremendous value of this shipment appeared in our increased ability to supply the needs of the battle front and even more in our ability to transfer troops rapidly from one portion of the front to another. The later move of the entire U. S. II Corps from the Tebessa region to northern Tunisia would have been completely impossible without the presence of these additional trucks. At the same time our railway engineers, under the leadership of Brigadier General Carl Gray, were working miracles in improving the decrepit French line leading to the front. When we went into North Africa the railway could daily deliver a maximum of 900 tons of supplies. By introducing Yankee energy and modern American methods of operation Gray increased the daily tonnage to 3000, and this before he received a single extra engine or boxcar from the United States.

Another particularly pleasing development was the steadily growing strength and efficiency of our air forces, and the construction of suitable operating fields and bases.[29] Still another was the speed with which the British forces in the desert opened up and began using the port in Tripoli, only recently captured.[30] We now had definite assurance that the advance of the Eighth Army would not be stopped, as it had been so often stopped before, by lack of supplies.

A final advantage that accrued to us during this period was opportunity for establishing our whole system of command on a sound and permanent basis in accordance with the arrangements made at

Casablanca. All air forces were integrated under Air Chief Marshal Tedder, with General Spaatz as his deputy; the ground command on the Tunisian front was placed under General Alexander.[31] The latter, freed from the necessity of commanding also a single army, the handicap under which General Anderson labored, was able to devote his entire attention to daily tactical co-ordination.

Just after the first of March, I replaced Fredendall with Patton as commander of the II Corps.[32] I had no intention of recommending Fredendall for reduction or of placing the blame for the initial defeats in the Kasserine battle on his shoulders, and so informed him. Several others, including myself, shared responsibility for our week of reverses. But morale in the II Corps was shaken and the troops had to be picked up quickly. For such a job Patton had no superior in the Army, whereas I believed that Fredendall was better suited for a training job in the States than he was for battle leadership. I recommended to General Marshall that Fredendall be given command of an army in the United States, where he became a lieutenant general.[33]

General Patton's buoyant leadership and strict insistence upon discipline rapidly rejuvenated the II Corps and brought it up to fighting pitch. Moreover, the troops were now fortified by battle experience and had a much higher appreciation of the value of training, discipline, and speed in action. Our losses in tanks, personnel, and equipment were rapidly made good and all the eastern airfields were again in our possession and occupied by our fighter craft.

Winter conditions of weather and terrain in the desert were much better than those in the north, and the Eighth Army, under General Montgomery, was able to continue its advance to the westward with the purpose of making junction with the right of our forces in Tunisia. It was foreseen that General Montgomery's principal battle to achieve this result would take place on the Mareth Line, a defensive position that had previously been constructed by the French along the Tunisian border and in which we now expected the Axis to make a determined defense.[34] To assist General Montgomery in this battle, General Alexander ordered the American II Corps to concentrate the bulk of its strength in the general area of Gafsa and to push eastward from that location so as to draw off as much of Rommel's forces as possible from the Eighth Army front. This maneuver had the desired effect, since Rommel could not afford to expose his line of communications and was forced to use a considerable portion of his strength to protect himself against this threat.

By the night of March 20, General Montgomery was ready to attack the Mareth Line.[35] The fighting was severe but by a brilliant and rapid switch of forces in the midst of the battle he succeeded in outflanking and surprising the enemy and drove him precipitately to the northward. The left flank of the Eighth Army soon joined up with Patton's II Corps, which had pushed aggressively to the eastward. At last all our troops were connected up in one single battle line.

I visited Montgomery soon after the Mareth battle. His Eighth Army was very colorful and probably the most cosmopolitan army to fight in North Africa since Hannibal. It included, in addition to English units, Highlanders, New Zealanders, Indians (including Gurkhas with their *kukris*—long, curved knives with which they beheaded their enemies), Poles, Czechs, Free French, Australians, and South Africans. Not all of these came as far as Tunisia. With the Eighth Army were American air squadrons, our first to see action in Africa against the Germans. They had participated in the campaign all the way from El Alamein.[36] I fortunately had a chance to talk with the pilots and crews during my visit to Montgomery; later I was able to send to them some of the soldier luxuries that they had been denied during the long trip across the desert.

In an effort to cut off the Germans retreating from Montgomery's front, General Alexander organized an attack to break through the pass at Fondouk and push eastward toward the sea. The left of the American II Corps was involved in this attack, but the entire operation was commanded by a British corps commander.[37] The only American division available for participation was one that had had only sketchy training and had been involved for many weeks in protection of our line of communications, thus missing the opportunity to work together as a unit. The task assigned the American unit was a difficult one and the attack failed. A break-through was finally accomplished by British formations, but it was not particularly effective because the Germans had made good their retreat to the northward. General Sir John Crocker, the British corps commander, severely criticized to press representatives the failure of the American division, and for almost the only time during the African operations definite British-American recrimination resulted.[38] It was disturbing, the more so because it was so unnecessary. With the help of Alexander, we quickly took steps to stop it. Nothing creates trouble between allies so often or so easily as unnecessary talk—particularly when it belittles one of them. A family squabble is always exaggerated beyond its true importance.

Although the outcome of this particular attack was disappointing, the rapid retreat of the Germans had the effect of shrinking the circumference of the enemy line, thus pinching out the American II Corps for employment elsewhere on the battle line.

Some discussion arose as to the suitability of the corps for participating effectively in the final battle. Alexander's staff felt that a large portion should be sent back to the Constantine area for additional training. Admittedly some of the troops were still relatively green. However, both Patton and I were confident that the corps was now ready to act aggressively and to take an important sector in the battle line. For one thing the troops were at last angry—not only because of the rough handling they had received, but more so because of insulting and slighting comments concerning the fighting qualities of Americans, originated by German prisoners and given some circulation within the theater.

I had a personal interview with Alexander to insist upon the employment of the entire II Corps, as a unit.[39] For this I had several reasons. In the first place, the bulk of the ground forces required by the Allies to defeat Germany would have to come from the United States. The need for battle training on a large scale was evident. Secondly, in all its prior battles the corps had been compelled to fight in small packets; never had it had a chance to exert its power as a unit. Thirdly, the morale of the corps had improved markedly since March 1 and it had a right to prove its own effectiveness as well as the quality of American arms.

Success would make the unit, and it would give a sense of accomplishment to the American people that they richly deserved in view of the strenuous efforts they had made thus far in the war. Out of victory participated in by both countries on a significant scale would come a sense of partnership not otherwise obtainable. The soldiers themselves were entitled to engage in an operation where for the first time conditions would favor instead of hamper and impede them. A real victory would give them a great élan for the sterner tests yet to come.

Alexander instantly concurred in my determination that the corps should be used in its entirety and as a unit. He proposed, and I agreed, that the best plan was to transfer the II Corps across the rear of the First Army and place it on the northern flank facing Bizerte. This involved a nicety in staff work in order to avoid entanglement with the British First Army's supply lines, but Anderson's and Patton's

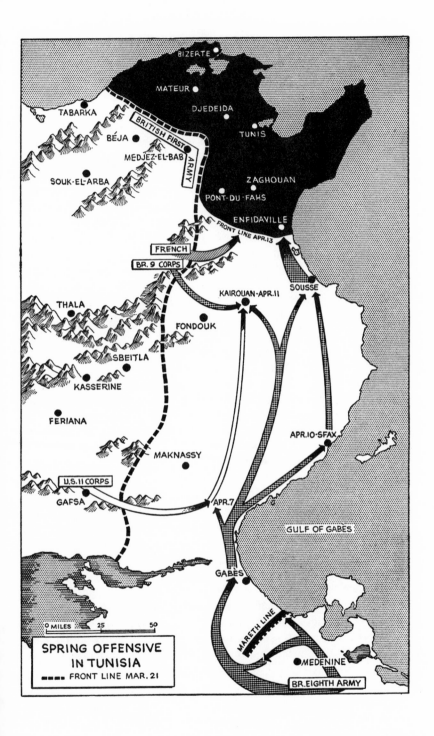

BIZERTE

MATEUR

DJEDEIDA

TABARKA

BÉJA

BRITISH FIRST

TUNIS

MEDJEZ-EL-BAB

SOUK-EL-ARBA

ZAGHOUAN

PONT-DU-FAHS

ENFIDAVILLE

FRONT LINE APR.13

FRENCH

BR. 9 CORPS

THALA

FONDOUK

KAIROUAN-APR.11

SOUSSE

SBEITLA

KASSERINE

FERIANA

APR.10-SFAX

MAKNASSY

U.S. II CORPS

APR.7

GAFSA

GULF OF GABES

GABES

0 MILES   25   50

MARETH LINE

MEDENINE

SPRING OFFENSIVE
IN TUNISIA
- - - - FRONT LINE MAR. 21

BR. EIGHTH ARMY

staffs worked out the details so efficiently that no confusion resulted.[40] It was a move that prewar staff colleges would have deemed an impossibility. But clockwork schedules and effective traffic control at crossroads characterized the whole movement.

At this time I made another change in the command of the II Corps. Major General Omar N. Bradley had reported to me in late February as an "inspector." Aside from his outstanding personal qualifications, he had gained much experience during the March and early April fighting. The compelling reason for the change was to give General Patton the opportunity to go back to Seventh Army Headquarters and finish preparations for the Sicilian invasion, which was to take place as soon as possible after the completion of the African campaign. A second and less important reason, and the one given out, since manifestly the whole truth could not be hinted at for the moment, was that the II Corps operations would from then on feature infantry rather than tank tactics and so the change of its commander from a tank technician to an infantry expert was logical. Bradley took command on April 15, 1943, after part of the corps was already in position in the north.[41]

In the meantime General Montgomery continued to advance northward, until finally he pushed up to the line of Enfidaville, where he came up against a very strong enemy position which effectively blocked his further progress.[42]

However, the stage was now almost completely set for the final all-out effort against the enemy position. Improving weather was eagerly seized upon by the air forces to harass the enemy's line of communications between Africa and Italy, and the Axis position grew more precarious. Under our growing air superiority our naval forces also pushed forward their bases and operations and added to the enemy's difficulties. Our ground troops were confident and anxious to wind up the whole affair. The enemy still held some depth in the mountainous areas on his western flank, and the first move was to launch assaults calculated to drive him back to the edge of the Tunisian plain. These began on April 23, and all along the line satisfactory advances were made. Co-ordination between air and ground forces was immeasurably better than at the beginning of the campaign, and all of our assaults took place with effective aerial help. Our superiority in artillery was giving us a further advantage.[43]

By the time Alexander reached, on the west, the line from which he wished to launch his final thrust, it had become apparent that further attacks from the south by the Eighth Army would be costly and indecisive because of the nature of the terrain along the Enfida- ville line. At the same time we confidently believed that the German would expect the main attack to be delivered by the Eighth Army, since that organization had established a brilliant reputation in its long pursuit across the Western Desert and the enemy would naturally expect us to use it for our knockout punch.

In the conviction, therefore, that the enemy would in any event keep strong forces in front of the Eighth Army, General Alexander quickly and secretly brought around from that flank several of the Eighth Army's best divisions and attached them to the British First Army. These arrangements were completed in time to begin the final assault on May 5.⁴⁴

The results were speedily decisive. On the left the American II Corps, with some detachments of French "Goumiers," advanced magnificently through tough going and captured Bizerte on the seventh. Just to the southward the British First Army, under General Anderson, carrying out the main effort, was in Tunis at approximately the same time that the II Corps reached Bizerte.

During the final days of the Tunisian campaign two local battles in the north, one in the British sector and one in the American, gripped the interest of the entire theater. Both positions were exceedingly strong naturally and fiercely defended, and both were essential to us in our final drive for victory. The position in the British sector was Longstop—the battles for its possession from the beginning to the end of the African campaign probably cost more lives than did the fighting for any other spot in Tunisia. In the American sector the place was Hill 609, eventually captured by the 34th Division, to the intense satisfaction, particularly, of the American high command. This division had been denied opportunity for training to a greater degree than any other, and its capture of the formidable 609 was final proof that the American ground forces had come fully of age.

Following immediately upon the break-through, Alexander sent armored units of the British First Army rapidly forward across the base of the Bon Peninsula, where we believed the Germans might attempt to retreat to make a last stand in the manner of Bataan.⁴⁵ Alexander's swift action, regardless of the many thousands of enemy still fighting in confused packets along the front of the First Army, destroyed this last desperate hope of the enemy. From then on the operations were of a mopping-up variety. Some fighting continued

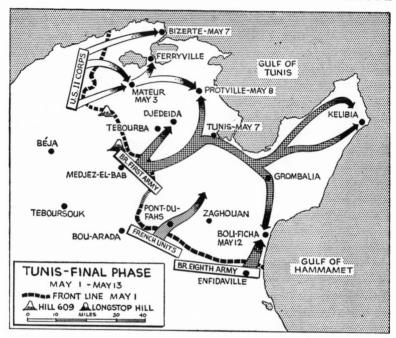

TUNIS-FINAL PHASE
MAY 1 - MAY 13
▬▬▬ FRONT LINE MAY 1
⛰HILL 609 ⛰LONGSTOP HILL
0   10   MILES   30   40

until the twelfth but by the following day, except for a few stragglers in the mountains, the only living Germans left in Tunisia were safely within prison cages. The number of prisoners during the last week of the campaign alone reached 240,000, of which approximately 125,000 were German. Included in these captures was all that was left of the Afrika Korps and a number of other crack German and Italian units.[46]

Rommel himself escaped before the final debacle, apparently foreseeing the inevitable and earnestly desiring to save his own skin. The myth of his and Nazi invincibility had been completely destroyed. Von Arnim surrendered the German troops, and Field Marshal Messe, in nominal command of the whole force, surrendered the Italian contingent. When Von Arnim was brought through Algiers on his way to captivity, some members of my staff felt that I should observe the custom of bygone days and allow him to call on me.

The custom had its origin in the fact that mercenary soldiers of old had no real enmity toward their opponents. Both sides fought for the love of a fight, out of a sense of duty or, more probably, for money. A captured commander of the eighteenth century was likely to be, for weeks or months, the honored guest of his captor. The tradition that all professional soldiers are really comrades in arms has, in tattered form, persisted to this day.

For me World War II was far too personal a thing to entertain such feelings. Daily as it progressed there grew within me the conviction that as never before in a war between many nations the forces that stood for human good and men's rights were this time confronted by a completely evil conspiracy with which no compromise could be tolerated. Because only by the utter destruction of the Axis was a decent world possible, the war became for me a crusade in the traditional sense of that often misused word.

In this specific instance, I told my Intelligence officer, Brigadier Kenneth Strong, to get any information he possibly could out of the captured generals but that, as far as I was concerned, I was interested only in those who were not yet captured. None would be allowed to call on me. I pursued the same practice to the end of the war. Not until General Jodl signed the surrender terms at Reims in 1945 did I ever speak to a German general, and even then my only words were that he would be held personally and completely responsible for the carrying out of the surrender terms.

The outcome of the Tunisian campaign was of course eminently satisfactory, but the high command was so busily engaged in preparation for the Sicilian attack that little opportunity was available for celebration. However, a Victory Parade was held in Tunis on the twentieth to mark the end of the Axis Empire in Africa.

The very magnitude of our victory, at least of our captures, served to intensify our difficulties in preparing for the Sicilian affair. We had more than a quarter of a million prisoners corralled in Tunisia, where poor communications made feeding and guarding difficult and rapid evacuation impossible.[47] But the end of the campaign did have the effect of freeing commanders and staffs from immediate operations and allowed them to turn their full attention to the matter next in hand. Preparatory planning had been going on ever since February in a special group attached to Allied Headquarters but operating under General Alexander. This group was now absorbed completely in General Alexander's staff and the whole process of preparation was vastly speeded up.

The Tunisian victory was hailed with delight throughout the Allied nations. It clearly signified to friend and foe alike that the Allies were at last upon the march. The Germans, who had during the previous winter suffered also the great defeat of Stalingrad and had been forced to abandon their other offensives on the Russian front in favor of a desperate defense, were compelled after Tunisia to think only of the protection of conquests rather than of their enlargement.

Within the African theater one of the greatest products of the victory was the progress achieved in the welding of Allied unity and the establishment of a command team that was already showing the effects of a growing confidence and trust among all its members. It is easy to minimize the obstacles that always obstruct progress in developing efficient command mechanisms for large allied forces. Some are easy to recognize, such as those relating to differences in equipment, training and tactical doctrine, staff procedures and methods of organization. But these are overshadowed by national prides and prejudices.

In modern war, with its great facilities for quickly informing populations of battlefield developments, every little difference is magnified, and a soldier fighting for his life is likely to be a very temperamental organism. Even tried veterans, normally selfless and serene, can react suddenly and explosively to a headline story favoring, in their opinion, another nationality. The problem is delicate, tricky, and important—but success in allied ventures can be achieved if the chief figures in the government and in the field see the necessities of the situation and refuse to violate the basic principle of unity, either in public or in the confidence of the personal contacts with subordinates and staffs. Immediate and continuous loyalty to the concept of unity and to allied commanders is basic to victory. The instant such commanders lose the confidence of either government or of the majority of their principal subordinates, they must be relieved.

This was the great Allied lesson of Tunisia; equally important, on the technical side, was the value of training. Thorough technical, psychological, and physical training is one protection and one weapon that every nation can give to its soldiers before committing them to battle, but since war always comes to a democracy as an unexpected emergency, this training must be largely accomplished in peace. Until world order is an accomplished fact and universal disarmament a logical result, it will always be a crime to excuse men from the types and kinds of training that will give them a decent chance for survival in battle. Many of the crosses standing in Tunisia today are witnesses to this truth.

Chapter 9

HUSKY

DURING THE FINAL WEEKS OF THE TUNISIAN campaign, particularly after the outcome could be definitely foreseen, major staffs were busy planning our next campaign. As directed by the Casablanca Conference, this was to be the capture of Sicily.[1] At the time of the conference, alternative missions for the Mediterranean forces were discussed by the Combined Chiefs of Staff. One of these was to assault Sicily with the least practicable delay; the other was to capture Sardinia and Corsica.

My own opinion, given to the conference in January, was that Sicily was the proper objective if our primary purpose remained the clearing of the Mediterranean for use by Allied shipping. Sicily abuts both Africa and Italy so closely that it practically severs the Mediterranean, and its capture would greatly reduce the hazards of using that sea route. On the other hand, if the real purpose of the Allies was to invade Italy for major operations to defeat that country completely, then I thought our proper initial objectives were Sardinia and Corsica. Estimates of hostile strength indicated that these two islands could be taken by smaller forces than would be needed in the case of Sicily, and therefore the operation could be mounted at an earlier date. Moreover, since Sardinia and Corsica lie on the flank of the long Italian boot, the seizure of those islands would force a very much greater dispersion of enemy strength in Italy than would the mere occupation of Sicily, which lies just off the mountainous toe of the peninsula.

This discussion served to focus attention once more upon the desirability of fixing, once and for all, ultimate objectives within the Mediterranean. It was completely normal that some differences in conviction should obtain—we were not yet far enough along in the process of defeating the Axis to produce crystal-clear and unanimous conclusions as to the specific actions that would obviously produce victory. General Marshall and I shared the belief that everything done in the Mediterranean should continue to be subsidiary to and in support of the main purpose of attacking across the Channel in early 1944. In this we were supported by some, but others held that, in war, opportunity should be exploited as it arises, and that if things went well in the "soft underbelly" we should not pause merely because we had made up our minds to conduct the cross-Channel operation. The doctrine of opportunism, so often applicable in tactics, is a dangerous one to pursue in strategy. Significant changes in the field of strategy have repercussions all the way back to the factory and the training center. They must be carefully scrutinized. Moreover, in the specific case, all the original reasons for adopting the cross-Channel operation as our basic strategic aim were still valid. However, even while adhering faithfully to this purpose there still remained important questions, then and later, as to the best methods of using the forces in the south for supporting the great projected attack of 1944.

At Casablanca the Sicily operation was decided upon for two reasons, the first of which was its great immediate advantage in opening up the Mediterranean sea routes. The second was that because of the relatively small size of the island its occupation after capture would not absorb unforeseen amounts of Allied strength in the event that the enemy should undertake any large-scale counteraction. This reason weighed heavily with General Marshall—moreover, this decision, in January 1943, avoided a commitment to indefinite strategic offensives in the area. Successful attack would advance our bomber bases still farther, but we would not necessarily be drawn into a campaign that would continuously devour valuable resources. The Combined Chiefs of Staff ordered that Alexander, in addition to serving as my deputy, should also be the ground commander of the Sicilian operation.[2]

The importance of Mediterranean bases for furthering our bombing campaign against central Germany was always a factor in the development of plans. During the spring of 1943 a project was developed in Washington for a special bombing effort from an African base against the Ploesti oil fields, the most important single source of natural oil available to the Axis.[3] It was worked out on an academic basis and a special staff group came from Washington to explain the plan to us.[4] Because of heavy defenses, the distance to the target—the fields were in Rumania—the nature of the terrain, and the alleged efficacy of "horizontal" bombing, the plan called for a single surprise attack, conducted at treetop height and with every crew briefed to attack a particular facility in the great installation. The originators of the plan had worked out mathematical probabilities in great detail and then provided strength on the basis of double the bombers deemed necessary. They calculated that the attack could achieve near perfection in its destructive results.

One feature to which we objected was the confidence placed in the efficacy of a single attack. Too often we had found that factories listed by our experts as destroyed were again working at full output within a matter of weeks or even days. We raised another question as to the advisability of the undertaking. The target selected was a great refinery, but our information led us to believe that the enemy had a surplus of refining capacity and that his true oil shortage was in production and distribution facilities. Our doubts and objections were not, however, decisive in the matter because the air units to be used were specially sent to us from the United States for the execution of this particular mission.

The attack was carried out, with great gallantry—five Medals of Honor were awarded—on August 1.[5] As usual, mathematical calculations could not win over unexpected conditions, but the effort was reasonably successful. This was the second American raid against Ploesti. While I was still chief of operations in the spring of 1942 a small detachment of big planes had taken off from Near East bases on a surprise attack, but nothing was accomplished and the planes were mainly lost. Some were interned when they had to come down in Turkey. The early attempt, called the Halverson Project (HALPRO), because of the name of its commander, did something to dispel the illusion that a few big planes could win a war.[6]

Development of the Sicilian plan, assigned the code name Husky, began in February. The major points to be decided were the strength of the attack, its timing, and its exact location. Manifestly we could not depend entirely upon the employment of troops that were then engaged in the Tunisian battle. To do this would force us to defer decisions respecting timing until after the final battle in Africa, and since this date could not be accurately predetermined, all other planning would have been indecisive and commanders and staffs could not have proceeded with confidence.

Considering the strength of the enemy garrison, we felt that some five or six divisions should be deployed in the initial landing. An invasion on this scale required the concentration of a very considerable number of landing craft and additional fighting vessels of the Navy.

During the spring months of 1943 we kept in constant communication with the Combined Chiefs of Staff to determine the amount of the resources upon which we could count and the time at which they could be made available. The United States staff found that it could send us a splendidly trained division, the 45th, properly loaded on convoys for the assault. In addition we had the 3d, which we did not plan to use in the Tunisian battle. Moreover, our plans called for the release of the U. S. 1st Division from the Tunisian battle area as quickly as success was sure. These three divisions, reinforced by the 2d Armored Division, still in Morocco, paratroop elements of the 82d Airborne Division, and Rangers were to make up the American portion of the assaulting forces.[7] On the British side it was determined to bring into the assault a Canadian division from England, while the Eighth Army was able, some time before the end of the Tunisian campaign, to detach part of its strength to prepare for the Sicilian assault.[8] These forces were to attack Sicily in early July, and all preparation was based upon the keeping of that target date. Because of the location of our troops and embarkation points, the convoys would converge upon the island from the east, the west, and the south.

Selection of the assaulting areas was a complicated problem. From the standpoint of ease of approach from our scattered ports, protection of our communications, and the nature of the coast line, the southeastern portions of the island looked favorable, yet the supply staffs were convinced that a force of the size contemplated could not be maintained over available beaches. Even assuming the early capture of Syracuse on the eastern coast of the island, the technical experts flatly stated that without additional ports the operation would be defeated by lack of reinforcements, ammunition, and other supplies. The alternative was to arrange the attack so as to gain quickly more points and ports of entry, but since strength in landing craft was limited, each of these attacks would be relatively weak. Experience up to that time led us largely to discount the quality of the defense to be put up by the Italian formations; however, in the coming operation they would be defending their own territory, which could easily make a great difference.

Our Intelligence staffs were vitally concerned with the strength of the German garrison. We felt—and later experience proved that our estimate was reasonable—that if the German garrison at the time of attack should be substantially greater than two fully manned and equipped divisions, then the assault as we were planning it was too weak and we would be wise to defer the operation until we could effect a greater concentration of our own forces.[9]

Because of the estimated inability to supply several assault divisions and their reinforcements over the southern and eastern beaches, we studied and tentatively adopted a plan that contemplated assault by echelon, beginning in the southeast, followed by a second one in the south, and a third in the vicinity of Palermo on the north coast.[10] The idea was that each would provide air cover for the following one and the result would be to give us a number of beaches and ports at the earliest possible date, thus facilitating supply.

The danger in such an operation was that failure in any particular assault would cancel out the following ones, and even if initial landings were successful, later concentration would be difficult, and we ran the risk of defeat in detail. This last possibility we did not consider serious unless before the attack could begin the German strength defending the garrison should reach the danger point, namely, substantially over two divisions. But the plan was complicated and that is always a disadvantage. At first, however, it appeared to be the only possible solution to the problem.

As time went on it was evident that the German was moving to stiffen up the garrison in Sicily, but our information led us to believe that he had not yet attained, or at least passed, what we considered to be the critical level.

No one really liked the plan for echelon attack. Its complications, dispersion, and successive rather than simultaneous assaults were cited as risks outweighing the chance of defeat through lack of port facilities. Montgomery, especially, always a believer in the power concept, desired to throw heavy forces into the southeastern portion of the island.[11] The supply staffs were again required to study the problem, and now they came to a more optimistic estimate than they had some weeks previously.

This change resulted from the unforeseen availability of a considerable number of LSTs and the quantity production of the "duck," an amphibious vehicle that proved to be one of the most valuable pieces of equipment produced by the United States during the war. Incidentally, four other pieces of equipment that most senior officers came to regard as among the most vital to our success in Africa and

Europe were the bulldozer, the jeep, the 2½-ton truck, and the C-47 airplane. Curiously enough, none of these is designed for combat.

With considerable quantities of improved equipment in sight, the supply staffs agreed that their estimates could be markedly revised upward, and plans were crystallized on the basis of the British forces moving against the eastern coast and the American against the eastern part of the southern coast.[12]

Before leaving this point, a word upon the "might-have-been" of the alternate plan. Some professionals and others have since vigorously asserted to me that if we had correctly evaluated the low combat value of the huge Italian garrison we would have stuck to the "encircling" plan and so overrun the island in ten to fifteen days rather than in the thirty-eight eventually required. Moreover, it is alleged, we would have captured the German core of the defending forces instead of merely driving it back into Italy. It is possible that with Syracuse, Gela, and Palermo quickly in our hands we might have been able to capture Messina, the key point, before the Germans could have concentrated sufficiently to defeat any of our attacks. But not even by hindsight can it be said with certainty that the whole Italian garrison would quit—I still believe that we were wise to concentrate as much as possible, and to proceed methodically to the conquest of an island in which the defending strength was approximately 350,000.[13] In any event the simple, simultaneous attack became the adopted plan.

To conduct the British portion of the attack General Alexander designated the Eighth Army under General Montgomery, while on the American side General Patton, who had been brought out of the Tunisian battle in the middle of April, was placed in command. General Alexander was to be in immediate charge of the ground assault; his headquarters was designated Fifteenth Army Group.[14]

While these plans were still in preparation, study indicated the desirability of first seizing the island of Pantelleria, lying roughly between Sicily and the northeastern coast of Tunisia. This island was popularly known as the "Gibraltar of the central Mediterranean" and was assumed by many to be unassailable. It possessed an airfield from which Axis planes were able to operate against us but, more than this, we badly needed the airfield ourselves in order to supply additional air support for the Sicilian attacks. Except for small numbers of P-38s, we were still using the short-range British Spitfires and American P-40s, and to bring their bases closer to their intended target would be of tremendous advantage.

Topographically Pantelleria presented almost dismaying obstacles to an assault. Its terrain was entirely unsuited to the use of airborne troops, while its coast line was so rocky that only through the mouth of the island's one tiny harbor was it possible to land troops from assault boats. We would obviously have to use an attack of a blasting nature; that is, the volume of fire on the point of attack would have to be so great that, in spite of the lack of surprise, our assaulting troops could get ashore and make good their position.

Many of our experienced commanders and staff officers strongly advised against attempting this operation, since any failure would have a disheartening effect on the troops to be committed against the Sicilian shore. However, Admiral Cunningham, in particular, agreed with me that the place could be taken at slight cost. We based our conviction upon the assumption that most Italians had had a stomachful of fighting and were looking for any good excuse to quit. We believed that if the island were subjected for several days and nights to an intensive air bombardment, denying the garrison any chance for sleep or rest, the assault, if supported heavily by naval gunfire, would be relatively easy. The garrison might even surrender beforehand.

We proceeded on this assumption, since our air force had now grown to the point where a bombardment of the kind contemplated could be readily carried out. Air Chief Marshal Tedder, General Spaatz, and the air forces became enthusiastic supporters of the project. In a period of six days and nights approximately 5000 tons of high explosives were dropped on the eastern portion of the island and in such a limited area that the concentrations achieved were greater than any we had previously attempted.[15]

In the actual outcome the capture of Pantelleria was so easy—the garrison surrendered on June 11, just as our troops were getting into their assault boats from the larger ships—that few people had any inkling of the doubts and fears that had to be overcome in launching the operation.[16] Indeed, objection had been so pronounced that I resolved to make a personal reconnaissance immediately prior to the assault date in order to determine for myself that the defenses were sufficiently softened to assure success. This reconnaissance took the form of a naval and air bombardment of the island two days prior to the attack, conducted so as to appear to the defenders to be a real assault and to simulate as nearly as possible the actual operation contemplated for D-day and H-hour.[17] Admiral Cunningham and I boarded a British cruiser at Bône one evening, and during that night steamed eastward at full speed to join the squadron assembly near Pantelleria. Cunningham told me that the whole area was mined except for a narrow channel we were following, which had been swept. This prompted me to ask, "Are there no floating mines about?" His answer was, "Oh yes, but at this speed the bow wave will throw them away from the ship. It would be just bad luck if we should strike one."

The squadron of some half-dozen cruisers and ten destroyers began the bombardment about eleven in the morning, while the planes came over in wave after wave to drop their bombs on selected targets. Reaction was weak and sporadic. Although all our ships pressed in close to shore, and small, speedy craft ran up almost to the edge of the mole, the ships suffered no damage. Cunningham and I were confirmed in our belief that little opposition would be offered to the attack and that we could have taken the island then if we had been accompanied by troops.

The Prime Minister, who was then visiting with me in Africa, was very anxious to go along on this operation. I evaded direct reply but would never have agreed to his going, on the grounds that it involved needless risk for a man of his importance. But I had a difficult time indeed explaining to him afterward that Admiral Cunningham and I had always intended to participate. Two years later he reminded me that I had been very unfair to him on that occasion, especially as he had a personal financial stake in the enterprise.

A small wager between us had grown out of his estimate that there were no more than 3000 Italians on the island. He offered to pay me five centimes each for all we captured in excess of that number. We took 11,000, and though I had naturally forgotten the joking wager, he paid up promptly, figuring out the exchange himself and remarking that at that rate (a twentieth of a cent each) he'd buy all the prisoners we could get.

With Pantelleria captured we immediately moved strong air elements onto its airfield.[18] In the meantime we further improved our air position by building a new field on the island of Gozo, just off Malta. On Malta itself was stationed every aircraft that its fields could possibly absorb.

In late May, a month before we were to attack Sicily, Prime Minister Churchill, with General Marshall and General Brooke, chief of the Imperial General Staff, came to my headquarters to discuss further the objectives of the Sicilian campaign, other than the mere capture of the island to assure free use of the Mediterranean sea route.[19] There was something to be said for closing down large-scale activity in the Mediterranean, once we had Sicily in our grasp, and saving everything for the main operation in northwest Europe.

Against this there were weighty considerations. To cease heavy attacks would eliminate all threat to the Germans on the southern front and would allow the enemy great freedom of action. In Europe, Allied ground forces would be completely unengaged from the summer of 1943 to early summer of 1944. We badly wanted the fine airfields of southern Italy. Finally, we wanted to keep up the pressure in the belief that Italy would soon crack and quit. Such an outcome would denude the Balkans of Italian garrisons and so force Germany to extend her forces still further.

Both Alexander and Montgomery were called to the conference, in which Admiral Cunningham, Air Chief Marshal Tedder, General Spaatz, and my chief of staff, "Beedle" Smith, also participated.[20] Mr. Churchill was at his eloquent best in painting a rosy picture of the opportunities that he foresaw opening up to us with the capture of Sicily. He insisted, in the conference discussions, that he had no intention of interfering with preparations for the cross-Channel attack in 1944, but he was concerned that I understand the desire of the two governments that the Allied forces should quickly exploit any opportunity arising out of the fall of Sicily. He was fearful that we would interpret our mission in such narrow fashion as to stop short with the capture of Sicily, regardless of circumstances.

Since a normal part of every battle is maximum exploitation of victory, I was personally in doubt as to just what the Prime Minister expected or desired. However, he did not propose in my hearing any campaign on a major scale, with the Balkans, or even northern Italy, as a minimum objective. He seemed honestly concerned in the quick capture of southern Italy but, so far as I knew, no more, at that moment.

In private conversation, however, Brooke told me that he would be glad to reconsider the cross-Channel project, even to the extent of eliminating that bold concept from accepted Allied strategy. He had commanded a corps during the short campaign on the Continent in 1940; both Alexander and Montgomery had served under him. Impulsive by nature, as became his Irish ancestry, he was highly intelligent and earnestly devoted to the single purpose of winning the war. When I first met him in November 1941 he seemed to me adroit rather than deep, and shrewd rather than wise. But gradually I came to realize that his mannerisms, which seemed strange to me, were merely accidental, that he was sincere and, though he lacked that ability so characteristic of General Marshall to weigh calmly the conflicting factors in a problem and so reach a rocklike decision, I soon found it easy to work with him. He did not hesitate to differ sharply and vehemently, but he did it forthrightly and honestly, and heated official discussion never affected the friendliness of his personal contacts or the unqualified character of his support. He must be classed as a brilliant soldier. So I listened carefully to the expression of his ideas at that moment.

He said that he favored a policy of applying our naval and air strength toward the blockading of Germany and the destruction of its industry but avoiding great land battles on the main fronts. He held the belief that in ground conflict in a large theater we would be at a great disadvantage and would suffer tremendous and useless losses. He wanted to open no larger front than one we could sustain in Italy. I do not know whether the Prime Minister agreed with the part of this opinion that favored the indefinite postponement of the cross-Channel invasion, but he did want to pour into Italy the maximum amount of Allied forces available in the Mediterranean.

Any suggestion or intimation of abandoning Overlord could always be guaranteed to bring Marshall and me charging into the breach with an uncompromising, emphatic refusal to consider such an idea for an instant. Not only did both of us still believe in, and frequently repeat, all the basic reasons for originally adopting the Overlord concept as our principal strategic effort in Europe, but we closely examined every proposal for committing troops elsewhere in the light of the eventual effect of weakening or strengthening prospects of success in Overlord. Both of us were willing to concede, and to strive for, the advantages that would flow from a successful invasion of southern Italy—but we resolutely refused to commit ourselves, or Allied troops, to an all-out campaign for winning the war through the Italian approach.

These and other reasons led to an agreement which, in effect, left exploitation of the Sicilian operation to my judgment—but expected me to take advantage of any favorable opportunity to rush into Italy —and which emphasized the great value of the Foggia airfields.[21] Since a major port was necessary to sustain us in Italy, the city of Naples was named as the other principal locality desired by the Allies.

At this conference long discussions were carried on regarding the desirability of bombing the marshaling yards near Rome. All agreed that the Eternal City should not be uselessly damaged—indeed, this was the policy we pursued with respect to all the relics of the ancient civilization of Italy—but it was common knowledge that the Germans were taking advantage of our restraint to use Rome as a principal link in their communication system. No final answer was then resolved but later we were authorized to bomb the yards, taking particular care to avoid damage to Rome and the Vatican City.[22]

The broad outline of the Sicilian campaign was announced to our press representatives one month before it took place.[23] This unprecedented step was taken, paradoxically, to maintain secrecy.

I felt I had to stop speculation by war reporters as to the future intentions of the Allied Force. I knew the Germans were watching us intently and it is astonishing how expert a trained Intelligence staff becomes in piecing together odd scraps of seemingly unimportant information to construct a picture of enemy plans. At the moment northern Africa was a hive of preparation for the Sicilian invasion. At every possible spot along the beaches we were holding exercises; ports were being stacked with needed supplies, and harbors and inlets were receiving landing craft. It seemed certain that if reporters seeking items of interest for their papers and radio networks should continue to report upon activities throughout the theater, the enemy would soon be able to make rather accurate deductions as to the strength and timing of our attack, even if we should be successful in concealing its location.

During periods of combat inactivity reporters have a habit of filling up their stories with speculation, and since after some months of experience in a war theater any newsman acquires considerable skill in interpreting coming events, the danger was increased that soon the enemy would have our plans almost in detail. I do not believe that speculation by self-styled military analysts in the homelands, far removed from a theater of operations, is of any great benefit to the enemy. These long-distance conclusions are based upon the sketchiest of information and are usually amusing rather than terrifying, although they become dangerous as they edge closer to the truth and give statistical information to substantiate ideas. But in an active theater it is an entirely different matter, and because of an inborn hatred of unexplained censorship and, more than this, because of the confidence I had acquired in the integrity of newsmen in my theater, I decided to take them into my confidence.

The experiment was one which I would not particularly like to repeat, because such revelation does place a burden upon the man whose first responsibility is to conceal the secret. But by making it I immediately placed upon every reporter in the theater a feeling of the same responsibility that I and my associates bore. Success was complete. From that moment onward, until after the attack was launched, nothing speculative came out of the theater and no representative of the press attempted to send out anything that could possibly be of any value to the enemy. After the operation was completed many correspondents told me of the fear they felt that they might be guilty of even inadvertent revelation of the secret. During the period of preparation they even became reluctant to discuss the subject among themselves, and invented the most elaborate code names to refer to items of equipment and to details of the projected operation.

Mouths fell open as I began the conference by telling the reporters that we would assault Sicily early in July, with the Seventh Army under General Patton attacking the southern beaches and the British Eighth Army under General Montgomery attacking the eastern beaches south of Syracuse. There was almost painful silence as I explained that General Alexander would be in command of both armies and that we were already conducting the preliminary air campaign to destroy the German air forces and to cut his sea and land communications as well as to soften his defenses. I told the press that we were conducting this air offensive in such a way as to lead the enemy to believe that we would attack the western end of the island. I informed them that we would use airborne troops in the operation on a much larger scale than had yet been attempted in warfare. The attack was carried out in exactly this fashion on the night of July 9.[24]

Because of the existence of splendid naval communications at Malta that place was chosen as our headquarters for the initial stages of the operation. Most of our air formations were crowded into the airfields of northeastern Tunisia, so the principal air headquarters had to remain in the vicinity of ancient Carthage. General Alexander, Admiral Cunningham, and I all went to Malta a day or so before the attack was scheduled, to be in position to take any action that might prove necessary.[25] We were guests of Field Marshal Lord Gort, governor of the island.

Malta then presented a picture far different from the one of a few months earlier, when it was still the target for a hostile air force that had little effective opposition. Malta had taken a fearful beating but the spirit of the defenders had never been shaken. As Allied air and naval support approached them through the conquest of North Africa, they rose magnificently to the occasion. By the time we found need for Malta's facilities its airfields were in excellent condition and its garrison was burning to get into the fight.

A story in connection with this preparation illustrates the amazement sometimes created by American organizations that have been indoctrinated in the mass production methods of the United States. This incident involved the construction of the airfield on the little island of Gozo, lying just off Malta. It was so ill favored in the matter of terrain that British field engineers, who depended to a great extent upon hand tools and light equipment, had given up any hope of producing a field there in time for use in the Sicilian campaign. Happily, just at the critical moment Air Marshal Park, in command of the air forces of the island, had as a visitor an American engineer who specialized in the construction of airfields.

Park told the engineer of this particular problem and after showing him the projected site asked for an estimate on the time it would take to construct an operational strip. The answer was a nonchalant "Ten days." This struck Park—who is a human dynamo himself—as so preposterous that he thought himself the victim of a joke. However, upon noting the thoughtful way in which the engineer was considering the problem, he asked: "When can you start?"

"As soon as my equipment can get here, which should take several days."

The upshot was that messages began to fly through the air, and thirteen days from the time the first American construction unit stepped on the island the first fighter plane was taking off from the strip.

To perform this seeming miracle the engineers had employed almost every type of modern earth-moving machinery to be found on any large construction job in the United States, equipment that British engineers envied but had never dreamed could be brought into such a remote part of an active theater of war. This story was told to me over and over again by British officers on the island whose admiration for the American engineers was scarcely short of awe. This fighter strip gave us an additional base from which to sustain our attack against Sicily.

The ship convoys bringing the troops to their allotted places had to come from ports stretched throughout the length of the Mediterranean. The timing and final maneuvering of the various naval columns had to be exactly performed in the narrow, mine-filled waters separating Sicily from the mainland and had to be done so as to keep the enemy in a state of confusion and indecision until the last moment. Admiral Cunningham, Admiral Hewitt, and all their subordinates performed the task faultlessly.

Everything was proceeding with seeming perfection until the actual day of the assault. Then the weather, which in that part of the Mediterranean is normally serene in summer, began to deteriorate so badly as to threaten our ability to land. Since the wind direction was generally from the west it was the southern beaches for which we were anxious. The eastern beaches would have the shelter of the island itself.

I spent some hours with Admiral Cunningham in his office, to which meteorological specialists brought frequent reports and forecasts. Naval personnel has a habit of referring to wind velocity in terms of "Force." In would come a man and say, "Force IV, sir," or "Force V, sir." For me this had to be translated into miles per hour, but I had no difficulty, watching Cunningham's face, in realizing that Force V was worse than Force IV. However, falling velocities were predicted for sundown and this cheered us, because if that tendency continued conditions by midnight should be satisfactory!

Some of us went outside for a short walk, but we watched the wind indicators fearfully, almost prayerfully, because the hour was fast approaching when it would be impossible to turn back assaulting forces from their intended landings. A message came from General Marshall: "Is the attack on or off?" My reaction was that I wish I knew! Evening approached with predictions indicating some slight improvement. We decided to proceed as planned, and I so radioed to General Marshall.[20] My feeling was that, even if the forces on the southern coast should find it necessary to delay landing, those on the east would surely get ashore and we would have less confusion and disadvantage than would result from any attempt to stop the whole armada.

But the evening wore on and the wind velocity increased alarmingly. There was nothing we could do but pray, desperately.

Chapter 10

SICILY
AND SALERNO

THE FIRST TROOPS SCHEDULED TO REACH THE island were the airborne contingents. The route of some of these lay directly across Malta and a number of us went out on the hilltops to watch them pass. In the wind and storm it was difficult for them to keep direction. Our plotting board in the air operations room showed that many planes and tows were blown far off course, but generally the columns kept on target and when the one we were watching had passed overhead, we returned to headquarters to await reports. Most of us turned in to catch a few hours of sleep.

The first messages in the morning were a mixture of good and bad. A number of the gliders participating in the airborne attack on the British front had been cast loose too far from their targets and the high wind had dropped some into the sea. We feared a heavy loss of life and, though statistics later showed that casualties were less than we feared, it was still a tragic incident. On both flanks the landings from the sea seemed to be proceeding well with only moderate opposition.[1]

On the southern front the parachutists had landed, although in certain instances far from their appointed landing grounds. We were almost amazed at the reports of progress in the American sector, where we had thought it possible Rear Admiral Alan Kirk, in command of the assault convoy, might even postpone the transfer to small boats for several hours, hoping for better weather conditions. It was so difficult for Admiral Cunningham to believe that landings in that area were feasible that he promptly took off in a destroyer to see what had happened. He came back and reported that the landings in the 45th Division sector constituted one of the finest exhibitions of seamanship it had been his pleasure to witness in forty-five years of sailoring.

As battle reports began to arrive it was evident that the enemy had been badly deceived as to the point of attack. His best formations were located largely on the western end of the island, which he had apparently believed we would select for attack because of its proximity to our own North African ports. His reaction was typical. He pushed east and south with his most mobile forces to attack the American 1st Division at Gela.[2] The division was not yet well ashore and these attacks seriously threatened to pierce through to the beach, but the enemy was short of supporting troops, particularly infantry and artillery. The gallant action of the 1st, supported steadfastly by an airborne formation and with assistance from naval gunfire, repulsed the counterattack after some hours of bitter touch-and-go fighting.

Believing that the enemy might persist in his counterattacks on this portion of our forces, I left Malta that night in a British destroyer to visit Patton and Hewitt, the ground and naval commanders directly concerned.[3] When I arrived the following morning the German was pulling back, presumably to strengthen his defenses in the critical Catania area. Everybody was in fine fettle, and though we in the destroyer saw little more of the fighting than sporadic gunfire, yet we got a good conception of the whole action on the south coast, and two accompanying pressmen, of whom John Gunther was one, picked up local color for their dispatches. I seized the chance to stop on the beach to send the Canadian division a message of welcome to the Allied command.

Up to that moment no amphibious attack in history had approached this one in size. Along miles of coast line there were hundreds of vessels and small boats afloat and antlike files of advancing troops ashore. Overhead were flights of protecting fighters.

The point we wanted to capture at the earliest possible moment was Messina, the enemy port in the northeastern end of the island, directly across the narrow strait from the Italian mainland. Through this port almost all enemy supplies would have to flow, and once it was secured the position of the garrison on the island would be hopeless. The enemy of course saw this simple truth as clearly as we and rapidly gathered up his forces to bar the progress of Montgomery, who was closest to Messina. In this effort the enemy was tremendously favored by the ground. Mount Etna dominates the whole northeast corner of the island and the Eighth Army's route to the northward lay over a narrow road along the seaward shoulder of the mountain. Montgomery's attack initially proceeded swiftly and quickly overran the

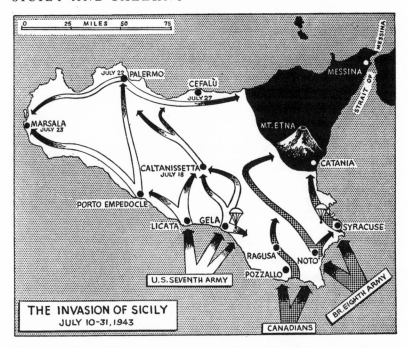

THE INVASION OF SICILY
JULY 10-31, 1943

eastern beaches to include the Nazi port of Syracuse, most important to our supply plan. From there toward Catania opposition grew increasingly stern. From July 17 onward the Eighth Army lay in the Catania plain facing the Mount Etna bastion with small prospect of penetrating the passes to the northward.⁴ Montgomery began to build up his reinforcements so as to throw an encircling column to the westward as his only hope of forcing his way onward to the ultimate goal.

The plain was infected with malaria. In no other area during the Mediterranean campaign did we suffer equal percentage losses from disease. At other points in Sicily we likewise had a serious casualty list from malaria, but Catania was the pesthole of the region.

Patton in the meantime pushed vigorously forward to the center of the island, while with his extreme left flank he threw mobile columns around the western perimeter of the island, entering Palermo within twelve days after the initial landing.⁵ His rapidity of movement quickly reduced the enemy ports to the single one of Messina; it broke the morale of the huge Italian garrison and placed Patton's forces in position to begin the attack from the westward to break the deadlock on the eastern flank.

Patton was a shrewd student of warfare who always clearly appreciated the value of speed in the conduct of operations. Speed of movement often enables troops to minimize any advantage the enemy may temporarily gain but, more important, speed makes possible the full exploitation of every favorable opportunity and prevents the enemy from readjusting his forces to meet successive attacks. Thus through speed and determination each successive advantage is more easily and economically gained than the previous one. Continuation of the process finally results in demoralization of the enemy. Thereupon speed must be redoubled—relentless and speedy pursuit is the most profitable action in war.

To insure rapidity of action all commanders, and troops, must recognize opportunities and be imbued with the burning determination to make the most of them. The higher commander must constantly plan, as each operation progresses, so to direct his formations that success finds his troops in proper position and condition to undertake successive steps without pause. Long periods of inaction for regrouping are justified only by sheer necessity. Veteran troops realize that by continuing the advance and attack against a shaken enemy the greatest possible gains are made at minimum cost. Speed requires training, fitness, confidence, morale, suitable transport, and skillful leadership. Patton employed these tactics relentlessly, and thus not only minimized casualties but shook the whole Italian Government so forcibly that Mussolini toppled from his position of power in late July.[6]

As the Seventh Army approached the western slopes of the Mount Etna highlands fighting became more and more severe. The Battle of Troina, conducted largely by the 1st Division, was one of the most fiercely fought smaller actions of the war.[7] The enemy launched twenty-four separate counterattacks during the battle. The ground was rocky and broken, with hidden areas difficult to clean out. Several days after the capture of the position our troops were astonished to find in one small valley a field of several hundred German dead, so far uncounted. They were victims of American artillery fire.

In the advance eastward from Palermo the left flank of the Seventh Army, following the coast line, made a series of small amphibious operations, the strength of the landings varying from one to two battalions.[8] A small naval task force under Rear Admiral Lyal A. Davidson and the troops advancing along the rocky coastal cliffs of Sicily achieved a remarkable degree of co-ordination and efficiency in carrying out these attacks. The only road was of the "shelf" variety,

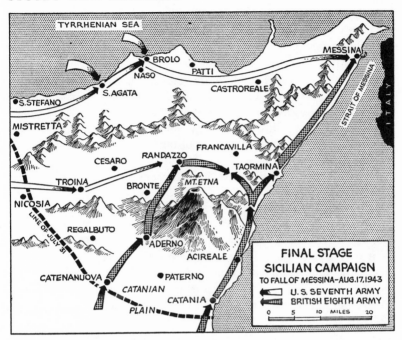

FINAL STAGE
SICILIAN CAMPAIGN
TO FALL OF MESSINA—AUG.17,1943
⬛ U. S. SEVENTH ARMY
⬛ BRITISH EIGHTH ARMY
0   5   10   MILES   20

a mere niche in the cliffs interrupted by numerous bridges and culverts that the enemy invariably destroyed as he drew back fighting. The advance along the coast line toward Messina by the Seventh Army was a triumph of engineering, seamanship, and gallant infantry action.

By the end of July the Italian garrison, except for a few small elements under the direct domination of their German overlords, had entirely quit, but along the great saw-toothed ridge of which the center was Mount Etna the German garrison was fighting skillfully and savagely. Panzer and paratroop elements here were among the best we encountered in the war, and each position won was gained only through the complete destruction of the defending elements.

Nevertheless, by the time the Seventh and Eighth Armies had closed up into position for their final assault against the Mount Etna bastion the Germans saw that the game was up and began the evacuation across the Strait of Messina.[9] Our bombers operated against this line of escape, but the narrowness of the strait allowed the enemy to get out most of the badly battered German garrison during hours of darkness.

Early on August 17 the U. S. 3d Division pushed into the town of

Messina.[10] A detachment from the Eighth Army soon after arrived and on that date the last remaining element of the enemy forces on the island was eliminated.

In the original study of the Sicilian operation Alexander had faintly hoped that the forces landing on the east of the island would quickly push to the northward, close to Messina. There they could effectively block the easy avenue for enemy evacuation, and would also be in a position to make a possible surprise landing across the narrow strait and thus assist in a speedy transfer of our troops to the Italian mainland later on.

Montgomery's operations on the east coast had begun auspiciously, and for a few days it looked as if Alexander's hope might be realized. But by the time Montgomery was ready to assault the natural defensive barriers running from Mount Etna to the sea the enemy had brought up too much strength. The chance for a *coup de main* passed, if it ever had existed. Thereafter the northward path of the Eighth Army was fully as difficult from the terrain viewpoint as was the eastward advance on the left of the Seventh Army. In addition the Eighth Army had to overcome the preponderance of enemy strength. On the cliffs facing the sea just to the eastward of Mount Etna, I saw an almost incredible feat of field engineering. The road, completely blown away through a gap of two hundred yards, presented nothing but a sheer cliff hundreds of feet in height. Across this gap the engineers built a trestle capable of supporting the heaviest army loads; it was another example of what troops in the field can do when they are faced with stark necessity.

Nevertheless, again there cropped up criticisms of Montgomery's "caution," which I had first heard among pressmen and airmen when he was conducting his long pursuit of Rommel across the desert. Criticism is easy—an unsuccessful attack brings cries of "butcher" just as every pause brings wails of "timidity." Such charges are unanswerable because proof or refutation is impossible. In war about the only criterion that can be applied to a commander is his accumulated record of victory and defeat. If regularly successful, he gets credit for his skill, his judgment as to the possible and the impossible, and his leadership. Those critics of Montgomery who assert that he sometimes failed to attain the maximum must at least admit that he never once sustained a major defeat. In this particular instance I went over all details carefully, both with Montgomery and with Alexander. I believed then, and believe now, that a headlong attack against the Mount Etna position, with the resources available in the middle of July, would have been defeated. And it is well to remember that caution and timidity are not synonymous, just as boldness and rashness are not!

Among the American leaders, Bradley had done so well in Sicily that when General Marshall, toward the end of August, asked my recommendation on the Army commander for the United States troops in Great Britain, I answered: "The truth of the matter is that you should take Bradley and moreover I will make him available on any date you select." Shortly thereafter General Bradley assumed his new duties in England.[11]

One of the valuable outcomes of the campaign was the continued growth and development of the spirit of comradeship between British and American troops in action. The Seventh Army, in its first campaign, had established a reputation that gained the deep respect of the veteran British Eighth, while on the American side there was sincere enthusiasm for the fighting qualities of their British and Canadian partners.

The operations brought to a high degree of efficiency the co-ordination among air, naval, and ground forces. The Navy, in its escorting, supporting, and maintenance functions, performed miracles and always in exact co-ordination with the needs and support of the other arms. The real preliminary to the assault was a vast bombing operation by air.[12] Entirely aside from its success in defeating the enemy air forces, it so badly battered the enemy communications in Sicily and southern Italy that the mobility of his forces was materially lowered and the supply of his troops was a most difficult process.

The development of this international and interservice spirit had begun with the establishment of a headquarters in London in July of the previous year. By the end of the Sicilian campaign it was so firmly established and so much a part of the daily lives of commanders and staffs that it was scarcely necessary longer to treat it as a problem.

It was during this campaign that the unfortunate "slapping incident" involving General Patton took place.[13] Patton, on a visit to base hospitals to see the wounded, encountered, in quick succession, two men who had no apparent physical hurts. Of the first one he met, Patton inquired why he was a patient in the hospital. To this the man replied, "General, I guess it's my nerves." Patton flew into a rage. He had, himself, been under a terrific strain for a period of many days. Moreover, he sincerely believed that there was no such thing as true "battle fatigue" or "battle neurosis." He always maintained that any man who began to show signs of breaking under battle conditions could by shock be restored to a sense of responsibility and to adequate performance of duty. At the moment, also, Patton was in a highly emotional state because of the sights he had seen and the suffering he had sensed among the wounded of the hospital. He broke out into a torrent of abuse against the soldier. His tirade drew protests from doctors and nurses, but so violent was his outbreak that they hesitated to intervene.

Within a matter of moments he met a second soldier under somewhat similar circumstances. This time his emotions were so uncontrollable that he swung a hand at the soldier's head. He struck the man's helmet, which rolled along the ground, and by this time doctors and nurses, overcoming their natural timidity in the presence of the commanding general, intervened between Patton and the soldier.

Both enlisted men were, of course, badly upset. One of them was seriously ill. Doctors later testified that he had a temperature of 102. Patton soon gained sufficient control of himself to continue his inspection and left the hospital. But throughout his visit he continued to talk in a loud voice about the cowardice of people who claimed they were suffering from psychoneuroses and exclaimed that they should not be allowed in the same hospital with the brave wounded men.

The story spread throughout the hospital and among neighboring units with lightning speed. I soon received an unofficial report from the surgeon commanding the hospital and only a few hours thereafter was visited by a group of newspaper correspondents who had been to the hospital to secure the details. Their report substantially corroborated the one I had already received from the doctor. The question became, what to do? In forward areas it is frequently necessary, as every battle veteran knows, to use stern measures to insure prompt performance of duty by every man of the organization. In a platoon or in a battalion, if there is any sign of hesitation or shirking on the part of any individual, it must be quickly and sternly repressed. Soldiers will not follow any battle leader with confidence unless they know that he will require full performance of duty from every member of the team. When bullets are flying and every man's safety and welfare depend upon every other man in the team doing his job, men will not accept a weakling as their leader. Patton's offense, had it been committed on the actual front, within an assaulting platoon, would not have been an offense. It would merely have been an incident of battle

—no one would have even noted it, except with the passing thought that here was a leader who would not tolerate shirking.

But because of the time and place of his action Patton's offense was a serious one, more so because of his rank and standing. Thus to assault and abuse an enlisted man in a hospital was nothing less than brutal, except as it was explained by the highly emotional state in which Patton himself then existed. His emotional tenseness and his impulsiveness were the very qualities that made him, in open situations, such a remarkable leader of an army. In pursuit and exploitation there is need for a commander who sees nothing but the necessity of getting ahead; the more he drives his men the more he will save their lives. He must be indifferent to fatigue and ruthless in demanding the last atom of physical energy.

All this I well understood, and could explain the matter to myself in spite of my indignation at the act. I felt that Patton should be saved for service in the great battles still facing us in Europe, yet I had to devise ways and means to minimize the harm that would certainly come from his impulsive action and to assure myself that it would not be repeated. I was then working intensively on plans for the invasion of Italy, and could not go immediately to Sicily. In these circumstances I sent to Sicily three different individuals in whose judgment, tact, and integrity I placed great confidence.[14] One of these I sent to see General Patton. Another went to visit the hospital in which the trouble occurred. Still a third was sent to visit the divisions of Patton's army to determine for himself the extent to which the story had spread among the troops and to determine their reaction. I not only wanted independent reports from several sources, but I wanted to accomplish the whole investigation as rapidly as possible.

As a result I determined to keep Patton. I first wrote him a sharp letter of reprimand in which I informed him that repetition of such an offense would be cause for his instant relief. I informed him, also, that his retention as a commander in my theater would be contingent upon his offering an apology to the two men whom he had insulted. I demanded also that he apologize to all the personnel of the hospital present at the time of the incident. Finally, I required that he appear before the officers and representative groups of enlisted men of each of his divisions to assure them that he had given way to impulse and respected their positions as fighting soldiers of a democratic nation.[15]

Patton instantly complied and I kept in touch with results again through a series of observers and inspectors.

In the meantime, as soon as I had determined upon my course of action, I called in to see me the group of reporters who had brought me the story of the occurrence. I explained to them in detail the action I had taken and the reasons for it. I read them the letter I had written to Patton and extracts from the letter he wrote me in reply. This, so far as I was then concerned, closed the incident.

On one point connected with the matter there has been considerable misapprehension. This was the assumption that censorship was applied. On the contrary, my staff and General Patton were told that under no circumstances was there to be any effort to suppress the story. These specific instructions, which I issued personally to a group of newspapermen, covered "indirect pressure" as well as direct censorship. They were flatly told to use their own judgment![16] That they voluntarily refused to write or speak about the matter is proved by the fact that two of the press representatives who made a detailed report to me of the affair returned to the United States within a few days after the occurrence. They were then no longer under the direct or indirect influence of Allied Headquarters. They were Demaree Bess and Quentin Reynolds.

However, the aftermath connected with this episode temporarily strained our usually splendid relations with the press. When, months later, the story finally reached Washington via the gossip route, a great public uproar immediately followed its broadcast by a commentator. To play fair with the pressmen in our own headquarters, my chief of staff decided to hold an informal press conference to supply any details of information that they might lack. My only instructions to him were, "Tell the full truth."

During this later conference a question was posed concerning disciplinary action against Patton, and the chief of staff replied that no reprimand had been administered, which was correct technically, since the reprimand had not been recorded in the official files. But it was factually wrong, and immediately the conference was over a reporter called me on the phone to protest what he called "the shabby treatment of the press." Instantly I issued orders for correction. But the damage was done and the story already in America; and this only ten minutes later! The chief of staff ruefully regretted his error; his self-blame was so great that it was clear he'd never again be guilty of that kind of error. Moreover, it emphasized to both of us the speed with which newspapermen acted. In dealing with them we plainly had to be right the first time.[17]

After the incident was all over my old friend George sent me a long letter in which the following appeared: "I am at a loss to find words with which to express my chagrin and grief at having given you, a man to whom I owe everything and for whom I would gladly lay down my life, cause to be displeased with me."

The results of the Sicilian campaign were more far-reaching than the mere capture of the enemy garrison. As already noted, the bombastic Mussolini was thrown out. Evidence of unrest and dissatisfaction throughout the Italian nation became more and more pronounced and it was obvious that Italy was seeking the easiest way out of the war. Mussolini's place as Premier was taken by old Field Marshal Pietro Badoglio.[18] The initial pronouncements of the latter indicated his government's purpose to continue in the war, but it was clear that this statement was made merely in the hope of placating the Germans and giving the Italians a chance to escape punishment from their arrogant ally.

The Italian hope of independently negotiating a surrender was slim indeed, because throughout the Italian governmental structure Mussolini had permitted or had been forced to accept the infiltration of countless Germans, all of whom were ready to pounce upon the first sign of defection and to take over the Italian nation in name as well as in fact. But in spite of German watchfulness the Italian Government attempted to reach us by sending an agent to Lisbon.[19] I sent there two of my most trusted staff officers, my chief of staff, General Smith, and my Intelligence officer, Brigadier, later Major General Kenneth Strong, to act as emissaries in arranging for the unconditional surrender of the Italian forces.

Then began a series of negotiations, secret communications, clandestine journeys by secret agents, and frequent meetings in hidden places that, if encountered in the fictional world, would have been scorned as incredible melodrama. Plots of various kinds were hatched only to be abandoned because of changing circumstances. One of these plots involved the landing of a large airborne force in the vicinity of Rome. At the last moment either the fright of the Italian Government or the movement of German reserves as alleged by the Italians—I have never known which—forced the cancellation of the project. But in the meantime Brigadier General Maxwell D. Taylor, later the gallant commander of the 101st Airborne Division, had been hurried secretly to Rome, where his personal adventures and those of his companion added another adventurous chapter to the whole thrilling story.[20] The risks he ran were greater than I asked any other agent or emissary to undertake during the war—he carried weighty responsibilities and discharged them with unerring judgment, and every minute was in imminent danger of discovery and death.

The Italians wanted frantically to surrender. However, they wanted to do so only with the assurance that such a powerful Allied force would land on the mainland simultaneously with their surrender that the government itself and their cities would enjoy complete protection from the German forces. Consequently they tried to obtain every detail of our plans. These we would not reveal because the possibility of treachery could never be excluded. Moreover, to invade Italy with the strength that the Italians themselves believed necessary was a complete impossibility for the very simple reason that we did not have the troops in the area nor the ships to transport them had they been there. Italian military authorities could not conceive of the Allies undertaking this venture with less than fifteen divisions in the assault waves. We were planning to use only three with some reinforcing units, aside from the two that were to dash across the Messina strait.[21]

These negotiations were still proceeding when, according to plan, Montgomery slipped two divisions across the Strait of Messina one night against no resistance and the Allied invasion of the continent of Europe was an accomplished fact.[22] This was on September 3—a date ten days later than I had hoped it could be done. Preparation for amphibious attack is time-consuming, but if we could have saved a few days in this instance our Salerno problem would have been much easier to solve. Nevertheless the timing was sufficiently good to permit us to use for the later main assault some of the landing craft that Montgomery had employed to get across the strait. He immediately started an advance up the toe of the boot with enemy forces cautiously delaying him and anxiously watching for our major move.

For a brief period following upon the expulsion of Mussolini we had ceased the intensity of our bombing raids against Italy. We publicized this as an opportunity for the new government to avoid further destruction in the country by accepting without delay our demands for unconditional surrender of their entire armed forces. This evoked an angry protest from London—again reminding us that a modern commander in the field is never more than an hour away from home capitals and public opinion. Actually the bombing delay was caused by the necessity of transferring air units and the bringing up of supplies; we were attempting to make a virtue out of a necessity. As quickly as

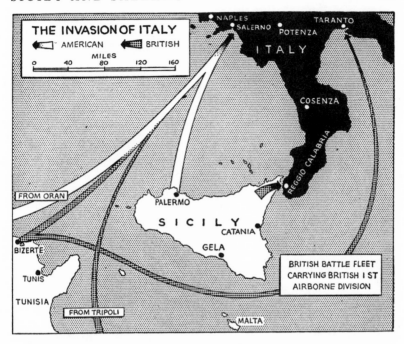

THE INVASION OF ITALY

AMERICAN   BRITISH

MILES

0   40   80   120   160

ITALY

NAPLES   TARANTO
SALERNO   POTENZA

COSENZA

REGGIO CALABRIA

FROM ORAN

PALERMO

S I C I L Y
CATANIA

BIZERTE

GELA

TUNIS

BRITISH BATTLE FLEET
CARRYING BRITISH 1 ST
AIRBORNE DIVISION

TUNISIA

FROM TRIPOLI

MALTA

we were again in position for using our air force at maximum effectiveness, we resumed our air campaign.

In the actual determination of tactical plans there arose a question on which there was sharp difference of opinion. One group held that our safest, even if less decisive, means of advancing into Italy was to follow along through the toe of the boot, after Montgomery had made the initial beachhead, and to work our way laboriously up the narrow winding roads toward the heart of the country. This scheme was safe, but it could offer no worth-while results. Indeed, once the enemy was sure that our major effort was to come from that direction, he could easily have bottled up our force on a number of mountainous positions where we would have been without opportunity to deploy and utilize our strength.

An invasion on a wider front was clearly indicated, and after examination of every spot of the beach from Rome to the toe of the boot, the bay of Salerno was selected. The greatest disadvantage of this plan was that its logic was obvious to the enemy as well as to us. Most of our pursuit planes were still handicapped by short range and Salerno Bay lay at about the extreme limit of their effective support for the landings. Besides, between the bay and the toe of the boot there were no other particularly favorable landing beaches, so we went into the operation with no illusions of surprising the opposition.

In the meantime negotiations for the Italian surrender had been dragging along. They were very intricate. They involved the still strong Italian fleet, the remnants of the Italian air forces, and Italian ground forces throughout the peninsula and in the Balkans. Above all they involved the feasibility of a surrender while the Germans so closely dominated the entire country. Finally it was agreed that the surrender would be effective on the evening of September 8 and that Badoglio and I should simultaneously announce the capitulation.[23] I chose that date because at midnight our Salerno attack would begin. All these long, and at times exasperating, negotiations were carried on for us by my chief of staff.

Everything was proceeding according to plan when, at noon on September 8, I received a message through clandestine channels to the effect that Badoglio had reversed his decision on the ground that we were too hasty and that the result would merely mean complete domination of Italy by the Germans and the sanguinary punishment of the individuals involved.[24] The matter had proceeded too far for me to temporize further. I replied in a peremptory telegram that regardless of his action I was going to announce the surrender at six-thirty o'clock as previously agreed upon and that if I did so without simultaneous action on his part Italy would have no friend left in the war.[25]

I was then in my advanced headquarters near Carthage. Badoglio's message was first received at main headquarters in Algiers and the staff, thrown completely off balance, radioed the Combined Chiefs of Staff for instructions at the same time that they forwarded the original message to me. Determined to proceed on my own judgment, I ordered the staff to cancel the message to the Combined Chiefs of Staff or if that could not be done to explain that I had already handled the matter myself. I announced the surrender at six-thirty that evening and Badoglio, in fear and trembling, finally decided an hour and a half later that he had to follow suit.[26]

This action did not by any means change our invasion plans. For some days we had known that the Italian garrison in the Salerno Bay area was being replaced by the best of the German troops and our Intelligence sections predicted a hard battle in the beachhead culminating in strong counterattacks somewhere between the fourth and the sixth day following the initial landing.

With the equivalent of four divisions in the assault, in addition to two which were already ashore but situated far to the southeastward, still in the toe of the boot, we were invading a country in which there were estimated to be eighteen German divisions.[27] Although follow-up troops would double the initial assault strength, in some respects the operation looked foolhardy; but it was undertaken because of our faith in the ability of the air forces, by concentrating their striking power, to give air cover and emergency assistance to the beachhead during the build-up period, and in the power of the Navy to render close and continuous gunfire support to the landing troops until they were capable of taking care of themselves.

The landing and succeeding operations developed almost identically to G-2 predictions. There was a sharp but relatively short fight in getting ashore and with minor exceptions the details of the actual landing proceeded well. The enemy, as was his custom, immediately began to counterattack and by the thirteenth had gathered up sufficient strength to make a major effort to throw us into the sea. During this period German propaganda was ridiculing the operation as a great mistake and pouring out over the radios of the world predictions of a complete defeat for the Allied invasion.

On the thirteenth the German attack struck in all its fury, and fierce fighting ensued for a considerable period.[28] The greatest pressure of the German attack came in the center and pushed forward to within two or three miles of the beach. The outlook became somewhat gloomy, particularly when the American 36th Division was struck from an unexpected direction and suffered heavy losses before it could extricate and recover itself. At one time it looked so probable that the invasion forces might be divided that General Clark made tentative plans for re-embarking his headquarters in order to control both sectors and to continue the battle in whichever one offered the greatest chance for success. This tentative plan, repeated to headquarters in garbled form, caused consternation because it seemed to indicate that commanders on the spot were discouraged and preparing to withdraw the whole force. This was actually not the case. General Clark and General Richard L. McCreery, commanding the British 10 Corps, never once faltered in their determination.

When General Clark led the Fifth Army into Salerno he had not previously participated in any of the fighting of World War II. He proved to be a fine battle leader and fully justified the personal confidence that had impelled me to assign him to such an important position. Later in the war, when General Alexander became the supreme commander in the Mediterranean, Clark was advanced to army group commander in Italy, an appointment which obviously meant that both British and American authorities were well satisfied with his performance.

Continued reports and reconnaissance on the thirteenth furnished the details of the German attack, and that day Air Chief Marshal Tedder was ordered to concentrate the full strength of his air force, to include every plane that could fly, in an attack upon sensitive spots in the German formations.[29] This great air attack was delivered with precision and effectiveness on the morning of the fourteenth. So badly did it disrupt the enemy's communications, supplies, and mobility that, with the aid of naval gunfire, the ground troops regained the initiative and thereafter German counterattacks were never in sufficient strength to threaten our general position.

But the hard fighting was not yet over. The two great initial objectives of the Italian invasion were the capture, first, of Naples as a satisfactory port from which to supply our troops, and, second, of the airfields at Foggia from which to supplement the air bombardment of central Europe, which up to that moment had been conducted almost exclusively from the British bases.

On the sixteenth I went to Salerno to examine into circumstances that seemed to indicate some lack of skill on the part of one or more of the American commanders. After careful investigation I felt it necessary to approve General Clark's recommendation for the relief of his American corps commander.

The relief of a combat leader is something that is not to be lightly done in war. Its first effect is to indicate to troops dissatisfaction with their performance; otherwise the commander would be commended, not relieved. This probable effect must always be weighed against the hoped-for advantage of assigning to the post another, and possibly untried, commander. On the other hand, really inept leadership must be quickly detected and instantly removed. Lives of thousands are involved—the question is not one of academic justice for the leader, it is that of concern for the many and the objective of victory.

Because of the distance of Salerno from our air bases in Sicily we were particularly anxious to capture the Foggia airfields speedily, and a number of plans had been previously studied in order to facilitate this operation.

With the completion of the Sicilian campaign we had begun the transfer of seven divisions, four American and three British, from the Mediterranean theater to Britain, in preparation for the great assault across the English Channel.[30] With these divisions unavailable for action in Italy, the only unit left that could be used for an expedition into the heel and lower leg of the Italian peninsula in the direction of Foggia was a British airborne division. Its indicated port of entry was Taranto, an Italian base that we hoped to obtain under the terms of the Italian surrender and one where German strength was almost nonexistent. If we could immediately place even small formations ashore we should be able to get the important airfields promptly and cheaply.

The prize to be won was great, but except for naval fighting ships our sea transport was assigned to the Salerno operation. Moreover, because of its lack of land transport and heavy equipment, the airborne division was not a particularly suitable formation to use on an invasion where a long land advance was necessary. Again we decided to gamble, and in this case a tremendous burden of responsibility was assumed by Admiral Cunningham. He unhesitatingly agreed to push his battle fleet directly into Taranto Harbor, discounting the possibility of treachery or destruction by mine fields, in order to carry the British 1st Airborne Division into the docks at that port. The operation was carried out as planned on September 9, but with the loss of one fine British cruiser and more than two hundred men she was carrying.[31] She was sunk by a mine in the harbor of Taranto.

A dramatic incident during the operation is told in the official report:

On the afternoon of 9th September the battleship *Howe* with four cruisers in company, carrying elements of the 1st British Airborne Division, steamed up the swept channel towards Taranto. Shortly before, the Taranto Division of the Italian Battle Fleet had emerged from the harbor. As the two fleets passed each other, there was a moment of tension. There was no guarantee that the Italian Fleet would observe the terms of surrender and would not, at long last, show fight. But the final challenge by Admiral Cunningham, delivered with the same cold nerve that had characterised all the actions of that great sailor, went unanswered. The Italian Fleet passed out of sight on its way to surrender.[32]

With this landing we were ashore on the Italian mainland in three places, Salerno, Taranto, and Reggio Calabria.

The fierce fighting in Salerno drew off enemy forces from in front of Montgomery and his advance to the northward speeded up. By the sixteenth his left made contact with Clark's right just south of Salerno Bay. Montgomery's right moved forward to join up with the airborne division which was pushing its way toward Foggia. Within a few days that great prize fell to us. Clark continued his battling toward Naples and on October 1, 1943, his forces triumphantly entered that city.[85]

The combination of engineers and sea salvage experts who had constantly amazed us with their exploits in the rehabilitation of harbors immediately went to work. All of their prior successes at Casablanca, Algiers, Oran, Bizerte, and Palermo were as nothing compared to the speed and efficiency with which they repaired the seemingly destroyed and useless harbor facilities at Naples. With the establishment of this base and with Foggia firmly in our grasp, we had accomplished the first major objectives of the Italian campaign. All later fighting in that area would have as its principal objective the pinning down of German forces far from the region of the major assault that was to take place the following year across the English Channel. A secondary purpose was of course to force the constant drain upon German resources of replacing losses and providing supplies over the tortuous and vulnerable Italian communications. A third purpose was political in nature: the constant threat against Rome and the Italian industrial centers to the northward would cause unrest through the Balkans and other portions of Europe, which would depress German morale and raise our own.

Fundamentally, however, the Italian campaign thereafter became a distinctly subsidiary operation, though the results it attained in the actual defeat of Germany were momentous, almost incalculable. It was obvious, however, that the Italian avenue of approach did not in itself offer a favorable route from which to attack decisively the German homeland. That could be done only across the English Channel and through France and the Low Countries.

Immediately after the surrender of Italy in early September there arose a situation in the eastern Mediterranean that not only caused us great concern but which will be argued pro and con for a long time to come. The important Dodecanese Islands were largely garrisoned by Italian troops and with the Italian surrender it was possible that all these islands could be taken almost without a fight. Provided that the Italian garrisons could then be persuaded to defend them for the Allies, it appeared that we could gain a tremendous strategic advantage in that area with almost no expenditure.

Thoroughly alive to this situation, the Middle East command, under General Sir Henry Maitland Wilson, promptly dispatched small detachments to these islands, among which were Leros and Rhodes, and an early success was secured.[34] However, it was quickly found that the Italian garrison had no stomach for fighting against anyone. If the islands were to be held the Allies had to provide the garrisons and these could come from nowhere except from the Allied Force then engaged in the bitter struggle in Italy.

The Prime Minister was anxious to provide support for the islands and my staff and I studied the problem with the greatest possible sympathy. We came to the conclusion that aside from some temporary air support there was nothing we could give. To detach too much of our air force and particularly to dispatch land forces to that area would be definitely detrimental—possibly fatal—to the battle in which we were then engaged, while the amount of strength these reinforcements could provide in the eastern Mediterranean would probably be insufficient to hold these important islands.

The insistence of the Prime Minister on undertaking something to help the Middle East was so great that we were directed to hold a conference with the commanders in chief of the Middle East.[35] They all came to meet us in Tunisia, where I had assembled my own commanders in chief of ground, sea, and air.

It was the simplest, most unargumentative of any similar conference I attended during the war. I outlined the entire situation as we saw it and announced the decision I had reached, which was to be final unless overridden by the Combined Chiefs of Staff. Its purport was that detachments from the Italian command were not warranted and that we could and would do nothing about the islands. Those islands, in my judgment, while of considerable strategic importance, did not compare in military value to success in the Italian battle. Every officer present agreed emphatically with my conclusions, even though it was a great disappointment to the Middle East commanders, while all of us knew that the decision would be a bitter one for the Prime Minister to accept. I reported these conclusions to the Combined Chiefs of Staff, who supported my decision.[36] The islands were quickly retaken by the enemy.

From the beginning of the conquest of Sicily we had been engaged in a new type of task, that of providing government for a conquered population. Specially trained "civil affairs officers," some American, some British, accompanied the assault forces and continuously pushed forward to take over from combat troops the essential task of controlling the civil population.

The American contingent had been trained in the school established at Charlottesville, Virginia. Later, groups of both British and American military government officers received further training in North Africa. They operated under the general supervision of a special section of my headquarters.[37]

Public health, conduct, sanitation, agriculture, industry, transport, and a hundred other activities, all normal to community life, were supervised and directed by these officers. Their task was difficult but vastly important, not merely from a humanitarian viewpoint, but to the success of our armies. Every command needs peace and order in its rear; otherwise it must detach units to preserve signal and road communications, protect dumps and convoys, and suppress underground activity.

The job was new to us but in spite of natural mistakes it was splendidly done. We gained experience and learned lessons for similar and greater tasks still lying ahead of us in Italy and Germany.

Chapter 11

CAIRO
CONFERENCE

WHILE THE SUMMER AND FALL FIGHTING WAS IN full swing we received word that the President and the Prime Minister and their staffs were preparing to hold another joint meeting, this time near Cairo.[1] Egypt was not then within the limits of our theater, but aside from insuring safe passages through our area we were called upon to provide secure places for preliminary meetings and for the accommodation of individuals. The usual swarm of United States Secret Service men preceded the President into every locality where he was expected to stop even briefly. They began with my staff the reconnaissance work that was intended to guarantee the safety of the President but which also, inevitably, advertised his coming.

The secret concerning plans for the conference leaked, apparently, either in Washington or London; and because of the great amount of comment inspired in the press of the world, including some embarrassingly accurate statements in the Cairo papers, the home governments became very much worried. Even after the principals were en route to the meeting place the home governments suggested a complete change in the program.[2] An urgent proposal came from the War Department to shift the meeting place to Malta or possibly even to Khartoum. Our responsibility in protecting and assuring the safety of the President and the Prime Minister was made heavier by the knowledge that every fanatical Nazi sympathizer was already notified as to their possible movements. After reflection I nevertheless made strong recommendations to the President against any change in plan. I believed that if we could not protect the meeting and its participants after we had made every conceivable defensive preparation, including heavily guarded enclosures and anti-aircraft defenses, then we would only be adding to the risk by making a sudden change to a place where we could not be well prepared. Almost any place would have been satisfactory for a surprise stop of one or two days. But when a meeting of several weeks' duration is planned, the only protection lies in thorough preparation.

The Prime Minister preceded the President into our area and I met Mr. Churchill at Malta, where we had a lengthy conference.[3] After considerable discussion he agreed with me as to the wisdom of adhering to the original plan for the meeting and he cabled the President to that effect.

The Prime Minister was accompanied by his military staff, and I had an opportunity to spend the day going over a number of subjects of interest to current and future operations.

Mr. Churchill, as always, was entertaining and interesting. I have never met anyone else so capable at keeping a dinner gathering on its toes. His comments on events and personalities were pointed and pungent, often most amusing. He looked forward with great enthusiasm to his meeting with the President, from whom, he said, he always drew inspiration for tackling the problems of war and of the later peace. He dwelt at length on one of his favorite subjects—the importance of assailing Germany through the "soft underbelly," of keeping up the tempo of our Italian attack and extending its scope to include much of the northern shore of the Mediterranean. He seemed always to see great and decisive possibilities in the Mediterranean, while the project of invasion across the English Channel left him cold. How often I heard him say, in speaking of Overlord prospects: "We must take care that the tides do not run red with the blood of American and British youth, or the beaches be choked with their bodies."

I could not escape a feeling that Mr. Churchill's views were unconsciously colored by two considerations that lay outside the scope of the immediate military problem. I had nothing tangible to justify such a feeling—I know, though, that I was not alone in wondering occasionally whether these considerations had some weight with him. The first of them was his concern as a political leader for the future of the Balkans. For this concern I had great sympathy, but as a soldier I was particularly careful to exclude such considerations from my own recommendations. The other was an inner compulsion to vindicate his strategical concepts of World War I, in which he had been the principal exponent of the Gallipoli campaign. Many professionals agreed that the Gallipoli affair had failed because of bungling in execution rather than through mistaken calculations of its possibilities. It sometimes seemed that the Prime Minister was determined in the second war to gain public acceptance of this point of view.

In the old palace of the Knights of Malta the Prime Minister presented Alexander and me each a specially designed medal sent to us by the King; no others identical to them were ever to be produced. The occasion was informal; one of the guests commented that such an event in the same palace, four hundred years earlier, would have called for days of jousting, pageantry, and roistering in the garrison.

I was called upon shortly to go meet the President, who was arriving by ship at Oran. At Oran we transferred Mr. Roosevelt to a plane and took him to a villa on the seashore in Tunisia, which by coincidence was locally known as the "White House." At that time the President seemed in good health and was optimistic and confident. He stayed over an extra day in Tunisia in order to visit battlefields of that area. While traveling through them he speculated upon the possible identity of our battlefields with those of ancient days, particularly with that of Zama. So far as either the President or I knew, that battlefield had never been positively identified by historians, but we were certain, because of the use of elephants by the Carthaginians, that it was located on the level plains rather than in the mountains, where so much of our own fighting took place. The President's liking for history and his frequent reference to it always gave an added flavor to conversation with him on military subjects. The same was true of George Patton and the Prime Minister.

I wandered off to inspect some burnt-out tanks while the President and his Wac driver had their lunch. When I returned he remarked, "Ike, if, one year ago, you had offered to bet that on this day the President of the United States would be having his lunch on a Tunisian roadside, what odds could you have demanded?" This thought apparently directed his mind to the extraordinary events of the year just past. He told me, first, what a disappointment it had been to him that our African invasion came just after, instead of just before, the 1942 elections. He spoke of Darlan, of Boisson and Giraud. He talked of Italy and Mussolini and of the uneasiness he had felt during the Kasserine affair. He told of instances of disagreement with Mr. Churchill, but earnestly and almost emotionally said, "No one could have a better or sturdier ally than that old Tory!" Mr. Roosevelt seemed to be enjoying himself sincerely, but his reminiscences were interrupted by a Secret Service man who approached to say, "Mr.

President, we've been here longer than I like. We should go on now."
The President grinned and said to me, "You are lucky you don't have
the number of bosses I have."

The Secret Service had objected strenuously to the battlefield tour
for the President but I felt so well acquainted with conditions that I
thought the trip was perfectly safe. Because of the fact that it was a
surprise move, executed without warning to anyone, it tended to add
to rather than detract from the degree of safety enjoyed by the President.

To give General Marshall and Admiral King some release from the
restrictions that inevitably accompany travel with a presidential party
I invited the two of them to stay at my little cottage in Carthage. Both
were outspokenly delighted to have the opportunity for a quiet evening, and both seemed to me to be in splendid health and spirits. In a
before-dinner conversation Admiral King brought up the subject of
future command of Overlord. He said that in early discussions between
the President and the Prime Minister it had apparently been agreed
that a British officer would be named to the post, possibly because an
American was already commanding in the Mediterranean. Later, when
the President came to realize that American strength in Overlord
would eventually predominate over British, he decided that public
opinion would demand an American commander. He so informed the
Prime Minister, who agreed although the agreement cost him some
personal embarrassment because he had already promised Alan
Brooke the command.[4]

At the same time the President had suggested to Mr. Churchill that
acceptance of this arrangement would logically throw the Mediterranean command to the British, where British Empire forces would be
expected to provide the bulk of the ground and naval strength. The
President had tentatively decided, King said, to give the Overlord command to Marshall, against the urgent and persistent advice of King
and others who dreaded the consequences of Marshall's withdrawal
from the Combined Chiefs of Staff.[5]

During the admiral's explanation General Marshall remained completely silent; he seemed embarrassed. Admiral King was generous
enough to say that only because I was personally slated to take Marshall's place in Washington could he view the plan with anything less
than consternation, but that he still felt it a mistake to be shifting the
key members of a winning team and declared he was going to renew
his arguments to the President.

While the Prime Minister had spoken of this matter a few days earlier at Malta, this was the first time I had heard any American discuss the Overlord command, except on the basis of rumor and speculation. Admiral King's story agreed in such exact detail with what the Prime Minister had told me that I accepted it as almost official notice that I would soon be giving up field command to return to Washington.

Incidentally, the Prime Minister, although he was disappointed that Brooke would not get the Overlord assignment, had spoken with considerable satisfaction over the prospect of Marshall's appointment. He said, "It is the President's decision; we British will be glad to accept either you or Marshall." Then he added, "Marshall's appointment will certainly insure that the American Government will put everything available into the enterprise." He hastily added that "they always did," but said that this development would tend to attract even greater intensity. With his usual concern for personal feelings, Mr. Churchill assured me that he was delighted with the results so far achieved in the Mediterranean, but felt I would understand the wisdom of transferring the Mediterranean to British command so long as an American was to have command of the major operation across the Channel.

On the morning following my talk with Admiral King, the President spoke briefly to me about the future Overlord command and I came to realize, finally, that it was a point of intense official and public interest back home. He did not give me a hint as to his final decision except to say that he dreaded the thought of losing Marshall from Washington. But he added, "You and I know the name of the Chief of Staff in the Civil War, but few Americans outside the professional services do." He then added, as if thinking aloud, "But it is dangerous to monkey with a winning team." I answered nothing except to state that I would do my best wherever the government might find use for me.

On the second day the President and his party departed for Cairo, leaving personal orders with me to join the conference in that city within two or three days. Accompanied by my principal commanders, except for Alexander, who was ill, we proceeded to Cairo to present our views concerning the forces in the Mediterranean.[6]

Trips such as these gave me an opportunity to provide a break for members of my personal staff. Since these individuals normally had little to do during my absence from headquarters, I would invite them, in such numbers as could be accommodated in my plane, to go with me on these journeys. Consequently they always greeted with considerable satisfaction news of an impending trip to a distant point because some four to six of them could count on a vacation to strange places and interesting sights. Officers, enlisted men, and Wacs seized a number of well-earned opportunities that otherwise could not have come to them.

So far as there was discernible any difference between the professional views of the British and American groups it appeared to me and to my associates at the Cairo Conference that the British still favored a vigorous and all-out prosecution of the Mediterranean campaign even, if necessary, at the expense of additional delay in launching Overlord; while the Americans declined to approve anything that would detract from the strength of the attack to be delivered across the Channel early in the following summer. The Americans insisted upon examining all projects for the Mediterranean exclusively in the light of their probable assistance to the 1944 cross-Channel attack; on the other hand, the British felt that maximum concentration on the Italian effort might lead to an unexpected break that would make the Channel operation either unnecessary or nothing more than a mopping-up affair.

The Prime Minister and some of his chief military advisers still looked upon the Overlord plan with scarcely concealed misgivings; their attitude seemed to be that we could avoid the additional and grave risks implicit in a new amphibious operation by merely pouring into the Mediterranean all the air, ground, and naval resources available. They implied that by pushing the Italian campaign, invading Yugoslavia, capturing Crete, the Dodecanese, and Greece, we would deal the Germans a serious blow without encountering the admitted dangers of the full-out effort against northwest Europe. My own staff, including its British members, and I continued to support the conclusions reached a year and a half previously that only in the cross-Channel attack would our full strength be concentrated and decisive results achieved.[7]

Because, later, the landing in Normandy was successfully accomplished without abnormal loss, it is easy to ignore the very real risks and dangers implicit in the plan. Had we encountered there a disastrous reverse, those who now criticize the concern with which some looked forward to the prospect would have been loudest in condemning the others who insisted upon the validity of the plan. One thing that opponents feared was a repetition of the trench warfare of World War I. The British had vivid and bitter memories of Passchendaele and Vimy Ridge. None of us wanted any repetition of those experiences. Moreover, the Dieppe raid of the summer of 1942 did not promise any easy conquest of the beaches themselves. That raid, carried out by a strong force of Canadians, had resulted in a high percentage of losses. From it we learned a number of lessons that we later applied to our advantage, but the price paid by the Canadians still rankled.[8]

Mindful of such past experiences, a number of persons, among them some Americans, were moved to consider the wisdom of avoiding the risks of a Channel crossing and, instead, to push the Italian and other campaigns in the Mediterranean to the limit of Allied ability.

However, I never at any time heard Mr. Churchill urge or suggest complete abandonment of the Overlord plan. His conviction, so far as I could interpret it, was that at some time in the indefinite future the Allies would have to cross the Channel. But he seemed to believe that our attack should be pushed elsewhere until the day came when the enemy would be forced to withdraw most of his troops from northwest Europe, at which time the Allies could go in easily and safely.

The view presented by the Allied Headquarters staff to the Cairo Conference was that the immediate and prescribed purposes of the Italian campaign had already been accomplished, namely the capture of a line covering the Foggia airfields, with Naples as a port to meet logistic needs. We agreed that the greatest possible support to the north European campaign would be rendered by the Allied armies in the Mediterranean if they could promptly advance to and be concentrated in the valley of the Po. From that region Allied forces could threaten to enter France over the mountainous roads of the Riviera. They could develop an equal threat to advance northeastward to Trieste and the Ljubljana Gap into Austria and would be in position also to launch, over the shortest possible water distances, amphibious operations either against southern France or across the Adriatic. But an advance to the Po, we believed, was possible during the winter of 1943–44 only in the event that the departure of troops from the Mediterranean to England be immediately halted and the Allied forces built up to maximum strength. We believed that with the troops then in sight there was no hope of attaining the valley of the Po before summer weather should again make possible air, land, and sea operations.[9]

This meant that a more modest objective had to be accepted in the Mediterranean, because to insure seizure of the Po Valley would necessitate withholding from the United Kingdom so many troops and so much vital equipment that the cross-Channel operation could not be undertaken in the spring of 1944.

My own recommendation, then as always, was that no operation should be undertaken in the Mediterranean except as a directly supporting move for the Channel attack and that our planned redeployment to England should proceed with all possible speed. Obviously a sufficient strength had to be kept in the Mediterranean to hold what we had already gained and to force the Nazis to maintain sizable forces in that area.

This was the program adopted by the Cairo Conference, and our shipment of troops and equipment to England continued without abatement.[10] The psychological value of the capture of Rome was, however, emphasized to us, particularly by the Prime Minister.

Again I had an opportunity for private talks with the President, at one of which he informally presented me with the Legion of Merit. His conversation revolved more around postwar problems than those of immediate operations. He gave me his ideas on the post-hostilities occupation of Germany and listened sympathetically to my contention that occupation should become a responsibility of civil agencies of government as soon as the exigencies of war might permit. He mentioned domestic politics only to say that, much as he'd like to go back to private life, it looked as if he'd have to stand again for the presidency.

One evening General Marshall asked me with some others to dinner. It was a splendid American dinner with turkey and all that goes with it. As the guests were leaving, one said to General Marshall, "Thank you very much for a fine Thanksgiving dinner." I turned around in complete astonishment and said, "Well, that shows what war does to a man. I had no idea this was Thanksgiving Day."

A personally pleasing incident of the Cairo trip was an order from the Chief of Staff that I take two days' rest and recreation. I employed them for a quick visit to Luxor, site of the ancient Egyptian city of Thebes, and a visit of a few hours to Jerusalem and Bethlehem. This was my first glimpse of these areas and the intense interest that I felt in viewing the remains of ancient civilizations came closer than had anything else during the war to lifting briefly from my mind the constant preoccupation with military problems.

Chapter 12

ITALY

THE PRESIDENT AND HIS GROUP OF ADVISERS went on to Teheran from Cairo, but I returned to my own theater. Forward headquarters were then in the process of moving to Caserta, a castle near Naples.[1] Plans were going ahead rapidly for moving the entire main headquarters to that location, a change that I felt necessary. By such a move I could be closer to the scene of operations. Moreover, our affairs in Africa were no longer so important because our need for the African ports would constantly diminish as shipments could be made directly from the homelands into captured Italian ports. Another reason for moving was to permit concentration of command and logistical systems solidly in proximity to the battle line. Finally, it is always a good thing to move a headquarters when its personnel begin to get so well "dug in" as they were in Algiers—when directing staffs become too much concerned with the conveniences of living they grow away from troops and from the real problems of war.

An immediate visit along the entire battle front convinced me again of the soundness of our view that winter operations in Italy would be accompanied by the utmost hardship and difficulty, especially as they would be undertaken without the constant support of our great asset, an overwhelming air force.[2] I felt that maintenance of morale would require careful control of operations and the best efforts of all commanders. Certainly I intended to be close by to help.

A new piece of equipment that we began receiving about this time was a godsend to us. It was the "tank-dozer." Whenever the German gave up even a foot of ground he made certain that every culvert and bridge on the miserable roads was blown out; every shelf road cut into the steep mountainsides was likewise destroyed. To restore these to some semblance of usefulness we had to use the ever-present bull-dozer. They had to work with, sometimes even in front of, our front lines in order that necessary supplies could be brought up to the troops and wounded could be evacuated.

The enemy countered this by hidden machine guns and other long-range light-caliber weapons, which, from the safety of a thousand yards' distance, picked off operating personnel and often destroyed the machines themselves. Some imaginative and sensible man on the home front, hearing of this difficulty, solved the problem by merely converting a number of Sherman tanks into bulldozers. These tanks were impervious to all types of small-arms fire and could not be destroyed except by shells from a large-caliber gun or by big mines. From that time on our engineering detachments on the front lines began to enjoy a degree of safety that actually led them to seek this kind of adventurous work. None of us could identify the individual responsible for developing this piece of equipment but had he been present he would have, by acclamation, received all the medals we could have pinned upon him.

A basic principle for the conduct of a supporting or auxiliary operation is that it be carried out as cheaply as possible. Since its purpose is to induce dispersion of hostile power, the operation, to be successful, must force a heavier relative drain upon enemy resources than upon our own. Obviously, however, there must be something valuable to the enemy under threat by the auxiliary operation, and our forces must be strong enough to sustain the threat. If these two conditions are not present the enemy can afford to ignore the whole effort.

For several reasons we were certain that the enemy would react to our threat and would sustain himself to the limit of his ability. The "conqueror complex" almost forced him to do so; just as it had induced him to keep pouring men and munitions into Tunisia long after there was any possible chance of salvaging the situation. On a smaller scale he had done the same in Sicily. Moreover, there was a very considerable psychological value to Rome, while the industrial resources of northern Italy were economically important to the German.

With our command of the sea and our communications firmly anchored in Naples it was much easier for us to sustain active operations in southern and central Italy than it was for the enemy, who had to bring in everything he used over the long, tortuous, and exposed lines through the Alps. Our problem became that of forcing the fighting, but with economy and caution so as to avoid unnecessary diversion of units and supplies that could be used in Overlord. We had to follow a plan that would avoid reverses, costly attacks, and great expenditures of supplies but which would continue to keep the enemy uneasy and, above all, would prevent him from reducing his Italian forces to reinforce his position in northwest Europe.

Carefully planned minor offensives, with success assured in each, comprised the campaign I expected to use during the winter; it was dictated by the objective and by the need to sustain morale amidst the inescapably miserable conditions of the Italian mountains.[3]

With the coming of autumn, wretched weather had overtaken us. American soldiers frequently referred, in terms of sarcastic disgust, to "sunny Italy." With railroads wrecked, bridges destroyed, and many sections of roads blown out, the advance was difficult enough even without opposition from the enemy. The country itself was ideal for defensive fighting. The terrain was cut up by rivers, large and small, which ran athwart the route of advance. Some of these were so winding that they had to be crossed several times.

The forward route of the 34th Division took it across the Volturno three times. One night the assistant commander, Brigadier General B. F. Caffey, was returning from the front with a jeep driver who remarked that he simply could not understand such a "crazy" country. Caffey asked him why he felt that way about Italy. The soldier's reply was a classic: "Why, every durn river in the fool country is named Volturno."

In the mountain passes the Germans constructed defenses almost impregnable to frontal attack. Yankee ingenuity and resourcefulness were tested to the limit. Shortly after the capture of Mount Camino, I was taken to a spot where, in order to outflank one of these mountain strongpoints, a small detachment had put on a remarkable exhibition of mountain climbing. With the aid of ropes a few of them climbed steep cliffs of great height. I have never understood how, encumbered by their equipment, they were able to do it. In fact I think that any Alpine climber would have examined the place doubtfully before attempting to scale it. Nevertheless, the detachment reached the top and ferreted out the location of the German company headquarters. They entered this and seized the captain, who ejaculated, "You can't be here. It is impossible to come up those rocks."[4]

The fronts of both the American Fifth and British Eighth Armies were difficult, although on the American sector the country was more mountainous. On Montgomery's front the principal factors of the problem during the late fall were the rivers, the mud, and the enemy. Nevertheless, all along the line slow but steady advances were made.[5]

On November 15, 1943, the Fifth Army was composed of the American 3d, 34th, 45th Infantry, 82d Airborne, and 1st Armored Divisions and the British 46th, 56th Infantry, and 7th Armored Divisions. However, the 1st Armored Division had not yet completed movement to Italy and the 82d Airborne and the 7th Armored Divisions were to be withdrawn soon for transfer to England. In Montgomery's Eighth Army there were six divisions, the 5th, 78th, 1st Canadian, 8th Indian, 2d New Zealand, and 1st Airborne Divisions.[6]

In the fall we made arrangements for the transfer of General Juin's French corps from North Africa to the Italian battlefield. To provide more strength for a campaign that I felt would be of great assistance to the later operation in northwest Europe, I suggested to Washington that the American contingent be reinforced by two or three new divisions, as soon as this should prove feasible.[7]

On December 2, 1943, a most regrettable and disturbing incident took place at the port of Bari. We were using that port to assist in the support of the Eighth Army and the large air forces we were rapidly building up in Italy. It was constantly crowded with ships and the port itself was located uncomfortably close to some of the enemy air bases just across the narrow Adriatic.

One night the port was subjected to a raid and we suffered the greatest single loss from air action inflicted upon us during the entire period of Allied campaigning in the Mediterranean and in Europe. We lost sixteen vessels, some of them loaded with extremely valuable cargo. The greatest damage arose from the fact that a fuel ship was struck and the escaping oil carried fiery catastrophe to many of the neighboring vessels. One circumstance connected with the affair could have had the most unfortunate repercussions. One of the ships was loaded with a quantity of mustard gas, which we were always forced to carry with us because of uncertainty of German intentions in the use of this weapon. Fortunately the wind was offshore and the escaping gas caused no casualties. Had the wind been in the opposite direction, however, great disaster could well have resulted. It would have been indeed difficult to explain, even though we manufactured and carried this material only for reprisal purposes in case of surprise action on the part of the enemy.[8]

An outcome of the unfortunate affair was the establishment of a

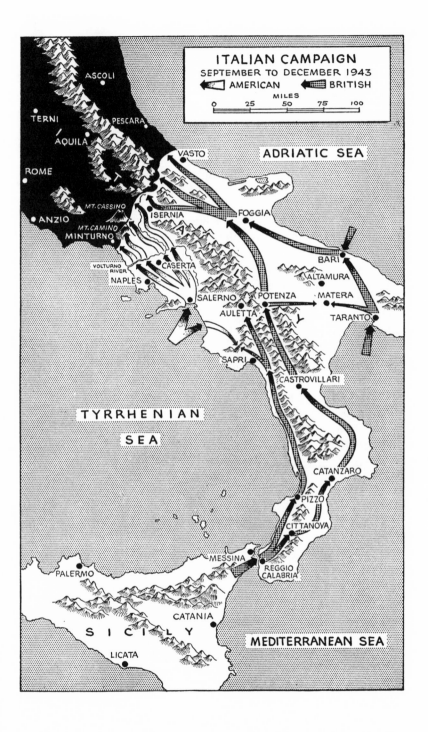

very much better informational and control machinery for anti-aircraft defense among the naval, ground, and air forces. It was the last serious blow that forces under my command suffered from the enemy air forces in the Mediterranean.

An incident connected with this affair illustrates clearly that war is always conducted in the realm of the possible and of the estimated rather than of the certainly known. It never pays to be too sure about the future! On the afternoon preceding the attack on Bari, Air Marshal Sir Arthur Coningham, commanding the British air forces supporting the Eighth Army, held a press conference. The German air forces had been so thoroughly defeated—almost eliminated from the immediate front—that Coningham estimated they had no power to intervene further in the operation. To the assembled press he stated flatly: "I would regard it as a personal affront and insult if the Luftwaffe should attempt any significant action in this area." The next morning he was definitely more than embarrassed. His newspaper friends did not, by any means, allow him to forget his arbitrary and unqualified statement of the day before.

By Christmas Day, the last time that I visited the Italian forces, our front generally ran along the line Ortona–Arielli–Orsogna–east bank of Sangro, Peccia, and Gorigliano rivers.[9] The long and costly battle for Mount Cassino began after I left the theater.

To the soldier at the front the high command's designation of an operation as "secondary" makes little difference. In this case it certainly meant no amelioration of his hardships. Heavy rains fell and the streams were habitually torrents. The weather grew colder day by day. Men and vehicles sank in the mud. But the dogged fighting was constant. The enemy's emplacements, often dug into solid rock, covered every approach—every foot of ground was gained only by weary maneuvers over mountain slopes and by blasting and digging the hostile gunners out of their shelters.

In early December, I had received word the President would return to the United States through our area. I went to Tunis to meet him.[10] A few hours before his arrival I received a somewhat garbled radiogram from General Marshall that discussed some administrative details incident to my forthcoming change in assignment. When he wrote the message General Marshall apparently assumed that I had already received specific information concerning the new assignment through staff channels. But, lacking such information, I was unable to deduce his meaning with certainty. The President arrived in midafternoon and was scarcely seated in the automobile when he cleared up the matter with one short sentence. He said, "Well, Ike, you are going to command Overlord."

Because I had to discuss with him, at once, details of his next day's plans, we had no opportunity, at the moment, to talk further about the new assignment, but I did manage to say, "Mr. President, I realize that such an appointment involved difficult decisions. I hope you will not be disappointed."

During the remainder of the afternoon we made arrangements to conduct the President to Malta and to Sicily. At the former place he wanted to award to Lord Gort and the island's garrison a Presidential Citation for the gallant defense of 1941 and 1942, while at the latter he wanted to inspect an American airfield and personally confer a decoration on General Clark.[11] Both these desires he accomplished but, owing to a delay at Malta because of mechanical difficulty with his plane, he could not continue on his homeward trip that day, as had been planned. The Secret Service men were irritated and fearful, but the President confided to me that he had made up his mind to stay at Carthage an extra night and if a legitimate reason for the delay had not been forthcoming he would have invented one. I remarked that I assumed the President of the United States would not be questioned in dictating the details of his own travel. He replied with considerable emphasis, "You haven't had to argue with the Secret Service!"

During his visit the President on several occasions discussed matters in connection with my imminent transfer to London. He said that, with the full concurrence of General Marshall, he had designated me to command Overlord because he felt that the time element permitted no further delay in naming a commander. He said also that he had originally planned to give that command to General Marshall, observing that senior officers might well rotate in sharing the burdens and honors of staff and command duty. However, after consideration he had decided that Marshall could not be spared from Washington and particularly from his post on the Combined Chiefs of Staff. The President said that it was Marshall's commanding presence on the Combined Staff that always inspired his own great feeling of confidence in the decisions of that body. He added that though the British would gladly accept Marshall as the Overlord commander the fact was that all the President's associates appeared pleased with the present decision.

The President was quite concerned with two points that did not seem particularly important to me, but to which both he and Mr. Harry Hopkins attached significance. The first of these was the timing of the announcement. It was finally decided that the President would do this from Washington; in the meantime my change in assignment would be a closely guarded secret.[12] The second point was my title as commander of Overlord. He toyed with the word "Supreme" in his conversation but made no decision at the moment. He merely said that he must devise some designation that would imply the importance the Allies attached to the new venture.[13]

A few days after the President's departure I received from General Marshall a scrap of paper that is still one of my most cherished mementos of World War II.

From the President to Marshal Stalin

The immediate appointment of General Eisenhower to command of Overlord operation has been decided upon

Roosevelt

Cairo, Dec. 7. 43

Dear Eisenhower, I thought you might like to have this as a memento. It was written very hurriedly by me as the final meeting broke up yesterday, the President signing it immediately.

G. C. M.

BOMBERS' HOLOCAUST

In Italy, "head-on attacks against the enemy on his mountainous frontiers would be slow and extremely costly." *Page 212.* Only by utter destruction of his strongholds could the battle toll be tolerable.

Smoke Pall Shrouds Cassino as Bombing Begins

BEYOND THE DUNE—EUROPE

"You will enter the continent of Europe and . . . undertake operations aimed at the heart of Germany and the destruction of her Armed Forces." *Page 225*

Assault Troops Hit Normandy Beach on D-day

For me the real value of this informal memorandum is in Marshall's postscript. Already in the fall of 1943 false and malicious gossip was circulating to the effect that Marshall and I had been conducting a private vendetta, the prize to be the command of Overlord. Many of my friends knew that I hoped to remain somewhere in the field rather than return to Washington for duty. Yet never had I, or General Marshall, stooped to the level of conniving for position in either peace or war. I had never, and I know he had not, expressed to anyone a personal preference for a particular assignment. In fact from the personal viewpoint I would have preferred, over anything else, to remain as the Mediterranean commander.

Marshall's thoughtfulness in sending me a memento he knew I would value was certainly not the action of a disgruntled and defeated opponent for a "job." While I have never discussed the matter directly with him, I have always been confident that it was his decision, more than anyone else's, that sent me to the Overlord post. Since I first met General Marshall at the beginning of the war I felt for him only intense loyalty and respect, and I had already informed the President of my conviction that no one could undertake the Overlord command with greater prospect of success than could Marshall. I believed then, and I believe now, that he would have been as pre-eminent in field work as he was in the complicated duties he encountered in Washington.

The honor and confidence implied by my selection for this critical post were, of course, tremendous, and of this I was well aware and appreciative. Nevertheless, there is always some degree of emotional letdown when a military commander in war is removed from one task to enter upon another. By the nature of his work he has become so intimately tied up with close friends and assistants and with innumerable intricate problems that he feels almost a resentful shock at facing again the problem of building up organizations, staffs, and plans necessary for the conduct of another operation. On top of this we were in the midst of active campaigning and I and all those I took with me were going, for a period of some months, from the scene of immediate and fierce action to one of study, investigation, and planning.

The command organization that existed in the Mediterranean at Christmastime, 1943, was the result of an evolutionary process, the beginnings of which were far back in the hectic London days of the summer and fall of 1942.

We had entered Africa in November 1942 with preconceived

notions of the areas in which British and American troops would be respectively employed. The command organization had been designed to fit the anticipated situation. The moment we found that the military requirements differed radically from those expected, we had to begin reorganization of command and staff. The lesson was plain that in the new venture we should avoid the necessity of major revision of the command structure in the midst of battle and should adopt one whose basic soundness and flexibility would meet any probable eventuality in combat.

Our Mediterranean experiences had reaffirmed the truth that unity, co-ordination, and co-operation are the keys to successful operations. War is waged in three elements but there is no separate land, air, or naval war. Unless all assets in all elements are efficiently combined and co-ordinated against a properly selected, common objective, their maximum potential power cannot be realized. Physical targets may be separated by the breadth of a continent or an ocean, but their destruction must contribute in maximum degree to the furtherance of the combined plan of operation. That is what co-ordination means.

Not only would I need commanders who understood this truth, but I must have those who appreciated the importance of morale and had demonstrated a capacity to develop and maintain it. Morale is the greatest single factor in successful war. Endurable comparisons with the enemy in other essential factors—leadership, discipline, technique, numbers, equipment, mobility, supply, and maintenance—are prerequisite to the existence of morale. It breeds most readily upon success; but under good leaders it will be maintained among troops even during extended periods of adversity. The methods employed by successful leaders in developing morale differ so widely as to defy any attempt to establish rules. One observation, however, always applies: in any long and bitter campaign morale will suffer unless all ranks thoroughly believe that their commanders are concerned first and always with the welfare of the troops who do the fighting. A human understanding and a natural ability to mingle with all men on a basis of equality are more important than any degree of technical skill.

I was happy to secure Air Chief Marshal Tedder as my deputy for Overlord. In the Mediterranean he had won the respect and admiration of all his associates not only as a brilliant airman but as a staunch supporter of the "allied" principle as practiced in that command. Authority was also granted to take along my chief of staff, General Smith, without whose services it would have been dif-

ficult to organize a staff for the conduct of a great allied operation.[14] I at first understood that originally either General Alexander or
General Montgomery was available for the command of the British
forces in the new venture. At that time I expressed a preference for
Alexander, primarily because I had been so closely associated with
him and had developed for him an admiration and friendship which
have grown with the years. I regarded Alexander as Britain's outstanding soldier in the field of strategy. He was, moreover, a friendly
and agreeable type; Americans instinctively liked him.[15]

The Prime Minister finally decided, however, that Alexander should
not be spared from the Italian operation, which would have an important effect on the one we were to undertake the following summer,
and from which he still hoped for almost decisive results. Consequently
General Montgomery was assigned to command the British forces in
the new operation, a choice acceptable to me.[16] General Montgomery
has no superior in two most important characteristics. He quickly develops among British enlisted men an intense devotion and admiration
—the greatest personal asset a commander can possess. Montgomery's other outstanding characteristic is his tactical ability in what
might be called the "prepared" battle. In the study of enemy positions
and situations and in the combining of his own armor, artillery, air,
and infantry to secure tactical success against the enemy he is careful,
meticulous, and certain.

I was particularly pleased to secure the services of Admiral Ramsay
as the naval commander in chief.[17] Admiral Cunningham had left us
some weeks earlier to become First Sea Lord of the Admiralty, but
Admiral Ramsay was a most competent commander of courage, resourcefulness, and tremendous energy. Moreover, all of us knew him
to be helpful and companionable, even though we sometimes laughed
among ourselves at the care with which he guarded, in British tradition
and practice, the "senior service" position of the British Navy.

On Christmas Eve we listened to the radio, having learned that
President Roosevelt was to make a significant speech. During that talk
he made the first public announcement of my transfer to command of
Overlord and included in the statement the designation of the title I
was to assume. The title was Supreme Commander, Allied Expeditionary Forces.[18] This sounded very imposing and inspired Commander
Butcher, my naval aide, to say that his major problem for the next
week or so would be to design proper stationery to carry my exalted
title.

The most significant of my final acts in the Mediterranean took place on Christmas Day, 1943. On that day I had just completed another tour along the front lines in Italy and I then took off for Tunisia, where I met the Prime Minister. Present with him were the new commander in chief of the Mediterranean, General Sir Henry Maitland Wilson, along with General Alexander and a number of staff officers. The matter for discussion was a proposed amphibious operation against Anzio. The operation could not be launched before January, after my departure, and my own conclusions on the matter were not decisive. Nevertheless, I was involved because of the fact that launching the attack would require a delay in the planned schedule for shipping certain landing craft to England. Consequently my concurrence in the project was sought.[19]

As the situation then stood in Italy it was apparent that a steady advance up the peninsula demanded a succession of outflanking operations by sea, preferably on both flanks. Head-on attacks against the enemy on his mountainous frontiers would be slow and extremely costly. The real question to be decided was whether the over-all interests of the Allies would be best served by allocating to the Italian operation sufficient resources to maintain momentum in the advance, or whether on the contrary we should content ourselves with minor, well-prepared attacks in the mountains with limited aims but with maximum economy in men and resources. Neither troops nor landing craft were immediately available in sufficient numbers to carry out large-scale operations on both flanks, and because of comparative ease in their later support such operations were more feasible on the western than on the eastern flank of Italy.

I agreed to the general desirability of continuing the advance but pointed out that the landing of two partially skeletonized divisions at Anzio, a hundred miles beyond the front lines as then situated, would not only be a risky affair but that the attack would not by itself compel the withdrawal of the German front. Military strategy may bear some similarity to the chessboard, but it is dangerous to carry the analogy too far. A threatened king in chess must be protected; in war he may instead choose to fight! The Nazis had not instantly withdrawn from Africa or Sicily merely because of threats to their rear. On the contrary, they had reinforced and fought the battle out to the end. In this case, of course, one of the principal objects was to induce the enemy to reinforce his Italian armies, but it was equally important that this be done in such a way that our own costs would be minimized. It was from the standpoint of costs that I urged careful consideration of the whole plan. I argued that a force of several strong divisions would have to be established in Anzio before significant results could be achieved. I pointed out also that, because of distance, rapid building up of the attacking force at Anzio would be difficult and landing craft would be needed long after the agreed-upon date for their release.

The Prime Minister was nevertheless determined to carry out the proposed operation. He and his staff not only felt certain that the assault would be a great and prompt success but they engaged to release the landing craft as quickly as the two divisions had been established on the beach. Although I repeated my warning as to the probable outcome, I accepted their firm commitments on the date of the release of these craft, which would be so badly needed in England, and agreed to recommend to the United States Chiefs of Staff that the equipment remain in the Mediterranean for an additional two weeks.[20]

In the final outcome the Anzio operation paid off handsomely but in its initial stages it developed exactly as my headquarters thought it would. In addition, the landing craft scheduled for transfer to the United Kingdom had to remain in the Mediterranean for a considerable length of time to provide rapid reinforcement for the hard-pressed troops at Anzio. Fortunately this circumstance did no harm to Overlord. But before real results were achieved the Anzio force had to be built up to more than six divisions and had to fight under adverse conditions for some four months. On the other hand, the move undoubtedly convinced Hitler that we intended to push the Italian campaign as a major operation and he reinforced his armies there with eight divisions. This was a great advantage to the Allies elsewhere.[21]

Facing an early transfer to London, I found myself entangled in a mass of terminal detail in the Mediterranean theater. I could not escape a feeling of uneasiness over the Anzio project and was disturbed to learn that my plan for concentrating the entire AFHQ in Caserta was to be abandoned. To me this decision seemed to imply a lack of understanding of the situation and of the duties of the highest commander in the field; regardless of preoccupation with multitudinous problems of great import, he must never lose touch with the "feel" of his troops. He can and should delegate tactical responsibility and avoid interference in the authority of his selected subordinates, but he must maintain the closest kind of factual and spiritual contact with them or, in a vast and critical campaign, he will fail. This contact requires frequent visits to the troops themselves. An allied commander finds that these visits to troops of other nationalities inevitably assume a regrettable formality—but he can and should avoid ceremony when visiting troops of his own country.

It was a simple affair to turn over to another responsibility for controlling operations. The great bulk of the staffs and principal subordinates would remain in the Mediterranean. They were familiar with plans and resources, as was the new commander, General Wilson of the British Army, who had been on duty in the eastern Mediterranean. He was present at the Christmas Day conference with the Prime Minister in Tunis, where every factor of our military situation was exhaustively reviewed. Mr. Murphy and Mr. Macmillan were to remain in their political capacities to assist General Wilson. Consequently I had no fear that his lack of acquaintanceship with the principal French officials, and with plans for arming French forces by the American Government, would cause him embarrassment.

On the administrative side, however, there was much to do. In addition to my Allied responsibilities I was, of course, the commander of American forces in the theater. Administration of such a force, with its eternal questions of supply, maintenance, replacement, promotion, demotion, and a voluminous correspondence with the War Department, is a very intricate and sometimes very personal process.

One of the first questions to be settled was the choice of the American officer who would now become deputy to General Wilson and who would therefore take over American administrative duties in the Mediterranean.

This brought up the problem of filling high American positions in both theaters—General Marshall and I of course wanted to place each man in the post where we felt his special qualifications could best assist in the prosecution of the war.

At that time my own ideas as to the best possible allocation of American commanders to the two theaters were given in a telegram sent to General Marshall on December 23, 1943:

In the early stages of Overlord I see no necessity for British and American Army Group Commanders. In fact, any such setup would be destructive of the essential coordination between Ground and Air Forces. When Army Group Commanders become necessary, I profoundly hope to designate an officer who has had combat experience in this War. My preference for American Army Group Commander, when more than one American Army is operating in Overlord, is General Bradley. One of his

Army Commanders should probably be Patton; the other, a man that may be developed in Overlord operations or, alternatively, somebody like Hodges or Simpson, provided such officer could come over to United Kingdom at an early date and accompany Bradley through the early stages of the operations.

To my mind, Bradley should be the United States Assaulting Army Commander, and become Army Group Commander when necessary.

I have sent to you at Washington a long letter outlining my ideas for the American Command setup, both here and in Overlord. I hope that letter will be awaiting you when you arrive in Washington, but I summarize it here for your immediate information. The American Theater Commander here in the Mediterranean should be Devers, leaving Clark free at the appropriate time to take complete charge of Anvil.[22]

My high opinion of Bradley, dating from our days at West Point, had increased daily during our months together in the Mediterranean. At my request he had come to Africa in February 1943 as a major general to assist me in a role that we called "Eyes and Ears."[23] He was authorized and expected to go where and when he pleased in the American zone to observe and report to me on anything he felt worthy of my attention. He was especially suited to act in such an intimate capacity, not only by reason of our long friendship, but because of his ability and reputation as a sound, painstaking, and broadly educated soldier. Soon after his arrival in Africa he was assigned as deputy commander in the U. S. II Corps, then fighting in the Tebessa area. He was promoted to command this corps on April 16, 1943, and demonstrated real capacity for leadership. He was a keen judge of men and their capabilities and was absolutely fair and just in his dealings with them. Added to this, he was emotionally stable and possessed a grasp of larger issues that clearly marked him for high office. I looked forward to renewal of our close association in the cross-Channel operation.

I foresaw some possibility of friction in advancing Bradley to the highest American ground command in Overlord because I was also planning to use Patton in that operation, provided he concurred in the new arrangement, which would involve a reversal of the relative positions the two men had held in the successful Sicilian campaign. Both were my intimate friends of many years' standing and I knew that each would loyally accept any assigned duty. I was hopeful, however, that Patton, who for certain types of action was the outstanding soldier our country has produced, would wholeheartedly support the plan I had in mind. I had a frank talk with him and was gratified to find that he thoroughly agreed that the role for which he personally was ideally suited was that of an army commander. At that moment he wanted no higher post. With these two able and experienced officers available for the cross-Channel operation, I foresaw little immediate need in the same organization for Lieutenant General Jacob L. Devers, then commanding United States forces in the United Kingdom. He had a reputation as a very fine administrator. In Africa these qualifications would be vastly important, whereas his lack of battle experience would not be critical because the American tactical operations in Italy would be under General Clark, commanding the U. S. Fifth Army. With these views the War Department agreed, and General Devers was ordered to the Mediterranean theater to serve as the senior American officer in that region.[24]

I also desired to take General Spaatz to England. By agreement reached in Cairo the American strategic bombers in the Mediterranean and in England were to be combined under Spaatz's single operational command, a circumstance that made it more than ever necessary that he should be in the United Kingdom, where the principal effort was to be mounted. This was arranged by bringing Lieutenant General Ira C. Eaker from the United Kingdom to the Mediterranean to serve as the air commander in chief in that theater. In the United Kingdom, Eaker's post as commander of the U. S. Eighth Air Force was given to General Doolittle.[25]

While engaged in all of these details and counting on getting away to England about the tenth of January, I received a Christmas telegram from General Marshall. He urged me to come immediately to Washington for short conferences with him and the President and for a brief breather before undertaking the new assignment. I protested, on the ground that time was vital and that, moreover, I could accomplish little by a visit to Washington until I had been in London at least long enough to familiarize myself with the essentials of the problems there. General Marshall did not agree. He advised me to "allow someone else to run the war for twenty minutes," and to come on to Washington.[26] Strictly speaking, my commanders were the Combined Chiefs of Staff but, realizing General Marshall's earnestness in the matter, I quickly cleared the point with the British side of the house and made ready to leave for the United States. After a week I planned to return briefly to Africa to complete the details of turning over the American command to General Devers, who had not yet arrived from London.[27] All this would consume time, the most precious element of all.

To provide guidance to the staff in London pending my arrival, I thought it necessary to send there someone who was acquainted with my general ideas. Fortunately General Montgomery was available to leave for England at once. He came to my headquarters for a conference and I told him that some weeks earlier I had seen a sketchy outline of the proposed attack across the Channel, brought to my office by Brigadier General William E. Chambers of the American Army.[28] I was doubtful about the adequacy of the tactical plan because it contemplated an amphibious attack on a relatively narrow, three-division front with a total of only five divisions afloat at the instant of the assault. I informed Montgomery, moreover, that in addition to being disturbed by the constricted nature of the proposed maneuver, I was also concerned because the outline I had seen failed to provide effectively for the quick capture of Cherbourg. I was convinced that the plan, unless it had been changed since I had seen it, did not emphasize sufficiently the early need for major ports and for rapid build-up.[29]

I directed him therefore to act, pending my arrival in London, as my representative in analyzing and revising the ground plan for the beach assault with special reference to the points on which I was uneasy.[30] I told him that he could communicate with me quickly and easily in Washington. I gave these views also to my chief of staff, General Smith, who was to proceed to London as soon as his successor was familiar with the nature of the intricate staff work of the Mediterranean headquarters.[31]

While I was taking care of these details in Italy and in Algiers, the Prime Minister had become seriously ill at Tunis. He had recovered sufficiently by the year's end to proceed as far as Marrakech, Morocco, where the doctors decided he would have to remain for several weeks in recuperation. He sent me an urgent message, asking me to a conference on my way to the United States. I joined him at that place on the afternoon of December 31.[32]

At this time the Anzio operation had been definitely agreed upon and the Prime Minister was, with his habitual energy and in spite of the serious threat to his health, devoting himself intensively to the task of unearthing every possible resource in order to strengthen the attack and to launch it at the earliest moment. He hoped it would immediately result in the overrunning of Italy, although I continued to voice doubts of such an optimistic outcome. The Prime Minister made the personal request that I allow General Smith to remain in the Mediterranean as chief of staff, but to this I could not agree. The relationship between a commander and his chief of staff is a very individual thing. That relationship differs with every commander and General Smith suited me so completely that I felt it would be unwise to break up the combination just as we were on the eve of the war's greatest venture. Moreover, I felt that General Wilson would have his own ideas about such an important member of his Mediterranean team and would be resentful if someone were forced on him from the outside, even by the head of his own government. The Prime Minister was obviously ill and badly run down, but he was so interested in the Anzio venture that the conference lasted until late in the evening.

We left Marrakech about 4:45 a.m. on New Year's Day, arriving in Washington at 1:00 a.m. the following morning. The trip was without incident except that a nervous battery of Portuguese anti-aircraft artillery tossed a few ineffective shots in our direction as we passed along the edge of one of the Azores Islands.[33]

Upon arrival in the United States I met with the War Department staff and later with the President. Mr. Roosevelt was temporarily ill with influenza but seemed quite cheerful and kept me at his bedside for more than an hour as we discussed a hundred details of past and future operations. As always he amazed me with his intimate knowledge of world geography. The most obscure places in faraway countries were always accurately placed on his mental map. He took occasion to brief me on his post-hostilities occupational plans for Germany. He definitely wanted the northwest section as the United States area but listened attentively as I voiced my objection to dividing Germany into "national sectors." I admitted all the difficulties of true joint occupation but said we should insist upon that plan as the only practicable one—and one, moreover, which would quickly test the possibilities of real "quadripartite action." I urged, again, that occupied territories be turned over, as quickly as possible, to civil authority. He seemed impressed but did not commit himself.

In none of the various talks I had with the President were domestic politics ever mentioned except casually. His son Elliott, whom I sometimes saw both in Africa and in England, likewise avoided politics as a subject of conversation except to refer to himself occasionally, in a jocular tone, as the "black sheep and reactionary of the family."

As I left the President I said, "I sincerely trust that you will quickly recover from your indisposition." He quickly replied, "Oh, I have not felt better in years. I'm in bed only because the doctors are afraid I might have a relapse if I get up too soon." I never saw him again.

During my short stay in the United States I had a treasured opportunity of going with my wife to see our son at West Point. Later I made a hasty trip to see my mother and brothers, my wife's parents, and a few other members of our families, all gathered for the occasion in the town of Manhattan, Kansas. These family visits were a rejuvenating experience—until then I had not fully realized how far war tends to carry its participants away from the interests, objectives, and concerns of normal life.

Of course my temporary removal from the preoccupations of war was far from complete. Telegrams arrived periodically from London, posing most serious questions and in certain instances asking me to make final determinations before I personally could familiarize myself with all the factors in the problem. However, I was pleased to find that Montgomery was definitely working on a plan for a five-division assault front, with two follow-up divisions afloat, and this knowledge kept me from worrying too much until I could reach the United Kingdom.

In the meantime a certain uneasiness developed in the British Government over the prevailing command situation in the Mediterranean. As long as I was nominally in command of all forces in that region there was a lack of decisiveness in the preparatory work for the Anzio attack, an attack which was to be executed after my own connection with the Mediterranean should be terminated. I learned that the individuals who would bear final responsibility felt some hesitancy in making decisions because my assignment had not yet been officially concluded. Therefore I instantly abandoned the plan for returning to Africa and recommended to General Marshall that prompt action be taken to terminate my connection with the theater and to place all authority in the Mediterranean in the hands of General Wilson. This involved a point of personal regret because I was thereby barred from going back to my old command to say thank you and good-by to all the people who had served with me loyally, efficiently, and devotedly. I had, however, already issued a final written farewell to the troops, predicting that we would meet again in the heart of the enemy homeland.

Chapter 13

PLANNING
OVERLORD

I LEFT THE UNITED STATES ON JANUARY 13 TO undertake the organization of the mightiest fighting force that the two Western Allies could muster. On the evening of the second day I was back in London. Now began again the task of preparing for an invasion, but by comparison with the similar job of a year and a half earlier, order had replaced disorder and certainty and confidence had replaced fear and doubt. Immediate subordinates included Air Chief Marshal Sir Arthur Tedder, Lieutenant General Omar Bradley, General Sir Bernard Montgomery, Lieutenant General Carl Spaatz, and Admiral Sir Bertram Ramsay, all tested battle leaders and all experienced in the problems of developing real allied unity in a large operation. Air Chief Marshal Sir Trafford Leigh-Mallory was assigned to the Allied forces, with the title of Air Commander in Chief. He had much fighting experience, particularly in the Battle of Britain, but had not theretofore been in charge of air operations requiring close co-operation with ground troops.

As on my first arrival in London in June 1942, I found headquarters staffs concentrated in the heart of the city, but this time I determined I would not be defeated in my plan to find a suitable site somewhere in the countryside. I found one, and there were protests and gloomy predictions. Once concentrated in the Bushey Park area, however, we quickly developed a family relationship that far more than made up for minor inconveniences due to distance from the seat of Britain's administrative organization.[1] My headquarters was officially called Supreme Headquarters, Allied Expeditionary Force, and taking the initials from the name, SHAEF was born.

The period of planning and preparing that then ensued will be studied in detail only by professionals and by technical schools. With respect to command and staff organization, there were several important points to consider. The first of these was determination of the most desirable composition of the headquarters staff. Ever since I had been appointed an Allied commander in July 1942, with command over ground, air, and naval forces, we had understood and studied certain desirabilities in a truly integrated staff with approximately equal representation from each of the ground, air, naval, and logistic organizations. I believed that under certain situations, where large task forces might have to carry on extensive operations at great distances from Supreme Headquarters, such a composition of the staff would be necessary. In the preparatory days of Torch in 1942 we had initially planned to organize in this way. We finally abandoned the idea as being expensive in personnel, and not necessary in our situation.

The scheme which we found most effective, where it was possible for all commanders to meet together almost instantly, was to consider the naval, air, and ground chiefs as occupying two roles. In the first role each was part of my staff and he and his assistants worked with us in the development of plans; in the second role each was the responsible commander for executing his part of the whole operation. This was the general system that we followed throughout the Mediterranean operation and I was convinced that, considering only the conditions of our theater, it should be adopted as the guide for the new organization, although certain exceptions were inescapable.

The first of these exceptions involved the air forces. It was desirable that for the preparatory stages of the assault and for proper support during the critical early stages of the land operation—until we had established ourselves so firmly that danger of defeat was eliminated—all air forces in Britain, excepting only the Coastal Command, should come under my control.[2] This would include the Strategic Air Forces, comprising the British Bomber Command under Air Chief Marshal Sir Arthur Harris, and the U. S. Eighth Air Force under General Doolittle. Some opposition quickly developed, partly from the Prime Minister and his chiefs of staff. The Strategic Air commanders were also unwilling to take orders from the Tactical Air commander of the expedition. Their objections, I felt sure, were not based upon personal reasons but upon a conviction that a Tactical Air commander, who is always primarily concerned with the support of front-line troops, could not be expected to appreciate properly the true role and capabilities of Strategic Air Forces and would therefore misuse them.[3]

A broader contention was that these great bomber units, with their ability to strike at any point in western Europe, should never be confined, even temporarily, to a role wherein their principal task would be to assist in a single ground operation. In answer we pointed out that the venture the United States and Great Britain were now about to undertake could not be classed as an ordinary tactical movement in which consequences would be no greater than those ordinarily experienced through success or failure in a battle. The two countries were definitely placing all their hopes, expectations, and assets in one great effort to establish a theater of operations in western Europe. Failure would carry with it consequences that would be almost fatal. Such a catastrophe might mean the complete redeployment to other theaters of all United States forces accumulated in the United Kingdom, while the setback to Allied morale and determination would be so profound that it was beyond calculation. Finally, such a failure would certainly react violently upon the Russian situation and it was not unreasonable to assume that, if that country should consider her Allies completely futile and helpless in doing anything of a major character in Europe, she might consider a separate peace.

My insistence upon commanding these air forces at that time was further influenced by the lesson so conclusively demonstrated at Salerno: when a battle needs the last ounce of available force, the commander must not be in the position of depending upon request and negotiation to get it. It was vital that the entire sum of our assault power, including the two Strategic Air Forces, be available for use during the critical stages of the attack. I stated unequivocally that so long as I was in command I would accept no other solution, although I agreed that the two commanders of the heavy bombing forces would not be subordinated to my Tactical Air commander in chief but would receive orders directly from me. This imposed no great additional burden on me because my deputy, Air Chief Marshal Tedder, was not only an experienced air commander, but in addition enjoyed the confidence of everybody in the air forces, both British and American.

We had no intention of using the Strategic Air Forces as a mere adjunct to the Tactical Air Command. On the contrary, we were most anxious to continue the destruction of German industry with emphasis upon oil. General Spaatz convinced me that, as Germany became progressively embarrassed by her diminishing oil reserves, the effect upon the land battle would be most profound and the eventual winning of the war would be correspondingly hastened.

My representations were accepted in early April and from that time until the critical phases of the campaign in France and Belgium were past Doolittle and Harris reported directly to me.[5] Strictly speaking, however, Leigh-Mallory's organization comprised only those air forces that were definitely allocated as a permanently integral part of the expeditionary forces. These were the British air forces supporting the Twenty-first Army Group, the Ninth Air Force supporting the U. S. Twelfth Army Group, and, later on, the American air forces that operated in support of the Sixth Army Group (French and American) in the south. His command included also large air transport, reconnaissance, and other special units.[6]

For control of ground forces no special appointment as "Ground Commander in Chief" was contemplated. Since our amphibious attack was on a relatively narrow front, with only two armies involved, one battle-line commander had to be constantly and immediately in charge of tactical co-ordination between the two armies in the initial stages. Montgomery was charged with this responsibility. But plans called for the early establishment of separate British and American army groups on the Continent and it was logical that, when these were in sufficient force to accomplish a decisive breakout and begin a rapid advance through western Europe, the land force in each natural channel of march should have its own commander, each reporting directly to my headquarters.[7] This plan would apply also to the army group which was later to invade France from the south. It would be completely confusing—a case of too many cooks—to place any headquarters intermediate between these three principal ground commanders and my own. As a consequence each of these three ground commanders was in effect to be a ground commander in chief for his particular zone and each would be supported by a tactical air force for day-by-day operations.

This point was thoroughly discussed and well understood by all long before the operation was undertaken. However, a number of British officers—but not including those in my own headquarters— were by tradition wedded to strict compliance with the "triumvirate" method of command, and believed that we should have a single ground commander, installed as a deputy in my headquarters.

Our team acquired an important member with the arrival of George Patton, whose transfer from the Mediterranean I had asked. Sometimes he would spend the evening with me at my quarters, and though this usually involved the certainty of sitting up till the wee hours of the morning, conversation with him was always so stimulating that it was difficult to remember that the work day began before dawn when operating under double daylight saving time.

I made a particular point of directing George to avoid press conferences and public statements.[8] He had a genius for explosive statements that rarely failed to startle his hearers. He had so long practiced the habit of attempting with fantastic pronouncements to astound his friends and associates that it had become second nature with him, regardless of circumstances. A speech he made to an American division shortly after his arrival in the United Kingdom caused more than a ripple of astonishment and press comment, and I well knew that it would be far easier to keep him for a significant role in the war if he could shut off his public utterances. He promised faithfully to do so.

Later in the spring, however, another storm broke around his head. Before a British gathering he expressed indiscreet and inappropriate opinions about the need for Great Britain and America to combine to run the world after the victory should be won.[9]

Because the memory of the Sicilian slapping incident was still fresh in the public mind the statement, widely publicized, attracted far more attention than it would otherwise have done. His public critics were confirmed in their conviction that he was totally unsuited to command an army. For the first time I began seriously to doubt my ability to hang onto my old friend, in whose fighting capacity I had implicit faith and confidence. However, my concern was not so much for his particular statements, which were the object of criticism at home, as it was for his broken promise with the resultant implication that he would never improve in this regard.

Investigation quickly revealed two points which influenced my decision. The first of these was that in advance of the meeting Patton had refused to make any speech and had merely, under the insistence of his hosts, risen to his feet to say a word or two in support of the purpose of the particular gathering. The second point was that he had been assured that the meeting was a private one, with no reporters present, and that no information concerning its details would be given to anyone.

In the meantime the incident had become one for an exchange of cablegrams with the War Department, but as usual the Secretary and the Chief of Staff left final decision to me, to be based completely upon my judgment as to the needs of battle.[10]

OVERLORD FORECAST

━━━━━━━ U.S. FRONT LINE   ▦▦▦▦▦▦ BRITISH FRONT LINE

◐➤ U.S. COMBAT DIVISION   ■ U.S. DIVISION ON DEFENSIVE LINE

⊕➤ BRITISH COMBAT DIVISION ▦ BRITISH DIVISION ON DEFENSIVE LINE

➤ PLANNED OFFENSIVE ATTACKS

DIVISIONS EXPECTED TO BE IN REST AREAS AND IN RESERVE ARE NOT SHOWN.

HEREFORD ●

GREAT BRITAIN

MARGAT

SOUTHAMPTON ●   BRIGHTON ●

PLYMOUTH

ENGLISH CHANNEL

DIEPPE ●

CHERBOURG

LE HAVRE

D+60   D+90   RO

THIS COMPOSITE OF EIGHT PLANNING
MAPS, PREPARED IN THE SPRING OF 1944
AT SHAEF, SHOWS THE CONSTRICTED
AND TEDIOUS CAMPAIGN THAT WOULD
HAVE BEEN REQUIRED FOR THE LIBER-
ATION OF FRANCE WITHOUT THE
SUPPORT OF ANVIL-DRAGOON, DRIVING UP
FROM THE SOUTHERN COAST. COMPELLED
TO MAINTAIN A LONG DEFENSIVE LINE
BELOW THE LOIRE, THE ALLIES WOULD
HAVE BEEN RESTRICTED TO LOCAL
OFFENSIVES AGAINST THE GERMANS.

ST. LÔ ●   CAEN ●

EVREUX ●

ARGENTAN ●

AVRANCHES ●   LAIGLE

ALENÇON ●

RENNES ●   LAVAL ●

F   R   A

LE MANS ●

LORIENT ●

D+60   D+90

ANGERS ●

D+60 TO D+90

ST. NAZAIRE ●

NANTES ●   SAUMUR   LOIRE R.   TOURS ●

CHOLET ●

D+120 TO D+330

0   25   50   75   100   125

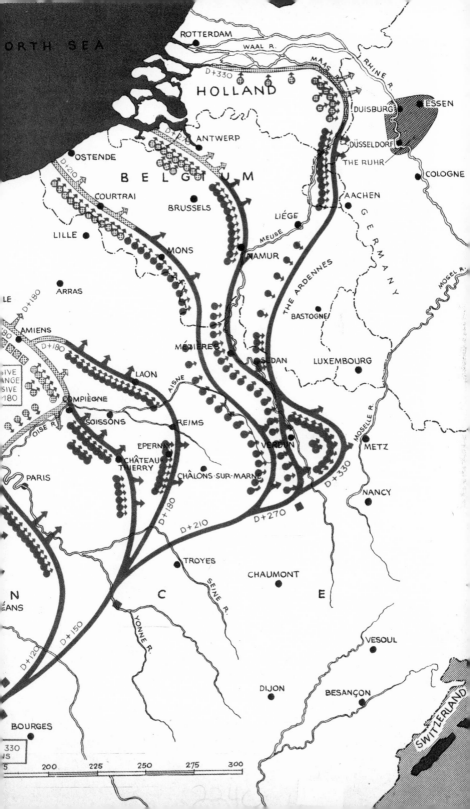

During my investigation George came to see me and in his typically generous and emotional fashion offered to resign his commission so as to relieve me of any embarrassment. When I finally announced to him my determination to drop the whole matter and to retain him as the prospective commander of the Third Army, he was stirred to the point of tears. At such moments General Patton revealed a side of his make-up that was difficult for anyone except his intimate friends to understand. His remorse was very great, not only for the trouble he had caused me but, he said, for the fact that he had vehemently criticized me to his associates when he thought I might relieve him. His emotional range was very great and he lived at either one end or the other of it. I laughingly told him, "You owe us some victories; pay off and the world will deem me a wise man."

It was important that a long-term strategic concept of the operation—of which the amphibious assault would be merely the opening phase—should develop early. The directive from the Combined Chiefs of Staff was very simple, merely instructing us to land on the coast of France and thereafter to destroy the German ground forces. Its significant paragraph read, "You will enter the continent of Europe and, in conjunction with the other Allied Nations, undertake operations aimed at the heart of Germany and the destruction of her Armed Forces." This purpose of destroying enemy forces was always our guiding principle; geographical points were considered only in relation to their importance to the enemy in the conduct of his operations or to us as centers of supply and communications in proceeding to the destruction of enemy armies and air forces.[11]

The heart of western Germany was the Ruhr, the principal center of that nation's wartime munitions industry. The second most important industrial area in western Germany was the Saar Basin. Within those two areas lay much of Germany's warmaking power.

Of the natural avenues for crossing the Rhine with large forces, one lay north of the Ruhr. Another good route passed through the Frankfurt area, while still farther southward, in the Strasbourg region, crossings were practicable. Of these feasible avenues the northern one was, from our viewpoint, the most important. One reason was that north of the Ruhr the terrain near the Rhine was of a more favorable nature for offensive action. Another was that in this region a relatively short advance from the Rhine would cut off the Ruhr and its war industries from the rest of Germany. A third consideration favoring the northern channel of operations was the perfect location, from a logistic viewpoint, of Antwerp, the finest port in northwest Europe. Seizure and use of that port would vastly shorten our lines of communication, and it was clear that when we once arrived on the borders of Germany logistic problems were going to be critical.

However, our hope of destroying Germany's final powers of resistance could not be attained merely by devoting all our resources to organizing a single thrust along a narrow channel following the northern coast. The problem remained that of destroying the German armed forces in the field and it was certain those forces would be encountered head on in whatever region the enemy felt his safety to be most greatly threatened. To employ offensively only a fraction of our forces anywhere on the front would have meant merely a head-on collision between our spearheads and all the defensive forces the enemy could muster. We wanted to bring all our strength against him, all of it mobile and all of it contributing directly to the complete annihilation of his field forces.

To avoid stalemate and to attain the position of power and mobility required to destroy the German forces, we planned, following upon any breakout, to push forward on a broad front, with priority on the left.[12] Thus we would gain, at the earliest possible date, use of the enormously important ports of Belgium. This advance would also overrun the areas in which we knew some mysterious "secret weapons" were being installed, and as the advance continued we would directly threaten the Ruhr. It was additionally planned, from the start, to advance in the direction of the Saar, so far as this would be possible after assuring the capture of the Belgian ports and the arrival of the left at a location to threaten the Ruhr.[13] The enemy would be sensitive about the safety of the Saar Basin, while our own forces, pushing in that direction, would soon connect with the invasion planned to come up from the south through the Rhone Valley.[14] This linking up of our whole front was mandatory and would have several great and early advantages. It would liberate France. It would open up for us a great additional line of communication to insure the rapid arrival of troops from America and the sufficiency of their supply. Finally, it would cut off whatever German troops might remain behind the point of junction and so eliminate them from the war. This would allow us to use all our troops in facing and fighting the enemy and would prevent the costliness of establishing long defensive flanks along which our troops could have nothing but negative, static missions.

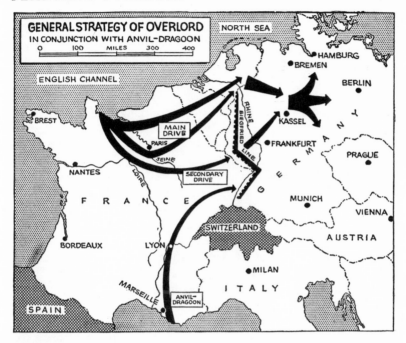

If all these movements should prove successful, we next had to look forward to the final destruction of the enemy, who would then, presumably, be defending the Siegfried Line and the Rhine River.

In May 1944 we calculated that with the ports of entry upon which we were counting we would probably have sixty-eight strong divisions available to us, not including divisions from the Mediterranean, when the time came to make our decisive thrusts across the Rhine. Allotting thirty-five of these to the advance on the axis, Amiens–Maubeuge–Liége–Ruhr, which, according to administrative estimates, was the maximum number that could be sustained along that channel of invasion, would leave us some thirty-three plus those introduced through the south of France for other operations along the long line from Wesel on the Rhine all the way south to Switzerland.[15] Consequently, unless we could eliminate the Siegfried, we would be able to do little more than to defend along the front south of the Ruhr. With all the advantages the enemy would thus enjoy, he could concentrate almost at will for strong counterattack.

However, this prospect would be completely changed provided we could gain the line of the Rhine substantially throughout its entire length. Once this was done we would enjoy a comparative degree of safety throughout the theater that would permit the assignment of offensive roles to practically our entire force instead of only to the thirty-five divisions that could be sustained along the one route north of the Ruhr.

There were other considerations dictating the wisdom of gaining the whole length of the Rhine before launching a final assault on interior Germany. Our objective was the destruction of the German armed forces. If we could overwhelmingly defeat the enemy *west* of the river it was certain that the means available to him for later defense of the Rhine would be meager indeed; Soviet forces had already entered Poland and much of the German strength would be tied down to meet future Russian offensives on the eastern front. Finally, if we could not destroy the German armies west of the Rhine obstacle, where our own supply lines would be as short as possible, how could we expect to do it east of the Rhine, where this advantage would not be ours? Generals Bradley and Patton, along with my entire staff, always concurred in these planning views for advances both through the Metz gap and north of the Ardennes.

Proceeding to the next step from this one, we reasoned that the Ruhr, which we expected to be defended by the strongest forces the enemy could provide, would be best reduced by a double envelopment. To achieve it we planned to make the northern attack as strong as the lines of communication would sustain, and the Frankfurt attack as strong as remaining resources would permit. We believed further that once these two attacks had joined in the vicinity of Kassel, east of the Ruhr, there would be no hope, in the military sense, remaining to Germany. In any event we believed that, once established in the Kassel region, we could easily thrust out offensively on our flanks. This would mean the end of the war in Europe.

All these successive moves with possible alternatives were the subjects of long discussions but the general plan approved as the outline of the operation we intended to conduct was:

Land on the Normandy coast.
Build up the resources needed for a decisive battle in the Normandy–Brittany region and break out of the enemy's encircling positions. (Land operations in the first two phases were to be under the tactical direction of Montgomery.)
Pursue on a broad front with two army groups, emphasizing the left to gain necessary ports and reach the boundaries of Germany and threaten

the Ruhr. On our right we would link up with the forces that were to invade France from the south.

Build up our new base along the western border of Germany, by securing ports in Belgium and in Brittany as well as in the Mediterranean.

While building up our forces for the final battles, keep up an unrelenting offensive to the extent of our means, both to wear down the enemy and to gain advantages for the final fighting.

Complete the destruction of enemy forces west of the Rhine, in the meantime constantly seeking bridgeheads across the river.

Launch the final attack as a double envelopment of the Ruhr, again emphasizing the left, and follow this up by an immediate thrust through Germany, with the specific direction to be determined at the time.

Clean out the remainder of Germany.

This general plan, carefully outlined at staff meetings before D-day, was never abandoned, even momentarily, throughout the campaign.[16]

The timing of the operation was a difficult matter to decide. At Teheran the President and the Prime Minister had promised Generalissimo Stalin that the attack would start in May but we were given to understand that any date selected in that period of the year would fulfill the commitments made by our two political leaders.[17]

In order to obtain the maximum length of good campaigning weather, the earlier the attack could be launched the better. Another factor in favor of an early attack was the continuing and frantic efforts of the German to strengthen his coastal defenses. Because of weather conditions in the Channel, May was the earliest date that a landing attempt could be successfully undertaken and the first favorable combination of tides and sunrise occurred early in the month. Thus early May was the original and tentatively selected target date.

Alarming Intelligence reports concerning the progress of the Germans in developing new long-range weapons of great destructive capacity also indicated the advisability of attacking early.

From time to time during the spring months staff officers from Washington arrived at my headquarters to give me the latest calculations concerning German progress in the development of new weapons, including as possibilities bacteriological and atomic weapons. These reports were highly secret and were invariably delivered to me by word of mouth. I was told that American scientists were making progress in these two important types and that as a result of their own experience they were able to make shrewd guesses concerning some of the details of similar German activity. All of this information was supplemented by the periodic reports of Intelligence agencies in

London. In addition, aerial photographs were scrutinized with the greatest care in order to discover new installations that would apparently be useful only in some new kind of warfare.

The finest scientific brains in both Britain and America were called upon to help us in evaluation and in making estimates of probabilities. Our only effective counteraction, during the preparatory months of 1944, was by bombing. We sent intermittent raids against every spot in Europe where the scientists believed that the Germans were attempting either to manufacture new types of weapons or where they were building launching facilities along the coast.[18]

During this long period the calculations of the Intelligence agencies were necessarily based upon very meager information and as a consequence they shifted from time to time in their estimates of German progress. Nevertheless, before we launched the invasion, Intelligence experts were able to give us remarkably accurate estimates of the existence, characteristics, and capabilities of the new German weapons.

Two considerations, one of them decisive in character, combined to postpone the target date from May to June. The first and important one was our insistence that the attack be on a larger scale than that originally planned by the staff assembled in London under Lieutenant General Frederick Morgan. He was an extraordinarily fine officer and had, long before my arrival, won the high admiration and respect of General Marshall. I soon came to place an equal value upon his qualifications. He had in the months preceding my arrival accomplished a mass of detailed planning, accumulation of data, and gathering of supply that made D-day possible. My ideas were supported by General Morgan personally but he had been compelled to develop his plan on the basis of a fixed number of ships, landing craft, and other resources. Consequently he had no recourse except to work out an attack along a three-division front, whereas I insisted upon five and informed the Combined Chiefs of Staff that we had to have the additional landing craft and other gear essential to the larger operation, even if this meant delaying the assault by a month. To this the Combined Chiefs of Staff agreed.[19]

Another factor that made the later date a desirable one was the degree of dependence we were placing upon the preparatory effort of the air force. An early attack would provide the air force with only a minimum opportunity for pinpoint bombing of critical transportation centers in France, whereas the improved weather anticipated for the month of May would give them much more time and better opportunity to impede the movement of German reserves and demolish German defenses along the coast line. The virtual destruction of critical points on the main roads and railroads leading into the selected battle area was a critical feature of the battle plan. Nevertheless, acceptance of the later date was disappointing. We wanted all the summer weather we could get for the European campaign.

Along with the general plan of operations we thoroughly considered means of deceiving the enemy as to the point and timing of attack. Our purpose was to convince him that we intended to strike directly across the Channel at its narrowest point, against the stronghold of Calais. In many ways great advantages would have accrued to us could we have successfully attacked in this region. Not only were the beaches the best along the coast, they were closest to the British ports and to the German border. The enemy, fully appreciating these facts, kept strong forces in the area and fortified that particular section of coast line more strongly than any other. The defenses were so strong that none of us believed that a successful assault from the sea could be made except at such terrific cost that the whole expedition might find itself helpless to accomplish anything of a positive character, after it got ashore. But we counted upon the enemy believing that we would be tempted into this operation, and the wide variety of measures we took for convincing him were given extraordinary credence by his Intelligence division.[20]

The complementary attack against southern France had long been considered—by General Marshall and me, at least—as an integral and necessary feature of the main invasion across the Channel. In the planning of early 1944, I supposed that all principal commanders and the Combined Chiefs of Staff were solidly together on this point. Our studies in London, however, soon demonstrated that, even with a June date of attack, the Allies did not have enough landing craft and other facilities to mount simultaneously both the cross-Channel and the Mediterranean attacks in the strength we wanted.[21]

The United States was at that time committed to offensive action in the Pacific and the necessary additional craft could not be diverted from that theater. In the face of this, General Montgomery proposed the complete abandonment of the attack on southern France, which then had the code name of Anvil. He wrote to me on February 21, 1944: "I recommend very strongly that we now throw the whole weight of our opinion into the scales against Anvil."[22] I refused to go along with this view.[23] But it became clear that there was no other recourse except to delay the southern attack for a sufficient time to permit ships and craft first to operate in Overlord and then to proceed to the Mediterranean for participation in that battle.[24] We concluded that this arrangement was not especially disadvantageous; at least it was far better than cancellation. The presence of Allied troops in the Mediterranean would prevent the German from completely evacuating his troops from southern France, while, if he gradually drained that area, our later advance from the south would be much speedier. Consequently we agreed upon the delay in the southern attack with the recommendation that it be made as soon after July 15 as was feasible.

Our scheme for employing the air force in preparation for the great assault encountered very earnest and sincere opposition, especially on the political level. To demolish the key bridges, freight yards, and main rail arteries of France would inevitably result in casualties among the French population. Even though we planned, in the case of large cities, to disrupt communications by bombing critical points surrounding the locality instead of within the highly populated centers, some statisticians calculated that the plan would cost at least 80,000 French lives. Such a catastrophe was of course likely to embitter the French nation; the Prime Minister and many of his subordinates insisted that some other way must be found to employ the air forces in support of the attack. The Prime Minister was genuinely shaken by the fearful picture presented to him by opponents of our idea, and his appeals to me were correspondingly urgent and appealing. He said, "Postwar France must be our friend. It is not alone a question of humanitarianism. It is also a question of high state policy."[25]

My own air commanders and I challenged the accuracy of the statisticians' figures. We anticipated losses of not more than a fraction of 80,000—particularly because we planned to issue both general and specific warnings to the inhabitants. We used every possible means repeatedly to tell the French and Belgians to move away from critical points in the transport system. More than this, preceding every raid we planned to warn inhabitants, by radio and by leaflet, to evacuate temporarily the areas selected for that attack. We could afford to give these definite warnings because of our knowledge that we had badly diminished the strength of the German Air Force and because also we knew that the enemy could not have anti-aircraft in sufficient quantities to cover, on short notice, every critical spot in the transportation system of France. The plan had to be so arranged

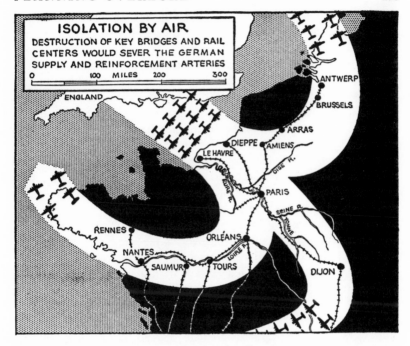

ISOLATION BY AIR
DESTRUCTION OF KEY BRIDGES AND RAIL
CENTERS WOULD SEVER THE GERMAN
SUPPLY AND REINFORCEMENT ARTERIES

that it did not, by its general pattern, reveal the area selected for assault. Consequently, in furtherance of our deception plans, we invariably chose some targets in the Calais area for heavy bombing simultaneously with every critical raid.[26]

The value and need of the bombing were argued long and earnestly and of course, sympathetically, because of human factors involved. Finally the Prime Minister and his government and General Pierre Joseph Koenig, the commander of the French Forces of the Interior, all agreed that the attacks had to be executed as laid down, with the hope that the measures we adopted for warning the population would be effective in minimizing casualties. In the outcome the efficacy of this preparatory bombing for the ground attack was clearly proved. Moreover, not only were the civilian casualties a mere fraction of those originally estimated, but the French nation as a whole calmly accepted their necessity and developed no antagonisms toward the Allied forces as a result of them. In addition to the work of the air forces against the transportation system of France we continued our steady pounding at German oil plants and other vital parts of its warmaking industry. Moreover, the air forces constantly sought to engage the Luftwaffe in battle with a view to wearing down its strength still more, before the crisis of the land battle should develop.[27]

In the meantime both ground and air staffs were constantly working on the perfection of measures for the co-ordination of ground and air in actual battle. We had long ceased to refer to "air support of the ground forces" and referred to our battles merely as "ground-air." This interdependence is a characteristic of modern battle. Ground forces must always be determined to gain and protect favorable localities from which the air can operate close up to the front lines, while on the other hand constant fighter-bomber support of ground forces must be accepted as a matter of routine. In several crises of the European campaign the air flew more than 10,000 combat sorties per day as its share of the ground-air battle.[28]

One of the most difficult problems, which invariably accompanies planning for a tactical offensive, involves measures for maintenance, supplies, evacuation, and replacement.

Prior to the late war it had always been assumed that any major amphibious attack had to gain permanent port facilities within a matter of several days or be abandoned. The development of effective landing gear by the Allies, including LSTs, LCTs, ducks, and other craft, did much to lessen immediate dependence upon established port facilities. It is not too much to say that Allied development of great quantities of revolutionary types of equipment was one of the greatest factors in the defeat of the plans of the German General Staff.[29]

Nevertheless, possession of equipment and gear that permit the landing of material on open beaches does not by any means eliminate the need for ports. This was particularly true in Overlord. The history of centuries clearly shows that the English Channel is subject to destructive storms at all times of the year, with winter by far the worst period. The only certain method to assure supply and maintenance was by capture of large port facilities.

Since the nature of the defenses to be encountered ruled out the possibility of gaining adequate ports promptly, it was necessary also to provide a means for sheltering beach supply from the effect of storms. We knew that even after we captured Cherbourg its port capacity and the lines of communication leading out of it could not meet all our needs. To solve this apparently unsolvable problem we undertook a project so unique as to be classed by many scoffers as completely fantastic. It was a plan to construct artificial harbors on the coast of Normandy.[30]

The first time I heard this idea tentatively advanced was by Admiral Mountbatten, in the spring of 1942. At a conference attended by a number of service chiefs he remarked, "If ports are not available, we may have to construct them in pieces and tow them in." Hoots and jeers greeted his suggestion but two years later it was to become reality.

Two general types of protected anchorages were designed. The first, called a "gooseberry," was to consist merely of a line of sunken ships placed stem to stern in such numbers as to provide a sheltered coast line in their lee on which small ships and landing craft could continue to unload in any except the most vicious weather. The other type, named "mulberry," was practically a complete harbor. Two of these were designed and constructed in Great Britain, to be towed piecemeal to the coast of Normandy. The principal construction unit in the mulberry was an enormous concrete ship, called a "phoenix," boxlike in shape and so heavily constructed that when numbers of them were sunk end to end along a strip of coast they would probably provide solid protection against almost any wave action. Elaborate auxiliary equipment to facilitate unloading and all types of gear required in the operation of a modern port were planned for and provided. The British and American sectors were each to have one of the mulberry ports. Five gooseberries were to be installed.

Experience in Mediterranean warfare had demonstrated that each of our reinforced divisions in active operation consumed about 600 to 700 tons of supplies per day. Our maintenance arrangements had to provide for the arrival of these amounts daily. In addition we had simultaneously to build up on the beaches the reserves in troops, ammunition, and supplies that would enable us, within a reasonable time, to initiate deep offensives with the certainty that these could be sustained through an extended period of decisive action. On top of all this we had to provide for bringing in the heavy engineering and construction material needed to re-establish and refit captured ports, to repair railways, bridges, and roads, and to build airfields. A further feature of the logistic plan, and a most important one, provided for the speedy removal of wounded from the beaches and their prompt transfer to the great array of hospitals in England.

In SHAEF my principal logistic officers were Lieutenant General Sir Humfrey Gale and Major General R. W. Crawford, both widely experienced and extremely able. The commander of the American logistic organization was Lieutenant General John C. H. Lee. He was an engineer officer of long experience, with a reputation for getting things done. Because of his mannerisms and his stern insistence upon the outward forms of discipline, which he himself meticulously observed, he was considered a martinet by most of his acquaintances. He was determined, correct, and devoted to duty; he had long been known as an effective administrator and as a man of the highest character and religious fervor. I sometimes felt that he was a modern Cromwell, but I was ready to waive the rigidity of his mannerisms in favor of his constructive qualities. Indeed, I felt it possible that his unyielding methods might be vital to success in an activity where an iron hand is always mandatory.

Special tactical problems anticipated in the initial attack were many, some of them most difficult of solution. The principal subordinate commanders and staff officers met with me frequently to discuss and fit together evolving plans; often experts and specialists of a variety of categories attended these meetings to give technical advice.

Constant advisers in all tactical and operational affairs were these officers in whom I reposed the greatest confidence. They were Major General Harold R. Bull, Brigadier General Arthur S. Nevins of the American Army and Major General J. F. M. Whiteley of the British.

At a secluded spot in eastern England the British Army constructed every type of tactical obstacle that the German might use in defending against our attack. The British built pillboxes, massive stone walls, and great areas of barbed-wire entanglements. They planted mine fields, erected steel obstacles for underwater and land use, and dug anti-tank ditches. Each of these was a replica of similar defenses we knew the Germans had already installed. Then the British set about the task of designing equipment that would facilitate destruction of these obstacles. They used the area for actual test of the equipment so developed and for trying out new battle techniques.[31]

An interesting example of this experimentation was a new method for using the Bangalore torpedo. This torpedo is nothing but a long tube filled with explosive. It is thrust out into a mine field and upon detonation explodes all the mines planted along its length. Thus is created a narrow path through the mine field, along which troops can advance and continue the attack while others in the rear come forward to clear up the remaining portions of the field. These torpedoes had long been used in warfare but the British developed a novel way of employing them. They did this by covering a Sherman tank with a series of pipes, each of which contained a Bangalore torpedo. The pipes pointed straight to the front and were, in effect, guns with light charges of black powder at the rear. As the tank advanced it automatically fired these makeshift guns in succession so that, as each of the torpedoes flew out in the air and exploded some thirty feet in front of the tank, it cleared a continuous path through the mine field. Each tank carried a sufficient number of torpedoes to clear a path approximately fifty yards long. The idea was that, instead of depending upon defenseless foot soldiers to do this hazardous work, it would be done by a tank crew, from the comparative safety afforded by its protecting armor. I never saw this particular piece of equipment used in action but it is an example of the methods by which we tried to ease the problem of the foot soldier. Transportable bridges to span anti-tank ditches, flame-throwing tanks, and flails, plows, and heavy rollers for destroying mines were other items constantly under development and test.

As always, the matter of the Army's morale attracted the constant attention of all senior commanders. Sometimes this attention had to be directed toward particular and specific points. For example, a columnist estimated that any attempt to land on the defended coast of northwest Europe would result in eighty to ninety per cent losses in the assaulting units. This irresponsible statement was sufficiently circulated to cause doubt and uneasiness in the command. Bradley and others immediately took occasion, during numerous visits to troops, to brand this statement for just what it was—a fearful, false, and completely misguided statement by someone who knew nothing of warfare or of the facts. Bradley predicted that the attacking losses would be no greater than in any other stiff battle of comparable size. We went so far as to give publicity to his estimate in the papers and used every other means available to us to prevent the doleful prediction from shaking the confidence of the troops.

The air plan, in both its preparatory and supporting phases, was worked out in minute detail, and as the spring wore on the results obtained in the preparatory phase were reviewed weekly. Reconnaissance by submarine and airplane was unending, while information was gathered from numbers of sources. The naval plan involved general protection, mine sweeping, escorting, supporting fire, and, along with all else, erection of artificial ports, repair of captured ports, and maintenance of cross-Channel supply. The coastal defenses were studied and specific plans made for the reduction of every strong point, every pillbox. Pictures were studied and one of the disturbing things these continued to show was the growing profusion of beach obstacles, most of them under water at high tide. Embarkation plans for troops, equipment, and supplies were voluminous, and exact in detail. Routes to ports, timings of departures and arrivals, locations, protection and camouflage of temporary camps, and a thousand related matters were all carefully predetermined and, so far as feasible, tested in advance.

Senior commanders used every possible moment in visiting and inspecting troops. Records left by a staff officer show that in four months, from February 1 to June 1, I visited twenty-six divisions, twenty-four airfields, five ships of war, and numerous depots, shops, hospitals, and other important installations. Bradley, Montgomery, Spaatz, and Tedder maintained similar schedules. Such visits, sandwiched between a seemingly endless series of conferences and staff meetings, were necessary and highly valuable.

Soldiers like to see the men who are directing operations; they properly resent any indication of neglect or indifference to them on the part of their commanders and invariably interpret a visit, even a brief one, as evidence of the commander's concern for them. Diffidence or modesty must never blind the commander to his duty of showing himself to his men, of speaking to them, of mingling with them to the extent of physical limitations. It pays big dividends in terms of morale, and morale, given rough equality in other things, is supreme on the battlefield.

As the time came for shifting our concentrations toward the ports, the southern portion of England became one vast camp, dump, and airfield. At our request the British Government stopped all traffic between this part of England and the remainder of the United Kingdom, just as it did between the United Kingdom and Eire, since enemy spies abounded in neutral Eire. The government even took the unprecedented step of arbitrarily stopping all diplomatic communications from the United Kingdom to foreign countries and drew down upon itself angry and prolonged protest.[32] Further, it withdrew from normal use its coastwise shipping so that we could employ these immensely valuable vessels for military purposes. This threw an almost impossible load on the already overworked railways. Passenger traffic practically ceased and even essential commodities were transported with difficulty. Construction of the great artificial harbors engaged the services of thousands of men and added indescribable congestion to already crowded ports and harbors.

The war-weary British public responded without a whimper to

these added inconveniences and privations. Sustained by the certainty that a decisive effort was in the offing and inspired by the example and leadership of Winston Churchill, people cheerfully accepted the need of using their own streets and roads at the risk of being run down, of seeing their fields and gardens trampled, of waiting in long queues for trains that rarely arrived, and of suffering a further cut in an already meager ration so that nothing should interfere with the movement of the soldiers and the mountains of supplies we so lavishly consumed.

After the abandonment of the May target date, the next combination of moon, tide, and time of sunrise that we considered practicable for the attack occurred on June 5, 6, and 7. We wanted to cross the Channel with our convoys at night so that darkness would conceal the strength and direction of our several attacks. We wanted a moon for our airborne assaults. We needed approximately forty minutes of daylight preceding the ground assault to complete our bombing and preparatory bombardment. We had to attack on a relatively low tide because of beach obstacles which had to be removed while uncovered. These principal factors dictated the general period; but the selection of the actual day would depend upon weather forecasts.[33]

If none of the three days should prove satisfactory from the standpoint of weather, consequences would ensue that were almost terrifying to contemplate.[34] Secrecy would be lost. Assault troops would be unloaded and crowded back into assembly areas enclosed in barbed wire, where their original places would already have been taken by those to follow in subsequent waves. Complicated movement tables would be scrapped. Morale would drop. A wait of at least fourteen days, possibly twenty-eight, would be necessary—a sort of suspended animation involving more than 2,000,000 men! The good-weather period available for major campaigning would become still shorter and the enemy's defenses would become still stronger! The whole of the United Kingdom would become quickly aware that something had gone wrong and national discouragement there and in America could lead to unforeseen results. Finally, always lurking in the background was the knowledge that the enemy was developing new, and presumably effective, secret weapons on the French coast. What the effect of these would be on our crowded harbors, especially at Plymouth and Portsmouth, we could not even guess.

It was a tense period, made even worse by the fact that the one thing that could give us this disastrous setback was entirely outside our control. Some soldier once said, "The weather is always neutral." Nothing could be more untrue. Bad weather is obviously the enemy of the side that seeks to launch projects requiring good weather, or of the side possessing great assets, such as strong air forces, which depend upon good weather for effective operations. If really bad weather should endure permanently, the Nazi would need nothing else to defend the Normandy coast!

A particularly difficult decision involved our planned airborne attack in the Cotentin Peninsula. The assault against the east coast of that peninsula, to take place on a beach called Utah, was included in the attack plan because of my conviction, concurred in by Bradley, that without it the early capture of Cherbourg would be difficult if not almost impossible. Unless we could soon seize Cherbourg, the enemy's opportunity for hemming us in on a narrow beachhead might be so well exploited as to lead to the defeat of the operations. Rapid and complete success on Utah Beach was, we believed, prerequisite to real success in the whole campaign.

The only available beach on the Cotentin Peninsula was, however, a miserable one. Just back of it was a wide lagoon, passable only on a few narrow causeways that led from the beaches to the interior of the peninsula. If the exits of these causeways should be held by the enemy our landing troops would be caught in a trap and eventually slaughtered by artillery and other fire to which they would be able to make little reply.

To prevent this, we planned to drop two divisions of American paratroopers inland from this beach, with their primary mission to seize and hold the exits of the vital causeways. The ground was highly unsuited to airborne operations. Hedgerows in the so-called "bocage" country are big, strong, and numerous. The coast lines that the vulnerable transport planes and gliders would have to cross were studded with anti-aircraft. In addition, there were units of mobile enemy troops in the area and these, aside from mounting anti-aircraft fire, would attempt to operate against our paratroopers and glider troops before they could organize themselves for action.[35]

The whole project was much argued from its first proposing, but Bradley and Major General Matthew Ridgway, our senior American airborne general, always stoutly agreed with me as to its necessity and its feasibility. At an early date it was approved for inclusion in plans and I supposed the matter settled, but it was to come up again in dramatic fashion, just before D-day.

CARGO FOR INVASION

". . . we had . . . to build up on the beaches
the reserves in troops, ammunition, and supplies
that would enable us, within a reasonable time,
to initiate deep offensives . . ." *Page 235*

Ships, Troops, Trucks, Supply Crowd French Beach

AXIS ALLY—MUD

"Some soldier once said, 'The weather is always neutral.' Nothing could be more untrue." *Page 240*. In Tunis, Italy, and across the Continent, mud was a formidable barrier to Allied advances.

Even the Jeep Succumbed to Italian Mud

The staffs that were developing, co-ordinating, and recording all these details were, of course, working in constant co-operation with numerous agencies and personalities in London and Washington. During the preparatory period an endless stream of staff officers from Washington visited our headquarters to provide information on the availability of needed items, confirm dates of shipment, discuss plans for personnel replacements, for security, for photographic coverage, and a thousand related items.

One of General Somervell's principal assistants, Major General LeRoy Lutes, remained with us in Britain several weeks, investigating arrangements for insuring the uninterrupted flow of supplies all the way from the factories in the United States to the front line. At various times we had conferences with such people as Mr. Eden and Mr. Bevin of the British Cabinet, with Mr. Stimson and Mr. Stettinius from Washington, with Mr. Winant, Mr. Harriman, and Mr. Biddle, American representatives in London, and with General de Gaulle, who came up from Africa for the purpose. These conferences had to do with every type of subject, including that of future plans for controlling the areas in which we intended to operate and for governing Germany and Austria once we should reach those countries.

During all this period my personal contacts with the Prime Minister were frequent and profitable. He took a lively interest in every important detail, and was able to lend us an effective hand when some of our requirements demanded extra effort on the part of overloaded British civil agencies.

Visits to Chequers always had business as their main purpose. But the countryside was so pleasant and peaceful that an occasional hour spent in strolling through the fields and woods was real recreation. Chequers was at one time occupied by Cromwell; its setting, architecture, and furniture were all historically interesting.

The Prime Minister would usually ask his guests to arrive during the late afternoon. Dinner would be followed by a short movie and then, at about 10:30 p.m., business conferences would begin. These sometimes lasted until three the next morning. Nearly always present were Mr. Eden and one or more of the British Chiefs of Staff. Every type of problem was discussed and often definite decisions reached. Operational messages arrived every few hours from the London headquarters, and Mr. Churchill always participated with the British Chiefs in the formulation and dispatch of instructions, even those that were strictly military, sometimes only tactical, in character.

In such conferences as these I came to admire and like many of the people with whom I was so often in contact. One of them was Air Chief Marshal Sir Charles Portal, Air Member of the British Chiefs of Staff. He was a profound military student—but with it all a man of action—and quiet, courteous, of strong convictions. It was a pleasure to discuss with him any problem of war, whether or not it pertained exclusively to his own field of the air. He enjoyed great prestige in British military and civil circles, as well as among the Americans of the Allied command. His distinguishing characteristic was balance, with perfect control of his temper; even in the most intense argument I never saw him show anger or unusual excitement.

Mr. Churchill, on the other hand, rarely failed to inject into most conferences some element of emotion. One day a British general happened to refer to soldiers, in the technical language of the British staff officer, as "bodies." The Prime Minister interrupted with an impassioned speech of condemnation—he said it was inhuman to talk of soldiers in such cold-blooded fashion, and that it sounded as if they were merely freight—or worse—corpses! I must confess I always felt the same way about the expression, but on that occasion my sympathies were with the staff officer, who to his own obvious embarrassment had innocently drawn on himself the displeasure of the Prime Minister.

As in most other British homes, there was a guest book in Chequers. Each guest was expected to sign it every time he entered the house. Once, on a trip to the southern coast, I dropped in at Chequers to see Mr. Churchill for ten minutes, after which I dashed for the door to continue the journey. Just as I gained the seat of my car I became aware that the family butler, in all his dignity, was standing by to speak to me. He said, "Sir, you have forgotten the book," and his solemn tone meant to me that he found it difficult to forgive my oversight. I corrected the omission and sped upon my way.

In spite of all his preoccupations, Mr. Churchill constantly evidenced an intensely human side. When London had to endure the "Little Blitz" of February 1944 he took frequent occasion to urge me to occupy one of the specially built underground shelters in London. He even went to the extent of having an entire apartment, complete with kitchen, living room, bedroom, and secret telephones, fixed up for me. While I never used or even saw the place, yet he never ceased to show great concern for my safety, although paying absolutely no attention to his own. His single apparent desire, during an air raid, was to visit his daughter Mary, then serving in an anti-aircraft battery protecting London.

In all our conferences Mr. Churchill clearly and concretely explained his attitude toward and his hopes for Overlord. He gradually became more optimistic than he had earlier been, but he still refused to let his expectations completely conquer his doubts. More than once he said, "General, if by the coming winter you have established yourself with your thirty-six Allied divisions firmly on the Continent, and have the Cherbourg and Brittany peninsulas in your grasp, I will proclaim this operation to the world as one of the most successful of the war." And then he would add, "And if, in addition to this, you have secured the port at Le Havre and freed beautiful Paris from the hands of the enemy, I will assert the victory to be the greatest of modern times."

Always I would reply, "Prime Minister, I assure you that the coming winter will see the Allied forces on the borders of Germany itself. You are counting only on our presently available thirty-six divisions. We are going to bring in ten additional from the Mediterranean, and through the ports we capture we shall soon begin to rush in an additional forty from the United States."

He doubted that we could get the elbow room to do all this in the summer and fall of 1944 and often observed, "All that is for later; my statement still holds." In reply to my insistence that the picture I painted him was not too rosy, even if the German continued to fight to the bitter end, he would smile and say, "My dear General, it is always fine for a leader to be optimistic. I applaud your enthusiasm, but liberate Paris by Christmas and none of us can ask for more."

On April 7, General Montgomery was ready, with co-operating air and naval staffs, to present the completed picture of the detailed plan for the ground assault against the beaches. A huge conference was arranged in St. Paul's School in London and there an entire day was spent in presentation, examination, and co-ordination of detail.[36]

The plan carried the troops straight southward against the shore of France with the Americans on the right, the British and Canadians on the left. The extreme right flank of the assault was against Utah Beach on the Cherbourg peninsula, the left flank at approximately the mouth of the river Orne. The entire front of attack was over sixty miles long.[37]

Since our desire was to bring up close to the battle lines large numbers of fighter bombers and to seize areas in which our great tank strength could operate most effectively, the plan provided for the early capture by the British Second Army of the open plains lying south of Caen.[38] To the right of that city the Americans were to advance southward from Omaha Beach abreast of the British, while farther right Major General J. Lawton Collins' corps, after landing on Utah, was to make its principal objective the early capture of Cherbourg.[39] Because large German forces were located in the Calais area it seemed probable that to preserve communications between that region and Normandy the enemy would concentrate heavily in the Caen area. It was certain also that he would make desperate efforts to hold Cherbourg and so deny us the use of that port. Nevertheless, we hoped that speed and surprise would gain for us early possession of the open ground outside Caen, while Bradley estimated that the Americans would take Cherbourg in from ten to thirty days, depending upon the degree of luck we might enjoy.

Montgomery's detailed plan also indicated the areas that he estimated we would probably be holding in successive periods following the assault. These estimates are shown on map "Overlord Forecast."

The anticipated development pictured in the phase lines was not, of course, an essential feature of the landing plan, since the first and great objective was to assault and capture a satisfactory and indestructible beachhead which we could build up as rapidly as possible for the later decisive battle for France. But progress predictions are always helpful to the supply staffs in order that they may plan their own operations according to a concept that gives some idea of the scope of responsibilities they will be called upon to meet. The predicted ninety-day line was actually reached slightly ahead of schedule, but those forecast for the earlier days of the operation proved impossible of attainment. Out of this circumstance developed some difficulties.

The air plan, already in execution, called for the progressive wearing down of the Luftwaffe and the destruction of critical points in the rail and highway systems so as to isolate the coastal areas selected for assault. For D-day the air forces were charged with the responsibility of demolishing selected targets in the enemy's coastal defenses, of providing overhead cover and rendering general fighter-bomber support as the troops progressed inland.[40]

The naval plan was complicated by the configuration and nature of the coastal area, which provided little sea room for maneuver, and by the density and extent of mine fields. Nevertheless, the whole program of mine sweeping, escorting, preliminary bombardment, gunfire support, and general protection against enemy surface and submarine forces was provided for in detail.[41] The logistic plan for transportation, care, and maintenance of troops and forwarding of supplies was fully as comprehensive as any of the others.

On May 15 a final conference was held at St. Paul's School under the supervision of SHAEF.[42] At this final meeting every principal member of the British Chiefs of Staff and the War Cabinet attended, as did also the King of England and Allied generals by the score. Field Marshal Smuts came with his old friend, Mr. Churchill. During the whole war I attended no other conference so packed with rank as this one. The purpose was to assure that any doubtful points of the earlier conference would be ironed out and corrected. It also served to bring to the attention of all commanders the broad purposes of the highest headquarters and to give to each a fully completed and rounded picture of the support he could expect. Instructions for the briefing of small units and their care during the period of moving to the ports were checked and confirmed. Secrecy was a dominating factor.

This meeting gave us an opportunity to hear a word from both the King and the Prime Minister. The latter made one of his typical fighting speeches, in the course of which he used an expression that struck many of us, particularly the Americans, with peculiar force. He said, "Gentlemen, I am hardening toward this enterprise," meaning to us that, though he had long doubted its feasibility and had previously advocated its further postponement in favor of operations elsewhere, he had finally, at this late date, come to believe with the rest of us that this was the true course of action in order to achieve the victory. The whole meeting was packed with dramatic significance. It not only marked the virtual completion of all preliminary planning and preparation but seemed to impart additional confidence as each of the scores of commanders and staff officers present learned in detail the extent of the assistance he would receive for his own particular part of the vast undertaking.

Before the actual assault, operational portions of SHAEF and Twenty-first Army Group Headquarters were set up at Portsmouth on the south coast. This was the region of our principal embarkation point, and here also the Navy had established a communication system that would keep us in touch, during the early hours of D-day, with the progress of each element in the great armada.

By the time the operational staffs had moved to Portsmouth, I felt that the only remaining great decision to be faced before D-day was that of fixing, definitely, the day and hour of the assault. However, the old question of the wisdom of the airborne operation into the Cherbourg peninsula was not yet fully settled in Air Chief Marshal Leigh-Mallory's mind. Later, on May 30, he came to me to protest once more against what he termed the "futile slaughter" of two fine divisions. He believed that the combination of unsuitable landing grounds and anticipated resistance was too great a hazard to overcome. This dangerous combination was not present in the area on the left where the British airborne division would be dropped and casualties there were not expected to be abnormally severe, but he estimated that among the American outfits we would suffer some seventy per cent losses in glider strength and at least fifty per cent in paratroop strength before the airborne troops could land. Consequently the divisions would have no remaining tactical power and the attack would not only result in the sacrifice of many thousand men but would be helpless to effect the outcome of the general assault.

Leigh-Mallory was, of course, earnestly sincere. He was noted for personal courage and was merely giving me, as was his duty, his frank convictions.

It would be difficult to conceive of a more soul-racking problem. If my technical expert was correct, then the planned operation was worse than stubborn folly, because even at the enormous cost predicted we could not gain the principal object of the drop. Moreover, if he was right, it appeared that the attack on Utah Beach was probably hopeless, and this meant that the whole operation suddenly acquired a degree of risk, even foolhardiness, that presaged a gigantic failure, possibly Allied defeat in Europe.

To protect him in case his advice was disregarded, I instructed the air commander to put his recommendations in a letter and informed him he would have my answer within a few hours. I took the problem to no one else. Professional advice and counsel could do no more.

I went to my tent alone and sat down to think. Over and over I reviewed each step, somewhat in the sequence set down here, but more thoroughly and exhaustively. I realized, of course, that if I deliberately disregarded the advice of my technical expert on the subject, and his predictions should prove accurate, then I would carry to my grave the unbearable burden of a conscience justly accusing me of the stupid, blind sacrifice of thousands of the flower of our youth. Outweighing any personal burden, however, was the possibility that if he were right the effect of the disaster would be far more than local: it would be likely to spread to the entire force.

Nevertheless, my review of the matter finally narrowed the critical points to these:

If I should cancel the airborne operation, then I had either to cancel the attack on Utah Beach or I would condemn the assaulting forces there to even greater probability of disaster than was predicted for the airborne divisions.

If I should cancel the Utah attack I would so badly disarrange elaborate plans as to diminish chances for success elsewhere and to make later maintenances perhaps impossible. Moreover, in long and calm consideration of the whole great scheme we had agreed that the Utah attack was an essential factor in prospects for success. To abandon it really meant to abandon a plan in which I had held implicit confidence for more than two years.

Finally, Leigh-Mallory's estimate was just an estimate, nothing more, and our experience in Sicily and Italy did not, by any means, support his degree of pessimism. Bradley, with Ridgway and other airborne commanders, had always supported me and the staff in the matter, and I was encouraged to persist in the belief that Leigh-Mallory was wrong!

I telephoned him that the attack would go as planned and that I would confirm this at once in writing. When, later, the attack was successful he was the first to call me to voice his delight and to express his regret that he had found it necessary to add to my personal burdens during the final tense days before D-day.[43]

There was, of course, much to do aside from merely waiting to make the final decision concerning the timing of the attack. We had visits from many important officials. One of our final visitors was General de Gaulle, with whom some disagreement developed, involving the actual timing and nature of pronouncements to be made to the French population immediately upon landing. General de Gaulle wanted to be clearly and definitely recognized by both the Allied governments as the ruler of France. He insisted that he alone had the right to give orders to the French population in directing the necessary co-operation with the Allied forces.[44]

President Roosevelt was flatly opposed to giving General de Gaulle this specific and particular type of recognition. The President then, as always, made a great point of his insistence that sovereignty in France resided in the people, that the Allies were not entering France in order to force upon the population a particular government or a particular ruler. He asserted, therefore, that our proclamations should show that we were quite ready to co-operate with any French groups that would participate in the work of destroying the German forces. He agreed that if any or all of these groups chose to follow De Gaulle we would operate through his command, but the President could not agree to forcing De Gaulle upon anyone else.[45]

The attempt to work out a plan satisfactory to De Gaulle and still remain within the limits fixed by our governments fell largely to the lot of our headquarters and occasioned a great deal of worry because we were depending on considerable assistance from the insurrectionists in France. They were known to be particularly numerous in the Britanny area and in the hills and mountains of southeast France. An open clash with De Gaulle on this matter would hurt us immeasurably and would result in bitter recrimination and unnecessary loss of life.

The staff thought the argument was, in a sense, academic. It was considered that, in the initial stages of the operation at least, De Gaulle would represent the only authority that could produce any kind of French co-ordination and unification and that no harm would result from giving him the kind of recognition he sought. He would merely be placed on notice that once the country was liberated the freely expressed will of the French people would determine their own government and leader. We had already, with the consent of our governments, accepted De Gaulle's representative, General Koenig, as the commander of the French Forces of the Interior, who was serving as a direct subordinate of mine in the Allied organization.

We particularly desired De Gaulle to participate with me in broadcasting on D-day to the French people so that the population, avoiding uprisings and useless sacrifice at non-critical points, would still be instantly ready to help us where help was needed. We worked hard, within the limits of our instructions, to win De Gaulle to our point of view, but although after the campaign was started he co-operated with us effectively, he did not meet our requests at the moment.[46]

A number of other details remained to be ironed out during the days at Portsmouth preceding D-day, but the big question mark always before us was the weather that would prevail during the only period of early June that we could use, the fifth, sixth, and seventh.

All southern England was one vast military camp, crowded with soldiers awaiting final word to go, and piled high with supplies and equipment awaiting transport to the far shore of the Channel. The whole area was cut off from the rest of England. The government had established a deadline, across which no unauthorized person was allowed to go in either direction. Every separate encampment, barrack, vehicle park, and every unit was carefully charted on our master maps. The scheduled movement of each unit had been so worked out that it would reach the embarkation point at the exact time the vessels would be ready to receive it. The southernmost camps where assault troops were assembled were all surrounded by barbed-wire entanglements to prevent any soldier leaving the camp after he had once been briefed as to his part in the attack. The mighty host was tense as a coiled spring, and indeed that is exactly what it was—a great human spring, coiled for the moment when its energy should be released and it would vault the English Channel in the greatest amphibious assault ever attempted.

We met with the Meteorologic Committee twice daily, once at nine-thirty in the evening and once at four in the morning. The committee, comprising both British and American personnel, was headed by a dour but canny Scot, Group Captain J. M. Stagg. At these meetings every bit of evidence was carefully presented, carefully analyzed by the experts, and carefully studied by the assembled commanders. With the approach of the critical period the tension continued to mount as prospects for decent weather became worse and worse.

The final conference for determining the feasibility of attacking on the tentatively selected day, June 5, was scheduled for 4:00 a.m. on June 4. However, some of the attacking contingents had already been ordered to sea, because if the entire force was to land on June 5, then some of the important elements stationed in northern parts of the United Kingdom could not wait for final decision on the morning of June 4.

When the commanders assembled on the morning of June 4 the report we received was discouraging. Low clouds, high winds, and formidable wave action were predicted to make landing a most hazardous affair. The meteorologists said that air support would be impossible, naval gunfire would be inefficient, and even the handling of small boats would be rendered difficult. Admiral Ramsay thought that the mechanics of landing could be handled, but agreed with the estimate of the difficulty in adjusting gunfire. His position was mainly neutral. General Montgomery, properly concerned with the great disadvantages of delay, believed that we should go. Tedder disagreed.

Weighing all factors, I decided that the attack would have to be postponed.[47] This decision necessitated the immediate dispatch of orders to the vessels and troops already at sea and created some doubt as to whether they could be ready twenty-four hours later in case the next day should prove favorable for the assault. Actually the maneuver of the ships in the Irish Sea proved most difficult by reason of the storm. That they succeeded in gaining ports, refueling, and readying themselves to resume the movement a day later represented the utmost in seamanship and in brilliant command and staff work.

The conference on the evening of June 4 presented little, if any, added brightness to the picture of the morning, and tension mounted even higher because the inescapable consequences of postponement were almost too bitter to contemplate.

At three-thirty the next morning our little camp was shaking and shuddering under a wind of almost hurricane proportions and the accompanying rain seemed to be traveling in horizontal streaks. The mile-long trip through muddy roads to the naval headquarters was anything but a cheerful one, since it seemed impossible that in such conditions there was any reason for even discussing the situation.

When the conference started the first report given us by Group Captain Stagg and the Meteorologic Staff was that the bad conditions predicted the day before for the coast of France were actually prevailing there and that if we had persisted in the attempt to land on June 5 a major disaster would almost surely have resulted. This they probably told us to inspire more confidence in their next astonishing declaration, which was that by the following morning a period of relatively good weather, heretofore completely unexpected, would ensue, lasting probably thirty-six hours. The long-term prediction was not good but they did give us assurance that this short period of calm weather would intervene between the exhaustion of the storm we were then experiencing and the beginning of the next spell of really bad weather.

The prospect was not bright because of the possibility that we might land the first several waves successfully and then find later build-up impracticable, and so have to leave the isolated original attacking forces easy prey to German counteraction. However, the consequences of the delay justified great risk and I quickly announced the decision to go ahead with the attack on June 6. The time was then 4:15 a.m., June 5. No one present disagreed and there was a definite brightening of faces as, without a further word, each went off to his respective post of duty to flash out to his command the messages that would set the whole host in motion.[48]

A number of people appealed to me for permission to go aboard the supporting naval ships in order to witness the attack. Every member of a staff can always develop a dozen arguments why he, in particular, should accompany an expedition rather than remain at the only post, the center of communications, where he can be useful. Permission was denied to all except those with specific military responsibility and, of course, the allotted quotas of press and radio representatives.

Among those who were refused permission was the Prime Minister. His request was undoubtedly inspired as much by his natural instincts as a warrior as by his impatience at the prospect of sitting quietly back in London to await reports. I argued, however, that the chance of his becoming an accidental casualty was too important from the standpoint of the whole war effort and I refused his request. He replied, with complete accuracy, that while I was in sole command of the operation by virtue of authority delegated to me by both governments, such authority did not include administrative control over the British organization. He said, "Since this is true it is not part of your responsibility, my dear General, to determine the exact composition of any ship's company in His Majesty's Fleet. This being true," he rather slyly continued, "by shipping myself as a bona fide member of a ship's complement it would be beyond your authority to prevent my going."

All of this I had ruefully to concede, but I forcefully pointed out that he was adding to my personal burdens in this thwarting of my instructions. Even, however, while I was acknowledging defeat in the matter, aid came from an unexpected source. I later heard that the King had learned of the Prime Minister's intention and, while not presuming to interfere with the decision reached by Mr. Churchill, he sent word that if the Prime Minister felt it necessary to go on the expedition he, the King, felt it to be equally his duty and privilege to participate at the head of his troops. This instantly placed a different light upon the matter and I heard no more of it.[49]

Nevertheless, my sympathies were entirely with the Prime Minister. Again I had to endure the interminable wait that always intervenes between the final decision of the high command and the earliest possible determination of success or failure in such ventures. I spent the time visiting troops that would participate in the assault. A late evening trip on the fifth took me to the camp of the U. S. 101st Airborne Division, one of the units whose participation had been so severely questioned by the air commander. I found the men in fine fettle, many of them joshingly admonishing me that I had no cause for worry, since the 101st was on the job and everything would be taken care of in fine shape. I stayed with them until the last of them were in the air, somewhere about midnight. After a two-hour trip back to my own camp, I had only a short time to wait until the first news should come in.

Chapter 14

D-DAY AND
LODGMENT

THE FIRST REPORT CAME FROM THE AIRBORNE units I had visited only a few hours earlier and was most encouraging in tone. As the morning wore on it became apparent that the landing was going fairly well. Montgomery took off in a destroyer to visit the beaches and to find a place in which to set up his own advanced headquarters. I promised to visit him on the following day.

Operations in the Utah area, which involved the co-ordination of the amphibious landing with the American airborne operation, proceeded satisfactorily, as did those on the extreme left flank. The day's reports, however, showed that extremely fierce fighting had developed in the Omaha sector. That was the spot, I decided, to which I would proceed the next morning.

We made the trip in a destroyer and upon arrival found that the 1st and 29th Divisions, assaulting on Omaha, had finally dislodged the enemy and were proceeding swiftly inland. Isolated centers of resistance still held out and some of them sustained a most annoying artillery fire against our beaches and landing ships. I had a chance to confer with General Bradley and found him, as always, stouthearted and confident of the result. In point of fact the resistance encountered on Omaha Beach was at about the level we had feared all along the line. The conviction of the German that we would not attack in the weather then prevailing was a definite factor in the degree of surprise we achieved and accounted to some extent for the low order of active opposition on most of the beaches. In the Omaha sector an alert enemy division, the 352d, which prisoners stated had been in the area on maneuvers and defense exercises, accounted for some of the intense fighting in that locality.[1]

During the course of the day I made a tour along all the beaches, finding opportunities to confer with principal commanders, including Montgomery. Toward evening and while proceeding at high speed along the coast, our destroyer ran aground and was so badly damaged that we had to change to another ship for the return to Portsmouth.

The next few days thoroughly taxed the soundness of the build-up plan that had been so patiently devised over many months. On the whole it stood the strain exceedingly well, but here and there emergency conditions of the battlefield demanded minor changes in plan and my location at Portsmouth enabled these to be executed swiftly and smoothly.

Unforeseen difficulties are always certain to develop in the execution of a plan of this kind; frequently they involve two or more of the services. They are easily enough handled if the high command is alert to the situation and in position instantly to make a decision that prevents the difficulty from assuming unnecessary proportions. For example, where planned naval schedules are exceeded, or loading and unloading facilities suffer damage, ships begin to pile up either in debarkation or embarkation points. This represents waste when time is vital and shipping is a bottleneck. Confusion is likely to develop unless someone with authority is in position to make necessary decisions quickly. To take care of this type of difficulty a staff agency, comprising representatives from all services, had been set up. Through it was satisfactorily handled the matter of insuring the availability and loading of troops and supplies at ports and co-ordinating these with the arrival and dispatch of ships. We had remarkably little trouble, once the difficult initial days were behind us.

We soon learned that strain had also been developing in Washington during the long preinvasion period of preparation. We were scarcely well on the beaches when General Marshall, Admiral King, General Arnold, and a group from their respective staffs arrived in England. I arranged to take them into the beachhead during the day of June 12. Their presence, as they roamed around the areas with every indication of keen satisfaction, was heartening to the troops. The importance of such visits by the high command, including, at times, the highest officials of government, can scarcely be overestimated in terms of their value to soldiers' morale. The soldier has a sense of gratification whenever he sees very high rank in his particular vicinity, possibly on the theory that the area is a safe one or the rank wouldn't be there.

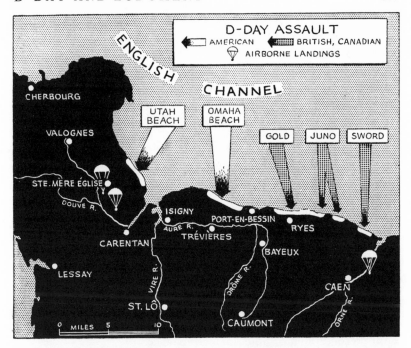

The period from D-day to our decisive breakout on July 25 was a definite phase of the Allied operation and has received the name "Battle of the Beachhead."

Interest in battles of the past, for soldier and civilian alike, often centers around points that were either of no great moment at the time of their happening or did not impress the actors as being so. An extraordinary amount of research and analysis, to say nothing of charge and countercharge, frequently concerns the originator of an idea; the detail in which developments conformed to preconceived plans; the inspiration for given decisions and the influence of particular individuals upon particular actions.

The Battle of the Normandy Beachhead proved no exception to this rule. A deal of froth and fury, as well as much painstaking and objective research, has been devoted to the support of individual theories concerning matters which, had they been recognized at the time as of special later value, might have been settled for all time by the maintenance of written record.

Fortunately most soldiers in war become very objective and the judgment of history does not seem as important, in the midst of battle, as does victory. Moreover, the lack of time and the demands upon the attention of all commanders and staff officers preclude the keeping of day-by-day and minute-by-minute accounts of everything that happens. Many significant actions are initiated by verbal contact, and frequently no record is kept. Battle orders, even for large formations, are often written after instructions have been issued in an exhaustive conference. Notes of the actual discussions do not exist. Moreover, later curiosity so often concerns itself with responsibility for thought and idea, rather than with events and results, that possibly even the most painstaking amanuensis could not leave any clear and unchallengeable account of all the occurrences that go to make up a campaign.

Concerning the origination of plans and decisions: it is my conviction that no commander could normally take oath that a particular plan or conception originated within his own mind. Preoccupation with the concerns of his command are such that it is impossible for any person later to say whether the first gleam of an idea that may eventually have developed into a great plan came from within his own brain or from some outside suggestion. One of his problems is to keep his mind open, to avoid confusing necessary firmness with stubborn preconception or unreasoning prejudice.

Another point: there is a vast difference between a definite plan of battle or campaign and the hoped-for eventual results of the operation. In committing troops to battle there are certain minimum objectives to be attained, else the operation is a failure. Beyond this lies the area of reasonable expectation, while still further beyond lies the realm of hope—all that might happen if fortune persistently smiles upon us.

A battle plan normally attempts to provide guidance even into this final area, so that no opportunity for extensive exploitation may be lost through ignorance on the part of the troops concerning the intent of the commander. These phases of a plan do not comprise rigid instructions, they are merely guideposts. A sound battle plan provides flexibility in both space and time to meet the constantly changing factors of the battle problem in such a way as to achieve the final goal of the commander. Rigidity inevitably defeats itself, and the analysts who point to a changed detail as evidence of a plan's weakness are completely unaware of the characteristics of the battlefield.

The Battle of the Beachhead was a period of incessant and heavy fighting and one which, except for the capture of Cherbourg, showed few geographical gains. Yet it was during this period that the stage was set for the later, spectacular liberation of France and Belgium. The struggle in the beachhead was responsible for many developments, both material and doctrinal, that stood us in good stead throughout the remainder of the war.

Knowing that his old antagonist of the desert, Rommel, was to be in tactical charge of the defending forces, Montgomery predicted that enemy action would be characterized by constant assaults carried out by any force immediately available from division down to battalion or even company size. He discounted the possibility that the enemy under Rommel would ever select a naturally strong defensive line and calmly and patiently go about the business of building up the greatest possible amount of force in order to launch one full-out offensive into our beach position. Montgomery's predictions were fulfilled to the letter.[2]

From the day we landed the battle never settled down, except in isolated spots, to anything resembling the trench warfare of the first World War. But it was the possibility of such an eventuality that we could never forget, particularly our British comrades with their memories of Vimy Ridge and Passchendaele.

Bradley had predicted that the capture of Cherbourg was going to be a rather nasty job and counted on speed and boldness as much as upon the strength of his assaulting forces to gain an early decision in that area. His estimate was "ten days if we are lucky, thirty if we are not." Among other things, all such predictions depended, of course, upon our success in maintaining the scheduled build-up. The landing tables provided in great detail for the daily and hourly arrival of given quantities of every kind of fighting unit, sandwiched in between the ammunition and other supplies which were required, not only for the daily operations but to provide the reserves to sustain continuous action once we should pass to the decisive stages of the battle.

On the eastward flank, the city of Caen did not fall to our initial rush as we had hoped and we were consequently unable to gain the ground south and southeast of that city where we had planned to make early exploitation of our tank and combat air strength. But the battling in that area reached a sustained and intensive pitch: Rommel defended tenaciously, and as the fighting progressed it became clear why it was necessary for him to do so.

To support the divisions in the attack area the enemy first drew into the battle zone all the troops he could spare from the Brittany Peninsula. Next he brought up divisions from the south of France and others from the Low Countries. His only remaining major reserves in northwest Europe not committed to the fighting were in and about Calais, in the German Fifteenth Army. To maintain connection with these troops he had to hold Caen. If he lost that city his two principal forces would be divided and could thenceforth operate together only if both executed a long withdrawal. So to Caen he hurried his strongest and best divisions, and made every possible preparation to hold it to the end.[3]

Our frustration in the attainment of our immediate tactical goals in the eastern sector involved no change in the broad purposes of the operational plan. It was merely another example of the age-old truth that every battle plan comprises merely an orderly commitment of troops to battle under the commander's calculations of desirable objectives and necessary resources, but always with the certainty that enemy reaction will require constant tactical adjustment to the requirements of the moment. As quickly as it became certain that the enemy intended at all costs to hang onto Caen as the hinge of his operations it instantly became to our advantage to keep him so preoccupied in that region that all other Allied operations would be facilitated.

On the far western flank General Collins' VII Corps initially attacked straight westward to cut the peninsula in two. He then turned swiftly toward Cherbourg but had also to establish on his southward flank a secure line to block any enemy reinforcements attempting to push into the peninsula.[4]

On June 12, 1944, the first flying bomb, known as V-1, reached London. The V-1 was a small pilotless airplane which flew at high speed on a predetermined course and terminated its flight by means of settings in its mechanism. It contained a large amount of explosive which detonated upon contact, and the blast effect was terrific.[5] The first V-2 was not used until early August. It was a rocket, shot into the air to a great height, which fell at such high speed that the first warning of its coming was the explosion. During flight it could not be heard, seen, or intercepted and for these reasons was never as terrifying as the V-1.

The V-2 bomb was particularly destructive when it fell directly into a structure of some kind. Owing to its speed, it penetrated deeply into the ground and its great explosive effect was exerted directly upward. As a consequence, when it fell into open spaces it was relatively ineffective, but so great was its explosive charge when it hit a building that destruction was almost complete.[6]

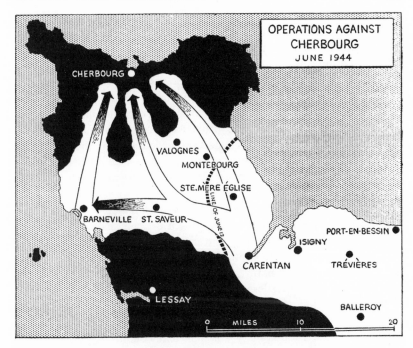

The development and employment of these weapons were undoubtedly greatly delayed by our spring bombing campaign against the places where we suspected they were under manufacture. Peenemünde, in Germany, was known to be one of the largest of the German experimental plants and periodically we sent large formations of bombers to attack that area. There were other places indicated to us as suspicious. One was Trondheim, in Norway, where we thought that the Germans were engaged in atomic development. We also bombed the suspected launching sites along the coast of northwestern Europe, where our reconnaissance photography showed numerous facilities and installations that could not be interpreted in terms of any known weapon. These areas were continuously hammered.[7]

The effect of the new German weapons was very noticeable upon morale. Great Britain had withstood terrific bombing experiences. But when in June the Allies landed successfully on the Normandy coast the citizens unquestionably experienced a great sense of relief, not only at the prospect of victory but in the hope of gaining some insurance against future bombings. When the new weapons began to come over London in considerable numbers their hopes were dashed. Indeed, the depressing effect of the bombs was not confined to the civilian population; soldiers at the front began again to worry about friends and loved ones at home, and many American soldiers asked me in worried tones whether I could give them any news about particular towns where they had previously been stationed in southern England.

It seemed likely that, if the German had succeeded in perfecting and using these new weapons six months earlier than he did, our invasion of Europe would have proved exceedingly difficult, perhaps impossible. I feel sure that if he had succeeded in using these weapons over a six-month period, and particularly if he had made the Portsmouth–Southampton area one of his principal targets, Overlord might have been written off.

Defensive measures against the V-1 soon attained a very high degree of efficiency, but even so, the threat of their arrival was always present at all hours of the day and night and in all kinds of weather. We in the field wanted to capture the areas from which these weapons were fired against southern England. However, it must be said to the credit of the British leaders that never once did one of them urge me to vary any detail of my planned operations merely for the purpose of eliminating this scourge.

On June 18, Montgomery still felt that conditions permitted the early capture of Caen. His directive of that date stated: "It is clear that we must now capture Caen and Cherbourg, as the first step in the full development of our plans. Caen is really the key to Cherbourg. . . ." In the same directive he gave the following instructions to the British Army: "The immediate task of this Army will be to capture Caen." The final sentence of that order was: "I shall hope to see both Caen and Cherbourg captured by June 24."³

On the left the German armor and defensive strength continued to defeat our intentions, but the port of Cherbourg fell on June 26, just twenty days after the landing. General Collins had conducted against it a relentless offensive and as a result of the operation justified his nickname, "Lightning Joe." The final assault was materially assisted by heavy and accurate naval gunfire.

In the matter of luck we had enjoyed a rough medium between Bradley's minimum and maximum estimates of the influence of this imponderable factor. Our good luck was largely represented in the degree of surprise that we achieved by landing on Utah Beach, which the Germans considered unsuited to major amphibious operations, and by the effective action of the two airborne divisions, the 82d and the

101st, which had landed almost in the center of the peninsula. Our bad luck was in the hurricane that struck us on June 19. It stopped for a period of four days nearly all landing activity on the beaches and therefore interfered seriously with every operation; it was so fierce in character as to render offensive fighting extremely difficult.

During that time sea communications between the United Kingdom and the Continent were completely interrupted and it was almost impossible to land an airplane on the small landing strips we had constructed in the bridgehead. The mulberry at Omaha Beach in the American sector suffered damage beyond repair. Great numbers of ships and small vessels were grounded or hurled onto the beach.[9]

Conditions would have been ideal for a German counterattack except for the prior effectiveness of the air forces' campaign of isolation. Here, as always, was emphasized the decisive influence of air power in the ground battle.

On the day of the storm's ending I flew from one end of our beach line to the other and counted more than 300 wrecked vessels above small-boat size, some so badly damaged they could not be salvaged.

When the storm struck, one American division, the 83d, was still lying in its ships just off the beach. Bulk unloading was out of the question and so during the entire storm the division underwent an extremely uncomfortable and trying experience. I visited the men of that division the day they finally got ashore and found a number of them still seasick and temporarily exhausted.

There was no sight in the war that so impressed me with the industrial might of America as the wreckage on the landing beaches. To any other nation the disaster would have been almost decisive; but so great was America's productive capacity that the great storm occasioned little more than a ripple in the development of our build-up.

With the capture of Cherbourg the work of port rehabilitation was started immediately. The Germans had accomplished major demolitions and had planted in the harbor and its approaches a profusion and variety of mines. Some of the new types of mines could be removed only by deep-sea divers, who had to descend to the bottom to disarm the mines. The work of the mine sweepers and the deep-sea divers in Cherbourg Harbor was dramatic and courageous.[10]

During the twenty days required by the U. S. VII Corps to capture Cherbourg, the fighting was continuous throughout the remainder of the front, with only local gains anywhere, and almost stalemate in the Caen sector. The sketch shows our lines on June 12 and 26.

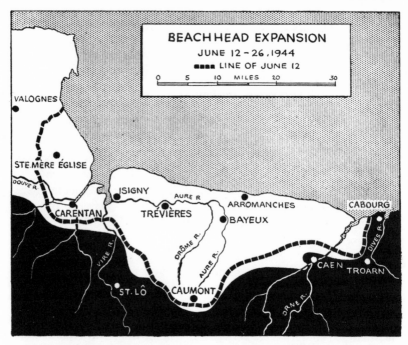

BEACHHEAD EXPANSION
JUNE 12 - 26, 1944
▰▰▰▰ LINE OF JUNE 12
0   5   10   MILES   20   30

VALOGNES

STE.MÈRE ÉGLISE

DOUVE R.

ISIGNY
AURE R
ARROMANCHES
CABOURG

CARENTAN
TRÉVIÈRES
BAYEUX

VIRE R.
DRÔME R.
AURE R.
DIVES R.
CAEN
TROARN

ST.LÔ
CAUMONT
ORNE R.

   Montgomery's tactical handling of the British and Canadians on the eastward flank and his co-ordination of these operations with those of the Americans to the westward involved the kind of work in which he excelled. He well understood the personal equation of the British soldier, and the morale of his forces remained high, in spite of frustrations and losses that could easily have shaken troops under a commander in whom they did not place their implicit trust.

   General Bradley displayed qualities of steadfastness, drive, professional skill, and a capacity for human understanding which became so obvious to his subordinates and his superiors alike that the American teamwork forged on the many battlefields of the Normandy beachhead was never thereafter seriously shaken. He was then commanding the First Army. Major General Elwood R. Quesada, a young and active air commander, was in charge of the tactical air groupments immediately supporting him. The mutual confidence they developed, the systems and methods they worked out for battlefield co-ordination, and the spirit they infused among all their subordinates, were in pleasing contrast to other cases that I had encountered early in the war. The Navy likewise fitted perfectly into the picture. The accomplishments in

Europe of the three United States services operating under unified command strongly influenced my determined advocacy of a similar type of organization in postwar Washington.

During the early stages of the battle my own life was one of almost incessant travel. A visit to Montgomery, Bradley, or to troops on the front would be immediately followed by a period of activity in the Portsmouth headquarters, where the work of co-ordinating and adjusting shipments and major phases of planning was interspersed with countless interviews and conferences. Along with this there was of course a constant need to visit formations still in England and destined for early entry into battle.

One incident, pleasing to me personally and indicative of General Marshall's constant thoughtfulness for his subordinates, was the arrival of my son in the theater about the middle of June. He graduated from West Point on D-day and, with General Marshall's approval, was given authority to spend his short graduation leave with me in the battle area, subject only to the proviso that he return to the United States in time to enter upon his advanced training by July 1. He traveled with me everywhere, and his sole disappointment was my refusal to interfere in the normal routine for a young graduate and assign him to one of the infantry divisions then in Europe.

Both the British and American forces were building up steadily in strength. In spite of the interruptions and destruction due to the great storm of the nineteenth, the delays imposed were only temporary and interfered little with the execution of final plans.

The steady arrival of fresh troops made it possible to keep up the offensive, but under unfavorable conditions of terrain and weather. On the east our purpose was now to contain the maximum amount of the German forces, on the west to make sufficient progress so that the final and co-ordinated drive to break out of the restricted beachhead could be delivered.[11]

Late June was a difficult period for all of us. More than one of our high-ranking visitors began to express the fear that we were stalemated and that those who had prophesied a gloomy fate for Overlord were being proved correct. A grave risk that always accompanies an amphibious undertaking against a continental land mass is finding itself sealed off in a beachhead. Adequate elbow room is a prerequisite to the build-up of troops and supplies necessary to a decisive, mobile battle.

When possibilities of supply and reinforcement, as well as terrain, favor the defense, there exists the chance that in spite of successful landing the battlefield may thus easily become a draining sore in the side of the attacker rather than the opening stages of a destructive campaign against the defender's main forces. This had been the Allied experience at Gallipoli in the first World War, an experience that was partially repeated, for some months in the early part of 1944, in the Anzio operation. Such a possibility had, of course, been thoroughly examined and planned against, long before D-day. Our greatest asset in defeating it lay in our air and sea power. With the first we were confident of disrupting enemy supply and communication, of impeding troop movements, and of beating down prepared defenses. Through sea power and the development of artificial ports we had a rugged and effective system of supply and reinforcement. We were confident, consequently, that in the build-up race we were sure to win. Beyond this, a possible countermove was the launching of a secondary amphibious and possibly airborne effort against the Brittany Peninsula.

Early planning placed a very great importance on the ports in that area, and we believed that, if the enemy should denude his defenses there in an effort to present an impregnable line in front of our Normandy landings, we could accomplish a surprise move into the Brittany region which would threaten to take him in flank and rear. In this connection we had already learned that the Germans never deliberately evacuated a port without leaving behind them a desolation and destruction that rendered rapid repair extremely difficult; therefore the particular spot we had decided upon as most useful for supply and maintenance purposes in Brittany was Quiberon Bay, a large, well-sheltered, but undeveloped harbor on the southern flank of the peninsula's base.

As June faded into July we closely watched the situation to determine whether or not a secondary landing would prove profitable to us. More and more I turned against it. One reason was that our air forces and our deceptive threats were preventing the Germans from building up an impregnable line in front of our Normandy forces. Moreover, I knew that any attempt to stage a secondary landing would occasion delay in the direct build-up of our forces and supplies on the main front. I still believed we would have to make major use of the Brittany ports, but I believed that by continuing our attacks we would get them sooner than by lessening the weight of our blows on the main front to allow the mounting of the secondary attack.

I spent much time in France, conferring frequently with General Bradley and General Montgomery concerning timing and strength of projected battle operations.[12] Such visits with Bradley were always enjoyable because he shared my liking for roaming through the forward areas to talk to the men actually bearing the burden of battle. Many of our personal conferences, throughout the war, were conducted during the trips we so often made together to the fighting troops.

A sergeant who accompanied me everywhere in France was a motorcycle policeman named Sidney Spiegel. His personal loyalty and his anxiety to protect and assist me knew no bounds. He was always particularly careful about his soldierly appearance, and no matter what the miserable conditions of road travel, he never delayed shining up his motorcycle and making of himself a model in soldierly appearance upon arrival at our destination. When finally we were separated I lost a devoted friend and a valued assistant.

During this period I kept up a written, telephonic, and radio correspondence with both Bradley and Montgomery. At the end of June the beachhead area was still too restricted to permit Supreme Headquarters to begin its move to France, but in order to be in constant touch with senior ground commanders I started my personal headquarters detachment to France during July. The battle for position and of building up reserves progressed at times with disappointing slowness and inspired the press in both Britain and America to sharp criticism. The writers could not, of course, know the facts. If everything in war were a matter of common knowledge there would be no opportunity to surprise an alert enemy.

In temporary stalemates, however, there always exists the problem of maintaining morale among fighting men while they are suffering losses and are meanwhile hearing their commanders criticized. The commentators' voices came into every squad and platoon over the tiny radios that soldiers would never abandon.

The effect of carping becomes more serious when soldiers find it also in letters from relatives at home who have been led to expect the impossible. Among green troops the problem is much more serious than among veterans. The attitude of the latter was well expressed in a remark made to me one day by a sergeant, who with his railway unit was waiting to go farther to the front in order to start some needed construction. He said, "General, on the map this job looked easy, but now the Heinies seem to have something to say about it. But there is nothing wrong with us that a good, rousing victory won't cure."

Chapter 15

BREAKOUT

THE FIRST CRITICAL OBJECTIVE OF THE NORmandy campaign, which was to establish a secure beachhead with adequate avenues of supply in the area between Cherbourg and the mouth of the Orne, was fully accomplished by the end of June.[1]

From the beginning it was the conception of Field Marshal Montgomery, Bradley, and myself that eventually the great movement out of the beachhead would be by an enormous left wheel, bringing our front onto the line of the Seine, with the whole area lying between that river and the Loire and as far eastward as Paris in our firm possession. This did not imply the adoption of a rigid scheme of grand tactics. It was merely an estimate of what we believed would happen when once we could concentrate the full power of our air-ground-naval team against the enemy we expected to meet in northwest France.

An important point in our calculations was the line from which we originally intended to execute this wheel. This part of our tactical prognostications did not work out and required adjustment. The plan, formally presented by Montgomery on May 15, stated: "Once we can get control of the main enemy lateral Granville–Vire–Argentan–Falaise–Caen, and the area enclosed in it is firmly in our possession, then we will have the lodgment area we want and can begin to expand."

This line we had hoped to have by June 23, or D plus 17.[2] In his more detailed presentation of April 7, Montgomery stated that the second great phase of the operation, estimated to begin shortly after D plus 20, would require the British Army to pivot on its left at Falaise, to "swing with its right toward Argentan–Alençon." This meant that Falaise would be in our possession before the great wheel began. The line that we actually held when the breakout began on D plus 50 was approximately that planned for D plus 5.

This was a far different story, but one which had to be accepted. Battle is not a one-sided affair. It is a case of action and reciprocal action repeated over and over again as contestants seek to gain position and other advantage by which they may inflict the greatest possible damage upon their respective opponents.

In this case the importance of the Caen area to the enemy had caused him to use great force in its defense. Its capture became a temporary impossibility or, if not that, at least an operation to be accomplished at such cost as to be almost prohibitive.

Naturally this development caused difficulties. Had we been successful in our first rush in gaining the open ground south of Caen, the advance of the Americans to the Avranches region might have become, instead of the dogged battle that it was, a mere push against German withdrawals. That is, greater initial success on our left should have made easier attainment, on our right, of a satisfactory jump-off line from which to initiate the great wheel.

As the days wore on after the initial landing the particular dissatisfaction of the press was directed toward the lack of progress on our left. Naturally I and all of my senior commanders and staff were greatly concerned about this static situation near Caen. Every possible means of breaking the deadlock was considered and I repeatedly urged Montgomery to speed up and intensify his efforts to the limit. He threw in attack after attack, gallantly conducted and heavily supported by artillery and air, but German resistance was not crushed.

Further, one must realize that when the enemy, by intensive action or concentration of forces, succeeds in balking a portion of our own forces, he usually does so at the expense of his ability to support adequately other portions of the field. In this instance, even though the breakout would now have to be initiated from farther back than originally planned, it was obvious that if the mass of enemy forces could be held in front of Caen there would be fewer on the western flank to oppose the American columns. This was indeed fortunate in view of the difficult type of country through which the Americans would have to advance. These developments were constantly discussed with Bradley and Montgomery; the latter was still in charge of tactical co-ordination of ground forces in the crowded beachhead.

By June 30, Montgomery had obviously become convinced, as Bradley and I already had, that the breakout would have to be launched from the more restricted line. His directive of that date clearly stated that the British Second Army on the left would continue its attacks to attract the greatest possible portion of enemy strength, while the American forces, which had captured Cherbourg four days before, would begin attacking southward with a view to final breakout on the right flank.[3] From that moment onward this specific battle plan did not vary, and although the nature of the terrain and enemy resistance combined with weather to delay the final all-out attack until July 25, the interim was used in battling for position and in building up necessary reserves.

This, of course, placed upon the American forces a more onerous and irksome task than had at first been anticipated. However, Bradley thoroughly understood the situation of the moment and as early as June 20 had expressed to me the conviction that the breakout on the right would have to be initiated from positions near St. Lô, rather than from the more southerly line originally planned. He sensed the task with his usual imperturbability and set about it in workmanlike fashion. He rationed the expenditure of ammunition all along the front, rotated troops in the front lines, and constantly kept his units and logistic elements in such condition as to strike suddenly and with his full power when the opportunity should present itself.

Complicating the problem of the breakout on the American front was the prevalence of formidable hedgerows in the bocage country. In this region the fields have for centuries past been divided into very small areas, sometimes scarcely more than building-lot size, each surrounded by a dense and heavy hedge which ordinarily grows out of a bank of earth three or four feet in height. Sometimes these hedges and supporting banks are double, forming a ready-made trench between them, and of course affording almost the ultimate in battlefield protection and natural camouflage. In almost every row were hidden machine gunners or small combat teams who were in perfect position to decimate our infantry as they doggedly crawled and crept to the attack along every avenue of approach.

Our tanks could help but little. Each, attempting to penetrate a hedgerow, was forced to climb almost vertically, thus exposing the unprotected belly of the tank and rendering it easy prey to any type of armor-piercing bullet. Equally exasperating was the fact that, with the tank snout thrust skyward, it was impossible to bring guns to bear upon the enemy; crews were helpless to defend themselves or to destroy the German.

In this dilemma an American sergeant named Culin came forth with a simple invention that restored the effectiveness of the tank and gave a tremendous boost to morale throughout the Army. It consisted merely in fastening to the front of the tank two sturdy blades of steel which, acting somewhat as scythes, cut through the bank of earth and hedges. This not only allowed the tank to penetrate the obstacle on an even keel and with its guns firing, but actually allowed it to carry forward, for some distance, a natural camouflage of amputated hedge.⁴

As soon as Sergeant Culin had demonstrated his invention to his captain it was speedily brought to the attention of General Walter M. Robertson of the 2d Division. He, in turn, demonstrated the appliance to Bradley, who set about the task of equipping the greatest possible number of tanks in this fashion so as to be ready for the coming battle. A feature of the incident from which our soldiers derived a gleeful satisfaction was that the steel for the cutting blades was obtained from the obstacles which the German had installed so profusely over the beaches of Normandy to prevent our landing on that coast.

However, we were still without this contrivance when the First Army began its tedious southward advance to achieve a reasonable jump-off line for the big attack. It was difficult to obtain any real picture of the battle area. One day a few of us visited a forward observation tower located on a hill, which took us to a height of about a hundred feet above the surrounding hedgerows. Our vision was so limited that I called upon the air forces to take me in a fighter plane along the battle front in an effort to gain a clear impression of what we were up against. Unfortunately, even from the vantage point of an altitude of several thousand feet there was not much to see that could be classed as helpful. As would be expected under such conditions, the artillery, except for long-range harassing fire, was of little usefulness. It was dogged "doughboy" fighting at its worst. Every division that participated in it came out of that action hardened, battle-wise, and self-confident.

Tactics, logistics, and morale—to these three the higher commanders and staffs devoted every minute of their time. Tactics to gain the best possible line from which to launch the great attack against the encircling forces. Logistics to meet our daily needs and to build up the mountains of supplies and to bring in the reserve troops we would need in order to make that attack decisive. And always we were concerned in morale because troops were called upon constantly to engage in hard fighting but denied the satisfaction of the long advances that invariably fill an army with élan. By July 2, 1944, we had landed in Normandy about 1,000,0ᴏᴜ men, including 13 American, 11 British, and 1 Canadian divisions. In the same period we put ashore 566,648 tons of supplies and 171,532 vehicles. It was all hard and exhausting work but its accomplishment paid off in big dividends when finally we were ready to go full out against the enemy. During these first three weeks we took 41,000 prisoners. Our casualties totaled 60,-771, of whom 8975 were killed.[5]

During the battling in the beachhead a particular development was our continued progress in the employment of air forces in direct support of the land battle. Perfection in ground-air co-ordination is difficult if not impossible to achieve.

When a pilot in a fighter bomber picks up a target on the ground below it is easily possible for him to mistake its identity. He may be ten to fifteen thousand feet in the air and unless visibility is perfect he may have difficulty in identifying the exact spot on the ground over which he is flying. In his anxiety to help his infantry comrades he may suddenly decide that the gun or truck or unit he sees on the ground belongs to the enemy, and the instant he does so he starts diving on it at terrific speed. Once having made his decision, his entire concentration is given to his target; his purpose is to achieve the greatest possible amount of destruction in the fleeting moment available to him. Only incessant training and indoctrination, together with every kind of appropriate mechanical aid, can minimize the danger of mistaken identification and attack on our own forces.

One method we used was to put an air liaison detachment in a tank belonging to the attacking unit. Each such detachment was given a radio capable of communicating with planes in the air, and through this means we not only helped to avoid accidents but were able to direct the airplane onto specific and valuable targets. The ground and air, between them, developed detailed techniques and mechanisms for improvement, with a noticeable degree of success.[6]

Accidents in the other direction were just as frequent. More than one friendly pilot attempting to co-operate with the ground troops has been greeted with a storm of small-arms fire and many returned to their bases bitterly complaining that the infantry did not seem to want friendly planes around. In the early days in Africa these accidents were almost daily occurrences; by the time we had won the Battle of the Beachhead they had practically ceased.

Within the high command a clear appreciation of the relationship between the strategic bombing effort in the German homeland and the needs of the land forces was essential if we were to work in common purpose and achieve the greatest possible result. As this appreciation developed among air as well as ground commanders, the early reluctance of such specialists as Air Chief Marshal Harris and General Doolittle, who commanded respectively the bomber forces of Great Britain and the U. S. Eighth Air Force, to employ their formations against so-called tactical targets completely disappeared. By the time the breakout was achieved, the emergency intervention of the entire bomber force in the land battle had come to be accepted almost as a matter of course.

To this general rule there was one notable exception. The U. S. 30th Division by unfortunate accident suffered considerable casualties from our own bombing effort, an incident that was repeated later in the campaign. To the end of the war the commander of this particular division insisted that when given attack missions he wanted no heavy or medium bombers to participate.[7]

It became necessary to specify a date on which the whole ground organization should take on its final form—that is, with each army group reporting directly to Supreme Headquarters. We planned to bring Patton's army into operation on August 1, and with this development the Twelfth Army Group, under Bradley's command, would be established in France. Command of the First Army would then pass to Lieutenant General Courtney H. Hodges, who, during the early battling, served as Bradley's deputy. However, what could not then be foreseen was the time required to effect the eventual breakout, the completion of the enemy's defeat in close fighting on the Normandy front, and the eventual sorting out of army groups, each into its own main channel of invasion.

Until this should come about and while all forces were operating toward the common purpose of destroying the German forces on our immediate front, it was clear that one battle commander should stay in co-ordinating authority over the whole line. Our estimate of the date that these conditions would prevail was September 1 and senior commanders were notified that on that date each army group would operate in direct subordination to Supreme Headquarters.[8] Fortunately my personal headquarters was located so conveniently to the headquarters of both Montgomery and Bradley that I could visit each easily.[9]

The July battling all along the front involved some of the fiercest and most sanguinary fighting of the war. On the American front every attack was channelized by swamps and streams and the ground was unusually advantageous to the defense. Many of Bradley's subordinates made names for themselves during this period, clearly establishing their right to be numbered among the best of America's tacticians. Our corps and division commanders, to say nothing of hundreds of more junior officers, generally demonstrated qualities of leadership and tactical skill that stamped them as top-flight battle leaders; the same was true in the armies of our Allies. And among our troops, whatever their nationality or flag, stubborn courage was an outstanding characteristic that boded inevitable defeat for the enemy.

Just after the middle of July the U. S. First Army attained, on its portion of the front, the line—St. Lô to the west coast—from which it could launch a powerful assault. At that moment the weather, which had been bad, grew abominably worse and for the following week all of us went through a period of agonizing tenseness. We had to draw plans to take advantage of the first favorable break in the weather, and yet we wanted to avoid the constant alerting and shifting of troops entailed by frequent initiation and postponement of orders. Earlier in the war the period would have had a most serious effect upon morale and efficiency, but the American troops had by this time become battle-wise and they passed through the ordeal of waiting like veterans.

Finally on July 25, seven weeks after D-day, the attack was launched, from the approximate line we had expected to hold on D plus 5, stretching from Caen through Caumont to St. Lô. A tremendous carpet, or area, bombing was placed along the St. Lô sector of the American front and its stunning effect upon the enemy lasted throughout the day. Unfortunately a mistake by part of the bombing forces caused a considerable number of casualties in one battalion of the 9th Division and in the 30th Division, and killed General McNair, who had gone into an observation post to watch the beginning of the attack. His death cast a gloom over all who had known this most able and devoted officer.[10]

Progress on the first day was slow, but that evening General Bradley observed to me that it was always slow going in the early phases of such an attack and expressed the conviction that the next day and thereafter would witness extraordinary advances by our forces. The event proved him to be completely correct. In the following week he slashed his way downward to the base of the peninsula, passing through the bottleneck at Avranches, and launched his columns into

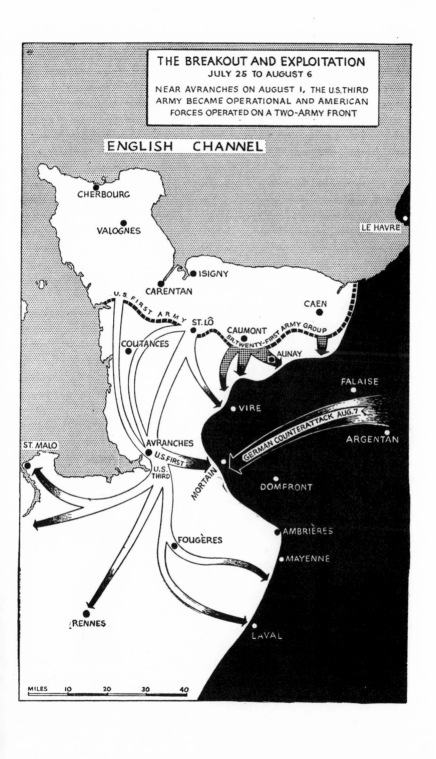

THE BREAKOUT AND EXPLOITATION
JULY 25 TO AUGUST 6

NEAR AVRANCHES ON AUGUST 1, THE U.S. THIRD
ARMY BECAME OPERATIONAL AND AMERICAN
FORCES OPERATED ON A TWO-ARMY FRONT

ENGLISH CHANNEL

CHERBOURG

VALOGNES

LE HAVRE

ISIGNY

CARENTAN

U.S. FIRST ARMY

ST. LÔ

CAUMONT

CAEN

BR. TWENTY-FIRST ARMY GROUP

COUTANCES

AUNAY

FALAISE

VIRE

GERMAN COUNTERATTACK AUG. 7

ST. MALO

AVRANCHES

U.S. FIRST

ARGENTAN

U.S.
THIRD

MORTAIN

DOMFRONT

AMBRIÈRES

FOUGÈRES

MAYENNE

RENNES

LAVAL

MILES   10   20   30   40

the rear of the German forces. At this moment, on August 1, General Patton, with Third Army Headquarters, was brought up into the battle to take charge of the operations on the First Army's right flank.[11] Montgomery, at the same time, still confronted by German defenses in depth, shifted his weight from Caen to his right at Caumont and drove for the high ground between the Vire and the Orne.

With a clean and decisive breakout achieved, Bradley's immediate problem became that of inflicting on the enemy the greatest possible destruction. All else could wait upon his exploitation of this golden opportunity, in the certainty that with the enemy destroyed everything else could quickly be set right. His scheme was to throw every unit he could spare elsewhere directly at the rear of the German forces still in place between Caen and the vicinity of Avranches. In effect, he hoped to encircle the enemy forces, which were still compelled to face generally northward against the Canadians and British.[12]

To carry out this general idea, the first change in original plans was in the reduction of the size of the force allocated for the capture of the Brittany Peninsula. Instead of committing to this mission the bulk of the Third Army, General Patton was directed to send back into that area only the VIII Corps, under Major General Troy H. Middleton.[13]

As the enemy saw the American First Army attack gather momentum to the southward and finally break through the Avranches bottleneck, his reaction was swift and characteristic. Chained to his general position by Hitler's orders as well as by the paralyzing action of our air forces, he immediately moved westward all available armor and reserves from the Caen area to counterattack against the narrow strip through which American forces were pouring deep into his rear. His attack, if successful, would cut in behind our breakout troops and place them in a serious position. Because our corridor of advance was still constricted the German obviously felt that the risks he was assuming were justified even though, in case of his own failure, the destruction he would suffer would be vastly increased. His attacks, which were thrown in at the town of Mortain, just east of Avranches, began on August 7.[14]

The air co-operation against the enemy attack was extraordinarily effective. The United States Ninth Air Force and the RAF destroyed hundreds of enemy tanks and vehicles. The Royal Air Force had a large number of Typhoons equipped with rocket-firing devices. These made low-flying attacks against the enemy armor and kept up a sustained assault against his forces that was of great help to the defending infantry.[15]

Bradley and I, aware that the German counterattack was under preparation, carefully surveyed the situation. We had sufficient strength in the immediate area so that if we chose merely to stand on the defensive against the German attack he could not possibly gain an inch. However, to make absolutely certain of our defenses at Mortain, we would have to diminish the number of divisions we could hurl into the enemy's rear and so sacrifice our opportunity to achieve the complete destruction for which we hoped. Moreover, by this time the weather had taken a very definite turn for the better and we had in our possession an Air Transport Service that could deliver, if called upon, up to 2000 tons of supplies per day in fields designated by any of our forces that might be temporarily cut off.

When I assured Bradley that even under a temporary German success he would have this kind of supply support, he unhesitatingly determined to retain only minimum forces at Mortain, and to rush the others on south and east to begin an envelopment of the German spearheads. I was in his headquarters when he called Montgomery on the telephone to explain his plan, and although the latter expressed a degree of concern about the Mortain position, he agreed that the prospective prize was great and left the entire responsibility for the matter in Bradley's hands. Montgomery quickly issued orders requiring the whole force to conform to this plan, and he, Bradley, and Lieutenant General Miles Dempsey, commanding the British Second Army, met to co-ordinate the details of the action.[16]

Another factor that justified this very bold decision was the confidence that both Bradley and I had now attained in our principal battle commanders. In Patton, who took command of the Third Army on the right immediately after the breakout was achieved, we had a great leader for exploiting a mobile situation. On the American left we had sturdy and steady Hodges to continue the pressure on the Germans, while in both armies were battle-tested corps and division commanders. They could be depended upon in any situation to act promptly and effectively without waiting for detailed instructions from above.

Bradley's judgment as to his ability to hold the Mortain hinge was amply demonstrated by events but the whole situation is yet another example of the type of delicate decision that a field commander is frequently called upon to make in war. Had the German tanks and infantry succeeded in breaking through at Mortain, the predicament of all troops beyond that point would have been serious, in spite of our ability partially to supply them by airplane. While there was no question in our minds that we could eventually turn the whole thing into a victory even if the German should succeed temporarily in this interruption of our communications, yet had the enemy done so the necessary retrograde movements of our own troops and the less satisfactory results achieved would have undoubtedly been publicly characterized as a lost battle.

There were many points of similarity between this situation and the one that developed some four months later in the Ardennes, which resulted in the Battle of the Bulge. In both cases our long-term calculations proved correct but in the one the German achieved temporary success, while at Mortain he was repulsed immediately and materially added to the severity of his own battle losses.

The enemy concentrated the bulk of his available armor at Mortain and continued his obstinate attack until August 12. By this time Bradley's planned movements were developing satisfactorily.

On General Bradley's directive, General Patton had sent the XV Corps, commanded by Major General Wade H. Haislip, straight southward to the town of Laval. East of Laval it turned north on Argentan. The XII Corps, under command of Major General Gilbert R. Cook, was ordered to advance on Orléans on the Third Army's south flank; and the XX Corps, commanded by Major General Walton H. Walker, was directed on Chartres. Later, the XIX Corps, under Major General Charles H. Corlett, also participated in the envelopment. The Canadian First Army was directed by Montgomery to continue to thrust southward on Falaise with a view to linking up with the Americans at Argentan, to close the net around the enemy forces still west of that point. Meanwhile the U. S. First Army and the British Second Army would both drive toward the trapped Germans to accomplish their rapid destruction.[17]

The enveloping movement from the south therefore had as its first objective the destruction or capture of the German forces in the Mortain–Falaise region, while at the same time there remained the opportunity for sweeping up remaining portions of the German First and Seventh Armies by directing an even wider employment toward the crossings of the Seine River. The operation assumed this over-all picture: Montgomery's army group was attacking generally southward against the old Normandy beachhead defenses, while Bradley's forces, with their left anchored near the position of the initial break-through,

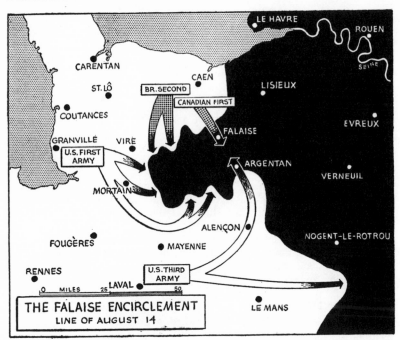

THE FALAISE ENCIRCLEMENT
LINE OF AUGUST 14

were carrying out the great envelopments intended to trap the entire German force still between his marching columns and the front of the British Twenty-first Army Group. In the meantime the Allied air forces kept up an incessant battering against any possible crossings of the Seine so as to impede the escape of any German forces that might try to cross to the north of that river before the trap could be closed. Perfection of co-ordination in such an operation is difficult to achieve.

By the night of August 13, the U. S. 5th Armored Division under General Oliver, a veteran of the African campaign, was in the outskirts of Argentan. The French 2d Armored Division under General Jacques LeClerc was near by and the U. S. 79th and 90th Divisions were in close support. The Germans were still fighting desperately just south of Caen, where by this time they had established the strongest defenses encountered throughout the entire campaign.[18] The Canadians threw in fierce and sustained attacks but it was not until August 16 that Falaise was finally captured. Caen, by then a heap of rubble, had been captured on July 9.[19]

By late July the enemy was bringing reinforcements across the

Seine as rapidly as he could. Five divisions entered the battle area during the week August 5–12 but, as before, they were unable to affect the outcome.

On August 13, I sent a personal message to the Allied command that, in part, read:

> Because this opportunity may be grasped only through the utmost in zeal, determination and speedy action, I make my present appeal to you more urgent than ever before.
>
> I request every airman to make it his direct responsibility that the enemy is blasted unceasingly by day and by night, and is denied safety either in fight or in flight.
>
> I request every sailor to make sure that no part of the hostile forces can either escape or be reinforced by sea, and that our comrades on the land want for nothing that guns and ships and ships' companies can bring to them.
>
> I request every soldier to go forward to his assigned objective with the determination that the enemy can survive only through surrender: let no foot of ground once gained be relinquished nor a single German escape through a line once established.[20]

With the great bulk of all the Allied forces attacking from the perimeter of a great half-circle toward a common center, the determination of the exact points on which each element should halt, in order not to become involved against friendly units coming from the opposite direction, was a tricky problem.

In this instance Bradley's troops, marching in the great wheel, had much farther to go to close the trap than did the British and Canadian troops. On the other hand, the latter were still faced up against prepared defenses and their movement was limited to the advances they could make through heavily defended areas. Montgomery kept in close touch with the situation but so rapid was the movement of the Americans that it was almost impossible to achieve the hour-by-hour co-ordination that might have won us a complete battle of annihilation.

Mix-ups on the front occurred, and there was no way to halt them except by stopping troops in place, even at the cost of allowing some Germans to escape. In the aggregate considerable numbers of Germans succeeded in getting away. Their escape, however, meant an almost complete abandonment of their heavy supply and was accomplished only by terrific sacrifices.

I was in Bradley's headquarters when messages began to arrive from commanders of the advancing American columns, complaining that the limits placed upon them by their orders were allowing Germans to escape. I completely supported Bradley in his decision that it was necessary to obey the orders, prescribing the boundary between the army groups, exactly as written; otherwise a calamitous battle between friends could have resulted.

In the face of complete disaster the enemy fought desperately to hold open the mouth of the closing pocket so as to save as much as he could from the debacle. German commanders concentrated particularly on saving armored elements, and while a disappointing portion of their Panzer divisions did get back across the Seine, they did so at the cost of a great proportion of their equipment. Eight infantry divisions and two Panzer divisions were captured almost in their entirety.

The battlefield at Falaise was unquestionably one of the greatest "killing grounds" of any of the war areas. Roads, highways, and fields were so choked with destroyed equipment and with dead men and animals that passage through the area was extremely difficult. Forty-eight hours after the closing of the gap I was conducted through it on foot, to encounter scenes that could be described only by Dante. It was literally possible to walk for hundreds of yards at a time, stepping on nothing but dead and decaying flesh.

In the wider sweep directed against the crossings of the Seine behind the German Army, the rapidly advancing Americans were also forced to halt to avoid overrunning their objectives and firing into friendly troops. The German again seized the opportunity to escape with a greater portion of his strength than would have been the case if the exact situation could have been completely foreseen.[21]

While the bulk of Bradley's forces was engaged in these great battles and overrunning France toward Paris, General Middleton's VIII Corps turned back to the westward to overrun the Brittany Peninsula and to capture the ports in that area. We were still of the belief that some use would have to be made of Quiberon Bay and possibly of Brest. Middleton was directed to capture these places as quickly as possible. He made a rapid advance and invested St. Malo, a small port on the north coast of the Brittany Peninsula. The garrison resisted fanatically but Middleton was able, with co-operating air and naval forces, to bring to bear enough power to reduce it by August 14, although remnants of the garrison held out for three more days in the citadel of the town. Middleton then pushed on to the westward and reached the vicinity of Brest. The commander of the German garrison there was named Ramcke, a formidable fighter.

Middleton vigorously prosecuted the siege but the defenses were strong and the garrison was determined. Any attempt to capture the place in a single assault would be extremely costly to us. Fortunately our prospects for securing better ports than Brest began to grow much brighter just after the middle of August, and in any event we had never counted on the use of that place so much as we had on Quiberon Bay. In these circumstances Middleton was directed to avoid heavy losses in the Brest area but was also directed to continue the pressure until the garrison should surrender.[22]

I visited him during the conduct of the siege and surveyed the defenses that we would have to overcome. He skillfully kept up a series of attacks, each designed to minimize our own losses but constantly to crowd the enemy back into a more restricted area, where he was intermittently subjected to bombing by our aircraft.

In the garrison was a contingent of German SS troops. Instead of concentrating them as a unit, General Ramcke distributed them among all other German formations in the defenses. In this way he used the fanaticism of the SS troopers to keep the entire garrison fighting desperately, because at any sign of weakening an SS trooper would execute the offender on the spot.

Brest fell on September 19. The harbor and its facilities had been so completely wrecked by our bombing and by German demolitions that we never made any attempt to use it.[23]

When the Allied armies finally completed their envelopment of the German forces west of the Seine the eventual defeat of the German in western Europe was a certainty. The question of time alone remained. A danger, however, that immediately presented itself was that our own populations and their governments might underrate the task still to be accomplished, and so might slacken the home-front effort, which could have the gravest consequences. I not only brought this danger to the attention of my superiors, but as early as August 15 held a press conference, predicting that there was one more critical task remaining to the Allied forces—the destruction of the German armies along the general line of the Siegfried and the Rhine.[24] This word of caution was swept away in the general rejoicing over the great victory, and even among the professional leaders of the fighting forces there grew an optimism, almost a lightheartedness, that failed to look squarely in the face such factors as the fanaticism of great portions of the German

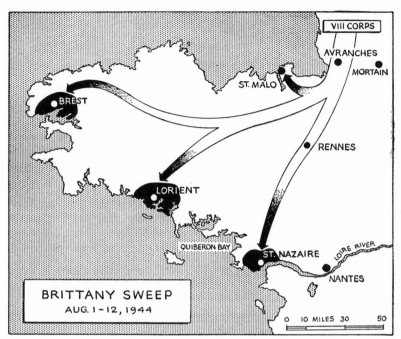

BRITTANY SWEEP
AUG. 1 - 12, 1944

0 10 MILES 30 50

Army and the remaining strength of a nation that was inspired to desperate action, if by no other means than the Gestapo and Storm Troopers, who were completely loyal to their master, Hitler.

Our new situation brought up one of the longest-sustained arguments that I had with Prime Minister Churchill throughout the period of the war. This argument, beginning almost coincidentally with the break-through in late July, lasted throughout the first ten days of August. One session lasted several hours. The discussions involved the wisdom of going ahead with Anvil, by then renamed Dragoon, the code name for the operation that was to bring in General Devers' forces through the south of France.

One of the early reasons for planning this attack was to achieve an additional port of entry through which the reinforcing divisions already prepared in America could pour rapidly into the European invasion. The Prime Minister held that we were now assured of early use of the Brittany ports and that the troops then in the Mediterranean could be brought in via Brittany, or even might better be used in the prosecution of the Italian campaign with the eventual purpose of invading the Balkans via the head of the Adriatic.[25]

To any such change I was opposed, and since the United States Chiefs of Staff, following their usual practice, declined to interfere with the conclusions of the commander in the field, I instantly became the individual against whom the Prime Minister directed all his argument. In brief he advanced the following points:

We no longer had any need of the port of Marseille and the line of communication leading northward from it. Troops in America could come in via Brittany.

The attack through the south of France was so far removed geographically from the troops in northern France that there was no tactical connection between them.

The troops to be used under General Devers in the southern invasion would have more effect in winning the war by driving forward in Italy and into the Balkans and threatening Germany from the south than they would by pursuing the originally planned line of action.

Our entry into the Balkans would encourage that entire region to flame into open revolt against Hitler and would permit us to carry to the resistance forces arms and equipment which would make the efforts of these forces more effective.

My own stand was defined generally as follows:

Experience of the past proved that we were likely to be vastly disappointed in the usefulness of the Brittany ports. Not only did we expect them to be stubbornly defended but we were certain they would be effectively destroyed once we had captured them. We did not expect this destruction to be so marked at Marseille because we knew that a large portion of the defending forces had already been drawn northward to meet our attacks. Capture should be so swift as to allow little time for demolition.

The distance from Brest to the Metz region was greater than the distance from Marseille to Metz. The railway lines connecting the two former points were much more tortuous and were more easily damaged than was the case with regard to the lines up the Rhone River.

Unless Marseille were captured, we would be unable to speed up the arrival of American divisions from the homeland.

The entry of a sizable force into southern France provided definite tactical and strategic support to our own operation.

First, it would protect and support the right flank as we continued our advance toward the heart of the German resistance. Secondly, by joining it to our own right flank we would automatically cut off all regions westward of that point, capture the enemy troops remaining back of the point of junction, and free all of France to assist us both passively and actively.

Without the Dragoon attack we would have to protect our right flank all the way from the base of the Brittany Peninsula to the most forward point of our attacking spearheads. This would have meant the immobilization of large numbers of divisions, stationed along the right merely to insure our own safety against raids by small mobile forces. These defending divisions could scarcely have participated in later aggressive action.

As yet we had secured as a permanent port only Cherbourg. The lines leading out of it were entirely incapable of maintaining our fighting forces along the front. Our maintenance and administrative position would never be equal to the final conquest of Germany until we had secured Antwerp on the north and Marseille or equivalent port facilities on our right. Once we had accomplished this, I was certain, we could marshal on the borders of Germany a sufficient strength, both in troops and in supplies, to launch final and decisive offensives that would knock Germany completely out of the war. Without such facilities we would inevitably outrun our maintenance capacity. We would then find ourselves in a position such as the British had so often experienced in their advances westward from Egypt, an experience that was repeated by Rommel when he finally attained the El Alamein line and was then unable to exploit his advantage.

Another factor was that the American Government had gone to great expense to equip and supply a number of French divisions. These troops naturally wanted to fight in the battle for the liberation of France. At no other point would they fight with the same ardor and devotion, and nowhere else could they obtain needed replacements for battle losses. These troops were located in Italy and North Africa, and the only way they could be brought quickly into the battle was through the opening in the south of France.

I firmly believed that the greatest possible concentration of troops should be effected on the great stretch between Switzerland and the North Sea, whence we would most quickly break into the heart of Germany and join up eventually with the Red forces advancing from the east.[26]

In sustaining his argument, the Prime Minister pictured a bloody prospect for the forces attacking from the south. He felt sure they would be involved for many weeks in attempts to reduce the coastal defenses and feared they could not advance as far northward as Lyon in less than three months. He thought we would suffer great losses and insisted that the battlefield in that region would become merely another Anzio. It is possible the Prime Minister did not credit the authenticity of our Intelligence reports, but we were confident that few German forces other than largely immobile divisions remained in the south. Consequently we were sure that the German defensive shell would be quickly pierced and that Devers' troops would pour northward at a rapid pace.

Although I never heard him say so, I felt that the Prime Minister's real concern was possibly of a political rather than a military nature.

He may have thought that a postwar situation which would see the Western Allies posted in great strength in the Balkans would be far more effective in producing a stable post-hostilities world than if the Russian armies should be the ones to occupy that region. I told him that if this were his reason for advocating the campaign into the Balkans he should go instantly to the President and lay the facts, as well as his own conclusions, on the table. I well understood that strategy can be affected by political considerations, and if the President and the Prime Minister should decide that it was worth while to prolong the war, thereby increasing its cost in men and money, in order to secure the political objectives they deemed necessary, then I would instantly and loyally adjust my plans accordingly. But I did insist that as long as he argued the matter on military grounds alone I could not concede validity to his arguments.

I felt that in this particular field I alone had to be the judge of my own responsibilities and decisions. I refused to consider the change so long as it was urged upon military considerations. He did not admit that political factors were influencing him, but I am quite certain that no experienced soldier would question the wisdom, strictly from the military viewpoint, of adhering to the plan for attacking southern France.[27]

As usual the Prime Minister pursued the argument up to the very moment of execution. As usual, also, the second that he saw he could not gain his own way, he threw everything he had into support of the operation. He flew to the Mediterranean to witness the attack and I heard that he was actually on a destroyer to observe the supporting bombardment when the attack went in.

In this long and serious argument the Prime Minister was supported by certain members of his staff. On the other hand, British officers assigned to my own headquarters stood firmly by me throughout.

Although in the planning days of early 1944, Montgomery had advocated the complete abandonment of the southern operation in order to secure more landing craft for Overlord, he now, in early August, agreed with me that the attack should go in as planned.

Coincidentally with this drawn-out discussion, Montgomery suddenly proposed to me that he should retain tactical co-ordinating control of all ground forces throughout the campaign. This, I told him, was impossible, particularly in view of the fact that he wanted to retain at the same time direct command of his own army group. To my mind and to that of my staff the proposition was fantastic. The reason for having an army group commander is to assure direct, day-by-day battlefield direction in a specific portion of the front, to a degree impossible to a supreme commander. It is certain that no one man could perform this function with respect to his own portion of the line and at the same time exercise logical and intelligent supervision over any other portion. The only effect of such a scheme would have been to place Montgomery in position to draw at will, in support of his own ideas, upon the strength of the entire command.

A supreme commander in a situation such as faced us in Europe cannot ordinarily give day-by-day and hour-by-hour supervision to any portion of the field. Nevertheless, he is the one person in the organization with the authority to assign principal objectives to major formations. He is also the only one who has under his hand the power to allot strength to the various major commands in accordance with their missions, to arrange for the distribution of incoming supply, and to direct the operations of the entire air forces in support of any portion of the line. The existence, therefore, of any separate ground headquarters between the supreme commander and an army group commander would have placed such a headquarters in an anomalous position, since it would have had the power neither to direct the flow of supply and reinforcement nor to give instructions to the air forces for the application of their great power.

Modern British practice had been, however, to maintain three commanders in chief, one for air, one for ground, one for navy. Any departure from this system seemed to many inconceivable and to invite disaster. I carefully explained that in a theater so vast as ours each army group commander would be the ground commander in chief for his particular area; instead of one there would be three so-called commanders in chief for the ground and each would be supported by his own tactical air force. Back of all would be the power of the supreme commander to concentrate the entire air forces, including the bomber commands, on any front as needed, while the strength of each army group would be varied from time to time depending on the importance of enemy positions to the progress of the whole force.

While my decision was undoubtedly distasteful to individuals who had been raised in a different school, it was accepted. In different form the question was raised at a later stage of the campaign, but the decision was always the same.[28]

In spite of such occasional differences of conviction, there was in our day-by-day operations, month after month, a degree of teamwork and intensive co-operation that made incidents such as I have described exceptional. When these exceptions arose they had to be thrashed out firmly and decisively and an answer given. The wonder is that so few of them ever became of a serious nature.

Field Marshal Montgomery, like General Patton, conformed to no type. He deliberately pursued certain eccentricities of behavior, one of which was to separate himself habitually from his staff. He lived in a trailer, surrounded by a few aides. This created difficulties in the staff work that must be performed in timely and effective fashion if any battle is to result in victory. He consistently refused to deal with a staff officer from any headquarters other than his own, and, in argument, was persistent up to the point of decision.

The harm that this practice could have created was minimized by the presence in the Twenty-first Army Group of a chief of staff who had an enviable reputation and standing in the entire Allied Force. He was Major General Francis de Guingand, "Freddy" to all his associates in SHAEF and in other high headquarters. He lived the code of the Allies and his tremendous capacity, ability, and energy were always devoted to the co-ordination of plan and detail that was absolutely essential to victory.

Montgomery is best described by himself in a letter he wrote to me shortly after the victory was won in Europe. He said:

Dear Ike:

Now that we have all signed in Berlin I suppose we shall soon begin to run our own affairs. I would like, before this happens, to say what a privilege and an honor it has been to serve under you. I owe much to your wise guidance and kindly forbearance. I know my own faults very well and I do not suppose I am an easy subordinate; I like to go my own way.

But you have kept me on the rails in difficult and stormy times, and have taught me much.

For all this I am very grateful. And I thank you for all you have done for me.

Your very devoted friend,

Monty[29]

In my reply I said, with complete truth:

Your own high place among military leaders of your country is firmly fixed, and it has never been easy for me to disagree with what I knew to be your real convictions. But it will always be a great privilege to bear evidence to the fact that whenever decision was made, regardless of your personal opinion, your loyalty and efficiency in execution were to be counted upon with certainty.[30]

Another interesting, if less pressing, discussion took place with Secretary Morgenthau. In a visit to our headquarters in early August 1944 he said that the rate of monetary exchange, to be eventually established in Germany, should be such as to avoid giving that country any advantage. I candidly told him that I had been far too busy to be specifically concerned with the future economy of Germany but that I had an able staff section working on the problem. This brought about a general conversation on the subject of Germany's future and I expressed myself roughly as follows.

"These things are for someone else to decide, but my personal opinion is that, following upon the conclusion of hostilities, there must be no room for doubt as to who won the war. Germany must be occupied. More than this, the German people must not be allowed to escape a sense of guilt, of complicity in the tragedy that has engulfed the world. Prominent Nazis, along with certain industrialists, must be tried and punished. Membership in the Gestapo and in the SS should be taken as *prima facie* evidence of guilt. The General Staff must be broken up, all its archives confiscated, and members suspected of complicity in starting the war or in any war crime should be tried. The German nation should be responsible for reparations to such countries as Belgium, Holland, France, Luxembourg, Norway, and Russia. The warmaking power of the country should be eliminated. Possibly this could be done by strict controls on industries using heavy fabricating machinery or by the mere expedient of preventing any manufacture of airplanes. The Germans should be permitted and required to make their own living, and should not be supported by America. Therefore choking off natural resources would be folly."

I emphatically repudiated one suggestion I had heard that the Ruhr mines should be flooded. This seemed silly and criminal to me. Finally, I said that the military government of Germany should pass from military to civil hands as quickly as this could be accomplished.

These views were presented to everyone who queried me on the subject, both then and later. They were eventually placed before the President and the Secretary of State when they came to Potsdam in July 1945.

Chapter 16

PURSUIT AND THE BATTLE OF SUPPLY

DURING THE PERIOD OF THE BATTLE OF THE Beachhead the enemy kept his Fifteenth Army concentrated in the Calais region. He was convinced that we intended to launch an amphibious attack against that fortress stronghold and as a result stubbornly refused to use those forces to reinforce the Normandy garrison. We employed every possible ruse to confirm him in his misconception; General McNair, for instance, was in the European theater so that we could refer to him, semipublicly, as an army commander, although his army was a phantom only. His name was kept on the censored list, but we took care to see that, in the United Kingdom, the secret was an open one. Thus any Axis agent would feel certain that knowledge of his presence was important information, to be passed promptly to the Germans who, we hoped, would interpret his "army's" mission to be an assault against the Pas de Calais front.

Finally the enemy began to obtain a clearer view of the situation; we quickly knew this. Identification of hostile units on the front is one of the continuous objectives of all battlefield Intelligence activities. From this information we daily constructed, normally with remarkable accuracy, the "Enemy Order of Battle," which revealed in late July that the German had started the divisions of the Fifteenth Army across the Seine to join in the battle. They were too late. Every additional soldier who then came into the Normandy area was merely caught up in the catastrophe of defeat, without exercising any particular influence upon the battle. In that defeat were involved, also, a number of divisions that the enemy had been able to spare from the south of France, from Brittany, from Holland, and from Germany itself. When the total of these reinforcements had not proved equal to the task of stopping us, the enemy was momentarily helpless to present any continuous front against our advance.

When General Patton's Third Army Headquarters came into action on August 1 our ground organization expanded to four armies. On the right was the U. S. Third Army under General Patton. Next to him the U. S. First Army under General Hodges. These two, forming the U. S. Twelfth Army Group, were under command of General Bradley. On the left was the British Twenty-first Army Group under General Montgomery. His group comprised the British Second Army under General Dempsey and the Canadian First Army under Lieutenant General Henry D. G. Crerar. The British air force supporting General Montgomery's army group was commanded by Air Marshal Coningham. General Bradley's army group was supported by the U. S. Ninth Air Force commanded by Major General Hoyt S. Vandenberg. Subordinate to General Vandenberg were Major General Otto R. Weyland, in charge of the Tactical Air Command supporting General Patton's Third Army, and General Quesada, who commanded the air units supporting Hodges' army.

In each of these armies and army groups the normal mission of the associated air forces was to carry out attacks requested by the respective ground commanders. However, all tactical air units were subordinate to Leigh-Mallory and consequently all, both American and British, could in emergency be employed as a mass against any target designated by SHAEF. A typical example of unified action was the work of the British air forces in helping to defeat the German attack against Mortain in Bradley's sector. Owing to this flexibility in command, the Tactical Air Forces were also available, when needed, to support the big bombers, even when the bombers were proceeding to penetrations deep within Germany.

By the end of August the approximate strength of the Allied forces on the Continent was twenty American divisions, twelve British divisions, three Canadian divisions, one French, and one Polish division. There were no more British divisions available, but in the United Kingdom were an additional six American divisions, including three airborne. The operational strength of all available air forces was approximately 4035 heavy bombers, 1720 light, medium, and torpedo bombers, and 5000 fighters. Added to all this was the Troop Transport Command, which, counting both American and British formations, numbered more than 2000 transport planes.[1]

Against a defeated and demoralized enemy almost any reasonable risk is justified and the success attained by the victor will ordinarily be measured in the boldness, almost foolhardiness, of his movements. The whole purpose of the costly break-through and the whirlwind attacks of the succeeding three weeks was to produce just such a situation as now confronted us; we had been preparing our plans so as to reap the richest harvest from the initial success. But the difficulties of supply, once our columns began their forward race, was a problem that required effective solution if we were to gain our full battle profit.

Our logistic formations had been confined in a very restricted area during the entire Battle of the Beachhead. The only operating ports were Cherbourg and the artificial port on the British beaches near Arromanches. The repair of Cherbourg had presented many difficulties. The harbor and approaches had to be cleared of hundreds of mines, many of them of new and particularly efficient types. We began using the port in July, but it did not reach volume production until the middle of August. The artificial port on the American beaches had been demolished in the June storm. From Arromanches and Cherbourg we had not been able to project forward the roads, railways, and dumps as we would have done had our breakout line actually been as far to the southward as the base of the Cotentin Peninsula, where we originally expected it to be. All our marching columns, therefore, had to be supplied from stocks located near the beaches and over roads and railways that had to be repaired as we advanced.

These meager facilities could not support us indefinitely and there was bound to be a line somewhere in the direction of Germany where we would be halted, if not by the action of the enemy, then because our supply lines had been strained to their elastic limit.

A reinforced division, in active operations, consumes from 600 to 700 tons of supplies per day. When battling in a fixed position, most of this tonnage is represented in ammunition; on the march the bulk is devoted to gasoline and lubricants, called, in the language of the supply officer, POL.[2]

With thirty-six divisions in action we were faced with the problem of delivering from beaches and ports to the front lines some 20,000 tons of supplies every day. Our spearheads, moreover, were moving swiftly, frequently seventy-five miles per day. The supply service had to catch these with loaded trucks. Every mile of advance doubled the difficulty because the supply truck had always to make a two-way run to the beaches and back, in order to deliver another load to the marching troops. Other thousands of tons had to go into advanced airfields for construction and subsequent maintenance. Still additional amounts were required for repair of bridges and roads, for which heavy equipment was necessary.

During the days that we were roped off in the beachhead we could not foresee the exact reaction of the enemy following upon a successful breakout on our right. His most logical move appeared to be a swinging of his troops back toward the Seine, to defend the crossings of that river. If he had chosen to do this he could undoubtedly have made a stubborn defense of that obstacle until our advancing troops were able to outflank him and force evacuation.

If we had been compelled to fight a general battle on the Seine our lines of communication would have been relatively short and the logistic problem would have been solved gradually, conforming to the pace that our own troops could advance. However, when the enemy decided, under Hitler's insistence, to stand where he was and to counterattack against the flank of our marching columns at Mortain the entire prospect was changed.

We grasped eagerly at the opportunity to swing in from the south against his rear in the attempt to accomplish a complete destruction of all his forces, because, if we were successful, then the intermediate battles that we had always calculated as possibilities on the Seine and on the Somme would not be fought and our problem became a calculation of the furthermost line we could hope to reach before we completely outran supply.

Consequently, while General Bradley was swinging the mass of his forces in toward the German rear it became necessary for me to review our entire plan of campaign to determine what major changes this new development would indicate as desirable.

The two most hopeful probabilities then presented to us were the early capture of Marseille, far in the south, and of Antwerp, in Belgium. Possession of this latter port, if usable, would solve our logistic problems for the entire northern half of our front. Not only was Antwerp the greatest port in Europe but its location, well forward toward the borders of Germany, would reduce our rail and truck haulage to the point where supply should no longer be a limiting factor in the prosecution of the campaign, at least in the northern sectors.

We hoped for the early use of Marseille because the Germans had already largely denuded that area of mobile divisions, and speedy capture should prevent extensive demolition. Final success in that region would afford the right flank of the Allies the best possible supply lines. Through that avenue would pour early reinforcements from the United States, and the capacity of the magnificent railway lines running up the valley of the Rhone was so great that after they were once operating we should have no great difficulty with the logistic support of any part of our lines south of the Luxembourg region.

To make full use of these two probabilities it was, of course, important that the right flank of our own armies join up as quickly as possible with General Devers' Sixth Army Group, which would be coming up from the south. At the same time we had to thrust toward the northeast with great strength. In this way we would, incidentally, quickly clear the area from which the V-1 and V-2 bombs had been consistently bombarding southern England. But the principal object was the early capture of Antwerp, with a line to the eastward thereof that would protect us in the use of that great port.

All this conformed to original plans except that the prospect of a speedy instead of a fighting advance promised early use of the ports farther north and lessened our dependence upon the Brittany ports. But the problem remaining to be determined was whether or not our supply system, handicapped as it had been through all the first seven weeks of the battle, could support our movements up to and including the accomplishment of these purposes.

All units were certainly going to be short of supply. The task was to allot deficits so as to avoid stopping troops before they had accomplished their main objectives, and this in turn meant that no formation could get one pound of supply over and above that needed for basic missions.

When action is proceeding as rapidly as it did across France during the hectic days of late August and early September every commander from division upward becomes obsessed with the idea that with only a few more tons of supply he could rush right on and win the war. This is the spirit that wins wars and is always to be encouraged. Initiative, confidence, and boldness are among the most admirable traits of the good combat leader. As we dashed across France and Belgium each commander, therefore, begged and demanded priority over all others and it was undeniable that in front of each were opportunities for quick exploitation that made the demands completely logical.

In the late summer days of 1944 it was known to us that the German still had disposable reserves within his own country. Any idea of attempting to thrust forward a small force, bridge the Rhine, and continue on into the heart of Germany was completely fantastic. Even had such a force been able to start with a total of ten or a dozen divisions—and it is certain no more could have been supported even temporarily—the attacking column would have gradually grown smaller as it dropped off units to protect its flanks and would have ended up facing inescapable defeat. Such an attempt would have played into the hands of the enemy.

The more the entire situation was studied the more it became clear that the plan arrived at through weeks and months of development was still applicable, even though the immediate conditions under which it would be executed did not conform to the detailed possibilities we had projected into the operation. Consequently I decided that we would thrust forward on our right to a point of junction with General Devers' forces, which we believed would be in the region of Dijon, while on the left Montgomery would be ordered to push forward as rapidly as possible, to make certain of securing a line that would adequately cover Antwerp. Bradley directed Hodges' First Army to advance abreast of the British formations, roughly in the general direction of Aachen, so as to make certain of success on our left.[3]

We hoped that this northeastward thrust would go so rapidly and that the collapse of the German would be so great that we might even gain, before the inevitable halt came about, a bridgehead over the Rhine which would immediately threaten the Ruhr.

It was under this general plan that the battling of the succeeding weeks took place.

While affairs on the front of the Twelfth and Twenty-first Army Groups were proceeding in such satisfactory fashion, Lieutenant General Alexander M. Patch's Seventh Army was achieving remarkable results in the south of France.[4]

At the conference of Allied war leaders at Teheran, in late 1943, the Western Allies had informed Generalissimo Stalin that a secondary movement into the south of France would be an integral part of our invasion across the Channel to establish the second front in Europe. However, in early 1944 the Allies were waging one campaign in Italy and were planning for the great adventure of Overlord. During all the first half of 1944, therefore, it was impossible for General Wilson, commanding in the Mediterranean, to secure estimates of what might be available for the Dragoon attack.

My decision in January that the Overlord attack must be carried out on a front of five divisions had made it impossible to launch the Dragoon attack simultaneously with the Overlord landing, as had been originally planned. A vast amount of study and telegraphic correspondence subsequently developed between the Combined Chiefs of Staff, General Wilson, and my headquarters concerning the wisdom of persisting in the plan. From the beginning I had been an ardent advocate of this secondary attack and never in all the long period of discussion would I agree to its elimination from our plans. In this position I was supported by General Marshall.[5]

All these arguments and discussions were now definitely things of the past and we were assured that very shortly there would be a force, to be constituted as General Devers' Sixth Army Group, of at least ten American and French divisions in southern France driving northward to join us and that these would be followed quickly by reinforcing divisions from the United States. There was no development of that period which added more decisively to our advantages or aided us more in accomplishing the final and complete defeat of the German forces than did this secondary attack coming up the Rhone Valley.

Because of the distance of General Patch's troops from my headquarters and the lack of communications, it had been arranged that General Wilson was to retain operational control of that force until it was possible for me to establish the machinery for command. This date we estimated as September 15. However, from the beginning of the southern invasion all battle fronts in France really became one, and all plans, both tactical and logistical, were devised upon the assumption that soon the whole would constitute one continuous order of battle. This we wanted to bring about quickly, and with the conclusion of the fighting on the Seine at the end of August, Bradley ordered Patton's Third Army to push eastward with a primary mission of linking up quickly with the Seventh Army to form a continuous front.[6]

The remainder of the Allied forces continued their generally northeastern direction of advance to liberate Belgium, seize Antwerp, and threaten the Ruhr. This advance was conducted on a wide front and involved many incidents of marches and battles that will be told only in detailed history. For example, the American VII and XIX Corps advanced so rapidly that in the vicinity of Mons, location of one of the great battles of the first World War, they trapped between them an entire German corps. After a fierce engagement 25,000 prisoners were taken. In ordinary times this would have been acclaimed as a great victory. But the times were far from ordinary and the incident passed almost unnoticed in the press.[7]

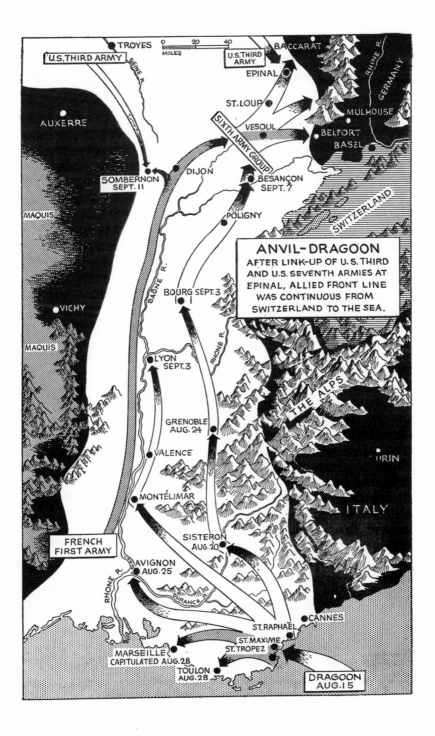

A special problem that became acute toward the end of August was that of determining what to do about Paris. During all preliminary operations we had been at great pains to avoid direct bombing of the French capital. Even in the process of destroying French communications we had, in the Paris region, done this by attacking railway bottlenecks outside rather than terminals inside the city. Pursuing the same general purpose, we wanted to avoid making Paris a battleground and consequently planned operations to cut off and surround the vicinity, thus forcing the surrender of the defending garrison. We could not know, of course, the exact condition and situation of the city's population. At the moment we were anxious to save every ounce of fuel and ammunition for combat operations, in order to carry our lines forward the maximum distance, and I was hopeful of deferring actual capture of the city, unless I received evidence of starvation or distress among its citizens.

In this matter my hand was forced by the action of the Free French forces inside Paris. Throughout France the Free French had been of inestimable value in the campaign. They were particularly active in Brittany, but on every portion of the front we secured help from them in a multitude of ways. Without their great assistance the liberation of France and the defeat of the enemy in western Europe would have consumed a much longer time and meant greater losses to ourselves. So when the Free French forces inside the city staged their uprising it was necessary to move rapidly to their support. Information indicated that no great battle would take place and it was believed that the entry of one or two Allied divisions would accomplish the liberation of the city.

For the honor of first entry, General Bradley selected General Le-Clerc's French 2d Division. The veterans of this organization had started at Lake Chad three years before, made an almost impossible march across the Sahara Desert, joined the Eighth Army to participate in the latter part of the African campaign, and now, on August 25, 1944, its commander received the surrender from the German general commanding the Paris garrison. It was a satisfying climax to an odyssey which, in its entire length, carried all the way from central Africa to Berchtesgaden in Germany.

However, before the Germans were completely subdued in Paris and the city restored to order, the American 4th Division had to be brought in. Fortunately the fighting involved no great material damage to the city. From our viewpoint the most significant of all these fortunate circumstances was that the bridges over the Seine were left intact.

Immediately after the capture of Paris, I notified General de Gaulle that I hoped he would quickly enter the capital; I desired that he, as the symbol of French resistance, should make an entrance before I had to go in or through it.

On the Saturday following the capture of the city I visited General Bradley's headquarters and there learned that General de Gaulle had already established his headquarters in one of the government buildings of Paris. I at once determined to push on into the city to make a formal call upon him. To present an Allied front, I advised Montgomery of my intention and asked him to accompany me. This he was unable to do because of the rapidly changing situation on his front, and so I contented myself, in this respect, with taking along my British military assistant, Colonel Gault.

On the forward journey Bradley and I made a slight detour around an area in which fighting was still in progress, but entered Paris quietly and secretly, as we supposed, before noon on Sunday, August 27. We went immediately to call on De Gaulle, who was already surrounded by the traditional Republican Guards in their resplendent uniforms. We visited General Gerow, at the headquarters of the American V Corps, and stopped to see General Koenig, who as a subordinate of SHAEF was commanding all the Free French Forces of the Interior. As we moved about the city word apparently got out that Bradley and I were in town and when we went past the Arc de Triomphe on the Etoile we were surrounded by a crowd of enthusiastic citizens. The exuberant greetings of the liberated population were a bit embarrassing and we made our way as quickly as possible to one of the exit gates and returned to Bradley's headquarters, near Chartres.[8]

While I was in the city General de Gaulle communicated to me some of his anxieties and problems. He asked for food and supplies. He was particularly anxious for thousands of uniforms for issue to the Free French forces, so as to distinguish between them and the disorderly elements who, taking advantage of temporary confusion, might begin to prey upon the helpless citizens. He also wanted additional military equipment, with which to begin organizing new French divisions.

A serious problem in view of the disorganized state of the city was the speedy establishment of his own authority and the preservation of order. He asked for the temporary loan of two American divisions to use, as he said, as a show of force and to establish his position firmly.

My memory flashed back almost two years, to Africa and our political problems of that time. There we had accepted the governmental organization already in existence and never during our entire stay had one of the French officials asked for Allied troops in order to establish or affirm his position as a local administrative authority. Here there seemed a touch of the sardonic in the picture of France's symbol of liberation having to ask for Allied forces to establish and maintain a similar position in the heart of the freed capital.

Nevertheless, I understood De Gaulle's problem, and while I had no spare units to station temporarily in Paris, I did promise him that two of our divisions, marching to the front, would do so through the main avenues of the city. I suggested that while these divisions were passing through Paris they could proceed in ceremonial formation and invited him to review them. I felt that this show of force and De Gaulle's presence on the reviewing stand would accomplish all that he sought. I declined personally to be present at this formation but told him that General Bradley would come back to the city and stand with him on the reviewing platform to symbolize Allied unity.

Because this ceremonial march coincided exactly with the local battle plan it became possibly the only instance in history of troops marching in parade through the capital of a great country to participate in pitched battle on the same day.

A section of the British press commented that "the Americans love a parade," and somewhat critically observed that British troops, also, had participated in the campaign to free France and that none of the Allies should seek to take the glory. No one in official position, however, misunderstood the circumstances or criticized the incident. Moreover, as soon as the offending papers learned of the reasons, they were quick to retract, but it was merely another instance of the necessity, in modern war, for a commander to concern himself always with the appearance of things in the public eye as well as with actual accomplishment. It is idle to say that the public may be ignored in the certainty that temporary misunderstandings will be forgotten in later victory.

A similar instance, involving the press of both America and Britain, occurred during August when a story appeared in American papers alleging that General Montgomery was no longer in a co-ordinating position with respect to the ground forces and that both he and General Bradley, on equal status, were already reporting directly to me. This was denied from SHAEF merely because the described arrangement was not yet in force. The press report was completely accurate although premature: the change had long been planned but was not to be put into effect until September 1.[9]

British newspapers greeted the story with great resentment, alleging that Montgomery had been demoted because of his success. The American press, on the other hand, hailed the story with considerable satisfaction because it indicated that the American troops, in their own channel of invasion, were now operating on a truly independent basis. The prompt denial from SHAEF consequently created confusion in America and General Marshall found it necessary to send me a telegram of inquiry on the point. I had to repeat at great length the exact details of our arrangements for the passing of command. I also allowed myself to express a certain amount of irritation by remarking in my telegram that "it wasn't enough for the public to obtain a great victory, the manner in which it was gained seemed to be more important." However, the reactions in both countries were completely normal. Were it not for the intensive patriotism and esprit that create this kind of nationalistic pride the task of organizing and maintaining armies in the face of continuing losses would be an impossible one. The incident became just one more profitable lesson in handling matters in which the public was certain to have great concern.

Complete wartime co-ordination and perfect co-operation can never be achieved between the press and military authorities. For the commander secrecy is a defensive weapon; to the press it is anathema. The task is to develop a procedure that takes into account an understanding of both viewpoints.

The press is primarily and properly concerned with providing information to the public at home. Civilian effort produces the fighting formations and the equipment necessary to achieve victory. Civilians are entitled to know everything about the war that need not remain secret through the overriding requirement of military security. Indeed, the commander in the field must never forget that it is his duty to cooperate with the heads of his government in the task of maintaining a civilian morale that will be equal to every purpose.

To do this effectively, the principal agency available to the commander is the body of press representatives in his theater. These represent every type of newspaper and periodical, radio chain, and photographic service, both motion and still. Some commanders resent the presence of this body of non-combatants, which sometimes grows to a considerable size; there was, at one time, a total of 943 within the European theater.

When I first met Generals Alexander and Montgomery in Africa they favored the imposition upon press representatives of strict rules and regulations, and their list of censorable items was long. They were aware that reporters were present in the theater of operations by the authority of the government, but so great was their concern for secrecy that they appeared to treat the press as a necessary evil rather than as a valuable link with the homeland and as an agency that could be of great assistance in the waging of a campaign.

There was a sound reason, particularly at the beginning of the war, for the British to evidence more reserve and conservatism in their treatment of the press than was reflected in the policies that American headquarters always favored. In the early days of the war, particularly when Britain stood alone in 1940 and 1941, the British had little with which to oppose the German except deception. They resorted to every type of subterfuge, including the establishment of dummy headquarters and the sending of fake messages in order to confuse the German as to the amount of military strength available and, more important than this, its disposition. Out of this necessity was born a habit that was later difficult to discard.

I believed that the proper attitude of the commander toward representatives of the press was to regard them as quasi staff officers; to recognize their mission in the war and to assist them in carrying it out. Normally the only justifiable excuse for censorship is the necessity to withhold valuable information that the enemy could not otherwise obtain. During the war I personally violated this general rule by imposing temporary political censorship in North Africa and by withholding advance notice of the eventual command arrangements in Normandy. Though my reasons, on both occasions, seemed valid to me, I never failed to regret what later proved to be a mistake.

In World War II the great body of the American and British press representatives comprised an intelligent, patriotic, and energetic group of individuals. They could, with complete safety and mutual advantage, be taken into the confidence of the commander. When this was done the press body itself became the best possible instrument for the disciplining of an individual who violated any confidence or code under which the group was operating. Throughout the campaigns in the Mediterranean and Europe, I found that correspondents habitually responded to candor, frankness, and understanding.

In the handling of the press, the American practice was to provide every facility that would permit an individual to go wherever he wanted, whenever he wanted. While this imposed upon us some additional administrative burdens, it paid off in big dividends because of the conviction in the minds of all that there was no attempt to conceal error and stupidity. These, when discovered, could be promptly aired and therefore did not grow into the festering sores that would have resulted from any attempt at concealment.

Censorship applied to the designation of units already committed to action denies the commander one of his greatest aids in the development and maintenance of morale among his own fighting troops. The combat soldier wants to be recognized; he wants to know that his sufferings and privations are known to others and, presumably, appreciated. Nothing seems to please him more than to find his own battalion, regiment, or division mentioned favorably in the press. To cover the whole under an umbrella of impersonality deprives the soldier of this satisfaction and is sooner or later reflected in open complaint. Moreover, any enemy worthy of the name quickly learns through front-line contacts the identity of all units opposing him. To pursue the ostrichlike policy of pretending the contrary merely enrages the press and does no good.

Under the policy adopted by the American forces in Europe, a great deal of responsibility devolves upon the accredited press representatives. One of these is to write fairly and with a sense of perspective. Some tend to become advocates and supporters of a particular unit or a particular commander. This becomes serious, in an allied command, when the bias has also a nationalistic tinge. Unpleasant incidents of course arose, and the fault was sometimes definitely with the press, just as at others it was with the commander. But when there is considered the enormous opportunity that existed for prejudiced reporting and for troublemaking between units, services, and whole peoples, it must be concluded that the press in the field measured up as well as any other group to the fundamental requirements of allied co-operation.

From August on, the friendly relationship between the press and the military was strengthened by the presence of Brigadier General Frank A. Allen, Jr., as my public relations officer. He had been a successful leader of an armored combat command in North Africa and France but I believed that his ability to maintain military security and at the same time to assure the public the information it wanted and needed would prove most valuable to the war effort. By his assignment to headquarters duty, although I lost a proved combat commander thereby, I was relieved of many worrisome problems.

The liberation of Paris on the twenty-fifth of August had a great impact on people everywhere. Even the doubters began to see the end of Hitler. By this time enemy losses were enormous. Since our landings three of the enemy's field marshals and one army commander had been dismissed from their posts or incapacitated by wounds. Rommel was badly wounded by one of our strafing planes on July 19. Some months later he committed suicide to escape trial for alleged complicity in the July 20 murder plot against Hitler. One army commander, three corps commanders, and fifteen division commanders had been killed or captured. The enemy had lost 400,000 killed, wounded, or captured. Half the total were prisoners of war, and 135,-000 of these had been taken in the month subsequent to July 25.

German matériel losses included 1300 tanks, 20,000 other vehicles, 500 assault guns, and 1500 pieces of artillery. In addition the German air forces had suffered extensively. More than 3500 of his aircraft had been destroyed and this in spite of the fact that the Luftwaffe had been seriously depleted before the invasion began.[10]

There was a definite drop in enemy morale. So far as prisoners were concerned this was more noticeable among the higher officers because they, with professional training, could see the inevitability of final defeat. But the Army as a whole had clearly not yet reached the stage of mass collapse and there was no question that the German divisions, given decent conditions, were still capable of putting up fierce resistance.[11]

With the capture of Paris we were substantially on the line that had been predicted before D-day as the one we would attain three to four months after our landing. Thus, in long-term estimate, we were weeks ahead of schedule, but in the important particular of supply capacity we were badly behind. Because almost the entire area had been captured in the swift movements subsequent to August 1, the roads, railway lines, depots, repair shops, and base installations, required for the maintenance of continuous forward movement, were still far to the rear of the front lines.[12]

When the German forces succeeded, in spite of defeat and disorder, in withdrawing significant numbers of their troops across the Seine, there still remained the hope of constructing another trap for them before they could reorganize and present an effective defensive front. Portions of the German Fifteenth Army still remained in the Calais area, where they would provide a stiffening core for the retreating troops of the First and Seventh Armies. It was considered possible that some resistance would be attempted along one of the natural defenses provided by the waterways of Belgium. A surprise vertical envelopment by airborne troops appeared to offer the best hope of encirclement if the enemy chose to make a stand.

As quickly as the defeat of the Germans on the Normandy front became certain, airborne forces were directed to prepare plans for drops in a number of successive positions, the appropriate spot to be selected when the developing situation should indicate the one of greatest promise. The mere paper planning of such operations was, while laborious, a simple matter. However, when actual preparation for a planned drop was undertaken, delicately balanced alternatives presented themselves. Preparation for airborne attack required the withdrawal of transport planes from supply purposes, and it was difficult, at times, to determine whether greater results could not be achieved by continuing the planes in supply activity.

Unfortunately this withdrawal of planes from other work had to precede an airborne operation by several days, to provide time for refitting equipment and for briefing and retraining of crews. In late August, with our supply situation growing constantly more desperate, and with all of us eagerly following combat progress in the search for another prospect of cutting off great numbers of the enemy, the question of the Transport Command employment came up for daily discussion. On the average, allowing for all kinds of weather, our planes could deliver about 2000 tons a day to the front. While this was only a small percentage of our total deliveries, every ton was so valuable that the decision was a serious one.

It appeared to me that a fine chance for launching a profitable airborne attack was developing in the Brussels area, and though there was divided opinion on the wisdom of withdrawing planes from supply work because of the uncertainty of the opportunity, I decided to take the chance. The Troop Carrier Command, on September 10, was withdrawn temporarily from supply missions to begin intensive preparation for an airborne drop in the Brussels area.[13] But it quickly became clear that the Germans were retreating so fast as to make the effort an abortive one. Except with rear guards, the Germans made no attempt to defend in that region at all.

All along the front we pressed forward in hot pursuit of the fleeing enemy. In four days the British spearheads, paralleled by equally forceful American advances on their right, covered a distance of 195 miles, one of the many fine feats of marching by our formations in the great pursuit across France. By September 5, Patton's Third Army reached Nancy and crossed the Moselle River between that city and Metz. Hodges' First Army came up against the Siegfried defenses by the thirteenth of the month and was shortly thereafter to begin the struggle for Aachen. Pushed back against the borders of the homeland, the German defenses showed definite signs of stiffening. On September 4, Montgomery's armies entered Antwerp and we were electrified to learn that the Germans had been so rapidly hustled out of the place that they had had no time to execute extensive demolitions. Marseille had been captured on August 28 and this great port was being rehabilitated.

These developments assured eventual solution of our logistical problem, which meant that within a reasonable time we would be in position to wage on the German border a battle of a scale and intensity that the enemy could not hope to match. However, there was much to be done before we could be in this fortunate position, and we had little remaining elasticity in our overstrained supply lines. On the south Patch's and Bradley's forces had to make a junction, and railway lines up the Rhone would have to be repaired. On the north we were faced by even greater difficulties.

Antwerp is an inland port connected with the sea by the great Scheldt Estuary. The German defenses covering these approaches were still intact and before we could make use of the port we had the job of clearing out those defenses.

The task on the north comprised three parts. We had to secure a line far enough to the eastward to cover Antwerp and the roads and railways leading out of it toward the front. We had to reduce the German defenses in the areas lying between that city and the sea. Finally, I hoped to thrust forward spearheads as far as we could, to include a bridgehead across the Rhine if possible, so as to threaten the Ruhr and facilitate subsequent offensives.

On Montgomery's flank the question for immediate decision became the priority in which these tasks should be taken up. As a first requisite our lines had to be advanced far enough to the eastward to cover Antwerp securely, else the port and all its facilities would be useless to us. This had to be done without delay; until it was accomplished the other tasks could not even be started. Equally clear was the fact that, until the approaches to the port were cleared, it was of no value to us. Because the Germans were firmly dug in on the islands of South Beveland and Walcheren, this was going to be a tough and time-consuming

RED BALL ROARS FORWARD

On Red Ball Highways "every vehicle ran at least twenty hours a day . . . allowed to halt only for necessary loading, unloading, and servicing." *Page 308*

Tank Transporters Rush Armored Supply

NAKEDNESS OF THE BATTLEFIELD

". . . each man feels himself so much alone, and each is prey to the human fear and terror that to move or show himself may result in instant death." *Page 314*

German 88 Pounds Paratroopers Near Arnhem

operation. The sooner we could set about it the better. But the question remaining was whether or not it was advantageous, before taking on the arduous task of reducing the Antwerp approaches, to continue our eastward plunge against the still retreating enemy with the idea of securing a possible bridgehead across the Rhine in proximity to the Ruhr.

While we were examining the various factors of the question, Montgomery suddenly presented the proposition that, if we would support his Twenty-first Army Group with all supply facilities available, he could rush right on into Berlin and, he said, end the war. I am certain that Field Marshal Montgomery, in the light of later events, would agree that this view was a mistaken one. But at the moment his enthusiasm was fired by the rapid advances of the preceding week and, since he was convinced that the enemy was completely demoralized, he vehemently declared that all he needed was adequate supply in order to go directly into Berlin.[14]

During early September, while returning from a visit to the forward areas, I suffered a minor injury incident to a forced landing on a beach. Caught in a sudden storm, we found it impossible to return to our own little landing strip near headquarters and had no place to land except on a neighboring beach. It was one of the beaches that the Germans had fortified before D-day, and had at one time been mined. This did not add to the comfort of our position but we tried to pull the plane far enough away from the water's edge to prevent its inundation by the rising tide. In doing so, I badly wrenched a knee. My pilot, Lieutenant Underwood, helped me across the beach while I kept an anxious eye on the smooth sand in front of us for any telltale signs of buried explosives. We reached a country road and started the long trek toward headquarters. It was a miserable walk through a driving rain but we had little hope of thumbing a ride because the back road we were traveling was rarely used by our soldiers. However, within a few minutes there came up behind us a jeep into which eight soldiers had managed to crowd.

We flagged them down and the occupants, instantly recognizing me, jumped out to help. They were obviously astounded to see the commanding general in such an out-of-the-way place and limping along in the rain. I asked them to take me to headquarters and so great was their concern that they practically lifted me into the front seat of the jeep. Then, careful to avoid crowding against my injured leg, they allowed no one else except the driver to sit in front. I still do not understand how all the rest of them piled in and on the jeep and managed to get my pilot aboard, but this they did.

For two days I was confined to bed and thereafter was forced, for a time, to carry a plaster cast on my leg. Press representatives noted my absence from headquarters and surmised that I was ill, possibly because of overwork. When a story to this effect appeared in the press I had to publish the details of the affair, with the hope that my wife would not magnify the seriousness of the accident pending receipt of my letter of explanation.

Travel was temporarily difficult, but to make sure that Montgomery would be completely informed as to our plans, I met him at Brussels on September 10.[15] Air Chief Marshal Tedder and General Gale were also present.

I explained to Montgomery the condition of our supply system and our need for early use of Antwerp. I pointed out that, without railway bridges over the Rhine and ample stockages of supplies on hand, there was no possibility of maintaining a force in Germany capable of penetrating to its capital. There was still a considerable reserve in the middle of the enemy country and I knew that any pencillike thrust into the heart of Germany such as he proposed would meet nothing but certain destruction. This was true, no matter on what part of the front it might be attempted. I would not consider it.

It was possible, and perhaps certain, that had we stopped, in late August, all Allied movements elsewhere on the front he might have succeeded in establishing a strong bridgehead definitely threatening the Ruhr, just as any of the other armies could have gone faster and farther, if allowed to do so at the expense of starvation elsewhere. However, at no point could decisive success have been attained, and, meanwhile, on the other parts of the front we would have gotten into precarious positions, from which it would have been difficult to recover.

General Montgomery was acquainted only with the situation in his own sector. He understood that to support his proposal would have meant stopping dead for weeks all units except the Twenty-first Army Group. But he did not understand the impossible situation that would have developed along the rest of our great front when he, having outrun the possibility of maintenance, was forced to stop or withdraw.

I instructed him that what I did want in the north was Antwerp working, and I also wanted a line covering that port. Beyond this I believed it possible that we might with airborne assistance seize a bridgehead over the Rhine in the Arnhem region, flanking the defenses of the Siegfried Line. The operation to gain such a bridgehead—it was assigned the code name Market-Garden—would be merely an incident and extension of our eastward rush to the line we needed for temporary security. On our northern flank that line was the lower Rhine itself. To stop short of that obstacle would have left us in a very exposed position, particularly during the period that Montgomery would have to concentrate large forces on the Walcheren Island operation.

If these things could be done, we would engage in no additional major advances in the north until we had built up our logistics in the rear. But we could and would carry out minor operations all along the great front to facilitate later great offensives. Montgomery was very anxious to attempt the seizure of the bridgehead.

At the September 10 conference in Brussels Field Marshal Montgomery was therefore authorized to defer the clearing out of the Antwerp approaches in an effort to seize the bridgehead I wanted. To assist Montgomery I allocated to him the First Allied Airborne Army, which had been recently formed under Lieutenant General Lewis H. Brereton of the United States Air Forces. The target date for the attack was tentatively set for September 17, and I promised to do my utmost for him in supply until that operation was completed. After the completion of the bridgehead operation he was to turn instantly and with his whole force to the capture of Walcheren Island and the other areas from which the Germans were defending the approaches to Antwerp. Montgomery set about the task energetically.[16]

With all of our affairs, except supply, in reasonably good order, the Combined Chiefs of Staff, in conference at Quebec, decided that it was no longer necessary for me to retain under my direct and personal command the two bomber forces stationed in Great Britain. They set up an arrangement whereby the strategic bombers were to be directly subordinate to the Combined Chiefs of Staff through the medium of a combined agency set up in London. From my own viewpoint, this was a clumsy and inefficient arrangement, but so far as our operation was concerned it made no difference whatsoever. This was because a paragraph was inserted in the directive which gave the demands of the supreme commander in Europe priority over anything else that the strategic bombers might be required to do. With this safeguard and unequivocal authority, I had no objection to the new arrangement regardless of my opinion of its awkwardness.[17]

Spaatz protested bitterly at the new command system for the strategic bombers until I showed him that it made no difference to me. Even Harris, who had originally been known as the individual who wanted to win the war with bombing alone and who was supposed to have derided the mobilization of armies and navies, had become exceedingly proud of his membership in the "Allied team." Here are extracts of a letter he wrote to me upon receipt of the order returning him to the direct control of the Combined Chiefs of Staff:

21st September 1944

My dear Ike:

Under the new dispensation I and my Command no longer serve directly under you. I take opportunity to assure you, although I feel sure that you will recognize that assurance as superfluous, that our continuing commitment for the support of your forces upon call from you will indeed continue, as before, to be met to the utmost of our skill and the last ounce of our endeavour. . . .

I wish personally and on behalf of my Command to proffer you my thanks and gratitude for your unvarying helpfulness, encouragement and support which has never failed us throughout the good fortunes and occasional emergencies of the campaign. . . .

We in Bomber Command proffer you not only our congratulations and our thanks, but our utmost service wherever and whenever the need arises. I hope indeed that we may continue the task together to its completion in our respective spheres.

Yours ever

Bert

All along the front we felt increasingly the strangulation on movement imposed by our inadequate lines of communication. The Services of Supply had made heroic and effective effort to keep us going to the last possible minute. They installed systems of truck transport by taking over main-road routes in France and using most of these for one-way traffic. These were called Red Ball Highways, on which trucks kept running continuously. Every vehicle ran at least twenty hours a day. Relief drivers were scraped up from every unit that could provide them and the vehicles themselves were allowed to halt only for necessary loading, unloading, and servicing.

Railway engineers worked night and day to repair broken bridges and track and to restore the operational efficiency of rolling stock. Gasoline and fuel oil were brought onto the Continent by means of

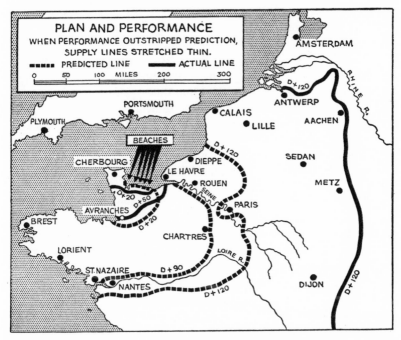

flexible pipe lines laid under the English Channel. From the beaches the gas and oil were pumped forward to main distribution points through pipe lines laid on the surface of the ground. Aviation engineers built landing strips at amazing speed, and throughout the organization there was displayed a morale and devotion to duty equal to that of any fighting unit in the whole command.

In the months succeeding the conclusion of hostilities I had many opportunities to review various campaigns with the leaders of the Russian Army. Not only did I talk to marshals and generals but on this subject I spent a considerable time with Generalissimo Stalin. Without exception, these Russian officers made one pressing demand upon me. It was to explain the supply arrangements that enabled us to make the great sweep out of our constricted beachhead in Normandy to cover, in one rush, all of France, Belgium, and Luxembourg, up to the very borders of Germany. I had to describe to them our systems of railway repairs and construction, truckage, evacuation, and supply by air.

They suggested that of all the spectacular feats of the war, even including their own, the Allied success in the supply of the pursuit across France would go down in history as the most astonishing. Possibly they were only being polite, but I nevertheless wished that they could have been heard by all the men who worked so hard during those hectic weeks to see that the front got every possible pound of ammunition, gasoline, food, clothing, and supplies.

Regardless, however, of the extraordinary efforts of the supply system, this remained our most acute difficulty. All along the front the cry was for more gasoline and more ammunition. Every one of our spearheads could have gone farther and faster than they actually did. I believed then and believe now that on Patton's front the city of Metz could have been captured. Nevertheless, we had to supply each force for its basic missions and for basic missions only.

On our right we connected up near Dijon with Patch's advancing forces on September 11, just twenty-seven days after the landing in southern France.[18] From that moment onward the only thing standing in the way of the ample supply of all our forces south of Metz was the repair of the railways leading up the Rhone Valley. As a result of the junction with Patch's forces, a considerable number of Germans were trapped in southwestern France. These began to give themselves up by driblets except in one instance, when 20,000 Germans surrendered in a single body.[19]

On the extreme left the attack against Arnhem went off as planned on the seventeenth. Three airborne divisions dropped, in column, from north to south. The northernmost one was the British 1st Airborne Division, while farther southward were the American 82d and 101st Airborne Divisions. The attack began well and unquestionably would have been successful except for the intervention of bad weather. This prevented the adequate reinforcement of the northern spearhead and resulted finally in the decimation of the British airborne division and only a partial success in the entire operation. We did not get our bridgehead but our lines had been carried well out to defend the Antwerp base.

The progress of the battle gripped the attention of everyone in the theater. We were inordinately proud of our airborne units but the interest in that battle had its roots in something deeper than pride. We felt it would prove whether or not the Germans could succeed in establishing renewed and effective resistance—on the battle's outcome we would form an estimate of the severity of the fighting still ahead of us. A general impression grew up that the battle was really a full-out attempt to begin, immediately, a drive into the heart of

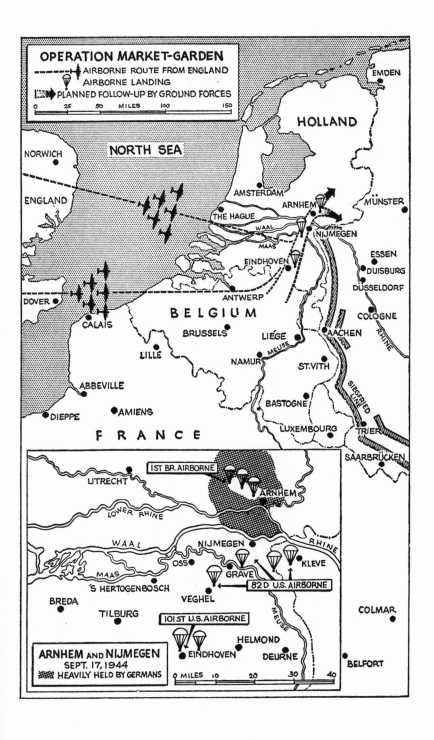

OPERATION MARKET-GARDEN

- ✈ AIRBORNE ROUTE FROM ENGLAND
- ⊻ AIRBORNE LANDING
- ⇒ PLANNED FOLLOW-UP BY GROUND FORCES

0   25   50   MILES   100   150

NORTH SEA

HOLLAND

EMDEN

NORWICH

ENGLAND

AMSTERDAM

THE HAGUE

ARNHEM

MÜNSTER

WAAL

NIJMEGEN

MAAS

EINDHOVEN

ESSEN

DUISBURG

DÜSSELDORF

ANTWERP

BELGIUM

COLOGNE

RHINE

DOVER

CALAIS

BRUSSELS

LIÉGE

AACHEN

LILLE

NAMUR

MEUSE

ST.VITH

SIEGFRIED LINE

ABBEVILLE

BASTOGNE

DIEPPE

AMIENS

LUXEMBOURG

TRIER

FRANCE

SAARBRÜCKEN

1ST BR. AIRBORNE

UTRECHT

ARNHEM

LOWER RHINE

WAAL

NIJMEGEN

RHINE

OSS

KLEVE

GRAVE

MAAS

82D U.S. AIRBORNE

'S HERTOGENBOSCH

VEGHEL

BREDA

101ST U.S. AIRBORNE

COLMAR

TILBURG

MEUSE

HELMOND

EINDHOVEN

DEURNE

BELFORT

ARNHEM AND NIJMEGEN
SEPT. 17, 1944
▨ HEAVILY HELD BY GERMANS

0   MILES   10   20   30   40

Germany. This gave a great added interest to a battle in which the circumstances were unusually dramatic.

When, in spite of heroic effort, the airborne forces and their supporting ground forces were stopped in their tracks, we had ample evidence that much bitter campaigning was still to come. The British 1st Airborne Division, in the van, fought one of the most gallant actions of the war, and its sturdiness materially assisted the two American divisions behind it, and the supporting ground forces of the Twenty-first Army Group, to take and hold important areas. But the division itself suffered badly; only some 2400 succeeded in withdrawing across the river to safety.[20]

It was now vital to avoid any further delay in the capture of Antwerp's approaches. Montgomery's forces were, at the moment, badly scattered. His front, in an irregular salient, reached to the lower Rhine. He had to concentrate a sizable force in the Scheldt Estuary and still provide investing troops at some of the small ports holding out along the coast. To insure him opportunity to concentrate for the Scheldt operation we sent him two American divisions, the 7th Armored, commanded by Major General Lindsay McD. Sylvester, and the 104th, commanded by Major General Terry Allen, a veteran of the Tunisian and Sicilian campaigns.

The American First Army, at the end of its brilliant march from the Seine to the German border, almost immediately launched the operations that finally brought about the reduction of Aachen, one of the gateways into Germany. The city was stubbornly and fiercely defended but Collins, with his VII Corps, carried out the attack so skillfully that by October 13 he had surrounded the garrison and entered the city. The enemy was steadily forced back into his final stronghold, a massive building in the center of the city. This was reduced by the simple expedient of dragging 155-mm. "Long Tom" rifles up to point-blank range—within 200 yards of the building—and methodically blowing the walls to bits. After a few of these shells had pierced the building from end to end the German commander surrendered on October 21, with the rueful observation, "When the Americans start using 155s as sniper weapons, it is time to give up!"[21]

In the south Devers' Sixth Army Group became operational and came under my command on September 15. The continuous front under control of SHAEF now extended from the Mediterranean in the south to the mouth of the Rhine, hundreds of miles to the north.

Devers' forces included the U. S. Seventh Army under Lieutenant

General Patch, and the French First Army under General de Lattre de Tassigny, previously under Patch's operational control. Bradley's army group comprised the First, Third, and the newly organized Ninth Army under Lieutenant General William H. Simpson.[22] Montgomery still had Dempsey's British Second Army and Crerar's Canadian First Army. The Allied Airborne Army, temporarily assigned to him, was directly subordinate to SHAEF.

In October we learned that Leigh-Mallory was needed in another theater of war. Although reluctant to lose him, our organization had, by that time, definitely crystallized and teamwork had been perfected to the point that I approved the transfer. He was killed shortly thereafter in an airplane accident, and thus passed one of the intrepid and gallant figures of World War II.

In the late summer SHAEF began moving from Granville, its initial location on the Continent, to Versailles, just outside Paris. In selecting a new location, I desired to find a suitable spot well east of Paris in order to avoid the congested metropolitan area in trips to the front. However, because of the location of main lines of signal communications and the lack of existing facilities in the areas east of Paris, the staff was forced, originally, to accept Versailles as the most suitable spot from which to operate. I established a forward command post just outside Reims, from which point I could easily reach any portion of the front, even on days when flying was impossible.

During the three months beginning September 1, I spent a great portion of my time in travel. The front was constantly broadening and distances were getting greater, so that every visit was time-consuming. Nevertheless, they were valuable and always worth the cost in time and effort. By adhering to this practice, I could visit commanders in their own headquarters, keep personal touch with problems as they arose, and, above all, gain a feel of the troops. Two months later, as winter approached, the winding roads leading into my little camp at Reims at times became impassable. One afternoon I was bogged down for three hours while waiting for a tractor to pull my car out of a ditch. This compelled me to rejoin the main headquarters at Versailles and from that time on travel became more difficult, except when flying conditions were good.

On one trip during the autumn I stopped briefly in a forward location to talk with several hundred men of a battalion of the 29th Infantry Division. We were all standing on a muddy, slippery hillside. After a few minutes' visit I turned to go and fell flat on my back.

From the shout of laughter that went up I am quite sure that no other meeting I had with soldiers during the war was a greater success than that one. Even the men who rushed forward to help pick me out of the mire could scarcely do so for laughing.

At times I received advice from friends, urging me to give up or curtail visits to troops. They correctly stated that, so far as the mass of men was concerned, I could never speak, personally, to more than a tiny percentage. They argued, therefore, that I was merely wearing myself out, without accomplishing anything significant, so far as the whole Army was concerned. With this I did not agree. In the first place I felt that through constant talking to enlisted men I gained accurate impressions of their state of mind. I talked to them about anything and everything: a favorite question of mine was to inquire whether the particular squad or platoon had figured out any new trick or gadget for use in infantry fighting. I would talk about anything so long as I could get the soldier to talk to me in return.

I knew, of course, that news of a visit with even a few men in a division would soon spread throughout the unit. This, I felt, would encourage men to talk to their superiors, and this habit, I believe, promotes efficiency. There is, among the mass of individuals who carry the rifles in war, a great amount of ingenuity and initiative. If men can naturally and without restraint talk to their officers, the products of their resourcefulness become available to all. Moreover, out of the habit grows mutual confidence, a feeling of partnership that is the essence of *esprit de corps*. An army fearful of its officers is never as good as one that trusts and confides in its leaders.

There is an old expression, "the nakedness of the battlefield." It is descriptive and full of meaning for anyone who has seen a battle. Except for unusual concentration of tactical activity, such as at a river crossing or an amphibious assault, the feeling that pervades the forward areas is loneliness. There is little to be seen; friend and foe, as well as the engines of war, seem to disappear from sight when troops are deployed for a fight. Loss of control and cohesion are easy, because each man feels himself so much alone, and each is prey to the human fear and terror that to move or show himself may result in instant death. Here is where confidence in leaders, a feeling of comradeship with and trust in them, pays off.

My own direct efforts could do little in this direction. But I knew that if men realized they could talk to "the brass" they would be less inclined to be fearful of the lieutenant. Moreover, it was possible that my example might encourage officers to seek information from and comradeship with their men. In any event I pursued the practice throughout the war, and no talk with a soldier or group of soldiers was ever profitless for me.

All these visits were, in addition, the occasion for serious discussion of problems, involving particularly replacements, ammunition, clothing, and equipment for winter weather and future plans. Staffs of all echelons are, of course, constantly working on these matters and, according to the manuals, all of the needs of troops are automatically supplied through the working of the staff systems. Nothing, however, can take the place of direct contact between commanders and this is far more valuable when the senior does the traveling, instead of sitting in his headquarters and waiting for subordinates to come back to him with their problems.

Morale of the combat troops had always to be carefully watched. The capacity of soldiers for absorbing punishment and enduring privations is almost inexhaustible so long as they believe they are getting a square deal, that their commanders are looking out for them, and that their own accomplishments are understood and appreciated. Any intimation that they are the victims of unfair treatment understandably arouses their anger and resentment, and the feeling can sweep through a command like wildfire. Once, in Africa, front-line troops complained to me that they could get no chocolate bars or anything to smoke, when they knew that these were plentifully issued to the Services of Supply. I queried the local unit commander, who said he had requisitioned these things time and again, only to be told that no transport was available to bring them to the front.

I merely telephoned to the rear and directed that until every forward airfield and front-line unit was getting its share of these items there would not be another piece of candy or a cigarette or cigar issued to anyone in the supply services. In a surprisingly short time I received a happy report from the front that their requisitions were being promptly filled.

One of these distressing affairs developed in the fall of 1944. The two items in shortest supply on the front seemed to be gasoline and cigarettes. A true report came out that in Paris there was a flourishing black market in both these articles, conducted by men of the SOS. We promptly put a group of inspectors on the job and uncovered all the sordid facts. That some men should give way to the extraordinary temptations of the fabulous prices offered for food and cigarettes was to be expected. But in this case it appeared that practically an entire unit had organized itself into an efficient gang of racketeers and was selling these articles in truck- and carload lots. Even so, the blackness of the crime consisted more in the robbery of the front lines than it did in the value of the thefts. I was thoroughly angry.[23]

However, I realized that a whole American unit had not suddenly become criminal. It was logical to believe that the sorry business had been started by a few crooks and others had been gradually drawn into it almost without conscious will and, once started, saw no easy way of getting out.

I instructed the law-enforcement staffs to push prosecution of the guilty—fortunately these were not so numerous as first reported—but that no sentence in the case would be finally approved until brought to my personal attention. When this was later done I explained my plan. This was to offer to each of the convicted men a chance to restore himself to good standing by volunteering for front-line duty. The sentences, which were severe, had already been published to the command, so the forward troops knew that the guilty were not escaping punishment. But now I was determined to give the offenders a chance. Most of them eagerly seized the opportunity, removed the stigma from their names, and earned honorable discharges. This same opportunity was not, however, extended to the officers who participated in the affair.

Because of the miserable conditions along the front we began to suffer a high percentage of non-battle casualties. Trench foot was one of the principal causes. Cure is difficult, sometimes almost impossible, but the doctors discovered that prevention was a relatively simple matter. Effective prevention was merely a matter of discipline: making sure that no one neglected the prescribed procedure. This was to remove the shoes and socks at least once daily and massage the feet for five minutes. To make certain that this was done properly the normal practice was to take the treatment in pairs; each man was to rub the feet of his partner five minutes by the clock. Nothing much; but as soon as we knew the answer and applied it rigorously in all affected areas we reduced the number of serious casualties by thousands per month.

The medical service was efficient; the ratio of fatalities per hundred wounded was, in the American Army of World War II, less than one half the ratio of World War I.[24] For this there were many reasons. Among them were penicillin and the sulfa drugs, early use of blood plasma, and an efficient system of evacuation, a great deal of it by air. With respect to the wounded, the job of the doctor is to get the man fit again for combat as quickly as possible, and where the wound is permanently disabling to get him quickly, safely, and comfortably to a hospital in the homeland. In both tasks the doctors, the nurse corps, and their associates did a remarkable job. Some wounded men returned several times from the hospitals to the front in a single year of campaigning. I have seen other men unloaded at base hospitals, hundreds of miles from the front, within hours of receiving a permanently disabling wound.

The soldier's welfare is always the business of commanders of all grades. But in the fall of 1944 it was of particular importance. The Allied soldier faced all the hardship and danger of ordinary battle, while the elements made his daily life almost unendurable. It was a struggle in housekeeping as well as against the enemy. Yet my associates and I were convinced of the necessity of maintaining the tempo of operations. The job was to maintain a punishing pace against the enemy, to build up our strength in troops and supplies throughout the fall and winter, and to be ready in the spring to deliver the final killing blows.

Commanders in the American Army were all of my own choosing. Ever since the beginning of the African campaign there had existed between General Marshall and me a fixed understanding on the point. He said, "You do not need to take or keep any commander in whom you do not have full confidence. So long as he holds a command in your theater it is evidence to me of your satisfaction with him. The lives of many are at stake; I will not have you operating under any misunderstanding as to your authority, and your duty, to reject or remove any that fails to satisfy you completely." General Marshall never violated this rule, and I, in turn, prescribed the same procedure for my senior subordinates.

Early in the Overlord operation Prime Minister Churchill and Field Marshal Brooke took occasion to inform me that they also were prepared, at any moment I expressed dissatisfaction with any of my principal British subordinates, to replace him instantly. Allied co-operation had come a long way since the first days of Torch!

We had splendid troops and fine commanders, both on the ground and in the air. More were arriving daily from the United States. All we needed, in addition to our growing strength, was supply in the forward areas. We were certain that by the time we could provide this we would have the strength needed to begin the final battles to finish off the enemy in the West.

As we pushed rapidly across western Europe the wildest enthusiasm greeted the advancing Allied soldiers. In France, Belgium, Holland, and Luxembourg the story was everywhere the same. The inhabitants were undernourished and impoverished, but the regaining of their individual liberty, of their right to talk freely with their neighbors and to learn of the outside world, seemed to overshadow, at least for the moment, their hunger and their privation. The people had lived in virtual captivity for more than four years.

During that period their trade with other nations had ceased, their industries were perverted to the use of the Nazis, and their daily lives were never free from fear of imprisonment and worse. Even their news of the outside world was filtered to them through Nazi-controlled newspapers and radios. On a clandestine basis they did, of course, receive some information from British and American broadcasting stations but such news could not be freely circulated to the whole population and those who listened were, if discovered, subject to stern punishment. With the coming of the Allies popular exuberance sometimes was so emotional as to embarrass our soldiers, but there was no room left for doubt concerning the people's great joy in deliverance from the Nazi yoke.

The re-established governments of western Europe co-operated wholeheartedly with the Allied high command. Labor and other assistance were made available to us so far as the capacity of each country would permit. There were, of course, dissident elements. Men who, with arms in their hands, had long served in the underground, who were accustomed by stealth and violence to accomplish their purposes of sabotage, did not easily adapt themselves again to the requirements of social order. In some cases they wanted to maintain and magnify their power, to become the dominant and controlling element in the liberated country. While these things caused some local, and at times worrisome, difficulty, they were overshadowed by the eagerness of the population to earn again, under free institutions, their own living.

Because France had been divided into occupied and unoccupied segments by the armistice of 1940 and because the underground in that country was not only strong but very aggressive, more than normal difficulties were encountered in the re-establishment of stability. However, as always, the French peasant was devoted to the soil and continued assiduously to attend his crops. In the cities there was greater confusion because Communist penetration in trade unions and elsewhere had created sharp political division within the country which was reflected in divided councils and some disunity, even, in the prosecution of the war. For example, great portions of the former underground, or, as they were called, Maquis, refused to enter the Army except as separate units. They insisted upon forming their own regiments and divisions under their own leaders.

Unless their demands were met, it was feared they might even maintain themselves in various parts of the country as armed bands ready to challenge the authority of the Central Provisional Government. Their plan could not be wholly accepted by the government because the manifest result would have been the establishment of two French armies, one serving under and loyal to the generally recognized government, the other responsible only to itself. However, the government developed a plan to accept the Maquis in units no larger than battalion size.

Thoughtful Frenchmen frequently discussed with me the reasons for their national collapse in 1940. In other countries an opinion prevailed that the French military debacle came about because of an excessive faith in the efficiency of the Maginot Line. I did not find any Frenchmen who agreed with this. They felt that the fortified line along the eastern border was necessary and served a good purpose in that it should have allowed the French Army to concentrate heavily on the northern flank of the line to oppose any German advances through Belgium. Militarily, they felt, their difficulties came about because of internal political weaknesses. One French businessman said to me, "We defeated ourselves from within; we tried to oppose a four-day work week against the German's six- or seven-day week."

In general, the liberated peoples were startlingly ignorant of America and the American part in the war. Our effort had been so belittled and ridiculed by Nazi propaganda that the obvious strength of the American armies completely amazed and bewildered the populations of western Europe. In numerous ways we tried to place before them the facts of the American position prior to our entrance in the war and our contribution thereafter to its waging. But so great was the chasm of ignorance that we were only partly successful. The job is yet far from done.

The war, moreover, did not purge France of its divisive influences. Apparently Communistic doctrines had flourished in great segments of the underground movement and with the coming of liberation the Communists, as a minority but a very aggressive body, began to weaken the national will to regain France's former position of power and prosperity in western Europe.

This partisan disunity in localities behind us did not affect the Allied military position; whatever their political affiliation, the liberated peoples were friendly to us. But there was a threatening physical weakness in our communications zone, stretching from the French coast to the front, that did endanger our future offensive operations. The lifeblood of supply was running perilously thin throughout the forward extremities of the Army.

ENGLISH CHANNEL

ATLANTIC
OCEAN

BREST

LE

ST LÔ

CAEN

AVRANCHES

CANADI
FIRST AF

BR. SECO

ARGENT

U.S. FIR

ALENÇON

LORIENT

U.S. THIRD ARMY

LAVAL

LE MANS

ST. NAZAIRE

NANTES

ANGERS

OR

LOIRE R

LIBERATION OF FRANCE

PATHS OF ALLIED ARMIES FROM NORMANDY
BREAK-THROUGH AND ANVIL-DRAGOON
LANDING TO DECEMBER 15, 1944.

POITIERS

F   R

ILE D'OLÉRON

ANGOULÊME

LIMOGES

BAY OF BISCAY

PÉRIGUEUX

BORDEAUX

DISINTEGRATION OF GER
IN SOUTHWESTERN FRAN
JUNCTION OF OUR TROOP

GARONNE

SANTANDER

BILBAO

BAYONNE

BURGOS

PAU

TOULOUSE

SPAIN

CARCASSONNE

50   100   MILES   200   300

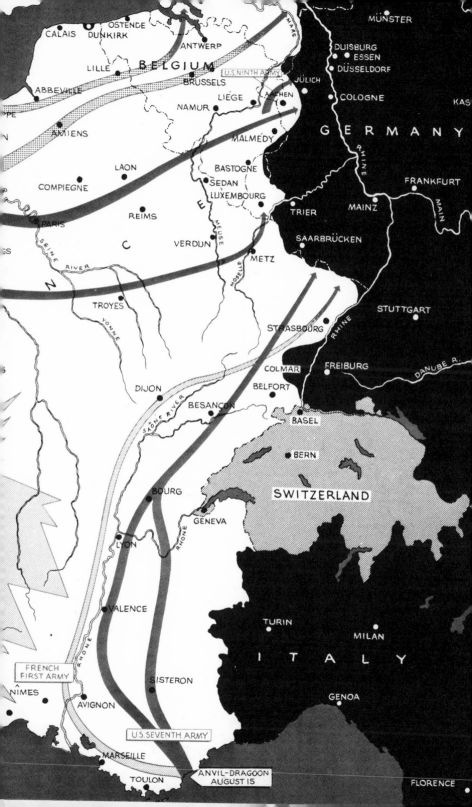

Chapter 17

AUTUMN FIGHTING ON GERMANY'S FRONTIER

IN SEPTEMBER OUR ARMIES WERE CROWDING UP against the borders of Germany. Enemy defenses were naturally and artificially strong. Devers' U. S. Seventh and French First Armies were swinging in eastward against the Vosges Mountains, which formed a traditional defensive barrier. In the north the Siegfried Line, backed up by the Rhine River, comprised a defensive system that only a well-supplied and determined force could hope to breach.

For the moment we were still dependent upon the ports at Cherbourg and Arromanches, and because of their limited capacity and the restricted communications leading out of them the accumulation of forward reserves was impossible. It was even difficult to maintain adequately the troops that were daily engaged in constant fighting for position along the front. This would continue to be true until we could get Antwerp and Marseille working at capacity. Of the former, Bradley wrote to me on September 21: ". . . all plans for future operations always lead back to the fact that in order to supply an operation of any size beyond the Rhine, the port of Antwerp is essential."[1] He never failed to see that logistics would be a vital factor in the final defeat of Germany.

With the advent of bad weather, road maintenance presented additional problems to the Services of Supply because of the shallow foundations of many of the European roads, particularly in Belgium. In numerous instances our heavily laden trucks broke completely through the surfaces of main highways and it seemed almost impossible to fill the resulting quagmires with sufficient stone and gravel to restore them to a semblance of usefulness.

To reduce dependence on roads we brought in quantities of railway rolling stock to replace that destroyed earlier in the war.[2] To do this expeditiously, railway engineers developed a simple scheme that was adopted with splendid results. Heavy equipment like railway cars can normally be brought into a theater only at prepared docks. Unloading is laborious because of the need for using only the heaviest kind of cranes and booms. Our engineers, however, merely laid railway tracks in the bottom of LSTs. They then laid railway lines down to the water's edge at the beaches of embarkation and debarkation and, by arranging flexible connections between ground tracks and those in the LSTs, simply rolled the cars in and out of the ships. But while waging and winning, during the autumn months, the battle of supply, we found no cessation of fighting along the front.

Our ground forces, while not yet at peak strength, continued constantly to increase. On August 1 our divisional strength on the Continent was thirty-five, with four American and two British divisions in the United Kingdom. By October 1 our aggregate strength on the Continent, including the Sixth Army Group which had advanced through the south of France, was fifty-four divisions, with six still staging through the United Kingdom.[3] All our divisions were short in infantry replacements, and in total numerical strength of ground forces the Germans still had a marked advantage. We were disposed along a line which, beginning in the north on the banks of the Rhine, stretched five hundred miles southward to the border of Switzerland. To the south of that country detachments were posted on the French-Italian border to guard against raids on our lines of communication by the Germans in Italy.

This meant that, counting all types of divisions—infantry, armored, and airborne—we could, on the average, deploy less than one division to each ten miles of front.

In view of all these conditions there was much to be said for an early assumption of the defensive in order to conserve all our strength for building up the logistic system and to avoid the suffering of a winter campaign. I declined to adopt such a course, and all principal commanders agreed with me that it was to our advantage to push the fighting.

One important consideration that indicated the advantage of keeping up our offensives to the limit of our troop and logistical capacity was the knowledge that in order to replace his great losses of July, August, and September the enemy was hastily organizing and equipping new divisions. In many instances he was compelled to bring these troops into the lines with but sketchy training. Initially they had a low order of efficiency, and attacks against them were far less costly than they would become later as these new enemy formations succeeded in perfecting their training and their defensive installations.

Intelligence agencies were required to make exhaustive daily analyses of enemy losses on all parts of the front. The purpose was to avoid attacks in those areas where the balance sheet in losses showed any tendency to favor the enemy. During this period we took as a general guide the principle that operations, except in those areas where we had some specific and vital objective, such as in the case of the Roer dams, were profitable to us only where the daily calculations showed that enemy losses were double our own.

We were certain that by continuing an unremitting offensive we would, in spite of hardship and privation, gain additional advantages over the enemy. Specifically we were convinced that this policy would result in shortening the war and therefore in the saving of thousands of Allied lives.

Consequently the fall period was to become a memorable one because of a series of bitterly contested battles, usually conducted under the most trying conditions of weather and terrain. Walcheren Island, Aachen, the Hurtgen Forest, the Roer dams, the Saar Basin, and the Vosges Mountains were all to give their names during the fall months of 1944 to battles that, in the sum of their results, greatly hastened the end of the war in Europe. In addition to the handicap of weather there was the difficulty of shortages in ammunition and supplies. The hardihood, courage, and resourcefulness of the Allied soldier were never tested more thoroughly and with more brilliant results than during this period.

The strength of our growing ground force was multiplied by the presence of a powerful and efficient air force.

Tactically, an air force possesses a mobility which places in the hand of the high command a weapon that may be used on successive days against targets hundreds of miles apart. Aerial bombardments are delivered in such concentrated form as to produce among defending forces a shock that is scarcely obtainable with any amount of artillery.

For pinpointing of accessible targets, the air was normally not so effective as artillery. Moreover, against general targets, air power did not destroy—it damaged. An industrial area was never eliminated by a single raid and, indeed, rarely obliterated beyond partial repair even by repeated bombings. Lines of communication were never, except in extended periods of good weather, completely severed beyond any hope of use. But the air did deplete the usefulness of anything it attacked and, given ideal flying conditions and when used in large concentrations, could carry this process of depletion to near perfection.

Air attack by a single combat plane is a fleeting thing, and the results achieved do not always conform to first estimates. Air reports of destroyed vehicles, particularly armored vehicles, were always too optimistic by far. This was not the fault of pilots. Each fighter-bomber airplane was equipped with a movie camera which automatically recorded the apparent results of every attack. The films were examined at bases and became the basis of "Air Claims," but we found that this method provided no accurate estimate of the damage actually inflicted. Exact appraisal could be made only after the area was captured by the ground troops.

For the delivery, in a single blow, of a vast tonnage of explosives upon a given area, the power of the air force is unique. Employment of large bombers in this role has the advantage of imposing no strain upon the forward lines of communication. Every round of ammunition that is fired from an artillery shell is unloaded at a main base and from there progresses to the front over crowded rail and road lines. After several handlings it is finally available for use at the gun site. The big bombers are stationed far in the rear; in our case they were in the United Kingdom. The bombs they used were either manufactured in that country or brought over from the United States in cargo ships. From factories or ports they went to appropriate airfields, and from there were delivered in one handling directly against the enemy.

The air can be employed in a variety of ways to forward the progress of the land battle. Its most common functions are to prevent interference with our ground forces by enemy airplanes, to render tactical assistance to attacking troops by fighter-bomber effort against selected targets on the front, and to facilitate capture of strongly defended points by heavy bombardment. In these close-support activities it has, of course, certain limitations. In Europe bad weather was the worst enemy of the air, and the unexpected advent of rain, fog, or cloud often badly disarranged a battle plan. In the middle of December bad weather prevented the air from discerning the concentration of unused German strength in the Ardennes, and made the air force of little use to us in the first week of that battle. Moreover, by its nature, the air cannot stay constantly at the front; each plane must return periodically to its base for refueling and servicing. This limited the number present at the front to a fraction of the total numbers available. Occasionally enemy planes could therefore strafe our front lines, even though in over-all numbers our air strength was relatively overwhelming.

The air force had other important uses. One of these was to attack the enemy's supply lines. Still another was that of increasing the decisiveness of the ground battle. Every ground commander seeks the battle of annihilation; so far as conditions permit, he tries to duplicate in modern war the classic example of Cannae. In the beginning of a great campaign, battles of annihilation are possible only against some isolated portion of the enemy's entire force. Destruction of bridges, culverts, railways, roads, and canals by the air force tends to isolate the force under attack, even if the severance of its communications is not complete.

In the fall of 1944 our air strength, in operational units, including the associated bomber strength, was approximately 4700 fighters, 6000 light, medium, and heavy bombers, and 4000 reconnaissance, transport, and other types.[4]

While this build-up was proceeding during the fall months there was, as originally planned, much to be done operationally. In the north, besides capturing the approaches to Antwerp, it was desirable to make progress toward closing the Rhine, because it was from this region that our heaviest attacks would be launched in the crossing of that river. Farther south, on Bradley's front, it was advantageous to conduct preliminary operations looking toward the final destruction of all German forces remaining west of the Rhine. Thus we would not only deplete the forces available for the later defense of the river but we would also secure the areas in the Saar region from which we planned to launch strong attacks in conjunction with those in the north, when we were ready to envelop the Ruhr.

In the fall fighting we again encountered our old enemy, the weather. The June storm on the beaches had established a forty-year record for severity. Again in the autumn the floods broke another meteorological record extending back over decades. By November 1 many of the rivers were out of their banks and weather conditions along the whole front slowed up our attacks. In spite of these conditions we proceeded with the general plan of building up great bases and communications to the borders of Germany, closing the

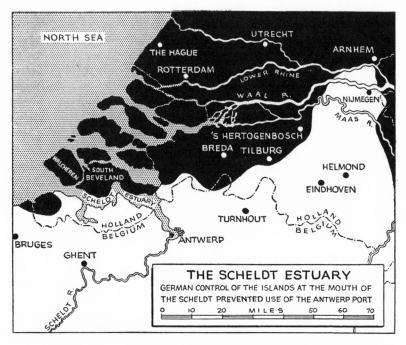

THE SCHELDT ESTUARY

GERMAN CONTROL OF THE ISLANDS AT THE MOUTH OF THE SCHELDT PREVENTED USE OF THE ANTWERP PORT

Rhine with initial emphasis on the left, preparing for the destruction of the German forces west of the river, throughout its length, and getting ready to launch the final assaults toward the heart of Germany.

Capture of the approaches to Antwerp was a difficult operation. The Scheldt Estuary was heavily mined, and the German forces on Walcheren Island and South Beveland Island completely dominated the water routes leading to the city. It was unfortunate that we had not been successful in seizing the area during our great northeastward reach in the early days of September.

Reduction of these strongholds required a joint naval, air, and ground operation. Montgomery gave General Crerar of the Canadian First Army responsibility for developing and executing the plans.[5] Preparatory work was started shortly after the city fell into our hands on September 4.

The only land approach to the hostile positions was by a narrow neck connecting South Beveland with the mainland, and the operation was worked out to include an attack westward along this isthmus, co-ordinated with an amphibious assault brought in by sea. The necessary forces for the attack could not be assembled until late October.

If I had not attempted the Arnhem operation, possibly we could have begun the Walcheren attack some two or three weeks earlier.

To the Canadian 2d Division was assigned the job of entering the neck, and from there attacking westward along the isthmus against the Germans on South Beveland. The troops were frequently forced to fight waist-deep in water against strong German resistance and it took them three days to reach the west end of the isthmus. But by October 27 the division had established itself on the island proper. The British 52d Division was landed on the south shore of South Beveland on the night of October 25–26. The two forces then fought forward in a converging attack to a juncture and by the thirtieth of the month South Beveland was entirely in our possession.

The defending garrison on Walcheren Island consisted of the troops that had escaped from South Beveland and of detachments from the German Fifteenth Army, which had originally been stationed in the Calais area.

The amphibious assault against Walcheren, on November 1, was carried out against some of the strongest local resistance we met at any coast line during the European operation. To provide supporting fire, only small naval vessels could be used but these unhesitatingly pushed in close to the Walcheren Island shore and persistently engaged heavy land batteries in order to assist the troops going ashore. Losses among the naval vessels were abnormally high but the courage and tenacity of the crews were responsible both for the successful landing and for minimizing losses among assaulting personnel.

A feature of this difficult campaign was a novel employment of big bombers to blow up portions of the dikes that held back the sea from the lower levels of the island. These breaches, permitting the sea to flood critical sections of the defenses, were of great usefulness in an operation that throughout presented unusual difficulties.[6]

Final German resistance on the island was eliminated by November 9, by which time some 10,000 enemy troops had been captured, including a division commander. The cost was high. For the entire series of operations in the area our own casualties, almost entirely Canadian and British, numbered 27,633. This compared to less than 25,000 in the capture of Sicily, where we defeated a garrison of 350,000.[7]

With this effort accomplished, we began the clearing of mines from the Scheldt Estuary. As usual the Germans had installed their mines in great profusion and the job, in spite of unremitting work on the part of the Navy, required two weeks for completion.

The first ships to begin unloading in Antwerp arrived there November 26. The Germans had begun launching V-1 and V-2 weapons against the city in mid-October. While the bombs were frequently erratic, as they had been in London, the V-2s caused considerable damage in the district. Numbers of civilians and soldiers were killed and communications and supply work were often interrupted, although usually only for brief periods. The civilian population of Antwerp sustained these attacks unflinchingly. One V-2 bomb struck a crowded theater and killed hundreds of civilians and an almost equal number of soldiers.

The enemy also employed large numbers of E-boats (a small, speedy type of surface torpedo boat) and tiny submarines to interfere with our use of Antwerp. These weapons we countered by energetic naval and air action. In spite of all difficulties, Antwerp quickly became the northern bulwark of our entire logistical system.

While this spectacular and gratifying operation was in progress on the northern flank, the rest of the front was far from quiet. On the Twenty-first Army Group front Montgomery succeeded in concentrating enough strength so that on November 15, immediately following the fall of Walcheren Island, he undertook an eastward drive. Winter conditions were now approaching and his advances were made over difficult country, but by December 4 he had cleared out the last German pocket west of the Maas, the same river which, farther south in Belgium and France, is called the Meuse.

Because of the extended front held by the Twenty-first Army Group it was impossible at the moment to launch further strong offensives in that area. Montgomery's army group had long since absorbed all the British Empire troops available in the United Kingdom, including the Canadian Army and the Polish division. Further reinforcement was impossible unless, as eventually happened, a few additional units could be brought up from the Mediterranean theater. The Americans were in a different position. Reinforcing divisions were rapidly coming from the United States, and as they reached the battle front they provided strength for the execution of important tasks and made it possible to broaden the American sector whenever necessary to provide opportunity for concentrations on the flanks.

Immediately south of the British area Bradley, on October 22, brought into line the U. S. Ninth Army under General Simpson.[3] On November 16, Bradley renewed his offensive toward the Rhine in the northern part of his sector. The attack was carried out by the

Ninth and First Armies and was preceded by a heavy bombing of the enemy and by artillery bombardment. Twelve hundred and four American and 1188 British heavy bombers participated, the operation being another example of the extent to which we were then using the heavy bomber to intervene effectively in the ground battle.[9]

These attacks initially employed fourteen divisions, and the number was soon increased to seventeen. Nevertheless, progress was slow and the fighting intense. On the right flank of this attack the First Army got involved in the Hurtgen Forest, the scene of one of the most bitterly contested battles of the entire campaign. The enemy had all the advantages of strong defensive country, and the attacking Americans had to depend almost exclusively upon infantry weapons because of the thickness of the forest. The weather was abominable and the German garrison was particularly stubborn, but Yankee doggedness finally won. Thereafter, whenever veterans of the American 4th, 9th, and 28th Divisions referred to hard fighting they did so in terms of comparison with the Battle of Hurtgen Forest, which they placed at the top of the list.[10]

In spite of numerous smaller battles of the same sanguinary character, in which units were pinned down for days as they dug out the defending garrisons, general progress continued until we reached the banks of the Roer River, where the Ninth Army arrived on December 3.

At the banks of the Roer we met a new kind of tactical problem. Farther up the river, at Schmidt, were great dams. They were of special defensive value to the German because, by operation of the floodgates in the dams, he could vary the water level below them. This made an immediate assault across the Roer River impossible, since any troops successful in crossing could be isolated by a flooding of the river and thereafter eliminated by the employment of German reserves.[11]

We first attempted the destruction of the dams by air. The bombing against them was accurate and direct hits were secured. However, the concrete structures were so massive that damage was negligible, and there was no recourse except to take them by ground attack. Because the dams were located in difficult mountain country the attack was certain to be slow and costly. After an attack by the 28th Division had failed to make satisfactory progress a heavy assault was started by the First Army December 13.

Meanwhile, south of the Ardennes Forest, the Third Army launched an attack on November 8. Its offensive was aimed generally at the Saar region and made excellent initial progress. North of Metz, bridge-heads were established across the Moselle, and shortly after the middle of November the leading troops crossed the German frontier. Metz was surrounded and cut off. The city surrendered November 22.[12] However, some of the forts in the vicinity held out stubbornly and it was almost the middle of December before the final one was reduced and mopped up.

In the right sector of the Third Army the advance quickly brought us up against some of the strongest sections of the Siegfried Line, those guarding the triangle between the Moselle and the Rhine. In this region the Siegfried comprised two general lines of defenses. The forward one was a continuous system of obstacles and pillboxes, but was of no great depth. In the rear was another line, of extraordinary strength. It featured a series of field forts, mutually supporting, arranged in a line more than two miles deep. These defenses slowed up the advance of the Third Army, and since their reduction required a vast amount of heavy artillery ammunition, the attacks there were suspended until additional logistical support could be provided.

Still farther south there was much fighting in Devers' Sixth Army Group. During September it advanced northward through the Rhone Valley and came in abreast of the Third Army line, facing eastward in the difficult Vosges Mountain area. Devers attacked that formi-dable barrier on November 14, in an attempt to penetrate into the plains of Alsace. Once we could secure this region Devers' forces could concentrate the bulk of their strength on the left and the de-fenders of the Saar would have to resist powerful attacks on two fronts.

The French First Army led the attack on Devers' front and breached the Belfort Gap within a week. Its leading troops quickly reached the Rhine. This turned the flank of the German position in the Vosges and forced a general withdrawal in front of the U. S. Seventh Army under General Patch. This force, attacking abreast of the French First Army, had found exceedingly tough going through the tortuous passes of the mountains. In Patch's army Major General Edward H. Brooks's VI Corps was on the right, and Major General Wade H. Haislip's XV Corps, formerly with Patton, was on the left. When the German withdrawal started because of the French success, these troops made rapid progress. The U. S. 44th Division captured Saarebourg on the twenty-first, and on the twenty-second our troops broke out into the Rhine plain. Strasbourg, on the banks of the Rhine, was entered by the French 2d Armored Division on the twenty-second of the month. The enemy, as was his habitual practice, launched a counterattack almost instantly. Initially, our advancing troops lost some ground but the 44th Division fought off the enemy and regained its positions. The 79th Division now came abreast of the 44th and the two of them made rapid progress toward Haguenau, which they took on December 12.[13]

During the progress of these attacks I visited Devers to make a survey of the situation with him. On his extreme left there appeared to be no immediate advantage in pushing down into the Rhine plain. I directed him to turn the left corps of Patch's army northward to bring it into line connecting with the right flank of Patton's army, on the western slopes of the Vosges. That corps was to support the Third Army in its attacks against the Saar, which were soon to be renewed.

On the remainder of Devers' front it was of course desirable to close up to the Rhine as rapidly as possible and then, by moving northward, to gain the river bank all the way northward to the Saar. However, I particularly cautioned Devers not to start this northward movement, on the east of the Vosges Mountains, until he had cleaned out all enemy formations in his rear.

Sometimes it is advisable to by-pass enemy garrisons and merely contain them until their isolation and lack of supply compel surrender. However, this procedure is normally applicable only if the enemy's troops are completely surrounded. Moreover, the method always immobilizes a portion of our own troops and it is never applicable when the pocket is in an area which we must use for offensive purposes or from which it can threaten our communications. I had gotten tired of dropping off troops to watch enemy garrisons in the rear areas, so I impressed upon Devers that to allow any Germans to remain west of the river in the upper Rhine plain, south of Strasbourg, would be certain to cause us later embarrassment.

General Devers believed that the French First Army, which had operated so brilliantly in breaking through the Belfort Gap and reaching the Rhine, could easily take care of the remnants of the German Nineteenth Army still facing them in the Colmar area. In describing the situation to me he said, "The German Nineteenth has ceased to exist as a tactical force." Consequently he estimated that he could carry out my instructions for the elimination of the Germans near

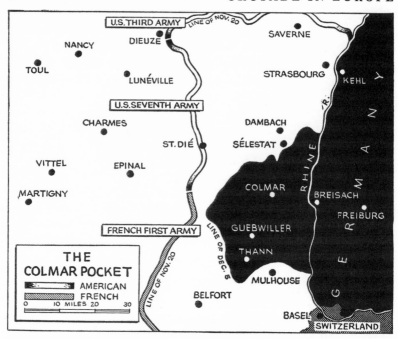

THE
COLMAR POCKET

AMERICAN
FRENCH
0   10 MILES 20   30

Colmar without the assistance of General Brooks's VI Corps. He had reason to feel justified in this estimate, particularly in view of the great defeats already inflicted on the German Army. He ordered the VI Corps to turn northward in the plain east of the Vosges, so that it could co-operate with the XV Corps, west of those mountains, in the attacks against the Saar.

Devers' estimate of the French First Army's immediate effectiveness was overoptimistic, while he probably underrated the defensive power of German units when they set themselves stubbornly to hold a strong position. The French Army, weakened by its recent offensive, found it impossible to eliminate the German resistance on its immediate front, and thus was formed the Colmar pocket, a German garrison which established and maintained itself in the defensible ground west of the Rhine in the vicinity of Colmar. The existence of this pocket was later to work to our definite disadvantage.[14]

The fighting throughout the front, from Switzerland, to the mouth of the Rhine, descended during the late fall months to the dirtiest kind of infantry slugging. Advances were slow and laborious. Gains were ordinarily measured in terms of yards rather than miles. Operations became mainly a matter of artillery and ammunition and, on the part of the infantry, endurance, stamina, and courage. In these conditions infantry losses were high, particularly in rifle platoons. The infantry, which in all kinds of warfare habitually absorbs the bulk of the losses, was now taking practically all of them. These were by no means due to enemy action alone. In other respects, too, the infantry suffered an abnormal percentage of casualties. Because of exposure the cases of frostbite, trench foot, and respiratory diseases were far more numerous among infantry soldiers than others. Because of depletion of their infantry strength, divisions quickly exhausted themselves in action. Without men to carry on the daily task of advance and maneuver under the curtain of artillery fire our offensive strength fell off markedly.

Aside from the problem of depleted unit strength, we found it difficult to find enough divisions to perform all the tasks that required immediate attention and still maintain the concentrations required for successful attacks.

As the infantry replacement problem became acute we resorted to every kind of expedient to keep units up to strength. Full reports were made to the War Department so that effort in the homeland would be concentrated on this need. We combed through our own organization to find men in the Services of Supply and elsewhere who could be retrained rapidly for employment in infantry formations. Wherever possible we replaced a man in service organizations by one from the limited-service category or by a Wac.[15] General Spaatz found that he could give us considerable help in this matter. Ten thousand men were transferred from his units to the ground forces. All these measures, however, failed to keep filled the ranks of the infantry formations. Realizing this, General Marshall sent me a suggestion that seemed to possess great merit. It was that the infantry of the trained divisions in the United States should be dispatched to us without waiting for the additional shipping needed to bring their artillery, trucks, and other heavy equipment. He and I hoped that in this way we could bring into line new regiments and give them valuable battle training by rotating them with the infantry of divisions already in the line. The principal purpose was to give the tired and depleted infantry of a veteran division opportunity to refit and rehabilitate itself while its place on the front was taken by one of the new full-strength regiments.[16]

In the outcome our hopes were not completely fulfilled. As the winter wore on our need for troops became so great and our long lines were so thinly manned that when the new regiments arrived each army commander frequently found it necessary, instead of replacing tired troops with the fresh ones, to assign a special sector to the new troops and to support them with such artillery from corps and army formations as he could scrape together for the purpose.

This situation was entirely unsatisfactory and a complete violation of the purpose for which the new regiments were rushed into the theater ahead of their heavy equipment. Nevertheless, the requirements of the front allowed us to do nothing else, and though wherever possible we returned to the original plan of rotation, we were never able to implement it in the manner intended. In the over-all result, however, the early arrival of these infantry units had a profound and beneficial effect. In particular crises of the campaign they allowed us to effect a concentration of veteran units which would otherwise have been impossible.

In both World Wars the infantry replacement problem plagued American commanders in the field. Only a small percentage of the manpower in a war theater operates in front of the light artillery line established by the divisions. Yet this small portion absorbs about ninety per cent of the casualties. Many of these casualties are soon fit to return to the front, but this creates another problem of great importance—particularly in maintaining morale.

Replacements, whether newly arrived from the homeland or recently discharged from hospitals, are normally processed to the front through replacement depots. Thus there is a great intermingling of veterans from numerous divisions and of others who have not seen action. When the need for replacements is acute, efficiency demands that all men available in depots be dispatched promptly to the place where most needed. Individual assignment according to personal preference is well-nigh impossible.

However, veterans always insist on returning to their own divisions, and when this cannot be done a definite morale emergency results. We tried, within the limits imposed by dire needs, to return veterans to their own units, but in emergency the rule had to be violated. In the fall of 1944 all such purposes had to be thrown overboard in the effort to supply men to the areas of most critical need.

Maintenance of morale was a problem of first importance. We had established a furlough plan which gave at least some men the opportunity to go back to Paris or London. We also established divisional centers in rear of the lines where a company or a battalion could occasionally get out of the fighting zone and the men could secure baths, warm beds, and a day or two of rest. In Paris we established an Allied Club in one of the city's largest hotels. It was reserved exclusively for enlisted men and was one of the most successful activities we had for the benefit of men who got an opportunity to visit the city. We depended upon the Red Cross and the USO for civilian aid in the matter of recreation and entertainment.[17]

During World War I the American Army had received recreation and entertainment assistance from a variety of civilian organizations. They were effective, but the many administrative difficulties arising out of contacts with so many different groups led the War Department at the beginning of World War II to insist that this work should be handled by two principal agencies. These were, in the recreational field, the Red Cross and, in the entertainment field, the USO. The services of these devoted people to soldiers in the field were beyond praise. The Red Cross operated clubs and coffee and doughnut wagons; it sent visitors to hospitals, wrote letters, furnished friendly counsel; and all in all was as successful in providing an occasional hour of homelike atmosphere for the fighting men as was possible in an area thousands of miles from America.[18]

In the same way the USO succeeded in giving the soldier an occasional hour or two of entertainment which he never failed to appreciate. I have seen entertainers carrying on their work in forward and exposed positions, sometimes under actual bombing attack. In rest areas, in camps, in bases, and in every type of hospital they brought to soldiers a moment of forgetfulness which in war is always a boon.

In the late fall, as we approached the borders of Germany, we studied the desirability of committing our air force to the destruction of the Rhine bridges, on which the existence of the German forces west of the river depended. If all of them could be destroyed, it was certain that with our great air force we could so limit the usefulness of floating bridges that the enemy would soon have to withdraw. We entertained no hope of saving these bridges for our own later use. It was accepted that once the enemy decided that he had to retreat he would destroy all the bridges, and our arrival would find none standing, unless by sheer accident.

Our reasons for declining to commit the air force against the bridges were based upon considerations of priority and effectiveness.

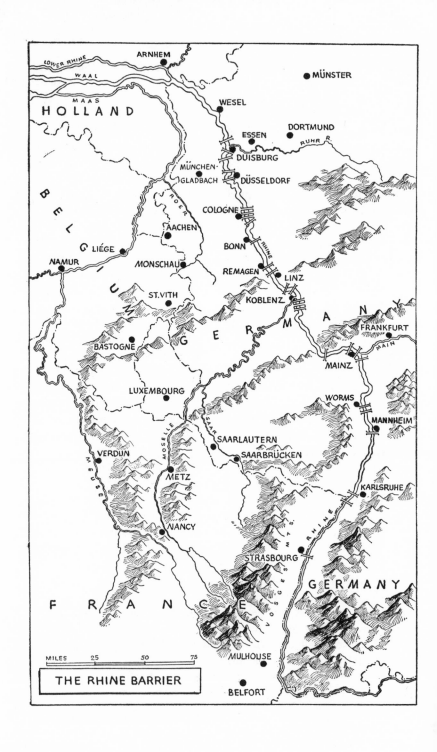

THE RHINE BARRIER

"... battles of annihilation are possible only against some isolated portion of the enemy's entire force. Destruction of bridges, culverts, railways, roads, and canals by the air force tends to isolate the force under attack . . ." *Page 325*

Ulm Rail Yards After December 1944 Raid

SUPREME OVER GERMANY

"By early 1945 the effects of our air offensive against the German economy were becoming catastrophic . . . there developed a continuous crisis in German transportation and in all phases of her war effort." *Page 368*

To destroy merely a few was of little use. A total of twenty-six major bridges, it was reported to me at that time, spanned the river; some twenty of them would have to be rendered useless or the effort would be only partially effective. Even with the best of flying conditions the task would require a prolonged and heavy bombing effort. But at that period of the year in Europe there rarely occurs a day of sufficiently good weather to allow pinpoint bombing from great heights, and enemy anti-aircraft was still so strong and so efficient that low-flying bombing was far too expensive. Consequently the only method we could employ against the bridges was blind bombing, through the clouds. The Air Staff calculated that destruction of the bulk of the bridges would require vastly more time and bomb tonnage than we could afford to divert from other vitally important purposes.[19]

One of the greatest of these other purposes was to deplete Germany's reserves of fuel oil. By this time the enemy was getting into precarious position with respect to this vital item of supply. The orders to the heavy bombers were to keep pounding all sources of oil, refineries, and distribution systems to the limit of their ability. This tactic had a great effect not only generally upon the entire war-making power of Germany but also directly upon the front. Every German commander had always to calculate his plans in terms of availability of fuel, and it was to our advantage to keep pounding away to increase the enemy's embarrassment.[20]

This air campaign against oil reserves tended to emphasize one of the great advantages we had enjoyed over the enemy in all the Mediterranean and European campaigning. It was in the matter of relative mobility. The American Army has always featured mobility in the organization and equipment of its forces. Before the advent of the motorcar our Army was proportionately stronger in cavalry than most other armies of the time. With the coming of the motor, the American Army eagerly seized upon it to gain added mobility. Our advantage in this direction was vastly increased by the mass production methods of American industry. There was certainly no other nation in the world that could have supplied, repaired, and supported the great fleet of motor transportation that the American armed forces used in World War II.[21]

Through late November and early December the badly stretched condition of our troops caused constant concern, particularly on Bradley's front. In order to maintain the two attacks that we then considered important we had to concentrate available forces in the vicinity of the Roer dams on the north and bordering the Saar on the south. This weakened the static, or protective, force in the Ardennes region. For a period we had a total of only three divisions on a front of some seventy-five miles between Trier and Monschau and were never able to place more than four in that region.[27] While my own staff kept in closest possible touch with this situation, I personally conferred with Bradley about it at various times. Our conclusion was that in the Ardennes region we were running a definite risk but we believed it to be a mistaken policy to suspend our attacks all along the front merely to make ourselves safe until all reinforcements arriving from the United States could bring us up to peak strength.

In discussing the problem Bradley specifically outlined to me the factors that, on his front, he considered favorable to continuing the offensives. With all of these I emphatically agreed. First, he pointed out the tremendous relative gains we were realizing in the matter of casualties. The daily average of enemy losses was double our own. Next, he believed that the only place in which the enemy could attempt a serious counterattack was in the Ardennes region. The two points at which we had concentrated troops of the Twelfth Army Group for offensive action lay immediately on the flanks of this area. One, under Hodges, was just to the northward; the other, under Patton, was just to the south. Bradley felt, therefore, that we were in the best possible position to concentrate against the flanks of any attack in the Ardennes area that might be attempted by the Germans. He further estimated that if the enemy should deliver a surprise attack in the Ardennes he would have great difficulty in supply if he tried to advance as far as the line of the Meuse. Unless the enemy could overrun our large supply dumps he would soon find himself in trouble, particularly in any period when our air forces could operate efficiently. Bradley traced out on the map the line he estimated the German spearheads could possibly reach, and his estimates later proved to be remarkably accurate, with a maximum error of five miles at any one point. In the area which he believed the enemy might overrun by surprise attack he placed very few supply installations. We had large depots at Liége and Verdun but he was confident that neither of these could be reached by the enemy.

Bradley was also certain that we could always prevent the enemy from crossing the Meuse and reaching the major supply establishments lying to the westward of that river. Consequently any such enemy attack, in the long run, would prove abortive.

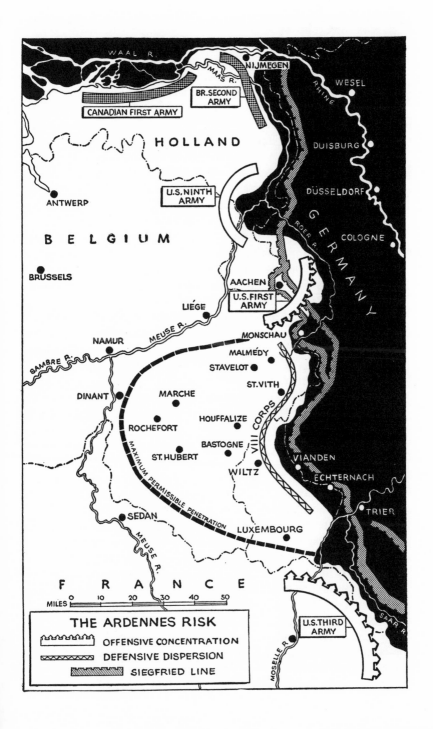

THE ARDENNES RISK

<table>
<tr><td>⌐⌐⌐⌐⌐⌐⌐⌐</td><td>OFFENSIVE CONCENTRATION</td></tr>
<tr><td>XXXXXXXXX</td><td>DEFENSIVE DISPERSION</td></tr>
<tr><td>////////////</td><td>SIEGFRIED LINE</td></tr>
</table>

Our general conclusion was that we could not afford to sit still doing nothing, while the German perfected his defenses and the training of his troops, merely because we believed that at some time before the enemy acknowledged final defeat he would attempt a major counteroffensive. Bradley's final remark was: "We tried to capture all these Germans before they could get inside the Siegfried. If they will come out of it and fight us again in the open, it is all to our advantage."

Both Bradley and I believed that nothing could be so expensive to us as to allow the front to stagnate, going into defensive winter quarters while we waited for additional reinforcements from the homeland.

The responsibility for maintaining only four divisions on the Ardennes front and for running the risk of a large German penetration in that area was mine. At any moment from November 1 onward I could have passed to the defensive along the whole front and made our lines absolutely secure from attack while we awaited reinforcements. My basic decision was to continue the offensive to the extreme limit of our ability, and it was this decision that was responsible for the startling successes of the first week of the German December attack.

In early December, General Patton, with his Third Army, was making preparations to renew the attack against the Saar, the assault to begin December 19. Patton was very hopeful of decisive effect; but, determined to avoid involvement in a long, inconclusive, and costly offensive, Bradley and I agreed that the Third Army attack would have to show tremendous gains within a week or it would be suspended. We knew of course that if it was successful in gaining great advantages the enemy would have to concentrate from other sectors to meet it, and therefore Patton's success would tend to increase our safety elsewhere. On the other hand, if we should get a considerable number of divisions embroiled in costly and slow advances we not only would be accomplishing little: we would be in no position to react quickly at any other place along the front.[23]

In the meantime the First Army's attack against the Roer dams had gotten off as scheduled on December 13, but relatively few divisions were engaged. Early in the month the weather, which had been intermittently bad, took a turn for the worse. Fog and clouds practically prohibited aerial reconnaissance and snows began to appear in the uplands, together with increasing cold.[24]

The German Sixth Panzer Army, which had appeared on our front, was the strongest and most efficient mobile reserve remaining to the enemy within his whole country. When it arrived on our front it was originally stationed opposite the left of the Twelfth Army Group, apparently to operate against any crossing of the Roer. When the American attacks on that front had to be suspended early in December, we lost track of the Sixth Panzer Army and could not locate it by any means available. At that time some Intelligence reports indicated a growing anxiety about our weakness in the Ardennes, where we knew that the enemy was increasing his infantry formations. Previously he had, like ourselves, been using that portion of the front in which to rest tired divisions.[25]

This type of report, however, is always coming from one portion or another of a front. The commander who took counsel only of all the gloomy Intelligence estimates would never win a battle; he would forever be sitting, fearfully waiting for the predicted catastrophes. In this case I later learned that the man who predicted the coming of the attack estimated, during its crisis, that the enemy had six or seven divisions of fresh and unused reserves ready to hurl into the fight.

In any event the fighting during the autumn followed the pattern I had personally prescribed. We remained on the offensive and weakened ourselves where necessary to maintain those offensives. This plan gave the German opportunity to launch his attack against a weak portion of our lines. If giving him that chance is to be condemned by historians, their condemnation should be directed at me alone.

Chapter 18

HITLER'S
LAST BID

ON DECEMBER 16, 1944, GENERAL BRADLEY CAME to my headquarters to discuss ways and means of overcoming our acute shortages in infantry replacements. Just as he entered my office a staff officer came in to report slight penetrations of our lines in the front of General Middleton's VIII Corps and the right of General Gerow's V Corps in the Ardennes region. The staff officer located the points on my battle map, and Bradley and I discussed the probable meaning.[1]

I was immediately convinced that this was no local attack; it was not logical for the enemy to attempt merely a minor offensive in the Ardennes, unless of course it should be a feint to attract our attention while he launched a major effort elsewhere. This possibility we ruled out. On other portions of the front either we were so strong that the Germans could not hope to attack successfully, or there was a lack of major objectives that he could reasonably hope to attain. Moreover, we knew that for a number of days German troop strength in the Ardennes area had been gradually increasing. It was through this same region that the Germans launched their great attack of 1940 which drove the British forces from the Continent, and France out of the war. That first attack was led by the same commander we were now facing, Von Rundstedt. It was possible that he hoped to repeat his successes of more than four years earlier. We had always been convinced that before the Germans acknowledged final defeat in the West they would attempt one desperate counteroffensive. It seemed likely to Bradley and me that they were now starting this kind of attack.

On the north of the critical region General Hodges' First Army, in

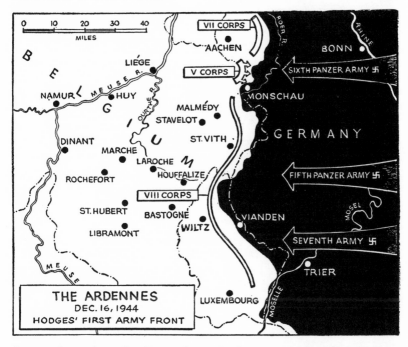

its attack against the Roer dams, had as yet engaged only four divisions. On the south of the Ardennes front General Patton was still concentrating and preparing for the renewed attack against the Saar which was to begin December 19.

Bradley and I were sufficiently convinced that a major attack was developing against the center of the Twelfth Army Group to agree to begin shifting some strength from both flanks toward the Ardennes sector. This was a preliminary move—rather a precaution— made in order to support the seventy-five-mile length of the VIII Corps front, providing our calculations as to German intentions should prove correct.

We called a number of the SHAEF staff into our conference room; among them were Air Chief Marshal Tedder, and Generals Smith, Bull, and Strong. The operational maps before us showed that on each flank of the Ardennes the bulk of a United States armored division was out of the front lines and could be moved quickly. On the north was the 7th Armored Division commanded by Major General Robert W. Hasbrouck. In Patton's army on the south was the 10th Armored Division under Major General William H. Morris, Jr.

We agreed that these two divisions should immediately begin to close in toward the threatened area, the exact destination of each to be determined later by Bradley. This meant postponement of preparations for the attack in the Saar and we knew that General Patton would protest. His heart was set on the new offensive, which he thought would gain great results. But to Bradley and me there now appeared to be developing the very situation that we had felt justified in challenging because of the location of our concentrations on the flank of the weak Ardennes front. We had always felt the risk to be justified by the conviction that in emergency we could react swiftly. The critical moment, in our judgment, was now upon us. In addition to directing these preliminary moves Bradley alerted all army commanders in his group to be ready to provide additional units for the battle that he expected to develop.[2]

With the staff we carefully went over the list of reserves then available to us. Among those most readily accessible was the XVIII Airborne Corps under General Ridgway, located near Reims. It included the 82d and the 101st Airborne Divisions, both battle-tested formations of the highest caliber. They had shortly before been heavily engaged in the fighting in Holland, and were not yet fully rehabilitated. Moreover, they were relatively weak in heavy supporting weapons, but these Bradley felt he could supply from the unthreatened portion of his long line.[3]

The U. S. 11th Armored Division had recently arrived and the 17th Airborne Division was in the United Kingdom ready to come to the Continent. The 87th Infantry Division could also be brought into the area within a reasonable time.

In the British sector, far to the north, Montgomery was preparing for a new offensive. At the moment he had one complete corps, the 30, out of the line.[4] With the resources available to us, we were confident that any attack the German might launch could eventually be effectively countered. But we were under no illusions concerning the weakness of the VIII Corps line or the ability of any strong attack to make deep penetrations through it. We agreed, therefore, that in the event the German advance should prove to be an all-out assault we would avoid piecemeal commitment of reserves. The temptation in such circumstances is always to hurl each individual reinforcement into the battle as rapidly as it can be brought up to the line. This habit was a weakness of Rommel's. In the face of a great attack it merely assures that each reinforcing unit is overwhelmed by the strength of the advance. We knew that even if we should finally succeed in this fashion in stopping the advance there would be nothing available for a decisive counterstroke. On the other hand, it would be necessary to assist the VIII Corps rapidly with sufficient forces so that it could withdraw its lines in orderly fashion and save the bulk of its own strength.[5]

We went over, again, the limit of the penetration that we could, if necessary, permit in that region without irretrievable damage to ourselves. This line covered the cities of Luxembourg and Sedan on the south, followed the Meuse River on the west, and covered Liége on the north. Farther back than this we would not go, and we would of course stop the enemy earlier if possible.[6]

One factor that caused us a special concern, even anxiety, was the weather. For some days our great air force had been grounded because of clouds and impenetrable fog. The air force was one of our greatest assets, and now, until the weather improved, it was practically useless. As long as the weather kept our planes on the ground it would be an ally of the enemy worth many additional divisions.

Following the conference, Bradley returned to his own headquarters in the city of Luxembourg, whence he kept in almost hourly contact with me by telephone during the next few critical days.

Bradley's first task was to bring up reinforcements to help in the withdrawal of the VIII Corps. In the meantime both Bradley's headquarters and my own would begin to gather up and assemble reserves for whatever action might be indicated as more exact information became available to us.

Middleton's divisions, employed along the front of the VIII Corps from north to south, were the 106th Division under Major General Alan W. Jones, the 28th Division under Major General Norman D. Cota, and the 4th Division under Major General Raymond O. Barton. The 9th Armored Division, under Major General John W. Leonard, was also part of Middleton's corps.[7]

The morning of December 17 it became clear that the German attack was in great strength. Two gaps were torn through our line, one on the front of the 106th Division, the other on the front of the 28th. Reports were confusing and exact information was meager, but it was clear that the enemy was employing considerable armor and was progressing rapidly to the westward. All Intelligence agencies of course worked tirelessly and we soon had a very good picture of the general strength of the German attack.

For the assault Von Rundstedt concentrated three armies. These were the Fifth and Sixth Panzer Armies and the Seventh Army. Included were ten Panzer and Panzer Grenadier divisions and the whole force totaled twenty-four divisions with their supporting troops. Some of this information did not become available until later in the battle, but by the evening of the seventeenth Intelligence agencies had identified seventeen divisions and were certain that at least twenty were involved in the operation.[8]

In two important points the enemy had gained definite surprise.[9] The first of these was in timing. In view of the terrible defeats we had inflicted upon him during the late summer and fall, and of the extraordinary measures he had been compelled to undertake in raising new forces, we had believed that he could not be ready for a major assault as early as he was. The other point in which he surprised us was the strength of the attack. The Sixth Panzer Army was the mobile reserve we had lost track of earlier, a fresh and strong unit only recently arrived on our front from Germany, but we had already badly mauled the Seventh Army and the Fifth Panzer.

In gaining this degree of surprise the enemy was favored by the weather. For some days aerial reconnaissance had been impossible, and without aerial reconnaissance we could not determine the locations and movements of major reserves in the rear of his lines. The strong artificial defenses of the Siegfried Line assisted the enemy to achieve strength in the attack. The obstacles, pillboxes, and fixed guns of that line so greatly multiplied the defensive power of the garrison that the German could afford to weaken long stretches of his front in order to gather forces for a counterblow.

Although with regard to the strength of the forces engaged on both sides the Kasserine affair was a mere skirmish in proportion to the Ardennes battle, yet there were points of similarity between the two. Each was an attack of desperation; each took advantage of extraordinary strength in a defensive barrier to concentrate forces for a blow at Allied communications and in the hope of inducing the Allied high command to give up over-all plans for relentless offensives.

Surprised as we were by the timing and the strength of the attack, we were not wrong in its location, nor in the conviction that it would eventually occur. Moreover, so far as the general nature of our reaction was concerned, General Bradley and I had long since agreed on plans.[10]

To carry out our general scheme successfully it was vitally necessary that the shoulders of our defenses bordering upon the German penetration be held securely. In the north the critical region was near Monschau, an area over which Gerow's American V Corps of the First Army was attacking toward the Roer dams at the moment the German offensive began. In Gerow's corps the veteran 2d Division under General Robertson and the new 99th Division under Major General Walter E. Lauer were initially struck by the German attack. Our lines were forced back by superior numbers. The 2d Division and portions of the 99th met the issue with great skill and during the ensuing three days fought one of the brilliant actions of the war in Europe. The attack caught the divisions while they were advancing toward the Roer dams. General Hodges, First Army commander, at first did not sense the extent of the threat and directed the American attacks to continue. But General Robertson, on the spot, soon sized up the situation and acted decisively.

Robertson had first to select a line on which his division could conduct an effective defense. The troops then had to occupy the line while under pressure, and ready themselves to receive heavy assaults. All this the division succeeded in doing, in the meantime gaining some added strength from portions of neighboring units, which were partially assimilated within the ranks of the 2d.[11]

The German threw heavy attacks against the division but the Americans stubbornly refused to give way. It is doubtful, however, that the 2d Division could have held out alone throughout the thirty-six hours before reinforcements reached its vicinity except for the courageous action of the 7th Armored Division at St. Vith.

When the 7th Armored Division came down from the northern flank on December 17 the situation was still far from clear. It pushed forward with the purpose of supporting the left of the VIII Corps and finally became semi-isolated in St. Vith, some fifteen miles south of Monschau. St. Vith was an important point on the road net of that area and necessary to the German spearheads attempting to push to the west. Joined there by remnants of the 106th and 28th Divisions, the 7th Armored hung grimly on in the face of repeated attacks. Its battle at St. Vith not only divided the German effort in the north but prevented quick encirclement of the Monschau position.

Finally the continued and heavy pressure of the Germans tended further to isolate the 7th Armored. A concentrated attack by several divisions on December 20 drove it to the west, in the area north of St. Vith. Consequently it was ordered to withdraw the next day to join the Allied lines which were now building up on the north flank of the German salient. But the great stand of the division had not only badly upset the timetable of the German spearheads: its gallant action had been most helpful to the 2d Division at the vitally important Monschau shoulder until the 1st Division, under Brigadier General Clift Andrus, and the 9th, under Major General Louis A. Craig, came up to its support. Thereafter, with these three proved and battle-tested units holding the position, the safety of our northern shoulder was practically a certainty.[12]

As early as December 17 the 82d and 101st Airborne Divisions were released from SHAEF Reserve to General Bradley. Immediately arrangements were made to utilize the 11th Armored Division, just arrived, and to begin the transfer to France of the 17th Airborne Division.[13]

General Lee, commanding the great Services of Supply organization, was directed, with available engineers and other detachments, to prepare to defend the crossings of the Meuse, including the blowing up of bridges if this should be necessary. The reason for this order was that the task was largely a precautionary and static one and I did not want to employ mobile divisions for this kind of work. The SOS responded promptly and within the American area began the work of providing strong defenses for the Meuse line. General Montgomery, in the British area, also took this early precaution to protect the dumps and depots in the rear.[14]

The German's advance, in spite of his failure at Monschau, was very rapid through the center of the break-through. As the advance continued it gradually began swinging to the north and northwest, and it was evident that the enemy's objective lay in that direction. We believed that his first purpose would be the capture of Liége. We reasoned that even if he had the more ambitious objective of Antwerp he would have to depend partially upon supplies he might capture at Liége. We arrived at this conclusion because from the beginning we had counted upon the German deficiency in supplies, particularly the difficulties he was certain to encounter in transporting them to the front. Consequently we believed that his continued advance would depend, almost regardless of countermeasures of our own, upon the capture of one of our great supply depots.

Even if the German had possessed as efficient a supply system as we—which he did not—he would still have found tremendous difficulty in supplying his spearheads over the miserable roads available,

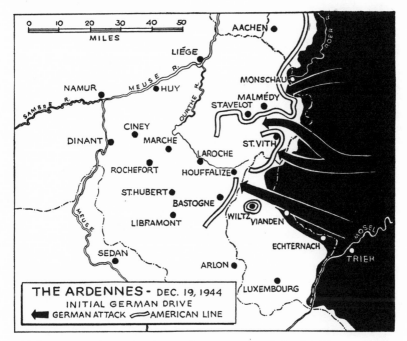

0   10   20   30   40   50
MILES

AACHEN

LIÉGE

NAMUR   MEUSE R. HUY   MONSCHAU

SAMBRE R.   MALMÉDY
                            STAVELOT

        CINEY
DINANT   MARCHE   ST. VITH

            LAROCHE
  ROCHEFORT   HOUFFALIZE

ST.HUBERT
      BASTOGNE   WILTZ
  LIBRAMONT   VIANDEN

                             ECHTERNACH

SEDAN   TRIER
            ARLON
                        LUXEMBOURG

THE ARDENNES - DEC. 19, 1944
INITIAL GERMAN DRIVE
◄ GERMAN ATTACK ⇐ AMERICAN LINE

which were at the same time, of course, crowded with his reinforcements pushing to the front.

So we were particularly careful about Liége, where there were vast
quantities of every kind of vital supplies, including fuel and food.
However, we were determined that the enemy would be stopped
short of that point, and in the outcome he never got close to Liége.
Subsequently we learned that Brussels and Antwerp were designated
by the Germans as the principal objectives for the assaulting troops.
Nevertheless, our reasoning was correct because lack of supply did become one of Von Rundstedt's major difficulties in the prosecution of
the offensive.[15]

On the seventeenth Bradley ordered the XVIII Airborne Corps
from reserve to the front with Bastogne its original destination. General Middleton, then in Bastogne, saw the great importance of the spot
and urged preparation to hold it. He conferred with Bradley by telephone, and although he stated that the place could soon be surrounded,
recommended that it be held. It became necessary to divert the 82d
Airborne Division to the north toward Stavelot, so the 101st, with
detachments of the VIII Corps, became the defenders of Bastogne.[19]

Developments were closely examined and analyzed all during December 17 and 18. By the night of the eighteenth I felt we had sufficient information of the enemy's strength, intentions, and situation, and of our own capabilities, to lay down a specific plan for our counteraction. On the early morning of December 19, accompanied by Air Chief Marshal Tedder and a small group of staff officers, I went to Verdun, where Generals Bradley, Patton, and Devers had been ordered to meet me.[17] As the conference started, with everyone around a long table, I remarked: "The present situation is to be regarded as one of opportunity for us and not of disaster. There will be only cheerful faces at this conference table." True to his impulsive nature, General Patton broke out with, "Hell, let's have the guts to let the ———— —— ———— go all the way to Paris. Then we'll really cut 'em off and chew 'em up." Everyone, including Patton, smiled at this one, but I replied that the enemy would never be allowed to cross the Meuse.

The situation was carefully reviewed and it was gratifying to find that every man present, whether a commander or staff officer, was cool and confident. I did not hear any remark that indicated hysteria or excessive fear.

In a situation of this kind there are normally two feasible lines of reaction for the defending forces, assuming that the high command does not become so frightened as to order a general retreat along the whole front. One is merely to build up a safe defensive line around the general area under attack, choosing some strong feature, such as a river, on which to make the stand. The other is for the defender to begin attacking as soon as he can assemble the necessary troops. I chose the second, not only because in the strategic sense we were on the offensive, but because I firmly believed that by coming out of the Siegfried the enemy had given us a great opportunity which we should seize as soon as possible. This was in my mind when I radioed Montgomery on the nineteenth, saying: "Our weakest spot is in direction of Namur. The general plan is to plug the holes in the north and launch co-ordinated attack from the south."[18] The following day I was more specific in another message to him: "Please let me have your personal appreciation of the situation on the north flank with reference to the possibility of giving up, if necessary, some ground in order to shorten our line and collect a strong reserve for the purpose of destroying the enemy in Belgium."[19]

I had already determined that it was not essential for our counterattack to begin on both flanks simultaneously. In the north, where the weight of the German attack was falling, we would be on the defensive for some days. But on the south we could help the situation by beginning a northward advance at the earliest possible moment. My immediate purpose at the Verdun meeting on the nineteenth was to make arrangements for the beginning of the southern assault.

It was Bradley's responsibility to outline the exact unit sectors, together with other local details of direction and co-operation. But because Devers' forces would have to extend their left in order to take over a part of Bradley's front and therefore allow him a greater opportunity for concentration, I had to make appropriate decisions, including those of general strength and timing.

We first determined the point to which we believed Devers could stretch his left without exposing the southern flank injudiciously. The next problem was to determine the amount of force Patton could gather up for a counterattack and the approximate time that it could begin. I did not want him to start until he was in sufficient force so that, once committed, he could continue gradually to crush in the southern flank of the developing salient. Once this was done, the German troops west of our point of attack would be effectively stopped, because east-west communications through the region were relatively meager. We estimated that Patton could begin a three-division attack by the morning of December 23, possibly by the twenty-second.

I issued verbal orders for these arrangements to be undertaken instantly, with the understanding that Patton's attack, under Bradley, was to begin no earlier than the twenty-second and no later than the twenty-third. It was agreed further that when Patton's forces had reached the Bastogne area they would continue on, probably in the general direction of Houffalize. Ample air support was promised the instant flying conditions should improve so that planes could take the air. Moreover, I informed the meeting that I would begin an arrangement for offensive action on the northern flank as quickly as the force of the German blow in that sector had spent itself.

It was arranged for Patton to concentrate his attacking corps of at least three divisions in the general vicinity of Arlon and from that point to begin the advance toward Bastogne. I personally cautioned him against piecemeal attack and gave directions that the advance was to be methodical and sure. Patton at first did not seem to comprehend the strength of the German assault and spoke so lightly of the task assigned him that I felt it necessary to impress upon him the need of strength and cohesion in his own advance.

We discussed the advisability of attempting to organize a simultaneous attack somewhat farther to the east, against the southern shoulder of the salient. It was concluded that future events might indicate the desirability of such a move but that for the moment we should, in that locality, merely insure the safety of the shoulder and confine our attacks to the sector indicated.

The directive issued at Verdun on December 19 established the outline of the plan for counteraction on the southern flank and was not thereafter varied.[20] When Patton issued his own attack order, he, as was customary with him, set an impossibly distant objective for his forces.[21] However, this hurt nothing because both Bradley and I were concerned only with a methodical advance to the Bastogne area, after which Bradley would determine the particular moves to follow.

The Colmar pocket had a definite and restrictive influence on the plans made that morning. Had that pocket not existed, the French Army could easily have held the line of the Rhine from the Swiss border northward to the Saar region, which would have released all of the American Seventh Army for employment northward of that point and so provided much greater strength for Patton's attack. However, the Colmar pocket stood as a threat to our forces in the Rhine plain east of the Vosges and it was consequently unwise and dangerous to take from that area all the troops that otherwise could have been spared.

Devers was instructed to give up any forward salient in his area that would permit saving troops and in case of an attack to give ground slowly on his northern flank, even if he had to move completely back to the Vosges. The northern Alsatian plain was of no immediate value to us. I was at that time quite willing to withdraw on Devers' front, if necessary, all the way to the eastern edge of the Vosges. But I would not allow the Germans to re-enter those mountains, and this line was definitely laid down as the one that must be held on Devers' front.[22]

These instructions were of course communicated to the French Army, since they implied the possibility of retrograde movement, and if this became extensive, even the city of Strasbourg might have to be temporarily abandoned. The French commander eventually relayed this information to Paris, where it caused great concern in military and governmental circles. General Juin, Chief of Staff of the

French Army, came to see me and urged all-out defense of Strasbourg. I told him that at that moment I could not guarantee the city's security but would not give it up unnecessarily.[23] The Strasbourg question was, however, to plague me throughout the duration of the Ardennes battle.

By the night of the nineteenth, at headquarters at Versailles, reports showed that the German attack was making rapid progress through the center of the salient and that the spearheads of the attack continued to swing to the northwest. The direction of the attack seemed more and more to indicate that the German plan was to cross the Meuse somewhere west of Liége and from there—we thought after surrounding Liége—to continue northwestward to get on the main line of communications of all our forces north of the breakthrough. The northern flank was obviously the dangerous one and the fighting continued to mount in intensity. Moreover, it appeared likely that the German might attempt secondary and supporting attacks still farther to the north in an effort to disperse our forces and accomplish a double envelopment of our entire northern wing. The Intelligence Division had some evidence that such supporting attacks were planned by the enemy.

The German attack had quickly gained the popular name of "Battle of the Bulge," because of the rapid initial progress made by the heavy assault against our weakly held lines, with a resulting penetration into our front that reached a maximum depth of some fifty miles.

This kind of battle places maximum strain upon an army in the field, from the highest general to the last private in the ranks. Its destructive moral effect falls most heavily, of course, upon the troop units that are struck by the attack. Confronted by overwhelming power, and unaware of the measures that their commanders have in mind for moving to their support, the soldiers in the front lines, suffering all the dangers and risks of actual contact, inevitably experience confusion, bewilderment, and discouragement.

In a different way, the pressure upon higher commanders is equally great. No matter how confident they may be of their ultimate ability to foil the enemy and even to turn the situation into a favorable one, there always exists the danger, when the enemy has the initiative, of something going wrong. The history of war is replete with instances where a sudden panic, an unexpected change of weather, or some other unforeseen circumstance has defeated the best-laid plans and brought reverse rather than victory. It would be idle and false to pretend that the Allied forces, in all echelons, did not suffer strain and

THE ARDENNES
MAXIMUM GERMAN PENETRATION

worry throughout the first week of the Ardennes attack. It would be equally false to overemphasize the extent and the effect.

No responsible individual in war is ever free of mental strain; in battles such as the one initiated by the German attack in the Ardennes, this reaches a peak. But in a well-trained combat force, everyone has been schooled to accept it. Hysteria, born of excessive fear, is encountered only in exceptional cases. In battles of this kind it is more than ever necessary that responsible commanders exhibit the firmness, the calmness, the optimism that can pierce through the web of conflicting reports, doubts, and uncertainty and by taking advantage of every enemy weakness win through to victory. The American commanders reacted in just this fashion.

Early in the battle, on December 22, I issued one of the few "Orders of the Day" I wrote during the war. In it I said:

By rushing out from his fixed defenses the enemy may give us the chance to turn his great gamble into his worst defeat. So I call upon every man, of all the Allies, to rise now to new heights of courage, of resolution and of effort. Let everyone hold before him a single thought—to destroy the enemy on the ground, in the air, everywhere—destroy him! United in this determination and with unshakable faith in the cause for which we fight, we will, with God's help, go forward to our greatest victory.[24]

North of the break-through three Allied armies and part of another occupied a great salient, extending in a rough semicircle over 250 miles of front. In the extreme north was the Twenty-first Army Group, facing northward and eastward along the lower Rhine and the Maas River. Next to the south was the U. S. Ninth Army, facing east. Next in line was that part of the U. S. First Army, now facing southward, which remained north of the penetration.

All the troops that could be spared from the First and Ninth Army fronts were being assembled to build up an east-west defensive line against the German assault. These two armies could, at that moment, provide no mobile reserve whatsoever.

There was, however, an available reserve in Montgomery's Twenty-first Army Group. It was the British 30 Corps, then out of the line and available for duty anywhere on our great semicircular line in the north, any part of which might be attacked by the enemy. Very definitely that salient had become one battle front, with a single reserve which might be called upon to operate in support either of the British and Canadian armies or of the American Ninth and First Armies. The depth of the German advances on the eighteenth and nineteenth had broken all normal communications between Bradley's headquarters at Luxembourg and the headquarters of the Ninth and First Armies. For this reason it was completely impossible for Bradley to give to the attack on the southern shoulder the attention that I desired and at the same time keep properly in touch with the troops in the north who were called upon to meet the heaviest German blows.

To this whole situation only one solution seemed applicable. This was to place all troops in our northern salient under one commander. The only way of achieving the necessary unity was to place Montgomery temporarily in command of all the northern forces and direct Bradley to give his full attention to affairs on the south. Because of my faith in the soundness of the teamwork that we had built up, I had no hesitancy in adopting this solution. I telephoned Bradley to inform him of this decision and then called Field Marshal Montgomery and gave him his orders.[25]

Late that evening Mr. Churchill telephoned to ask how the battle was going. I gave him the outline of the countermeasures already directed and informed him of the temporary command setup. He remarked that my plan would make the British reserve instantly available for use wherever needed, regardless of previously defined zones, and said, "I assure you that British troops will always deem it an honor to enter the same battle as their American friends."

The command plan worked and there was generally universal acceptance of its necessity at the time.

Unfortunately, after the battle was over a press conference held by Montgomery, supplemented by a number of press stories written by reporters attached to the Twenty-first Army Group, created the unfortunate impression among Americans that Montgomery was claiming he had moved in as the savior of the Americans. I do not believe that Montgomery meant his words as they sounded, but the mischief was not lessened thereby.

This incident caused me more distress and worry than did any similar one of the war. I doubt that Montgomery ever came to realize how deeply resentful some American commanders were. They believed that he had deliberately belittled them—and they were not slow to voice reciprocal scorn and contempt. However, the accusations and recriminations that flew about the command for a period were directed not at the military soundness of the original decision but at the interpretations the Americans placed upon Montgomery's press conference and the news stories out of his headquarters. It was a pity that such an incident had to mar the universal satisfaction in final success.[26]

At the same time a portion of the British press revived the old question of a single ground commander. Field Marshal Montgomery believed in this as a matter of principle; he even offered to serve under Bradley if I would approve. I was opposed as a matter of principle and continued to reject the proposition. Even General Marshall, on December 30, telegraphed me on this point, saying:

They may or may not have brought to your attention articles in certain London papers proposing a British deputy commander for all your ground forces and implying that you have undertaken too much of a task yourself. My feeling is this: under no circumstances make any concessions of any kind whatsoever. I am not assuming that you had in mind such a concession. I just wish you to be certain of our attitude. You are doing a grand job, and go on and give them hell.[27]

On New Year's Day, I replied:

You need have no fear as to my contemplating the establishment of a ground deputy. Since receipt of your telegram I have looked up the articles in the British papers to which you refer. Our present difficulties are being used by a certain group of papers and their correspondents to advocate something that they have always wanted but which is not in fact a sound organization. In the present case the German attack did not involve an army group boundary but came exactly in the center of a single group command. The emergency change in command arrangements, that is, the placing of one man in charge of each flank, was brought about by the situation, since the penetration was of such depth that Bradley could no longer command both flanks, while the only reserves that could be gathered on the north flank had to be largely British. Consequently single control had to be exercised on the north and on the south.[28]

The defense of Bastogne was not only a spectacular feat of arms but had a great effect upon the outcome of the battle. Bastogne lay in the general path of the sector of advance of the German Fifth Panzer Army. The orders of that army, we later found, directed that Bastogne be by-passed if defended and that the leading troops rush on to the west and then swing north to join in the major attack.

When on December 17 the XVIII Airborne Corps with its two divisions had been released to General Bradley and directed toward Bastogne, it was not in anticipation of the battle that developed in that area but merely because Bastogne was such an excellent road center. Troops directed there could later be dispatched by the commander on the spot to any region he found desirable. These troops were pushing toward the front on the eighteenth when the situation became so serious on the northern front that General Bradley diverted the leading division, the 82d, toward the left, but the 101st continued on to its original destination in Bastogne. It began closing in there on the night of December 18. During that night and on the nineteenth, while the Germans were occupying themselves with isolated detachments of the troops that manned the original defensive line, the division prepared to defend Bastogne. At the time of the Verdun conference on the morning of the nineteenth we did not know whether Bastogne was yet surrounded, but the strength and direction of advance of German troops in that area indicated that it quickly would be.

Consequently the 101st Division prepared for all-round defense, and although the assaulting armored divisions of the Germans by-passed it to participate in the attack to the northwest, the division was under constant pressure from other German units from that moment onward until relieved.

The situation on the northern front of the German attack remained critical for some days. On December 21 the remnants of the 7th Armored Division and its supporting detachments were withdrawn from their exposed position near St. Vith after they had withstood the day before a terrific assault from overwhelming forces. Fighting on the northern flank continued desperate on the succeeding days. As soon as Montgomery took charge he began to organize an American force to lead a later counteroffensive on that flank.

General Collins, with his VII Corps, was selected for this task but, for some days, as rapidly as divisions could be assigned to him they were sucked into the battle to prevent enemy advances at critical points.

Fighting kept up on this scale until the twenty-sixth, and from all available evidence it appeared that the German was going to make at least one more great effort to break through our lines in that region.

On the south Bradley had gotten off his attack on the morning of December 22. Progress was extremely slow and because of the snow-choked roads and fields maneuvers were difficult. The initial attack was made by the III Corps, in which were the 4th Armored Division with the 80th and 26th Divisions. It was the kind of fighting that General Patton distinctly disliked. It was slow, laborious going, with a sudden break-through an impossibility. Several times during the course of this attack General Patton called me to express his disappointment because he could go no faster; at the Verdun conference on the morning of the nineteenth he had implied, or even predicted, that he would get into Bastogne in his first rush. I replied that as long as he was advancing I was quite satisfied. He was doing exactly what I expected, and although I knew that his early attacks were meeting only the defensive divisions of the German Seventh Army, terrain and climatic conditions were so bad that a faster advance could not be expected.[29]

One of the breaks in our favor occurred December 23. This was a sudden, temporary clearing of the weather in the forward areas which released our air forces to plunge into the battle. From that moment onward, with some interruptions owing to bad weather, our battle-tested ground-air tactical team began again to function with its accustomed efficiency. The air forces bombed sensitive spots in the German communications system, attacked columns on the road, and sought out and reported to us every significant move of the hostile forces. German prisoners taken thereafter invariably complained bitterly about the failure of their Luftwaffe and the terror and destruction caused by the Allied air forces.

On the twenty-sixth Patton at last succeeded in getting a small column into Bastogne but he did so by a narrow neck along his left flank that gave us only precarious connection with the beleaguered garrison. It was after that date that the really hard fighting developed around Bastogne, both for the garrison itself and for the relieving troops.

I had planned to go to see Montgomery on the twenty-third but air travel in the rear areas was still not advisable and travel by road was slow and uncertain. It was unwise for me to leave headquarters on a trip that might keep me absent for several days. Fortunately telephone and radio communications with both him and Bradley remained satisfactory and I was able to keep in close touch with the situation. Nevertheless, I decided to make a night run by railway to Brussels to see Montgomery and to return immediately upon completion of the conference. The train I expected to use was bombed by the Germans on the night of the twenty-sixth, but another was hurriedly made up and I got away on the twenty-seventh.

The trip was further complicated by the extraordinary fears entertained by the Security Corps that enemy murderers were circulating in the area with the hope of killing Montgomery, Bradley, and me, and possibly others.[30] The report was astonishing. For several months I had been driving everywhere around France with no more protection than that provided by an orderly and an aide who habitually rode in the car with me. The story was brought to me on December 20 by a very agitated American colonel who was certain that he had complete and positive proof of the existence of such a plot. He outlined it in great detail and his conclusions were supported by other members of the Security Staff. I discounted the murder theory but agreed to move my quarters closer to headquarters. I had been living in the town of St. Germain, in a house which Von Rundstedt had previously occupied. I was convinced that the Germans had too much need of their men to use them in roaming over a wide area in search of their intended victims, each of whom could presumably be replaced. I was irritated at the insistence of the Security Corps that I definitely circumscribe my freedom of movement, but I found that unless I conformed reasonably to their desires they merely used more men for protective measures.

Consequently I promised to move out of headquarters only when necessary, provided they would cut down protective detachments to the utmost, so that soldiers could be used on the battle line and not in trailing me around. They promised that this period of watchfulness would terminate December 23, but when I started to Brussels on December 27, I found the railway station swarming with Military Police and armed sentries. I sharply queried the security officers about this use of men but they assured me that they had merely assembled in the station individuals who were normally on duty in that vicinity. However, after we were well started on our journey I found that a squad of soldiers was accompanying me. At every stop—and these were frequent because of difficulties with ice and snowbanks— these men would jump out of the train and take up an alert position to protect us.

I remarked to the junior officer in charge of the detail that I would consider it miraculous if any ambitious German murderer could determine in advance that he would find his prospective victim on a particular railway train, at a given moment, at a given spot in Europe. I told him to keep his men inside and to avoid exposing them to the bitter cold. He agreed in principle but so greatly impressed was he by the strictness of the orders he had received that I doubt that I saved any of the men from useless and futile activity.

It was almost noon on the twenty-eighth before I made contact with Montgomery. Roads were so bad that automobile travel was impossible and our train had to proceed by a long, roundabout, secondary line all the way to Hasselt, where I met Montgomery. He gave me the details of the recent attacks against the northern line, showed me the position of his general reserve, and said that he was again beginning to assemble Collins' corps, with which to initiate the Allied offensive from the northern flank. He intended to drive in the general direction of Houffalize.

At that meeting we had no positive information that indicated a German intention to cease his attacks in the north. Montgomery was certain from information available to him—and this information was correct at the time it was received—that the German intended to make at least one more full-blooded attack against the northern line. Montgomery was confident of beating off this attack and he wanted to get his reserve ready to follow in on the heels of the Germans as they were repulsed. This plan, of course, would seize the best possible conditions under which to initiate a great counterblow, the only difficulty with it being that its timing depended upon the action of the enemy. I discussed with him the possibility that the German might not attack again in the north but he felt that this was a practical certainty. If the enemy should not renew the assault, Montgomery said, he could use the time in reorganizing, re-equipping, and refreshing his troops. At that time the first task was to make sure of the integrity of our northern lines. The German was still far south of any area in which he could cause us major damage and the only thing we had to fear was a clean break-through by fresh troops arriving on that front.

We agreed that the best thing to do in this situation was to strengthen the front, reorganize units, and get thoroughly ready for a strong counterblow, in the meantime constantly preparing to beat off any German attack that might be launched. We agreed also that if no such German attack was launched Montgomery would begin his own offensive on the morning of January 3.

In the outcome there was no further German attack because of a change in enemy plans which concentrated his troops in the Bastogne area. The Allied troops on the northern flank used the intervening time to good advantage and on the morning of January 3 passed over to the offensive, in accordance with the plan adopted December 28.[31]

I returned to my own headquarters on the twenty-ninth. By that time the security people were beginning to believe that their fear of the murder scheme had been exaggerated. While they continued to surround me with greater security measures than they had employed before the beginning of the offensive, I could at least now depart from my headquarters without a whole platoon of MPs riding in accompanying jeeps and scout cars.

On December 26, Patton had established tenuous contact with the garrison of Bastogne, while on the north the Germans had just been repulsed from a very determined, and what proved to be their final, major attack on that flank. By this time the garrison at Bastogne was proving to be a serious thorn in the side of the German high command. As long as it was in our hands, the German corridor to the westward was cut down to the narrow neck lying between Bastogne on the south. and Stavelot on the north. Through this neck there was only one east-west road that was worthy of the name. On the twenty-sixth the German began to concentrate strong forces for an attack upon the Bastogne area. Enemy troops were shifted from the northern front and additional strength was brought up from his rear areas.[32]

In the meantime, however, we had brought up the 11th Armored Division and moved the 17th Airborne Division to the Continent. These, with the 87th Division, were stationed close to the Meuse and held in position to determine their area of greatest usefulness. Because of the continued attacks of the Germans on the northern flank between December 20 and 26 it appeared possible that our new formations would be best used on that flank. However, during the twenty-seventh it became clear that the German was now throwing his principal effort against Bastogne, and on the twenty-eighth I released the new divisions for Bradley's use. The 11th and 87th were used to support Patton's left flank just to the westward of Bastogne, but so difficult were the icy, snowy roads that these new troops accomplished little. By the end of the month Middleton's VIII Corps was reconstituted and back in the fight, joining in the northward attacks toward Bastogne. The Germans persisted in their attacks against the Bastogne area from the north and never ceased their assaults until the night of January 3.[33]

During the progress of the December fighting there was no letup in our planning for the resumption of the general offensive. On December 31, I forwarded to Montgomery and Bradley an outline plan to cover operations until we should reach the Rhine all along the front from Bonn to the northward.[34]

As the Battle of the Ardennes wore on the Germans began diversionary attacks in Alsace. They were not in great strength but because we had weakened ourselves in that area the situation had to be carefully watched. I told Devers he must on no account permit sizable formations to be cut off and surrounded.[35]

The French continued to worry about the safety of Strasbourg. On January 3, De Gaulle came to see me. I explained the situation to him and he agreed that my plan to save troops in that region was militarily correct. However, he pointed out that ever since the war of 1870 Strasbourg had been a symbol to the French people; he believed that even its temporary loss might result in complete national discouragement and possibly in open revolt. He was very earnest about the matter, saying that in extremity he would consider it better to put the whole French force around Strasbourg, even at the risk of losing the entire Army, than to give up the city without a fight. He brought a letter saying that he would have to act independently unless I made disposition for last-ditch defense of Strasbourg. I reminded him that the French Army would get no ammunition, supplies, or food unless it obeyed my orders, and pointedly told him that if the French Army had eliminated the Colmar pocket this situation would not have arisen.

At first glance De Gaulle's argument seemed to be based upon political considerations, founded more on emotion than on logic and common sense. However, to me it became a military matter because of the possible effect on our lines of communication and supply, which stretched completely across France, from two directions. Unrest, trouble, or revolt along these lines of communication would defeat us on the front. Moreover, by the date of this conference the crisis in the Ardennes was well past. We were now on the offensive within the salient, and while I wanted to send to Bradley's front all the troops we could spare elsewhere, the motive was now to increase the decisiveness of victory, not to stave off defeat. I decided to modify my orders to Devers. I told General de Gaulle that I would immediately instruct Devers to withdraw only from the salients in the northern end of his line and to make disposition in the center to hold Strasbourg firmly. No more troops would be taken away from the Sixth Army Group. This modification pleased De Gaulle very much, and he left in a good humor, alleging unlimited faith in my military judgment.[36]

Mr. Churchill was, by chance, in my headquarters when De Gaulle came to see me. He sat in with us as we talked but offered no word of comment. After De Gaulle left he quietly remarked to me, "I think you've done the wise and proper thing."

During the battle the Luftwaffe attempted to operate on a more intensive scale than at any time since the early days of the campaign. On January 1 the German Air Force came out in the strongest attack it had attempted against us in months. Its principal targets were Allied airfields, particularly those lying near the Bulge and to the northward thereof. During the course of the day the Germans destroyed many of our planes, most of them on the ground. Reaction of our own fighter planes was swift, and although we took quite a severe, and partially needless, loss the enemy paid with almost half of his entire attacking force.[37]

Two days later, January 3, the First Army, spearheaded by the VII Corps, began its attacks on the northern flank and all danger from the great German thrust had disappeared. From that moment on it was merely a question of whether we could make sufficient progress through his defenses and through the snowbanks of the Ardennes to capture or destroy significant portions of his forces.

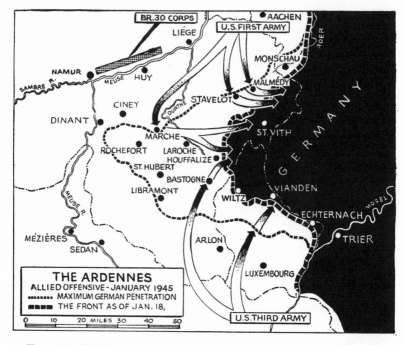

THE ARDENNES
ALLIED OFFENSIVE · JANUARY 1945
▪▪▪▪▪▪▪ MAXIMUM GERMAN PENETRATION
▰▰▰▰ THE FRONT AS OF JAN. 18,

0   10   20 MILES 30   40   50

From both flanks we continued attacks in the direction of Houffalize, where we joined up January 16. However, the advance had been so slow and so intensely opposed by the enemy that most of the enemy troops to the westward of the closing gap had succeeded in withdrawing. Upon arrival at Houffalize both armies turned generally eastward to drive the Germans beyond their initial lines. At this time the First Army again came under General Bradley's command. The U. S. Ninth Army on the left flank of the American forces I assigned temporarily to Twenty-first Army Group because of a plan we were developing for the crossing of the Roer and for a converging operation against the Rhine crossing in the northern sector.[38] I hoped to launch this assault by February 8–10, and since Montgomery's forces were still stretched back along the line to the vicinity of Antwerp the only way I could provide the necessary two armies for the assault was to employ the U. S. Ninth Army.

The losses on both sides in the Battle of the Ardennes were considerable. Field commanders estimated that in the month ending January 16 the enemy suffered 120,000 serious casualties. In view of the fact that after the war German commanders admitted a loss of about 90,000, this estimate of our own would seem to be fairly accurate. In addition to personnel losses the enemy suffered serious casualties in tanks, assault guns, planes, and motor transport. These we estimated at the time as 600 tanks and assault guns, 1600 planes, and 6000 other vehicles.[39] In the Ardennes battle our ground forces employed, for the first time in land battles, the new "proximity fuse." It was an invention that added immensely to the effectiveness of our artillery.

Our own losses were high, with the 106th Infantry Division suffering the worst. Because of its exposed position it was not only in the fight from the start, but many men were isolated and captured. The 28th Division was likewise roughly handled and the 7th Armored took serious losses during its gallant defense of St. Vith. Altogether, we calculated our losses at a total of 77,000 men, of whom about 8000 were killed, 48,000 wounded, and 21,000 captured or missing. Our tank and tank destroyer losses were 733.[40]

The projected attack for February 8–10 was to be merely the beginning of a series of blows that we were planning to complete the destruction of the Germans west of the Rhine. I wanted to pass to the general offensive as quickly as possible because I was convinced that in the Battle of the Bulge the enemy had committed all of his remaining reserves. I counted on a greatly weakened resistance from that moment onward, both because of losses suffered by the Germans and because of the widespread discouragement that I felt sure would overtake his armies. Moreover—and this was very important—the Russians had opened their long-awaited and powerful winter offensive on January 12. Already we had reports that it was making great progress and it was obvious that the quicker we could attack the more certain we would be that the German could not again reinforce his west front in an effort to avoid defeat.

Chapter 19

CROSSING
THE RHINE

ALL DURING THE BATTLE OF THE BULGE WE CON-
tinued to plan for the final offensive blows which, once started, we
intended to maintain incessantly until final defeat of Germany.
Operations were planned in three general phases, beginning with
a series of attacks along the front to destroy the German armies west
of the Rhine. The next phase would comprise the crossing of that
river and establishment of major bridgeheads. Thereafter we would
initiate the final advances that we were sure would carry us into the
heart of Germany and destroy her remaining power to resist.[1]

Somewhere during this final advance we would meet portions of
the Red Army coming from the east and it now became important
to arrange closer co-ordination with the activities of the Red Army.
During earlier campaigns we had been kept informed of the general
intentions of the Soviet forces by the Combined Chiefs of Staff. This
provided sufficient co-ordination between the two forces so long as
the two zones of operations were widely separated. Now, however,
the time had come to exchange information of plans as to objectives
and timing.

In early January 1945, with the approval of the Combined Chiefs
of Staff, I sent Air Chief Marshal Tedder to Moscow to make necessary arrangements for this co-ordination. He was accompanied by
Major General Harold R. Bull and Brigadier General T. J. Betts, two
able American officers from the SHAEF staff. Air Chief Marshal
Tedder was authorized to give the Russian military authorities full
information concerning our plans for the late winter and spring, and
was to obtain similar information concerning Russian projects.[2]

We already knew that the Russians were contemplating an early westward attack from their positions around Warsaw, on the Vistula. We understood that the Russians had effected concentrations for an offensive by the first of the year, but because of conditions of terrain and, more particularly, because of thick blankets of fog and cloud that interfered with air operations, they were holding up the attack until conditions should be more favorable. We learned through the Combined Chiefs of Staff, however, that even if these conditions failed to show improvement the Russian attack would be launched no later than January 15. It began on January 12 and made remarkable progress.

Air Chief Marshal Tedder and his associates arrived in Moscow just after this attack began. The Generalissimo and the Russian military authorities received them with the utmost cordiality and there was a full and accurate exchange of information concerning future plans. The Generalissimo informed our mission that even if the attacks then in progress should fail to reach their designated objectives the Russians would keep up a series of continuous operations that would, at the very least, prevent the German from reinforcing the western front by withdrawing forces from the Russian zone.[3]

As a further result of this initial effort the Combined Chiefs of Staff authorized me to communicate directly with Moscow on matters that were exclusively military in character. Later in the campaign my interpretation of this authorization was sharply challenged by Mr. Churchill, the difficulty arising out of the age-old truth that politics and military activities are never completely separable.[4]

In modern war the need for co-ordination between two friendly forces that are attacking toward a common center is far more acute than it was in the days when fighting was confined to the ground, along a narrow band of territory defined by the range of small arms and field guns. Today the fighter bombers supporting an attacking army constantly range over the enemy lines, sometimes hundreds of miles in his rear. Their purpose is to find and destroy hostile headquarters, dumps, depots, and bridges and to attack reserve formations. Long before the two friendly armies themselves can make contact there arises a delicate problem in co-ordination to prevent unfortunate accidents and misunderstandings between allied but separated forces.

Recognition of friend or foe on the battlefield is never easy. In our own War Between the States, where one side was clad in blue and the other in gray, more than one sharp fight took place between units of the same army. In modern war, where all uniforms are de-

signed with the idea of blending with the countryside, where the mass
formations of the nineteenth century are never seen, and where the
speeds of airplanes and vehicles afford observers only a fleeting
instant for decisive action, the problem is difficult to solve. These
matters would demand more and more detailed attention as our advance progressed. But in January 1945 we needed primarily to know
the timing and direction of the next Russian attack and to lay the
groundwork that would permit future battlefield co-operation.

By early 1945 the effects of our air offensive against the German
economy were becoming catastrophic. Our great land advances had
effectively disrupted the enemy's air warning and defense system and
had overrun many places—particularly the western European ports
where submarine nests were located—which had formerly diverted
much of our bombing effort from targets in the heart of Germany.
Another advantage that our strategic bombers now enjoyed was
better protection from accompanying fighters. Groups of fighters
could be located at forward fields near the Rhine and, in spite of their
comparatively short range, could operate over almost any target in
Axis territory.

By this time also the air had achieved remarkable success in de--
pleting the German oil reserves. For many months the enemy's oil
resources had been one of the principal objectives of strategic bomb--
ing and as the effects of this offensive accumulated there developed
a continuous crisis in German transportation and in all phases of her
war effort. It had a definite influence upon the ground battles. Germany found it increasingly difficult to transfer reserve troops and
supplies from one front to another, while her troops in every sector
were constantly embarrassed by lack of fuel for vehicles. The effect
was felt also by the Luftwaffe, in which training of new pilots had
to be sharply curtailed because of fuel shortage.[5]

During the long winter fighting our Intelligence staffs began to
bring us disturbing information that the Germans were making great
progress in the development of jet airplanes. Our air commanders
were of the opinion that if the enemy could succeed in putting
these planes into the air in considerable numbers he would quickly
begin to exact insupportable losses from our bombers operating over
Germany. Our own development of jet planes was progressing in
the United States and in Great Britain but we were not yet far enough
along to count on squadrons of them during the spring campaign.

Our only possible recourse was to attempt by our bombing effort to delay German production of this new weapon. The air forces knew that extra-long runways were required for the employment of the jet plane and whenever they found a German field with such a runway they kept it under intermittent but repeated bombardment. In addition they sought out every area where they believed these planes were under construction. This caused some diversion from our objective of depleting oil reserves but by January 1945 we had such air strength and efficiency that we could afford it without material damage to our primary mission. The effect of our bombing effort against jet production was at least partially successful because the German never succeeded in employing a sufficient number of the new planes to damage us materially.[6]

Information concerning all these things was gathered by our Intelligence services, which daily presented to me their calculations and conclusions. These emphasized the mounting difficulties of the German war machine and encouraged me and all my associates to believe that one more great campaign, aggressively conducted on a broad front, would give the death blow to Hitler Germany.

I found, among some of the higher military officials of Britain, a considerable and, to me, surprising opposition to my plan.

The relationship maintained by the American Chiefs of Staff with their commanders in the field differed markedly from that which existed between similar echelons in the British service. The American doctrine has always been to assign a theater commander a mission, to provide him with a definite amount of force, and then to interfere as little as possible in the execution of his plans. The theory is that the man in the field knows more of the tactical situation than someone removed by several thousand miles from the scene of action; and that if results obtained by the field commander become unsatisfactory the proper procedure is not to advise, admonish, and harass him, but to replace him by another commander.

On the other hand, the British Chiefs in London maintained throughout the war the closest kind of daily contact with their own commanders in the field and insisted upon being constantly informed as to details of strength, plans, and situation. This habit may have been based upon sound reasons of which I knew nothing, but it was always a shock to me, raised in the tradition of the American services, to find that the British Chiefs regularly queried their commanders in the field concerning tactical plans. For example, the British commander was required to submit to London a daily report covering

every item of information that in our service would only in exceptional circumstances go higher than a local army headquarters.

My own practice throughout the war was merely to submit to
Washington and London brief daily situation reports called "Cositin-
treps" (combined situation and intelligence reports).

When I completed my final plan in January 1945 my friend Field
Marshal Brooke informally but very earnestly presented serious objections. His questions were directed against what he called the planned
dispersion of our forces. He maintained that we would never have
enough strength to mount more than one full-blooded attack across
the Rhine. Consequently, he said, in order to assure ourselves of the
strength to sustain such an attack we should, as the situation then
stood, pass to the defensive on all other parts of the line.[7]

Dispersion is one of the greatest crimes in warfare, but as with
all other generalities the proper application of the truth is far more
important than mere knowledge of its existence.

In the situation facing us in January, the German enjoyed the
great advantage of the Siegfried defenses in the area northward from
the Saar, inclusive. As long as we allowed him to remain in those
elaborate fortifications his ability was enhanced to hold great portions
of his long line with relatively weak forces, while he concentrated
for spoiling attacks at selected points. This meant that a large proportion of the Allied Force would be immobilized in a protective
role, with only that portion on the offensive that could be maintained
north of the Ruhr. In that single zone of advance we could not
logistically sustain more than thirty-five divisions.[8]

If, however, we should first, in a series of concentrated and powerful attacks, destroy the German forces west of the Rhine, the effect
would be to give us all along the great front a defensive line of equal
strength to the enemy's. We calculated that with the western bank
of the Rhine in our possession we could hurl some seventy-five reinforced divisions against the German in great converging attacks. If
we allowed the enemy south of the Ruhr to remain in the Siegfried,
we would be limited to a single offensive by some thirty-five divisions.

A second advantage of our plan would be the depletion of the
German forces later to be met at the crossings of the Rhine obstacle.
Moreover, the effect of the converging attack is multiplied when it
is accompanied by such air power as we had in Europe in the early
months of 1945. Through its use we could prevent the enemy from
switching forces back and forth at will against either of the attacking

columns and we could likewise employ our entire air power at any moment to further the advance in any area desired.

I laboriously explained to Field Marshal Brooke that, far from dispersing effort, I was conducting the campaign so that when we were ready to initiate the final invasion of Germany on the other side of the Rhine we could bring such a concerted and tremendous power against him that his collapse would quickly follow. The decisive advantage in gaining the Rhine River along its length was to increase drastically the proportion of the Allied forces that could be used offensively.

I did not wholly convince him. He said, "I wish that the Twelfth Army Group were deployed north of the Ruhr and the British forces were in the center," implying that my plans were drawn up on nationalistic considerations.

To this I retorted: "I am certainly no more anxious to put Americans into the thick of the battle and get them killed than I am to see the British take the losses. I have strengthened Montgomery's army group by a full American army, since in no other way can I provide the strength north of the Ruhr that I deem essential for the rapid execution of my plans. I have not devised any plan on the basis of what individual or what nation gets the glory, for I must tell you in my opinion there is no glory in battle worth the blood it costs."

Field Marshal Brooke expressed the hope that things would work out as I believed they would; but he was apparently doubtful of Allied ability to destroy the German forces between us and the Rhine River by a succession of crushing blows.

At the same time there was again suggested to me the establishment of an over-all "ground commander" to operate directly under SHAEF. I repudiated this suggestion, as I always had before. I was certain that our plans for the completion of the German defeat were the best that could be devised. Entirely aside from my feeling that the proposed arrangement would be futile and clumsy, I was determined to prevent any interference with the exact and rapid execution of those plans.[9]

In early January, I learned that the President, the Prime Minister, and their staffs were again to meet with Generalissimo Stalin, this time at Yalta. General Marshall proceeded separately from the rest of the American group into Europe, and I arranged to meet him secretly at Marseille. I went there on January 25 and we had a long talk about the situation as we then saw it.

In Washington he had heard rumblings of the British Staff's dissatisfaction with our plans and had also heard the proposal that a single ground commander be set up. I explained our situation and outlined the exact steps by which we planned the defeat of Germany. He was in full agreement.[10]

At that time, however, there was one miscalculation in our plans, based upon faulty technical information. The engineers had made many studies of the Rhine River, based upon statistics covering a long period. They had reported to me that successful assaults could probably not be made over the Rhine until about the first of May. This opinion was so forcibly expressed that in my own mind I had accepted the necessary delay and was planning not to start our major assaults across the river until about that time. This did not, of course, affect any part of our plans that were to be executed before the time came to cross the river. Later our technical advice on this point was markedly changed and we found that it was feasible to cross the river, establish bridges, and maintain ourselves long before the first of May.

General Marshall was so impressed by the soundness of the whole plan that he suggested I send my chief of staff, General Smith, to Malta to participate in a conference that was to take place there between the President, the Prime Minister, and their respective staffs before they went on to Yalta. He remarked: "I can, of course, uphold your position merely on the principle that these decisions fall within your sphere of responsibility. But your plan is so sound that I think it better for you to send General Smith to Malta so that he may explain these matters in detail. Their logic will be convincing."[11] I was glad to agree because I well knew that with General Marshall backing me up there would be no danger of interference with our developing plans.

Field Marshal Brooke's arguments in the matter were founded in conviction. There was no petty basis for his great concern. This was proved by the fact that only a few weeks later, when the destruction of the German armies west of the Rhine had been accomplished and he stood with me on the banks of the river to witness the crossing by the Ninth Army and the Twenty-first Army Group, he turned to me and said: "Thank God, Ike, you stuck by your plan. You were completely right and I am sorry if my fear of dispersed effort added to your burdens. The German is now licked. It is merely a question of when he chooses to quit. Thank God you stuck by your guns."[12]

The operational schedule for the first phase of our strategic plan—

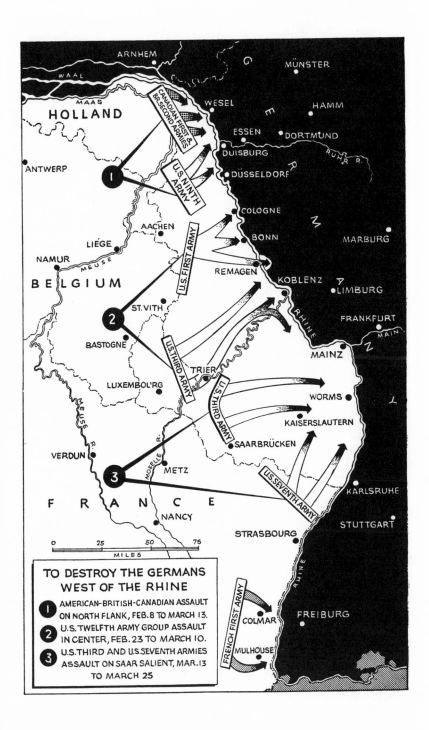

TO DESTROY THE GERMANS WEST OF THE RHINE

1. AMERICAN-BRITISH-CANADIAN ASSAULT ON NORTH FLANK, FEB. 8 TO MARCH 13.
2. U.S. TWELFTH ARMY GROUP ASSAULT IN CENTER, FEB. 23 TO MARCH 10.
3. U.S. THIRD AND U.S. SEVENTH ARMIES ASSAULT ON SAAR SALIENT, MAR. 13 TO MARCH 25

destruction of the enemy strength west of the Rhine—contemplated three major assaults. The first would be by the Twenty-first Army Group at the northern flank of our lines; the second, by Bradley's group in the center; and the third, a converging attack by Bradley and Devers to eliminate the enemy garrison in the Saar Basin.

As soon as the First and Third Armies had joined forces at Houffalize on January 16, 1945, Montgomery returned to specific preparation for the first of these three attacks.[13] West of the Rhine the Siegfried Line extended southward from the confluence of that river with the Maas, down to include the defenses of the Saar Basin. Immediately south of the Saar a few German detachments remained in the Alsace plain, while farther south we were plagued by the Colmar pocket.

In January, with the Germans recoiling from their disastrous adventure in the Ardennes, I turned my attention again to Colmar. The existence of this German position in a sensitive part of our lines had always irritated me and I determined that it was to be crushed without delay. The French First Army began attacks against it on the twentieth of January but these, handicapped by bad weather, made little progress. There were two French corps surrounding the pocket, but in my determination to get rid of this annoyance once and for all I gave additional strength to Devers so that he could support the French with an entire United States corps of four divisions. He assigned the XXI Corps under Major General Frank W. Milburn to the task, with the 3d, 28th, and 75th Infantry Divisions and the French 5th Armored Division. Later the 12th Armored Division and French 2d Armored Division were also used in the XXI Corps zone. With the American corps as the spearhead, the two French corps and the American attacked simultaneously. German defenses quickly disintegrated. Colmar surrendered February 3 and by the ninth of the month such Germans as survived in that region had been driven across the Rhine. In this operation the enemy suffered more than 22,000 casualties and heavy losses in equipment.[14]

In the planned campaign against German forces confronting our units the first attack was to be carried out by the Canadian Army of the Twenty-first Army Group, and the U. S. Ninth Army, temporarily attached to Montgomery. The Canadians were to attack south and southeast across the Maas River, while Simpson's Ninth Army would cross the Roer to advance northeastward. This would bring a converging effort upon the defending forces and drive them rapidly back to the Rhine.

In this region were some of the best combat troops the enemy had remaining to him. They included his First Paratroop Army, in which men and units had been trained to a high degree of skill and hardihood. An additional difficulty on Simpson's front was the enemy's continued possession of the Roer dams, through which he was enabled to prevent successful assault across the Roer River. Bradley therefore ordered Hodges' First Army to capture the dams at the earliest possible date. The attack against them was launched by the V Corps on February 4. After hard fighting the First Army captured them within six days. Even then our difficulties with the dams were not over because the Germans blocked the spillway gates in such position as to insure that overflow from the reservoirs would keep the river at flood stage for some days.[15]

As Montgomery began preparing for his offensive he naturally wanted the U. S. Ninth Army built up to the greatest possible strength. He recommended that Bradley be ordered to stop attacking with the First and Third Armies through the Ardennes region so as to save troops for greater concentration farther north. I declined to do this. I was certain that the continued attacks in the Ardennes would tend to keep the enemy's forces away from the northern sector. More important than this, I was very anxious to push the American lines forward in the Ardennes region so that when the time should come to participate in major destructive attacks the troops would be in excellent position from which to start the move. I was sure that we could gain the line I wanted without interfering with the timely build-up of the Ninth Army.

Montgomery and I agreed on the proper timing for his initial attack. Originally we had wanted to make a simultaneous assault by the Canadians and Americans, both of whom could be ready to attack by February 10. However, neither Montgomery nor I felt it wise to wait until the flood waters of the Roer receded. He proposed, and I approved, that the Canadian attacks should begin as quickly as possible, even if a period of two weeks or more had to intervene before the American Army could join in the operation.[16]

The Canadian Army jumped off February 8. It made satisfactory initial gains but the troops quickly found themselves involved in a quagmire of flooded and muddy ground and pitted against heavy resistance. Progress was slow and costly and opposition became stiffer as the Germans began moving their forces from the Roer into the path of the Canadian advance. Montgomery was not too displeased by this transfer of German weight because of the promise it held that, once the American attack began, it would advance with great speed.[17]

I visited General Simpson's Ninth Army during this period and found it keyed up and well prepared for the attack. If Simpson ever made a mistake as an army commander, it never came to my attention. After the war I learned that he had for some years suffered from a serious stomach disorder, but this I never would have suspected during hostilities. Alert, intelligent, and professionally capable, he was the type of leader that American soldiers deserve. In view of his brilliant service, it was unfortunate that shortly after the war ill-health forced his retirement before he was promoted to four-star grade, which he had so clearly earned.

Simpson's army comprised three corps. The XVI, under Major General J. B. Anderson, was on the left. On the right was the XIX under Major General Raymond S. McLain. McLain was a National Guard officer who had entered the war as a brigadier general in command of the artillery of the 45th Division. Later he took over the 90th Division during the hard fighting just following the breakout in late July. His leadership of that division was so outstanding that when General Corlett, commanding the XIX Corps, suffered a breakdown in health, McLain was advanced to command of that corps. The center corps of Simpson's army was the XIII under Major General Alvan C. Gillem, Jr.[18]

In the days following upon the Canadian attack in the north the Americans could do little except watch the river and be ready to attack as soon as receding floods permitted the bridging of that obstacle. It was two weeks after General Crerar's Canadians began the attack that this became possible. Simpson set his attack for the morning of the twenty-third.

Preceded by a violent bombardment, the Ninth Army got off as scheduled and succeeded in crossing the river. Initially the troops encountered great difficulties, particularly because of hostile artillery fire upon their floating bridges and because of destruction in the city of Jülich, caused by our aerial and artillery bombardment. The advancing units had to pass through this city, and in order to get vehicles through, it was first necessary to bring up bulldozers to shove a path through the heaps of rubble. Major General Charles H. Gerhardt's 29th Division, veterans of the Normandy assault in the preceding June, performed splendidly as did the 30th, 102d, and 84th Divisions, also in the initial assault. These three divisions were commanded by Major Generals Leland S. Hobbs, Frank A. Keating, and Alexander R. Bolling respectively. In spite of delays, Simpson's forces made fine progress, partially as a result of the prior transfer of German forces from this front to the Canadian battlefield. In less than a week the Ninth Army captured München-Gladbach. This was the largest German city we had captured in the war up to this time.

While going into the city with Simpson, shortly after its capture, I saw my first jet plane. It was a German fighter, flying very high. Every anti-aircraft gun in the area immediately opened intensive fire and within a few seconds fragments of exploded shells were dropping around us. For the only time in the war I put on a steel helmet. The alternative was to stop the jeep and get under it for protection. In Africa one of our finest officers had been struck by a falling shell fragment and so severely wounded that he was hospitalized for more than a year. Fortunately the hostile plane found the area uncomfortable and quickly left.

The German forces in the area were now feeling the effect of the powerful converging attack and began to retreat toward the Rhine. By March 3, Simpson's left corps, the XVI, had swung forward, joined the Canadians, and was driving toward the river. The whole area was rapidly cleared of the enemy. In this battle, because of the proximity of the defending Germans to their bridges over the Rhine, we did not succeed in capturing the same proportions that we did in later assaults.

With the Rhine's west bank cleared in the northern sector it became Montgomery's task to prepare for an early assault across the river. For that operation he would need greater strength than the Twenty-first Army Group could possibly provide. Consequently I directed the Ninth Army to remain attached to him.[19] As those forces turned their attention to preparation for the crossing, events to the southward were proceeding remarkably well.

When Simpson began his assault on February 23 it was the signal for Bradley, in the center of our long line, to begin a series of attacks which were brilliantly managed and swiftly conducted. He then had two armies under his operational command, the First on the left, the Third on the right. As a result of the late January and early February fighting along the fronts of these two armies they had secured good positions from which to make a major assault. Bradley's first move was made by Hodges, who sent forward the VII Corps, the left of his

First Army, simultaneously with Simpson's attack. The first mission of the VII Corps was to support Simpson's right as the Ninth Army moved to the assault. Success in this move would tend to uncover the right flank of the Germans to the southward and as quickly as this happened the VII Corps was to turn to its right to attack the Germans in flank. The remainder of Hodges' army, facing eastward, would then take up the assault. Still farther to the south Patton would then begin to attack in the effort to cut off and surround the Germans and to capture or destroy them in place.[20]

Everything went like clockwork. The VII Corps, on Simpson's right, was quickly able to begin its southward attacks, and from that moment on success attended us everywhere along the front.

The VII Corps first overcame heavy opposition near the Erft Canal. It continued a spectacular advance and on March 5 was on the outskirts of Cologne. We had calculated that this city would be stubbornly defended, as Aachen had been. However, the hastily trained and astonished defending troops were by no means the equal of those we had met earlier in the campaign. By the afternoon of the seventh of March, Collins had taken over the whole of the city. Since we had estimated that his corps would be engaged there for a period of days in a heavy siege, the quick capture had the effect of providing us with additional divisions to exploit other victories to the south.[21]

While Collins' VII Corps was making these great advances Hodges launched the III and V Corps southeastward toward the Rhine. The III Corps reached the river at Remagen on March 7. Here it encountered one of those bright opportunities of war which, when quickly and firmly grasped, produce incalculable effect on future operations. The assaulting Americans found the Ludendorff Bridge over the Rhine was still standing at Remagen.

The Germans had, of course, made elaborate advance preparations to destroy the Rhine bridges. The Ludendorff Bridge was no exception. However, so rapid was the advance of the American troops and so great was the confusion created among the defenders that indecision and doubt overtook the detachment responsible for detonation of the charges under the bridge. Apparently the defenders could not believe that the Americans had arrived in force and possibly felt that destruction of the bridge should be delayed in order to permit withdrawal of German forces which were still west of the river in strength.

The 9th Armored Division, under General Leonard, was leading the advance toward the bridge. Without hesitation a gallant detachment of

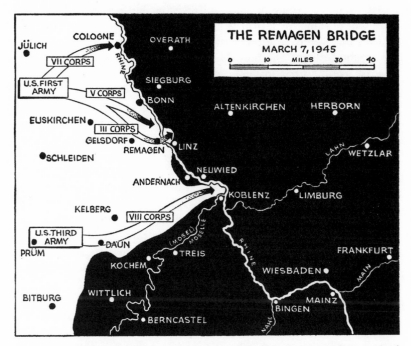

Brigadier General William M. Hoge's Combat Command B rushed the bridge and preserved it against complete destruction, although one small charge under the bridge was exploded.[22]

This news was reported to Bradley. It happened that a SHAEF staff officer was in Bradley's headquarters when the news arrived, and a discussion at once took place as to the amount of force that should be pushed across the bridge. If the bridgehead force was too small it would be destroyed through a quick concentration of German strength on the east side of the river. On the other hand, Bradley realized that if he threw a large force across he might interfere with further development of my basic plan. Bradley instantly telephoned me.

I was at dinner in my Reims headquarters with the corps and division commanders of the American airborne forces when Bradley's call came through. When he reported that we had a permanent bridge across the Rhine I could scarcely believe my ears. He and I had frequently discussed such a development as a remote possibility but never as a well-founded hope.

I fairly shouted into the telephone: "How much have you got in that vicinity that you can throw across the river?"

He said, "I have more than four divisions but I called you to make sure that pushing them over would not interfere with your plans."

I replied, "Well, Brad, we expected to have that many divisions tied up around Cologne and now those are free. Go ahead and shove over at least five divisions instantly, and anything else that is necessary to make certain of our hold."

His answer came over the phone with a distinct tone of glee: "That's exactly what I wanted to do but the question had been raised here about conflict with your plans, and I wanted to check with you."

That was one of my happy moments of the war. Broad success in war is usually foreseen by days or weeks, with the result that when it actually arrives higher commanders and staffs have discounted it and are immersed in plans for the future. This was completely unforeseen. We were across the Rhine, on a permanent bridge; the traditional defensive barrier to the heart of Germany was pierced. The final defeat of the enemy, which we had long calculated would be accomplished in the spring and summer campaigning of 1945, was suddenly now, in our minds, just around the corner.

My guests at the dinner table were infected by my enthusiasm. Among them were veterans of successful aerial jumps against the enemy and of hard fighting in every kind of situation. They were unanimous in their happy predictions of an early end to the war. I am sure that from that moment every one of them went into battle with the élan that comes from the joyous certainty of smashing victory.

By March 9 the First Army had enlarged the Remagen bridgehead area until it was more than three miles deep. It took the enemy a considerable time to recover from his initial surprise and confusion, and by the time he could bring up reinforcements against our bridgehead troops we were too strong to fear defeat. As usual the enemy attacked piecemeal with every unit as soon as it could arrive in the area but such feeble tactics were unable to combat our steady enlargement of the hold we had on his vitals.

From the day we crossed the river the enemy initiated desperate efforts to destroy the Ludendorff Bridge. Long-range artillery opened fire on it and the German Air Force concentrated every available plane for bombing attacks upon the structure. None of these was immediately successful and we continued to pour troops across the bridge, but at the same time we established floating Treadway bridges.

The Treadway bridge was one of our fine pieces of equipment, capable of sustaining heavy military loads. It was comparatively easy to transport and was quickly installed. After General Collins and his VII Corps crossed the Rhine he was of course concerned with getting his floating bridges established as quickly as possible. He called in his corps engineer, Colonel Mason J. Young, and said: "Young, I believe you can put a bridge across this river in twelve hours. What kind of a prize do you want me to give you for doing it in less time than that?" Young reflected a second and then said, "I don't want anything but if you can promise a couple of cases of champagne to my men we shall certainly try to win them." "All right," said Collins, "I'll get the champagne if you get me a bridge in less than twelve hours."

In ten hours and eleven minutes the 330-yard bridge was completed and the first load crossed the river.[23] Collins gladly paid off. I heard that even this creditable record was later broken.

The accumulated effects of the German effort against the Ludendorff Bridge finally began to weaken it seriously. After the fifth day, by which time our Treadways were fully capable of sustaining the troops on the far side, we ceased using the Ludendorff structure. American engineers, however, stubbornly and persistently continued the effort to strengthen the weakened members of the bridge so that it would be of future use. In this they failed. On March 17 the center span—the one which had been damaged by the unsuccessful German attempt to blow the bridge on March 7—fell into the river. It carried with it a number of our fine engineers, some of whom we were unable to rescue from the icy waters of the river.[24]

The diversion of five divisions to seize the Remagen bridgehead in early March did not modify or interfere with the development of the plan for destroying the German armies north of the Moselle. All during February the Third Army was engaged in necessary preparation for its attack toward the Rhine. Middleton's VIII Corps advanced east beyond Prüm and Major General Manton S. Eddy's XII Corps captured Bitburg. The XX Corps, under General Walker, eliminated resistance in the Saar–Moselle triangle by February 23, and a bridgehead was established over the Saar. The Siegfried defenses were penetrated and Trier was captured March 2. Two days later the XII Corps secured bridgeheads over the Kyll River.[25]

This was the signal for the main advance of the Third Army to begin. The VIII Corps attacked toward the northeastward and, breaking through all German resistance, reached Andernach on the Rhine on March 9, where it soon joined up with the First Army. The XII Corps launched a simultaneous attack northeastward along the northern bank of the Moselle and reached the Rhine March 10. Both these corps made great captures of enemy supplies and equipment and, as their spearheads joined up along the Rhine, they surrounded entire combat units of the enemy.[26]

The stunning victories by the First and Third Armies completed the second step in the planned destruction of the German forces west of the Rhine. There now remained only the great hostile garrison in the Saar Basin. These troops were situated in a huge triangle that had its base along the Rhine, with the two sides meeting in a point seventy-five miles to the west. The northern leg of this triangle was protected by the Moselle River and the southern by some of the strongest sections of the Siegfried Line. In retrospect it is difficult to understand why the German, as he saw his armies north of the Moselle undergo complete collapse and destruction, failed to initiate a rapid withdrawal of his forces in the Saar Basin, in order to remove them from their exposed position and employ them for defense of the Rhine.

More than once in prior campaigns we had witnessed similar examples of what appeared to us sheer tactical stupidity. I personally believed that the cause was to be found in the conqueror complex: the fear that to give up a single foot of ravished territory would be to expose the rotten foundation on which was built the myth of invincibility. Some of my staff thought that in the Saar the Germans were influenced to stand where they were by their faith in the defensive strength of the Moselle and the Siegfried Line. In addition the enemy was probably ignorant of the strength of the Seventh Army lying to the south of the Saar salient.

Such reasons as these would imply a woeful stupidity on the part of the German commanders and staffs. When free to act, they had proved their capacity too often for me to believe that the failure to pull back their exposed troops was a military decision—it was more of Hitler's intuition in action!

During the first two acts of the month-long drama before the Rhine, I required Devers' army group, except for the reduction of the Colmar pocket, to remain essentially on the defensive. In the meantime we had built up his American Seventh Army, under General Patch, to the unusual strength of fourteen divisions, not including one French division, the 3d Algerian. The stage was set for the third act.

Bradley was poised to strike at the nose of the triangular salient and at its northern base; Devers was ready to crush in its southern side.

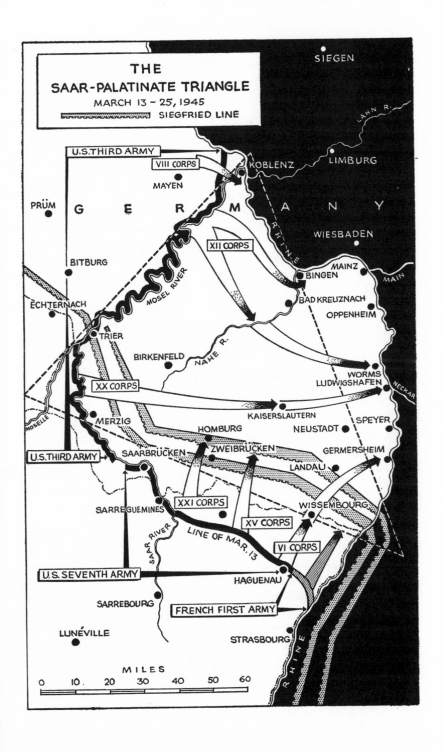

The plan called for the American Seventh Army to launch a power-ful assault in the direction of Worms. It was to penetrate the Siegfried Line and seize a bridgehead over the Rhine. Bradley was to launch an attack across the lower reaches of the Moselle so as to thrust deep into the rear of the forces facing the Seventh Army. Thus we expected by converging attacks to cut off the German forces and prevent their retreat across the Rhine. At the same time that these two attacks were launched at the base of the salient the nose would be struck by the right flank of the Third Army.[27]

The attack began March 15. The southern and western attacks met stiff opposition in the enemy's strong defenses but made good progress, so much so that the entire German attention seemed centered on these two great attacks. This made the assault of the XII Corps, across the lower Moselle, very effective. The corps began crossing the river March 14 and during the entire operation never met heavy and or-ganized resistance. This may have been because the Germans ex-pected the corps to push northward down the Rhine, to join the forces east of the river in the Remagen bridgehead. In any event the Germans were completely surprised when the XII Corps leaped straight southward in one of the war's most dramatic advances, to strike deeply into the heart of the Saar defenses.[28]

The enemy position quickly became hopeless. All around the perimeter of the salient the Americans battered their way forward while Eddy's XII Corps effectively blocked almost every possible avenue of escape. Patton did not even pause when his forces reached the Rhine, but threw Major General Stafford Irwin's 5th Division across the river without formal preparation of any kind. Irwin's losses were negligible and on March 23 his division was well established in this second Allied bridgehead.[29]

Mopping up in the Saar was speedily accomplished and by March 25 all organized resistance west of the Rhine had ended.

All these operations were carried out in the now familiar pattern of air-ground partnership. Our powerful air force ranged far and wide and attacked important targets en masse, almost paralyzing the German power to maneuver and destroying quantities of vital sup-plies and equipment. While the weather was not ideal for air opera-tions, it was never sufficiently bad to ground the air force completely.

On Washington's Birthday the Allied air forces had staged an opera-tion on such a vast scale as to be almost unique, even in an area where battle-front sorties had sometimes run as high as well over 10,000 in a single day. The operation was called Clarion and its purpose was to deliver one gigantic blow against the transportation system of Germany, with specific targets specially selected so as to occasion the greatest possible damage and the maximum amount of delay in their repair. Nine thousand aircraft, coming from bases in England, France, Italy, Belgium, and Holland, took part in the attack, and the targets were located in almost every critical area of Germany. Reaction was weak; the Luftwaffe was apparently unable to present an effective defense because of the widespread nature of the blow. It was a most imaginative and successful operation and stood as one of the highlights in the long air campaign to destroy the German warmaking power.

One of the notable features of the late winter campaign was the extraordinary conformity of developments to plans. Normally, in a great operation involving such numbers of troops over such vast fronts, enemy reaction and unforeseen developments compel continuous adjustment of plan. This one was an exception. The precision was due primarily to the great Allied air and ground strength; secondly to the fighting qualities of the troops and the skill of their platoon, battalion, and divisional leaders; and thirdly to the growing discouragement, bewilderment, and confusion among the defenders. Part of the price of the Battle of the Bulge was paid off by Hitler in the crushing defeats he suffered in February and March 1945.

All troops went into battle with orders to seize a bridgehead over the Rhine whenever the slightest opportunity presented itself, and all were alerted to the remote possibility of seizing a standing bridge. Our good fortune at Remagen hastened the end of Germany but had no real effect upon the battles then raging west of the river.

One slight change in plans occurred during the Saar battle. The boundary between Bradley's and Devers' army groups ran directly through the battlefield. This was deliberately arranged so as to obtain the full converging power of the Seventh and Third Armies on that stronghold. As the battle developed it became possible for Patton's Third Army to move against objectives in Patch's Seventh Army zone that Devers found it impossible to engage. Happening to be on the spot at the moment, I authorized appropriate boundary adjustments, specifying particularly close interarmy liaison. This involved also the transfer of an armored division from the Seventh to the Third Army.[30] The insignificance of this slight change illustrates the accuracy with which staffs had calculated the probabilities.

During the month-long campaign our captures of German prisoners averaged 10,000 per day. This meant that the equivalent of twenty full divisions had been subtracted from the German Army, entirely aside from normal casualties in killed and wounded. The enemy suffered great losses in equipment and supplies, and in important areas of manufacture and sources of raw materials.[31]

We had by this time a logistic and administrative organization capable of handling such numbers of prisoners and these captives interfered only temporarily with troop maneuvers and offensives. We had come a long way from the time in Tunisia when the sudden capture of 275,000 Axis prisoners caused me rather ruefully to remark to my operations officers, Rooks and Nevins: "Why didn't some staff college ever tell us what to do with a quarter of a million prisoners so located at the end of a rickety railroad that it's impossible to move them and where guarding and feeding them are so difficult?"

By March 24 there was in the Remagen bridgehead an American army of three full corps, poised, ready to strike in any direction. Farther to the south the Third Army had made good a crossing of the Rhine and there was now in that region no hostile strength to prevent our establishing further bridgeheads almost at will.

Just to the north of the Remagen bridgehead ran the Sieg River, which flanked the Ruhr region on the south. So vital was the safety of the Ruhr to the German warmaking capacity that the enemy hastily assembled along the Sieg all of the remaining forces that he could spare from other threatened areas in the west, because the German assumed that we would strike directly against the Ruhr from Remagen.[32]

In this situation Hitler resorted to his old practice of changing senior commanders: Von Rundstedt was relieved from command, destined to take no further part in the war. Von Rundstedt, whom we always considered the ablest of the German generals, had been in command in the west when the landings were made June 6. Unable to drive the Allies back into the ocean, as ordered by Hitler, he had been relieved within three weeks after the landing and replaced by Von Kluge. When the latter fared no better than his predecessor Hitler again determined to make a change and called Von Rundstedt back into action. We understood at the time that the immediate cause of this second transfer was a belief that Von Kluge had participated in the July 20 plot against Hitler's life.

Hitler now determined to bring Field Marshal von Kesselring up from Italy.

Chapter 20

ASSAULT AND ENCIRCLEMENT

WHILE MONTGOMERY, ON THE NORTH, WAS waging the first of the February and March battles for the destruction of the German forces before the Rhine, additional Canadian and British strength began transferring from the Mediterranean to the Twenty-first Army Group. The move was called Operation Goldflake, and involved a Canadian corps from Italy and a British division from the Middle East. A large proportion of these troops landed at Marseille and cut across the entire network of Allied communications to reach their position on the northern flank. The difficult move was handled smoothly and skillfully by the staffs. No interference with front-line supply and maintenance occurred. Thus while Bradley and Devers, farther south, were delivering the blows that freed the west bank of the Rhine, Montgomery, in the north, could count on early reinforcement as he completed his preparations for forcing a crossing of the river.

Montgomery was always a master in the methodical preparation of forces for a formal, set-piece attack. In this case he made the most meticulous preparations because we knew that along the front just north of the Ruhr the enemy had his best remaining troops, including portions of the First Paratroop Army.

His assault was planned on a front of four divisions, two in the Twenty-first Army Group and two in the attached Ninth Army. Supporting these divisions was an airborne attack by the American 17th Airborne Division and the British 6th Airborne Division. Normal use of airborne forces was to send them into battle prior to the beginning of ground attack so as to achieve maximum surprise and create confusion among defending forces before the beginning of the ground assault. In this instance Montgomery planned to reverse the usual sequence. He decided to make the river crossing under cover of darkness, to be followed the next morning by the airborne attack. It was also normal to drop airborne forces at a considerable distance in rear of the enemy's front lines, where their landing would presumably meet little immediate opposition and so give them time to organize themselves to overrun headquarters, block movement of reserves, and create general havoc. But in this operation the two divisions were to drop close to the front lines, merely far enough back so that they would not be within the zone of our own artillery fire. From those positions they were to wreck the enemy's artillery organization and participate directly in the tactical battle. Elaborate arrangements were made for the use of smoke to provide artificial concealment for the river crossing and a great array of guns was assembled to support it.[1]

The Rhine was a formidable military obstacle, particularly so in its northern stretches. It was not only wide but treacherous, and even the level of the river and the speed of its currents were subject to variation because the enemy could open dams along the great river's eastern tributaries. Special reconnaissance and warning detachments were set up to guard against this threat. Because of the nature of the obstacle the crossing resembled an assault against a beach, except that the troops, instead of attacking from ship to shore, were carried into the battle from shore to shore.

Study of conditions indicated the great desirability of naval participation in the attack. We needed vessels of sufficient size to transport tanks with the leading assault waves, and so the Navy began the transfer to the front of landing boats known as LCMs and LCV(P)s. Part of these were brought up by waterways but many of them had to be hauled over the roads of northern Europe. Special trailers were constructed for the purpose and these small ships, some of them 45 feet in length and 14 feet wide, were successfully transported overland for participation in the attack.

The Twenty-first Army Group's organic strength when the assault began was fifteen divisions. With the two airborne divisions and Simpson's Ninth Army there were twenty-nine divisions and seven separate brigades under Montgomery's operational command that day.[2] Not all of these, however, could immediately be committed to the eastward thrust, since Montgomery had to protect his long left flank, stretching westward along the Rhine River to the North Sea. Additional Empire troops, from the Mediterranean, were on the way to join him.

The assault, on the night of March 23–24, was preceded by a violent artillery bombardment. On the front of the two American divisions two thousand guns of all types participated. General Simpson and I found a vantage point in an old church tower from which to witness the gunfire. Because the batteries were distributed on the flat plains on the western bank of the Rhine every flash could be seen. The din was incessant. Meanwhile infantry assault troops were marching up to the water's edge to get into the boats. We joined some of them and found the troops remarkably eager to finish the job. There is no substitute for a succession of great victories in building morale. Nevertheless, as we walked along I fell in with one young soldier who seemed silent and depressed.

"How are you feeling, son?" I asked.

"General," he said, "I'm awful nervous. I was wounded two months ago and just got back from the hospital yesterday. I don't feel so good!"

"Well," I said to him, "you and I are a good pair then, because I'm nervous too. But we've planned this attack for a long time and we've got all the planes, the guns, and airborne troops we can use to smash the Germans. Maybe if we just walk along together to the river we'll be good for each other."

"Oh," he said, "I meant I *was* nervous; I'm not any more. I guess it's not so bad around here." And I knew what he meant.

Our preparations for the crossing north of the Ruhr had been so deliberately and thoroughly made that the enemy knew what was coming. We anticipated strong resistance, since we would achieve surprise only by the timing and strength of the assault. In particular we thought that the enemy would have a great number of guns trained on the river and the eastern banks and would attempt to stop our troops at the water's edge with gunfire.

This kind of resistance, however, was not encountered. The two American divisions making the assault on the Ninth Army front, the 30th and the 79th, suffered a total of only thirty-one casualties during the actual crossing. The divisions were under the command of General Anderson of the XVI Corps.[3]

Throughout the remainder of the night we received a series of encouraging reports. Everywhere the landings appeared completely successful. We were encouraged to believe that we could very quickly achieve such an eastward advance that the communications leading into the Ruhr would be cut.

With the arrival of daylight I went to a convenient hill from which to witness the arrival of the airborne units, which were scheduled to begin their drop at ten o'clock. The airborne troops were carried to the assault in a total of 1572 planes and 1326 gliders; 889 fighter planes escorted them during the flight, and 2153 other fighters provided cover over the target area and established a defensive screen to the eastward.[4]

Fog and the smoke of the battlefield prevented a complete view of the airborne operation but I was able to see some of the action. A number of our planes were hit by anti-aircraft, generally, however, only after they had dropped their loads of paratroopers. As they swung away from the battle area they seemed to come over a spot where anti-aircraft fire was particularly accurate. Those that were struck fell inside our own lines, and in nearly every case the crews succeeded in saving themselves by taking to their parachutes. Even so, our loss in planes was far lighter than we had calculated. Operation Varsity, the name given to the airborne phase of this attack, was the most successful airborne operation we carried out during the war.[5]

During the morning I met the Prime Minister with Field Marshal Brooke. Mr. Churchill always seemed to find it possible to be near the scene of action when any particularly important operation was to be launched. On that morning he was delighted, as indeed were all of us. He exclaimed over and over, "My dear General, the German is whipped. We've got him. He is all through." The Prime Minister was merely voicing what all of us felt and were telling each other. It was on that morning also that Field Marshal Brooke expressed his own tremendous pleasure that the operations of February and March had been carried through as planned by SHAEF.[6]

About noon of March 24 it was necessary for me to rush down to Bradley's headquarters to confer on important phases of his own operations. After I left, the Prime Minister persuaded the local commander to take him across the Rhine in an LCM. He undoubtedly derived an intense satisfaction from putting his foot on the eastern bank of Germany's traditional barrier. Possibly he felt the act was symbolic of the final defeat of an enemy who had forced Britain's back to the wall five years before. However, had I been present he would never have been permitted to cross the Rhine that day.

As was normal with us, the air force participated intensively in the attack. For a number of days preceding March 23 we placed a continuous air bombardment upon a wide variety of targets in the area.

Chief among these targets were enemy airfields, with particular attention given every field from which we believed the Germans could operate a jet plane. Starting on March 21, we constantly drenched all these fields with bombs. The runways were effectively cratered and planes were destroyed on the ground. These measures were decisive: on the day of the attack the Allied air force flew about 8000 sorties and saw fewer than 100 enemy planes in the air.[7] During all this time we were favored with excellent weather; visibility was perfect.

During March 24 we also conducted diversionary air operations in order to prevent the concentration of enemy fighters at the point of attack. A hundred and fifty bombers of the Fifteenth Air Force, located in Italy, flew fifteen hundred miles to attack Berlin. Other air forces from Italy raided airfields in the south. Long before this time the RAF Bomber Command, originally designed for night bombing only, had begun to participate regularly in daylight attacks. With the protection provided by our great array of fighters, it could operate safely during hours of daylight and its accuracy was vastly increased. On the twenty-fourth it came over to attack rail centers and oil targets in and near the Ruhr.[8]

The March 24 operation sealed the fate of Germany. Already, of course, we had secured two bridgeheads farther to the south. But in each of those cases surprise and good fortune had favored us. The northern operation was made in the teeth of the greatest resistance the enemy could provide anywhere along the long river. Moreover, it was launched directly on the edge of the Ruhr and the successful landing on the eastern bank placed strong forces in position to deny the enemy use of significant portions of that great industrial area.

In the meantime events farther south had been proceeding swiftly. Bradley's first purpose was to secure a firm lodgment in the Frankfurt region from which an advance in strength would be undertaken toward Kassel. At this latter point we expected to join up with Montgomery's attack on the north of the Ruhr and so complete the envelopment of that area.

From the moment that General Patton pushed the U. S. 5th Division across the Rhine on the night of March 22 he had continued steadily to build up his bridgehead. By the evening of March 24 it was nine miles long and six miles deep, and the attacking troops had taken 19,000 prisoners. The entire XII Corps was now across the river and its 4th Armored Division pushed forward so rapidly that on March 25 it captured intact the bridges over the Main at Aschaffenburg.[9]

The Remagen bridgehead, ever since its establishment, had continued to expand in spite of repeated piecemeal attacks by the German. General Hodges had thrown the III, V, and VII Corps into that area. By the twenty-sixth, German detachments on the northern flank of the bridgehead had been driven back across the Sieg, where they confidently expected to receive a major assault.[10] However, the German was to suffer still another great surprise in the Remagen area. As soon as American forces had begun to establish themselves firmly in the Remagen bridgehead Bradley and I had started to develop our plans for deriving the greatest usefulness from this development.

We had always planned, on Bradley's front, to make our main crossings in the region where Patton had seized his bridgeheads, since this was the most suitable area from which to launch the southern prong of the great double offensive that was expected to surround the Ruhr. From Remagen we could of course turn the First Army to the north and northeast to assault the Ruhr directly. This would, however, involve frontal attack across the Sieg and would not accomplish the great and complete encirclement of that area which was an essential feature of our basic plan. Consequently Bradley and I had early decided to launch the troops out of the Remagen bridgehead to the southeastward to join up with Patton near Giessen.[11] Bradley would then have his force concentrated and we were certain that his further success would be swift and sure.

On the twenty-sixth of March the advance out of the Remagen bridgehead began. The V Corps, now under Major General Clarence R. Huebner, thrust rapidly to the southeast and overran Limburg. These great converging thrusts by Hodges and Patton completed the demoralization of the enemy in that region.

Middleton's VIII Corps, of the Third Army, was still west of the Rhine, lying along a stretch north of Braubach where, because of the rugged banks, bridging operations against an enemy looked almost impossible. Nevertheless, the VIII Corps made the attempt and, in spite of some sharp initial resistance, was successful. It was thus able to push forward directly and join in the great advance. Frankfurt was cleared by March 29 and armored spearheads were thrust forward in the direction of Kassel.[12]

Still farther south, in the Sixth Army Group, Patch's Seventh Army joined the attack. While that army had been engaged in the Saar operation the Rhine defenses in its region were considered sufficiently strong to require the use of airborne troops in order to assure a suc-

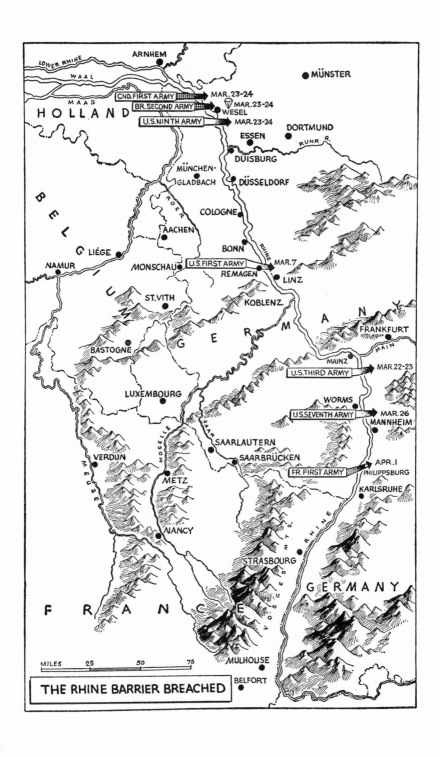

THE RHINE BARRIER BREACHED

cessful river crossing. For this purpose the U. S. 13th Airborne Division was directed to plan an attack. However, so great was the confusion of the enemy following his collapse in the Saar that the airborne assault was found unnecessary. General Haislip's XV Corps, of the Seventh Army, forced a crossing of the river near Worms on March 26. Enemy detachments at the water's edge presented stubborn opposition but it was quickly overcome and the XV Corps completed the crossing on the twenty-seventh.[13] The Seventh Army immediately took up the advance and after linking up with the Third Army pushed on quickly to capture Mannheim.[14] The final crossing of the Rhine against resistance was made by the French Army at Philippsburg April 1.[15] From there the French were subsequently to strike southeastward in the direction of Stuttgart and clear the eastern bank of the Rhine all the way to the Swiss border.

We now had crossings over the Rhine in every main channel we had selected for invasion. The ease with which these were accomplished and the light losses that we suffered incident to them were in great contrast to what certainly would have happened had the Germans, during the winter, withdrawn from the west bank and made their decisive stand along the river. It is a formidable obstacle and the terrain all along the eastern bank affords strong defensive positions. Frontal assaults against the German Army, even at the decreased strength and efficiency available to it in early 1945, would have been a costly business.

We owed much to Hitler. There is no question that his General Staff, had it possessed a free hand in the field of military operations, would have foreseen certain disaster on the western bank and would have pulled back the defending forces, probably no later than the beginning of January. At that time the abortive attack in the Ardennes was a proven failure and the participating German troops were being driven back in defeat. Moreover, on January 12 the Russians began a great offensive that was to carry them all the way from the Vistula to the Oder, within thirty miles of Berlin.

Militarily, the wise thing for the German to do at that moment would have been to surrender. His position was hopeless and even if he could have saved nothing on the political front he could have prevented the loss of thousands on the field of battle and avoided further destruction of his cities and industries.

So long as he chose to continue the fight, possibly in the desperate hope that the Allies would fall out among themselves and consequently fail to complete the conquest, he should instantly have taken up in the west his strongest possible defensive line, the Rhine River, and gathered up everything he could to use as a central reserve. Even that procedure could have offered him no hope of eventual success, if for no other reason than the fact that our tremendous air force was now daily pulverizing the resources in his dwindling territory on an almost unendurable scale. But it was the only method that would have given him a chance to prolong hostilities and it now became clear that there could be no other reason to continue the war. Even Hitler, fanatic that he was, must have had lucid moments in which he could not have failed to see that the end was in sight. He was writing an ending to a drama that would far exceed in tragic climax anything that his beloved Wagner ever conceived.

So far as the Allies were concerned the situation was somewhat like the one that followed upon the breakout in Normandy eight months earlier. There were, however, important differences. We now had present a ground and air strength satisfactorily disposed to brush aside any resistance that we would encounter and there was no Siegfried Line off in the distance for the enemy to man. Far more important was the health and strength of our logistical organization. Lying just behind the Rhine were stocks of equipment and supplies. Close by were the service organizations so necessary to provide for the rapid advance of troops and their constant maintenance. As quickly as we crossed the Rhine we installed floating bridges and they were soon supplemented with fixed types. The first semipermanent railway bridge was built at Wesel, in the northern sector. There, on one of the widest stretches of the river, American engineers constructed a bridge over which ran our first railroad train, less than eleven days after the capture of the site.[16]

With our forces everywhere crossing the Rhine and with so much of the German strength lost in the wreckage of the Siegfried Line, the second great phase of our spring campaign was completed. It was then necessary to review the situation and prescribe the movement of forces to accomplish the third phase, the final destruction of German military power and the overrunning of German territory.

The first step in this movement remained the encirclement of the Ruhr. This had always been a major feature of our plans and there was nothing in the situation now facing us to indicate any advantage in abandoning the purpose. On the contrary, it now appeared that this double envelopment would not only finally and completely sever the industrial Ruhr from the remainder of Germany but would result in the destruction of one of the major forces still remaining to the enemy.

When the enemy failed to eliminate the Remagen bridgehead in the early days of March he began frantically to build up the southern defenses of the Ruhr along the Sieg River. In the same way, when Montgomery catapulted across the Rhine in the northern sector on March 24, the Germans hurriedly began to establish a line along the northern flank of the Ruhr region. The double envelopment would therefore surround these defending forces, tear a wide gap in the center, and open a path across the country to the eastward.

I already knew of the Allied political agreements that divided Germany into post-hostilities occupational zones. The north-south line allotted by that decision to the British and American nations ran from the vicinity of Lübeck, at the eastern base of the Danish peninsula, generally southward to the town of Eisenach and on southward to the Austrian border.[17]

This future division of Germany did not influence our military plans for the final conquest of the country. Military plans, I believed, should be devised with the single aim of speeding victory; by later adjustment troops of the several nations could be concentrated into their own national sectors.

A natural objective beyond the Ruhr was Berlin. It was politically and psychologically important as the symbol of remaining German power. I decided, however, that it was not the logical or the most desirable objective for the forces of the Western Allies.[18]

When we stood on the Rhine in the last week of March we were three hundred miles from Berlin, with the obstacle of the Elbe still two hundred miles to our front.

The Russian forces were firmly established on the Oder with a bridgehead on its western bank only thirty miles from Berlin. Our logistic strength, which included an ability to deliver to forward elements some 2000 tons of supplies by air transport every day, would sustain our spearheads thrusting across Germany. But if we should plan for a power crossing of the Elbe, with the single purpose of attempting to invest Berlin, two things would happen. The first of these was that in all probability the Russian forces would be around the city long before we could reach there. The second was that to sustain a strong force at such a distance from our major bases along the Rhine would have meant the practical immobilization of units along the remainder of the front. This I felt to be more than unwise; it was stupid.

There were several other major purposes, beyond the encirclement of the Ruhr, to be accomplished quickly.

It was desirable to thrust our spearheads rapidly across Germany to a junction with the Red forces, thus to divide the country and effectually prevent any possibility of German forces acting as a unit. It was important also to seize the town of Lübeck in the far north as quickly as possible. By so doing we would cut off all German troops remaining in the Danish peninsula as well as those still in Norway. Such a thrust would also gain us northern ports in Germany through the capture of either Bremen or Hamburg, or both. This would again shorten our line of communications.

Equally important was the desirability of penetrating and destroying the so-called "National Redoubt."[19] For many weeks we had been receiving reports that the Nazi intention, in extremity, was to withdraw the cream of the SS, Gestapo, and other organizations fanatically devoted to Hitler, into the mountains of southern Bavaria, western Austria, and northern Italy. There they expected to block the tortuous mountain passes and to hold out indefinitely against the Allies. Such a stronghold could always be reduced, by eventual starvation if in no other way. But if the German was permitted to establish the Redoubt he might possibly force us to engage in a long-drawn-out guerrilla type of warfare, or a costly siege. Thus he could keep alive his desperate hope that through disagreement among the Allies he might yet be able to secure terms more favorable than those of unconditional surrender. The evidence was clear that the Nazi intended to make the attempt and I decided to give him no opportunity to carry it out.

Another Nazi purpose, somewhat akin to that of establishing a mountain fortress, was the organization of an underground army, to which he gave the significant name of "Werewolves." The purpose of the Werewolf organization, which was to be composed only of loyal followers of Hitler, was murder and terrorism. Boys and girls as well as adults were to be absorbed into the secret organization with the hope of so terrifying the countryside and making so difficult the problem of occupation that the conquering forces would presumably be glad to get out.

The way to stop this project—and such a development was always a possibility because of the passionate devotion to their Führer of so many young Germans—was to overrun the entire national territory before its organization could be effected.

With these several considerations in mind I determined that as soon as the Twelfth and Twenty-first Army Groups could complete the Ruhr envelopment our next major advances would comprise three essential parts.

The first would be a powerful thrust by Bradley directly across the center of Germany. By following this route his armies would traverse the central plateau of the country. Thus he would cross the rivers near their headwaters where they do not constitute the serious obstacles that they do in the northern German plain near the sea. To assure Bradley of enough strength to drive uninterruptedly across the country the U. S. Ninth Army was to be returned to his command.[20] Additionally we organized for Bradley's group a new army, the Fifteenth, under the command of General Gerow, which was to have two principal functions. It was to take over matters of military government in rear of advancing troops. It would also provide the necessary Allied strength on the western bank of the Rhine facing the Ruhr to prevent any of the Germans in that region from raiding important points on our supply lines west of the river. Gerow was furthermore charged with the command of the U. S. 66th Division, which, hundreds of miles to the westward, was still containing the German garrisons in the Biscay ports of St. Nazaire and Lorient.[21]

Bradley's advance with his three armies was to begin as soon as he had made sure that the German forces in the Ruhr could not interfere with his communications. I had no intention of conducting a bitter, house-to-house battle for the destruction of the Ruhr garrison. It was a thickly populated region with no indigenous sources of food supply. Hunger alone could certainly bring about eventual capitulation and spare the Allies great numbers of casualties.

The second and third parts of the general plan visualized, following upon Bradley's junction with the Russians somewhere along the Elbe, a rapid advance on each of our flanks. The northern thrust would cut off Denmark; the southern one would push into Austria and overrun the mountains west and south of that country. In the early stages of Bradley's advance the Sixth Army Group on the south and the Twenty-first Army Group on the left would advance generally in support of Bradley's main thrust, making as much progress as possible in the direction of their final objectives.

In turn, once Bradley had achieved his mission in the center, he would support Montgomery on the north and Devers on the south, as they undertook the final advances planned for them.

This general plan was presented to Generalissimo Stalin.[22]

Under the arrangement made in January and approved by the Combined Chiefs of Staff, I thought that I was completely within the scope of my own authority and responsibility in communicating this plan to the Generalissimo. However, we quickly found that Prime Minister Churchill seriously objected to my action. He disagreed with the plan and held that, because the campaign was now approaching its end, troop maneuvers had acquired a political significance that demanded the intervention of political leaders in the development of broad operational plans. He apparently believed that my message to the Generalissimo had exceeded my authority to communicate with Moscow only on purely military matters. He was greatly disappointed and disturbed because my plan did not first throw Montgomery forward with all the strength I could give him from the American forces, in the desperate attempt to capture Berlin before the Russians could do so. He sent his views to Washington.[23]

The Prime Minister knew, of course, that, regardless of the distance the Allies might advance to the eastward, he and the President had already agreed that the British and American occupation zones would be limited on the east by a line two hundred miles west of Berlin. Consequently his great insistence upon using all our resources in the hope of assuring the arrival of the Western Allies in Berlin ahead of the Russians must have been based on the conviction that great prestige and influence for the Western Allies would later derive from this achievement.

I had no means of knowing what his true reasons were but the protest immediately initiated an exchange of a series of telegrams, beginning with a message from General Marshall on March 29. In that message he informed me that the British Chiefs of Staff were concerned both as regarded the procedure which I had adopted in communicating with the Generalissimo and with what they called my change of plan. The British Chiefs informed Marshall that my main thrust should cross the plains of north Germany because by this means we could open German ports in the west and north. They pointed out that this would also to a great extent annul the U-boat war, and we should be free to move into Denmark, open a line of communication with Sweden, and liberate for our use nearly 2,000,000 tons of Swedish and Norwegian shipping.[24]

Receipt of this information inspired the following:

From Eisenhower to Marshall, dated March 30:

Frankly the charge that I have changed plans has no possible basis in fact. The principal effort north of the Ruhr was always adhered to with the object of isolating that valuable area. Now that I can foresee the time that my forces can be concentrated in the Kassel area I am still adhering to my old plan of launching from there one main attack calculated to accomplish, in conjunction with the Russians, the destruction of the enemy armed forces. My plan will get the ports and all the other things on the north coast more speedily and decisively than will the dispersion now urged upon me by Wilson's message to you.[25]

After sending this preliminary message we drew up, for General Marshall's information, a complete digest of our plan and dispatched it by following radio:

From Eisenhower to Marshall, dated March 30:

This is in reply to your radio.

The same protests except as to "procedure" contained in that telegram were communicated to me by the Prime Minister over telephone last night.

I am completely in the dark as to what the protests concerning "procedure" involve. I have been instructed to deal directly with the Russians concerning military co-ordination. There is no change in basic strategy. The British Chiefs of Staff last summer protested against my determination to open up the Frankfurt route because they said it would be futile and would draw strength away from a northern attack. I have always insisted that the northern attack would be the principal effort in that phase of our operations that involved the isolation of the Ruhr, but from the very beginning, extending back before D-day, my plan, explained to my staff and senior officers, has been to link up the primary and secondary efforts in the Kassel area and then make one great thrust to the eastward.

Even cursory examination of the decisive direction for this thrust, after the link-up in the Kassel area is complete, shows that the principal effort should under existing circumstances be toward the Leipzig region, where is concentrated the greater part of the remaining German industrial capacity, and to which area the German ministries are believed to be moving. My plan does not draw Montgomery's British and Canadian forces to the southward. You will note that his right flank will push forward along the general line Hanover–Wittenberge. Merely following the principle that Field Marshal Brooke has always emphasized, I am determined to concentrate on one major thrust and all that my plan does is to place the U. S. Ninth Army back under Bradley for that phase of operations involving the advance of the center from Kassel to the Leipzig region, unless, of course, the Russian forces should be met on this side of that area. Thereafter, that position will be consolidated while the plan clearly shows that Ninth Army may again have to move up to assist the British and Canadian armies in clearing the whole coast line to the westward of Lübeck.

After strength for this operation has been provided, it is considered that we can launch a movement to the southeastward to prevent Nazi occupation of a mountain citadel.

I have thoroughly considered the naval aspects of this situation and clearly recognize the advantages of gaining the northern coast line at an early date. It is for this reason that I have made that objective the next one to be achieved after the primary thrust has placed us in a decisive position. The opening of Bremen, Hamburg, and Kiel involves operations against the Frisian Islands and Heligoland and extensive mine sweeping. All this and operations into Denmark and Norway form part of a later phase.

May I point out that Berlin itself is no longer a particularly important objective. Its usefulness to the German has been largely destroyed and even his government is preparing to move to another area. What is now important is to gather up our forces for a single drive and this will more quickly bring about the fall of Berlin, the relief of Norway, and the acquisition of the shipping and the Swedish ports than will the scattering around of our effort.

As another point I should like to point out that the so-called "good ground" in northern Germany is not really good at this time of year. That region is not only badly cut up with waterways, but in it the ground during this part of the year is very wet and not so favorable for rapid movement as is the higher plateau over which I am preparing to launch the main effort.

To sum up:

I propose, at the earliest possible moment, in conjunction with the Soviets to divide and destroy the German forces by launching my main attack from the Kassel area straight eastward toward the heart of what remains of the German industrial power until that thrust has attained the general area of Leipzig and including that city, unless the Russian advance meets us west of that point. The second main feature of the battle is to bring Montgomery's forces along on the left and as quickly as the above has been accomplished to turn Ninth Army to the left to assist him in cleaning out the whole area from Kiel and Lübeck westward.

After the requirements of these two moves have been met, I will thrust columns southeastward in an attempt to join up with the Russians in the Danube Valley and prevent the establishment of a Nazi fortress in southern Germany.

Naturally, my plans are flexible and I must retain freedom of action to meet changing situations. Maximum flexibility will result from a concentration of maximum force in the center.[26]

An interesting sidelight on the foregoing telegram is that it was originally drafted, in my headquarters, by one of my British assistants.

From Marshall to Eisenhower, dated March 31:

British Chiefs of Staff sent from London to Combined Chiefs today their views on your plan.

They deny any desire to fetter the hand of the Supreme Commander in the field but mention wider issues outside the purvue of SCAEF (U-boat war, Swedish shipping, political importance of saving thousands of Dutchmen from starvation, importance of move into Denmark and liberating Norway) and request delay in the submission of further details to Deane [head of the Military Mission in Moscow] until you hear from the CCS.

The U. S. Chiefs replied today in substance as follows: SCAEF's procedure in communicating with the Russians appears to have been an operational necessity. Any modification of this communication should be made by Eisenhower and not by the CCS. The course of action outlined in SCAEF plan appears to be in accord with agreed strategy and SCAEF's directive, particularly in light of present developments. Eisenhower is deploying across the Rhine in the north the maximum number of forces which can be employed. The secondary effort in the south is achieving an outstanding success and is being exploited to the extent of logistic capabilities. The U. S. Chiefs are confident that SCAEF's course of action will secure the ports and everything else mentioned by the British more quickly and more decisively than the course of action urged by them.

The battle of Germany is now at a point where it is up to the Field Commander to judge the measures which should be taken. To deliberately turn away from the exploitation of the enemy's weakness does not appear sound. The single objective should be quick and complete victory. While recognizing there are factors not of direct concern to SCAEF, the U. S. Chiefs consider his strategic concept is sound and should receive full support. He should continue to communicate freely with the Commander in Chief of the Soviet Army.[27]

Later, on April 7, I included the following in my final radio on the subject to General Marshall:

The message I sent to Stalin was a purely military move taken in accordance with ample authorizations and instructions previously issued by the Combined Chiefs of Staff. Frankly, it did not cross my mind to confer in advance with the Combined Chiefs of Staff because I have assumed that I am held responsible for the effectiveness of military operations in this theater and it was a natural question to the head of the Russian forces to inquire as to the direction and timing of their next major thrust, and to outline my own intentions.

We are now holding up a message to the mission in Russia, the purpose of which is to establish some concrete arrangement for mutual identification of air and ground troops and to suggest a procedure to be followed in the event our forces should meet the Russians in any part of Germany, each with an offensive mission. It is critically important that this question be settled quickly on a practical basis.[28]

The outcome of all this was that we went ahead with our own plan. So earnestly did I believe in the military soundness of what we were doing that my intimates on the staff knew I was prepared to make an issue of it.

The only other result of this particular argument was that we thereafter felt somewhat restricted in communicating with the Generalissimo and were careful to confine all our communications to matters of solely tactical importance. This situation I did not regard as too serious, particularly because the United States Chiefs of Staff had staunchly reaffirmed my freedom of action in the execution of plans that in my judgment would bring about the earliest possible cessation of hostilities.

Chapter 21

OVERRUNNING GERMANY

THE INDUSTRIAL IMPORTANCE OF THE RUHR TO Germany had been greatly diminished even before we surrounded it. Not only had the factories of the region been the targets of many heavy bombing raids but in February 1945 the Allied air force had initiated an interdiction program designed to cut the communication lines leading from the Ruhr into the heart of Germany. That operation had been markedly successful and we knew that the Germans were having great difficulty in transporting munitions from the Ruhr to the armies still remaining in the fields. As a consequence of the threats now developing on both sides of that area and because of its greatly diminished usefulness, it would have seemed logical for the Germans to withdraw their military forces for use in opposing our forward advances. Certainly it should have been clear to the German General Staff that when once the Ruhr was surrounded there would be lost not only its industries but whatever military forces might be jammed into its defenses. Nevertheless, the Germans once again stood in place.

Bradley's forces on the south and Montgomery's in the north fought steadily toward their appointed meeting place near Kassel. The resistance to Simpson's Ninth Army, which was on the right of Montgomery's army group, was more stubborn than that encountered by the First and Third Armies advancing out of the Frankfurt area. As a result, the southern arm of our pincers swung well around the eastern and northeastern flanks of the Ruhr to meet Simpson's advancing columns in the vicinity of Lippstadt, near Paderborn.

By April 1, just one week after the Twenty-first Army Group had crossed the Rhine in the Wesel sector, the junction was complete, the Ruhr was surrounded, and its garrison was trapped.

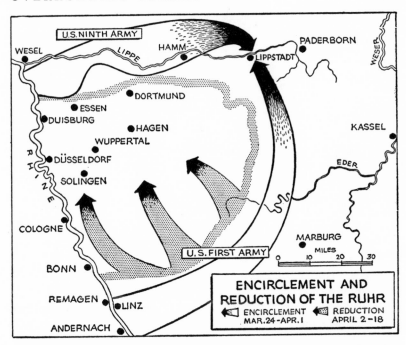

ENCIRCLEMENT AND
REDUCTION OF THE RUHR

◄─ ENCIRCLEMENT   ◄─ REDUCTION
MAR. 24 - APR. I   APRIL 2 - 18

The Germans had now suffered an unbroken series of major defeats. Beginning with the bloody repulse in the enemy's abortive Ardennes assault, the Allied avalanche had continued to inflict upon him a series of losses and defeats of staggering proportions. There was no atom of reason or logic in prolonging the struggle. In both the east and the west strong forces were now operating in the homeland of Germany. The Ruhr, the Saar, and Silesia were all lost to the enemy. His remaining industries, dispersed over the central area of the country, could not possibly support his armies still attempting to fight. Communications were badly broken and no Nazi senior commander could ever be sure that his orders would reach the troops for whom they were intended. While in many areas there were troops capable of putting up fierce and stubborn local resistance, only on the northern and southern flanks of the great western front were there armies of sufficient size to do more than delay Allied advances.

On March 31, I issued a proclamation to the German troops and people, urging the former to surrender and the latter to begin planting crops. I described the hopelessness of their situation and told them that further resistance would only add to their future miseries.

My purpose was to bring the whole bloody business to an end. But the hold of Hitler on his associates was still so strong and was so effectively applied elsewhere, through the medium of the Gestapo and SS, that the nation continued to fight.

When Bradley reached the Kassel region his problem was a double-headed one. He first had to compress the Ruhr defenders into a small enough pocket so that they could be contained with a few divisions and effectively prevented from interfering with his own communications. His second job was to organize his three armies for a main advance across the central plateau of Germany in the direction of Leipzig.

His three front-line armies were, from north to south, Simpson's Ninth, Hodges' First, and Patton's Third. He had a total of forty-eight divisions, the largest exclusively American force in our history.[1]

Field Marshal Model commanded the German forces in the Ruhr pocket. He first attempted to break out of the encirclement by an attack toward the north, and he was defeated. A similar attempt toward the south was equally abortive, and the German garrison had nothing to look forward to except eventual surrender. Bradley kept hammering back the enemy lines and on April 14 the Americans launched a local attack that split the pocket in two. Two days later the eastern half collapsed. On the eighteenth the whole remaining garrison surrendered. Originally we had estimated we would capture about 150,-000 of the German Army in the Ruhr. In the final count the total reached 325,000, including 30 general officers. We destroyed twenty-one divisions and captured enormous quantities of supplies. Hitler must have hoped that the siege of the Ruhr would be as stubbornly contested as was that of Brest, but within eighteen days of the moment the Ruhr was surrounded it had surrendered with an even greater number of prisoners than we had bagged in the final Tunisian collapse almost two years earlier.[2]

In the meantime Bradley had rapidly organized his forces for the eastward drive. By the time the Ruhr garrison surrendered, some of his spearheads had already reached the Elbe, a hundred and fifty miles from Kassel.[3] Bradley's advance was conducted on a broad front. On the south the Third Army struck in the direction of the Czecho-slovakian border and toward the city of Chemnitz just north of that country. It reached that area April 13–14.[4] On Patton's left the First Army attack began April 11 and made rapid progress against scattered resistance. On the fourteenth the 3d Armored Division of Collins' VII Corps reached Dessau, practically on the Elbe.[5] This corps, which had been in the original assault against the Normandy beaches and soon thereafter had captured Cherbourg, had fought all the way across northwest Europe from the coast of France to the river Elbe.

April 12 I spent with George Patton. Before the day ended, the scenes I saw and news I heard etched the date in my memory. In the morning we visited some of Patton's scattered corps and divisions, which were pushing rapidly eastward in a typical Patton thrust, here and there surrounding and capturing isolated detachments of the disintegrating enemy. There was no general line of resistance, or indeed even any co-ordinated attempt at delay. However, some of the local enemy detachments stubbornly defended themselves and we saw sporadic fighting throughout the day.

General Patton's army had overrun and discovered Nazi treasure, hidden away in the lower levels of a deep salt mine.[6] A group of us descended the shaft, almost a half mile under the surface of the earth.

At the bottom were huge piles of German paper currency, apparently heaped up there in a last frantic effort to evacuate some of it before the arrival of the Americans. In one of the tunnels was an enormous number of paintings and other pieces of art. Some of these were wrapped in paper and burlap, others were merely stacked together like cordwood.

In another tunnel we saw a hoard of gold, tentatively estimated by our experts to be worth about $250,000,000, most of it in gold bars. These were in sacks, two 25-pound bars to each sack. There was also a great amount of minted gold from the different countries of Europe and even a few millions of gold coins from the United States.

Crammed into suitcases and trunks and other containers was a great amount of gold and silver plate and ornament obviously looted from private dwellings throughout Europe. All the articles had been flattened by hammer blows, obviously to save storage space, and then merely thrown into the receptacle, apparently pending an opportunity to melt them down into gold or silver bars.

Attention had been originally drawn to the particular tunnel in which all this gold was stored by the existence of a newly built brick wall in the center of which was a steel safe door of the most modern type. The safe door was so formidable that heavy explosive charges would certainly have been necessary for its demolition. However, to an American soldier who inspected it the surrounding brick wall did not look particularly strong, and he tested out his theory with a mere half stick of TNT. With this he blew an enormous hole completely through the obstruction and the hoard was exposed to view. We speculated as to why the Germans had not attempted to provide a concealed hiding place for the treasure in the labyrinth of tunnels instead of choosing to attempt its protection by a wall that could easily have been demolished by a pickax. The elaborate steel door made no sense to us at all, but an American soldier who accompanied me remarked, "It's just like the Germans to lock the stable door but to tear out all its sides." Patton's story of the incident that led to the exploration of the mine was in itself intriguing.

It is probable, of course, that sooner or later the mine would have been carefully searched by the captors. But according to Patton, except for the instincts of human decency on the part of two Americans, we might not have discovered it until much of it had been more securely hidden away. The story was this:

In the little neighboring town the advancing Americans had established a curfew law. Any civilian in the streets after dark was instantly picked up for questioning. One evening a roving patrol in a jeep saw a German woman hurrying along the street after curfew and stopped to speak to her. She protested that she was rushing off to get a midwife for her neighbor, who was about to have a child. The American soldiers decided to check on the story, being quite ready to help if it should prove to be correct. They took the German woman into their jeep, picked up the midwife, and returned to the accouchement, which was all as described by the German woman. The soldiers, still helpful, remained long enough to return the German woman and her midwife friend to their homes. As they were going along the street they passed the mouth of one of the salt mines of that region and one of the women remarked, "That's the mine in which the gold is buried."

This remark excited the curiosity of the soldiers and they questioned the women sufficiently to learn that some weeks earlier great loads of material had been brought from the east to be put into the mine. The soldiers reported the story to their superiors, who in turn sought out some of the German officials of the mining corporation and the whole treasure fell into our hands.

The same day I saw my first horror camp. It was near the town of Gotha. I have never felt able to describe my emotional reactions when I first came face to face with indisputable evidence of Nazi brutality and ruthless disregard of every shred of decency. Up to that time I had known about it only generally or through secondary sources. I am certain, however, that I have never at any other time experienced an equal sense of shock.

I visited every nook and cranny of the camp because I felt it my duty to be in a position from then on to testify at first hand about these things in case there ever grew up at home the belief or assumption that "the stories of Nazi brutality were just propaganda." Some members of the visiting party were unable to go through the ordeal. I not only did so but as soon as I returned to Patton's headquarters that evening I sent communications to both Washington and London, urging the two governments to send instantly to Germany a random group of newspaper editors and representative groups from the national legislatures. I felt that the evidence should be immediately placed before the American and British publics in a fashion that would leave no room for cynical doubt.[7]

The day of April 12 ended on a note of dramatic climax. Bradley, Patton, and I sat up late talking of future plans, particularly of the selection of officers and units for early redeployment to the Pacific. We went to bed just before twelve o'clock, Bradley and I in a small house at Patton's headquarters, and he in his trailer. His watch had stopped, and he turned on the radio to get the time signals from the British Broadcasting Corporation. While doing so he heard the news of President Roosevelt's death. He stepped back into the house, woke up Bradley, and then the two of them came to my room to tell me the shocking news.

We pondered over the effect the President's death might have upon the future peace. We were certain that there would be no interference with the tempo of the war because we already knew something of the great measures afoot in the Pacific to accomplish the smashing of the Japanese. We were of course ignorant of any special or specific arrangements that President Roosevelt had made affecting the later peace. But we were doubtful that there was any other individual in America as experienced as he in the business of dealing with the other Allied political leaders. None of us had known the President very well; I had, through various conferences, seen more of him than the others, but it seemed to us, from the international viewpoint, to be a most critical time to be forced to change national leaders. We went to bed depressed and sad.

With some of Mr. Roosevelt's political acts I could never possibly agree. But I knew him solely in his capacity as leader of a nation at war—and in that capacity he seemed to me to fulfill all that could possibly be expected of him.

During the First Army's advance more than 15,000 of the enemy were cut off in the Harz Mountains. The defenders fought stubbornly and held out until April 21. The country was exceedingly difficult. The week-long fighting to reduce the pocket and to beat off other German troops who attempted to relieve the garrison was of a bitter character.[8] Still farther to the north Simpson's Ninth Army kept equal pace with the advance in the center and the south. By April 6 the Ninth had established a bridgehead over the formidable Weser River and thereafter dashed for the Elbe, which it reached just south of Magdeburg April 11. The next day the 2d Armored Division of the Ninth Army achieved a small bridgehead over the Elbe, ten miles below. Establishment of another small bridgehead by the 5th Armored Division of the XIII Corps north of Magdeburg was thwarted when the enemy blew the bridge. In this sector the enemy appeared to be willing to abandon the country west of the Elbe but savagely opposed any attempt to cross the river. The Germans immediately counterattacked the bridgehead of the 2d Armored Division, which was abandoned April 14. A crossing farther south by the 83d Division was maintained.[9]

Almost coincidentally with our arrival on the Elbe the Red Army launched a powerful westward drive from its positions on the Oder. The attack was on a front of more than two hundred miles. The Red drive made speedy progress everywhere. Its northern flank pushed in the direction of the Danish peninsula, the center toward Berlin, and the southern flank toward the Dresden area. On April 25 patrols of the 69th Division of the V Corps met elements of the Red Army's 58th Guards Division on the Elbe. The meeting took place at Torgau, some seventy-five miles south of Berlin. The V Corps, like the VII, had participated in the initial assault on the beaches of Normandy and it seemed eminently fitting that troops of one of these corps should be first to make contact with the Red Army and accomplish the final severance of the German nation.[10] The problem of liaison with the Russians grew constantly more important as we advanced across central Germany. The pressing questions were no longer those of major strategy but had become tactical in character. One of the principal difficulties was that of mutual identification.

Because of differences in language front-line radios were useless as a means of communication between the two converging forces.

The only solution to the problem seemed to lie in timely agreements upon markings and procedures. As early as the beginning of April the air forces of the Western Allies and the Russians had come into contact, with some unfortunate results. Shots had been exchanged between Red aircraft and our own, and the danger of major clashes continued to increase. The task of organizing a system of recognition signals was laborious and was not fully accomplished until April 20. However, both sides had already agreed upon restraining lines for the use of their air forces, and by the exercise of care, accompanied by a considerable degree of good fortune, no really serious errors took place.[11]

It was also agreed between ourselves and the Russians that when troops of the two converging forces met local commanders would arrange satisfactory junction lines between the two, based upon local and operational considerations. For the general junction line between the two forces we were anxious to have an easily identified geographical feature. For this reason the agreed-upon line, in the center of the front, followed the Elbe and Mulde rivers. It was understood that the withdrawal of our forces to their occupation zone would take place at whatever future date might be agreed upon by our respective governments.

While this decisive advance was taking place in the center the Twenty-first Army Group on the north and the Sixth on the south were both carrying out the operations assigned to them.

In the north Montgomery's Twenty-first Army Group advanced toward Bremen and Hamburg and pushed a column forward to the Elbe to protect the northern flank of Bradley's advance. Montgomery's eastward advance was carried out mainly by the British Second Army, while the Canadian Army thrust northward through Arnhem to clear northeast Holland and the coastal belt eastward toward the Elbe. The eastward advance of the British Second Army, with three corps in the front line, reached the Weser April 6 and the Elbe April 19. At Bremen the British Army encountered an enemy force determined to resist to the bitter end. The British 30 Corps reached the outskirts of the city April 20, but a week of bitter fighting was necessary before Bremen finally surrendered.[12]

Likewise, the northward advance of the Canadian Army on Montgomery's left initially encountered some desperate resistance. However, satisfactory advances were made all along the line and Arnhem was captured April 15. The fall of Arnhem was the signal for the enemy in that sector to withdraw into the Holland fortress behind flooded areas which posed a serious obstacle to an advance into western Holland.

Montgomery believed, and I agreed, that an immediate campaign into Holland would result in great additional suffering for that unhappy country whose people were already badly suffering from lack of food. Much of the country had been laid waste by deliberate flooding of the ground, by bombing, and by the erection of German defenses. We decided to postpone operations into Holland and to do what we could to alleviate suffering and starvation among the Dutch people.[13]

The mission of Devers' Sixth Army Group during the early days of April was to protect the right flank of Bradley's advance. To carry out this mission Devers organized a methodical advance by Patch's Seventh Army on his left and the French First Army on his right.[14]

Initially the opposition on the front of the Sixth Army Group was general and, despite the debacle in the north and the daily losses of battle, the Germans continued stubbornly to resist. When the Seventh Army reached the Neckar River it had to fight hard to establish a crossing and then required a week to reduce the garrison in the town of Heilbronn. The German troops in this region were not so seriously demoralized by the great Allied advances of February and March as were those who had borne the brunt of our attacks. On April 7 the 10th Armored Division made a thrust in the direction of Crailsheim but German reaction was so speedy and strong that the division had to withdraw hastily from its exposed position. The XV Corps reached Nürnberg April 16 but again several days of fighting were necessary before the defenses of the city finally collapsed.[15]

Resistance in the French sector was not so strong. After some sharp fighting in the immediate vicinity of the Rhine the French advance became rapid.

The French Army, of course, went into the attack under the orders of General Devers, who was responsible for the allocation of army boundaries, routes of supply, and all the other administrative arrangements necessary for troop maintenance throughout his army group. These boundaries placed the city of Stuttgart in Patch's Seventh Army zone, because the supply routes of the Americans would necessarily run through that place. The city was captured by the French, who afterward refused to evacuate to permit its use by Patch. So unyielding were the French in their assertion that national prestige was involved that the argument was referred to me. I instructed Devers to stand firm and to require compliance with his plan. The French still proved obstinate and referred the matter to Paris. Not content with this, General de Gaulle continued to maintain an unyielding attitude on the governmental level in his reply to a sharply worded message from the President of the United States on the subject. In the meantime I had warned the French commander that under the circumstances it was necessary for me to inform the Combined Chiefs of Staff that I could no longer count with certainty on the operational use of any French forces they might be contemplating equipping in the future. This threat of a possible curtailment of equipment for the French forces proved effective, and the French finally complied.[16]

A somewhat similar instance occurred on the French-Italian border, where there was a tiny bit of territory to which the French and Italians had each asserted moral and legal rights of possession. In that region I had made a boundary arrangement with Field Marshal Alexander, and this agreement was violated by the French in their anxiety to strengthen their claims to the disputed piece of territory.[17]

The French position in the war was, of course, not an easy one. Once known as the foremost military power of Europe, their Army as well as their pride had been shattered in the great debacle of 1940. Consequently when the Torch invasion of 1942 again gave patriotic Frenchmen an opportunity to join in the fight against the Nazis they were sensitive to all questions of national pride and honor. Added to this was their bitter hatred of the Nazi, a hatred which seemed to be intensified against some of their own former political and military leaders. On top of all this was the uncertain basis on which rested De Gaulle's authority and that of the governmental organization he had installed in France. A further factor was the complete dependence of the French Army, and indeed of considerable portions of the population, upon American supplies. This was an additional irritant to their pride and, although they constantly insisted upon the need for greater amounts of every kind of equipment and matériel, they were naturally galled by the realization that without those supplies they were completely helpless. All this tended to make them peculiarly sensitive and therefore difficult to deal with when they could find in any question, no matter how trivial, anything that they thought involved their national honor. Nevertheless, America's investment in the French forces paid magnificent dividends.

In the African campaign the French were helpful but extremely weak. So far as heavy fighting was concerned they first took a significant part in the war in Italy. In late 1943 and early 1944 the French corps in that theater did excellent work. Moreover, they performed brilliantly in the invasion of southern France, in the penetration of the Vosges Mountains, and the advance to the upper Rhine. Their efficiency rapidly fell off with the arrival of winter weather in late 1944 because of the large proportion of African native troops in their Army, who were unable to endure the cold and exposure incident to campaigning in a European winter. In the spring of 1945, however, during the final operations of the war, the French Army advanced gallantly and effectively to occupy great portions of southern Germany. At the same time they conducted a ground and air campaign against the Germans on the Bay of Biscay that resulted in the liberation of Bordeaux and the island of Oléron. This operation had been repeatedly postponed since the autumn of 1944 because of more urgent demands elsewhere. The battle commenced on April 14; a week later the Gironde had been cleared to the sea; by May 1, Oléron had fallen. When inspired, the French are great fighters.

Among the French were numbers of important individuals who never caused the slightest trouble; men whose breadth of vision and understanding of the issues at stake made them splendid allies. I personally liked General de Gaulle, as I recognized in him many fine qualities. We felt, however, that these qualities were marred by hypersensitiveness and an extraordinary stubbornness in matters which appeared inconsequential to us. My own wartime contacts with him never developed the heat that seemed to be generated frequently in his meetings with many others.

Giraud was my friend. He was a fighting man and thoroughly honest and straightforward. His complete lack of interest in political matters, however, obviously disqualified him for any political post in his country's service. Generals Juin, Koenig, Koeltz, and innumerable junior officers were courageous, honest, and capable professionals. The names of Generals Mast and Bethouart and their associates who first risked their lives in order to bring about restoration of France through Allied intervention in Africa will always live as symbols of the highest kind of patriotism and greatness of character.

With Bradley's army group firmly established on the Elbe, the stage was now set for the final Allied moves of the campaign. The enemy was split into independent commands in the north and south and had no means of restoring a single front against either the Russians or ourselves. With his world collapsing about him, the German soldier lost all desire to fight. Only in isolated instances did commanders succeed in maintaining cohesion among their units. During the first three weeks of April the Western Allies captured more than a million prisoners.[18]

Even before the Allied advance across central Germany began, we knew that the German Government was preparing to evacuate Berlin. The administrative offices seemed to be moving to the southward, possibly, we thought, to Berchtesgaden in the National Redoubt. Continuation of the movement was no longer possible after Bradley's speedy advance barred further north-south traffic across the country. We knew also that Hitler had been unable to go south and that he was making his last stand in Berlin. Nevertheless, the strong possibility still existed that fanatical Nazis would attempt to establish themselves in the National Redoubt, and the early overrunning of that area remained important to us.[19] In the north also there remained weighty reasons for speeding up the planned attack in the direction of Lübeck.

The Lübeck advance would capture the last remaining submarine bases of the German and would effectively eliminate the final vestiges of that once serious menace.

We could not predict the action of the German occupation forces in Denmark. It was possible they would choose to defend that region stubbornly and in that event we planned to conduct a lightning campaign against them.

In early April, Montgomery had estimated that, to carry out the mission assigned him, he would need no strength beyond the seventeen divisions then in his Twenty-first Army Group. I offered him additional logistic assistance by reserving for him a portion of the capacity of the American railroad bridge at Wesel. This help he declined.[20] But as the operations developed on his flank, he found his troops rapidly used up and in the interests of speed asked for additional strength and supply assistance. Both I was glad to provide. I attached temporarily to Montgomery's force the U. S. XVIII Airborne Corps under General Ridgway. It was to operate in a ground role to support Montgomery's attack. But we were also prepared, in the event the Germans in Denmark should decide to fight to a finish, to provide additional strength for an airborne attack to cross the Kiel Canal.

When Bremen finally fell to Montgomery's force April 26, the resistance in his front became markedly weaker. He quickly transferred his main effort to the sector of the British 8 Corps, which launched an attack across the Elbe April 29. The U. S. XVIII Corps made a simultaneous crossing somewhat to the south and provided right-flank protection to the British Second Army in its further advances.

On May 1 the 11th Armored Division of the British 8 Corps began a brilliant dash across Schleswig-Holstein to the Baltic and entered Lübeck on the afternoon of May 2. This sealed off the enemy in Denmark and also prevented any of the defeated forces in Germany from withdrawing into that country.

Montgomery now rapidly consolidated his gains all along his front and on May 3 the U. S. XVIII Corps made contact with the Russians in Montgomery's sector. With Berlin in flames and the northern flank of the Red Army attack sweeping in our direction across Germany, all resistance collapsed. Swarms of Germans streaming back from the Russian front now began giving themselves up to the Anglo-American armies. American troops standing on the Elbe daily received these prisoners by the thousands.

On Montgomery's left his Canadian Army had, in the meantime, continued its successful operations and rapidly cleaned up its entire front except that it made no attempt to turn back into western Holland, where the German Twenty-fifth Army was entrenched.

We knew that conditions in Holland had been steadily deteriorating and, after the advance of our armies had isolated the area from Germany, the Dutch situation became almost intolerable. Judging from the information available to me, I feared that wholesale starvation would take place and decided to take positive steps to prevent it. I still refused to consider a major offensive into the country. Not only would great additional destruction and suffering have resulted but the enemy's opening of dikes would further have flooded the country and destroyed much of its fertility for years to come. I warned General Blaskowitz, the German commander in Holland, to refrain from opening any more dikes and pointed out to him that nothing he could do in Holland would impede the speedy collapse of Germany.[21]

The Nazi High Commissioner in Holland, Seyss-Inquart, offered a local solution by proposing a truce. If the Allied forces would refrain from any westward advance into Holland no further flooding would take place in the country and the Germans would co-operate in the introduction of relief supplies. My military superiors had already given me a free hand in the matter and I accordingly sent my chief of staff, General Smith, to meet Seyss-Inquart on April 30. They agreed upon methods of introducing food and supplies, which the Allies had already accumulated for the purpose. Large-scale deliveries began immediately. Even before this we had been sending small amounts of food into the country by free parachute. General Smith carried to Seyss-Inquart a warning that I would tolerate no interference with the relief program and that if the Germans were guilty of any breach of faith I would later refuse to treat them as prisoners of war. I considered that continued occupation of Holland by the Germans was senseless and that any further repressive acts for which they were responsible should be punished. At the conference General Smith also proposed that the German commander Blaskowitz should surrender his forces at once. Seyss-Inquart reported, however, that as long as the German Government held out Blaskowitz could under no circumstances capitulate.[22]

Simultaneously with all these operations on the north equally decisive movements were progressing in the south. The principal line of advance was southeast down the Danube Valley toward Linz, with the purpose of joining up with the Russians in Austria. Since Bradley's offensive in the center had already gained its objectives we had the Third Army available to conduct this drive while the Sixth Army Group gave its entire attention to overrunning the Redoubt area farther to the south and west. In order to make certain of Devers' rapid advance we assigned to him the U. S. 13th Airborne Division, to use whenever he deemed advisable. So rapid, however, were the ground advances that the 13th Airborne Division was not needed and, as it turned out, this was the only American division to enter Europe that never engaged in active battle.[23]

The advance of the Third Army down the Danube began April 22. The enemy made an attempt at defense at Regensburg but both the III and XX Corps quickly established bridgeheads across the Danube east and west of the city and advanced rapidly down the river. The XII Corps's 11th Armored Division plunged ahead on May 5 to receive the surrender of the German garrison at Linz in Austria.[24]

With his main forces pushing down the Danube, Patton's Third Army was now reinforced by the V Corps from Hodges' army. Patton directed the V to push eastward into Czechoslovakia. The corps captured Pilsen May 6. In this area the Russian forces were rapidly advancing from the east and careful co-ordination was again necessary. By agreement we directed the American troops to occupy the line Pilsen–Karlsbad, while south of Czechoslovakia the agreed line of junction ran down the Budějovice–Linz railroad and from there along the valley of the Enns River.[25]

The final major move of Patch's Seventh Army in Devers' army group began April 22. On the right flank the XV Corps moved down the Danube and turned southward to strike at Munich, the place of origin of the Nazi movement. That great city was captured April 30. On May 4 the 3d Division of the same corps captured Berchtesgaden. Other troops occupied Salzburg. The defenses of the entire sector disintegrated.[26]

The XXI and VI Corps of the Seventh Army crossed the Danube April 22 and advanced steadily toward the National Redoubt. On May 3, Innsbruck was taken and the 103d Division of the VI Corps pushed on into the Brenner Pass. There, on the Italian side of the international boundary, this American division of the Allied command met the American 88th Division of the U. S. Fifth Army, advancing from Italy. My prediction of a year and a half before that I would meet the soldiers of the Mediterranean command "in the heart of the enemy homeland" was fulfilled.

Throughout the front principal objectives in all sectors were attained by the end of April or their early capture was a certainty. The great advances had the effect of multiplying many of the administrative, maintenance, and organizational problems with which we constantly had to wrestle. Again a tremendous strain was placed upon our supply lines. Distance alone would have been enough to stop our spearheads had we been dependent solely upon surface transport, efficient as it was. Distant and fast-moving columns were sometimes almost solely dependent upon air supply, and during April we kept 1500 transport planes constantly working in our supply system. They became known as "flying boxcars" and were never more essential than in these concluding stages of the war. Besides these planes we stripped and converted many heavy bombers to the same purpose. During the month of April the air forces delivered to the front lines 60,000 tons of freight, in which was included 10,000,000 gallons of gasoline.[27]

Our troops were everywhere swarming over western Germany and there were few remaining targets against which the air force could be directed without danger of dropping their bombs on either our own or the Russian troops. In the late days of the war, however, the air

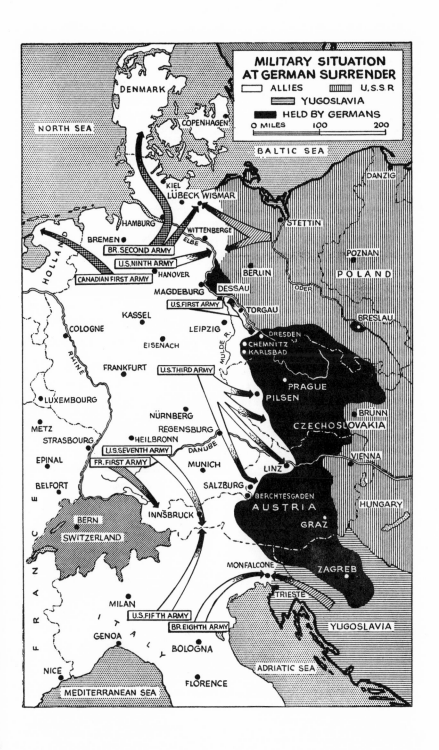

force carried out two important bombing raids. One was by British Bomber Command against the fortress island of Heligoland, which was attacked in order to help Montgomery in case he found it necessary to assault across the Kiel Canal.[28] The other one was by the U. S. Eighth Air Force against Berchtesgaden. That stronghold and symbol of Nazi arrogance was thoroughly pounded with high explosives. The bombing took place when we still thought the Nazis might attempt to establish themselves in their National Redoubt with Berchtesgaden as the capital. The photo reconnaissance units brought back pictures that showed our bombers had reduced the place to a shambles; from them we derived a gleeful and understandable satisfaction.[29]

On each return trip from the front our transports and converted bombers brought back planeloads of recaptured Allied prisoners. These men were concentrated at convenient camps for rehabilitation and early transfer to the homelands. Near Le Havre, in one camp alone, called Lucky Strike, we had at one time 47,000 recovered American prisoners. The British had similar camps at various places in northwest France and Belgium. The recovery of so many prisoners in such a short space of time presented delicate problems to the Medical Corps, to the Transport Service, and indeed to all of us. In many instances the physical condition of the prisoners was so poor that great care had to be exercised in their feeding. The weaker ones were hospitalized and for a period our hospitals were crowded with men whose joy at returning to their own people was almost pathetic, but who at the same time were suffering so badly from malnutrition that only expert care could save them. Some of the Americans had been prisoners since the early battles in Tunisia in December 1942. On the British side we recovered men who had been captured at Dunkirk in 1940.

One day I had an appointment to meet five United States senators. As they walked into my office I received a telegram from a staff officer, stating that a newspaper article alleged the existence at the Lucky Strike camp of intolerable conditions. The story said that men were crowded together, were improperly fed, lived under unsanitary conditions, and were treated with an entire lack of sympathy and understanding. The policy was exactly the opposite. Automatic furloughs to the States had been approved for all liberated Americans and we had assigned specially selected officers to care for them.

Even if the report should prove partially true it represented a very definite failure to carry out strict orders somewhere along the line.

I determined to go see for myself and told my pilot to get my plane ready for instant departure. I turned to the five senators, apologized for my inability to keep my appointment, and explained why it was necessary for me to depart instantly for Lucky Strike. I told them, however, that if they desired to talk with me they could accompany me on the trip. I pointed out that at Lucky Strike they would have a chance to visit with thousands of recovered prisoners of war and that at no other place could they find such a concentration of American citizens. They all accepted with alacrity.

In less than two hours we arrived at Lucky Strike and started our inspection. We roamed around the camp and found no basis for the startling statements made in the disturbing telegram. There were only two points concerning which our men exhibited any impatience. The first of these was the food. It was of good quality and well cooked but the doctors would not permit salt, pepper, or any other kind of seasoning to be used because they were considered damaging to men who had undergone virtual starvation over periods ranging from weeks to years. The senators and I had dinner with the men and we agreed that a completely unseasoned diet was lacking in taste appeal. However, it was a technical point on which I did not feel capable of challenging the doctors.

The other understandable complaint was the length of time that men were compelled to stay in the camp before securing transportation to America. This was owing to lack of ships. Freighters, which constituted the vast proportion of our overseas transport service at that stage of the war, were not suited for transportation of passengers. These ships lacked facilities for providing drinking water, while toilet and other sanitary provisions were normally adequate only for the crew. The men did not know these things and it angered them to see ships leaving the harbor virtually empty when they were so anxious to go home.

So pleased did the soldiers seem to be by our visit that they followed us around the camp by the hundreds. When we finally returned to the airplane we found that an enterprising group had installed a loud-speaker system, with the microphone at the door of my plane. A committee of sergeants came up and rather diffidently said that the men would like to see and hear the commanding general. There were some fifteen to twenty thousand in the crowd around the plane.

In hundreds of places under almost every kind of war condition I had talked to American soldiers, both individually and in groups up to the size of a division. But on that occasion I was momentarily at a loss for something to say. Every one of those present had undergone privation beyond the imagination of the normal human. It seemed futile to attempt, out of my own experience, to say anything that could possibly appeal to such an enormous accumulation of knowledge of suffering.

Then I had a happy thought. It was an idea for speeding up the return of these men to the homeland. So I took the microphone and told the assembled multitude there were two methods by which they could go home. The first of these was to load on every returning troopship the maximum number for which the ship was designed. This was current practice.

Then I suggested that, since submarines were no longer a menace, we could place on each of these returning ships double the normal capacity, but that this would require one man to sleep in the daytime so that another soldier could have his bunk during the night. It would also compel congestion and inconvenience everywhere on the ship. I asked the crowd which one of the two schemes they would prefer me to follow. The roar of approval for the double-loading plan left no doubt as to their desires.

When the noise had subsided I said to them: "Very well, that's the way we shall do it. But I must warn you men that there are five United States senators accompanying me today. Consequently when you get home it is going to do you no good to write letters to the papers or to your senator complaining about overcrowding on returning ships. You have made your own choice and so now you will have to like it."

The shout of laughter that went up left no doubt that the men were completely happy with their choice. I never afterward heard of a single complaint voiced by one of them because of discomfort on the homeward journey.

The war's end was now in sight. The possible duration of hostilities could be measured in days; the only question was whether the finale would come by linking up throughout the gigantic front with the Red Army and the forces from Italy, or whether some attempt would be made by the German Government to capitulate.

Some weeks before the final surrender we received intimations that various individuals of prominence in Germany were seeking ways and means of accomplishing capitulation. In no instance did any of these roundabout messages involve Hitler himself. On the contrary, each sender was so fearful of Nazi wrath that he was as much concerned in keeping secret his own part in the matter as he was in achieving the surrender of the German armies.

One early hint of German defection was a feeler that came through the British Embassy in Stockholm. Its stated purpose was to arrange a truce in the west; this was an obvious attempt to call off the war with the Western Allies so that the German could throw his full strength against Russia. Our governments rejected the proposal.[30]

Another came out of Switzerland, under mysterious circumstances, from a man named Wolff. There was apparently afoot a plot to surrender to Alexander the German forces in Italy.[31] Our own headquarters had nothing to do with this particular instance but we were kept informed because of the definite signs of weakening determination on the part of higher German officials. Receipt of any such tip or of a bona fide message always caused a terrific amount of work and involved much care because of the numbers of nations involved on the Allied side, each of which was naturally concerned that its own interests be fully protected. In the Wolff incident the Western Allies, although proceeding in good faith to determine the authenticity of the message and the authority of the man who initiated it, incurred the suspicion of the Soviets. A great deal of explanation was necessary and it put us definitely on notice to be careful if any such message should reach us.

The first direct suggestion of surrender that reached SHAEF came from Himmler, who approached Count Bernadotte of Sweden in an attempt to get in touch with Prime Minister Churchill.[32] On April 26, I received a long message from the Prime Minister, discussing Himmler's proposal to surrender the western front. I regarded the suggestion as a last desperate attempt to split the Allies and so informed Mr. Churchill. I strongly urged that no proposition be accepted or entertained unless it involved a surrender of all German forces on all fronts. My view was that any suggestion that the Allies would accept from the German Government a surrender of only their western forces would instantly create complete misunderstanding with the Russians and bring about a situation in which the Russians could justifiably accuse us of bad faith. If the Germans desired to surrender an army, that was a tactical and military matter. Likewise, if they wanted to surrender all the forces on a given front, the German commander in the field could do so, and the Allied commander could accept; but the only way the *government* of Germany could surrender was unconditionally to all the Allies.

This view coincided with the Prime Minister's, and he and the President promptly provided full information to Generalissimo Stalin, together with a statement of their rejection of the proposal.

However, until the very last the Germans never abandoned the attempt to make a distinction between a surrender on the western front and one on the eastern. With the failure of this kind of negotiation German commanders finally had, each in his own sector, to face the prospect of complete annihilation or of military surrender.

The first great capitulation came in Italy. Alexander's forces had waged a brilliant campaign throughout the year 1944 and by April 26, 1945, had placed the enemy in an impossible situation. Negotiations for local surrender began and on April 29 the German commander surrendered. All hostilities in Italy were to cease May 2.

This placed the German troops just to the north of Italy in an equally impossible situation. On May 2 the German commander requested the identity of the Allied commander he should approach in order to surrender and was told to apply to General Devers. He was warned that only unconditional surrender would be acceptable. This enemy force was known as Army Group G and comprised the German First and Nineteenth Armies. They gave up on May 5, with the capitulation to be effective May 6.[33]

Far to the north, in the Hamburg area, the German commander also saw the hopelessness of his situation. On April 30 a German emissary appeared in Stockholm to say that Field Marshal Busch, commanding in the north, and General Lindemann, commanding in Denmark, were ready to surrender as quickly as the Allied advance reached the Baltic. We were told that the Germans would refuse to surrender to the Russians but that, once the Western Allies had arrived at Lübeck and so cut off the forces in that region from the arrival of fanatical SS formations from central Germany, they would immediately surrender to us. Montgomery's forces arrived in Lübeck May 3. By then, however, a great change in the governmental structure of Germany had taken place.

Hitler had committed suicide and the tattered mantle of his authority had fallen to Admiral Doenitz. The admiral directed that all his armies everywhere should surrender to the Western Allies. Thousands of dejected German soldiers began entering our lines. On May 3, Admiral Friedeburg, who was the new head of the German Navy, came to Montgomery's headquarters. He was accompanied by a staff officer of Field Marshal Busch. They stated that their purpose was to surrender three of their armies which had been fighting the Russians and they asked authority to pass refugees through our lines. Their sole desire was to avoid surrender to the Russians. Montgomery promptly refused to discuss a surrender on these terms and sent the German emissaries back to Field Marshal Keitel, the chief of the German high command.

I had already told Montgomery to accept the military surrender of all forces in his allotted zone of operations. Such a capitulation would be a tactical affair and the responsibility of the commander on the spot. Consequently, when Admiral Friedeburg returned to Montgomery's headquarters on May 4 with a proposal to surrender all German forces in northwest Germany, including those in Holland and Denmark, Montgomery instantly accepted. The necessary documents were signed that day and became effective the following morning.[34] When Devers and Montgomery received these great surrenders they made no commitments of any kind that could embarrass or limit our governments in future decisions regarding Germany; they were purely military in character, nothing else.

On May 5 a representative of Doenitz arrived in my headquarters. We had received notice of his coming the day before. At the same time we were informed that the German Government had ordered all of its U-boats to return to port. I at once passed all this information to the Russian high command and asked them to designate a Red Army officer to come to my headquarters as the Russian representative in any negotiations that Doenitz might propose. I informed them that I would accept no surrender that did not involve simultaneous capitulation everywhere. The Russian high command designated Major General Ivan Suslaparov.[35]

Field Marshal von Kesselring, commanding the German forces on the western front, also sent me a message, asking permission to send a plenipotentiary to arrange terms of capitulation. Since Von Kesselring had authority only in the West, I replied that I would enter into no negotiations that did not involve all German forces everywhere.[36]

When Admiral Friedeburg arrived at Reims on May 5 he stated that he wished to clear up a number of points. On our side negotiations were conducted by my chief of staff, General Smith. The latter told Friedeburg there was no point in discussing anything, that our purpose was merely to accept an unconditional and total surrender.

Friedeburg protested that he had no power to sign any such document. He was given permission to transmit a message to Doenitz, and received a reply that General Jodl was on his way to our headquarters to assist him in negotiations.

To us it seemed clear that the Germans were playing for time so that they could transfer behind our lines the largest possible number of German soldiers still in the field. I told General Smith to inform Jodl that unless they instantly ceased all pretense and delay I would close the entire Allied front and would, by force, prevent any more German refugees from entering our lines. I would brook no further delay in the matter.

Finally Jodl and Friedeburg drafted a cable to Doenitz requesting authority to make a complete surrender, to become effective forty-eight hours after signing. Had I agreed to this procedure the Germans could have found one excuse or another for postponing the signature and so securing additional delay. Through Smith, I informed them that the surrender would become effective forty-eight hours from midnight of that day; otherwise my threat to seal the western front would be carried out at once.

Doenitz at last saw the inevitability of compliance and the surrender instrument was signed by Jodl at two forty-one in the morning of May 7. All hostilities were to cease at midnight May 8.[37]

After the necessary papers had been signed by General Jodl and General Smith, with the French and Russian representatives signing as witnesses, General Jodl was brought to my office. I asked him through the interpreter if he thoroughly understood all provisions of the document he had signed.

He answered, *"Ja."*

I said, "You will, officially and personally, be held responsible if the terms of this surrender are violated, including its provisions for German commanders to appear in Berlin at the moment set by the Russian high command to accomplish formal surrender to that government. That is all."

He saluted and left.

Chapter 22

VICTORY'S
AFTERMATH

UNDER THE TERMS OF THE SURRENDER DOCU-
ment the heads of the German armed services were required to
appear in Berlin on May 9 to sign a ratification in the Russian headquarters. The second ceremony was, as we understood it, to symbolize the unity of the Western Allies and the Soviets, to give notice to
the Germans and to the world that the surrender was made to all,
not merely to the Western Allies.[1] For this reason we were directed to
withhold news of the first signing until the second could be accomplished.

In order that American and British newsmen could have the full
story of the Reims surrender, we invited a number to be present at
the ceremony. In accepting the invitation they agreed to withhold
publication until the story could be officially given out under the
agreements among the Allies. One American reporter published the
story before the release hour, which infuriated other newsmen who
kept faith. The incident created a considerable furor, but in the outcome no real harm was done, except to other publications.[2]

The Western Allies were invited and expected to participate in the
signing at Berlin, but I felt it inappropriate for me personally to go.
The Germans had already appeared in the Allied Headquarters to
accomplish their unconditional surrender and I thought the ratification
in Berlin should be a Soviet affair. Consequently I designated my
deputy, Air Chief Marshal Tedder, to represent me at that ceremony.
It was difficult business to make all the detailed arrangements concerning timing, the numbers and classifications of individuals allowed
to attend, and the routes to be followed by our planes over Russian-
occupied territory. However, these were accomplished and Tedder

kept the appointment, accompanied by two or three planeloads of officers, enlisted men, Wacs, and press representatives.[3] Some months later I saw in Moscow a movie film portraying the highlights of the Berlin ceremony. No mention was made in the film of the prior surrender at Reims.

My "Victory Order of the Day" looked forward with hope to co-operative solutions of postwar problems. After thanking the troops and the home fronts for their unfailing support I said:

The route you have traveled through hundreds of miles is marked by the graves of former comrades. Each of the fallen died as a member of the team to which you belong, bound together by a common love of liberty and a refusal to submit to enslavement. Our common problems of the immediate and distant future can be best solved in the same conceptions of co-operation and devotion to the cause of human freedom as have made this Expeditionary Force such a mighty engine of righteous destruction.

Let us have no part in the profitless quarrels in which other men will inevitably engage as to what country, what service, won the European war. Every man, every woman, of every nation here represented has served according to his or her ability, and the efforts of each have contributed to the outcome. This we shall remember—and in doing so we shall be revering each honored grave, and be sending comfort to the loved ones of comrades who could not live to see this day.[4]

We had no local victory celebrations of any kind, then or later. When Jodl signed we merely went to bed for some much-needed rest, to get up the next day and tackle the multitude of tasks that followed upon the cessation of hostilities. Thereafter, however, all our work was done in the satisfying knowledge that the carnage in Europe had ended. Our problems were difficult but we were spared casualty lists.

The most intricate and pressing of our immediate problems was redeployment.

Ever since 1941 the global strategy of the Allies had insisted upon defeat of Germany before undertaking an all-out concerted offensive against the Japanese. The German surrender on May 7 marked the accomplishment of the first and greatest Allied objective.

Now it was time to turn with all speed to the second. Throughout the world Allied forces were released for operations against the oriental end of the Axis. Russia was still officially at peace with the Japanese but, according to the information furnished us, Generalissimo Stalin had told President Roosevelt at Yalta that within three months from the day of the German surrender the Red Army would join in the attack against Japan.

Against divided hostile forces more than one leader of the past has successfully employed mobility and surprise to concentrate his own forces first against one isolated portion of the enemy and, after defeating it, turned with overwhelming power to the destruction of the second. Never before, however, had this simple method of war been applied on a scale broader than continental in scope. But the conception was just as correct globally as it was locally, and the Allied leaders responsible for its application in World War II were not dismayed because the planned redeployment against the second enemy involved the transport of millions of men and unlimited quantities of equipment from Europe halfway around the world to Japan.

Russian redeployment meant the shifting of large forces from west to east over the long Trans-Siberian Railway. Because only the one railroad system was available, that task was laborious and would take time to accomplish. But for the Western Allies the transfer of their European armies and air forces to the Asiatic theater was a stupendous undertaking, involving hundreds of ships operating over sea routes ten thousand miles long.

As early as February 1945 we had begun to develop plans to accomplish this move. There was continuous consultation between members of my staff and the War Department. By V-E Day, schedules, priorities, and organizational preparation were sufficiently advanced for us to begin the mass transfer to the Pacific.

Several factors made still harder a problem that was at best a very complex business. Adequate strength had to be maintained in Europe for the occupation of conquered Germany. The immediately critical requirements in the Asiatic theater were for service units, while our own need for these same units was more acute than ever before if we were speedily to accomplish the shipment of combat divisions to the Far East. Even greater difficulty grew out of our policy of equalizing the burdens of combat service among the millions of individuals in the command.

On the day of the surrender there were, in the great Allied Force, more than 3,000,000 Americans under my command. This force included sixty-one U. S. divisions, all except one of which had participated in actual battle.[5]

Men with the longest battle service were to be assigned to occupation duty or sent home; others were to go on to the Pacific. Many of our divisions were veterans of eleven months' continuous fighting, while some, among them the 1st, 3d, 9th, 36th, and 45th Infantry Divisions and the 82d Airborne and 2d Armored Divisions, had entered the war in the Mediterranean campaign. The older ones had fought with only brief interruptions for two and a half years. The 34th Infantry and 1st Armored Divisions, still in the Mediterranean theater, had done likewise.

To make necessary adjustments required wholesale transfers from many of the veteran divisions and the filling up of vacancies by men with shorter battle service. At the same time we had to be extremely careful to preserve the efficiency of units; to have sent to the Pacific whole divisions of near recruits would have been senseless.

The individual soldier's eligibility for duty or discharge was determined by an elaborate point system, based on credits for length of service, length of time overseas, decorations, parenthood, and age. Application of the system was tedious, but probably no better plan could have been devised to accommodate the conflicting considerations of fairness to the individual and the efficiency of units. An added difficulty arose when the War Department found it advisable to change the "critical point" score. This created additional work, to say nothing of confusion and some discontent.[6]

Our administrative machine in Europe had to be thrown into reverse. Bases, fields, depots, ports, roads, and railways were geared up to push men and supply forward into the heart of Germany. They had, figuratively, to face about and begin operating in the other direction. Supplies and munitions were scattered throughout western Europe and through much of Italy and northern Africa. These had to be collected, inventoried, packaged, and shipped. Speed was the primary consideration.

So vast and urgent was this single undertaking that we set up a special headquarters with no other responsibility than to guide, supervise, and expedite the movement. That headquarters was formally established on April 9, a full month before the German surrender.[7]

Because of his unequaled experience in the handling of vast bombing campaigns, General Spaatz was relieved from duty in our theater and sent to the Pacific. An experienced army commander was also desired in the Far East. General Hodges, whose First Army had accomplished its final task in Europe when it reached the Elbe, was selected. He was not only completely competent and experienced but, among our army commanders, could be earliest spared from our theater. He departed from the battle front for the Pacific, by way of the United States, before the surrender date in Europe.

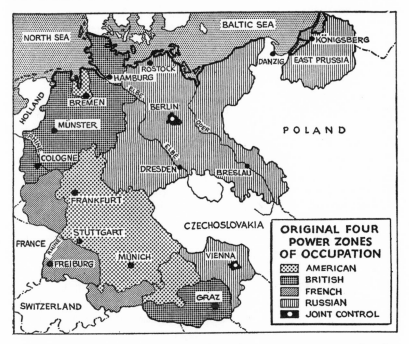

ORIGINAL FOUR
POWER ZONES
OF OCCUPATION

AMERICAN
BRITISH
FRENCH
RUSSIAN
JOINT CONTROL

This problem, big as it was, did not by any means comprise the bulk of the work devolving upon the American forces and responsible commanders. With the end of hostilities the Western Allies had to begin making arrangements for breaking up the great combat force into its national elements. The governments had rejected my repeated recommendation that the Western Allies occupy their portion of Germany on a unified basis. My plan was considered politically inexpedient, although I urged that, since occupation would be a residual task of the war and would require armies of the Western Allies for its accomplishment, there could be no reasonable objection to the maintenance, in western Germany, of the same Allied organization that had attained victory. The question was, however, clearly a political one, and our governmental leaders believed that my plan would be subject to unfortunate misinterpretation by the Soviet Union.[8]

Separation meant that we had to sort out all our complicated and highly integrated staffs, organizations, and procedures in order to meet the new requirements of national administration and responsibility. Almost all French and some British supply depended upon American stocks and facilities. With the anticipated end of Lend-Lease, detailed accounting systems had to be established in order to handle this work on a business instead of a war basis.

Military government had quickly to be installed over the recently overrun sections of Germany. Add to all this the never-ending volume of administrative detail incident to the control of the vast Allied Force in the West and it is easy to understand the remark of an overworked staff officer who said: "I always thought that when the Germans finally surrendered I would celebrate by going on a big binge. Now I'm taking aspirin every day—without the fun of looking back on the binge!"

We were so preoccupied in the daily grind of work that we were largely unaware of the enthusiasms sweeping our own countries.

My own failure to estimate popular reaction was typical of many others. Shortly after the German surrender it occurred to me that 1945 would mark the thirtieth anniversary of the graduation of my classmates and myself from West Point, and I planned a brief and private celebration for those of us who were serving in Europe. I believed that we could fly to the United States, spend one day at West Point's graduation exercises, and be back on duty in Germany with a total absence of only three days. I thought that by doing this quietly no one in the United States except people at West Point would know about it until we were back again in Frankfurt. I developed a high-pressure enthusiasm for the project and suggested that each of my twenty classmates in Europe should send a secret message to his wife asking her to meet him for a one-day reunion at West Point.

While I was planning to carry out this idea we received word from Washington that, because circumstances prevented American units in Europe from returning to the United States to appear in the traditional parades of victorious troops, General Marshall wanted me to pick representative officers and enlisted men for return in groups of some fifty each, for a short tour of our country. He felt that through these representative celebrations America would have a chance to pay tribute to her fighting men in Europe.

These orders knocked my personal scheme out of the picture. I think that all the men who were selected to go home to participate in the series of celebrations during the month of June 1945 experienced a feeling of amazement and astonishment at the enthusiasm with which they were greeted.

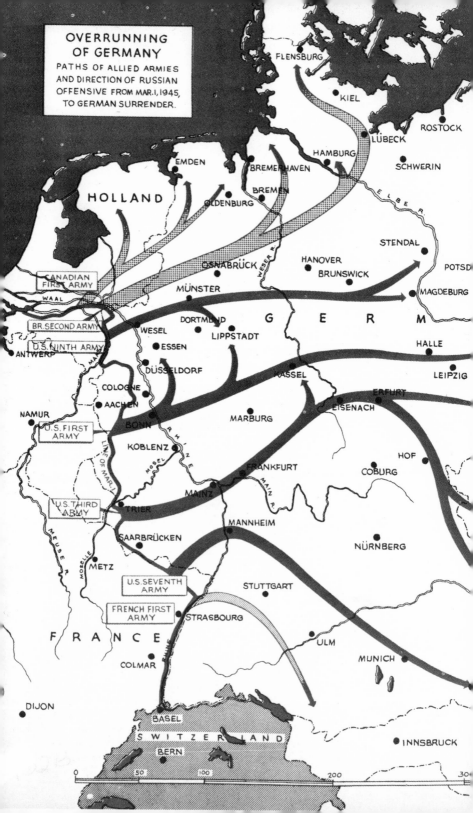

For every man the experience was inspiring and heartwarming. The generosity, cordiality, and hospitality poured out upon those groups by the people of the United States were overpowering. For me, it was a far cry from the modest one-day reunion I had so hopefully planned for a June day at West Point. The interlude was a happy one; but a quick return to the grind of work was inescapable. During the months succeeding V-E Day I went to various European capitals for similar celebrations, among them London, Paris, Brussels, The Hague, and Prague; other invitations I found it impossible to accept. My later visits to Moscow and Warsaw did not involve "victory celebrations."

At the Moscow Conference attended by Secretary Hull in 1943 it had been agreed among the three principal Allies to establish immediately a European Advisory Commission in London. This body was to begin the study of postwar political problems of Europe and to make appropriate recommendations to the governments.[9]

Beginning early in 1944, the Commission worked in London and agreed on recommendations for future surrender terms for Germany and upon national zones of occupation, along with machinery for joint control. The United States military adviser to the Commission, Brigadier General Cornelius Wickersham, later became my deputy in organizing the United States group of the Control Council.[10]

Under the protocols developed by the European Advisory Commission each of the four Allies was to be responsible for the occupation of a portion of Germany and the military government of that country was to be entrusted to a quadripartite council, to be composed of the four military commanders, with a co-ordinating committee to assist them. The control authority was to include, also, groups of officers and civilians with specific missions relating to the disarmament and demobilization of the German armed forces, political and economic affairs, legal, financial, and labor questions, and other activities in military government of a conquered country.[11]

While SHAEF existed the British and American efforts in military government were combined. The British had established a training school in England similar to ours at Charlottesville, Virginia. The latter school had already furnished the American contingent of the military government organization in Sicily and Italy.

Final training of the officers needed for military government in the American Zone in Germany was conducted in England. We established in SHAEF a general staff division charged with co-ordination of the whole effort. It was headed by Lieutenant General A. E. Grasett, of the British Army, and Brigadier General Julius C. Holmes, of the American Army.[12]

Our first military government experience in Germany was gained at Aachen before the crossing of the Rhine. This showed us the kind of problem that we were apt to meet later on when the occupation had extended deep into Germany. The situation was new and difficult, and became more acute because of our policy of non-employment of Nazis for any governmental work. In much of our necessary public utility work it was only the local Nazis who had sufficient knowledge to be of assistance. The question at once arose as to whether we should use them or non-Nazis, who knew little or nothing about the particular facility. It was difficult, but as quickly as possible we got rid of party members and trained others for necessary operation of public works, public utilities, sanitary service, posts, telegraphs, and telephones.

The life of a military government officer was never dull. Usually he had been commissioned in the Army because of his administrative or technical background. But with the housekeeping of a whole town or city on his shoulders, the officer had to meet every conceivable kind of problem in human relations, to keep local peace and order while ferreting out those wanted by the Allies for trial, to begin restoration of productive activity while carrying out his share of broad Allied policy as it was given to us from Washington in a document known as JCS/1067.[13] He was often forced, in the beginning, to act as a referee in personal feuds. As soon as the Germans learned of our de-Nazification program every complaint by an individual against another was on the basis of "He is a Nazi." In the chaos of postwar Germany errors were inescapable, and this applied to features of general policy as well as to details of execution by local functionaries. But by and large, the military government group of Americans did a remarkable job—one that reflected their sincerity and intelligence as well as the soundness of their special training.

Lieutenant General Lucius Du B. Clay came to Europe in April 1945 to act as my deputy for the military government of Germany. For a brief period, earlier in the war, he had performed invaluable services in the European theater in our logistics system. From the beginning he agreed with me that a civil agency of government should eventually take over the control of Germany, and his whole organization was definitely separated from the military staff. In this way we were prepared to turn over military government to the State Department with no necessity for complete reorganization.[14] General Clay later succeeded General McNarney as American commander in Germany, and always maintained this distinction in organization. More than any other two individuals, Clay and Wickersham deserve credit for the initial establishment of American Military Government in Germany—a performance that, in view of the frustrations, obstacles, divided counsels and responsibilities, and difficulties in postwar Allied co-operation, must be classed as brilliant.

By agreement on the political level, SHAEF went out of existence on July 14. To mark the occasion I sent a final message of thanks and good-by to the entire command. For the first time in three years I ceased to be an Allied commander. Thenceforth my responsibilities were American only.[15]

My personal staff was now joined by Lieutenant Colonel James Stack. Sergeant major in the 3d Division when I was with it at Fort Lewis, later commissioned and transferred to the Operations Division, where he became executive officer, Colonel Stack had served as my personal representative at the War Department throughout the Mediterranean and European campaigns.

Preliminary agreements for an initial meeting of the Allied Council in Berlin were accomplished with difficulty. Complications included differences in language and laborious methods of communication, the lack of intimate contacts between senior commanders, and the destruction in the city of Berlin which so stringently restricted accommodations. It was not until June 5 that we progressed far enough with all these tortuous negotiations to hold the first formal meeting of the Allied commanders in Berlin.[16]

The purpose was merely to sign our basic proclamation, a document announcing the formation of the Council and assumption of joint responsibility for the administration of Germany. We thought that the papers in the case had been completely agreed upon before we went to Berlin, but when we reached there we discovered that there were questions which the Russians still considered unsettled.

The meeting was arranged for the middle of the afternoon and before it began I seized the opportunity to call at Marshal Zhukov's headquarters to present him with the Chief Commander grade of the Legion of Merit, awarded him by the American Government. I thought Marshal Zhukov an affable and soldierly-appearing individual.

When I got back to my own temporary quarters in Berlin I found that there was an unexpected delay in convening the meeting, at which Marshal Zhukov was to act as host. This was annoying, as I had to return to Frankfurt that evening. Through the long afternoon hours we waited, but the English-speaking liaison officer from Zhukov's headquarters could give us no explanation for the delay. Finally, late in the afternoon, I determined to force the issue. Because I knew that all the documents to be handled had been previously studied and revised by each of the governments concerned, I could see no valid reason for a delay that began to look deliberate. I therefore asked the liaison officer to inform Marshal Zhukov that, much to my regret, I should be forced to return to Frankfurt unless the meeting began within thirty minutes. However, just as the messenger was ready to depart word came that we were expected at the conference room, to which we all instantly repaired. The marshal tendered an explanation for the delay, saying that he had been awaiting final Moscow instructions on an important point. The rest of us accepted the statement in good part and the Berlin Council got off to a start in an atmosphere of friendly cordiality.

The circular conference table was the largest I have ever seen. Each national delegation was assigned a ninety-degree quadrant at the table. The commanders were surrounded by a crowd of military and political assistants, photographers, newsmen, and others who seemed merely to be present. My political adviser was Robert Murphy, of North African days. Mr. Vishinsky, who had attracted considerable publicity some years earlier as the prosecutor in Russian purge trials, was Marshal Zhukov's first political adviser. There were four copies of each of the documents before us and each copy had to be signed by all four Council members; after some little discussion on minor details of wording the laborious business was completed.[17]

It then developed that Marshal Zhukov had arranged an elaborate banquet for his guests, but I was not prepared to spend the night in Berlin. Moreover, I had allowed so many people to accompany me to Berlin that there was no possibility of taking care of them in the cramped quarters allotted us. I therefore told Zhukov that I would have to go back to Frankfurt that evening, sufficiently early to land before dark. He asked me to compromise by coming to the banquet hall for a toast and to hear the Red Army choir sing two songs. He promised me a speedy trip through the city to the airfield, saying he would go along himself to see that there was no delay.

Because of the marshal's hospitable gesture toward his Allies I regretted my inability to stay. The singing of the Red Army chorus was remarkable, and the table was piled with Russian delicacies. Before I left Marshal Zhukov announced that he had just received a message from Moscow instructing him, with the approval of Generalissimo Stalin, to confer upon Field Marshal Montgomery and me the Russian Order of Victory, a Soviet decoration that had never previously been given to a foreigner. The marshal asked me when I should like to have the decoration presented and I invited him to visit my headquarters at Frankfurt for the ceremony. He accepted and I was pleased when Montgomery tactfully suggested that since he had served throughout the European campaign under my command he would also like to receive his decoration in my headquarters.

I invited Zhukov to bring to the ceremony at Frankfurt a number of staff assistants and to stay as long as he pleased, with the assurance of a warm welcome. He replied that he would come on June 10 and would be accompanied by no more than ten staff officers, but could stay for the day only. Consequently I planned a state luncheon for him and his party. Just a few hours before his arrival I received a telegram saying that in addition to the ten staff officers he was bringing five officer bodyguards. An officer bodyguard was a functionary of whom I had never heard and I was somewhat puzzled as to what to do with five at a luncheon. I directed the mess officer to keep his arrangements flexible and said I would let him know what to do after the marshal arrived.

We met Zhukov at the airport with a guard of honor and the United States Army Band, and we then, with an interpreter, got into my car for the trip back to headquarters. I promptly brought up the question of the proper place for officer bodyguards at a luncheon. I told him that he could have them seated immediately around him, standing behind him, or at the far end of the table. When all this was interpreted to him he blurted out: "Please tell the general he can put them wherever he pleases. I brought them along because I was told to do so." That settled the question of the officer bodyguards very satisfactorily.

The luncheon at Frankfurt was a great success. It was a beautiful summer day and we first took our guests to a large gallery, open to the sky, where wines and pre-luncheon refreshments were served. For this interval we had arranged a parade of a large segment of our Air Force, on the assumption that Marshal Zhukov would consider it a compliment. From nearby fields we brought over hundreds of fighter planes, followed by bombers ranging in size from the lighter types on up to the heaviest equipment we possessed. In the bright sunlight it was a tremendous show and Zhukov seemed much impressed.

Conforming to the Russian custom, as far as we knew it, the luncheon period included a series of toasts. The marshal was an accomplished speaker, or at least he sounded so to us, and the sentiments he expressed through the interpreter were complimentary to the Allies and hopeful of success in our co-operative purposes. Everybody had his turn at offering a toast—British, Americans, Russians, and French. We must have risen to our feet at least a dozen times but I noticed that most of the Americans soon followed my example and filled their glasses with water, colored only sufficiently with red wine to give the drink an appropriate appearance.

The decorations presented to Montgomery and me were among the few I have seen that have great intrinsic rather than exclusively sentimental and symbolic value. Designed in the form of a star, each contains some eighty or ninety diamonds surrounding a group of synthetic rubies, in the center of which is a small enameled representation of the Kremlin.

On the part of Zhukov and his assistants there was discernible only an intense desire to be friendly and co-operative. Looking back on it, that day still seems to have held nothing but bright promise for the establishment of cordial and close relations with the Russians. That promise, eventually lost in suspicion and recrimination, was never to be fulfilled. But so far as the friendly association between Marshal Zhukov and myself was concerned, it continued to grow until the moment I left Europe in November 1945. That friendship was a personal and individual thing and unfortunately was not representative of a general attitude.

From the record of Russian contacts with the Western Allies during the war, Generals Smith, Clay, and I believed in the early summer of 1945 that success in joint government of Germany would be measured almost exclusively by the degree to which the Western Allies, both generally and locally, overcame Russian suspicion and distrust. There was a vast gulf to be bridged between governmental systems, and manifestly it could never be crossed unless, on highest political levels, mutual confidence and trust were achieved. But, assuming that the heads of states would be reasonably successful, a great respon-

sibility still devolved upon us in Berlin. We were in daily and hourly
contact with problems on which unanimous agreements had to be
reached—and we felt that a record of local achievement would have
a happy and definite effect upon the whole question of whether Communism and democracy would find a way to get along together in the
same world. Consequently, in personal as well as in official relationships, we spared no pains or trouble to demonstrate good faith, respect, and friendly intent.

At the time, however, the difficult problem of displaced persons
pressed more immediately on my attention than my personal relations with the Russians. A displaced person was defined as a civilian
outside the national boundaries of his or her country by reason of war,
who was desirous but unable to return home or find a home without assistance, or who was to be returned to enemy or ex-enemy territory.[18]

Hundreds of thousands were quickly evacuated. These were in addition to prisoners of war and were those civilians who had homes somewhere in Europe and desired to return to them at once. We organized
camps to take care of these classes temporarily and fed them while we
worked out transportation plans.[19]

But those that we soon came to designate particularly as Displaced
Persons, DPs for short, did not include these easily dispersible thousands. The truly unfortunate were those who, for one reason or another, no longer had homes or were "persecutees" who dared not return home for fear of further persecution. The terror felt by this last
group was impressed on us by a number of suicides among individuals
who preferred to die rather than return to their native lands. In some
instances these may have been traitors who rightly feared the punishment they knew to be in store for them. But in many other cases they
belonged to the oppressed classes and saw death as a far less terrifying
thing than renewed persecution.

The Allies had, on the political level, worked out formulas for
distinguishing between displaced persons who were to be returned
to their own countries and those who were to be cared for by the
occupying powers. These policies and agreements we first tried to
apply without deviation, but we quickly saw that their rigid application would often violate the fundamental humanitarian principles we
espoused. Thereafter we gave any individual who objected to return
the benefit of doubt.[20]

Of all these DPs the Jews were in the most deplorable condition.
For years they had been beaten, starved, and tortured. Even food,

clothes, and decent treatment could not immediately enable them to shake off their hopelessness and apathy. They huddled together—they seemingly derived a feeling of safety out of crowding together in a single room—and there passively awaited whatever might befall. To secure for them adequate shelter, to establish a system of food distribution and medical service, to say nothing of providing decent sanitary facilities, heat, and light was a most difficult task. They were, in many instances, no longer capable of helping themselves; everything had to be done for them.[21]

Other groups of unreturnables included former citizens of the Baltic States—Estonia, Latvia, and Lithuania—which had been incorporated into the U.S.S.R. Thousands of the Balts we found in western Germany were classified as stateless; they had fled because of a record of opposition to the seizure of their countries and could not return. They were relatively healthy, strong, and quite ready to work to improve their buildings and surroundings. Along with these were also Poles, Ukrainians, Rumanians, Yugoslavs, and others.[22]

As soon as the news spread about eastern Europe that the Western Allies were treating displaced persons with consideration, additional thousands began seeping into our zones. Facilities were always over-crowded, food could be issued only at a subsistence level, and in spite of everything we could do progress was slow.

As usual, individuals with no responsibility in the matter, their humanitarian impulses outraged by conditions that were frequently beyond help, began carrying to America tales of indifference, negligence, and callousness on the part of the troops. Generally these stories were lies. The thousands of men assigned to the job of rescuing the DPs and organizing relief for them were Americans. They were given every facility and assistance the Army could provide, and they were genuinely concerned in doing their utmost for these unfortunate of the earth. But because perfection could not be achieved some so-called investigators saw a golden chance for personal publicity. They did so at the expense of great numbers of Americans who labored night and day to alleviate the average lot of people who had suffered so much that they seemed at times beyond suffering.

With commanders and members of my staff I made frequent visits to these camps. We would spend hours in each, discovering at first hand what was needed or most desired, and supplying these when-ever possible.

In the months since, great improvements have gradually been

THESE WERE HITLER'S ELITE

" . . . within eighteen days of the moment the Ruhr was surrounded it had surrendered with an even greater number of prisoners than we had bagged in the final Tunisian collapse . . ."
Page 406

Nazis Taken Prisoner in the Ruhr Pocket

DOUBLE-LOADED FOR HOME

This plan required "one man to sleep in the daytime so that another could have his bunk during the night. . . . I never afterward heard of a single complaint . . ." *Page 422*

The Queen Elizabeth Brings Them Home

made; but the problem is not yet solved. Of all the distressing memories that will forever live with American veterans of the war in Europe, none will be sharper or more enduring than those of the DPs and of the horror camps established by the Nazis.

The first business meeting of the Berlin Council was held on July 10. Chairmanship of the Council was to rotate monthly and a fine spirit was initially noticeable. Differences of opinion developed but most of these involved details of procedure or method, and in the prevailing co-operative atmosphere none of them seemed to threaten great difficulty.

In early July we received word that the Potsdam Conference would soon convene. Again we had to prepare accommodations and protection for the reception of VIPs (soldiers' language for Very Important Persons), but in this instance my task was limited to that of receiving and caring for the American delegation only. I went to Antwerp to meet the cruiser on which President Truman and Secretary Byrnes came to Europe. There I had an opportunity to discuss with them a few points which I thought important.

First, I urged that civilian authority take over military government of our portion of Germany at the earliest possible date. I pointed out to the President and the Secretary that, while the Army would obviously have to stay in control until order was assured, the government of individuals in their normal daily lives was not a part of military responsibility. I felt that no matter how efficiently and devotedly the Army might apply itself to this task, misunderstandings would certainly arise. In the long run American concepts and traditions would be best served by the State Department's assuming over-all responsibility in Germany, using the American Army there merely as an adjunct and supporter of civil authority and policy. In principle both the President and the Secretary emphatically agreed with me and I was encouraged to believe that this development would come about within a period of a few months.[23]

When I returned to the United States in late 1945 as Chief of Staff of the Army, I continued to urge the wisdom of this move upon Secretary Byrnes, but learned that he had undergone a change of heart. Though always agreed in principle, he would not agree to implement the idea because of the administrative and financial burdens that would thus be placed upon the State Department.

Another item on which I ventured to advise President Truman involved the Soviets' intention to enter the Japanese war.[24] I told him that since reports indicated the imminence of Japan's collapse I deprecated the Red Army's engaging in that war. I foresaw certain difficulties arising out of such participation and suggested that, at the very least, we ought not to put ourselves in the position of requesting or begging for Soviet aid. It was my personal opinion that no power on earth could keep the Red Army out of that war unless victory came before they could get in. However, I did not then foresee the future relentless struggle born in ideological antagonisms, or the paralysis of international co-operation because of that struggle. I merely feared serious administrative complications and possible revival of old Russian claims and purposes in the Far East that might prove very embarrassing to our own country.

A third suggestion I made to the President was that we preserve some flexibility in the termination of Lend-Lease arrangements with the French and British. I was unfamiliar with the exact provisions of the law covering the matter, but I knew that the mere cessation of hostilities did not instantly and appreciably lessen French and British need for quantities of food and supplies from us, upon which they had counted with confidence. I thought that arbitrary and sudden termination of the agreement should be avoided in favor of a scheme that would give those countries a chance for prompt readjustment.

I informed the President of my belief that we should handle the German economy, and particularly the problem of reparations, in such a way as to insure Germans an opportunity to make a living, provided they were ready to work. Of this readiness there was no doubt. From the day we entered Germany the willingness of the ordinary citizen to work from dawn to dark for a meager living was noticeable. Even before we crossed the Rhine, I had seen German women and their children in the fields, under sporadic gunfire, spading the ground and planting seed in order to produce some semblance of a crop that year.

Clay and I were convinced that rehabilitation of the Ruhr was vital to our best interests. Nowhere else in Europe were there coal deposits equal in quality and so easily workable. And already it was apparent that coal would be the key to successful administration of Occupied Germany. Without coal, transportation could not be restored and without transportation the whole country would remain paralyzed. I told the President that unless we emphasized Ruhr rehabilitation Germany would soon be starving. Americans, of course, would never permit even their former enemies to starve and would voluntarily assume the costly task of feeding them. But I thought that this financial burden could be prevented. It appeared to me that if Ruhr coal production were pushed and transportation restored Germany could soon be exporting products of light industry not in any way related to the banned war industries. Payment for these would enable her to buy and import from others enough food stocks to meet inevitable shortages.

At Potsdam, I called several times upon various members of the American delegation, but because the European war was over I did not participate in the conference either as an official witness or as an adviser.

I had a long talk with Secretary Stimson, who told me that very shortly there would be a test in New Mexico of the atomic bomb, which American scientists had finally succeeded in developing. The results of the successful test were soon communicated to the Secretary by cable. He was tremendously relieved, for he had apparently followed the development with intense interest and felt a keen sense of responsibility for the amount of money and resources that had been devoted to it. I expressed the hope that we would never have to use such a thing against any enemy because I disliked seeing the United States take the lead in introducing into war something as horrible and destructive as this new weapon was described to be. Moreover, I mistakenly had some faint hope that if we never used the weapon in war other nations might remain ignorant of the fact that the problem of nuclear fission had been solved. I did not then know, of course, that an army of scientists had been engaged in the production of the weapon and that secrecy in this vital matter could not have been maintained. My views were merely personal and immediate reactions; they were not based upon any analysis of the subject. In any event it was decided that unless Japan surrendered promptly in accordance with the demands communicated to the Japanese Government from Potsdam the plan for using the atomic bomb would be carried out.[25]

While the President was in Germany he expressed a desire to inspect some American troops. I arranged for him to come into the American area and by good fortune the 84th Division was selected as one of those he was to see. In that division his cousin, Colonel Louis Truman, was chief of staff; and so the meeting was not only a pleasant official experience for the President but held a nice personal touch as well.

One day when the President was riding with General Bradley and me he fell to discussing the future of some of our war leaders. I told him that I had no ambition except to retire to a quiet home and from there do what little I could to help our people understand some of the great changes the war had brought to the world and the inescapable responsibilities that would devolve upon us all as a result of those changes. I shall never forget the President's answer. Up to that time I had met him casually on only two or three occasions. I had breakfasted with him informally and had found him sincere, earnest, and a most pleasant person with whom to deal. Now, in the car, he suddenly turned toward me and said: "General, there is nothing that you may want that I won't try to help you get. That definitely and specifically includes the presidency in 1948."

I doubt that any soldier of our country was ever so suddenly struck in his emotional vitals by a President with such an apparently sincere and certainly astounding proposition as this. Now and then, in conversations with friends, jocular suggestions had previously been made to me about a possible political career. My reaction was always instant repudiation, but to have the President suddenly throw this broadside into me left me no recourse except to treat it as a very splendid joke, which I hoped it was. I laughed heartily and said: "Mr. President, I don't know who will be your opponent for the presidency, but it will not be I." There was no doubt about *my* seriousness.

The co-operative note, on the international political level, which marked the end of the Potsdam Conference was echoed on the levels of military administration. In all our dealings with the Russian authorities in Berlin we were particularly careful to carry out to the letter every commitment and engagement, even where these were only implied or understood. During the months of August, September, and October there prevailed, locally, a general attitude that encouraged us to believe that eventual full success was possible. This does not imply an absence of annoying details. On the contrary, there were many occasions when patience wore thin in the attempt to achieve the unanimous agreements necessary to progress of any kind. Normally the British and ourselves were in general agreement, although naturally we had occasional sharp differences. With the French we always differed on the basic question of centralized German government—we on the affirmative and the French on the negative. But with the Soviet authorities, in addition to the same occasional basic differences, there seemed to be an unending stream of paltry details to provide reason or excuse for complaint and consequent explanation.

One of the subjects concerning which the Soviet authorities wrote us frequent letters of complaint was what they claimed to be unauthorized flights of American airplanes over Russian-occupied Germany. For flights in and out of Berlin the Russians had allotted us a narrow corridor, within the limits of which all our planes were supposed to stay. Often a new pilot, unfamiliar with the country, got slightly outside the established boundaries; and in cloudy weather even the most experienced pilot might violate the agreement, technically and temporarily. Periodically the Russians submitted to us a detailed list of these alleged violations, in such numbers that specific investigation was completely futile.

All we could do was urge all air units to be careful in this regard, but finally I went to Marshal Zhukov and told him that I thought these inconsequential and unintentional violations were far too petty to engage the constant attention of us both. I remarked that in each case he had to write a letter, which I then had laboriously to answer. He instantly agreed that they were minor matters and should not take up our time, but he explained that all these violations were reported to Moscow by the Russian anti-aircraft organization. This organization, he said, was separate from the other ground forces, and not under his command. When these reports reached the capital they were sent back to him and he was then required to ask for a reply from me. It seemed an astonishing sort of system but somewhat in line with what we considered to be the Russian practice of overcentralization. In any event I told Marshal Zhukov to keep sending the letters and that I would keep sending him the same stereotyped replies. He said that was quite satisfactory.

We encouraged the exchange of social visits, particularly between Americans and Russians, and these affairs seemed to be thoroughly enjoyed by both sides. The Russians love entertainment and genuinely appreciate any kind of music; so the jokes, companionship, and the orchestras at a dinner made all these occasions successful.

We learned another lesson when at the Council of Foreign Ministers in London sharp official differences reportedly developed between Secretary Byrnes and Mr. Molotov. Instantly a strained and stiff attitude became apparent among the Russians in Berlin. Red Army officers who had already accepted dinner invitations from Americans either sent their regrets or failed to keep the engagement. Formerly pleasant faces clouded up; it seemed that no Russian was any longer allowed to smile at, or talk pleasantly with, an American. This lasted for some days, but then, just as mysteriously as it had begun, it completely disappeared. However, its occurrence did not affect Marshal Zhukov and me. We continued our friendly association and conducted our business on that basis.

During those months of the summer and early fall I maintained contacts and friendships with many of my British wartime associates. The British War Office allowed me to keep, until the last of August, my personal British military assistant, Colonel James Gault. He was a devoted, loyal, and efficient officer who for more than two years daily took on his own shoulders a multitude of detailed, sometimes exasperating problems which otherwise would have fallen to me.

Another Briton, with whom I still had occasional conferences and who had been a stalwart support in the most trying days of war, was General Sir Hastings Ismay. One of the prominent military figures in Great Britain, he was the immediate associate of Mr. Churchill in the latter's capacity as Defense Minister. Ismay's position as head of the secretarial staff to the War Cabinet and the British Chiefs of Staff was, from the American point of view, a critical one because it was through him that any subject could at any moment be brought to the attention of the Prime Minister and his principal assistants. It was fortunate, therefore, that he was devoted to the principle of Allied unity and that his personality was such as to win the confidence and friendship of his American associates. He was one of those men whose great ability condemned him throughout the war to a staff position. Consequently his name may be forgotten; but the contributions he made to the winning of the war were equal to those of many whose names became household words.

When Mr. Churchill's political party was defeated in the British summer elections of 1945 and he ceased to be Prime Minister he decided to go on a short vacation. He had withstood well the wear and tear of his great responsibilities throughout the war years, but now, with official responsibilities ended, Mr. Churchill wanted and needed a short rest. I was pleased and honored that he asked me to put him up; his suggestion implied that he felt for me some little fraction of the great respect, affection, and admiration I had developed for him. I made arrangements for his vacation in one of the pleasantest parts of our theater. I have always felt myself fortunate that I could, as his personal host for a few days, repay in a small way part of the debt I owe him for staunch support and unwavering courtesy, to say nothing of personal hospitality.

I sometimes saw Field Marshal Brooke, General Frederick Morgan, Air Chief Marshal Tedder, Sir Andrew Cunningham, Field Marshal Montgomery, and others of the British service heads and high commanders with whom I had served during the war. All were my good friends. Strangely enough our conversations rarely turned backward, in the habit of old soldiers, to incidents of the war. Even then we seemed to sense that the future problems of peace would overshadow even the great difficulties we had to surmount during hostilities. Consequently our talk nearly always dealt with the probabilities of the future: particularly the prospects for establishing clear and mutually observed understandings between the Western Allies and the Soviets.

During those months we had also at our headquarters a constant stream of visitors from the United States. Among these were congressional committees and various official and semiofficial bodies gathering material on the conduct of the war or informing themselves as to details of current administration. These visitors we were always delighted to have. We gave them every needed facility for the conduct of their investigations and explorations, and opened up to them every kind of information in our possession. They, on their part, always brought us news of the homeland, and frequently were good enough to carry personal letters from families at home to members of the command. This, in particular, was a distinct kindness on their part, for letters sent through them would take only one or two days for delivery, whereas in the ordinary mail, because of its volume, two or three weeks were sometimes required.

Chapter 23

OPERATION
STUDY

IN THE SUMMER OF 1945, ALTHOUGH OUR MAIN effort was redeployment of troops, establishment of occupation, and execution of many minor tasks directly connected with our mission, we were also occupied in a professional sequel to the war—the study and evaluation of its lessons.

The material confronting us was monumental in its bulk, and in its content unique. The campaigns in the Mediterranean and in Europe had no prior parallel in the history of warfare; throughout them, the United States Army had engaged in operations without comparable precedent since its establishment in 1775.

For the operations in Africa and Europe there had been involved the organization of a vast ground force. Built around forty-seven infantry divisions and their artillery, it included sixteen armored divisions and four airborne divisions, a mountain division, four seaborne brigades for the operation of landing craft, besides amphibious and combat engineer units, brigade, and separate battalions of anti-aircraft units, field artillery and tank destroyer battalions by the score. Equally stupendous was the growth of American air strength in those two theaters; between our entry into the war and the German surrender our fighter planes had won superiority over the Luftwaffe and our bombers had penetrated every defense which the German had raised against them.

Intercontinental communications, transport and administrative systems were established and a military government structure was built to control millions of enemy nationals. Conduct of operations required co-ordination with the civil ministries of foreign nations organized differently from our own, combined staff work with Allied armies, new methods of strategic command within our own military establishment, and diplomatic negotiations seldom entrusted to a combat force. No prewar definition of the Army's mission could adequately have forecast the scope or ramifications of its job against the European Axis. From study of both achievements and mistakes much could be learned.

Purely military operations constituted a vast and continuous offensive, prolonged over many months, that required assessment and evaluation of its lessons. The task set for the Allied Force was one of the most difficult ever to confront an army in the field. From North Africa through Sicily and Italy and the assault against *Festung Europa,* our units had to land on beaches, fight many days without the support of even a mediocre port, make good their positions against superior ground forces, and finally build up a strength that could accomplish the complete destruction of the enemy.

In all the campaigns, and particularly in western Europe, our guiding principle was to avoid at any cost the freezing of battle lines that might bog down our troops in a pattern similar to the trench warfare of World War I. At times in the conduct of any continental campaign there develops a strain upon supply lines that largely prohibits the continuance of heavy, decisive attacks; during such periods a certain degree of stabilization is unavoidable. But the Allied forces did not permit these periods of stabilization to develop into the long, dreary, and wasteful battles that bled Europe white in World War I. The combination of fire power, mobility, and air power that we used to accomplish our purpose had to be scrutinized so that the principles underlying its effective use might be incorporated into our military doctrine.

In addition to amphibious assault on an unprecedented scale, our forces had surmounted natural and fortified barriers that were believed invulnerable. In Africa, Sicily, and Italy the terrain we encountered was fitted by nature for defensive operations. In the Tunisian hills, on the shoulder of Mount Etna, and in the Apennines there were scores of vital points where a battalion could stop an army's advance. In western Europe the Rhine throughout its length, reinforced on the north by the easily inundated Netherlands, had been for twenty centuries the most formidable barrier to military operations against the German lands. All those natural obstacles were overcome.

Beyond that in western Europe the Allied armies twice battered their way through fortifications that had been designed with the greatest tactical and engineering skill. To break through either the Westwall or the Siegfried Line was outstanding in military annals; to smash them both in the space of ten months was a matchless achievement for the participating troops.

It is easy to deprecate the value of fixed defenses and fortifications. The Chinese Wall, the Roman Wall, and the Maginot Line all failed, eventually, in their defensive purposes. However, on any given section of front, any unit that is on the defensive and has the advantage of carefully prepared defenses enjoys a tremendous superiority over its exposed opponents.

Against the Westwall we used surprise in our choice of the landing area and a tremendous concentration of power on a narrow front to achieve the initial penetration. The defensive fortifications lacked depth. Once they were broken in the lodgment area, our air and sea power assured us use of the beaches for build-up. The German, moreover, was largely isolated by destruction of his communications lines and bridges across the Seine and Loire; our reinforcements poured in while his numbers were with difficulty maintained.

The Siegfried Line was more formidable. Its defenses included great mine fields, intricate networks of obstacles, tank ditches, concealed concrete blockhouses, and heavily fortified machine-gun nests, supported by artillery and auxiliary weapons, connected by a superlative communications system, backed up by a dependable line of supply over which could be moved rapidly reinforcements and munitions. In certain areas the defensive fortifications were several miles in depth. At others, river obstacles were utilized.

The task of penetrating and breaking through such fortifications presented the most serious, almost terrifying, problems to the attacking troops. Nothing is easy in war. Mistakes are always paid for in casualties and troops are quick to sense any blunder made by their commanders. Even though in the winter of 1945 some stretches of the Siegfried were held by hastily formed and inadequately trained defensive troops, its penetration on a large scale and the practical obliteration of the defending forces was a tribute not only to the extraordinary fighting qualities of the Allied soldiers and units, but to the determination and professional skill of their divisional, corps, army, and army group commanders.

The Allied Force that stood on the Elbe on May 8, 1945, was the most powerful military machine ever assembled. Its left flank rested on the Baltic Sea and its right in the Alps. Behind it were armadas of planes whose numbers were greater than all the air forces of the world a few years before. Its line of supply and communications was a vast network that covered France and the United Kingdom and extended into every community of the homelands. Its strength was supported by still another victorious host. To the south, pouring through the Alpine passes that had been the traditional avenues of classic warfare, were the million veterans of the Italian campaign under Alexander, backed also by immense air power and sea power and transoceanic supply lines. When these two forces came to a halt with the German surrender, their combined might was overwhelming evidence of democracy's might—a visible lesson of war.

Victory in the Mediterranean and European campaigns gave the lie to all who preached, or in our time shall preach, that the democracies are decadent, afraid to fight, unable to match the productivity of regimented economies, unwilling to sacrifice in a common cause.

The first and most enduring lesson of the Mediterranean and European campaigns was the proof that war can be waged effectively by a coalition of nations. Historic difficulties had been overcome and the grave doubts that had existed on this point even as late as the fall of 1942 had been completely dispelled. Governments and their subsidiary economic, political, and military organizations had combined into one great effort in which no major difficulty could be traced to diverging national interest.

Allied effectiveness in World War II established for all time the feasibility of developing and employing joint control machinery that can meet the sternest tests of war. The key to the matter is a readiness, on highest levels, to adjust all nationalistic differences that affect the strategic employment of combined resources, and, in the war theater, to designate a single commander who is supported to the limit. With these two things done, success rests in the vision, the leadership, the skill, and the judgment of the professionals making up command and staff groups; if these two things are not done, only failure can result.

In World War II, America and Great Britain, whose forces fought side by side in so many battles of the ground, sea, and air, understood and applied these truths. In the later stages of the war French forces likewise participated in this joint effort, as did detachments of numerous countries whose homelands had been previously overrun by the enemy.

Co-operation with the Soviet forces was, unhappily, not so close.

But her forces were widely separated, geographically, from those of the Western Allies, and the flaw in over-all teamwork did not impair the march to victory. Even so, if that country could have been as closely knit into the team as were the others, victory would probably have been achieved earlier and the peace would have rested on a more secure foundation.

Although Allied unity, and the ways and means of attaining it, constituted the principal war lesson, we within the Army were primarily concerned with the lessons that affected purely military concepts and principles. If every engagement could be studied, while the memory of it was still fresh in the minds of those who fought it, and both its tactical achievements and errors were subject to direct scrutiny, we could add an immense store of factual knowledge to the science of warfare—the speedy attainment of military victory at minimum expense in lives.

For this purpose we organized immediately after the cessation of hostilities a large board of the most experienced and at the same time most progressive officers we could find. The board was originally headed by General Gerow, who was later replaced by General Patton.[1]

In order that the War Department might have permanently available all the facts, so far as we could unearth them, and the opinions of the men most experienced in the actual business of fighting and of battlefield maintenance and administration, the board was provided with every possible facility and was given all the time it desired for the completion of its task.

Foremost among the military lessons was the extraordinary and growing influence of the airplane in the waging of war. The European campaign almost daily developed new and valuable uses for air power. Its effect in the weakening of German capacity was decisively felt on both fronts, the Allied and the Russian. Beyond this, the airplane was a valuable logistics agent, particularly during our speedy dashes across France in the fall of 1944 and across Germany in the spring of 1945; without it those pursuits could never have proceeded with such speed nor could they have accomplished such remarkable results.

The important road center of Bastogne could not have been held by the 101st Division during the German counteroffensive in December 1944 except for the airplanes that delivered 800,000 pounds of supplies to the division during the critical days between the twenty-third and twenty-seventh of December.[2] During our largest airborne operation, known as Varsity, in support of Montgomery's crossing of the Rhine River on March 24, 1945, 1625 airplane and 1348 glider sorties carried into battle more than 22,000 troops and almost 5,000,000 pounds of equipment.[3] The airplane became also a most valuable means of obtaining information of the enemy, not only at his major bases but along the actual battle front. Airplane photography searched out even minute details of defensive and offensive organization and our techniques were developed to the point that information so derived was available to our troops within a matter of hours.

The combination of an overwhelming air force and the great mobility provided by the vehicular equipment of the Army enabled us to strike at any chosen point along a front of hundreds of miles.[4] Our flexibility was nowhere better illustrated than during the German counteroffensive in the Ardennes when Patton's army ceased its preparations for an eastward attack, changed front, and undertook a movement extending over sixty to seventy miles at right angles to its former direction of advance. In less than seventy-two hours from the time Patton's staff had its orders an entire corps of his army had initiated a new attack.[5]

In dozens of ways scientists and inventors transformed the face of war. In landing on beaches we had the great advantage of new types of naval equipment and even tanks that could swim ashore after being launched into the water many hundreds of yards from the beach. Before the end of the war we were employing in great numbers recoilless weapons of very light weight that delivered projectiles of tremendous force.[6]

While we studied the effect on the conduct of war of new vehicles, new weapons, new systems of transport and communications, at the same time we re-examined the role of the fundamental agent in military success—the individual soldier.

The trained American possesses qualities that are almost unique. Because of his initiative and resourcefulness, his adaptability to change and his readiness to resort to expedient, he becomes, when he has attained a proficiency in all the normal techniques of battle, a most formidable soldier. Yet even he has his limits; the preservation of his individual and collective strength is one of the greatest responsibilities of leadership.

Veteran organizations are normally more capable than those entering battle for the first time. However, experience in fighting does not engender any love of the battlefield; veterans have no greater desire to enter the bullet-swept areas than have green troops. They do become more skillful in the utilization of every advantage offered by fire power, maneuver, and terrain. They acquire a steadiness that is not shaken by the confusion and destruction of battle. But when kept too long in the fight they not only become subject to physical and mental weariness; the most venturesome and aggressive among them—the natural leaders—begin to suffer an abnormally high percentage of losses. Consequently the periodical relief of units from the front lines is mandatory to the preservation of efficiency.

In Italy and in northwest Europe we were frequently unable to do this and sometimes regiments and battalions had to remain in line for excessive periods. Some divisions bore far more than their share of combat; the 34th, 45th, 3d, and 1st Divisions led in the number of days in battle, with total days in combat between 438 and more than 500; they also suffered relatively high casualties.[7]

The effect of prolonged combat is always bad. If a unit is brought out of line before the processes of physical and mental fatigue have gone too far and before its losses have become excessive it can, with the assimilation of new recruits, be ready for re-entry into battle far sooner than one that has been kept in line too long. Moreover, the periodic rests for the front-line soldier have a splendid effect upon morale—and in any kind of warfare troop morale is always a decisive factor.

Early in the North African campaign it became evident that the emotional stamina and spiritual strength of the individual soldier were as important in battle success as his weapons and training. Combat neuroses among the troops developed on an alarming scale as the intensity of our offensives increased.

At the war's beginning the average Army officer, both regular and civilian, placed too much faith in a surface discipline based solely upon perfection in the mechanics of training. Commanders are habitually diffident where they are called upon to deal with subjects that touch the human soul—aspirations, ideals, inner beliefs, affection, hatreds. No matter how earnestly commanders may attempt to influence a soldier's habits, his training, his conduct, or extoll the virtues of gallantry and fortitude, they shyly stop short of going into matters which they fear may be interpreted as "preaching."

A profound understanding of philosophy is not necessarily a part of the equipment of a successful military leader. Yet as certainly as a national army neglects the need for a simple, commonly held understanding of the nation's welfare and the individual's relationship to the whole, so certainly will victory be attained only at added cost and by so much will victory itself be jeopardized.

No proof of the subject's importance is needed by those who visited both the hospitals and reclassification centers in the rear of an army and the combat lines at the front. In the combat regions a visitor was invariably inspired by the capacity of the Allied soldier to perform his duty quietly and efficiently, enduring hardship and privation, and hourly facing danger with a determination and confidence, often even a cockiness, that seemed never to desert him. Whether he was American, British, Canadian, French, or Pole in his national allegiance, he inspired all who knew him.

In the rear, hospital and camp facilities were necessarily set aside for those suffering from self-inflicted wounds, from hysteria and psychoneuroses and from venereal disease, sometimes, according to the doctors, deliberately contracted. Their number, percentage-wise, was small, but in the aggregate, large. It is profitable for a commander to visit these places, to talk with individuals, to understand something of the bewilderment, the fear, the defeatism that afflict men who are essentially afraid of life, though believing they are afraid of death. An astonishing number of these individuals react instantly and favorably to a single word of encouragement. More than one has said to me, immediately upon discovering another's interest in him, "General, get me out of here; I want to go back to my outfit." Harshness normally intensifies the disease, but understanding can do much to cure it and in my opinion, if applied in time, can largely prevent it.

In war, time is vital. There is much to be done. Visible evidences of efficiency, noted in perfection of techniques and deportment, are so easy to observe that officers of all grades cannot or do not give sufficient attention to the *individual*. Yet attention to the individual is the key to success, particularly because American manpower is not only our most precious commodity—it will, in any global war, always be in short supply.

Our service schools have a definite duty to instruct officers in this field. Regardless of any progress made in the country's educational institutions, the Army's business is success in war—and the Army cannot safely neglect any subject that experience has shown to be important to that success.

All the developments in method, equipment, and destructive power that we were studying seemed minor innovations compared to the revolutionary impact of the atom bomb. None was used in the European theater and none was ever planned for use there. However, even without the actual experience of its employment, the reports that reached us after the first one was used at Hiroshima on August 6 left no doubt in our minds that a new era of warfare had begun.

In an instant many of the old concepts of war were swept away. Henceforth, it would seem, the purpose of an aggressor nation would be to stock atom bombs in quantity and to employ them by surprise against the industrial fabric and population centers of its intended victim. Offensive methods would largely concern themselves with the certainty, the volume, and the accuracy of delivery, while the defense would strive to prevent such delivery and in turn launch its store of atom bombs against the attacker's homeland. Even the bombed ruins of Germany suddenly seemed to provide but faint warning of what future war could mean to the people of the earth.

I felt and hoped that this latest lesson, added to all the others that six years of unremitting war had brought to the world, would convince everyone everywhere that the employment of force in the international field should of necessity be abjured. With the evidence of the most destructive war yet waged by the people of the earth about me, I gained increased hope that this development of what appeared to be the ultimate in destruction would drive men, in self-preservation, to find a way of eliminating war. Maybe it was only wishful thinking to believe that fear, universal fear, might possibly succeed where statesmanship and religion had not yet won success.

SURVIVING BOMBS AND HITLER

But no edifice, however sacred, will survive atomic war. "Even the bombed ruins of Germany . . . provide but faint warning of what future war could mean to the people of the earth." *Page 456*

The Cathedral Stands Amid Cologne's Rubble

PARTNERS IN VICTORY

"The Russians are generous. They like to give presents and parties . . . the ordinary Russian seems to me to bear a marked similarity to what we call an 'average American.'" *Pages 473–74*

East and West Celebrate at Torgau

Chapter 24

RUSSIA

THE UNITED STATES AND RUSSIA EMERGED FROM the war the two most powerful nations of the globe. This fact affected every detail of American official routine in conquered Germany, for any prolonged struggle between the two powers would hopelessly complicate our local problems and might even nullify our costly victory. But there was involved far more than efficiency in German administration or political control.

What permanence the new-won peace might have; what stature the United Nations could attain; even what the future course of civilization would be—the answers to these questions now clearly involved, as an important factor, the ability of East and West to work together and live together in one world.

In the past relations of America and Russia there was no cause to regard the future with pessimism. Historically, the two peoples had maintained an unbroken friendship that dated back to the birth of the United States as an independent republic. Except for a short period, their diplomatic relations had been continuous. Both were free from the stigma of colonial empire building by force. The transfer between them of the rich Alaskan territory was an unmatched international episode, devoid of threat at the time and of any recrimination after the exchange. Twice they had been allies in war. Since 1941 they had been dependent each on the other for ultimate victory over the European Axis.

Ideologically, however, they were in diametric opposition; the United States was devoted to a social and political order based upon individual liberty and human dignity; Russia, dedicated to the dictatorship of the proletariat, seemed in Western eyes to be engulfed in a form of statism under the absolute direction of a few men. By the same token, it is probable that to them our adherence to a system based upon personal liberty was actually a political immaturity that permitted exploitation of the masses. Out of this cleavage between the governmental systems of two great powers there might develop in the world two hostile camps whose differences would ultimately provoke another holocaust of war. Should the gulf, however, be bridged practically by effective methods of co-operation, the peace and unity of the world would be assured. No other division among the nations could be considered a menace to world unity and peace, provided mutual confidence and trust could be developed between America and the Soviets.

Obstacles, doubts, fears of failure in American-Soviet relations, there were on every side. But the alternative to success seemed so terrifying to contemplate that all of us on occupation duty sought every possible avenue through which progress might be achieved.

Berlin, we were convinced, was an experimental laboratory for the development of international accord. There the West was joined with the East in the task of reorganizing a highly complex economy and re-educating a numerous people to political decency so that Germany, purged of its capacity and will for aggression, might be restored to the family of nations.

If in that endeavor there could be developed friendly ways and means of solving our local differences and problems, a long step forward would be taken toward the friendly settlement of world problems. Overshadowing all goals for us Americans was the contribution we locally might make toward establishing a working partnership between the United States and Russia. My persistence in this effort and my faith also in the ultimate success of the United Nations were both rooted in my experience as supreme commander.

In that capacity I had seen many nations work out a fixed unity of purpose, despite all the divergences in aim and outlook and way of life that characterized them as individuals and independent states. The combat direction of their military power and the commitment of their armies to battle—the most jealously guarded tokens of national sovereignty—they delegated to single authority. While they retained administrative control of their military forces, from the appointment of commanders to the establishment of troop rations, the Allied command was a single engine in its battle mission—the winning of war. Direction by committee, in which unanimity had to be achieved before unified action could be taken, was abandoned in favor of a single commander representing all the nations engaged.

During the war it was demonstrated that international unity of purpose and execution could be attained, without jeopardy to any nation's independence, if all were willing to pool a portion of their authority in a single headquarters with power to enforce their decisions. In the formation of the new United Nations and of the Allied organization for the control of Germany, this lesson had not yet been accepted. Its application would have meant some form of limited, federated world government which, while conforming to the Western Allies' battle-front experience as providing the only sure way to success, was politically unacceptable to any of the great nations concerned. The insistence on retention of the veto during the United Nations Conference at San Francisco in June 1945 was based on the traditional but obsolete concept that international purposes could be decided only by unanimous action in committee. In Berlin the same unanimity was required on even minor matters.

Our chief hope, therefore, was to build among those engaged in the German occupation a friendly acceptance of each other as individuals striving peacefully to attain a common understanding and common purpose—our mutual good. Once that spirit could be developed in Berlin, it would spread beyond Germany to our own capitals. The international good feeling manifested at Potsdam, between the heads of states, was a favorable start. If we could learn at the conference tables to conduct our business as friends, we could eventually live together as friends and ultimately work together in world partnership. A *modus vivendi* between East and West was our first objective.

The President and his staff left Germany for the United States on August 2. A few days later I was informed from Washington that Generalissimo Stalin had sent me an invitation to visit Russia. This was a renewal of an invitation that originally had come to me in early June, when I could not accept because of a necessary appearance in the United States under War Department orders. With this invitation came an expression of my government's hope that I could accept.

The Generalissimo suggested that a particular date to be included in my visit was August 12, a day set aside for a National Sports Parade in Moscow. I was pleased at this chance to see a country that I had never before visited, but I was even more pleased by the implication that the Soviet Government was as interested in developing friendly contacts as we were. I promptly accepted and was informed that

Marshal Zhukov would be my official host for my stay in Russia and would accompany me from Berlin to Moscow.[1]

When news of my impending visit got around headquarters, literally scores of individuals submitted personal requests to go with me. Out of consideration for Moscow's limited accommodations I took on this journey only General Clay and my old friend Brigadier General T. J. Davis. As an aide for this one trip, I wanted my lieutenant son John, who had been serving, for some months, in the European theater. His commander approved. Master Sergeant Leonard Dry, who served with me all through the war, also was in the party.

Upon arrival in Moscow we were housed at the American Embassy with my good friend Averell Harriman, who was then ambassador. His hostess was his charming daughter Kathleen. During a long war association I had formed a high opinion of Mr. Harriman's abilities and public-spirited attitude and was delighted to have him as my mentor and guide during an important visit to a country in which I was a complete stranger.

Our first conference was with General Antonov, Chief of Staff of the Red Army. He took me into his war room and explained the dispositions of the Red armies in the Far East and showed me the exact plan of campaign, which had been initiated only a few days before. Everywhere in the Manchurian area things were going according to plan and Antonov was confident of a quick and easy victory. We discussed military subjects until late in the evening, all in an atmosphere of greatest cordiality and mutual confidence.

The following morning was the appointed time for the big Sports Parade. This was staged in the Red Square, a paved area of considerable acreage. The only people present were the specially invited guests of the government and the performers. Estimates as to the number of the latter varied between twenty and fifty thousand. I calculated that the lower figure was more nearly correct than the higher one.

Public attendance was not permitted and the whole area was well guarded by military personnel. The several hundred spectators were allotted spaces on a stadiumlike structure, which had no seating arrangements of any kind. Everyone had to stand. Just after we had arrived at the raised section of concrete reserved for the American ambassador and his party, General Antonov came to say that Generalissimo Stalin had extended to me an invitation to join him on top of Lenin's tomb, provided I should like to do so. Since I was in the

company of the American ambassador, whose prestige as representative of the President was important, I was doubtful as to the
propriety of deserting him to join the Generalissimo. The necessity of
saying everything through an interpreter denied me any opportunity
to ask General Antonov, on a personal basis, for further details, and
I momentarily hesitated. However, he relieved the situation by giving
me the remainder of the Generalissimo's message, which was: "The
Generalissimo says that if you would like to come he also invites
two of your associates, if you would like to bring them." I turned to
consult quickly with the ambassador. He said that the invitation was
precedent-making; to the best of his knowledge, no other foreigner
had ever been invited to set foot on top of Lenin's tomb. Realizing,
therefore, that a special courtesy was intended, I quickly told General
Antonov that I would be happy indeed to accept and that the associates I wanted were the ambassador and, the head of the United States
Military Mission to Moscow, Major General John R. Deane. My
thought was that if there was any local prestige to be gained, then the
people to whom it would be most useful were the ambassador and his
assistant.[2]

We stood for five hours on the tomb while the show went on. None
of us had ever witnessed anything remotely similar. The groups of
performers were dressed in the colorful costumes of their respective
countries and at times thousands of individuals performed in unison.
Every kind of folk dance, mass exercise, acrobatic feat, and athletic
exhibition was executed with flawless precision and, apparently, with
greatest enthusiasm. The band was said to number a thousand pieces,
and it played continuously, presumably by sections, during the entire
five-hour performance.

The Generalissimo showed no sign of fatigue. On the contrary, he
appeared to enjoy every minute of the show. He invited me to his
side and, through an interpreter, we conversed intermittently during
the entire period of the show.[3]

He evinced great interest in the industrial, scientific, educational,
and social achievements of America. He repeated several times that
it was necessary for Russia to remain friends with the United States.
Speaking through the interpreter, he said in effect: "There are many
ways in which we need American help. It is our great task to raise
the standards of living of the Russian people, which have been seriously damaged by the war. We must learn all about your scientific
achievements in agriculture. Likewise, we must get your technicians

to help us in our engineering and construction problems, and we want to know more about mass production methods in factories. We know that we are behind in these things and we know that you can help us." This general trend of thought he pursued in many directions, whereas I had supposed that he would content himself merely with some general expression of desire to co-operate.

At that time Marshal Zhukov was patently a great favorite with the Generalissimo. Zhukov was included in every conversation I had with Stalin and the two spoke to each other on terms of intimacy and cordiality. This was highly pleasing to me because of my belief in the friendliness and co-operative purpose of Marshal Zhukov.

The Generalissimo turned the conversation to the work of the Berlin Council and remarked that it was important not only because of its specific task but because it provided a testing ground to determine whether great nations, victors in a war, could continue to co-operate effectively in the problems of peace.

This thought coincided exactly with the convictions Clay and I held, but we thought also that one of the impediments to greater progress in Berlin was the apparent necessity for Zhukov to refer every new question, no matter how trivial, to Moscow. In the early days of the Council I had noted that, whereas Zhukov frequently seemed to be in agreement with some logical proposal of local import, he could apparently never give an immediate answer on his own authority. This led me to explore the remote possibility that I might be able to do something about it.

Knowing that everything my associates and I did and said was reported instantly to Moscow, and knowing also that national pride would impel the Russians to watch the comparative prestige and authority of their Berlin representative, I had adopted a simple plan which I hoped would have some effect. It was merely to take occasion, whenever possible, to make sure that Marshal Zhukov was aware of the degree of independence accorded me by my Washington superiors in dealing with all matters that did not violate approved policy. Whenever I had anything to discuss with Marshal Zhukov I made an opportunity to see him, usually just before or after a formal meeting of the Berlin Council. I then outlined the suggestion, which normally served the best interests of the Russians as well as of ourselves, and placed it before him in terms of a definite proposal. Then I would remark rather casually: "If this project looks well to you, I am ready to put it into effect whenever you say. If you want some time for study, or if you would like to refer the matter to Moscow, I am quite content to await your answer. But I am ready to act instantly."

Once or twice he was fortunately prompted to ask: "What will your government say about this?" to which I would reply, "If I sent such small details to Washington for decision I would be fired and my government would get someone who would handle these things himself."

Whether or not this personal campaign had any effect I do not know, but as time went on Marshal Zhukov began to exhibit a greater independence in action than he had at first been able to exercise. He discarded the practice of keeping his political adviser by his side and we would meet with no one present except an interpreter. Moreover, he became much more prone to say yes or no to a proposal than merely to ask for a delay in order to consider it.

So while standing on Lenin's tomb, when the Generalissimo brought up the matter of the Berlin Council, I decided to follow up my Berlin campaign. I said to the Generalissimo: "Of course Marshal Zhukov and I get along splendidly. This is because great and powerful countries like yours and mine can afford to give their proconsuls in the field a sufficient amount of authority to achieve accord in local details and administrative matters. Smaller or weaker countries might possibly find it impossible to do this and difficulties would arise. But because Marshal Zhukov and I have such great leeway in reaching agreement we two usually overcome the little obstacles we encounter."

The Generalissimo agreed with me emphatically. He said, "There is no sense in sending a delegate somewhere if he is merely to be an errand boy. He must have authority to act."

A final remark of the Generalissimo's while we were watching the sports spectacle was that mass athletics and exercises were fine because of their effect upon the populace. He said, "This develops the war spirit. Your country ought to do more of this," and then he added: "We will never allow Germany to do this." At that moment we were still at war with the Japanese.

During the few days we had in Moscow we went to a football game attended by 80,000 enthusiastic rooters. We visited the subway, of which the Russians are very proud, and went to one of their art galleries. We spent an afternoon in the Stormovik airplane factory and another day at state and collective farms. Everywhere we saw evidence of a simple, sincere, and personal devotion to Russia—a patriotism that was usually expressed in the words, "But this is for Mother

Russia and therefore it is not hard." A group of workers in the Stormovik factory told me that their work week during the war was eighty-four hours, and they proudly stated that the factory's attendance record was something over ninety-four per cent. Many of the workers were women and children, and it is difficult to see how, with their meager rations and serious lack of transportation facilities, they could have maintained such a record. The same was true on farms.

The social highlight of the Moscow trip was dinner at the Kremlin. In the glittering dining hall there was an array of Red Army marshals, with Mr. Molotov present, and a number of Foreign Office officials to act as interpreters. Officers of my party attended, as did the ambassador and General Deane. Toasts were many, each of them directed to the spirit of co-operation and teamwork that had been gradually evolved during the war. After dinner we saw a movie. It was a picture of the Russian operations to capture Berlin, in which battle, the interpreter told me, they had used twenty-two divisions and an enormous concentration of artillery. I expressed an interest in the picture and the Generalissimo promptly said he would give me a copy. I suggested that I should also like a picture of himself and he forgot neither detail. Within a few days I received in Berlin the complete movie film together with a generously inscribed photograph of the Generalissimo.

He asked that I extend to General Marshall an expression of his personal regret for an act of what he termed personal rudeness during the progress of the war. He said that once he had received from General Marshall a piece of information concerning the enemy that later turned out to be false and occasioned some embarrassment to the Red armies. In his irritation, he said, he sent a sharp radio message to General Marshall, but later regretted this because of his confidence that Marshall was acting in good faith. He earnestly charged me with the errand of conveying his expressions of regret to the Chief of Staff.[4]

Throughout our stay Marshal Zhukov and other Russian officials pressed me to designate the spots I should like to visit. They said there was no place, even if it took us as far as Vladivostok, that I could not see. My time was limited but before leaving Moscow I did want to see the museum in the Kremlin. Upon expression of this desire, a visit was immediately arranged and I was invited to bring with me such aides or assistants as I might wish. It is possible that my hosts had in mind only the little group who accompanied me from Berlin but when the time came for the visit I found that almost the entire American Embassy staff had volunteered to act as aides-de-camp that day. None of them had ever been permitted to visit the Kremlin and so I laughingly agreed to class them all as temporary aides. The entire party of some fifty or sixty people spent the afternoon viewing accumulated treasures of the czars.[5] Jewelry, gorgeously incrusted costumes, flags, and decorations of every description filled the great halls and constituted a magnificent display.

While walking through the Kremlin grounds we passed the largest-caliber gun I have ever seen; the inside diameter of the barrel appeared to be over thirty inches. It was an eighteenth-century relic. As we walked away from it my son musingly remarked, "I suppose that was the weapon which, two hundred years ago, made future wars too horrible to contemplate."

On the night before we left Moscow the American ambassador gave a reception for the visiting party. It was a stag affair and Russian guests were mainly individuals from the Foreign Office and the armed services. There were the usual toasts, followed by a supper, in the midst of which the ambassador received an urgent call to come to the Foreign Office at once. Suspecting that he might obtain news of a Japanese surrender, momentarily expected, Mr. Harriman asked me to do my best to hold all the guests until he returned. This proved to be quite a task because the ambassador was kept at the Foreign Office much longer than he had anticipated. However, by enlisting help from a number of American friends who devised new toasts, some of them even set to the tunes of the orchestra, we managed to entertain the guests and keep the bulk of them until Mr. Harriman returned.

He walked to the middle of the room and announced the Japanese surrender, which brought a joyous shout of approval from all the Americans present.[6] But I noted that old Marshal Budenny, who was standing at my side, did not seem to exhibit any great enthusiasm. I asked him whether he was not glad the war was over and he replied, "Oh yes, but we should have kept going until we had killed a lot more of those insolent Japanese." The marshal seemed to be a most congenial, humane, and hospitable type but at the same time he seemed to have no concern that even one day's continuance of war meant death or wounds for additional hundreds of Russian citizens.

During the war I had heard much of the magnificent defense of

Leningrad in 1941 and 1942. I expressed a desire to visit that city briefly. In the siege of Leningrad 350,000 civilians, according to the Russian records, died of starvation. Many more were killed and wounded. These figures were constantly recited to our visiting party by civilian officials of Leningrad who joined the military commanders to act as our local hosts. The extraordinary suffering of the population and the length of time that the city endured the rigors and privations of the battle combined to make the operation one of the memorable sieges of history; certainly it is without parallel in modern times. All of us were struck by the fact that in speaking of Leningrad's losses every citizen did so with a tone of pride and satisfaction in his voice. The pride, of course, was understandable in view of the heroic endurance that had defeated the enemy at that vital point; but it was more difficult to grasp the reasons for satisfaction, even though it was explained to us that the city, by paying such a tremendous price, had proved itself "worthy of Mother Russia."

The mayor of the city had us for luncheon with a number of civil and military leaders of the region. Russian artists were there to entertain us. We listened to vocal and instrumental music, to dramatic recitations—which, of course, we could not understand—and watched some beautiful dancing. I remarked to my host that I was struck by the universal respect for artists in Russia and the extraordinary appreciation that everyone, from highest to lowest, seemed to have for art in all its forms. My host replied that any Russian would cheerfully go hungry all week if by doing so he could, on Sunday, visit an art gallery, a football game, or the ballet.

During the toasting period at the Leningrad luncheon my son, who had heretofore escaped the ordeal, was called upon by Marshal Zhukov for a toast. Later John told me that during the entire visit he had been fearing such a challenge and had prepared himself for it as well as he could. He rose to his feet and after remarking that as a young lieutenant he was not accustomed to associate with marshals of the Soviet Union, mayors of great cities, and five-star generals, he said in effect: "I have been in Russia several days and have listened to many toasts. I have heard the virtues of every Allied ruler, every prominent marshal, general, admiral, and air commander toasted. I have yet to hear a toast to the most important Russian in World War II. Gentlemen, will you please drink with me to the common soldier of the great Red Army."

His toast was greeted with greater enthusiasm and shouts of approval than any other I heard during the days when we heard so many. Marshal Zhukov was particularly pleased and said to me that he and I must be getting old when we had to wait for a young lieutenant to remind us "who really won the war."

The return trip from Leningrad to Berlin became unpleasant when the weather turned bad. During our flights through Russia our agreements required us to use a Russian navigator. Their navigators seemed quite skillful in orienting themselves by terrain features in the countryside, with which they were very familiar. Apparently, they were not so proficient in celestial navigation and would never give us authority to fly at a greater height than would permit them to see the ground. On this particular trip the ceiling dropped so low that, finally, we were skimming along at treetop level in our four-engine transport. This was too much for my pilot, Major Larry Hansen, who pretended for a moment that he could not understand the broken English of the Russian navigator, and quickly pulled the ship up to the top of the clouds. From then on we had a normal and easy flight to Berlin.

During our hours on the plane Marshal Zhukov and I frequently discussed the campaigns of the war. Because of his special position for several years in the Red Army he had had a longer experience as a responsible leader in great battles than any other man of our time. It seems that he was habitually sent to whatever Russian sector appeared at the moment to be the decisive one. By his descriptions of the composition of the Russian Army, of the terrain over which it fought, and of his reasons for his strategic decisions, it was clear that he was an accomplished soldier.

The marshal was astonished when I told him that each of our divisions, with its reinforcing battalions, was maintained at a strength of 17,000. He said that he tried to maintain his divisions at about 8000, but that frequently, in a long campaign, some would be depleted to a strength of 3000 to 4000.

Highly illuminating to me was his description of the Russian method of attacking through mine fields. The German mine fields, covered by defensive fire, were tactical obstacles that caused us many casualties and delays. It was always a laborious business to break through them, even though our technicians invented every conceivable kind of mechanical appliance to destroy mines safely. Marshal Zhukov gave me a matter-of-fact statement of his practice, which was, roughly, "There are two kinds of mines; one is the personnel mine and the other is the vehicular mine. When we come to a mine field our infantry attacks exactly as if it were not there. The losses we get from personnel mines we consider only equal to those we would have gotten from machine guns and artillery if the Germans had chosen to defend that particular area with strong bodies of troops instead of with mine fields. The attacking infantry does not set off the vehicular mines, so after they have penetrated to the far side of the field they form a bridgehead, after which the engineers come up and dig out channels through which our vehicles can go."

I had a vivid picture of what would happen to any American or British commander if he pursued such tactics, and I had an even more vivid picture of what the men in any one of our divisions would have had to say about the matter had we attempted to make such a practice a part of our tactical doctrine. Americans assess the cost of war in terms of human lives, the Russians in the over-all drain on the nation. The Russians clearly understood the value of morale, but for its development and maintenance they apparently depended upon over-all success and upon patriotism, possibly fanaticism.

As far as I could see, Zhukov had given little concern to methods that we considered vitally important to the maintenance of morale among American troops: systematic rotation of units, facilities for recreation, short leaves and furloughs, and, above all, the development of techniques to avoid exposure of men to unnecessary battlefield risks, all of which, although common practices in our Army, seemed to be largely unknown in his.

However, he agreed with me that destruction of enemy morale must always be the aim of the high command. To this end nothing is so useful as the attainment of strategic surprise; a surprise that suddenly places our own forces in position to threaten the enemy's ability to continue the war, at least in an important area. This effect is heightened when accompanied by the tactical surprise that arouses the fear in the enemy's front-line units that they are about to be destroyed. Time after time in the campaigns in the Mediterranean and in Europe we successfully achieved surprise in either the strategic or tactical field, sometimes in both. We suffered tactical surprise in the strength and timing of the German attack in the Battle of the Bulge in December 1944. In this instance, however, the probability and the general location were foreseen to the extent that reaction had been planned and could be effectively executed. Nevertheless, the early effect on morale of front-line troops was noticeable.

The basic differences between American and Russian attitudes in the handling of men were illustrated on another occasion. While talking to a Russian general I mentioned the difficult problem that was imposed upon us at various periods of the war by the need to care for so many German prisoners. I remarked that they were fed the same rations as were our own soldiers. In the greatest astonishment he asked, "Why did you do that?" I said, "Well, in the first place my country was required to do so by the terms of the Geneva Convention. In the second place the German had some thousands of American and British prisoners and I did not want to give Hitler the excuse or justification for treating our prisoners more harshly than he was already doing." Again the Russian seemed astounded at my attitude and he said, "But what did you care about men the Germans had captured? They had surrendered and could not fight any more." However, these statements did not necessarily mean that the Russians were cruel or were innately indifferent to human life.

The experience of Russia in World War II was a harsh one. The year 1941 saw the entire western portion of that country overrun by the Nazis. From the region of the Volga westward, almost everything was destroyed. When we flew into Russia, in 1945, I did not see a house standing between the western borders of the country and the area around Moscow. Through this overrun region, Marshal Zhukov told me, so many numbers of women, children, and old men had been killed that the Russian Government would never be able to estimate the total. Some of their great cities had been laid waste and until November 1942 there seemed to be little hope that their desperate defense could hold off the enemy until their industries could be rehabilitated and the Western Allies could get into the war in force.

All this would have embittered any people; it would have been completely astonishing if the Russians had not had a more direct and personal vindictiveness toward the Germans and a sterner attitude toward the realities of war than was the case in countries far removed from the scene of hostilities.

Even in their successful offensives they paid a terrible price for victory. The most costly form of warfare, and the one in which the diminishing power of the offensive soonest manifests itself, is the tactical advance by superior forces that gradually gains ground against a flexible and skillful defense. The enemy constantly readjusts his forces so as to compel successive and expensive attacks against the same troops in prepared positions and, as the maintenance factor begins seriously to enter the problem, the enemy may reverse original relative values in both moral and material strength. In the early Russian counteroffensives of the war Zhukov had been compelled to employ his armies in this expensive method. It was not until the final months of the war that the Soviets began, in a military sense, to gain the great rewards paid for by their earlier severe sacrifices. Proud of their victories, the Russians always remembered with bitterness their cost.

I know that in my personal reactions, as the months of conflict wore on, I grew constantly more bitter against the Germans, particularly the Hitler gang. On all sides there was always evidence of the destruction that Hitler's ruthless ambition had brought about. Every battle, every skirmish, demanded its price in broken bodies and in the extinction of the lives of young Allied soldiers.

During the war hundreds of brokenhearted fathers, mothers, and sweethearts wrote me personal letters, begging for some hope that a loved one might still be alive, or, at the very least, for some additional detail as to the manner of his death. Every one of these I answered, and I know of no more effective means of developing an undying hatred of those responsible for aggressive war than to assume the obligation of attempting to express sympathy to families bereaved by it. Possibly, therefore, I had a more sympathetic understanding of the Russian attitude than would have been possible before the beginning of the war.

Marshal Zhukov showed little interest in measures that I thought, after Allied experience in North Africa and Europe, should be taken to protect the foot soldier and to increase his individual effectiveness. The efficiency of ground units is markedly affected by the success of a commander in getting his men onto the battle line without the fatigue of long and exhausting marches and under such conditions as to provide them protection from the sporadic fires that always harass the rear areas. Certain of our special formations habitually rode to battle in lightly armored vehicles and the percentage of losses among these, as compared to the percentage of losses among the fighting units of the normal infantry divisions, clearly indicated to me the desirability of devising ways and means whereby all troops could go into battle under similarly favorable circumstances. The Russians, however, viewed measures to protect the individual against fatigue and wounds as possibly too costly. Great victories, they seemed to think, inevitably require huge casualties.

To return the courtesy extended to me by the Russian Government, the American War Department, with the approval of President Truman, promptly invited Marshal Zhukov to pay a visit to America. An immediate acceptance was returned and we thought that the marshal would soon depart for the United States.[7] He asked that General Clay or I go along with him so that he might have a friend in my country, just as he had accompanied me during my trip to Russia. I had to tell him that because of special circumstances and problems at the moment I could not do this, but I arranged for General Clay to go with him. Marshal Zhukov also asked if my son could accompany him as an aide. I told him that John would be honored to do so and that, moreover, I would be glad to send him in the Sunflower, the C-54 that I regularly used.[8] This delighted him. He had already ridden through Russia in the plane and had great confidence in it and the crew. He said something to the interpreter which was given to me as, "With the general's plane and the general's son along, I know I shall be perfectly safe."

Unfortunately the marshal soon fell ill. At the time there was some speculation as to whether it was diplomatic illness, but when I next saw him at a meeting of the Control Council in Berlin he gave the appearance of a man who had gone through a serious siege of ill-health. In any event this served to postpone his visit until the approach of winter weather and he then expressed a desire to go to our country in the spring.[9] Before that time arrived the Russians had apparently no further interest in sending one of their marshals to spend a week or ten days in America.

I saw Marshal Zhukov for the last time November 7, 1945. It was a Soviet holiday, in honor of which he gave a large reception in Berlin, inviting to it the senior commanders and staff officers of all the Allies. The weather turned bad and flying was impossible. The other two commanders in chief canceled their engagements but, knowing that I was soon to be ordered home, I determined to attend the ceremony, although to do so I had to make a night trip by train, followed by a long automobile trip during the day.

When I arrived Marshal Zhukov, with his wife and a number of his senior assistants, was standing in the receiving line. He greeted me and then promptly deserted the receiving line. He took his wife by the arm, and the three of us, with an interpreter, retired to a comfortable room where were refreshments of all kinds. We talked for two hours.

The tenor of the marshal's conversation was that he believed that we in Berlin had done something to help in the difficult problem of promoting understanding between two nations so diverse in their cultural and political conceptions as were the United States and the Soviet Union. He felt that we could accomplish still more. He talked at length about the new United Nations and remarked: "If the United States and Russia will only stand together through thick and thin success is certain for the United Nations. If we are partners there are no other countries in the world that would dare go to war when we forbade it."

The marshal seemed to be a firm believer in the Communist concept. He said that, as he saw it, the Soviet system of government was based upon idealism, and ours upon materialism. In expanding his idea of this difference he remarked—and introduced an apology because of his criticism—that he felt our system appealed to all that was selfish in people. He said that we induced a man to do things by telling him he might keep what he earned, might say what he pleased, and in every direction allowed him to be largely an undisciplined, unoriented entity within a great national complex.

He asked me to understand a system in which the attempt was made to substitute for such motivations the devotion of a man to the great national complex of which he formed a part. In spite of my complete repudiation of such contentions and my condemnation of all systems that involved dictatorship, there was no doubt in my mind that Marshal Zhukov was sincere.

Another slight incident at that final meeting illustrated again how frequently things that we would probably consider inconsequential and scarcely worth noticing can become important in the eyes of individuals whose background from childhood has differed sharply from our own. The reverse, also, is probably true. The marshal told me that a book written by an American about Russia stated that Marshal Zhukov was shorter by two or three inches than his wife, and that he had two sons. This story irritated him because he saw in it personal disparagement and belittlement. He and his wife stood up for a moment and he said, "Now you see what kind of lies some of your writers publish about us." And he added, "Also, we have no sons. We have two daughters."

He referred to a picture of the Generalissimo published by one of our magazines. This was not a personal photograph but was a likeness of a painted portrait that hung in one of the Berlin night clubs. The magazine picture had been taken in such a way that, with seeming intent, the Generalissimo's portrait was photographed in most unfortunate and undignified surroundings. This literally infuriated the marshal. He turned to me and said: "If a picture of you like this one should appear in a Russian magazine, I would see that the magazine ceased operations at once. It would be eliminated. What are you going to do?"

This called for me to describe the free press of America, but after an earnest and, I thought, eloquent attempt I found that I had made no impression whatsoever. The marshal merely repeated, "If you are Russia's friend you will do something about it."[10]

Similarly I tried to make him see the virtues of free enterprise. Firmly believing that without a system of free or competitive enterprise, individual political freedom cannot endure, I showed him that, so far as I was concerned, complete state ownership necessarily would involve complete dictatorship, and that the effort to escape all dictatorial rule was the reason for America's founding and growth. He merely smiled.

Even after I returned to the United States the marshal and I continued, until April 1946, to correspond on our accustomed friendly terms. In the spring of that year he was relieved from his Berlin command and I have never since heard from him directly. It was rumored that he was out of favor—that for some reason he had fallen from the high place he held in Russian affections and popular esteem during the late months of the war.

One of the speculative reasons given for his virtual disappearance was his known friendship with me. I cannot believe that such was the case because, in spite of that friendship, he always seemed to be profoundly convinced of the essential rectitude of the Communist theory. He knew that I was an uncompromising foe of Communism because I believed that it was synonymous with dictatorship; he would listen patiently when I said that I hated everything that smacked of statism, and that our whole Western tradition was devoted to the idea of personal liberty. But his own adherence to the Communistic doctrine seemed to come from inner conviction and not from any outward compulsion.

The Russians are generous. They like to give presents and parties, as almost every American who has served with them can testify. In his generous instincts, in his love of laughter, in his devotion to a comrade, and in his healthy, direct outlook on the affairs of workaday life, the ordinary Russian seems to me to bear a marked similarity to what we call an "average American."

The existence of a personal friendship and understanding with Marshal Zhukov did not, however, eliminate the incidents and conflicts which were always irritating and exasperating members of my staff. Occasionally these were serious. Every railway train and every automobile that we sent into Berlin had to pass through Russian territory. Several times these were molested or even robbed by roving bands of individuals wearing the uniform of the Russian Army.

Because of the difference in languages no one had available the instrument of direct and personal conversation to alleviate the intensity of the ensuing arguments. Misunderstandings arose over the implementation of the Potsdam agreement, particularly as it applied to reparations. While Clay and I had always fought for the rehabilitation of the Ruhr and the development of an economy in western Germany sufficient to support the population, we likewise insisted that every firm commitment of our government should be properly and promptly executed. We felt that for us to be guilty of bad faith in any detail of operation or execution would defeat whatever hope we had of assisting in the development of a broad basis of international cooperation.

The policy of firm adherence to the pledged word of our government was first challenged shortly after the close of hostilities. Some of my associates suddenly proposed that when so requested by the Russians I should refuse to withdraw American troops from the line of the Elbe to the area allocated to the United States for occupation. The argument was that if we kept troops on the Elbe the Russians would be more likely to agree to some of our proposals, particularly as to a reasonable division of Austria. To me, such an attitude seemed indefensible. I was certain, and was always supported in this attitude by the War Department, that to start off our first direct association with Russia on the basis of refusing to carry out an arrangement in which the good faith of our government was involved would wreck the whole co-operative attempt at its very beginning.

I always felt that the Western Allies could probably have secured an agreement to occupy more of Germany than we actually did. I believe that if our political heads had been as convinced as we were at SHAEF of the certainty of early victory in the West they would have insisted, at Yalta, upon the line of the Elbe as the natural geographic line dividing the eastern and western occupation areas. Although in late January 1945 we were still west of the Rhine, and indeed had not yet demolished the Siegfried Line, my staff and I had informed our superiors that we expected to proceed rapidly to great victories.[11] Except for a fear that we could advance no farther eastward, there would seem to have been little reason for agreeing to an occupational line no deeper into Germany than Eisenach. This, however, is pure speculation. I have never discussed the matter with any of the individuals directly responsible for the decision.

In any event the Berlin record of those late summer and early autumn months of 1945 represents the peak of postwar cordiality and co-operation that we were ever able to achieve with the Soviet officials. In broader fields, on highest levels, misunderstandings continued to grow and these were inevitably reflected in the local German scene. It is possible, also, that this process worked in reverse.

Americans at that time—or at least we in Berlin—saw no reason why the Russian system of government and democracy as practiced by the Western Allies could not live side by side in the world, provided each respected the rights, the territory, and the convictions of the other, and each system avoided overt or covert action against the integrity of the other. Because implicit in Western democracy is respect for the rights of others, it seemed natural to us that this "live and let live" type of agreement could be achieved and honestly kept. That was probably the most for which we ever really hoped. But even such a purely practical basis for living together in the world has not been achieved.

What caused the change—not necessarily in the realm of ultimate purpose but definitely in the apparent desire for a pragmatic approach to co-operation—may possibly never be clearly understood by any of us. But two and one half years of growing tension have shattered our dream of rapid progress toward universal peace and the elimination of armaments. Seriously and soberly, aware of our strengths and our weaknesses, sure of our moral rectitude, we must address ourselves to the new tensions that beset the world.

The implications of the failure to eliminate aggression and to co-operate effectively are as full of meaning for the world as were the dictatorial and arbitrary acts in the late 1930s of Hitler, Mussolini, and Hirohito. The name of almost every small country of eastern Europe is a reminder to us of the lost objectives so bravely stated in the Atlantic Charter, even before Pearl Harbor Day. Fear, doubt, and confusion are the portion of those who fought and won the war with the fervent prayer that at last this was the war to end wars.

Volumes have been, and more volumes will be, written on the collapse of world co-operation and the true significance of the events that accompanied the tragedy. For us, all their words will amplify one simple truth. Freedom from fear and injustice and oppression will be ours only in the measure that men who value such freedom are ready to sustain its possession—to defend it against every thrust from within or without.

The compelling necessities of the moment leave us no alternative to the maintenance of real and respectable strength—not only in our moral rectitude and our economic power, but in terms of adequate military preparedness. To neglect this, pending universal resurgence of a definite spirit of co-operation, is not only foolish, it is criminally stupid. Moreover, present-day weakness will alarm our friends, earn the contempt of others, and virtually eliminate any influence of ours toward peaceful adjustment of world problems. The lessons of 1914 and 1939 remain valid so long as the world has not learned the futility of making competitive force the final arbiter of human questions.

Military preparedness alone is an inadequate answer to the problem. Communism inspires and enables its militant preachers to exploit injustices and inequity among men. This ideology appeals, not to the Italian or Frenchman or South American as such, but to men as human beings who become desperate in the attempt to satisfy common human needs. Therein it possesses a profound power for expansion. Wherever popular discontent is founded on group oppression or mass poverty or the hunger of children, there Communism may stage an offensive that arms cannot counter. Discontent can be fanned into revolution, and revolution into social chaos. The sequel is dictatorial rule. Against such tactics exclusive reliance on military might is vain.

The areas in which freedom flourishes will continue to shrink unless the supporters of democracy match Communist fanaticism with clear and common understanding that the freedom of men is at stake; meet Communist-regimented unity with the voluntary unity of common purpose, even though this may mean a sacrifice of some measure of nationalistic pretensions; and, above all, annul Communist appeals to the hungry, the poor, the oppressed, with practical measures untiringly prosecuted for the elimination of social and economic evils that set men against men.

As a world force, democracy is supported by nations that too much and too often act alone, each for itself alone. Nowhere perfect, in many regions democracy is pitifully weak because the separatism of national sovereignty uselessly prevents the logical pooling of resources, which would produce greater material prosperity within and multiplied strength for defense. Such division may mean ideological conquest.

The democracies must learn that the world is now too small for the rigid concepts of national sovereignty that developed in a time when the nations were self-sufficient and self-dependent for their own well-being and safety. None of them today can stand alone. No radical surrender of national sovereignty is required—only a firm agreement that in disputes between nations a central and joint agency, after examination of the facts, shall decide the justice of the case by majority vote and thereafter shall have the power and the means to enforce its decision. This is a slight restriction indeed on nationalism and a small price to pay if thereby the peoples who stand for human liberty are better fitted to settle dissension within their own ranks or to meet attack from without.

Here is the true, long-term assurance that democracy may flourish in the world. Physical means and skillful organization may see it safely through a crisis, but only if basically the democracy of our day satisfies the mental, moral, and physical wants of the masses living under it can it continue to exist.

We believe individual liberty, rooted in human dignity, is man's greatest treasure. We believe that men, given free expression of their will, prefer freedom and self-dependence to dictatorship and collectivism. From the evidence, it would appear that the Communist leaders also believe this; else why do they attack and attempt to destroy the practice of these concepts? Were they completely confident in the rectitude and appeal of their own doctrine, there would be no necessity for them to follow an aggressive policy. Time would be the only ally they needed if Communism as a spiritual force and moral inspiration appealed more to mankind than do individual rights and liberties. We who saw Europe liberated know that the Communistic fear that men will cling to freedom is well founded. It is possible that this truth may be the reason for what appears to be an aggressive intent on the part of the Communists to tear down all governmental structures based upon individual freedom.

If the men and women of America face this issue as squarely and bravely as their soldiers faced the terrors of battle in World War II, we would have no fear of the outcome. If they will unite themselves as firmly as they did when they provided, with their Allies in Europe, the mightiest fighting force of all time, there is no temporal power that can dare challenge them. If they can retain the moral integrity, the clarity of comprehension, and the readiness to sacrifice that finally crushed the Axis, then the free world will live and prosper, and all peoples, eventually, will reach a level of culture, contentment, and security that has never before been achieved.

ACKNOWLEDGMENTS

MILLIONS, IN UNIFORM AND OUT, WERE RESPON-
sible for the military accomplishments recounted in this book. In this
sense, they wrote the story and no enumeration of collaborators is
possible. But in a personal sense I am deeply indebted to a group of
close friends for the assistance that allowed me quickly to concentrate
and edit wartime notes, memoranda, and memories into a single narrative of my experiences in World War II. Among them the Hon.
Joseph E. Davies, former ambassador to the U.S.S.R.; my wartime
chief of staff, now Ambassador, Walter B. Smith; and Brigadier General Edwin Clark, formerly a valuable assistant of mine in SHAEF,
were primarily responsible for persuading me that I should undertake
the task at all. Without their insistence and urging there would certainly have been no collection of notes and memoranda from which
to start. Brigadier General Arthur S. Nevins and Kevin McCann,
who rose from private to lieutenant colonel during the war, were
indispensable assistants throughout the preparation of the book, once
the decision to write it had been made. To these, especially, and to all
those who served on my staff at various periods during and after the
war, my grateful thanks for what may be good herein; my apologies
for what is bad.

FOOTNOTES

CHAPTER 1: Prelude to War

1. Strength Accounting Branch, Adjutant General's Office, Department of the Army; U. S. Navy, Bureau of Naval Personnel; U. S. Coast Guard, Treasury Department.

2. *The Campaign in Poland*, 1939, Department of Military Art and Engineering, U. S. Military Academy, 1943.

3. General George C. Marshall, C. of S., U.S.A., *Biennial Report to the Secretary of War*, July 1, 1939–June 30, 1941, pp. 1, 2, and Chart 1; and *Munitions for the Army*, a five-year report on the procurement of munitions by the War Department under the direction of the Under Secretary of War.

4. Marshall, op. cit., pp. 4–9.

5. The bill for extension was passed on August 12 by the House with only one vote to spare. "There were—yeas 203, nays 202, not voting 27." *Congressional Record*, Vol. 87, Part 7, p. 7074.

6. Marshall, op. cit., Charts 1 and 2 (facing p. 34).

7. *History of the Second Army*, Study No. 16, Historical Section, Army Ground Forces, pp. 23–26.

8. *Second Army vs. First Army, Critiques,* General McNair's Papers, Files 354.2/2 and 354.2/3, Adjutant General's Office.

9. The Pearl Harbor attack time was about 0700, December 7. Clark Field, Luzon, was attacked at 1220, December 8 (local time), or about 1620, December 7 (Hawaiian time). *Army Air Action in the Philippines and Netherlands East Indies*, 1941–42, AAFRH-11, Assistant Chief of Air Intelligence, p. 35.

CHAPTER 2: Global War

1. Of the seven carriers and one escort carrier in the U. S. Navy on December 7, 1941, three carriers were in the Pacific. The *Saratoga* was en route to San Diego, the *Enterprise* and the *Lexington* were with Task Force 8 in the Solomons. *Disposition of Vessels in United States Navy*, December 7, 1941, Office of Naval Records.

2. Marshall, *Biennial Report,* July 1, 1941–June 30, 1943, p. 8.

3. Strengths were as follows: U. S. Army (exclusive of Philippine Scouts)—approximately 10,000, Philippine Scouts—12,000, U. S. Air Force—8000. Estimate Pacific Section, Historical Division, War Department Special Staff, after consideration of a number of conflicting sources.

4. Memo Report, National Guard Bureau, Department of the Army, January 3, 1946.

5. *The War Reports of General George C. Marshall, General H. H. Arnold, Admiral Ernest J. King,* p. 332.

6. Fleet Admiral Ernest J. King, U.S.N., *United States Navy at War, 1941–45,* Official Reports, pp. 39, 42.

7. *The United States at War,* Historical Reports on War Administration, Bureau of the Budget, No. 1, p. 237.

8. Colonel Julian F. Barnes, *Report of Organization and Activities of U. S. Forces in Australia,* December 7, 1941–June 30, 1942, AGO.

9. *Minutes of the Joint Board Meetings,* December 8, 9, 10, P & O Files, Department of the Army.

10. Strength Accounting Branch, AGO, STM-30, January 1, 1948, pp. 37, 40–41.

11. Memo, WPD for C. of S., February 28, 1942; subject: Strategic Conceptions and Their Application to the Southwest Pacific, Exec. 4, P & O Files, Department of the Army.

12. *Target: Germany, The Army Air Forces' Official Story of the VIII Bomber Command's First Year over Europe,* published in co-operation with *Life Magazine* by Simon and Schuster, New York, 1943, p. 27.

13. Memo, WPD for TAG, January 17, 1942; subject: Command in Far East, WPD 4560-9, AGO.

14. Radio message, Fort Mills to TAG, March 26, reports the arrival of three of these submarines at Corregidor. AG 381 (3–26–42).

15. WPD 4630-28 and 4630-29, AGO.

16. *History of the United States Army Forces in the South Pacific Area,* Historical Branch G-2, HQ U. S. Army Forces, Middle Pacific, p. 723.

17. A discussion of the telegram and the reply thereto is contained in Secretary Stimson's *Diary,* February 9, 1942.

18. Arcadia Conference, December 24, 1941–January 14, 1942. *Proceedings of the American-British Joint Chiefs of Staff Conference,* ABC-337 Arcadia, December 24, 1941, AGO.

19. ABC-1 Conversations, January 29, 1941–March 27, 1941. *United States-British Staff Conversations,* March 27, 1941, WPD 4402-89, AGO.

20. Memo, WPD for C. of S., February 28, 1942; subject: Strategic Conceptions and Their Application to the Southwest Pacific, Exec. 4, P & O Files, Department of the Army.

21. Samuel Eliot Morison, *History of United States Naval Operations in World War II,* Vol. I, p. 317, and Appendix 1, p. 410.

22. "General Wavell left Delhi January 5, 1942, by air, arrived Batavia on January 10, took over command 1200 hrs GMT, 15 January." ABDACOM, General Staff, India, p. 2, AGO.

CHAPTER 3: Command Post for Marshall

1. *WD Circular No. 59,* March 2, 1942, AGO.
2. ". . . there were insufficient facts on which to base strategic estimates; and there were no trained personnel for either strategic or combat intelligence." *A History of the Military Intelligence Division,* MID, WDGS, MI 725/1, AGO.
3. German War Records transmitted to the War Department from the European Theater. German Documents Section, Historical Division, Special Staff, Department of the Army.
4. President Quezon left Corregidor by submarine on February 20, 1942, arriving in the Southern Islands on February 22. In April he traveled by bomber to Australia and finally arrived in the United States on May 8. *The Sixth Annual Report of the United States High Commissioner to the Philippine Islands,* pp. 10, 11.
5. OPD 320.2, Middle East, AGO.
6. Military Planning and Intelligence Division, Office of the Chief of Transportation, Department of the Army.
7. WPD 4510 and 4511, AGO.
8. Ibid.
9. Memo, C. of S., GHQ, for C. of S., January 15, 1942; subject: Future Operations, WPD 4511-49, AGO.
10. King, *United States Navy at War,* pp. 79–82.
11. *Statistics Relating to the War Effort of the United Kingdom,* presented by the Prime Minister to Parliament, November 1944, pp. 20, 21.
12. Marshall memorandum, no addressee, April 2, 1942, presented to C. of S. on April 1, 1942; subject: Operations in Western Europe, Exec. 1, OPD Files, Department of the Army.
13. The plan was also approved by the President on April 1. Secretary Stimson's *Diary,* April 2, 1942.
14. Message CM-IN-2050, April 8, 1942, AGO.
15. Minutes of meeting held on April 14, 1942, WDSCA 381 (4-17-42), Section 5, AGO.

CHAPTER 4: Platform for Invasion

1. *The Administrative and Logistical History of the European Theater of Operations,* Part II, Vol. I, p. 22.
2. *The Special Observer Group Prior to the Activation of the European Theater of Operations,* Historical Section, European Theater of Operations, p. 14.
3. Marshall, *Biennial Report,* July 1, 1941–June 30, 1943, p. 33.
4. OPD 371 ETO (6-19-42), subject: Commanding General USAFBI designated as Commanding General, European Theater, AGO.
5. "The Service whose operations are of the greater importance for the accomplishment of a joint mission has paramount interest in such an operation." *Joint Action of the Army and Navy,* Chapter II, Par. 8.

6. Generals Eisenhower and Clark left by air for London on June 23. *OPD Diary,* June 23, 1942.

7. OPD 371 ETO, AGO.

8. Order of Battle for divisions is shown in SHAEF daily G-3 summaries, beginning June 6, 1944, AGO.

   SC-A1-9, Allied vs. Axis Air Strength Report, Statistical Control Division, Office of Management Control, Army Air Forces. Figures of combat planes actually with squadrons. Total inventory figures are considerably higher.

   Ships and landing craft are shown in *Allied Naval Commander Expeditionary Force Report* to the Supreme Allied Commander, AEF, pp. 29, 32.

9. *The Seventh United States Army Report of Operations,* France and Germany, 1944–45, Vol. I, map facing p. 47, "Final Plan Anvil."

10. Webster, *A History of the United States Army Forces, Northern Ireland,* pp. 35, 36.

11. Admiral Stark assumed his duties on April 30, 1942. *The Administrative and Logistical History of the European Theater of Operations,* Part II, Vol. I, p. 135.

12. "In June 1942, Major General Mark W. Clark assumed command, the Corps was reinforced, and on July 1, 1942, sailed from the New York Port of Embarkation." *A Brief History of the II Corps,* p. 7.

13. "General Spaatz was named as commander of the VIII Air Force on May 2, 1942, but did not arrive in the Theater until July." *History of the VIII Air Force,* Vol. I, p. 105.

14. An example was *A Short Guide to Great Britain,* War and Navy Departments, Washington, D.C., Special Service Division, Army Service Forces, U. S. Army.

15. Letter, General Eisenhower to General J. C. H. Lee, July 20, 1942. General Eisenhower's personal files (deposited in Adjutant General's Office, Department of the Army). Circulars 34 and 69, HQ ETOUSA, August 25, 1942, and October 30, 1942, AGO.

16. *Target: Germany,* p. 28.

17. "There was never any doubt in the minds of those airmen as to the ability of the Forts and Libs, given sufficient numbers, to penetrate to the heart of Germany unescorted and in daylight." Ibid., p. 59.

18. Theoretical range of the P-39 was 900 miles (est.) and that of the P-40 was 950 miles. A-4, U. S. Air Forces, official figure for the P-40, estimated figure for the P-39.

19. *Manual of Bomber Command Operations,* 1942, Air Ministry War Room.

20. *HQ VIII Bomber Command Narrative of Operations,* Day Operation, 13 June 1943.

21. *Target: Germany,* p. 60.

22. ". . . Captain the Lord Louis Mountbatten, who was promoted . . . and on the 18th March 1942, Acting Vice-Admiral, when his title was changed to Chief of Combined Operations." *Combined Operations,* 1940–42, Ministry of Information, p. 52.

23. *Operation Overlord Report and Appreciation,* Appendix M, OPD Files, Department of the Army.

24. Marshall, *Biennial Report,* July 1, 1941–June 30, 1943, pp. 27, 42.

25. Ibid., pp. 41, 42.

26. Memo from the President for the Hon. Harry L. Hopkins, General Marshall, Admiral King, subject: Instructions for London Conference, July 1942, July 16, 1942, WDSCA 381 (7-16-42), AGO.

27. Memorandum by the CCS, subject: Operations in 1942/1943, July 24, 1942 (SGS AFHQ 337.21), AGO.

28. General Eisenhower was officially informed on August 14. Annex I to the Minutes of Chiefs of Staff Committee, War Cabinet, August 14, 1942, in *History of AFHQ,* Part I, p. 3.

CHAPTER 5: Planning Torch

1. Message 1027, General Eisenhower to General Marshall, August 10, 1942, and Message 3204, August 11, in reply, AGO.

2. *Diary, Office of the Commander-in-Chief,* maintained on instructions of General Eisenhower by Harry C. Butcher, naval aide (deposited in Adjutant General's Office, Department of the Army).

3. Marshall, *Biennial Report,* July 1, 1941–June 30, 1943, p. 18.

4. "On the Atlantic side, only seven non-consecutive days in a month afford even reasonably good conditions for landing." Message 1406, General Handy to General Marshall, August 23, 1942, AGO.

5. "We are impressed with the disadvantages of elimination of the landing on the west coast." Message 2834, General Marshall to General Eisenhower, August 1, 1942, AGO.

6. "Bône received 2000 high-explosive bombs during the seven weeks from December 13 to February 1, 1943." Allied Force Headquarters, *Commander-in-Chief's Dispatch,* North African Campaign, 1942–43 (370.2), p. 28.

7. Message 1480, General Eisenhower to General Marshall, August 25, 1942, AGO.

8. Allied Force Headquarters, *Commander-in-Chief's Dispatch,* p. 4.

9. Memorandum for General Marshall, Survey of Strategic Situation, July 23, 1942, General Eisenhower's personal files.

10. Message R-1573, General Marshall to General Eisenhower, October 5, 1942, AGO.

11. Marshall, *Biennial Report,* July 1, 1941–June 30, 1943, pp. 19–20.

12. Allied Force Headquarters, *Commander-in-Chief's Dispatch,* p. 17.

13. General Patton arrived London August 9, 1942, departed August 20. *Diary, Office C-in-C,* pp. 107, 143.

14. Message 3103, General Marshall to General Eisenhower, August 8, 1942, AGO.

15. Letter, General Eisenhower to General Marshall, September 21, 1942, General Eisenhower's personal files.

16. *Diary, Office C-in-C,* p. 255.

17. *The Battle of Britain, An Air Ministry Record of the Great Days from August 8 to October 31, 1940,* pp. 5, 12.

18. Message R-553, General Marshall to General Eisenhower, September 9, 1942, AGO.

19. *Diary, Office C-in-C,* p. 231.

20. General Noguès, French Resident General in Morocco, was minister to Sidi Mohammed Ben Youssef, Sultan of Morocco.

21. Colonel J. C. Holmes, U.S.A., minutes of London meeting with Mr. Murphy, *Diary, Office C-in-C,* pp. 232–36.

22. Allied Force Headquarters, *Commander-in-Chief's Dispatch,* pp. 14, 15.

23. Holmes, minutes of London meeting with Mr. Murphy, *Diary, Office C-in-C,* pp. 232–36.

24. *History of the Twelfth Air Force,* Vol. I., pp. 19–23.

25. Allied Force Headquarters, *Commander-in-Chief's Dispatch,* pp. 6–8; also *History of the Twelfth Air Force,* Vol. I, pp. 11–26.

26. *Diary, Office C-in-C,* p. 115.

27. Message 1186, General Eisenhower to General Marshall, August 15, 1942, AGO.

28. *Diary, Office C-in-C,* Book III, p. Gib.-1.

29. Ibid., pp. Gib.-12, 13.

CHAPTER 6: Invasion of Africa

1. Allied Force Headquarters, *Commander-in-Chief's Dispatch,* p. 6.

2. "Msg. from Admiral Hewitt, just in, says operation proceeding on schedule. Good news." *Diary, C-in-C,* Book III, p. Gib.-23.

3. Allied Force Headquarters, *Commander-in-Chief's Dispatch,* p. 12.

4. The commander was Major Walter M. Oakes, C.O., 2d Battalion, 39th Infantry. Letter from Major General Charles W. Ryder to C-in-C, Allied Forces; subject: Brief Report of Operations of Eastern Assault Force, November 19, 1942, AGO.

5. Ibid.

6. Memo (s) to Commander, U. S. Naval Forces in Europe, from Captain Jerauld Wright, U.S.N., December 7, 1942; subject: Report on Operation Minerva, AG AFHQ 370.2–53, AGO.

7. Message, London to AGWAR, September 22, 1942 (CM-IN-9484), AGO.

8. Message 113, General Eisenhower to AGWAR, ABFOR, November 7, 1942, AGO.
   "Regardless of the outcome of your negotiations with Giraud, we wish you to know that the stand you have taken meets with our complete approval." Extract from message, CCS to General Eisenhower, November 8, 1942, AGO.

9. Lieutenant General F. N. Mason MacFarlane's minutes of meeting, Gen-

eral Eisenhower with General Giraud, November 8, 1942, *Diary, Office C-in-C,* Book V, A-147-A-152.

10. Messages from General Eisenhower, November 8, 1942, *OPD Diary,* November 9, 1942.

11. Ibid., November 8 and 10, 1942.

12. *Outline History of the II Corps,* 1918–45, AGO 202.0, p. 2.

13. Allied Force Headquarters, *Commander-in-Chief's Dispatch,* pp. 12, 13.

14. *Diary, Office C-in-C* Book III, p. Gib.-67.

15. Ibid., p. Gib.-30.

16. Ibid., pp. Gib.-50–53.

17. Ibid., p. Gib.-57.

18. Message, General Clark to General Eisenhower, November 12, 1942 (no reference number indicated), Ibid., facing p. Gib.-57.

19. William L. Langer, *Our Vichy Gamble,* Alfred A. Knopf, New York, 1947, pp. 315, 316.

20. Message 425, General Eisenhower to General Marshall, November 12, 1942, AGO; also *OPD Diary,* November 15, 1942.

21. Ibid., November 11, 1942.

22. Allied Force Headquarters, *Commander-in-Chief's Dispatch,* p. 16.

23. Colonel William Stirling, British Army, minutes of meeting, General Eisenhower with Admiral Darlan, November 13, 1942, *Diary, Office C-in-C,* Book III, pp. Gib.-83, 84.

24. Message 1160, General Eisenhower to General Marshall, November 23, 1942, AGO.

25. Message 527, General Eisenhower to CCS, November 14, 1942, AGO.

26. Langer, op. cit., pp. 63, 375. *The O.N.I. Weekly,* December 2, 1942, pp. 5, 21, 22.

27. "Vichy has directed Admiral Esteva to resist the Allies and cooperate with the Axis." *OPD Diary,* November 17, 1942.

28. Marshall, *Biennial Report,* July 1, 1941–June 30, 1943, p. 23.

29. Message 644, General Eisenhower to General Clark, November 15, 1942; Press Conference, President Roosevelt, November 17, 1942, *Diary, Office C-in-C,* Book III, pp. Gib.-87, 89.

30. Lieutenant General K. A. N. Anderson, excerpt from a dispatch submitted to the Secretary of State for War on June 7, 1943, extracted from *Supplement,* London *Gazette,* November 5, 1946.

31. Message 539, C-in-C to CCS, November 25, 1942, AGO.

32. The attempt to seize Dakar was made on July 8, 1940. Roger W. Shugg and Major H. A. de Weerd, *World War II,* Infantry Journal Press, Washington, D.C., 1946, p. 149.

33. Message 882, General Eisenhower to General Marshall, November 30, 1942, AGO.

34. Message R-3796, General Marshall to General Eisenhower, December 1, 1942, AGO.

35. *Diary, Office C-in-C,* Book IV, pp. A-38, A-39, A-51, A-56.

CHAPTER 7: Winter in Algiers

1. Field Marshal Sir B. L. Montgomery, *El Alamein to the River Sangro*, pp. 13–30.

2. Allied Force Headquarters, *Commander-in-Chief's Dispatch*, p. 18.

3. Anderson, op. cit.

4. Ibid.

5. Allied Force Headquarters, *Commander-in-Chief's Dispatch*, p. 19.

6. Message from General Eisenhower reporting five consecutive Axis night air raids on Algiers, *OPD Diary*, November 26, 1942.

7. Anderson, op. cit.

8. *History of the Twelfth Air Force*, Vol. II, pp. 5, 6.

9. Anderson, op. cit.

10. Allied Force Headquarters, *Commander-in-Chief's Dispatch*, pp. 21, 22.

11. Ibid.

12. *Diary, Office C-in-C*, Book IV, p. A-112.

13. Ibid., p. A-111.

14. Allied Force Headquarters, *Commander-in-Chief's Dispatch*, p. 24.

15. "Orders were issued on November 15 for the movement of French troops from Algiers and Constantine eastward." Message from General Eisenhower, *OPD Diary*, November 19, 1942.

16. Anderson, op. cit.

17. *II Corps—Report of Operations, Tunisia*, January 1–March 15, 1943, AGO 202.03, pp. 1, 2.

18. Ibid., Appendix A, Status of Strength.

19. "The mission of the II Corps as defined by AFHQ was the protection of the right flank of the Allied Forces in Tunisia." Ibid., p. 3.

20. Allied Force Headquarters, *Commander-in-Chief's Dispatch*, pp. 24–26; also Message 3457, General Eisenhower to AGWAR, December 29, 1942, AGO.

21. Anderson, op. cit.

22. Allied Force Headquarters, *Commander-in-Chief's Dispatch*, pp. 31–34.

23. Anderson, op. cit.

24. *II Corps—Report of Operations, Tunisia*, p. 3.

25. *OPD Diary*, December 27, 1942.

26. Message from Ulio to General Eisenhower for Murphy from Secretary Hull, AFHQ incoming Message 140, December 12, 1942.

CHAPTER 8: Tunisian Campaign

1. Messages from General Eisenhower report Axis air attack on Casablanca. *OPD Diary*, January 1 and 3, 1943.

2. General Marshall and Admiral King visited Algiers January 24–26, 1943. *Diary, Office C-in-C,* Book V, pp. 183, 186.

3. Allied Force Headquarters, *Commander-in-Chief's Dispatch,* pp. 25, 28–30.

4. Minutes JCS meeting with the President in preparation for the Casablanca Conference, January 7, 1943, confirm this attitude of President Roosevelt. OPD Exec. Files, Department of the Army.

5. The rearmament committee was established promptly after the Casablanca Conference. Allied Force Headquarters, *Commander-in-Chief's Dispatch,* p. 30.

6. Marshall memorandum, no addressee, April 2, 1942; subject: Operations in Western Europe, 5 Exec. 1, OPD Files, Department of the Army.

7. The President's unconditional surrender formula is mentioned in Minutes JCS meeting, January 7, 1943. OPD Exec. 10, Item 45, Department of the Army.

8. Allied Force Headquarters, *Commander-in-Chief's Dispatch,* p. 40.

9. Marshall, *Biennial Report,* July 1, 1941–June 30, 1943, p. 43.

10. Anderson, op. cit.

11. Ibid.

12. Notes on Constantine Conference, *Diary, Office C-in-C,* Book V, p. A-160.

13. Ibid. "It is inadvisable," said the C-in-C, "to risk our presently smaller force to flank attacks from Rommel on the south and Von Arnim on the north. The Fredendall force must be held as a mobile reserve." Also extract of letter, Eisenhower to Anderson, January 26, 1943, "C. to protect your right (south) flank, I deem it essential that you keep the bulk of the 1st Armored Division well concentrated." AFHQ, G-3 Div. Ops 58/2.1 Ops in Tunisia, AGO.

14. Extract from minutes of meeting, C-in-C and G.O.C., First Army, 1000 hours, February 1, 1943: "The Commander-in-Chief gave the following rulings: ". . . 1st Armored Division must be kept and used concentrated." AFHQ, G-3 Div. Ops 58/2.1, Ops in Tunisia, AGO.

15. *II Corps—Report of Operations, Tunisia,* p. 7.

16. *II Corps. A Brief History,* pp. 17, 18.

17. Message 255, General Eisenhower to General Marshall, February 15, 1943, AGO.

18. "At daylight on the 14th of February, the enemy attacked our positions in front of Faid." *II Corps—Report of Operations, Tunisia,* p. 7.

19. General Eisenhower's memorandum for record, February 25, 1943, General Eisenhower's personal files.

20. Anderson, op. cit.

21. Oral report, C. of S., Twelfth Air Force, to General Eisenhower, recorded in *Diary, Office C-in-C,* Book V, pp. 247–48.

22. Anderson, op. cit.

23. Memo, Brigadier Whitely for General Rooks, January 22, 1943, and memo, General Rooks for C/S, January 22, 1943, AFHQ, G-3 Div. Ops 58/2.1 Ops in Tunisia, AGO.

24. *II Corps After Action Reports,* February 14–23, AGO.
25. Allied Force Headquarters, *Commander-in-Chief's Dispatch,* p. 41.
26. *II Corps—Report of Operations, Tunisia,* p. 2 and overlay opposite p. 2.
27. *Diary, Office C-in-C,* Book V, p. A-197.
28. Message 71814, C. of S., ASF to CG, SOS, USAFIME for Somervell, January 28, 1943, AGO.
29. *History of the Twelfth Air Force,* Vol. II, pp. 26–34.
30. Tripoli was captured January 23, 1943, and the harbor was in use by February 3. Montgomery, op. cit., p. 44.
31. AFHQ G.O. 20, effective February 21, 1943, AGO.
32. General Patton assumed command on March 5, 1943. *Outline History of the II Corps,* p. 2.
33. Ibid.
34. Montgomery, op. cit., p. 57.
35. Ibid., pp. 60–68.
36. Interview with Lieutenant Colonel C. V. Whitney, Archives of the AAF Historical Office, 616.101, April 1943, pp. 12, 13.
37. The 34th Division was under command of 9 British Corps for the Fondouk operation. *II Corps—Report of Operations, Tunisia,* p. 9.
38. Message 5940, General Marshall to General Eisenhower, April 14, 1943, and General Eisenhower's reply, 4330, April 15, AGO.
39. Ibid.
40. Anderson, op. cit.
41. *II Corps. A Brief History,* p. 18.
42. Montgomery, op. cit., pp. 75, 76.
43. *II Corps—Report of Operations to Capture Bizerte and Surrounding Territory,* April 23–May 9, 1943, p. 5.
44. Montgomery, op. cit., p. 76.
45. Anderson, op. cit.
46. *OPD Diary,* May 18, 1943, Message CM-IN-11238.
47. Ibid., May 25, 1943.

CHAPTER 9: Husky

1. Marshall, *Biennial Report,* July 1, 1941–June 30, 1943, Casablanca Conference, p. 43.
2. Field Marshal the Viscount Alexander of Tunis, *The Conquest of Sicily, Despatch,* July 10–August 17, 1943, p. 1.
3. *The Ploesti Mission of 1 August, 1943,* Assistant Chief of Air Staff, Intelligence, Historical Division, pp. 23–25.
4. Ibid., pp. 25–26. "On May 24 [1943] Col. Jacob E. Smart presented the matter to General Eisenhower."
5. Ibid., pp. 80–101.

6. The Halverson raid was executed on June 12, 1942. Ibid., pp. 14–19.
7. *Report of Operations of the United States Seventh Army in the Sicilian Campaign,* pp. a-6, 7.
8. Major General Sir Francis de Guingand, *Operation Victory,* Hodder and Stoughton, London, 1947, p. 269. Montgomery, op. cit., pp. 85–89.
9. Alexander of Tunis, op. cit., p. 3.
10. Ibid., pp. 3–7; also *Report of Operations of the United States Seventh Army in the Sicilian Campaign,* p. a-4 and Plate 1.
11. De Guingand, op. cit., pp. 272–81. Montgomery, op. cit., pp. 85–89.
12. Alexander of Tunis, op. cit., pp. 10, 11.
13. Ibid., p. 17.
14. Ibid., pp. 18–20.
15. *History of the Twelfth Air Force,* Vol. III, p. 11.
16. Report on surrender of Pantelleria, Lieutenant Commander G. A. Martelli, R.N., *Diary, Office C-in-C,* Book VI, pp. A-495–A-498.
17. Ibid., pp. A-459–A-464.
18. *History of the Twelfth Air Force,* Vol. III, p. 9.
19. *Diary, Office C-in-C,* Book VI, pp. A-427–A-430.
20. Notes on conference held June 3, 1943, Ibid., pp. A-451–A-453.
21. Marshall, *Biennial Report,* July 1, 1943–June 30, 1945, p. 11.
22. Railroad yards at Rome were bombed on July 19 and again on August 13, 1943. *History of the Twelfth Air Force,* Vol. III, pp. 51, 52.
23. *Diary, Office C-in-C,* Book VI, pp. A-481–A-483.
24. Alexander of Tunis, op. cit., pp. 20, 21.
25. General Eisenhower arrived at Malta on July 8, 1943. *Diary, Office C-in-C,* Book VII, p. A-535.
26. Message 123, General Eisenhower to General Marshall, July 9, 1943, AGO.

CHAPTER 10: Sicily and Salerno

1. Messages 128, 130, 131, all July 10, 1943, and Message 140, July 11, 1943, General Eisenhower to AGWAR and USFOR, AGO.
2. *Report of Operations of the United States Seventh Army in the Sicilian Campaign,* pp. b-4–6.
3. Notes on General Eisenhower's visit to Sicilian beaches, *Diary, Office C-in-C,* Book VII, pp. A-576–A-581.
4. De Guingand, op. cit., pp. 296–300.
5. *Report of Operations of the United States Seventh Army in the Sicilian Campaign,* p. b-10.
6. King Victor Emmanuel announced on July 25, 1943, the resignation of Prime Minister Mussolini and his cabinet. *United States and Italy,* 1936–46, Documentary Record, Department of State, p. 44.

7. *Report of Operations of the United States Seventh Army in the Sicilian Campaign,* pp. b-14–16.

8. Ibid., pp. b-18–20, 22.

9. Ibid., pp. b-16, 20.

10. Ibid., p. b-22. De Guingand, op. cit., p. 306.

11. Message W8528, General Eisenhower to General Marshall, August 28, 1943, AGO.

12. *History of the Twelfth Air Force,* Vol. III, pp. 15–22, 29.

13. Memoranda relative to the incident, *Diary, Office C-in-C,* Book VII, p. A-656; Book VIII, pp. A-673, A-678, A-716, A-914–A-922.

14. Message W-6017, General Eisenhower to General Marshall, November 24, 1943, AGO.

15. Ibid.

16. Résumé of the handling of the incident in respect to press and radio representatives, *Diary, Office C-in-C,* Book VIII, pp. A-914–A-922.

17. Ibid.

18. *United States and Italy,* pp. 44, 219.

19. Message 4488, General Devers to General Eisenhower, August 17, 1943, AFHA incoming, AGO.

20. General Taylor's companion was Colonel Gardner, U. S. Air Forces. Brief outline of their visit to Rome is contained in account of Brigadier Strong's (AFHQ-G-2) press conference about September 8, 1944, *Diary, Office C-in-C,* Book VIII, pp. A-768–A-770.

21. *Salerno, American Operations from the Beaches to the Volturno,* September 9–October 6, 1943, MID, War Department, pp. 7–9. *History of the Fifth Army,* January 5–October 6, 1943, Vol. I, pp. 25–30.

22. De Guingand, op. cit., p. 317.

23. Notes relative to armistice terms, *Diary, Office C-in-C,* Book VIII, p. A-723.

24. Ibid., p. A-723.

25. Message, General Eisenhower to Marshal Badoglio, September 8, 1943, Ibid., p. A-737.

26. New York *Herald Tribune,* September 9, 1943.

27. *Salerno,* p. 9.

28. Ibid., pp. 54–80. *Fifth Army History,* Vol. I, pp. 37–41.

29. *Salerno,* p. 74.

30. Marshall, *Biennial Report,* July 1, 1943–June 30, 1945, p. 11.

31. Montgomery, op. cit., pp. 127, 128.

32. *Supreme Commander's Dispatch, Italian Campaign,* September 3, 1943, to January 8, 1944, p. 39.

33. *Fifth Army History,* Vol. I, p. 47.

34. Message, General Eisenhower to CCS, October 11, 1943, AGO.

35. Ibid. Also message from the Prime Minister quoted in *Diary, Office C-in-C,* Book VIII, p. A-847.

36. Notes relative to the conference with commanders-in-chief, Middle East, and Message, Prime Minister, on subject, Ibid., pp. A-849, 850.

37. Marshall, *Biennial Report*, July 1, 1943–June 30, 1945, pp. 90, 91.

CHAPTER 11: Cairo Conference

1. *Sextant Conference*, November 22–December 7, 1943, papers and minutes of the Sextant and Eureka Conferences, Office U. S. Secretary, Office CCS, AGO, pp. 377–511.

2. Message, Admiral King to General Eisenhower, November 17, 1943, outlined in *Diary, Office C-in-C*, Book IX, p. A-901.

3. General Eisenhower's memorandum for record, Ibid., pp. A-929, 930.

4. Report on Admiral Cunningham's conversation with General Eisenhower, October 8, 1943, Ibid., p. A-848.

5. Admiral King's conversation with General Eisenhower on Overlord command briefed, Ibid., p. A-907.

6. *Sextant Conference*, minutes of meeting, November 26, 1943, AGO.

7. Ibid; also General Eisenhower's memorandum for record, *Diary, Office C-in-C*, Book IX, pp. A-932–A-933.

8. *The Dieppe Raid* (combined report), Combined Operations Headquarters, 1942, AGO.

9. General Eisenhower's memorandum for record, *Diary, Office C-in-C*, Book IX, pp. A-932–A-933.

10. CCS 426/1, December 6, 1943, AGO.

CHAPTER 12: Italy

1. *Diary, Office C-in-C*, Book IX, p. A-948.

2. General Eisenhower's visits to the front in latter part of December 1943 reported, Ibid., pp. A-949, A-954, A-956, A-957.

3. *The Winter Line*, Military Intelligence Division, U. S. War Department, p. 1.

4. The assault on the Camino feature described, Ibid., pp. 15–28.

5. Ibid., pp. 1–7 and Map No. 2. De Guingand, op. cit., pp. 328–34.

6. *History of the Fifth Army*, Vol. II, p. 8 and Map No. 1. Field Marshal Montgomery, op. cit., pp. 131–39.

7. The U. S. 88th and 85th Divisions were sent to the theater and entered the line in March and April 1944. In the fall of 1944 the U. S. 91st Division, the 92d (one of the Army's two Negro divisions), and a Brazilian division arrived. Marshall, *Biennial Report*, July 1, 1943–June 30, 1945, pp. 22, 23.

8. Commander Walter Karig, U.S.N.R., with Lieutenant Earl Burton, U.S.N.R., and Lieutenant Stephan L. Freeland, U.S.N.R., *Battle Report, The Atlantic War*, Farrar and Rinehart, Inc., New York, 1946, pp. 274–78.

9. Montgomery, op. cit., p. 149 and Map 16. *Operations in Sicily and Italy,* Department of Military Art and Engineering, U. S. Military Academy, 1945, pp. 64–66 and Map 13.

10. General Eisenhower met the President on December 7, 1943. *Diary, Office C-in-C,* Book IX, pp. A-937, A-938.

11. Ibid., pp. A-938, A-939.

12. Ibid., p. A-941.

13. The combined Chiefs of Staff informed General Eisenhower on December 10, 1943, that their recommended title, Supreme Commander Allied Expeditionary Force, had the Prime Minister's approval but not as yet the President's. Message Out 3623, AGO.

14. General Eisenhower's insistence on retaining General Smith as his C. of S. is recorded in *Diary, Office C-in-C,* Book IX, p. A-946.

15. "If the British would give him to me I would like to have Alexander." Extract letter, General Eisenhower to General Marshall, December 17, 1943, General Eisenhower's personal files.

16. Montgomery, *Despatch* submitted to the Secretary of State for War, British Information Service, New York, December 1946, pp. 5, 6.

17. Ibid., p. 5.

18. "The President proudly announced the appointment of General Eisenhower as Supreme Commander Allied Expeditionary Forces." New York *Times,* December 25, 1943.

19. General Sir Henry Maitland Wilson, *Report by the Supreme Allied Commander, Mediterranean Theater,* to the CCS on the Italian campaign, January 8, 1944–May 10, 1944, p. 6.

20. Ibid., pp. 7, 8.

21. Prior to the Salerno assault it was estimated there were 18 German divisions in Italy. "At this time [after Anzio] Kesselring had some 26 divisions in Italy." *Operations in Sicily and Italy,* p. 76.

22. Message 187, General Eisenhower to General Marshall, December 23, 1943, AGO.

23. Message 2-90175, General Marshall to General Eisenhower, January 11, 1945, refers to Generals Bradley, Bull, and Bonesteel as successive "Eyes and Ears," AGO.

24. Messages 5810, General Marshall to General Eisenhower, December 28, 1943, and W8781, General Eisenhower to General Marshall, December 29, 1943, AGO.

25. Message 8792, General Eisenhower to General Marshall, December 29, 1943, AGO.

26. Ibid., and Message 5898, General Marshall to General Eisenhower, December 29, 1943, AGO.

27. *Diary, Office C-in-C,* Book X, p. A-981.

28. General Eisenhower's memorandum for record, February 7, 1944, Ibid., p. A-1062.

29. General Eisenhower's early views as to the necessity for strengthening the assault were shared by other leaders. At the Quadrant Conference held

in Quebec the Prime Minister stated: "The Overlord plan seems sound but should be strengthened," and General Marshall said, "There is a possibility that an attack on the inside of the Cotentin Peninsula would be included in the initial assault if more landing craft could be made available." Minutes of the 2d Meeting, *CCS Quadrant Conference,* August 23, 1943, AGO.

30. Field Marshal the Viscount Montgomery of Alamein, *Normandy to the Baltic,* Hutchinson & Co. Ltd., London, 1947, pp. 5, 6.

31. Messages W8550 and W8781, General Eisenhower to General Marshall, December 25 and 29, 1943, respectively, AGO.

32. *Diary, Office C-in-C,* Book X, p. A-981.

33. Ibid., p. A-982.

CHAPTER 13: Planning Overlord

1. Notes relative to moving headquarters to Bushey Park, *Diary, Office C-in-C,* Book X, pp. A-997, A-1053, A-1081; Book XI, p. 1126.

2. Memorandum, General Eisenhower to Air Chief Marshal Tedder, February 29, 1944, Ibid., Book X, p. 1120.

3. Ibid., Book XI, pp. 1121, 1122.

4. Letters, Air Chief Marshal Portal to General Eisenhower with inclosures, March 7, 9, 1944, Ibid., pp. 1126–30.

5. Messages B-316, March 21 and S-50310, April 12, 1944, General Eisenhower to General Marshall, AGO. Air Chief Marshal Sir Trafford Leigh-Mallory, *Despatch* to the Supreme Commander, AEF, pp. 2, 3.

6. Ibid., pp. 1–4.

7. Montgomery, *Despatch,* p. 5.

8. General Eisenhower's instructions to General Patton relative to public statements, *Diary, Office C-in-C,* Book X, p. A-1017.

9. Ibid., Book XI, p. 1229.

10. Messages W-28234, April 27, and W-29722, April 29, General Marshall to General Eisenhower; S-50908, April 28, S-50965, April 30, S-51128, May 3, General Eisenhower to General Marshall; W-30586, May 2, General McNarney to General Eisenhower; also letter, Secretary Stimson to General Eisenhower, May 5, AGO.

11. The directive is quoted in *Report by the Supreme Commander to the Combined Chiefs of Staff on the Operations in Europe of the AEF,* June 6, 1944–May 8, 1945, pp. vi, vii.

12. De Guingand, op. cit., pp. 410–13, also Map 47.

13. Ibid., pp. 412, 413.

14. *The Seventh United States Army Report of Operations,* France and Germany, 1944–45, Vol. I, pp. 57–70.

15. SHAEF/18008/plans, subject: Post Neptune—Courses of action after the capture of the lodgment area, Sec. I, May 4, 1944, and approved with changes by General Eisenhower, May 27, 1944, AGO.

16. *Report by the Supreme Commander.*

17. Minutes of the 3d Plenary Session, Teheran, November 30, 1943, *Sextant Conference,* November–December 1943, AGO.

18. Leigh-Mallory, *Despatch,* pp. 8, 33–36.

19. Message, General Eisenhower to CCS, *Diary, Office C-in-C,* Book X, pp. A-1007–A-1009.

20. Montgomery of Alamein, *Normandy to the Baltic,* pp. 36, 37.

21. *The Seventh United States Army Report of Operations,* Vol. I, pp. 10–14, 23–26.

22. Letters, General Montgomery to General Eisenhower, February 19, 21, 1944, advocated abandoning Anvil. General Eisenhower's personal files of correspondence with General Montgomery.

23. Letter, General Eisenhower to General Montgomery, February 21, 1944, General Eisenhower's personal files.

24. Marshall, *Biennial Report,* July 1, 1943–June 30, 1945, p. 30.

25. Letters relative to aerial bombardment of French railroad centers, Prime Minister Churchill and General Eisenhower, April 3 and 5, 1944, General Eisenhower's personal files.

26. Leigh-Mallory, *Despatch,* Pars. 30, 95, 100, 103d, 495.

27. Marshall, *Biennial Report,* July 1, 1943–June 30, 1945, pp. 30–32.

28. SHAEF G-3 War Room Daily Summaries, February 22, 1945, March 23, 25, 1945, AGO. *Third Report of the Commanding General of the Army Air Forces to Secretary of War,* November 12, 1945, p. 17.

29. Marshall, *Biennial Report,* July 1, 1943–June 30, 1945, Our Weapons, pp. 95–100.

30. Karig, et al., op. cit., pp. 343–57.

31. Notes on the experimental work of the British 79th Armored Division are contained in *Diary, Office C-in-C,* Book X, pp. A-1022–A-1026.

32. Letter, Prime Minister Churchill to General Eisenhower, May 31, 1944, Ibid., Book XII, pp. 1322, 1323.

33. De Guingand, op. cit., pp. 367, 368, 372.

34. Ibid., pp. 372–74.

35. *Ninth Air Force Invasion Activities,* April through June 1944, Historical Division, Ninth Air Force, 533.04B, pp. 40–43. Leigh-Mallory, *Despatch,* Pars. 217–26.

36. De Guingand, op. cit., pp. 356–62.

37. Marshall, *Biennial Report,* July 1, 1943–June 30, 1945, pp. 32, 33.

38. "Because we failed in the initial phases to gain the ground which was needed in the vicinity of Caen, the development of all the preselected sites could not be started" (underlining supplied). Leigh-Mallory, *Despatch,* Par. 427.

39. *First United States Army Report of Operations,* October 20, 1943–August 1, 1944, Book I, p. 56.

40. Leigh-Mallory, *Despatch,* Pars. 25–35.

41. Karig, et al., op. cit., pp. 300–08.

42. Notes regarding the final review of plans for Overlord, *Diary, Office C-in-C,* Book XI, p. 1254.

43. Copy of Air Chief Marshal Leigh-Mallory's letter to General Eisenhower and the reply thereto, Ibid., pp. 1307–09, 1344.

44. Henry L. Stimson and McGeorge Bundy, *On Active Service in Peace and War,* Harper and Brothers, New York, 1948, pp. 545–47.

45. Ibid., pp. 545–51.

46. Letter, Prime Minister Churchill to General Eisenhower, May 31, 1944, and General Eisenhower's reply, June 1, 1944; also report of telephone conversation, General Eisenhower to General Smith, June 5, 1944, *Diary, Office C-in-C,* Book XII, pp. 1322–24, 1333.

47. De Guingand, op. cit., pp. 372, 373.

48. "The actual decision was confirmed and made final this morning [June 5] at 4:15 after all the weather dope had been assembled. The tentative decision was made at the meeting last night, subject to review of latest weather information at this morning's meeting." Extract from notes on D-day decision, *Diary, Office C-in-C,* Book XII, p. 1331.

49. Notes regarding the Prime Minister's desire to accompany the invasion assault, Ibid., pp. 1320, 1321, 1328.

CHAPTER 14: D-day and Lodgment

1. *First United States Army Report of Operations,* Book I, p. 48.

2. A brief analysis of Rommel's defensive plan and dispositions, Montgomery *Despatch,* pp. 7–13.

3. De Guingand, op. cit., p. 396.

4. *First United States Army Report of Operations,* Book I, pp. 56–63.

5. "About 25 pilotless aircraft came across the channel last night [June 12] and 19 are known to have hit land, 4 in the London Area." Note re V-1, *Diary, Office C-in-C,* Book XII, p. 1365; also pp. 1371, 1378, 1379, 1396, 1398.

6. Notes relative to the V-2 bomb, Ibid., p. 1498; Book XIII, pp. 1561, 1572, 1615. SHAEF Cositintrep, August 1, 1944, AGO.

7. Leigh-Mallory, *Despatch,* Pars. 33, 169–82. *Ninth Air Force Invasion Activities,* pp. 1, 2.

8. Letter Orders, M502, to Generals Bradley and Dempsey, Tac. Hq., 21st Army Group, June 18, 1944, General Eisenhower's personal files.

9. Karig, et al., op. cit., pp. 343–57.

10. Ibid., pp. 370, 371.

11. Montgomery, *Despatch,* p. 30.

12. Lieutenant Colonel James F. Gault, British Army, aide to General Eisenhower, memorandum relative General Eisenhower's visit to France, July 1–5, 1944, notes that this trip is the general's sixth trip to France. *Diary, Office C-in-C,* Book XII, inclosure following p. 1433.

CHAPTER 15: Breakout

1. Marshall, *Biennial Report,* July 1, 1943–June 30, 1945, p. 34.

2. De Guingand, op. cit., Map 43, p. 359.

3. Letter Orders, M505 to Generals Bradley and Dempsey, Tac. Hq., 21st Army Group, June 30, 1944, General Eisenhower's personal files.

4. *First United States Army Report of Operations,* Book I, p. 122.

5. SHAEF G-3 War Room Daily Summaries 26, 28, 29, 30, July 2, 4, 5, 6, 1944, AGO.

6. Leigh-Mallory, *Despatch,* Pars. 287, 288, 296.

7. *First United States Army Report of Operations,* Book I, p. 99.

8. *Report of Operations, Final After Action Report, 12th Army Group,* Vol. 5, p. 38.

9. Trévières, near which General Eisenhower's personal headquarters was located, is approximately equidistant from Bayeux, St. Lô, and Isigny.

10. "The leading Battalion of the 47th Infantry, 9th Division, and the 120th Infantry of the 30th Division suffered severe casualties, and direct hits were received on certain of the artillery Battalion installations. The 743d Tank Battalion attached to the 30th Division likewise received heavy casualties." *First United States Army Report of Operations,* Book I, p. 99. General McNair's death is reported in Marshall, *Biennial Report,* July 1, 1943–June 30, 1945, p. 35.

11. *After Action Report, Third United States Army,* August 1, 1944–May 9, 1945, Vol. I, p. 16.

12. General Eisenhower's memorandum concerning visit to General Bradley's headquarters, August 8, 1944, *Diary, Office C-in-C,* Book XIII, p. 1579.

13. Message S-57189, General Eisenhower to General Marshall, August 9, 1944, AGO.

14. *First United States Army Report of Operations,* Vol. I, pp. 5–13.

15. Leigh-Mallory, *Despatch,* Pars. 288–95.

16. 21st Army Group General Operational Situation and Direction, M-518, August 11, 1944, General Eisenhower's personal files.

17. 12th Army Group's Letter of Instructions, No. 4, August 8, 1944. *Report of Operations, Final After Action Report, 12th Army Group,* Vol. V, pp. 77, 78.

18. *After Action Report, Third U. S. Army,* Vol. I, Map, p. 31.

19. Montgomery, *Despatch,* pp. 30, 39.

20. General Eisenhower's Order of the Day, August 13, 1944, quoted in full in *Diary, Office C-in-C,* Book XIII, pp. 1596, 1597.

21. General Bradley reviews the 21st–12th Army Group boundary situation in his letter to General Eisenhower, September 10, 1944, General Eisenhower's personal files.

22. *Ninth United States Army Operations,* Brest-Crozon, September 1944, Vol. I, pp. 16, 17.

23. Ibid., pp. 26–28.

24. Notes on General Eisenhower's press conference of August 15, 1944, *Diary, Office C-in-C,* Book XIII, pp. 1599, 1600.

25. Record of the conversations with Prime Minister Churchill regarding Dragoon, formerly Anvil, and cables on the subject, Ibid., pp. 1573–76.

26. General Eisenhower's memorandum for record, Ibid., pp. 1578, 1579.

27. Letters, General Eisenhower to Prime Minister Churchill and to General Marshall, August 11, 1944, General Eisenhower's personal files.

28. Letter, General Eisenhower to Field Marshal Montgomery, October 13, 1944, General Eisenhower's personal files.

29. Letter, Field Marshal Montgomery to General Eisenhower, June 7, 1945, General Eisenhower's personal files.

30. Letter, General Eisenhower to Field Marshal Montgomery, June 8, 1945, General Eisenhower's personal files.

CHAPTER 16: Pursuit and the Battle of Supply

1. SHAEF G-3 War Room Daily Summary, September 1, 1944, AGO. *SC-AI-9, Allied vs. Axis Air Strength Report.* Figures shown for combat planes are planes actually with squadrons; total inventory was much larger.

2. *Staff Officers' Field Manual,* Organization, Technical and Logistical Data, F.M. 101–10, AGO.

3. General Eisenhower's directive for the operations is recorded in *Diary, Office C-in-C,* Book XIII, pp. 1642, 1643.

4. The Seventh Army landed on the south of France on August 15. *The Seventh United States Army Report of Operations,* Vol. I, pp. 101–49.

5. The story of the entire planning period for Anvil, later called Dragoon, Ibid., Vol. I, pp. 1–26, 45–57.

6. Ibid., pp. 271, 283–84.

7. *First United States Army Report of Operations,* Vol. I, pp. 33–38.

8. Lieutenant Colonel James F. Gault, memorandum report on the visit to Paris, *Diary, Office C-in-C,* Book XIII, pp. 1638–40.

9. Message CPA-90230, General Eisenhower to General Marshall, August 19, 1944, AGO.

10. General Eisenhower's report to the CCS of enemy losses up to late August and released to the press August 31, 1944, is recorded in *Diary, Office C-in-C,* Book XIII, pp. 1650, 1651.

11. SHAEF G-2 Report on Enemy Morale, Ibid., pp. 1653, 1654.

12. A discussion of the supply difficulties is contained in *Report by the Supreme Commander,* pp. 59, 60.

13. *440th Troop Carrier Group History,* D. S. Europe, p. 60.

14. Message M-160, Field Marshal Montgomery to General Eisenhower, September 4, 1944, General Eisenhower's personal files.

15. Message, General Eisenhower to CCS and principal commanders, on or about September 12, 1944, contains résumé C-in-C's decisions following Brussels conference, *Diary, Office C-in-C,* Book XIII, pp. 1702–04.

16. Montgomery, *Despatch,* p. 49.

17. Directive, CCS to General Eisenhower, reference Strategic Bomber Forces, *Diary, Office C-in-C,* Book XIII, pp. 1720–22.

18. *The Seventh United States Army Report of Operations,* Vol. I, pp. 271, 284.

19. Ibid., p. 272. *Ninth United States Army Operations,* Vol. II, pp. 1–15.

20. The battle of Arnhem is outlined in De Guingand, op. cit., pp. 416–19.

21. *First United States Army Report of Operations,* Vol. I, pp. 57–62.

22. U. S. Ninth Army became operational at 1200 hrs., September 5, 1944. *Report of Operations, Final After Action Report, 12th Army Group,* Vol. V, p. 38.

23. *The Administrative and Logistical History of the European Theater of Operations,* Part XI, Basic Needs of the ETO Soldier, Vol. II, pp. 128–39.

24. Marshall, *Biennial Report,* July 1, 1943–June 30, 1945, Price of Victory Section, pp. 108, 109.

CHAPTER 17: Autumn Fighting on Germany's Frontier

1. Extract, memorandum, General Bradley to General Eisenhower, September 21, 1944, General Eisenhower's personal files.

2. "Over 900 locomotives and a third of the rolling stock used had to be shipped over from Allied sources." *Report by the Supreme Commander,* p. 60.

3. *Order of Battle of the United States Army,* World War II, European Theater of Operations, Office of the Theater Historian, pp. 573, 574. SHAEF G-3 Daily War Room Summary, October 2, 1944, AGO.

4. *SC-A1-9, Allied vs. Axis Air Strength Report* for October 30, 1944, AGO. Figures shown are planes actually with squadrons; total inventory figures are considerably larger.

5. Montgomery, *Despatch,* pp. 50, 51.

6. Ibid., p. 50.

7. Casualty figures for the Sicilian campaign, exclusive of Royal Air Force and Royal Navy casualties (not readily available), totaled 23,428. Statistical Section, Historical Division, War Department Special Staff.

8. *Ninth United States Army Operations,* IV, Offensive in November, Vol. I, 4th Information and Historical Service, p. 1.

9. *Report of Operations, Final After Action Report, 12th Army Group,* Vol. V, p. 42. *First United States Army Report of Operations,* Vol. I, p. 73.

10. Ibid., pp. 165–68.

11. *First United States Army Report of Operations,* Vol. I, pp. 95–97.

12. *After Action Report, Third United States Army,* Vol. I, pp. 127–38.

13. *The Seventh United States Army Report of Operations,* Vol. II, pp. 397–422.

14. Letter, General Eisenhower to General Marshall, January 12, 1945, General Eisenhower's personal files.

15. Marshall, *Biennial Report,* July 1, 1943–June 30, 1945, Manpower Balance Section, pp. 101–07.

16. Message W-50676, General Marshall to General Eisenhower, October 22, 1944, AGO.

17. *Report of the General Board,* United States Forces, European Theater, Live Entertainment, Study No. 117, and Special Service Clubs, Study No. 121, AGO.

18. *Operations Reports MB-858, Adm. 20 A,* American Red Cross, AGO.

19. A discussion of the Air Staff's exploration of the possibility of destroying the thirty-one Rhine bridges is contained in *Report by the Supreme Commander,* p. 84.

20. The attack on oil is summarized in *The United States Strategic Bombing Survey* (European War), September 30, 1945, pp. 8–10.

21. Marshall, *Biennial Report,* July 1, 1943–June 30, 1945, pp. 182, 183, 186. SHAEF G-3 War Room Daily Summary 337, May 9, 1945, shows 630, 601 vehicles unloaded on the Continent for the American Twelfth and Sixth Army Groups, only, by May 8, 1945, AGO.

22. Marshall, *Biennial Report,* July 1, 1943–June 30, 1945, p. 44.

23. "In the meantime operations in the South will go forward so long as the prospects continue good." Extract, Message S-69334 (SCAF 141), General Eisenhower to the CCS, December 3, 1944, AGO.

24. *First United States Army Report of Operations,* Vol. I, pp. 95–98.

25. Ibid., G-2 Estimate No. 37, Hq. First U. S. Army, December 10, 1944, and Records of Intelligence, December 12, 14, 15, pp. 100–03. *After Action Report, Third United States Army,* Vol. I, pp. 164, 165.

CHAPTER 18: Hitler's Last Bid

1. Report of General Eisenhower's and General Bradley's consideration of the first news concerning the German offensive, *Diary, Office C-in-C,* Book XIV, p. 1893.

2. Notes regarding the decision to order in the 7th and 10th Armored Divisions and to alert the army commanders, Ibid., p. 1893.

3. Movement of the 82d and 101st Airborne Divisions is reported in *Report of Operations, Final After Action Report, 12th Army Group,* Vol. V, p. 43, and SHAEF G-3 War Room Daily Summaries for 19 and 20 December 1944, AGO.

4. Field Marshal Montgomery's use of the British 30 Corps is discussed in De Guingand, op. cit., pp. 429, 432, 433.

5. General Eisenhower's memorandum of December 23, 1944, on the considerations involved and his decisions during the early days of the Ardennes battle, *Diary, Office C-in-C,* Book XIV, pp. 1906–09.

6. Message S-71400, General Eisenhower to Generals Bradley and Devers, December 18, 1944, AGO.

7. *First United States Army Report of Operations,* Vol. I, pp. 104, 105.

8. Ibid., pp. 103–06, including Situation Map No. 9.

9. De Guingand, op. cit., pp. 427, 428.

10. General Eisenhower's memorandum, December 23, 1944, on early phase, Ardennes battle, *Diary, Office C-in-C*, Book XIV, pp. 1906–09.

11. *First United States Army Report of Operations*, Vol. I, pp. 97, 98, 104–07.

12. Ibid., pp. 105–14, including Situation Maps Nos. 9 and 10.

13. General Eisenhower's memorandum, December 23, 1944, *Diary, Office C-in-C*, Book XIV, p. 1908.

14. Ibid., p. 1909; also Message, Field Marshal Montgomery to General Eisenhower, December 23, 1944, General Eisenhower's personal files.

15. *First United States Army Report of Operations*, Vol. I, chart facing p. 104; also Montgomery of Alamein, *Normandy to the Baltic*, pp. 224–27.

16. *Report of Operations, Final After Action Report, 12th Army Group*, Vol. V, p. 43.

17. Minutes of conference at Verdun, December 19, 1944, *Diary, Office C-in-C*, Book XIV, pp. 1902, 1903.

18. Message SCAF 149, General Eisenhower to CCS and Commanders, December 19, 1944, AGO.

19. Message (number not recorded), General Eisenhower to General Montgomery, December 20, *Diary, Office C-in-C*, Book XIV, p. 1898.

20. General Eisenhower's directive, December 20, 1944, confirming oral orders issued December 19, Ibid., pp. 1897, 1898.

21. *After Action Report, Third United States Army*, Vol. I, p. 172.

22. *The Seventh United States Army Report of Operations*, Vol. II, pp. 579, 580.

23. General Juin's visit and General Eisenhower's attitude at that time regarding the defense of Strasbourg are reported in General Eisenhower's letter, January 2, 1945, addressed to General de Gaulle, General Eisenhower's personal files.

24. General Eisenhower's Order of the Day is quoted in full in *Diary, Office C-in-C*, Book XIV, p. 1910.

25. *Report of Operations, Final After Action Report, 12th Army Group*, Vol. V, p. 43. De Guingand, op. cit., pp. 428, 429.

26. Ibid., pp. 434, 435. Letters, General Eisenhower to General Marshall and to Field Marshal Sir Alan Brooke, February 9 and February 16, 1945, respectively, General Eisenhower's personal files.

27. Message W-84337, General Marshall to General Eisenhower, December 30, 1944, AGO.

28. Message S-73275, General Eisenhower to General Marshall, January 1, 1945, AGO.

29. *Report of Operations, Final After Action Report, 12th Army Group*, Vol. V, p. 44. *After Action Report, Third United States Army*, Vol. I, pp. 176–81.

30. Notes relative to the German plan for assassination of Allied military leaders, *Diary, Office C-in-C*, Book XIV, pp. 1899, 1900.

31. Letter, with enclosed outline plan, General Eisenhower to Field Marshal Montgomery, December 31, 1944, outlines General Eisenhower's inten-

tions as given to Field Marshal Montgomery on December 28, 1944, General Eisenhower's personal files.

32. *After Action Report, Third United States Army,* Vol. I, p. 181.

33. Ibid., pp. 183–88, 203–08.

34. Letter, with enclosed outline plan, General Eisenhower to Field Marshal Montgomery, copy to General Bradley, December 31, 1944, General Eisenhower's personal files.

35. "As to units East of the main position [the Vosges], their integrity must not be endangered." Extract SHAEF message received by Sixth Army Group, January 2, 1945, *6th Army Group History,* Chapter V, p. 108.

36. Message W-87149, General Marshall to General Eisenhower, January 5, 1945; S-73871, General Eisenhower's reply, January 6, 1945, AGO.

37. "There were heavy enemy strafe/bomb attacks against 16 airfields in Brussels area and 168 of our aircraft have been reported lost on the ground." Extract SHAEF G-3 War Room Daily Summary 210, January 2, 1945, AGO.

38. *Report of Operations, Final After Action Report, 12th Army Group,* Vol. V, p. 44.

39. Message S-75872 (SCAF 179), General Eisenhower to General Marshall, January 20, 1945, AGO. *Report by the Supreme Commander,* p. 79.

40. The difference between casualty figures for United States troops (excluding Sixth Army Group) and British and Canadian troops on last reports as of January 15, 1945, and December 15, 1944, show 10,733 killed, 42,316 wounded, 22,636 missing, or a total of 75,685. Not all of these casualties were due to the Ardennes battle. SHAEF G-3 Daily War Room Summaries 197 and 226, December 20, 1944, and January 20, 1945, AGO.

CHAPTER 19: Crossing the Rhine

1. Message S-75871 (SCAF 180), General Eisenhower to CCS, January 20, 1945, AGO.

2. *Report by the Supreme Commander,* p. 83.

3. Ibid.; also letters, Mr. Harriman to General Eisenhower, January 17, 1945, and Marshal Stalin to General Eisenhower, January 15, 1945, General Eisenhower's personal files.

4. Messages W-60507, March 29; W-61337, March 31; W-64244 and W-64349, April 6, 1945; all General Marshall to General Eisenhower. FWD-18331, FWD-18345, March 30, and FWD-18707, April 7, 1945, all General Eisenhower to General Marshall, AGO.

5. *The United States Strategic Bombing Survey,* p. 9.

6. The effect of Allied bombing on enemy aircraft production is outlined in *Third Report of the Commanding General of the Army Air Forces,* pp. 10–16.

7. Message W-89338, General Marshall to General Eisenhower, January 10, 1945, and General Eisenhower's reply, S-74437, January 10, 1945, AGO.

8. Message S-74461, General Eisenhower to General Marshall, January 10, 1945, AGO.

9. This suggestion for an over-all ground commander came from the British Chiefs of Staff. Message W-88777, General Marshall to General Eisenhower, January 8, 1945, AGO. General Eisenhower's views regarding an over-all ground commander are outlined in *Report by the Supreme Commander*, pp. 85, 86.

10. Marshall, *Biennial Report*, July 1, 1943–June 30, 1945, p. 46. Notes on conference with General Marshall, January 28, 1945, *Diary, Office C-in-C*, Book XIV, pp. 2008, 2009.

11. General Eisenhower's plan is contained in Message S-75871 (SCAF 180) to CCS, January 20, 1945, AGO. Messages from General Smith relative to the presentation and discussion of the plan at Malta are quoted in *Diary, Office C-in-C*, Book XV, pp. 2033, 2034.

12. Letter, General Eisenhower to General Marshall, March 26, 1945, General Eisenhower's personal files.

13. Montgomery, *Despatch*, pp. 54–59.

14. *6th Army Group History*, Chapter VI; also Chapter VII, p. 169.

15. *First United States Army Report of Operations*, Vol. I, pp. 155–59.

16. Letter, Field Marshal Montgomery to General Eisenhower, M-547, January 19, 1945, and General Eisenhower's reply, January 21, 1945, General Eisenhower's personal files.

17. Montgomery, *Despatch*, p. 58. Message, Field Marshal Montgomery to General Eisenhower, quoted in *Diary, Office C-in-C*, Book XV, p. 2050.

18. SHAEF G-3 War Room Daily Summaries, February through April 3, 1945, AGO. Montgomery of Alamein, *Normandy to the Baltic*, Map 40, facing p. 233.

19. Message FWD-17822 (SCAF 231), General Eisenhower to Army Group and First Allied Airborne Army Commanders, March 13, 1945, AGO.

20. *Report of Operations, Final After Action Report, 12th Army Group*, Vol. V, pp. 46, 47, and Letter of Instructions No. 16, pp. 122–24.

21. SHAEF G-3 War Room Daily Summaries 263, February 24, 1945, to 275, March 8, 1945, AGO.

22. Ibid., 265, February 26, to 276, March 9, 1945. Message FWD-17645 (SCAF 223), General Eisenhower to Combined Chiefs of Staff, March 8, 1945, AGO. *Report of Operations, Final After Action Report, 12th Army Group*, Vol. V, p. 47.

23. The rapid construction of the bridge by VII Corps engineers under Colonel Young is described by General Eisenhower in letter to General Marshall, March 26, 1945, General Eisenhower's personal files.

24. *Report of Operations, Final After Action Report, 12th Army Group*, Vol. V, p. 47.

25. *After Action Report, Third United States Army*, Vol. I, pp. 253–92.

26. Ibid., pp. 293–300.

27. Message FWD-17655 (SCAF 224), General Eisenhower to Generals Bradley and Devers, March 8, 1945, AGO. Letter of Instructions No. 11, Hq. 6th Army Group, March 10, 1945, *6th Army Group History*, Vol. VIII, pp. 218–20. *Report of Operations, Final After Action Report, 12th Army Group*, Vol. V. p. 47.

28. *After Action Report, Third United States Army,* pp. 305–09. *The Seventh United States Army Report of Operations,* Vol. III, pp. 715, 737–38.

29. *After Action Report, Third United States Army,* Vol. I, p. 313.

30. *The Seventh United States Army Report of Operations,* Vol. III, p. 720.

31. SHAEF G-2 Summary, *Diary, Office C-in-C,* Book XV, pp. 2140–46.

32. SHAEF G-2 Summary, Ibid., p. 2141.

CHAPTER 20: Assault and Encirclement

1. Montgomery, *Despatch,* pp. 59–63. *Conquer, The Story of Ninth Army, 1944-45,* pp. 226–43.

2. SHAEF G-3 War Room Daily Summary 293, March 26, AGO. Montgomery, *Despatch,* pp. 62, 63.

3. In *Conquer,* p. 243, it is stated that 2070 guns supported the XIV Corps. This number, however, included anti-aircraft, tank, and tank destroyer guns, as well as the field artillery. Total casualties for the day were reported as 498. *Conquer,* p. 247. Letter, General Eisenhower to General Marshall, March 26, 1945, reports the assault-crossing casualties, General Eisenhower's personal files.

4. Statistics on the planes and gliders employed, prepared by the Air Force and First Allied Airborne Army, are contained in *Report by the Supreme Commander,* p. 100.

5. Ibid., pp. 100, 101.

6. Letter, General Eisenhower to General Marshall, March 26, 1945, General Eisenhower's personal files.

7. SHAEF G-3 War Room Daily Summaries 289, 290, 291, 292, March 22-25, 1945, AGO.

8. Ibid., 291, 292, March 24, 25, 1945, AGO.

9. *After Action Report, Third United States Army,* Vol. I, pp. 315, 316.

10. *First United States Army Report of Operations,* Vol. I, pp. 43–46.

11. Memorandum of instructions to General Bradley, March 9, 1945, General Bull, G-3 Division, SHAEF, *Diary, Office C-in-C,* Book XV, p. 2105.

12. *After Action Report Third U. S. Army,* Vol. I, p. 324.

13. *The Seventh United States Army Report of Operations,* Vol. III, pp. 741–55.

14. Mannheim was occupied by the 44th Division on March 29. Ibid., pp. 763, 764.

15. SHAEF G-3 War Room Daily Summary 299, April 1, 1945, AGO.

16. *Conquer,* p. 314.

17. Marshall, *Biennial Report,* July 1, 1943–June 30, 1945, pp. 92, 93.

18. General Eisenhower's reasons for his decision against an advance with Berlin as the major objective are outlined in his message FWD-18710 to General Marshall, April 7, 1945, AGO.

19. SHAEF G-2 Summary and Joint Intelligence Committee Report quoted in *Diary, Office C-in-C,* Vol. XV, pp. 2106, 2107, 2114, 2115.

20. Message FWD-18475 (SCAF 261), General Eisenhower to Army Group Commanders, April 2, 1945, AGO.

21. *Report of Operations, Final After Action Report, 12th Army Group*, Vol. V, pp. 48, 49.

22. Message FWD-18264 (SCAF 252), General Eisenhower to Military Mission to Moscow, Personal to Marshal Stalin, March 28, 1945, AGO.

23. Prime Minister Churchill's views relative to General Eisenhower's message to Marshal Stalin are outlined in Message W-60507, General Marshall to General Eisenhower, March 29, 1945, AGO.

24. Ibid.

25. Message FWD-18331, AGO.

26. Message FWD-18345, AGO.

27. Message W-61337, AGO.

28. Message FWD-18707, AGO.

CHAPTER 21: Overrunning Germany

1. SHAEF G-3 War Room Daily Summary 302, April 4, 1945, AGO.

2. *Report of Operations, Final After Action Report, 12th Army Group*, Vol. V, p. 50.

3. Ninth Army's 2d Armored Division reached the Elbe on April 11, 1945. *Conquer*, p. 298.

4. SHAEF G-3 War Room Daily Summary 313, April 15, 1945, AGO.

5. Ibid., 314, April 16, 1945.

6. *After Action Report, Third United States Army*, Vol. II, p. 33.

7. Letter, General Eisenhower to General Marshall, April 15, 1945, General Eisenhower's personal files. Message FWD-19461, General Eisenhower to General Marshall, April 19, 1945, AGO.

8. *Report of Operations, Final After Action Report, 12th Army Group*, Vol. V, p. 50. *First United States Army Report of Operations*, Vol. I, pp. 78, 79.

9. *Conquer*, pp. 290–304.

10. *First United States Army Report of Operations*, Vol. I, pp. 83, 84.

11. Messages FWD-18616 (SCAF 264), April 5, 1945, and FWD-18966 (SCAF 274), April 11, both General Eisenhower to CCS; FWD-19003 (SCAF 275), April 12, 1945, FWD-19274 (SCAF 282), April 15, 1945, FWD-19390 (SCAF 284), April 17, 1945, and FWD-19611 (SCAF 292), April 21, 1945, all General Eisenhower to Military Mission to Moscow; also WX-66731 (FACS 176), April 11, 1945, and W-70884 (FACS 191), April 21, 1945, to General Eisenhower from the CCS, AGO.

12. Montgomery, *Despatch*, p. 66.

13. De Guingand, op. cit., pp. 437–40.

14. *6th Army Group History*, Chapter IX, April 1945, pp. 246–50.

15. SHAEF G-3 War Room Daily Summaries 303, April 5–320, April 22, 1945, AGO.

16. *6th Army Group History*, Chapter IX, April 1945, pp. 273, 281, 282. Messages FWD-20127 (SCAF 319), April 28, 1945, and FWD-20425 (SCAF 328), General Eisenhower to CCS, AGO. Message, President Truman to General de Gaulle, and General de Gaulle's reply, quoted in *Diary, Office C-in-C*, Book XV, under date May 3, 1945.

17. Messages FWD-21506 (SCAF 393), May 15, and FWD-22095 (SCAF 408), May 21, 1945, General Eisenhower to CCS, AGO.

18. SHAEF G-2 Summary, *Diary, Office C-in-C*, Book XV, under date April 22, 1945.

19. Ibid. A discussion of the Redoubt area is contained in *Report by the Supreme Commander*, pp. 112, 113.

20. General Eisenhower's proffered assistance to Field Marshal Montgomery for the advance on Lübeck is outlined in his letter to Field Marshal Brooke, April 27, 1945, General Eisenhower's personal files.

21. Messages FWD-19751 (SCAF 300), April 23, 1945, General Eisenhower to CCS; FWD-19833 (SCAF 305), April 24, and FWD-19940 (SCAF 307), April 25, 1945, both General Eisenhower to Military Mission to Moscow; FWD-20047 (SCAF 314), April 27, 1945, General Eisenhower to CCS; W-72082 (FACS 194), April 24, and W-72737 (FACS 199), April 25, 1945, both CCS to General Eisenhower, AGO.

22. General Smith's memorandum for General Eisenhower, subject: Meeting with German Representatives in Holland, May 1, 1945, *Diary, Office C-in-C*, Book XV, under date May 1, 1945.

23. *6th Army Group History*, Chapter IX, April 1945, pp. 274–88.

24. *After Action Report, Third United States Army*, Vol. I, pp. 360–87.

25. Ibid., pp. 387–91.

26. *The Seventh United States Army Report of Operations*, Vol. III, pp. 813–37, 852–56.

27. Statistics compiled in May 1945 on April Air Supply are quoted in *Report by the Supreme Commander*, p. 113.

28. SHAEF G-3 Daily War Room Summary 317, April 19, 1945, AGO.

29. SHAEF G-3 Daily War Room Summary 324, April 26, 1945, AGO.

30. British report of Bernadotte's conference with Himmler referred to in Message W-73250, General Marshall to General Eisenhower, April 26, 1945, AGO. The proposal is outlined in *Report by the Supreme Commander*, p. 118.

31. Ibid.

32. Ibid.; also Messages W-73283, April 26, 1945, General Marshall to General Eisenhower, and FWD-20032, April 27, 1945, in reply, AGO.

33. Message FWD-20535 (SCAF 334), May 4, 1945, General Eisenhower to CCS, AGO. *6th Army Group History*, Chapter 10, May 1945, pp. 8–23.

34. De Guingand, op. cit., pp. 453, 454.

35. Messages FWD-20608 (SCAF 338), May 4, and FWD-20625 (SCAF 340), May 5, 1945, both General Eisenhower to CCS, AGO.

36. Message FWD-20635 (SCAF 341), May 5, 1945, General Eisenhower to Military Mission to Moscow, CCS, AGO.

37. Messages FWD-20692 (SCAF 345), May 5; FWD-20704 (SCAF 346), May 5; FWD-20713 (SCAF 347), May 5; FWD-20714 (SCAF 348), May 6; FWD-20797 (SCAF 354), May 6; and FWD-20800 (SCAF 357), May 7, 1945—all to CCS and/or Military Mission to Moscow, from General Eisenhower, AGO.

CHAPTER 22: Victory's Aftermath

1. Messages FWD-20804 (SCAF 359), FWD-20813 (SCAF 361), FWD-20862 (SCAF 365), and FWD-20898 (SCAF 366), all May 7, 1945, General Eisenhower to Military Mission to Moscow, and to CCS for information; also FWD-20809 (SCAF 360), May 7, 1945, General Eisenhower to CCS, AGO.

2. Messages FWD-20851 (SCAF 364), May 7, and FWD-20911, May 8, 1945, General Eisenhower to Military Mission to Moscow, and General Marshall, respectively, AGO.

3. John R. Deane, *The Strange Alliance,* Viking Press, New York, 1947, pp. 174–80; also *Diary, Office C-in-C,* Book XV under date May 8, 1945.

4. General Eisenhower's order of the day is quoted in full in *6th Army Group History,* Chapter X, May 1945, pp. 33, 34.

5. SHAEF G-3 War Room Daily Summary 36, May 8, 1945, AGO. *Redeployment,* Occupation Forces in Europe Series, 1945–46, Office of the Chief Historian, European Command, Chart I, facing p. 35, AGO.

6. Marshall, *Biennial Report,* July 1, 1943–June 30, 1945, pp. 115–16.

7. *Redeployment,* p. 68.

8. Letters, General Eisenhower to General Marshall, May 27 and September 25, 1944, General Eisenhower's personal files.

9. *Toward the Peace Documents,* Department of State, United States of America, Publication 2298, The Moscow Conference, pp. 4, 5.

10. *Civil Affairs,* Occupation Forces in Europe Series, 1945–46, Office of the Chief Historian, European Command, U. S. Group Central Council, pp. 80, 81, AGO.

11. Ibid., Allied Control Council and Chain of Command, pp. 94–96.

12. Ibid., Organization of the G-5 Division, SHAEF, etc., pp. 8–14.

13. JCS/1067 is published in *Department of State Bulletin,* Vol. XIII, 1945, pp. 596–607.

14. General Eisenhower's views relative to the separation of civil government from the Army's occupational duties are outlined in his letters to the President, October 26, and to General Marshall, October 13, 1945. General Eisenhower's personal files.

15. Message S-96883 (SCAF 478), July 12, 1945, General Eisenhower to all headquarters and offices concerned, announces dissolution SHAEF effective July 14, AGO.

16. Marshall, *Biennial Report,* July 1, 1943–June 30, 1945, pp. 93, 94.

17. Ibid.

18. *Occupation Forces in Europe Series,* "Displaced Persons," 1945–46, Office of the Chief Historian, European Command, pp. 1–3, AGO.

19. Ibid., pp. 30, 31, 55–62.

20. Ibid., "Repatriation," pp. 47, 48; also pp. 66, 67.

21. Ibid., pp. 74–77.

22. Ibid., pp. 70–73.

23. Reference is made to the conversations on the subject of turning over Military Government to civil authority, during the period of the Potsdam Conference, in General Eisenhower's letter to the President, October 26, 1945. General Eisenhower's personal files.

24. A comprehensive discussion of the Russians' attitude toward the Japanese war and factors involved is contained in Deane, op. cit., pp. 223–76.

25. Secretary Stimson discusses the atomic bomb and mentions that the New Mexico test occurred on July 16 during the Potsdam Conference in *On Active Service in Peace and War,* pp. 612–26, 637.

CHAPTER 23: Operation Study

1. The General Board was established by General Order 128, Hq. ETO, U. S. Army, June 17, 1945, as amended by General Order 182, August 7, 1945, to prepare a factual analysis of the strategy, tactics, and administration employed by the United States forces in the European theater, AGO.

2. SHAEF G-3 War Room Daily Summaries 201, December 24; 202, December 25; 204, December 27; and 205, December 28, 1945, AGO.

3. Montgomery of Alamein, *Normandy to the Baltic,* p. 257. Statistics on planes and gliders are noted in *Report by the Supreme Commander,* p. 100.

4. Marshall, *Biennial Report,* July 1, 1943–June 30, 1945, pp. 95, 98, 99, 100.

5. *After Action Report, Third United States Army,* Vol. I, pp. 176–81.

6. Marshall, *Biennial Report,* July 1, 1943–June 30, 1945, Our Weapons Section, pp. 95–100.

7. Report prepared by Historical Division, War Department, for Office of Secretary of War, 052 (March 28, 1947), Combat Days for Divs., Historical Division, Special Staff, Department of the Army.

CHAPTER 24: Russia

1. Message S-15377, General Eisenhower to General Marshall, August 3, 1945, AGO.

2. Deane, op. cit., pp. 215, 216.

3. Ibid., pp. 216–17.

4. General Eisenhower transmitted Generalissimo Stalin's expression of regret to General Marshall in letter dated August 16, 1945. General Eisenhower's personal files.

5. Deane, op. cit., p. 218.

6. Ibid., p. 219.

7. Message M-25591, General Deane (Military Mission to Moscow) to General Eisenhower, September 18, 1945, General Eisenhower's personal files.

8. Message S-25539, General Eisenhower to General Marshall, September 28, 1945, AGO.

9. Message CC-17792, General Clay to General Marshall, October 19, 1945, AGO.

10. Another discussion of the freedom of the press by General Eisenhower and Marshal Zhukov is mentioned in Deane, op. cit., p. 219.

11. Messages S-75871 (SCAF 180), General Eisenhower to CCS, January 20, 1945, and message (no number recorded), General Smith to General Eisenhower, *Diary, Office C-in-C,* Vol. XV, pp. 2033, 2034.

APPENDICES

A. ALLIED ORDER OF BATTLE FOR FINAL OFFENSIVE

SIXTH ARMY GROUP (Devers)
> 2d French Armored Division (Le Clerc)
> 27th French Alpine Division (Molle)
> 1st French Infantry Division (Garbay)

First French Army (De Tassigny)
> 9th French Colonial Infantry Division (Valluy)
> I French Corps (Bethouart)
>> 1st French Armored Division (Sudre)
>> 4th French Mountain Division (De Hesdin)
>> 14th French Infantry Division (Salan)
> II French Corps (De Montsabert)
>> 5th French Armored Division (De Vernejoul)
>> 2d Moroccan Division (Carpentier)
>> 3d Algerian Division (Gillaume)

Seventh U. S. Army (Patch)
> 103d U. S. Infantry Division (McAuliffe)
> 36th U. S. Infantry Division (Dahlquist)
> 44th U. S. Infantry Division (Dean)
> VI U. S. Corps (Brooks)
>> 100th U. S. Infantry Division (Burress)
>> 10th U. S. Armored Division (Morris)
>> 63d U. S. Infantry Division (Hibbs)
> XV U. S. Corps (Haislip)
>> 3d U. S. Infantry Division (O'Daniel)
>> 45th U. S. Infantry Division (Frederick)
>> 14th U. S. Armored Division (Smith)

XXI U. S. Corps (Milburn)
    42d U. S. Infantry Division (Collins)
    4th U. S. Infantry Division (Blakely)
    12th U. S. Armored Division (Allen)

TWELFTH ARMY GROUP (Bradley)
  Third U. S. Army (Patton)
    70th U. S. Infantry Division (Barnett)
  VIII U. S. Corps (Middleton)
    89th U. S. Infantry Division (Finley)
    87th U. S. Infantry Division (Culin)
    65th U. S. Infantry Division (Reinhart)
  XII U. S. Corps (Eddy)
    71st U. S. Infantry Division (Wyman)
    26th U. S. Infantry Division (Paul)
    11th U. S. Armored Division (Dager)
    90th U. S. Infantry Division (Earnest)
  XX U. S. Corps (Walker)
    80th U. S. Infantry Division (McBride)
    6th U. S. Armored Division (Grow)
    76th U. S. Infantry Division (Schmidt)
    4th U. S. Armored Division (Hoge)
  First U. S. Army (Hodges)
    20th U. S. Armored Division (Ward)
  III U. S. Corps (Van Fleet)
    99th U. S. Infantry Division (Lauer)
    7th U. S. Armored Division (Hasbrouck)
    9th U. S. Infantry Division (Craig)
    28th U. S. Infantry Division (Cota)
    5th U. S. Infantry Division (Irwin)
  V U. S. Corps (Huebner)
    9th U. S. Armored Division (Leonard)
    2d U. S. Infantry Division (Robertson)
    69th U. S. Infantry Division (Reinhardt)
  VII U. S. Corps (Collins)
    1st U. S. Infantry Division (Andrus)
    3d U. S. Armored Division (Hickey)
    104th U. S. Infantry Division (Allen)
  XVIII U. S. Airborne Corps (Ridgway)

THE ALLIED AIR-GROUND T

SUPREME HEADQUARTERS

SIXTH ARMY GROUP

TWELFTH ARMY

FRENCH FIRST ARMY	SEVENTH U.S. ARMY	THIRD U.S. ARMY	FIRST U.S. ARMY	FI U.

| I FRENCH CORPS
II FRENCH CORPS | VI U.S. CORPS
XV U.S. CORPS
XXI U.S. CORPS | VIII U.S. CORPS
XII U.S. CORPS
XX U.S. CORPS | III U.S. CORPS
V U.S. CORPS
VII U.S. CORPS
XVIII U.S. AIRBORNE CORPS | XX
XX |

| 2 ARMORED DIVISIONS
I MOUNTAIN DIVISION
3 INFANTRY DIVISIONS | 3 ARMORED DIVISIONS
6 INFANTRY DIVISIONS | 3 ARMORED DIVISIONS
8 INFANTRY DIVISIONS | 4 ARMORED DIVISIONS
12 INFANTRY DIVISIONS | 2 AIR
I INF |

GROUP AND ARMY RESERVE
I ALPINE DIVISION
5 INFANTRY DIVISIONS

GROUP AND ARMY RE
4 INFANTRY DIVISIO
2 ARMORED DIVISIO

FIRST TACTICAL AIR FORCE

NINTH U.S. AIR

FIRST FRENCH AIR CORPS	XII TACTICAL AIR COMMAND	XIX TACTICAL AIR COMMAND	IX TACTICAL AIR COMMAND	XXI AIR

SUPPLY SERVICES
BRITISH AND AMERICAN SUPPLY SERVICES AND SUPPORTING UNITS WERE
UNDER DIRECTION OF THEIR OWN NATIONAL FORCES CO-ORDINATED BY SHAEF.

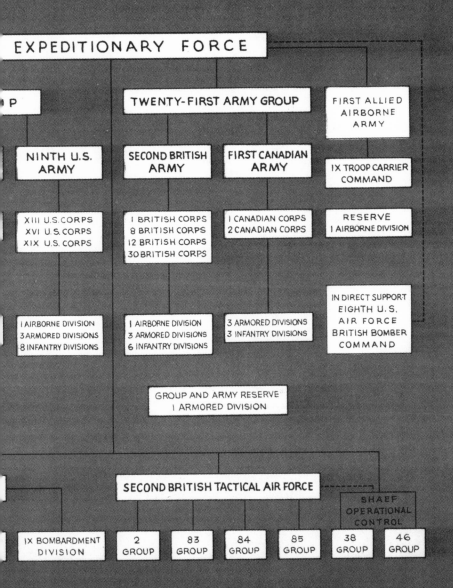

FOR THE FINAL OFFENSIVE

EXPEDITIONARY FORCE

P	TWENTY-FIRST ARMY GROUP		FIRST ALLIED AIRBORNE ARMY

NINTH U.S. ARMY	SECOND BRITISH ARMY	FIRST CANADIAN ARMY	IX TROOP CARRIER COMMAND

XIII U.S. CORPS XVI U.S. CORPS XIX U.S. CORPS	I BRITISH CORPS 8 BRITISH CORPS 12 BRITISH CORPS 30 BRITISH CORPS	I CANADIAN CORPS 2 CANADIAN CORPS	RESERVE I AIRBORNE DIVISION

I AIRBORNE DIVISION 3 ARMORED DIVISIONS 8 INFANTRY DIVISIONS	I AIRBORNE DIVISION 3 ARMORED DIVISIONS 6 INFANTRY DIVISIONS	3 ARMORED DIVISIONS 3 INFANTRY DIVISIONS	IN DIRECT SUPPORT EIGHTH U.S. AIR FORCE BRITISH BOMBER COMMAND

GROUP AND ARMY RESERVE
I ARMORED DIVISION

SECOND BRITISH TACTICAL AIR FORCE

SHAEF
OPERATIONAL
CONTROL

IX BOMBARDMENT DIVISION	2 GROUP	83 GROUP	84 GROUP	85 GROUP	38 GROUP	46 GROUP

BASIS: SHAEF G-3 SUMMARY # 309, APRIL 11, 1945
SHAEF A-3 OPERATIONAL SUMMARY, APRIL 6, 1945

8th U. S. Infantry Division (Moore)
78th U. S. Infantry Division (Parker)
97th U. S. Infantry Division (Halsey)
86th U. S. Infantry Division (Melosky)
13th U. S. Armored Division (Wogan)
Fifteenth U. S. Army (Gerow)
66th U. S. Infantry Division (Kramer)
106th U. S. Infantry Division (Stroh)
16th U. S. Armored Division (Pierce)
XXII U. S. Corps (Harmon)
82d U. S. Airborne Division (Gavin)
101st U. S. Airborne Division (Taylor)
94th U. S. Infantry Division (Malony)
XXIII U. S. Corps (Balmer)
Ninth U. S. Army (Simpson)
29th U. S. Infantry Division (Gerhardt)
XIII U. S. Corps (Gillem)
5th U. S. Armored Division (Oliver)
84th U. S. Infantry Division (Bolling)
102d U. S. Infantry Division (Keating)
XVI U. S. Corps (Anderson)
79th U. S. Infantry Division (Wyche)
8th U. S. Armored Division (Devine)
95th U. S. Infantry Division (Twaddle)
75th U. S. Infantry Division (Anderson)
35th U. S. Infantry Division (Baade)
17th U. S. Airborne Division (Miley)
XIX U. S. Corps (McLain)
83d U. S. Infantry Division (Macon)
2d U. S. Armored Division (White)
30th U. S. Infantry Division (Hobbs)

TWENTY-FIRST ARMY GROUP (Montgomery)
79th British Armored Division (Hobart)
Second British Army (Dempsey)
1 British Corps (Crocker)
8 British Corps (Barker)
15th British Infantry Division (Barber)

11th British Armored Division (Roberts)
6th British Airborne Division (Bols)
12 British Corps (Ritchie)
7th British Armored Division (Lyne)
53d British Infantry Division (Ross)
52d British Infantry Division (Hakewell-Smith)
30 British Corps (Horrocks)
3d British Infantry Division (Whistler)
43d British Infantry Division (Thomas)
51st British Infantry Division (McMillan)
Guards Armored Division (Adair)
First Canadian Army (Crerar)
1 Canadian Corps (Foulkes)
49th British Infantry Division (Rawlins)
5th Canadian Armored Division (Hoffmeister)
2 Canadian Corps (Simonds)
Polish Armored Division (Maczek)
2d Canadian Infantry Division (Matthews)
3d Canadian Infantry Division (Keefler)
4th Canadian Armored Division (Vokes)

FIRST ALLIED AIRBORNE ARMY (Brereton)
13th U. S. Airborne Division (Chapman)
IX Troop Carrier Command (Williams)
52d Troop Carrier Wing (Clark)
53d Troop Carrier Wing (Beach)
50th Troop Carrier Wing (Chappell)

FIRST TACTICAL AIR FORCE (Webster)
XII Tactical Air Command (Barcus)
First French Air Corps (Geradet)

NINTH U. S. AIR FORCE (Vandenberg)
IX Tactical Air Command (Quesada)
XIX Tactical Air Command (Weyland)
XXIX Tactical Air Command (Nugent)
IX Bombardment Division (Anderson)

SECOND BRITISH TACTICAL AIR FORCE (Coningham)
   83 Group (Broadhurst)
   84 Group (Hudleston)
   85 Group (Steele)
   2 Group (Embry)
   38 Group (Scarlett-Streathfield)
   46 Group (Darvall)

C. THE GERMAN GROUND FORCES

THE GERMAN COMBAT DIVISIONS WERE OF several types. The principal ones were:

Infantry divisions, consisting after D-day of three infantry regiments of two battalions each, with an authorized strength of approximately 12,000 officers and men.

Panzer Grenadier divisions, comprising two motorized infantry regiments of two battalions each, a motorized artillery regiment, and six battalions of supporting troops, with an authorized strength of approximately 14,000 officers and men.

Panzer divisions, corresponding to our armored divisions, consisting of two Panzer Grenadier regiments, a tank regiment, a Panzer artillery regiment, and five battalions of supporting troops, plus service troops, a personnel total of 14,000 officers and men.

Within the German forces a sharp distinction was made between the Wehrmacht, or ordinary army units, and the Schutzstaffel units which bore the prefix SS. The latter originally enrolled only specially selected members of the Nazi party, constituting a political and military elite which enjoyed special favors and privileges not accorded the Wehrmacht. The SS units were considerably stronger in both complement and fire power than comparable army units. Combat attrition and the frantic recruiting of replacements reduced the political and racial "purity" of the SS toward the end of the war but its troops continued until the end the most fanatical German fighters.

Equally fanatical in their resistance were the Volksgrenadier (People's Infantry) divisions, organized in September 1944; the personnel of these was interchangeable with the SS divisions. The use of the words "People's" and "Grenadier"—an honorary name bestowed upon the infantryman by Hitler in 1942—signified that these outfits were composed of elite fighters chosen for the defense of Germany in a mortal emergency. Although the Volksgrenadier divisions usually numbered less than 10,000 in personnel, they were extremely strong in automatic weapons, particularly submachine guns, and consequently could put up effective last-ditch resistance. This composition contrasted sharply with that of the Volkssturm units organized later in the war.

Strongest of the various types of infantry were the parachute divisions, part of the ground combat forces, but controlled by the German Air Force. These were carefully selected, well-trained and -equipped crack infantry divisions, with only a small percentage of the troops trained as parachutists. Because they had an authorized strength of 16,000 officers and men and a larger allotment of machine guns than the normal infantry divisions, the parachute troops were the best fitted of the German units for stout resistance on an extended and open front.

Assault troops and units that had distinguished themselves in combat were given the honorary title "Sturm." Only a few divisions were so honored. In the closing months of the war, however, this distinction was given for morale purposes to the frantically organized groups of old men and young boys who were known as the Volkssturm (People's Assault) troops.

Troops chosen for a special assault mission or one of a desperate character were usually formed into battle groups known by the name of their commander, e.g., Kampfgruppe Stoeckel. These varied from less than company to division strength and rarely remained independent for more than a month, but often retained as an honorary award for successful performance their battle-group designation even after their incorporation into a larger unit. Toward the end of the war they lost their specific-mission character and usually were composed of remnants of badly mauled regiments.

GLOSSARY

OF MILITARY CODE NAMES

THE CODE NAMES DESIGNATING MILITARY PROJ-
ects or operations in World War II were primarily intended as a
security measure against enemy intelligence agencies, although convenience of reference was an important by-product. For this purpose,
roughly ten thousand common nouns and adjectives, non-descriptive
of operations and geography, were compiled early in the war under
the direction of the American Joint Chiefs of Staff. After selection, the
alphabetical order of the words was scrambled, the list was published
in a classified catalogue, and blocks of words were assigned to each
theater of operations and to the Zone of the Interior in the United
States. Local headquarters in each theater later added to this original
list code names that either were not restricted to common nouns and
adjectives or were descriptive of the designated operation. Not to be
confused with code names are title abbreviations formed from initial
letters: COSSAC (Chief of Staff to the Supreme Allied Commander);
SHAEF (Supreme Headquarters, Allied Expeditionary Force);
PLUTO (Pipe Line under the Ocean).

Following is a list of selected code names, including some theater
additions to the original catalogue, and their definitions; in the case
of operations which were executed, the date the operation was started
is given.

Code Name	Definition	Operation Initiated
ANVIL	Allied operation in Mediterranean against south-ern France in 1944 (name was changed to Dragoon).	August 15, 1944

Code Name	Definition	Operation Initiated
APOSTLE I	Operation for the return to Norway following the surrender of Germany and the cessation of all organized resistance in Europe.	May 10, 1945
APOSTLE II	Operation for the return to Norway following the surrender of all German forces in Norway and the cessation of armed resistance in that country while German resistance continued elsewhere.	
ARCADIA	Roosevelt-Churchill Conference, Washington, December 1941–January 1942.	
ARGONAUT	Malta and Yalta Conferences: Roosevelt and Churchill, Malta; Roosevelt, Churchill, and Stalin, Yalta; January–February 1945.	
ASHCAN	Special detention center for captured civilians of political status equivalent to that of Von Papen.	
AVALANCHE	Amphibious assault against Naples—U. S. Fifth Army Salerno landings.	September 9, 1943
BAYTOWN	Invasion of Italian mainland opposite Messina —British Eighth Army.	September 3, 1943
BODYGUARD	Allied over-all strategic deception plan.	
BOLERO	Operation of transferring American forces from the United States to the United Kingdom.	
BRIMSTONE	Operation for the capture of Sardinia.	
CHOKER I	Airborne operation against the Siegfried Line in vicinity of Saarbrücken, Germany.	
CHOKER II	Airborne operation for crossing the Rhine in vicinity of Frankfurt, Germany.	
CLARION	Operation by Allied air forces designed to paralyze the German transportation system.	February 22, 1945
CORKSCREW	Operation against Pantelleria, Italy.	Mid-June 1943
CORONET	Planned operation against Honshu, Japan.	
CROSSBOW	Air attacks against V-bomb and rocket sites.	
DRAGOON	Allied operation in Mediterranean against southern France (previously called Anvil).	August 15, 1944
ECLIPSE	Plans and preparations for operations in Europe in event of German collapse after the launching of Overlord.	
EFFECTIVE	Planned airborne operation by the First Allied Airborne Army to seize the airfield in the Bisingen, Germany, area.	
EUREKA	Teheran Conference: Roosevelt, Churchill, Stalin; November 26–December 2, 1943.	
EXCELSIOR	Philippine Islands.	
FANFARE	All operations in the Mediterranean area.	

Code Name	*Definition*	*Operation Initiated*

FRANTIC   England-to-Russia air shuttle bombing.

GARDEN   Land operation in connection with Market.   September 17,
GOLD   The Asnelles beach for Overlord assault landing.   1944

GOLDFLAKE   Movement of Canadian corps from MTO   Early February
to ETO.   1944

GOOSEBERRY   One of the artificial harbors off the coast
of France in Operation Overlord. (There were
five in number, which later formed the two major
harbors, the Mulberries.)

GRENADE   Operation by U. S. Ninth Army northeast to-   February 23,
ward the Rhine with right flank on the general   1945
line Jülich–Neuss.

GYMNAST   Early planned operations against northwest
Africa; originally American only and outside the
Mediterranean, later enlarged to include British
and assault within Mediterranean.

HANDS UP   Planned air-sea operation for establishment
of a port in Quiberon Bay.

HOBGOBLIN   Pantelleria Island, Mediterranean Sea.

HORRIFIED   Sicily.

HUSKY   Invasion of Sicily.   July 10,
INDEPENDENCE   Operation to open the port of Bor-   1943
deaux, later changed to Venerable.

INFATUATE   Operation to capture Walcheren Island and   November 1,
free Scheldt approaches to Antwerp.   1944

JUBILANT   Planned airborne operations by First Allied
Airborne Army under Eclipse conditions to safeguard and supply Allied prisoner-of-war camps.

JUBILEE   Combined Allied raid on Dieppe, France.   August 19,
JUNO   The Courseulles beach for Overlord assault landing.   1942

LUMBERJACK   Operations north of the Moselle between   February 23,
Cologne and Koblenz, Germany.   1945

MAGNET   United States forces in northern Ireland.

MAJESTIC   Planned operation against Kyushu, Japan.

MARKET   Airborne operation to seize the bridges at   September 17,
Grave, Nijmegen, and Arnhem.   1944

MULBERRY   Major artificial harbor for Overlord. (Please
refer to Gooseberry.)

NEPTUNE   Actual operations within Overlord to be used
instead of Overlord only in communications and
documents which disclosed directly or by inference:
(a) target area, (b) precise date of the assault,
or (c) the total scale of the assault.

Code Name	Definition	Operation Initiated
NESTEGG	Occupation of Channel Islands either after surrender of local German garrison or after evacuation of islands by Germans.	May 9, 1945
OCTAGON	Quebec Conference: Roosevelt, Churchill; September 1944.	
OMAHA	The St. Laurent beach for Overlord assault landing.	
OVERLORD	Plan and operation for the invasion of France in spring of 1944.	June 6, 1944
PANTALOON	Naples, Italy.	
PHOENIX	Concrete barges used in Overlord artificial harbors.	
PLUNDER	The entire operation of crossing the Rhine north of the Ruhr.	March 23, 1945
QUADRANT	Quebec Conference: Roosevelt, Churchill; August 1943.	
RANKIN A	Plan to return to Continent in event of the weakening of German strength and morale prior to Overlord target date.	
RANKIN B	Plan to return to Continent if Germany withdrew from France and/or Norway.	
RANKIN C	Plan to return to Continent in the event of unconditional surrender.	
RED BALL	The one-way express traffic route for motors from beachheads to troops and return in Overlord.	
ROUNDUP	Planned operation against the coast of France. (Replaced by the code name Overlord.)	
SEXTANT	Cairo Conference: Roosevelt, Churchill, Chiang Kai-shek; November–December 1943.	
SLEDGEHAMMER	A planned landing on the Continent to secure a limited bridgehead in the event of a weakening of German morale or the necessity of securing diversion of enemy troops from eastern front.	
SOAPSUDS	The bombing of Ploesti, Rumania.	August 1, 1943
SWORD	The Douvres beach for Overlord assault landing.	
TERMINAL	Potsdam Conference: Truman, Churchill, Stalin; July 17–August 2, 1945.	
TORCH	Allied landings on the west and northwest coasts of Africa.	November 8, 1942
TRIDENT	Washington Conference: Roosevelt, Churchill; May 1943.	

Code Name	Definition	Operation Initiated
UNDERTONE Operation by Sixth Army Group south of Moselle to close on the Rhine from Koblenz southward.		March 15, 1945
UTAH The Varreville beach for Overlord assault landing.		
VARSITY First Allied Airborne Army operation north and northwest of Wesel.		March 23, 1945
VENERABLE Operation by the French Army Detachment of the Atlantic to open the port of Bordeaux.		April 14, 1945
VERITABLE First Canadian Army's operation southeast between the Rhine and the Meuse to the general line Xanten–Geldern.		February 8, 1945
WILDFLOWER Great Britain.		

INDEX

student of warfare, 176; Verdun conference, 350; Wac office manager, 133
Peacetime training, 119
Pearl Harbor attack, 3, 13–14, 17, 22, 31, *map*, 20
Peccia River, 206
Peenemünde, Germany, 259
Penicillin, 316
Pensacola Convoy, arrival at Brisbane, 22
"Persecutees" (displaced persons), 439
Pershing, General John J., 121
Persian Gulf, 28
Personal characteristics, importance in warfare, 75
Personnel: mines, 467–68; selection, 41; transport of, 30
Pétain, Marshal Henri Philippe, 105, 107, 109
Peyrouton, Marcel, 130, 131
Philippeville, Algeria, 118
Philippine Islands: air attack, 14; air communications, 21; blockade running, 25; commonwealth organization, 15; danger, 19, 20; defense, 15, 17, 24; government in exile, 39; Japanese attack, 17–18; MacArthur, 4, 23; *map*, 20; military training, 15; morale building, 22; neutralization, 26; reinforcements, 21; Scouts, 17
Philippsburg, Germany, 394; *map*, 393
Philosophy, understanding of, 454
"Phoenix" (concrete ship), 235
Photography: aerial, 230, 453; reconnaissance units, 420
Pillboxes, 236, 237, 330
Pilotless aircraft, 258
Pilsen, Czechoslovakia, 417; *map*, 419
Pilsen–Karlsbad (junction line), 418
Pinpoint bombing, 230, 323, 337
Pipe line: Alaska, 42; English Channel, 309
Planning process, 75, 256
Ploesti oil fields, Rumania, 160, 161
Po River, 199
POL (supplies of gasoline and lubricants), 290
Poland: German assault, 2; Germany, overrunning, *map*, following 432; invasion, 5, *map*, following 432; Montgomery's army group, 151, 328; national allegiance, 455; Soviet forces, 228; stateless citizens, 440; troops in invasion (1944), 53
Politics: and military activities, 88, 367; and racial relationships, 129; and social order (U. S.), 457; function of governments, 80

Popp, Sergeant, 133
Portal, Air Chief Marshal Sir Charles, 27, 242
Port Lyautey, Morocco, 103; *map*, 102
Ports: artificial, 237, 264; Cherbourg, 261; French North Africa, 115; mulberry, 235, 261; need for, 234; refitting captured, 235
Portsmouth, England, 245
Portsmouth–Southampton area, German target, 260
Portugal: anti-aircraft artillery, 218; plans for attack, 43
Positive action, 119
Potsdam Conference, 287, 441, 443, 444, 459, 474
Pound, Admiral Sir Dudley, 27
Power concept, 163
Prague, Czechoslovakia: bombing, *map*, 64; victory celebrations, 433
Precision bombing, 65
President, safety of, 193
Press. See Newspapers
Prince of Wales (British ship), 103
Prisoners: Allied recaptured, 420, 422; British recaptured, 420; care of, 469; German, 156, 294, 302, 406, 415, 416; handling numbers of, 386; Pantelleria, 166; Rhine crossing, 391; Ruhr, 406; Tunisia, 157; Walcheren Island, 327
Proletariat, dictatorship of, 457
Prolonged combat, effect of, 454
Propaganda: Free French, 113; German, 187, 319
Prüm, Germany, 381
Psychoneuroses, 455
Public: concern in army matters, 298, 299; mind, state of, 65; reaction to dissipation of U. S. Army, 121

Quebec Conference, 307
Queen Mary (ship), 30
Quesada, Major General Elwood R., 262, 289
Quezon, President Manuel, 15, 26, 39
Quiberon Bay, Brittany, 264, 279, 280

Racial and political relationships, confused nature of, 129
Radio communication: African campaign, 98; Algiers, 104
Rae, Nana, 133
Raff, Colonel Edson D., 125
Railways: Algiers to Tunis, 116; bottlenecks, attacking, 296; Brest, 282; Budĕjovice–Linz, 418; Casablanca–Oran, 79; Marseille–Metz, 282; North Africa, 149; repairs and con-